Barcode in Back

THE OXFORD HANDBOOK OF

COMPUTER MUSIC

THE OXFORD HANDBOOK OF

COMPUTER MUSIC

Edited by

ROGER T. DEAN

OXFORD
UNIVERSITY PRESS
2009

OXFORD
UNIVERSITY PRESS

Oxford University Press, Inc., publishes works that further
Oxford University's objective of excellence
in research, scholarship, and education.

Oxford   New York
Auckland   Cape Town   Dar es Salaam   Hong Kong   Karachi
Kuala Lumpur   Madrid   Melbourne   Mexico City   Nairobi
New Delhi   Shanghai   Taipei   Toronto

With offices in
Argentina   Austria   Brazil   Chile   Czech Republic   France   Greece
Guatemala   Hungary   Italy   Japan   Poland   Portugal   Singapore
South Korea   Switzerland   Thailand   Turkey   Ukraine   Vietnam

Published by Oxford University Press, Inc.
198 Madison Avenue, New York, New York 10016

www.oup.com

Oxford is a registered trademark of Oxford University Press.

Library of Congress Cataloging-in-Publication Data
The Oxford handbook of computer music / edited by Roger T. Dean.
p.   cm.
Includes bibliographical references and index.
ISBN 978-0-19-533161-5
1. Computer music—History and criticism.   I. Dean, R. T.
ML1380.O9 2009
786.76—dc22   2008046594

1   3   5   7   9   8   6   4   2
Printed in the United States of America
on acid-free paper

CONTENTS

....

Contributors

Freya Bailes, University of Western Sydney
Michael Casey, Dartmouth College
Nick Collins, University of Sussex
Roger T. Dean, University of Western Sydney
Paul Doornbusch, Victoria University, Wellington
Alan Dorin, Monash University
Alice Eldridge, Monash University
Simon Emmerson, De Montfort University
James Harley, University of Guelph
Douglas Keislar, Berkeley
Leigh Landy, De Montfort University
Peter Lennox, University of Derby
George E. Lewis, Columbia University
Peter Manning, University of Durham
Jon McCormack, Monash University
Peter McIlwain, Monash University
Daniel Müllensiefen, Goldsmiths, University of London
Pauline Oliveros, Rensselaer Polytechnic Institute
Garth Paine, University of Western Sydney
Marcus T. Pearce, Goldsmiths, University of London
Tim Perkis, Berkeley
Palmyre Pierroux, University of Oslo
Jøran Rudi, University of Oslo
Noam Sagiv, Brunel University
Wayne Siegel, Royal Academy of Music, Aårhus
Mary Simoni, University of Michigan
Hazel Smith, University of Western Sydney
Atau Tanaka, University of Newcastle
Geraint A. Wiggins, Goldsmiths, University of London
Trevor Wishart, Durham University
David Worrall, University of Canberra

THE OXFORD HANDBOOK OF

COMPUTER MUSIC

....

CHAPTER 1

INTRODUCTION: THE MANY FUTURES OF COMPUTER MUSIC

....

ROGER T. DEAN

COMPUTER music offers possibilities for music-making that can hardly (if at all) be achieved through other means. These possibilities commune between real-time creation in improvisation or other forms of interactive performance, production of scores for others to perform, and acousmatic composition. Broadly, we use *acousmatic* to refer to pre-fixed digital sound structures ready for acoustic diffusion through loudspeakers without performers energizing conventional musical instruments to make sounds.

In this brief introduction, I give some perspectives on the scope and futures of computer music, indicating how the topics are addressed within the book. Computer music has passed its 50th anniversary and is part of a slightly longer tradition of electroacoustic music. This book provides a broad introduction to the whole electroacoustic field and its history (see part I and the appendix in particular), but its explicit emphasis is on computer music in the period since the 1980s during which the Yamaha DX7 synthesizer and the availability of desktop (and later laptop) computers at prices individuals could afford meant that the practice of computer music was no longer restricted to those who could access a mainframe computer. Many composers and improvisers, like myself, first gained access to computer music opportunities in this period of the 1980s. Hence, the breadth of activity expanded until the present in part because the field of participants widened and in part because of the rapid acceleration in central processing unit (CPU) speed and therefore of the power of computers for real-time sound generation. Chapter 2, by Douglas Keislar, and the appendix, by Paul Doornbusch, provide interesting timelines of these issues of CPU speed.

1. THE APPEAL OF COMPUTER MUSIC

A. For Musicians

For many years, it seemed as if computer music could only usefully be the domain of the composer willing to await the generation of the sounds programmed (as described in chapters of part I). Such a composer can be said to operate "out-of-time," in contrast to those who use computers in "real-time" performance. But, these out-of-time composers also used the computer to assist the generation of scores for live instrumental performers (see chapter 5) as well as for the making of acousmatic sound. One of the appeals was the apparent potential of computers to generate any conceivable sound and to realize performances of precision or complexity not feasible as a human performance. Many parts of the book address computer music composition, notably chapters 5, 7, and 9, by James Harley, Trevor Wishart, and Simon Emmerson, respectively. Possibly the most influential composer within computer music was Iannis Xenakis, and Harley discusses his works, juxtaposing them with contributions from Karlheinz Stockhausen and other pioneers. The long-standing prejudice that electronic music did not sound sufficiently "human" was progressively overcome; furthermore, computational and perceptual analyses of what those prejudices identified (e.g., slowing of tempi at phrase boundaries, relationships between pitch and performed intensity) could then be applied in software for composition and its realization, such as Director Musices. So when desired, aspects of this particular range of human features could appear in computer music. The realization of computer music scores is discussed here particularly by Emmerson and by Douglas Keislar (chapter 2).

However, some remarkably powerful real-time performing vehicles, such as the Music Mouse, appeared along with the Macintosh computer in the '80s; by the '90s, real-time midi-manipulation (e.g., using the software MAX on such computers) and later digital sound manipulation (using MSP or many other platforms) became widespread, fluent, and stable. One of the appeals of computers in real-time music-making is the possibility that the computer can itself enter a dialogue with other musicians, as discussed in chapters 6, 18, 19, and 20, and in chapters 8, 21, and 22 by Tim Perkis, George Lewis, and Pauline Oliveros, respectively. Another is that the computer can generate or manipulate events long after some initiation point, and that this can be done either in a way that the performers control or without their foreknowledge of the nature of the impending events.

Some contemporary opportunities in computer music include "soundspotting" (see chapter 20 by Michael Casey), in which rapid identification of features of incoming streams of sound is used to find related features in stored databases of other sounds so that the stored materials can be used in performance in a variety of controlled and performable ways. Such principles of relating different materials can operate in real-time intermedia performance also and are among the topics discussed by Nick Collins, in chapter 17 on laptop music-making; by Jon McCormack and colleagues, in chapter 18's context of A-life (artificial life) and generative approaches to computer music; and by Noam Sagiv and colleagues in chapter 15. In chapter 10, Wayne Siegel considers dance and computer music, on the basis of long experience, and other aspects of the conversion of bodily or other gestures into computer music are considered by Garth Paine (chapter 11) and by Atau Tanaka (chapter 12).

Although all the chapters in this book operate at a sophisticated technical level that should not offend the sensibility of a professional computer music composer, the book is not focused on computer music techniques, software, and so on. It is about computer music itself; thus, it is throughout intended to stimulate the listener at large, especially those with modest prior experience of the work.

B. For Listeners and Users

Is computer music just another form of music, like Balinese music or Western classical music, or does it have some particular appeals or difficulties? As mentioned, it is unlike all previous musics in at least one respect: its capacity to generate and utilize, in principle, any sound. For most people even now, computer music thus presents unfamiliar components, articulated into meaning structures that need to be penetrated or, according to your perspective, that the listener is free to envisage. Broadly, there is similarity between the process of an Indian classical musician becoming engaged with the music of John Coltrane and of someone approaching computer music from a position of unfamiliarity. What is required is the capacity to recognize sonic features and their recurrence, since music is one of the most repetitive of the temporal arts, and then to construct meaning therefrom.

As Freya Bailes and I have shown recently (chapter 23), most listeners have a remarkable ability both to recognize and to co-relate computer-manipulated sounds. For example, we found that they identified close connections between speech sounds, manipulated speech sounds, and what we call NoiseSpeech, which is manipulated so extensively there are no remaining detectable phonemes: all these sounds are readily perceived as speechlike. Speech is characterized by vast rates of change in spectral quality compared with classical music or even with computer music at large. Yet, we even found that noise on which an invariant set of speech formants is superimposed is still heard as speechlike and qualifies as NoiseSpeech. Identifying sonic continuities and categories is an important facility for the listener seeking to gain meaning from their sonic exposure.

Such listener ability for construction of semiotic fields is useful in our approach to the long tradition of computer music using the voice, as discussed by Hazel Smith in chapter 14. It will also be useful in the more practical aspects of sonification, the representation of data for informational purposes of more objective kinds, as discussed by David Worrall in chapter 16. As he notes, an extension of these informational intents provides ideas by which the traditions of sonification and of computer music can interact.

Even given these widespread capacities to hear structure and extract meaning from sound, our involvement and enjoyment of computer music is necessarily influenced by our cultural and educational experience. Thus, Mary Simoni discusses gender discrimination within and about the music (chapter 24), and Jøran Rudi and Palmyre Pierroux analyze current processes in computer music education, with particular reference to their decade-long experience with interactive school study in Norway (chapter 26). Leigh Landy provides an optimistic outlook on the future for creation and appreciation of computer music and does so in the broadest possible artistic and sociopolitical contexts of digital culture (chapter 25).

2. Some Editorial Principles and Practices in This Book

I have invited (and cajoled) authors always from the ranks of those highly qualified to write on their topics, but also, in a few cases, in such a way as to create interaction among them. Thus, we have an expert on the psychology of synesthesia contributing to an article on algorithmic intermedia processes; one on the processes of imaging and imagining music joining a discussion of empirical approaches to the perception of computer-generated sound; and several contributions involving exchanges between computer science, modeling, generative algorithms, A-life, and music. Chapters also address sociocultural and educational issues. The authors originate from most parts of the world in which computer music has been important (notably North America, Europe, Australasia, and Asia), with the exception of South America.

As some of the authors may have lived to regret, I have interacted closely with them: first in providing some specific suggestions on which to base the range of ideas they cover and then in proposing editorial changes and additions once a draft was received. The authors have also had to put up in some cases with incessant pressure from me such that all articles could be completed reasonably efficiently. Timely book production has also been a consistent objective of our enthusiastic and supportive commissioning editor at Oxford University Press, Norm Hirschy.

I was quite clear in my approach to several authors, such as those writing in the opening part, that there would and should be overlap in the topics they addressed with those of other chapters. By seeking distinct approaches from these authors, I am happy that we achieved complementarity in the descriptions of individual events or developments. Thus, Keislar provides a perceptively conceptualized analysis of the development of computer music in the broad context of music at large; this is complemented by the "machine" emphasis I requested of Doornbusch and the "software" emphasis I asked of Peter Manning. I take responsibility for the points of overlap, of which I edited a few (with the authors' approval), cross-referenced some (as editor, I added several of the cross-references in the book), and purposely retained several more.

Another set of tangential and occasionally overlapping views are provided by the four personal statements (in the two sections titled "Sounding Out"), which complement the more conventional thematic review chapters. In inviting these informal statements, I indicated that I was seeking some expression of the most pressing thoughts about computer music these eminent musicians were digesting and developing at the time. They were given complete freedom regarding minimum length or breadth of topics to be addressed. I think you will agree the results are a distinctive and stimulating component of the book.

I would also like to thank Paul Doornbusch for his unstinting work on the chronology in the appendix, which I believed should be a component of such a book but which I anticipated researching and compiling myself, with some trepidation. I was very glad that he agreed to develop this into what I consider a useful and informative document. No chronology can be complete, and every chronology in an area of interest should be seen as challengeable. Paul's is already the most substantial and probably the most balanced currently available, and it is hoped he can develop it as a continuing resource.

3. Outlook

My purpose in editing this book has been to facilitate access to computer music for the listener and for the future and to bring together the range of compositional, theoretical, and practical issues that a practitioner can always benefit from considering. We are at a point in the history of this endeavor at which the opportunities are endless, and in most cases, one can actually readily envisage a means to fulfill them (the fulfillment of course may take immense effort). This has not always been the case in music composition and improvisation, and I hope some of the excitement of this moment will come across to our readers. If so, my contributors deserve the highest credit. You will not have great difficulty in finding substantial works by all the composers and improvisers discussed in the book, legitimately available without charge on the Internet, or finding examples of all the creative techniques and technologies described. Again, such an opportunity has not always existed in relation to music. I hope you enjoy the exploration the book encourages, and that it leads you to experience future performances and the many high-quality commercial recordings now available.

PART I

SOME HISTORIES OF COMPUTER MUSIC AND ITS TECHNOLOGIES

CHAPTER 2

··

A HISTORICAL VIEW OF COMPUTER MUSIC TECHNOLOGY

··

DOUGLAS KEISLAR

A single chapter on the history of computer music technology can hardly do justice to its topic. The most comprehensive volume on computer music techniques (Roads 1996a) was billed as a tutorial yet occupied 1,200 pages, a significant number of which examined the history and antecedents of these techniques. Recent book-length historical treatments of electronic music, encompassing computer music, include those by Chadabe (1997) and Manning (2004). Accordingly, the present chapter necessarily gives but a glimpse at some of the major mileposts. In lieu of extensive detail, it proffers a conceptual framework, a way of thinking about this multifarious field.

We start by discussing terminology. The term *computer music* arose in the context of 20th-century developments in Western art music. In the 20th century, the very term *music*, formerly understood to be straightforward and unambiguous, was subjected to stretching and questioning on a number of fronts owing to new musical directions such as serialism, aleatoric composition, percussion-only works, noise, and electronic sound. The compound noun *computer music* has its ambiguities, and it substantially overlaps with other terms such as *electronic music* and *electroacoustic music*. Difficulties with all these terms have been discussed by Manning (2004, pp. 403–404) and Landy (2007, pp. 9–17), among others. We can distinguish two main usages of the term computer music: (1) a musical genre or category, analogous to the symphony, jazz combo, and the like, in which the computer plays a part in composition, performance, or sonic realization; and (2) a technical discipline, analogous to computer graphics, that encompasses many aspects of the computer's use in applications related to music. Landy's discourse is not unusual in confining the scope of the term computer music to the first meaning. The present book also is oriented primarily toward this first definition, but it is informative to consider the second. Technical capabilities often stimulate aesthetic directions and vice versa. We focus here on technologies that directly enhance musical creation (as opposed to music scholarship, education, commerce, etc., as well as scientific endeavors), but as we shall see, even this limited scope is ultimately broader than might be expected.

The specific technical fields falling under the rubric of computer music can be gleaned by reading publications such as the *Proceedings of the International Computer Music Conference, Computer Music Journal*, and the aforementioned textbook by Roads (1996a). Areas relevant to computer music include not only music composition and computer science but also music theory, music representation, digital signal processing, acoustics, psychoacoustics, and cognitive science, to name but a few. Writers such as Pope (1994) have proposed taxonomies of the field. The keyword index at the ElectroAcoustic Resource site (http://www.ears.dmu.ac.uk/), also published in Landy (2007), hierarchically lists various relevant disciplines of study.

Kassler and Howe (1980) briefly characterized computer music technologies as replacements for conventional human musical activities, an approach akin to the more general writings of the media theorist Marshall McLuhan (1964). The next section of this chapter charts a course influenced by both these sources. Although it treats musical technologies prior to the computer, it forms an essential backdrop to the ensuing discussion, because its analytical perspectives and terminology reappear throughout the chapter. After that section, we examine the development of the computer as a musical instrument, broadly speaking, and then the means by which human musicians have operated this "instrument." Next, we consider the computer as a musician itself, whether composer or performer. The chapter concludes with a synopsis of some trends in the 20th and 21st centuries.

1. Antecedents: Abstraction, Disjunction, and Proliferation in Music Technology

Music-making involves a chain or network of relationships among musicians, musical technologies, and listeners. The historical development of music technology can be broadly viewed as a chronological series of abstractions and disjunctions that affect these linkages, as shown in table 2.1. Some of the abstractions represent instances of McLuhan's "extensions of man," in which a technology extends the reach or power of a human faculty, and some of the disjunctions represent instances of his "self-amputations," in which the technology replaces the use of a human faculty. A disjunction (i.e., decoupling) may permit the interjection of a new intermediary between the separated entities. Likewise, a pair of disjunctions around an entity in a chain may permit its disintermediation (i.e., bypass) or elimination, typically by the conjunction of the two entities it formerly separated. Either case—intermediation or disintermediation—may effect a proliferation of some capability or some musical feature. The proliferation sometimes results from a one-to-many mapping. Changes in music technology can clearly alter musicians' interactions with their instruments, but such changes may also profoundly affect musicians' interactions with each other and may transform music itself.

The prototypical music technology was the ancient musical instrument, which in the case of pitched instruments served as an abstraction of the singing voice. Advancement of technology led to instruments that were increasingly removed from human physiology, such as keyboard instruments, whose progenitor, the hydraulis, was invented in the 3rd century B.C.E. With keyboards, the controller's separation from the sound generators allows the latter to consist of pipes, strings, bars, or whatnot: there is a one-to-many mapping from performance technique to timbre. Also, the keyboard's pitch representation replaces the linear frequency distribution occurring along a pipe or string with logarithmic frequency, which corresponds better to human perception. These mappings were precursors to the arbitrary mappings enabled by computer technology. For that matter, one can consider the lever, central to the keyboard mechanism, as a prototype of mapping.

Self-playing mechanized musical instruments represent important predecessors of computer music. They effect a disintermediation of the performer; the "score" becomes directly conjoined to the instrument. The ancient Greeks had the technological means to construct such automata and may have done so. The first description of an automated instrument, an organ, is found in *The Book of Ingenious Devices* by the Banú Músà brothers (Hill 1979). These scholars worked in Baghdad's House of Wisdom in the 9th century C.E.—as did the mathematician al-Khwārizmī, from whose name the term *algorithm* derives. Automatic musical instruments of all sorts appeared with increasing frequency in Europe during the 18th and 19th centuries. The quintessential composer for an automated instrument was Conlon Nancarrow (1912–1997), whose studies for player piano exhibit a fascination with transcending the physiological and cognitive limitations of human pianists. This liberation of the composer from the constraints of performers' abilities figures prominently as a recurrent theme in music technology, particularly in computer music.

Analog electronic instruments were direct ancestors of computer music technology. The electronic musical instrument can be viewed as an abstraction of the acoustic instrument, one that can further decouple the control interface from the sound generator, permitting a proliferation of timbres as well as of possible

Table 2.1 An interpretive summary of some major developments in music technology prior to the computer

Technology	Introduced in	Added role	Abstraction	Disjunction	Proliferation	One-to-many mapping
Musical instrument	Prehistory	Instrumentalist, instrument builder	of voice	of sound production from body	of sounds: increased range of timbre, pitch, duration, loudness	of performer to sound generators (in some instruments)
Keyboard	Antiquity, Middle Ages			of control mechanism from sound generators (pipes, strings, etc.)	of timbres; of simultaneous pitches; increased range of duration and loudness (organ)	of performance skill to instruments and timbres
Music notation	Antiquity (symbolic); Middle Ages (graphic, with pitch axis)	Composer	of performance	of musical conception from sonic realization (temporally); of composer from instrument (performer is intermediary)	of the composition across space and time; of the composition's complexity, texture (polyphony), and duration	of one musician (composer) to many (performers); of one composition to many performances of it
—	—	Conductor (an outcome of notation-enabled complexity)	(conductor is an abstraction of the performer, a meta-performer)	of composer from performer (conductor is new intermediary); of performers' parts from the conductor's score	of parts (texture)	of one performer's (the conductor's) gestures to multiple voices or instruments
Mechanically automated musical instruments	Middle Ages, becoming more		of performer	of performer from score and instrument, which are now directly conjoined and the	of identical performances across time and (later, with mass production) across space; increased ranges of	

	common in 18th and 19th centuries			performer eliminated	musical parameters, sometimes exceeding human limitations	of performer to multiple audiences
Sound recording	Late 19th to early 20th century	Sound engineer	(a "concretion" of the score; captures the concrete performance rather than the abstract composition)	of performer from audience; of performance in time (editing); in musique concrète, elimination of performer and instrument	of identical performances across time and space	
Electrical transmission of sound (e.g., broadcast radio)	Early 20th century		of acoustical transmission	of performer from audience	of performance across space	
Electronic musical instruments	20th century	With synthesizer, composer or performer can become a builder of virtual instruments (patches)	of acoustic musical instruments	of control mechanism from sound generator; in theremin, a complete physical decoupling of performer from instrument	of timbres; of possible controllers; increased ranges of all musical parameters	of performer to multiple audiences
Electronic sound processing (reverb and spatialization)	20th century		of room	of sound source from original position and space; of listener from physical space		

The fourth row does not present a new technology, only another human role that resulted from the technology in the previous row.

controllers. Analog electronic instruments have a rich history in the 20th century (Rhea 1972, Roads 1996b, Chadabe 1997, Davies 2001). Two particularly noteworthy electrical devices were Thaddeus Cahill's colossal telharmonium and Lev Termen's theremin, first demonstrated publicly in 1906 and 1920, respectively. The telharmonium's sound was created by tonewheels (as in the later Hammond organ) and transmitted over telephone wires to listeners. This distribution mechanism foreshadowed Internet "radio" by virtue of having pre-dated broadcast radio. The theremin was notable for achieving the first tactile disjunction of the performer from the instrument. The theremin player moved his or her hands in the air without touching the instrument. However, this physical decoupling was not accompanied by an arbitrary mapping of gesture to sonic result; the distance of each hand from one of two antennae tightly controlled the frequency or amplitude, respectively, of a monotimbral signal.

What we now think of as analog sound synthesis was originally accomplished in the electronic music studios of the 1950s using custom collections of signal-processing modules such as oscillators, filters, and modulators. In the mid-1960s, Robert Moog and Donald Buchla each introduced modular analog synthesizers. In such instruments, the previously separate modules are housed together and interconnected using voltage control, in which one module's output modifies an input parameter of another module. (As discussed in the section "Digital Sound Synthesis," this notion of interconnected units had already been introduced in computer music software, albeit in a more abstract form and with sound generation that was much too slow for live performance.) The analog sequencer that appeared in the 1960s as a synthesizer module allowed one to store a repeatable sequence of control voltages. These could, for example, specify the pitches of a series of notes; therefore, the sequencer functioned analogously to the player piano roll, conjoining the "score" to the instrument and disintermediating the performer. The modular synthesizer's configurability lets the composer or performer construct new virtual instruments (synthesis "patches"), conceptually disintermediating the instrument builder by assuming that role. Similarly, one can consider the designer of the synthesizer itself to be a builder of meta-instruments.

One of the most dramatic of all technologies affecting music is sound recording. Recording made its debut with Édouard-Léon Scott de Martinville's phonautograph, patented in 1857; however, this device lacked a corresponding playback mechanism. In 1877, Thomas Edison invented the first practical technology for both recording and playback: the phonograph. Magnetic wire recorders were invented in 1898, and the Magnetophon tape recorder appeared in 1935. Phonograph disks, wire recorders, and tape recorders were all used in composition before 1950. Sound recording formed the sine qua non of musique concrète, the school of composition based on assemblage of recorded sounds, which Pierre Schaeffer (1910–1995) pioneered in his 1948 composition *Étude aux Chemins de Fer*.

"Tape music" disintermediates both the performer and the musical instrument. Working directly with sound, alone in a studio and unconcerned with performers' interpretation or skills, the composer becomes more like the visual artist. The impact of recording on music composition was similar to that of photography on visual art. However, the visual arts had already been primarily representational of the physical world; the camera as the ultimate representational tool stimulated painters to explore increasingly nonliteral representation and ultimately abstraction. By contrast, music had always been largely abstract; sound-recording technology introduced literal representation of the physical world. Music gained the ability to play with levels of allusion to this world, to juxtapose fragments of it, and to transform them. With tape recording, time itself could be disjoined and rejoined in an arbitrary fashion. In conjunction with electronic processing, recording technology endowed the already-rich timbres of the physical world with the new trait of plasticity.

Moreover, in conjunction with sound synthesis, recording technology gave the composer a new degree of control over the parameters of music. Whereas the musique concrète of midcentury Paris focused on sculpting sound from real-world sources, the contemporaneous *elektronische Musik* championed by Karlheinz Stockhausen (1928–2007) in Köln (Cologne) focused on constructing sound from the raw building blocks of acoustics, such as sine waves and noise. The frequencies, durations, and amplitudes of sounds could all be arbitrarily controlled and combined in ways not possible with traditional instruments. An interest in this degree of control stemmed naturally from the concerns of the serialist school of composition that Arnold Schoenberg (1874–1951) had founded earlier in the century.

Space also became a parameter for manipulation, through the use of multichannel playback to position a sound in the perceived space according to its level in each channel. A number of composers used this spatialization technique in the 1950s. It was put to dramatic effect by Stockhausen, who during the composition of *Kontakte* (1960) projected sounds from a rotating speaker that he recorded quadraphonically. The result is a dynamic swirling of sound around the audience, who listens to the recording while seated amid four loudspeakers. The midcentury composers also used artificial reverberators. Reverberation and spatialization techniques tend to disjoin sounds perceptually from both the space in which they were originally recorded and the space where the recording is heard. Room acoustics may represent the primary form of natural (acoustic) signal transformation, of which these specific electronic techniques are an abstraction (as suggested in table 2.1), but more generally, electronic signal processing leads to a proliferation of possible sonic transformations, most of which involve effects other than spatial imagery.

The technology of computer music incorporates and extends the capabilities of previous tools and previous human roles. As discussed in the rest of this chapter, the general-purpose nature of computer technology enables abstractions, disjunctions, and remappings at all points in the music-making process, including all the ones from earlier stages of music technology and more. With the exception, in most cases, of transducers (microphones, speakers, and, more generally, sensors, controllers, and actuators), all the elements can become virtual, that is, nonphysical (decoupled from hardware). The computer culminates the process of disjunction from the body that was begun with the instrument. While this separation might seem dismal from a certain humanistic perspective (especially in light of McLuhan's harsh term "amputation"), its important converse is a perspective that sees human energy spreading out beyond the body into the world, infusing it with potentially positive new manifestations of creativity. (The amputations are optional and temporary, being reversible, and the disjunctions enable new forms of connectedness, such as online musical collaboration.) The challenge for technological development is to stay cognizant of what may have been lost (e.g., a somatically intimate connection to sound) and to investigate how to regain it. Indeed, such considerations underlie much recent research, especially on controllers; some losses can be attributed to the relatively primitive state of tools in a young field, tools that will continue to improve.

Computer technology represents the generalization of "tool" or "instrument," by which the tool's domain can extend into all areas of human endeavor and the tool can be continually adapted (if not adapt itself) to solve new problems. A host of implications ensue, among them not only new horizons in musical practice but also challenges to preconceptions about art, creativity, and human identity. In computer music, the computer can function as an abstraction of the instrument, the musician, or both. We now examine these abstractions more closely.

2. The Computer as Musical Instrument

In 1963, Max Mathews (b. 1926), the electrical engineer who has been dubbed "the father of computer music," published an influential paper in *Science*, "The Digital Computer as a Musical Instrument." This article summarized some of the groundbreaking research and development in computer-generated sound at the Bell Telephone Laboratories in New Jersey. Mathews (see fig. 2.1) had invented digital sound synthesis: the numerical construction of sounds "from scratch." To this day, the use of the computer as an instrument—that is, a sound generator—remains at the heart of the multifaceted field we call computer music.

Still, many musicians rely less on synthesis than on the playback and processing of digitally recorded sound. Playback of prerecorded sounds and real-time processing of live sounds allow external sound input to become part of a musical instrument. The instrument now may encompass both kinds of transducer (i.e., the microphone and the loudspeaker, which are themselves abstractions of the ear and the voice) as well as abstractions of these transducers (e.g., input or output of symbolic music data rather than audio). Thus, after examining digital sound synthesis, we discuss digital recording and processing and then the implications of all these audio technologies for the craft of composition.

Figure 2.1 Max Mathews, standing amid the units of the IBM 7094 mainframe computer at Bell Labs around 1965. (Courtesy of Max Mathews.)

A. Digital Sound Synthesis

The earliest productions of musical sound by computer—in 1950 or 1951 in Australia (see the appendix) and England (*Computer Music Journal* 2004)—represented noteworthy technical achievements, but they were severely constrained in timbre as they relied on the machines' "system beep" facilities. This work did not result in any significant participation by composers, and until recently it remained unknown to the computer music community that subsequently developed worldwide.

True digital sound synthesis, availing itself of the computer's general-purpose nature to construct arbitrary sounds, awaited the introduction of digital-to-analog converters (DACs) in the 1950s. Max Mathews began research into digital sound synthesis in 1957 with his colleagues at Bell Laboratories, producing that year MUSIC I, the first of his computer programs for digital sound synthesis. MUSIC III, a system for interconnecting virtual modules like digital oscillators and filters, appeared in 1960. This approach was similar to the modular analog synthesizer (which appeared later in the decade) but was implemented purely in software. Owing to processor speeds, the synthesis could not be real time. In other words, it took much longer to create a sound than to play it back—a limitation not overcome for years.

Special-purpose, real-time digital synthesizers (separate musical instruments) became available in the mid-1970s. Digital synthesis on dedicated musical instruments attained wide distribution following the introduction of Yamaha's DX7 in 1983. By the late 1990s, the microprocessors in general-purpose desktop computers were fast enough for real-time sound synthesis. Of course, the computational speed of a synthesis algorithm depends on the algorithm's complexity and how efficiently it is implemented, as well as how many voices (i.e., instances of the algorithm) are running simultaneously. However, even the most demanding families of synthesis techniques are now feasible for real-time implementation. As in the past, much of the craft in designing sound synthesis algorithms involves finding computational shortcuts that have minimally adverse perceptual effects.

Many early digital synthesis algorithms were, like the typical analog synthesizer, subtractive: a timbrally rich waveform is filtered to remove its frequency components in a possibly time-varying manner. Additive synthesis, in which a spectrum is instead constructed by adding a sine wave oscillator for each of its component frequencies, was available, but its greater realism came at a much greater computational expense. John Chowning (b. 1934) at Stanford University discovered an entirely different method, frequency modulation (FM) synthesis (Chowning 1973), an efficient technique that remained popular for the next quarter century, until increased processor speeds rendered its efficiency moot. Most sound synthesis techniques can be used to emulate a desired musical sound with some degree of success, and in doing so they must approximate the acoustical waveform that reaches the ear, but the most fully virtual family of techniques, known as physical modeling (e.g., Smith 1992), goes back to the origin and explicitly emulates the acoustics within the instrument. This approach allows a virtual instrument to be played with the same kind of controls as the real instrument, with potentially striking realism. Current computers are also able to achieve comparable realism through real-time additive synthesis, given a database that stores all the timbral variants needed for a performance and given rules for joining these together in natural-sounding phrasing. Eric Lindemann's Synful Orchestra (http://www.synful.com) illustrates this approach applied to the emulation of orchestral instruments. Although realism might seem to be a moot criterion for composers who avoid imitative sounds, the significance of emulation is discussed under "Implications" in this section of the chapter.

B. Digital Sound Recording and Processing

The use of digital sound recording in composition postdated that of digital sound synthesis. Although analog-to-digital converters (ADCs) existed in the 1950s, other technical barriers to digital audio recording existed, such as limited computer memory and the need for error correction. The first commercial digital audio recorders were introduced in the mid-1970s. In the mid-1980s, after the introduction of the CD format in 1982, Sony introduced the digital audiotape (DAT) format, which became popular in the computer music community, as did direct-to-disk technologies enabled by affordable ADCs for personal computers in the late 1980s.

Once digital recording became practical, digital editing, mixing, and processing fell into place, and the methods of musique concrète could be transferred to the computer music studio. Digital signal processing in computer software enabled the development of many new techniques for transforming sound that in the analog realm had been impractical or of inferior quality. For instance, the phase vocoder, a frequency domain tool for audio analysis and resynthesis, permitted high-quality time stretching without pitch shifting and vice versa (Moorer 1978, Dolson 1982). Digital sound processing blurred the lines between synthesized and natural sound. In wavetable synthesis, for example, one period of a recorded waveform (a split second of audio) is stored in a numerical table for playback by an oscillator. With increases in computer memory, this early technique gave way to what was sometimes called *sampling synthesis*, in which a recorded note's entire duration could be stored for greater realism. As another example of the aforementioned blurring, granular techniques, which manipulate tiny snippets of sound in massive quantities (Roads 1978), can be applied equally to recorded or synthesized sound—often with perceptually similar results.

Chowning (1971) conducted the first research on the placement of sounds in a computer-generated virtual space, incorporating the simulation of reverberation and moving sound sources. He then employed these techniques in his own quadraphonic compositions. Other techniques such as ambisonics (Gerzon 1973) were invented for mathematically specifying spatial position, with the goals of greater flexibility in loudspeaker placement and listener position.

C. Implications

The synthesis, recording, and processing of sound by computer engendered a proliferation of new musical possibilities, further freeing composers from the constraints of human performers. The computer's increased precision, power, fidelity, flexibility, extensibility, and reproducibility augmented analog technologies' impact on music. The computer offered not only unlimited textural complexity and arbitrarily complicated yet precise rhythms but also unprecedented control and resolution in parameters such as pitch, timbre, and spatial location. The increased resolution implied the availability not only of discrete increments that were finer than previously possible but also of continuous trajectories along these musical dimensions.

Consider the proliferation of possibilities for pitch. The use of microtonal scales and arbitrary tuning systems, so long a challenge for acoustical instruments, became trivial with computer software, in which any frequency can be specified as easily as any other, and tuning is both precise and stable. (Some early analog instruments, notably the telharmonium, explicitly accommodated new tuning systems, but the oscillators in analog synthesizers typically suffer from frequency drift.)

Regarding computers' proliferation of timbres, Mathews realized early on that computers could, in principle, create any sound. He also recognized that the main limitation was humans' understanding of how to produce a desired sound: the field of psychoacoustics (the connection between the physics and the perception of sound) had, and still has, much to learn. As a result, psychoacoustical topics arose frequently in early computer music research. Using computer-synthesized sound, the recently introduced concept of timbre as a multidimensional space could be explored in research and in musical practice (Grey 1975, Wessel 1979). Additive synthesis made it possible to morph between timbres—an example of the trajectories mentioned. Also, it became clear that temporal variations in the amplitude or frequency of spectral components within a single tone could be critical for timbre. Understanding and manipulating sound at this microscopic level enriches the composer's vocabulary. As Chowning (2005) said, digital synthesis lets the musician not only compose with sound but also compose the sound itself.

Similarly, the parameter of space is uniquely tractable through computer technology. Although sonic liveliness can be achieved in the analog domain through multichannel recording and through dynamic routing to multiple loud-speakers during playback, computers grant the composer complete control of spatial imagery. Just as digital sound synthesis creates virtual instruments, so does digital positioning in multiple channels, along with carefully simulated reverberation, create a virtual space.

Digital sound synthesis also promotes a conjunctive blurring of the boundaries between musical dimensions that are normally thought of as distinct. For example, in the 1969 composition *Mutations* by Jean-Claude Risset (b. 1938), selected frequency components are first heard as distinct pitches but then fused in a unitary timbre (see fig. 2.2). Similarly, composers can harness the acoustical connections between timbre and tuning, as in some early experiments at Bell Labs and in Chowning's 1977 composition *Stria*. Also, *Stria* exhibits formal unity through self-similarity at multiple timescales. Computer sound generation allowed Chowning to apply the golden ratio (which itself expresses the self-similar relation $a+b$: $a = a{:}b \approx 1.618{:}1$) to FM synthesis parameters, spectral structure, and musical intervals in addition to overall form. This unification across temporal levels recalls Stockhausen's theoretical writing and early analog electronic music, for example, *Studie II* from 1954. Stockhausen was intrigued by a continuum of time that would span timbre, pitch, rhythm, and form.

In the same vein, digital processing of recorded sound allows the composer to play with a continuum between natural- and synthetic-sounding timbres (eroding the old ideological divide between elektronische Musik and musique concrète) and between recognizable and unrecognizable sound sources. Schaeffer was interested in disjoining sounds from their sources, focusing perception on their timbral

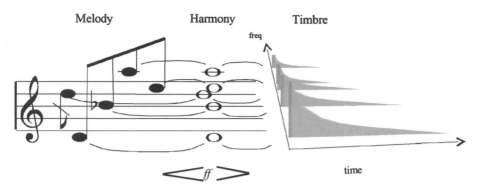

Figure 2.2 An excerpt from *Mutations* (1969) by Jean-Claude Risset, illustrating the use of computer sound synthesis to bridge pitch and timbre. Pitches first heard melodically are sustained as a harmony. Then a gong-like sound enters, containing the same frequencies, which however are now perceptually blended into a single note. (Courtesy of John Chowning.)

characteristics instead of their identities in the physical world. The term *musique concrète* has today been largely superseded by *acousmatic music*, a term with an explicitly disjunctive connotation that derives from the *akousmatikoi*, disciples of Pythagoras who listened to him from behind a veil. One way to veil the identity of a sound is to granulate it, to apply disjunction at a microscopic level. Granular synthesis and other microsound techniques (Roads 2001) became increasingly popular in the last decade or two, notably among composers of acousmatic music. As pointed out by Roads (2001, p. 340), these techniques foster a new conception of music. The traditional intervallic mode of musical thinking, concerned with numerical scales and proportions in precise parameters such as pitch and duration, gives way to a morphological mode of thinking in which sharp definition is replaced by fuzzy, supple, and ambiguous materials. It is not difficult to view these ideas through the lens of postmodernism or to compare them to an Einsteinian versus a Newtonian universe.

Computers are in fact excellent tools for both morphological and intervallic approaches, the latter including note-based musical conceptions. Notes are a disjunctive type of musical material at an intermediate timescale: the music consists of a sequence of discrete, measurable units, typically with abrupt changes in pitch from note to note. Composers in the acousmatic tradition, in particular, sometimes dismiss note-based music as lying outside the arena of interest for electroacoustic music, especially when the sounds are modeled after traditional instruments. However, it is important to understand the rationale for studying conventional features of music when undertaking technological research, regardless of their presence in particular styles of contemporary composition. As a case in point, consider the emulation of traditional instruments, which has figured heavily in sound synthesis research (Risset 1969, Chowning 1973, Smith 1992, and many others), as already implied by the discussion of realism in synthesis techniques (see "Digital Sound Synthesis"). A complaint is sometimes heard that such work should instead focus on novel timbres. The response to this argument is twofold. First, one can much better assess the success of a technique when gauging its results against a familiar reference point. Emulating the well known is often more complicated than emulating the little known, placing higher demands on the system. (Consider a "Turing test" in which the human subject has to judge whether text comes from a human or a computer, with two cases: one with the words in the subject's native language and the other with them in a completely unfamiliar language.) Second, and more germanely for the composer, the knowledge gained by refining the emulative technique will often inform a more sophisticated construction of brand-new sounds. Similarly, as we discuss under the heading "The Computer as Composer," the emulation of traditional musical styles has held an important position in algorithmic composition. The complaint about that research direction and the response to the complaint are directly analogous to those about the emulation of traditional instruments.

3. Human Control of the Digital "Instrument"

Having discussed the development of the computer as an instrument and its implications for composition, we now turn to the musician's connection to this instrument. The era of computer music extends from the 1950s to the present, a period that is roughly bisected by the appearance, within a matter of months of each other, of three paradigm-shifting technologies. The musical instrument digital interface (MIDI) protocol was introduced in 1983, as was the first affordable digital synthesizer, the Yamaha DX7. In January 1984, the first commercially successful computer with a graphical user interface—the Apple Macintosh—was launched, and it soon became especially popular among musicians as it was easy to use and could be connected to synthesizers via MIDI. For the first half of the history of computer music, therefore, users interacted with the computer via punch cards or, later, typed commands, and most had no access to real-time digital sound synthesis, having to wait, often for many hours, to hear the fruits of their labor. Music creation with the computer was almost exclusively a cerebral activity, a welcoming realm for composers perhaps, but not for performers.

In the second half of the computer music era, the two new aspects of musician-computer interaction—the graphical and the real time—made musical production less disjunct from the body. The visual representation and manual manipulation of virtual objects, combined with real-time sound synthesis or processing, come close to a natural experience for the musician. Logical next steps might involve paradigms that have been introduced in computer music but not yet widely deployed, such as haptic controllers with a realistic "feel" (Cadoz et al. 1984, Nichols 2002) and virtual reality technologies (Bargar 1993).

We divide the following discussion into tools for the composer and tools for the performer, recognizing that the boundary is not rigid: some tools may be used by both, and the two roles may overlap. In improvisation, the performer assumes some or all of the role of a composer. This discussion emphasizes software rather than hardware.

A. The Composer's Interface

As mentioned, for decades the primary interface for composers of computer music was textual input. Typically, a composer used a special-purpose computer language for music. Sometimes, a general-purpose programming language for which music routines had been written was used.

The software engineer who develops sound synthesis tools can be considered an abstraction of the traditional instrument builder. A composer who assumes this role disintermediates that engineer. Many computer music composers have reveled in the freedom to build their own virtual instruments and even to build languages for building instruments. However, there is a continuum of involvement available to the composer, ranging from writing languages, to writing programs, to creating algorithms, to simply tweaking parameters of existing algorithms (analogous to twiddling knobs on an analog synthesizer). At the very end of this continuum is the composer served by a technical assistant, a model available at large institutions like the Institut de Recherche et Coordination Acoustique/Musique (IRCAM), founded by Pierre Boulez (b. 1925). The last scenario is enviable for the composer who has no technical inclination, and its presence is unsurprising in a society like that of France, where support for the arts is widely considered a necessity rather than a luxury. The opposite end of the scale, the musician-cum-hacker, may be emblematic of societies with a do-it-yourself ethos and a cultural history that celebrates the pioneer.

Tool development and creative ideas are mutually influential. When the composer is also a programmer (or hardware developer), or if the engineer works closely with the user, it is more likely that creative musical goals will inform the tool's design. Otherwise, musicians are likely to be frustrated by the assumptions of the tools they are provided. (MIDI is a common example [Moore 1988].) However, it is also true that composers find inspiration in the implications of preexisting tools: much music has been written that was inconceivable without the specific technology the composer employed. We now turn our attention to some specific types of tool, with an emphasis on those having programmatic interfaces.

The MUSIC-N Languages

Mathews conceived of sound synthesis software as a twofold abstraction: of the orchestra and of the score. The "orchestra" was a collection of "instruments," and the instrument in turn was an interconnected set of "unit generators," that is, signal-processing modules (see fig. 2.3). The "score" was computer code that contained specifications of the notes that the instruments would play. In early sound synthesis languages, the instruments were also defined (as connections between unit generators) within the score. Later, the orchestra-score dichotomy became more explicit, with the code defining the instruments typically stored in one file (the orchestra file) and the note list in another (the score file). Mathews's MUSIC III, created in 1960, was the first in a long lineage of synthesis languages based on the paradigm of the unit generator. (See Roads 1996a, pp. 789–790 and

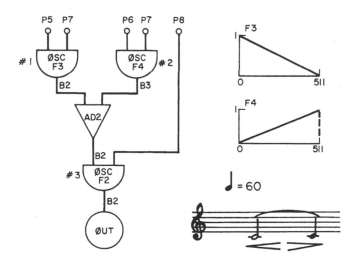

```
 1   INS 0 3 ;
 2   ØSC P5 P7 B2 F3 P30 ;
 3   ØSC P6 P7 B3 F4 P29 ;
 4   AD2 B2 B3 B2 ;
 5   ØSC B2 P8 B2 F2 V1 ;
 6   ØUT B2 B1 ;
 7   END ;
 8   GEN 0 1 3 .999 0 0 511 ;
 9   GEN 0 1 4 0 0 .999 511 ;
10   GEN 0 1 2 0 0 .99 50 .99 205  −.99 306  −.99 461 0 511 ;
11   NØT 0 3 2 0 2000 .0128 6.70 ;
12   NØT 2 3 1 2000 0 .0256 6.70 ;
13   TER 3 ;
```

Figure 2.3 A simple example of a MUSIC V software "instrument." *Top left:* a block diagram showing the interconnected unit generators that create the sound. *Top right:* Two functions, for diminuendo and crescendo. *Middle right:* The music to be synthesized. *Bottom:* The MUSIC V "score" for synthesizing the music; it contains both the instrument definition (lines 1–7) and the list of notes (11–12). (Reproduced from Mathews [1969], p. 59. Used with the permission of the MIT Press.)

807–808 for a list of these MUSIC-N languages.) Perhaps the most influential was MUSIC V, described by Mathews in his 1969 book, and the most widespread was Csound (Vercoe 1985a, Boulanger 2000), still in active use today.

The part of the MUSIC-N languages that abstracted the traditional score allowed the composer to list the notes in the composition along with the per note parameters for the instrument that would play that note. Depending on the language, different degrees of algorithmic control were available for generating the notes and their parameters. However, a score-generating language can lie outside the arena of MUSIC-N, and it can be conjoined to something other than sound synthesis software. For example, a note list can be translated into MIDI data for controlling hardware synthesizers, or it can be translated into music notation for human performers to read. The very first composition language to be developed, Robert Baker and Lejaren Hiller's MUSICOMP from 1963, is in the latter category. We return to the subject of algorithmic composition in a subsequent section ("The Computer as Composer").

Later Textual Languages

More recent languages for music programming offered increased flexibility. Nyquist (Dannenberg 1997) dissolved the separation between the score and the orchestra and between control signals and audio signals. Like some previous languages, it also gave the user access to all the features of a general-purpose programming language (in this case, LISP). SuperCollider (McCartney 2002) consists of an object-oriented language for composition and a real-time sound synthesis server that client applications can access over a network. There are a number of other noteworthy sound synthesis packages accessed from a general-purpose programming language such as C++ or LISP.

ChucK (Wang and Cook 2003) is a recent text-based language for real-time sound synthesis. Having a special syntax for manipulating the flow of time, its temporal model diverges from that of MUSIC-N. ChucK is designed to be useful for "on-the-fly" programming, which in a performance context is often referred to as "live coding." Live coding takes advantage of the virtualization of the instrument to eliminate the old temporal disjunction between the roles of instrument builder and performer. In live coding, their roles merge, as though Stradivarius were building violins on stage as he played them. Furthermore, both these roles are merged with that of the composer: the live coder is an improvising programmer of sound.

Graphical Patching Languages

Graphical patching languages take MUSIC-N's idea of interconnected units and render it less abstract through visual, manually manipulable representations of modules and their connections. For many composers, these environments represented a crucial advance in musician-computer interfaces as the user interface was reminiscent of a modular analog synthesizer. Graphical patching languages can also support some of the algorithmic logic characteristic of a general-purpose textual programming language, but in a form accessible to the less technically inclined musician. Roads (1996a, p. 753) and Puckette (2002) traced a bit of the history of these environments, starting with the MITSYN (Multiple Interactive Tone Synthesis System) graphical patching program that was developed at the Massachusetts Institute of Technology (MIT) by 1970. The best-known graphical patching language for music is Miller Puckette's Max program, which dates from the mid-1980s. Early versions of Max provided only control data, in the form of MIDI, but real-time audio signal processing and synthesis were added to a special-purpose version around 1990 and to the commercial version in 1997, as well as to an open source variant, Pure Data (Puckette 1997).

Puckette (2002) stressed that the most important influence on Max was in fact not graphical patching but the real-time scheduling of parallel control tasks found in Mathews's RTSKED program. (The Max software is named after Mathews.) Much of the appeal of Max is indeed its real-time nature; it is a tool for performers as well as composers. Similarly, Scaletti (2002) stressed that her environment Kyma, which among other features includes graphical patching of signal-processing modules, is not a graphical language, but rather a language offering multiple means for viewing and manipulating data.

Nonprogrammatic Software

For lack of space, we gloss over the numerous software packages with nonprogrammatic user interfaces. (See Roads [1996a] for historical summaries and publications such as *Electronic Musician* for in-depth descriptions of newer software.) After the introduction of MIDI and the graphical user interface, a number of commercial MIDI sequencers, synthesis patch editor/librarians, sound editors, and simple algorithmic composition programs appeared. As microprocessors got faster and hard disks more capacious, audio playback, audio editing, and signal processing were added to sequencers and other software, leading to a new generation of digital audio workstations (DAWs), which originally required special-purpose hardware but eventually were implemented in software. (The DAW can be thought of as a functionally extended virtual mixing console.) Similarly, faster microprocessors allowed synthesizer functionality to be implemented in software as virtual instruments, which typically provide graphical and MIDI control of simulations of older acoustic, analog, and digital musical instruments. The notion of interconnected signal-processing modules has been extended to plug-ins, modules that are accessed transparently across the boundaries of different software packages.

Of course, the user interface to which composers are most accustomed is traditional Western music notation. The input and output of music notation dates back to experiments by Hiller and Baker in 1961. Most notation software is used for creating printed output, often with supplementary auditioning via MIDI. However, some compositional software, such as OpenMusic and PWGL (Patch-Work Graphical Language), integrates music notation with a graphical patching environment.

Multimedia

Algorithmic approaches to the control of sound (audio, MIDI, etc.) can cross over into the control of visuals (images, video, lighting, etc.). The same software and even the same algorithm may control both sound and image, in but one example of a one-to-many mapping of functionality using computers. The term *visual music* is often used to describe such techniques and, more generally, visual arts that emulate music's dynamism and abstractness. The Jitter software package for the Max environment has been used in this manner (Jones and Nevile 2005). Visual data can be derived from audio data and vice versa. The term *sonification* refers to the mapping of nonaudio data into sound. This term originated outside music, referring to practical techniques for data display with the goal to help the listener understand the information in the nonaudio data. However, the idea has inspired many composers, whose goal is instead an aesthetically rewarding sonic result. Some pieces based on this kind of mapping have employed natural phenomena such as magnetic fields, coastlines, or molecular vibrations, while others have used technological sources such as network delays or the code for Web pages.

B. The Performer's Interface

Whereas the first half of the computer music era was dominated by the composer, the second half has witnessed the ascent of the performer. There had already been a long history of performers participating in analog electronic music. Most often, they simply performed on conventional acoustic instruments alongside a tape recorder that played back electronic sounds. "Tape music" was for years the main outlet for computer music as well—often pieces were conceived for the tape recorder alone, but music for performer plus "computer-generated tape" was not uncommon. However, live analog electronics also played an important role in the 20th century. Here, the performer could interact with the machine (see, e.g., Chadabe 1997). After the introduction of MIDI synthesizers, computer music quickly expanded into this interactive domain. The present discussion examines performers' interaction with computers from the standpoint of connectivity. First, we briefly look at types of input to the performer, then ways of capturing output from the performer to feed to the computer, and finally interconnections that are more complex.

Input to the Performer

When playing along with a computer, the performer usually simply listens to the generated sound and responds accordingly, just as in conventional performance with other musicians. However, electronics can explicitly cue the performer. In the analog domain, performers sometimes wore headphones to hear tape-recorded cues. The composer Emmanuel Ghent (1925–2003) in the 1960s was the first to use the computer to cue performers in this way (Roads 1996a, p. 680). Visual cues can also be given. Of course, the canonical input to the performer is a visual score in traditional music notation. More recently, composers have used real-time updating of various sorts of computer-displayed notation to effect interactivity between the computer and the performer (Freeman 2008).

Output from the Performer

The electronic capture of performers' gestures has become an especially rich field of study in the 21st century. The annual international conference, New Interfaces for Musical Expression (NIME), had its inception in 2001. In addition to the NIME proceedings, refer to the textbook on controllers by Miranda and Wanderley (2006) and to the article by Jordà (2004). We consider here three categories of output: performance on traditional acoustic instruments or voice, performance with new controllers, and performance analogous to the traditional conductor's.

Performances by singers and traditional instrumentalists can be captured as audio and video and analyzed to create control data for sound generation. Alternatively, the addition of sensors allows the performer's gestures and motions to be measured more directly. The technological extension of traditional instruments turns them into "hyperinstruments," as they are called by Tod Machover of the MIT Media Laboratory. (This idea recalls McLuhan's "extensions of man" but applied to the tool rather than to the human, adding an additional layer of abstraction.)

There is a large body of work on alternative controllers, that is, new performance interfaces (see chapter 11 this volume, and the previously mentioned references). The great variety of such systems, and the present chapter's emphasis on software, preclude a satisfactory treatment here. However, a key point is that the introduction of computer technology bestowed the instrument designer with the option of a complete disjunction between the controller and the synthesis engine. Within this gap can lie one or more software layers that map the physical gestures to synthesis parameters or to higher-level musical events in a thoroughly flexible fashion. These include going beyond the one-to-one mapping of traditional instruments, where each note requires a separate gesture, to a one-to-many mapping in which a gesture can trigger a complex set of events. Given the disjunction between player and sound generation, an important direction in controller design is to mimic what Moore (1988) called the "control intimacy" of traditional instruments. Minimizing the temporal latency between gesture and sonic result is crucial (Moore 1988, Wessel and Wright 2002).

There is a fuzzy boundary between interfaces for instrumentalists and interfaces for conductors. Mathews was interested long ago in the metaphor of "conducting" electronic instruments. The GROOVE (Generated Real-Time Output Operations on Voltage-Controlled Equipment) system (Mathews and Moore 1970) was a hybrid digital/analog system that included a CONDUCT program; in the late 1980s, Mathews developed his Radio Baton controller, which was still not designed for traditional conducting. For a nonmetaphorical conductor, the technology exists to conduct music in real time through video- or sensor-based capture of traditional conducting gestures. The conducting gestures can control real-time sound synthesis, or they can control an audio recording by modifying its timing and dynamics through digital signal processing (Lee et al. 2006).

Networked Performance

Performers using networked computers can collectively control the generation of synthesized music. Conceptually, this is not necessarily distant from four-hand piano. However, networked performers can also control each other's instruments, perhaps only subtly modifying a certain parameter while allowing the performer of each instrument to retain overall control or perhaps changing each other's performances more drastically. This interdependent sort of performance represents a relatively new paradigm in music, a new kind of conjunction of musicians and of instruments. The League of Automatic Music Composers pioneered interdependent computer performance in the late 1970s (Bischoff et al. 1978). Weinberg (2005) proposed a taxonomy for such performance, in which control can be centralized or decentralized and interaction can be sequential or simultaneous (see fig. 2.4). The network can, of course, be the Internet. Viewed from another perspective, the Internet can serve as a point of disjunction, allowing performers to be decoupled in space from each other as well as from their audience.

The audience can become part of the composition, providing input to the computer system and thereby becoming (to some extent) performers and even composers themselves. Their input can affect both automatic sound synthesis and, via real-time updates to performance instructions, human sound production (Freeman 2008).

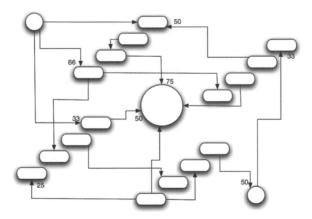

Figure 2.4 One example of a complex topology of networked performers, from Weinberg (2005). The circles represent computers serving as hubs, and the oblong shapes represent computers or digital instruments played by performers. The latter are arranged here in staircase patterns that indicate sequential operations, with one player's actions followed by another's. The numbers specify how much influence is exerted in a particular connection. (Used with the permission of MIT Press.)

C. Implications

The technology of computer music continues the older trends in music technology discussed in this chapter. Through a new intermediary, the computer, composers can avail themselves of new sonic possibilities and new levels of abstraction. The computer also permits the disintermediation of human performers and their instruments, with all their cognitive and physical constraints. In this case, the composer regains direct contact with sonic production and, in principle, gains unlimited control over the result. Conversely, the composer can relinquish control by only specifying the score algorithmically at a high level, for example, or by creating sound installations that vary depending on current conditions, including observers' actions. This release of control has many precedents in music, such as figured bass in the Baroque era and aleatoric composition in the 20th century.

With the computer, human physiology can be removed from the process of musical creation. However, given the physiological substrates of music, it is quite certain that musical performance will never become obsolete. Instead, humans will continue to find new expressive ways to map physical gestures into sonic results. Although the computer can certainly disintermediate the human performer, it is equally possible to disintermediate only the instrument, allowing the performer to transcend the limitations of conventional instruments.

Just as the composer can, in a sense, become a performer (directly creating the sound), the performer can, in a sense, become a conductor: controlling the sound in real time without being bound by the need to develop virtuosic technique on one or more conventional musical interfaces. The intrinsic idiosyncrasies of the instrument can vanish, to be replaced by whatever idiosyncratic mappings serve the performer's imaginative needs. Just as the computer frees the composer from a one-to-one mapping between compositional indication (notes on paper) and sonic result (sounding notes), so it frees the performer from a necessarily one-to-one mapping between gesture and sound. Like the composer (operating out of real time), the performer (operating in real time) can control arbitrarily complex musical processes. Composers and performers often play with the ambiguity and potential confusion between the expected conventional mappings or roles and newly possible ones. As a result, the clarity and theatricality of gesture become more important. The performer tends toward the dancer. Similarly, the dancer equipped with sensors can become a musical performer, controlling the music—or, as Siegel and Jacobsen (1998) say, "dancing the music."

4. THE COMPUTER AS MUSICIAN

The previous section was titled "Human Control of the Digital 'Instrument.'" What about interactivity? To the extent that the human musician's interaction with the computer cannot be termed "control," the computer is in at least one sense autonomous, and it starts to make sense to refer, at least metaphorically, to the computer as a musician. Of course, the ultimate control of the computer lies with the human who has programmed the computer. But, given the possible inclusion of machine-learning techniques and other forms of software complexity, the computer's behavior might not be predicted by its programmer. The threshold of autonomy is fuzzy. When does algorithmic composition software stop being just a human composer's tool and start becoming a composer itself? When does an instrument—or "hyperinstrument"—stop being just a human performer's tool and start becoming a performer itself?

A. The Computer as Composer

Even in his 1963 article on the "computer as a musical instrument," Mathews discussed other researchers' and composers' use of the computer for automated composition rather than for sound synthesis. Those people included Lejaren Hiller (1924–1994), James Tenney (1934–2006), and others. The book by Hiller and Isaacson (1959) includes the complete score for the world's first "serious" computer-generated composition, their *Illiac Suite for String Quartet*, constructed from September 1955 to November 1956 and published in 1957. (A short computer-generated song in a popular style, created in 1956 by two other programmers, is shown in Ames [1987].) Each of the *Illiac Suite's* four movements is the result of a different "experiment," with different musical results. The first two movements involve conventional counterpoint; the last two illustrate modern experimental styles. Thus, this early piece of computer-composed music illustrates two different aspects of algorithmic composition that have since been extensively developed: (1) emulation of a traditional style, as a sort of validation of the software's ability to solve a well-known musical problem; and (2) composition in a contemporary style, generally in service of a particular composer's aesthetic and creative needs. In the former category, significant contributions were made by investigators such as Schottstaedt (1984), Ebcioğlu (1985), Hörnel and Menzel (1998), and especially Cope (1996, 2004). (Some of these investigators are composers to whom category 2 also applies.) In the latter category, there are too many composers to list, but for this historical essay, special note must be made of the pioneers Iannis Xenakis (1922–2001), Gottfried Michael Koenig (b. 1926), and Herbert Brün (1918–2000), in addition to Hiller (who also collaborated with John Cage, 1912–1992) (see chapter 5, this volume).

In the category of style emulation, the software by David Cope (b. 1941), called Experiments in Musical Intelligence (1996), deserves special mention, not for the controversy it has engendered through its mimicking of famous classical composers, but for the number of years the composer has put into refining his software and for the sheer volume of the musical corpus it has produced. Counting individual movements as separate works, Cope calculated that he had created over a thousand finished compositions with his software. It seems likely that many of these works could pass a Turing test for all but the most musically knowledgeable listeners (see fig. 2.5). Regardless of one's view of these particular pieces, or of style emulation in general, the work is thought provoking because the future will certainly see many more such efforts of increasing sophistication, not all using Cope's methods, and because even Cope's techniques are not constrained to traditional styles. He has applied them to his own musical style, which

Figure 2.5 An excerpt from the first movement of David Cope's Emmy-Beethoven Symphony. (Used with the permission of David Cope and Spectrum Press.)

demonstrates that style emulation can be relevant to the second category of algorithmic composition mentioned.

The advent of computer-aided algorithmic composition of that second type represented a logical continuation of mathematical and formalized procedures in 20th-century music, such as serialism, Xenakis's stochastic composition, and Cage's chance music. Most composers of computer music who employ algorithmic compositional techniques would assert that in the case of their compositions, the computer is not a composer, only a compositional aid. There is indeed a spectrum of involvement available, ranging from simple calculations that solve a small musical problem or generate a bit of source material for further human manipulation, to systems that are intended to run as stand-alone generators of entire pieces, as was the case for each movement of the *Illiac Suite*. Composers of computer music have used a wide variety of algorithmic approaches. Representative categories include formal grammars, stochastic algorithms, genetic and other evolutionary algorithms, cellular automata, neural nets and other machine-learning techniques, and expert systems. Overviews of algorithmic composition include those by Ames (1987), Loy (1989), Roads (1996a), Chadabe (1997), and Essl (2007). Ariza (2005) has proposed a taxonomy of algorithmic composition systems.

B. The Computer as Performer

In considering a computer to be a "performer," there are several dimensions for classification. One can categorize the system based on its inputs and outputs; for example, it might accept keyboard and mouse events but not audio as input, and it might produce audio and video as output but not MIDI. One can examine what produces the sound: the computer itself, external synthesizers (e.g., via MIDI), physical musical instruments (via actuators), or humans (e.g., by automated conducting). One can also consider whether the machine is represented anthropomorphically, whether just through visual appearance or also through functional, robotic simulations of human body parts. Most important, though, one can assess the degree of "intelligence" the system exhibits. Does it have knowledge of musical conventions and styles in terms of either composition or performance practice (such as expressive deviation from metronomic timing)? Does it "listen" to other performers and react as a human musician might? Can it learn about music by listening to it? Can it improvise? Or, does it simply play back data that has been fixed in advance of the performance, oblivious of what might be going on around it? If it does more than the last, it exhibits some degree of what Rowe (2001) and others call machine musicianship. (Also see Jordà [2004] for an analytical discussion that treats intelligent and interactive systems within the framework of digital instruments.)

Robotics and Animated Characters

The computer that controls the playing of physical musical instruments represents a refinement of the old tradition of mechanical instruments, discussed in the section on antecedents. The player piano of a century ago has become a MIDI piano such as the Yamaha Disklavier (introduced in the 1980s), with the software-based MIDI sequence serving as an abstraction of the piano roll. Other instruments, conventional or innovative, can similarly be fitted with computer-controlled actuators (Kapur 2005). Musical robots have become increasingly so-phisticated, with Japanese efforts taking the lead. In 1985, researchers at Japan's Waseda University startled the computer music community by demonstrating WABOT-2, an anthropomorphic robot musician that had not only fingers to play an organ keyboard but also "eyes" (a camera) that read conventionally notated sheet music (Roads 1986). More recently, the Waseda group demonstrated an anthropomorphic robot flutist, complete with artificial lungs and lips (Solis et al. 2006). Other researchers are focusing on integrating machine musicianship into robots that can improvise (Weinberg and Driscoll 2006).

Indeed, the software challenges of machine musicianship are more broadly pertinent to computer music than are robot mechanics. Furthermore, anthropo-morphism is often more motivated by psychology than by functional necessity. However, anthropomorphism can also be obtained without robotics, through on-screen characters. As an example, Bos et al. (2006) implemented a virtual conduc-tor that directs a human ensemble whose players watch the animated character's traditional conducting patterns on a computer monitor. This virtual conductor incorporates machine-listening techniques, so it can react to the playing of the musicians it is conducting.

Machine Recognition of Music

There are numerous applications of machine recognition of music, whether the music takes the form of audio, sheet music, MIDI, or something else. Computer accompaniment of human performers, in the classical vein where the music is fully notated, required the development of score-following techniques (Dannenberg 1985, Vercoe 1985b). In these, the "score" was some computer representation of the music rather than traditional musical notation, and the computer "listened" to a human soloist. Actual optical music recognition (OMR), having sheet music as input, originated with research at MIT in the 1960s and became commercially available in the 1990s. Although designed for other musical applications, OMR can be incorporated in live performance, as prefigured by the WABOT-2 system.

More crucial than the ability to read music is the ability to hear it and parse what is heard into musical units. On the part of a computer, this ability is generally called *automatic transcription* (Moorer 1975, Klapuri and Davy 2006), a term that suggests but does not require traditional notation as the output. Real-time recog-nition of previously unknown music, combined with some musical knowledge, would permit the computer to improvise. Such a task is simplified when the input is MIDI rather than audio. Once the musical units, such as notes, are recognized, there are many paths the computer could take in response. For example, it could select harmonies to accompany an input melody, or it could improvise by extend-ing the melody further, as in the case of François Pachet's Continuator (Pachet

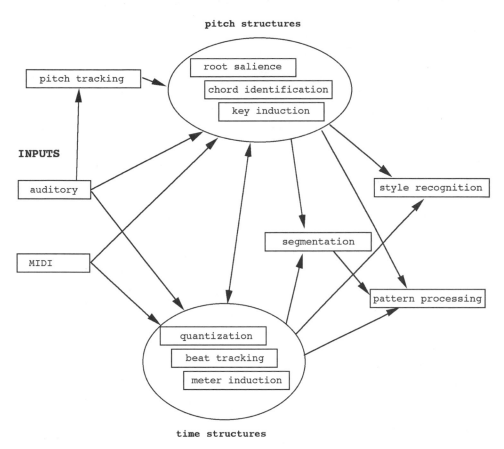

Figure 2.6 The overall architecture of a machine-musicianship system, from Rowe (2001). (Used with the permission of MIT Press.)

2002). Figure 2.6, from Rowe (2001), shows a typical architecture for a machine musicianship system in which the inputs are either MIDI or audio.

Expression

Traditional notation specifies music with symbols that are perfectly quantized in pitch and time. The score says to play a quarter-note A on the fourth beat, not to play 441 Hz for 0.8 s starting at 0.08 s after the beat, with a vibrato rate of 5.1 Hz and a deviation of ±3 Hz. A crucial part of a musician's knowledge consists of understanding how to render the music with expressive deviations from the putative regularity of the abstract symbols, based on the musical context and style. Machine musicianship benefits from research that quantifies and makes explicit these normally intuitive and implicit rules. Such research at Stockholm's Kungliga Tekniska Högskolan (KTH), or Royal Institute of Technology, has resulted in over 60 publications (http://www.speech.kth.se/music/performance/). The KTH rules for expressive performance have been embedded in MIDI sequencers (Friberg et al. 2000) and can accommodate real-time updates similar to conducting (Friberg 2006).

C. Implications

Research areas such as OMR, automatic transcription of musical audio, and other types of music information retrieval (MIR) were developed primarily for nonperformance applications, but they can be turned to creative use in performance, as other technical areas have been, especially if real-time implementations are possible. The goal of machine musicianship encourages "computer music," in the sense of a creative practice, to harness the wide-ranging resources of "computer music," in the sense of a technical field.

Computer performance can range from the trivial, with the machine exhibiting no more intelligence than a tape recorder, to the complex, with the computer interacting with human musicians, playing in a way that listeners consider expressive, and improvising. However, simply matching human performance may be more interesting to science than to art. As Nancarrow's work for player piano demonstrates, composers may find machine performance of music to be of most interest when the machine does something that human performers cannot.

As for machine composition, Cope's prolific experiments point to a future in which the validity of computers' musical output is no longer at issue. Just as the intermediary of notation led to the development of a new musical role, the meta-performer (i.e., the conductor), so has the intermediary of the computer led to a new role that we could call the meta-composer. Instead of working directly on a composition, the meta-composer (the prime example thus far being Cope) works with an automated or semiautomated system that can produce many more compositions than a human could in one lifetime working unaided. This again is an example of abstraction, disjunction, one-to-many mapping, and proliferation. The composer removes himself or herself from the details of creating a specific composition while producing a great many compositions, just as the conductor does not perform on a specific instrument but at a high level controls them all. To state that this new paradigm exists is not to denigrate the creative art of composers who work otherwise, including without a computer, or to claim that human postprocessing cannot improve the output of automated systems. However, a reflexively negative response would invite comparison with historical reactions to the Copernican revolution and similar upsets. Moreover, limitations of current computer models are hardly cause for a self-satisfied proclamation of some uniquely human ability that must lie beyond the reach of automata; similar claims in the past have fallen victim to advances in science and technology, and computer music is a young field.

5. CONCLUSION

Contemplating what Chadabe (1997, p. 21) called the "great opening up of music to all sound," as well as Schoenberg's modernist application of algorithms in the creative process, it is clear that the 20th century fundamentally redefined music. The new definition subsumed, rather than eliminated, the old. An important contributor to the redefinition was the introduction of electronically generated or captured sound, culminating in computer music technology, which has likewise expanded the definition of the musical instrument.

Similarly, the 21st century is fundamentally redefining the musician in a way that subsumes the old definition. There are several parts to this redefinition (all of which continue trends from the 20th century):

1. *The composer*: The interjection of arbitrarily complex algorithms into the compositional process allows the composer to operate on the music at as high or as low a level as desired. Whereas the traditional composer operates on the same level as the performer, writing the individual notes that the performer will play, the composer who uses algorithms may work at a higher level. At the high end of the scale, the composer can become what we have referred to as a meta-composer. At a lower level, in creating synthesis models and fashioning sounds directly, the composer takes on the roles of the instrument builder and performer.

2. *The performer*: The completion of the process of disjoining the control interface from the sound generator means that human musicianship need not be so focused on developing physical dexterity and can focus on higher-level control with flexible mapping of gesture to sonic result—the instrumentalist tends to become a conductor. Performers may develop and perfect their own individual interfaces and mappings. Performers may be networked together and control each other's performances.

3. *The public*: The ubiquity of sufficiently powerful computer hardware and the availability of sufficiently flexible software help to democratize music-making, allowing people with less training to craft and perform music. (Even a young schoolchild can use the GarageBand software, for example.) This is not to say that the amateur's musical output will be as sophisticated as the trained musician's, only that the amateur's output can achieve a previously inconceivable degree of polish. This is because the expert's musical knowledge and control have been virtualized, that is, abstracted and disjoined from the person and moved into the tools. Also, the disjunction between control and sound generation allows the network, such as the Internet, to act as an intermediary, conjoining users across space in collaborative music-making. Similarly, the flexible mapping of control information afforded by computer technology means that an audience can participate in a performance in numerous ways, directly affecting the rendering and even the composition of the music that the computer or the human performers play.

4. *The machine*: The ongoing advances in machine musicianship suggest that the term *musician* will increasingly be used metaphorically to refer to automated processes. When people habitually use a metaphorical term, the

sense of metaphor diminishes, so it is entirely possible, if not likely, that the word *musician* will come to refer, in common usage, to either a human or an automated entity. Anthropomorphic robots and on-screen characters, while unnecessary in principle, will probably accelerate the adoption of the new meaning.

Paradoxically, the ability of the computer to mimic, transform, and in some respects exceed conventional human music-making could serve to refocus humans' concern on the corporeal and emotional aspects of music—bringing to a full circle the process of disjunction that began with the externalization of sound production from the body. However, the arts do not follow preordained paths, and the subjective aspects of human experience are not off-limits for computer modeling, so such prognostication would simply be speculative. It is more likely that such a trend would intersect with others in different directions.

In summary, the historical development of music technology can be viewed as human creativity's drawing on the primal act of singing and proliferating it out from the body through a multitude of ingenious devices. These started with musical instruments and included tools to extend music across space and time. There is a web of interrelationships among musicians and these devices. As the generalization of the tool, computer technology can be inserted at any juncture in this network, augmenting or replacing instruments or musicians through disjunctions and new conjunctions. The resulting profusion of potential physical and virtual interconnections holds the seeds of countless sonic manifestations, which collectively constitute the musically possible. From these, it is the role of the artist to extract the musically meaningful.

Acknowledgments: In addition to this volume's editor (Roger Dean), the following individuals provided helpful suggestions after reading an earlier draft of this chapter: Thom Blum, Tim Perkis, Curtis Roads, and Robert Rowe.

BIBLIOGRAPHY

Ames, C. 1987. Automated composition in retrospect: 1956–1986. *Leonardo* 20(2): 169–185.

Ariza, C. 2005. Navigating the landscape of computer-aided algorithmic composition systems: a definition, seven descriptors, and a lexicon of systems and research. In *Proceedings of the International Computer Music Conference.* San Francisco: International Computer Music Association, pp. 765–772.

Bargar, R. 1993. Virtual sound composition for the CAVE. In *Proceedings of the 1993 International Computer Music Conference.* San Francisco: International Computer Music Association, p. 154.

Bischoff, J., R. Gold, and J. Horton. 1978. Microcomputer network music. *Computer Music Journal* 2(3): 24–29.

Bos, P., D. Reidsma, Z. M. Ruttkay, and A. Nijholt. 2006. Interacting with a virtual conductor. In *Proceedings of 5th International Conference on Entertainment Computing.* Lecture Notes in Computer Science 4161. Berlin: Springer Verlag, pp. 25–30.

Boulanger, R., ed. 2000. *The Csound Book: Perspectives in Software Synthesis, Sound Design, Signal Processing, and Programming.* Cambridge: MIT Press.

Cadoz, C., A. Luciani, and J. Florens. 1984. Responsive input devices and sound synthesis by simulation of instrumental mechanisms: The Cordis system. *Computer Music Journal* 8(3): 60–73.

Chadabe, J. 1997. *Electric Sound: The Past and Promise of Electronic Music.* Upper Saddle River, NJ: Prentice-Hall.

Chowning, J. 1971. The simulation of moving sound sources. *Journal of the Audio Engineering Society* 19: 2–6.

Chowning, J. 1973. The synthesis of complex audio spectra by means of frequency modulation. *Journal of the Audio Engineering Society* 21(7): 526–534.

Chowning, J. 2005. Composer le son lui-même. In *Portraits Polychromes no. 7: John Chowning,* ed. E. Gayou. Paris: Michel de Maule, pp. 25–30.

Computer Music Journal. 2004. Editor's note, in DVD Program Notes. [Includes a transcription of Frank Cooper's 1994 audio commentary on the production of computer music in Manchester in 1951. The music and commentary appear on the accompanying disc.] *Computer Music Journal* 28(4): 126–127.

Cope, D. 1996. *Experiments in Musical Intelligence.* Madison, WI: A-R Editions.

Cope, D. 2004. *Virtual Music: Computer Synthesis of Musical Style.* Cambridge: MIT Press.

Dannenberg, R. 1985. An on-line algorithm for real-time accompaniment. In *Proceedings of the International Computer Music Conference 1984.* San Francisco: International Computer Music Association, pp. 193–198.

Dannenberg, R. 1997. Machine tongues XIX: Nyquist, a language for composition and sound synthesis. *Computer Music Journal* 21(3): 50–60.

Davies, H. 2001. Electronic instruments. In *The New Grove Dictionary of Music and Musicians,* vol. 8, 2nd ed., ed. S. Sadie. London: Macmillan, pp. 67–107.

Dolson, M. 1982. "A tracking phase vocoder and its use in the analysis of ensemble sounds." Ph.D. thesis, California Institute of Technology.

Ebcioğlu, K. 1985. An expert system for Schenkerian synthesis of chorales in the style of J. S. Bach. In *Proceedings of the 1984 International Computer Music Conference.* San Francisco: International Computer Music Association, pp. 135–142.

Essl, K. 2007. Algorithmic composition. In *The Cambridge Companion to Electronic Music,* ed. N. Collins and J. d'Escrivan. Cambridge: Cambridge University Press, pp. 107–125.

Freeman, J. 2008. Extreme sight-reading, mediated expression, and audience participation: real-time music notation in live performance. *Computer Music Journal* 32(3): 25–41.

Friberg, A. 2006. pDM: An expressive sequencer with real-time control of the KTH music performance rules. *Computer Music Journal* 30(1): 37–48.

Friberg, A., V. Colombo, L. Frydén, and J. Sundberg. 2000. Generating musical performances with Director Musices. *Computer Music Journal* 24(3): 23–29.

Gerzon, M. 1973. Periphony: With-height sound reproduction. *Journal of the Audio Engineering Society* 21(1): 2–10.

Grey, J. M. 1975. "An exploration of musical timbre." Ph.D. thesis, Stanford University.

Hill, D., trans. and comm. 1979. *The Book of Ingenious Devices (Kitáb al-Hiyal) by the Banú (sons of) Músà bin Shákir.* Dordrecht, Netherlands: Reidel.

Hiller, L. A., and L. M. Isaacson. 1959. *Experimental Music: Composition with an Electronic Computer.* New York: McGraw-Hill.

Hörnel, D., and W. Menzel. 1998. Learning musical structure and style with neural networks. *Computer Music Journal* 22(4): 44–62.

Jones, R., and B. Nevile. 2005. Creating visual music in Jitter: Approaches and techniques. *Computer Music Journal* 29(4): 55–70.

Jordà, S. 2004. Instruments and players: Some thoughts on digital lutherie. *Journal of New Music Research* 33(3): 321–341.

Kapur, A. 2005. A history of robotic musical instruments. In *Proceedings of the International Computer Music Conference*. San Francisco: International Computer Music Association, pp. 21–28.

Kassler, M., and H. Howe. 1980. Computers and music. In *The New Grove Dictionary of Music and Musicians*, vol. 4, 1st ed., ed. S. Sadie. London: Macmillan, pp. 603–615.

Klapuri, A., and M. Davy. 2006. *Signal Processing Methods for Music Transcription*. New York: Springer.

Landy, L. 2007. *Understanding the Art of Sound Organization*. Cambridge: MIT Press.

Lee, E., T. Karrer, and J. Borchers. 2006. Toward a framework for interactive systems to conduct digital audio and video streams. *Computer Music Journal* 30(1): 21–36.

Loy, D. G. 1989. Composing with computers: A survey of some compositional formalisms and music programming languages. In *Current Directions in Computer Music Research*, ed. M. V. Mathews and J. R. Pierce. Cambridge: MIT Press, pp. 291–396.

Manning, P. 2004. *Electronic and Computer Music*. Rev. and expanded ed. New York: Oxford University Press.

Mathews, M. 1963. The digital computer as a musical instrument. *Science* 142(3592): 553–557.

Mathews, M. 1969. *The Technology of Computer Music*. Cambridge: MIT Press.

Mathews, M., and F. R. Moore. 1970. GROOVE—a program to compose, store, and edit functions of time. *Communications of the ACM* 13(12): 715–721.

McCartney, J. 2002. Rethinking the computer music language: SuperCollider. *Computer Music Journal* 26(4): 61–68.

McLuhan, M. 1964. *Understanding Media: The Extensions of Man*. Cambridge: MIT Press.

Miranda, E. R., and M. Wanderley. 2006. *New Digital Musical Instruments: Control and Interaction beyond the Keyboard*. Middleton, WI: A-R Editions.

Moore, F. R. 1988. The dysfunctions of MIDI. *Computer Music Journal* 12(1): 19–28.

Moorer, J. A. 1975. "On the segmentation and analysis of continuous musical sound by digital computer." Ph.D. thesis, Stanford University.

Moorer, J. A. 1978. The use of the phase vocoder in computer music applications. *Journal of the Audio Engineering Society* 26(1/2): 42–45.

Nichols, C. 2002. The vBow: A virtual violin bow controller for mapping gesture to synthesis with haptic feedback. *Organised Sound* 7(2): 215–220.

Pachet, F. 2002. The Continuator: Musical interaction with style. In *Proceedings of the 2002 International Computer Music Conference*. San Francisco: International Computer Music Association, pp. 211–218.

Pope, S. T. 1994. Editor's notes: A taxonomy of computer music. *Computer Music Journal* 18(1): 5–7.

Puckette, M. 1997. Pure Data. In *Proceedings of the International Computer Music Conference*. San Francisco: International Computer Music Association, pp. 224–227.

Puckette, M. 2002. Max at seventeen. *Computer Music Journal* 26(4): 31–43.

Rhea, T. 1972. "The evolution of electronic musical instruments in the United States." Ph.D. thesis, George Peabody College, Nashville, TN.

Risset, J.-C. 1969. *An Introductory Catalogue of Computer Synthesized Sounds*. Murray Hill, NJ: Bell Telephone Laboratories.

Roads, C. 1978. Automated granular synthesis of sound. *Computer Music Journal* 2(2): 61–62.

Roads, C. 1986. The Tsukuba Musical Robot. *Computer Music Journal* 10(2): 39–43.

Roads, C. 1996a. *The Computer Music Tutorial.* Second printing (pbk.). Cambridge: MIT Press.

Roads, C. 1996b. Early electronic music instruments: Time line 1899–1950. *Computer Music Journal* 20(3): 20–23.

Roads, C. 2001. *Microsound.* Cambridge: MIT Press.

Rowe, R. 2001. *Machine Musicianship.* Cambridge: MIT Press.

Scaletti, C. 2002. Computer music languages, Kyma, and the future. *Computer Music Journal* 26(4): 69–82.

Schottstaedt, W. 1984. *Automatic Species Counterpoint.* Stanford Technical Report STAN-M-19, Stanford University, Palo Alto, CA.

Siegel, W., and J. Jacobsen. 1998. The challenges of interactive dance: An overview and case study. *Computer Music Journal* 22(4): 29–43.

Smith, J. 1992. Physical modeling using digital waveguides. *Computer Music Journal* 16(4): 74–91.

Solis, J., K. Chida, K. Taniguchi, S. Hashimoto, K. Suefuji, and A. Takanishi. 2006. The Waseda flutist robot WF-4RII in comparison with a professional flutist. *Computer Music Journal* 30(4): 12–27.

Vercoe, B. 1985a. *Csound: A Manual for the Audio-processing System.* Program documentation. Cambridge: MIT Media Lab.

Vercoe, B. 1985b. The synthetic performer in the context of live musical performance. In *Proceedings of the International Computer Music Conference 1984.* San Francisco: International Computer Music Association, pp. 199–200.

Wang, G., and P. Cook. 2003. ChucK: A concurrent and on-the-fly audio programming language. In *Proceedings of the 2003 International Computer Music Conference.* San Francisco: International Computer Music Association, pp. 219–226.

Weinberg, G. 2005. Interconnected musical networks: Toward a theoretical framework. *Computer Music Journal* 29(2): 23–39.

Weinberg, G., and S. Driscoll. 2006. Toward robotic musicianship. *Computer Music Journal* 30(4): 28–45.

Wessel, D. 1979. Timbre space as a musical control structure. *Computer Music Journal* 3(2): 45–52.

Wessel, D., and M. Wright. 2002. Problems and prospects for intimate musical control of computers. *Computer Music Journal* 26(3): 11–22.

CHAPTER 3

EARLY HARDWARE AND EARLY IDEAS IN COMPUTER MUSIC: THEIR DEVELOPMENT AND THEIR CURRENT FORMS

PAUL DOORNBUSCH

THE great adventure of music in the 20th and 21st centuries is the use of computers. There have been enormous challenges to overcome for the pioneers of computer music, from original and unique technical requirements to new aesthetics. The result of these developments is now a dominant musical activity. There are many ideas and events in the early practice of computer music that are still evident today in one guise or another.

There is no linear trajectory or chronology to the history of computer music; it consists of a disparate conglomerate of discrete events. However, it is this milieu of events that makes computer music possible. There have always been those musicians and composers who engage with the latest technical advances, whether they are drawn steel strings, advanced mechanical instrument construction possibilities, or general-purpose machines such as the computer. These people have imaginative, creative uses for the technology, and they use it to expand their creativity.

While now routine, there was a time when the use of computers to make music was, if not exactly outrageous, then certainly highly unusual and controversial. This seems incongruous when we realize that composers and musicians have *always* embraced new technology to creative ends. While some traditionalists still find the use of computers in music abhorrent, to others it is an inevitable development of sublime beauty. For the enthusiastic, computer music still maintains an aura of a particular aesthetic and technical possibilities. For most others, computers in music are a ubiquitous fact, from CD playback to digital recording, editing, and production techniques.

Whatever the case, it was mostly a trail of small and uncoordinated steps that led to this use of computers in music. Often enough, a technical development in one area would spur a creative development in another, and sometimes a creative need would encourage a technical response. These developments were usually not seen at the time as scientific, artistic, or commercial. Ideas relating to complex compositional techniques, sound synthesis, musical instrument design, microtonality, and the enthralling power of the computation machine all contributed to a climate in which something called "computer music" emerged.

However incomplete this narrative must be, as a complete treatment would take a book, some of it will be of intentional developments, but other parts will be engineering advances, which were sometimes accidentally useful in a musical context. Oscillators and waveform generators, noise generators, filters, random number generators, numerical techniques, algorithm development, and so on are all examples of technical developments that found use in musical contexts. It is easy, from this artistic and historically distant standpoint, to devalue computer music's initial buzzes, squawks, and arcana as irrelevant. Nevertheless, an examination conscious of how the current artistic, scientific, and consumer-oriented reality has been shaped by the past, and still expresses many of the initial ideas from the past, would do well to note the achievements, effort, and dedication of these pioneers for it is their achievements that are the basis for what we have today.

1. Early Machines, Developments, and the First Steps in Computer Music

Early computer music developments were bound to the early machines on which they occurred. These computers were much more primitive than what is commonplace today and were what are now called mainframe computers. Typically, they occupied a large room, used vacuum tubes (valves) or discrete transistors as logic devices, were very slow by today's standards, and often ran in a time-share environment in which users submitted their program, or *job*, and returned later (usually the next day) to collect the output of their program. They did not have screens to interact with the user; they were typically controlled by a console with switches, lights, and buttons; and the data and programs were stored on punched-paper tape, punched cards, or magnetic tapes mounted on tape drives the size of large refrigerators. Memory was typically cathode ray tubes, mercury delay lines, magnetic core memory, and so on and usually only a few kilobytes. Mainframes and the slightly more friendly mini-computers were the typical computer until the very early 1980s.

Australia's CSIRAC (Council for Scientific and Industrial Research Automatic Computer) was the first computer to play music,[1] but through a series of conser-vative administrative decisions and missed opportunities it contributed little to what we now know as computer music. CSIRAC was developed by the Australian Commonwealth organization CSIR (Council for Scientific and Industrial Re-search), and it played music publicly in November 1951 at Australia's first comput-ing conference, although the musical programming of CSIRAC had been occurring for about a year or more. CSIRAC, now regarded as the fourth or fifth all-electronic digital computer in the world, was programmed by Geoff Hill to play popular tunes of the day, "Colonel Bogey," "Girl with Flaxen Hair," and so on. In 1957, another programmer, Tom Cherry, extended the music programming on CSIRAC and developed a program that would take a "score" tape (punched-paper tape) as input to be performed. CSIRAC was one of the very earliest computers and making it play music was a feat. Some of CSIRAC's details are as follows: it used over 2,000 "valves"; required 30 kW to run; had 768 ten-bit words of memory (one word was equal to 2 "bytes") and 2,048 words of disk storage; had a major-cycle frequency of 0.001 MHz and a computational power of about 0.0005 millions of instructions per second (MIPS); occupied 45 m² and weighed 7,000 kg.

CSIRAC, a primitive computer, had limited interaction possibilities, and one of them was a loudspeaker used by sending raw pulses from the serial bus to make what the programmers called a "blurt." This was used to indicate that a program had terminated or as a debugging aid to indicate the part of the program being executed. A few pulses were sent to the speaker to make the sound. Hill, Australia's first software engineer, came from a musical family and had perfect pitch. It would have been natural for him to ponder if the blurt could be turned into a steady tone by sending pulses to the speaker at a regular period. This was not as simple as it sounds because CSIRAC was a low-speed (1-kHz major clock), serial architecture computer, and each of the memory locations in the mercury acoustic delay line memory took a different *time* to access. Thus, programming pulses to arrive at the loudspeaker with a regular period (to make a steady tone) took considerable programming gymnas-tics and cunning. Only the few best programmers were able to achieve this in the fifteen years of CSIRAC's service. Because the sound generation mechanism was not using a digital-to-analog converter (DAC), there were no variable sound synthesis possibilities. One important characteristic of the musical activity was that it was all real time, and it was possible to make limited changes in tempo and pitch from the console while the piece was playing. It would be many years before computer music was again a real-time activity. Unlike the computers that immediately followed it, CSIRAC was operated by a single user who sat at the console and interacted with it, much like today's personal computers (PCs).

CSIRAC, developed as a scientific tool, found some use as a musical instrument but because of the lack of managerial enthusiasm for the activity, composers were never involved; thus, the musical activity was not developed further. There were early attempts by the engineers to do more with the music, but funding was directed elsewhere, and the computing activities were slowly reduced until CSIRAC was transferred from Sydney to Melbourne in 1955 and resumed service at The University of Melbourne. Musical activity also occurred there, particularly with a new program by Cherry, but there was a general ignorance of the significance of the development, and Percy Grainger, an adventurous local composer, was never put in touch with the machine despite regularly walking past the computation laboratory.

The real groundbreaking phase of computer music developments began at Bell Laboratories, where Max Mathews, with the support of John Pierce, developed the MUSIC-N family of music programming languages. Bell Labs, with vast research resources, was interested in sound research and computers for telephony usage; while related to this, the music activity was unofficial. It was in 1957 when Mathews finished MUSIC I, which was a basic sound-generating program for the International Business Machines (IBM) 704 mainframe. A key hardware development that was useful for Mathews was the DAC, which was not available on CSIRAC. Today, DACs are built into every computer and allow for digital information to be turned into analog voltage and sound. The IBM 704 had 4,096 words (of 36 bits) of magnetic core memory, hardware floating-point support, magnetic tape storage (5 megabits per tape), and magnetic "drum" storage and could perform over 4,000 multiplications per second or almost 40,000 simpler operations per second. It was considered an important and leading-edge machine.

The MUSIC-N languages developed from MUSIC I in 1957 to MUSIC V in 1968, and each new version included a number of advances, many of which are still evident in music software. MUSIC I was a monophonic program with only triangle waves for sound output, but importantly it took as input a *score* file of instructions of what to play. This is similar to what happened with CSIRAC in Melbourne at the same time; the Music Programme would play a score tape (of punched paper) in real time. MUSIC II in 1958 was a little more advanced, but MUSIC III (for the IBM 7094), in 1959, was a major step forward and introduced the important concept of modularity with the unit generator or UGen. This is the sort of nitty-gritty idea that in hindsight seems unreasonably wise for its day, along with the score and orchestra files for sound events and sound synthesis, respectively, and the table lookup oscillator. A UGen is a predefined unit of functionality, such as an oscillator, envelope generator, filter, audio input or output, and so on. UGens are combined in the orchestra file to make *instruments*, which create the sounds for the events defined in the score file. Some UGens take audio input, and they all take control input.

All of the MUSIC-N programs up to and including MUSIC IV were written in assembly language that was machine specific. This means that when the computer changed, the software had to be rewritten. MUSIC V was written in 1968 for the IBM System/360, but it was written in FORTRAN, a popular high-level language that was portable. The IBM S/360 was the first machine to standardize on 8-bit bytes and 32-bit words, and while it came in many variants, it typically had about 4 MB of disk storage, 4–8 KB of core memory, tape storage, and punched-card readers. This FORTRAN version of MUSIC became popular with researchers and universities as Mathews gave it away and it was relatively easy to make it work on many other and different computers. Later, MUSIC 10 was developed from this version to run on the Digital Equipment Corporation's (DEC) PDP-10 mainframe computers. However, while achievable, this was not trivial as the program was stored on over 3,000 punched cards.

While the popularity and availability of MUSIC V was a great advance in computer music, it was still very difficult to use. Often, computers were not available, a composer had to take a box of punched cards of the score and orchestra files to a computing facility where the job would be run, usually overnight because it could take many hours to compute a minute of audio. If there was an error, it would need to be corrected and resubmitted. Once the program ran properly, the composer would be handed a magnetic tape, but this was a digital tape of *samples*. Then, the composer would usually have to go to another facility, perhaps a long drive away, to have the digital tape played through a DAC and recorded to an analog tape. Only then, several days to several weeks after finishing the program, would the end result be heard.

One of the key decisions made by Mathews and Pierce at an early stage was to have composers and musicians involved in the program. They had met Milton Babbitt in 1959 along with Vladimir Ussachevsky, James Tenney, Otto Leuning, and later Edgard Varèse. James Tenney joined Bell Labs in 1961 to work on psycho-acoustics, but in reality he worked on computer music and stayed until 1964. The input from musicians greatly helped shape the development of the MUSIC-N languages. For example, composers wanted polyphony, variable tunings, flexible and variable timbres and timing, and so on. This directed the software development effort. Tenney was the first recognized composer to work at Bell Labs, and he produced some of the important work there, including *Analog #1: Noise Study* (1961) and *Four Stochastic Studies* (1962). *Analog #1: Noise Study* used MUSIC III to synthesize various kinds of controlled noise, and the form is also realized with a random number method. The *Four Stochastic Studies* required that he write a computer program, PLF 2, to compose them.

The MUSIC-N languages have been very influential because of their extremely elegant concepts: the UGen concept, the orchestra file that takes (time-varying) parameters for the sound synthesis, the score file that defines the timed events with the sounds from the orchestra file, and the table lookup oscillator. Indeed, the plug-ins of today are logically very similar to a MUSIC-N instrument: both output sounds in samples, and these may be mixed and controlled with pitch and duration commands; also they both take parameters (automation) to modify the sounds. Another influence is with the Moving Picture Experts Group 4 (MPEG-4) specification for the Structured Audio Orchestra Language (SAOL), a language for synthesis and signal processing that borrows greatly from MUSIC-N.

Another important development, at about the same time as MUSIC-N, took place at the University of Illinois, where Lejaren Hiller and Leonard Isaacson worked on computer-assisted algorithmic composition. In 1955, Hiller and Isaacson undertook the first experiments in computer-generated music by applying musical rules and later randomness. Hiller and Isaacson used the ILLIAC I computer, which was similar in some ways to CSIRAC, with 2,800 valves or vacuum tubes, storage of 1,024 (40-bit) words in memory (5 KB), magnetic drum storage of 12,800 (40-bit) words (64 KB), and punched-paper tape use.

Hiller asked the important question, "Why would anyone want to make music with a computer?" The answer he supplied is that because computers are excellent at organizing and selecting data, and this is similar to at least some aspects of composition, so computers should be useful for composition. After some initial experimentation with writing parts of the ILLIAC String Quartet, he concluded that the most successful results were obtained using controlled randomness and applying general abstractions to compositional problems rather than applying music theory rules. This idea was enthusiastically used (and separately arrived at) by Iannis Xenakis at about the same time and later by Gottfried Michael Koenig. Of course, there were no graphical displays or MIDI (Musical Instrument Digital Interface); musical information was coded as numbers and entered into programs via punched cards or punched-paper tape. The output would be printed (possibly after being first output to tape) as numbers representing notes and durations and then transferred to musical notation by hand.

2. COMPUTING ARCHITECTURES AND HOW THEY CHANGED MUSIC

Part of the history of computer music is also the history of computing because hardware and software developments in the computing world directly affected the computer music world. As discussed, the nature of computing in its early days—mainframe computers in time-share facilities, punched-card inputs, and fanfold printouts or (nine-track) digital magnetic tape output—was also part of the nature of computer music. These limitations of the technology, and the lack of what is now called "user friendliness," had a direct impact on what sort of computer music was created. This is also true as computing developed, and a brief overview of computing architectures will help this discussion. The performance of computers, especially older and larger machines, is difficult to quantify in modern terms.

Often, there were architectural differences (e.g., overlapping instruction execution and memory accesses) that allowed for performance greater than the "cycle time," memory access time, or central processing unit (CPU) speed would simplistically indicate. To give an approximate idea of the performance, there will be ratings of millions of instructions per second (MIPS) for some computers. While these are sometimes controversial measurements, seen as flawed or misleading and often meaningless, they are only an approximate indication of relative performance and sufficiently illustrative for the current purpose.

A. Mainframe Computer

A mainframe is a very large computer, typically these days with many CPUs and large storage capacity, along with large data input and output (I/O) capability. Mainframes have always had large word sizes of, typically, 32–36 bits, and large storage capacity (initially many megabytes of data, even if it was relatively slow magnetic tape), and as much central memory as possible, from a few kilobytes at the beginning. These are what governments and large companies use for their data processing. They have very secure operating systems, and while the CPU may be no faster than what is now in a PC, the data processing capacity is vastly superior because of the I/O speed (i.e., much faster memory, disk, and network access). This of course makes them very expensive and large, requiring temperature-controlled rooms and so on. Mainframes from the 1960s included very advanced concepts in their architecture that have taken several decades to appear in PCs today. Mainframes typically have proprietary operating systems that may be arcane for programming, but their reliability, security, and I/O capacity makes them attractive in certain situations, such as banking, for which some mainframes have operated for ten years without interruption, even when undergoing maintenance or upgrades.

The first computers were basically mainframes, even if they did not initially have a time-sharing operating system. Examples of mainframe computers are the IBM 704 (1954), IBM 1401 (1959), IBM 7040 (1961), IBM S/360 (1967), IBM zSeries (current), and many computers from the likes of Honeywell, Control Data Corporation, Burroughs, Amdahl, Hitachi, and so on. Today, mainframes are mostly used to serve data to other computing systems. As an indication of the performance of some of these machines, an IBM 704 was capable of 0.006–0.04 MIPS, and the IBM S/360 came in different configurations from about 0.025 to 1.25 MIPS. By the mid-1970s, mainframes were typically capable of a performance of about 1–5 MIPS.

B. Minicomputers

Minicomputers were developed in the 1960s and became popular in the 1970s. Minicomputers were smaller than mainframes and took up one or two electrical cabinets, about the size of one or two large refrigerators. They were smaller than mainframe computers in others ways, such as being 8- or 16-bit computers and having lower memory, storage, and I/O capability. The first minicomputer, the PDP-1, was developed by DEC. Because they were relatively low cost, minicomputers were popular and found their way into university computing and research departments as well as industry and commerce.

There were many new computing applications developed on minicomputers, and music applications were no exception. The DEC PDP-11, PDP-15, and VAX-11/780 computers became a staple in universities, and the MUSIC-N languages made a natural progression to them. With the differing configurations available, there was a range of performance for all of these machines, but the PDP-11s were capable of about 0.3–1 MIPS, and the VAX-11/780s were capable of about 0.5–1 MIPS. Minicomputers also developed sophisticated operating system environments, which were multiuser and multitasking—UNIX was developed on, and for, minicomputers. DEC, IBM, Hewlett-Packard, Honeywell-Bull, Data General, and others all manufactured minicomputers for many years. However, with the rise in power of the microprocessor and the PC, minicomputers were not widespread for so long.

C. Microcomputers and Personal Computers

The microprocessor—a single integrated-circuit processor—is the main processing unit of the microcomputer and the PC. Semiconductor fabrication progress and miniaturization allowed the development of a small microprocessor on a single chip in the very early 1970s. These were very limited, but by the mid-1970s generally useful microprocessors were readily available. Because they were small and inexpensive, computers built around these microprocessors were regarded in their early years as little more than toys or curiosities for hobbyists. Often sold as kits and with as little as a few hundred bytes of memory, they also usually had no I/O devices other than switches and lights and used cassette tapes for storage. The KIM-1, for example, had an 8-bit 6502 microprocessor that operated at 1 MHz, 1,024 bytes of memory, a cassette interface for storage (very slow), a hexadecimal keypad for input, no power supply or case, and a cost of U.S. $245 in 1975. Many single-purpose business machines were developed around microprocessors (e.g., the dedicated word processor), but these were eventually supplanted by the PC. As semiconductor memory became less expensive, along with floppy disk storage and the increasing power of microprocessors, these small machines became popular as home devices; such computers were the Apple II, Commodore 64, Atari, BBC Micro, Tandy TRS-80, and so on. These used a microprocessor from either Intel (typically an 8080), Motorola (often the 6502 or 6800), or Zilog (Z80) and had a simple operating system that allowed for program launching and directory/file listing. IBM entered the microcomputer market relatively late in 1981 with the IBM personal computer (PC), based on the Intel 8088 microprocessor. In the early to mid-1980s, microcomputers from, for example, IBM, were capable of about 0.25 MIPS, while the Apple Macintosh was capable of about 0.5 MIPS. The term *personal computer* has replaced the term *microcomputer*, and they have developed remarkably from their humble beginnings, to the point at which now PCs are the dominant computing force, with PC technology affecting and now appearing in mainframes and supercomputers. Now PCs have the power to process many millions of complex mathematical operations a second (5,000–50,000 MIPS), far outstripping mainframes and minicomputers of just a few years ago. This has had remarkable consequences for computer music.

Musicians and composers usually like to hear the results of their work as they do it. However, in the time of mainframe computers, computer music was an arduous activity, and it sometimes took weeks to hear the results, but the allure of computer music was so strong they persevered. A step closer to the real-time ideal was taken with the development of minicomputers. Barry Vercoe ported MUSIC-IV to the IBM S/360 and later, in the early 1970s, ported that version of MUSIC to the PDP-11 minicomputer. In the process he consolidated several branches and variations of the MUSIC-N programs and enhanced them with the addition of "control rate" (*k-rate*) capability. The concept of control rate is a rate of change lower than the sampling rate, that is utilized for parameter change in defined instruments. This is useful for computational efficiency because signals that control parameters (such as filter cutoff frequency) need not be calculated at the full sampling rate. The PDP-11s used 16-bit words and had a time-sharing operating system (UNIX), which made them attractive to university departments because they offered enough utility and precision for many tasks even if they were not always the fastest computers available. Thus, they were relatively plentiful in universities, and this special and extended version of the MUSIC IV language, called MUSIC 11, became available to a much wider community of users through its portability, the popularity of the platform, and the spirit of generosity engendered by Mathews and others who freely gave away their software. Along with Vercoe's earlier MUSIC 360 for the IBM mainframes, this meant that MUSIC V and variants were the dominant computer music software throughout the 1970s, and DEC PDP computers (along with some IBM mainframes) were the dominant general computer music platform, although all MUSIC programs and derivatives typically required significant memory resources due to their using long lists of instructions in their processing.

The popularity of minicomputers also encouraged the adoption of the C programming language and the UNIX operating system, which stimulated the development of software to run on them. The C language is a highly portable language, and UNIX was rewritten in C in its early days to encourage its adoption. Both UNIX and C were widely adopted by universities around the world that had minicomputers. The multiuser and multitasking capabilities of UNIX encouraged its use, and its system of using small programs, which could be interconnected to perform a complex task or create a larger system, was popular and highly influential.

At the University of California at San Diego (UCSD) in the late 1970s at the Computer Audio Research Laboratory (CARL), F. Richard Moore developed CMUSIC, a computer music system based on the UNIX approach. Rather than a single monolithic system like MUSIC V, Moore developed CMUSIC as a number of smaller programs that could be interconnected, one feeding another, to create a larger functional whole. In many respects, the smaller functional programs in CMUSIC are the same as, or similar to, the UGens in MUSIC V. CMUSIC was written in the C language so that it was portable, and it was open source so it was adopted by many universities. CMUSIC also allowed for easy expansion of the system through defining its application programming interface so that anyone could add their own functional units. While now outdated as an environment, because CMUSIC was written in C and open source, elements of it exist in many current computer music systems. CMUSIC was also another step along the way to what we now call plug-ins and plug-in architectures.

A similar development to CMUSIC is Paul Lansky's Cmix. Developed at Princeton University in 1982, Cmix is a *library* of C functions to mix sound files as well as process and manipulate them. As Cmix is not an environment but a software library, it required building programs in C to use. However, it is still in use today as RTCmix (Real Time Cmix) and most popularly as an external object for the Max/MSP (Max Signal Processing) environment.

In the mid-1980s, Vercoe, at the Massachusetts Institute of Technology (MIT), worked on rewriting MUSIC 11 in C. During the translation, and while updating it, Csound was created. Thus, Csound is a direct descendant of MUSIC V and is still in use today because it is in the public domain. Csound includes the concepts of MUSIC V and adds some of its own, such as spectral processing opcodes (UGens in MUSIC-N). Vercoe has continued to develop derivatives of Csound, including one version that runs on specialized digital signal-processing (DSP) hardware (Analog Devices's SHARC DSP processors), and newer opcodes for DSP effects such as real-time pitch shifting, dynamics manipulation, and others.

The development of PCs, particularly the Apple II, IBM PC, and Atari computers, brought basic computer music possibilities within the reach of the average musician. The Apple II used a 6502 microprocessor running at 1 MHz and was capable of 0.025 MIPS, had 4 KB of RAM (random-access memory) expandable to 48 KB, and had optional 5.25-inch floppy disks in 1977. The IBM PC in 1981 used an 8088 microprocessor running at 4.77 MHz, achieving 0.25 MIPS, and it came with 16 KB of memory expandable to 640 KB and two 5.25-inch floppy disk drives. Software was quickly developed, and by the early to mid-1980s, with the Apple Macintosh (1984) and IBM XT (1983) with hard disk, there were finally viable PCs for advanced music. The IBM XT was the same as the IBM PC, but it came with 128 KB of RAM and included a 10-MB hard disk and a single floppy disk. The Apple Macintosh, a radical machine in 1984, had a 68000 microprocessor running at 8 MHz achieving about 0.5 MIPS and came with 128 KB of RAM expandable to 256 KB, a single 3.5-inch floppy disk, a graphical display, and a mouse. The Macintosh was the first consumer PC with a graphical operating system for user interaction. The Atari ST was introduced in 1985, and with its 68000 processor and graphical display, it was mostly similar to the Macintosh, but it was cheaper and had integrated MIDI support. The introduction of MIDI at about the same time as the Macintosh and IBM XT allowed computers to communicate with sound synthesis hardware.

The increasing speed of PCs through the 1980s and 1990s led to more musical and sound possibilities. Computers were fast enough by the early 1990s that with some extra hardware they were able to manipulate sound in an editor. This was the birth of the digital audio workstation (DAW) so common today. Digital audio workstations were, and still are, used extensively to create computer music, most of which is for fixed media—tape music is what it used to be called. The precision editing, lossless bounces of multiple tracks, and other features of the DAW enabled composers to achieve a degree of quality and control that they could never achieve with analog tape machines and razor-blade editing. In addition, there were tools that allowed for the processing of sound in complex ways, even if it took the computer some time to complete the process. SoundHack by Tom Erbe and AudioSculpt from IRCAM (Institut de Recherche et Coordination Acoustique/Musique) were two of the most significant of these tools, along with Csound. They allowed for a range of processing functions by reading an input sound file, applying the process, and writing another sound file. This process could take several hours to complete. Of the range of processing functions offered, it was usually the phase vocoder that was most popular, and its processing formed the basis of many computer music pieces.

By the mid- to late 1990s, PCs were fast enough (about 300–400 MIPS) that Csound, the fundamental non-real-time application, could run in real time, directly synthesizing sound to the audio output of the computer from the supplied orchestra and score files or indeed via MIDI input. This was a remarkable event at the time and was seen as a breakthrough development. Thus, in about forty years, the MUSIC programs had matured into Csound, and the process of working with them had changed from weeks of batch processing to instantaneous, real-time results. The concept of UGens being assembled into instruments, all driven from a score file, is not far removed from the modern concept of software synthesizer plug-ins (or DSP processes) being driven in real-time from a MIDI score in a sequencer application. However, there is also a long history of hardware synthesizers that also feeds into this.

3. MORE PERSONAL COMPUTER MUSIC DEVELOPMENTS

By the mid- to late 1980s, other paradigms for computer music were being developed that would have a profound impact on how computer music was practiced. There was a push to develop computer languages that could interface with synthesizers, such as MIDI LOGO and MIDI LISP at IRCAM. In 1986, while at IRCAM, Miller Puckette developed a graphical language for controlling the 4X synthesizer through MIDI. This ran on a Macintosh, and the particular revolution of the Patcher environment was that people could build a program without typing text, instead graphically connecting functional boxes. This allowed composers to program the 4X and to control it in real time via the Macintosh and MIDI. David Zicarelli had been to IRCAM soon after this to talk about his early algorithmic music application (M) for the Macintosh, and Puckette talked with him about commercializing Patcher. Named after Max Mathews, in 1989 Opcode Max was released as the commercial product. It was immediately received as a revolutionary product for generating, managing, and manipulating MIDI data, and Max has continued to develop through the intervening years.

By the early 1990s, PCs had increased in power significantly. The Macintosh IIfx shipped with a 33-MHz Motorola 68030 CPU and 68882 FPU, 4 MB of RAM expandable to 128 MB, a 3.5-inch floppy disk, a SCSI (small computer system interface) hard disk from 40 to 160 MB in size, and a graphical user interface. An equivalent IBM PC (or "clone") had an Intel 80486 CPU running at 33 MHz, 4 MB of RAM expandable to 640 MB, a 160-MB hard disk, a 5.25-inch floppy disk, and a graphical user interface. With this increase in the power of computers through the early 1990s, there was the imagination to do more synthesis and audio manipulation on them without additional specialized hardware. With the miniaturization of specialized DSP chips and computers with standard expansion buses, it was possible to build a plug-in card with DSP units on it that would perform similar to a rack of equipment just a decade earlier. This led to several developments.

As well as the introduction of specialized audio DSP cards and editing applications by the likes of Digidesign, IRCAM became interested in this approach to replace the now-aging 4X synthesizer. IRCAM chose the NeXT computer as the basis for its IRCAM Signal Processing Workstation (ISPW) in 1990. The NeXT computer was of similar power to the Macintosh IIfx, but with a different bus, improved graphics, a more sophisticated graphical operating system based on UNIX, and a very sophisticated software development environment. With the addition of some specialized DSP hardware and a new version of Max called Max/FTS (Faster Than Sound) that was developed by Puckette with DSP objects that could generate and manipulate audio signals, the ISPW offered the type of development environment that would later dominate much of the computer music world.

By the mid-1990s, PCs had reached a high level of performance. Intel Pentium CPUs were shipping at speeds of 166 MHz (200–300 MIPS), systems had more RAM and faster hard disks and even better graphics capabilities and an improved graphical user interface (Windows 95). Apple's computers were similarly powerful, with the Power Macintosh 7600 having a 200 MHz PowerPC 604 RISC CPU, 16 MB of RAM expandable to 1GB and a 2GB hard disk. This ever-increasing power of PCs and UNIX workstations led people to imagine a version of Max that would run on a system without additional DSP hardware.

Puckette left IRCAM around 1994, and one of his first projects at UCSD was to develop the programming environment Pure Data (Pd), which was released in 1997. Pd functioned and looked almost the same as Max, and it handled control, audio, and video data equally (i.e., pure-ly data) on an SGI UNIX workstation without specialized hardware. An open source project, Pd has thrived ever since, has a very strong user community today, and has been ported to many different platforms, including Windows, Macintosh, and various open source operating systems such as Linux.

By the mid-1990s, it looked like the Macintosh PowerPC platform would be capable of performing DSP functions without hardware assistance. This was evident with Steinberg GmbH's development of the VST (Virtual Studio Technology) plug-in specification for audio processing on the host processor. In 1997, Zicarelli developed a new version of Max with DSP objects based on Pd. This addition was called MSP, which stands for Max Signal Processing, or Miller S. Puckette. Max/MSP is the commercial counterpart to Pd, and it also has a strong user community. Most users found that Max/MSP was easier to learn than Pd, although the patching-object paradigm is similar in both. Pd and Max/MSP have diverged as they matured, also leaving behind vestiges of the ISPW, and the current version of Max (version 5) includes many user interface changes and enhancements that obscure the common heritage of these environments. The utility of the Max and Pd environments allows for fairly intuitive development of real-time audio manipulation systems, and the resultant popularity has led to others that typically have higher-level functional blocks, such as Native Instrument's Reaktor and Plogue's Bidule software.

Other environments and languages also emerged with the increase in PC power in the 1990s. Most of these are text based and aimed at more real-time processes. Among these, Nyquist by Roger Dannenberg has proven influential. Nyquist is based on, and is a superset of, the LISP programming language, and working with it is highly interactive. The additions to LISP are many primitives to allow for audio synthesis and manipulation. Because it is primarily text based (although a graphical environment also became available later), it is perhaps less "musician friendly" than more graphical systems, but the interactivity of the language offers users immediate rewards. In Nyquist, the user defines "sounds" for sound synthesis and manages the events that make the sound. It also supports MIDI and audio and file I/O. Nyquist sounds are functionally similar to instrument definitions in Csound. One of the key differences between Nyquist and the MUSIC-N languages is that Nyquist does not separate sound synthesis from event playback in the same way as the MUSIC-N languages. This is a more highly integrated and interactive environment than many others, for example, Csound in its early incarnations. More recently, Nyquist has been able to program plug-ins for the audio editor Audacity, bringing another degree of utility to the programming language, and the inclusion of the language SAL (Simple Algorithmic Language, also available in Common Music) is useful for those uncomfortable with LISP. A graphical front end to Nyquist, jNyqIDE, has been written in Java and is also available for download.

Another advanced sound programming language and environment is SuperCollider, initially released by James McCartney in 1996. During its history, SuperCollider has undergone several major changes, both to the language syntax and to how it functions. Of use to scientists as well as computer musicians, SuperCollider offers an environment for real-time synthesis and performance. The syntax of the language is unique, visually similar to C or C++ but with the object-oriented structure of Smalltalk and aspects of other programming languages such as Nyquist. SuperCollider became an open source project in 2002, and as of version 3, it was functionally split between the user interface client (sclang) and the sound synthesis server (scsynth). The two parts communicate via Open Sound Control (OSC). This has several immediate benefits. Because OSC is a networked communication protocol, it means that several computers can run sound synthesis servers, thus effectively giving the environment unlimited resources. The other benefit is that other OSC-capable environments, for example, Max/MSP, can be used to drive the synthesis engine. SuperCollider has also developed a strong user community, and because of its real-time ability and interactive nature, it has been used for the recently emerged practice of *live coding* performance, by which the performers, on stage with computers, write code on stage (with the audience typically having a projected view of the computer screen) to create a piece of music.

With computers in the 21st century having plenty of power for audio synthesis (gigahertz CPU speeds and gigabytes of RAM), more people became attracted to live coding as a performance practice, whereby sound synthesis code is written and modified in real time as a major part of the performance, and several languages were developed to accommodate this. Live coding largely completes the transition of computer music practice from the historical model of writing the code, compiling and running it, and waiting to hear the results to an immediate and interactive experience. Computer music languages such as ChucK and Impromptu were developed with live coding in mind. Initially developed in 2003 by Ge Wang and Perry Cook at Princeton University, ChucK is generally considered to have a more familiar syntax than SuperCollider, although it is still unique. The ChucK operator "⇒" is used to enforce left-to-right precedence of actions, and ChucK has a strong concept of temporal flow. This enables accurate concurrent and sequential control over synthesis operations. The Impromptu language, developed by Andrew Sorensen in 2005, is somewhat different in several ways. Impromptu is based on the Scheme language, itself a dialect of the LISP language, and this makes it particularly elegant for constructing functions that are evaluated (executed) immediately or at a particular time. Another important feature of Impromptu for live coding is the ability to redefine functions and remap symbols at run time, making live modification of running code particularly natural. Impromptu also has a networked environment whereby multiple users can share and modify each other's code, making an ensemble performance of modifying shared running code possible. Both ChucK and Impromptu have no concept of a control rate, which was initially developed for computational efficiency and is no longer appropriate, as they tightly integrate sound synthesis with event generation and handling, and because modern CPU power has reduced the computational need for it. In addition to audio synthesis possibilities, both Impromptu and ChucK include graphics and video primitives that make them suitable for live coding video performances.

4. HARDWARE DIGITAL SYNTHESIZERS AND HOW THEY DEVELOPED

Analog synthesis existed for years before digital computers entered the world of music. Starting as far back as the Telharmonium at the end of the 19th century, through instruments by Leon Theremin, Hugh Le Caine, and Percy Grainger, and including the work of Karlheinz Stockhausen at the WDR studios and the RCA Synthesizer, analog synthesis by the 1960s was well established and soon to break into the mainstream with synthesizer manufacturers in America such as Robert Moog and Donald Buchla. However, one of the first advances in analog synthesis was the use of computers to control it.

Digital control of analog synthesizers is a concept that goes back the RCA Mark II Electronic Music Synthesizer (installed at the Columbia-Princeton Electronic Music Center [EMC] in 1957). Uniquely for its day, the RCA Mark II Synthesiser had two punched-paper tapes with a 4-bit, electromechanical, digital control system for most aspects of the analog synthesis circuitry. A little later, in the early 1960s several people were experimenting with building semicommercial-to-commercial analog synthesizers, including Moog and Buchla in America and Peter Zinovieff in London. These systems included a variety of analog control systems to send control voltages (CVs) around the system, sometimes with timing control via a device called a sequencer. In the late 1960s, Zinovieff had developed such complex sequencing requirements that he realized he needed a computer. At his Putney studio, Zinovieff installed a DEC PDP-8 and learned to program it so that he could use it to control the analog synthesis system. The PDP-8 was quite primitive, with 4K 12-bit words of memory, only eight instructions, and the possibility of paper-tape, magnetic-tape, and disk storage. Such a limited system was probably not capable of direct sound synthesis or running a MUSIC variant, but it was adequate for sequencing and synthesizer control.

At about the same time, in 1969, the Coordinated Electronic Music Studio (CEMS) system was conceived by Joel Chadabe and built by Moog. This was a programmable analog synthesis system that had an automated matrix mixer and a digital clock. It was installed at the Electronic Music Studio at the State University of New York at Albany. Similarly, in the mid-1970s at the Sonology Institute in Holland, Jo Scherpenisse interfaced the DEC LSI-11 so that the hand-built analog studio could be controlled digitally. Also in Stockholm, Sweden, at the Electronic Music Studio (EMS) in 1976, there was a PDP-15 controlling a collection of oscillators, filters, ring modulators, and a mixer. It was not long before this became more common, and in 1975 the newly established company Sequential Circuits had, as one of its first products, an analog CV sequencer controlled and programmed with a microprocessor. Thus, it was the hybrid of analog sound synthesis technology combined with digital control systems, which dominated synthesis for a time as digital circuitry was still very expensive to design and produce and was often too slow for real-time general-purpose digital synthesis, although some specific exceptions are mentioned here.

The PDP-15s mentioned had typical capabilities for mid-1970s minicomputers. They had 8K to 32K 18-bit words of memory storage, two magnetic tape drives capable of holding about 180,000 words each, and one or two disk drives of size about 0.5 megawords (just over 1 MB) and often had a variable clock rate, from very slow, for debugging, up to about 250 KHz to 1 MHz depending on the details of the model. While the lower-specified machines were suitable for composition data manipulation and synthesizer control, they were usually too slow and limited for general-purpose direct digital synthesis. Most digital synthesis until the early 1990s required specialized and purpose-built digital hardware to perform adequately.

Digital synthesis in hardware, or real-time digital synthesis, as opposed to the software developments such as MUSIC-N that were not real time, began with specialized hardware add-ons to computer systems or very efficient software algorithms. In 1972 and 1973, Barry Truax developed POD4, POD5, and POD6 at the Sonology Institute, and these programs ran on the PDP-15. The PDP-15 at Sonology had minimal mass storage and was unsuitable for running MUSIC V or similar software, and this encouraged a creative and different approach. Truax's POD (Poisson distribution) programs were composition software, and POD6 was the first to perform real-time frequency modulation (FM) synthesis in 1973, requiring only a DAC on the PDP-15 as it is a particularly efficient synthesis technique. POD5 performed fixed-waveform synthesis in real time. It also produces sounds in the range of 60 to 8,000 Hz, with sampling rates between 30 and 47 KHz and with the options of amplitude modulation and two-channel output. Truax continued developing POD at Simon Fraser University in Canada for the next several years.

In 1974, Luciano Berio, then head of electronic music at IRCAM in Paris, started discussions with Giuseppe Di Giugno in Naples about creating a digital synthesizer. Di Giugno joined IRCAM in 1975 and developed the 4 series of digital synthesizers. The 4A in 1976 was quite limited, although it did offer a large number of oscillators for the day. By 1977, Di Giugno had a much improved 4B synthesizer, and the 4C in 1978 had abstracted concepts of the interconnection of oscillators or objects, modularity, and algorithms, such that the 4C was used successfully by many composers. This work culminated in the 4X in 1981, intended as a flexible universal synthesizer and DSP processor. This was a very successful development that was used for many years in composition and performance. It was marketed for a time, but the price tag of $100,000 was beyond the reach of most institutions, let alone individuals.

At the University of Toronto, William Buxton developed a program called SSSP (Structured Sound Synthesis Program) on a PDP-11 minicomputer in the late 1970s; by 1978, it had 16 digital oscillators that could generate eight waveforms and be used for FM synthesis, additive synthesis, waveshaping, and fixed-waveform synthesis. There was also a VOSIM (Voice Simulator) mode for the oscillators and SSSP also had a high-resolution graphical display for interaction, making the user interface advanced for the day. Many of the developments and advances of this system were in its graphical control and real-time interaction capabilities.

In parallel developments, at the Sonology Institute, Werner Kaegi and Stan Templaars developed the VOSIM oscillator, which was an arbitrary waveform generator. While initial versions were based on analog technology, Jo Scherpenisse built digital hardware versions and interfaced them to the PDP-15 in the early to mid-1970s. Among the sonic possibilities of VOSIM oscillators are that they could produce a variety of voicelike sounds that were unique. There are now VOSIM patches for Pd and Max/MSP, a VOSIM opcode in Csound, and VOSIM patches for synthesizers like the Clavia G2.

Koenig, in 1972, designed and started implementing a digital synthesis technique called Sound Synthesis Program (SSP), although he started planning it many years earlier. An interactive system, SSP used compositional selection principles to assemble individual elements of waveforms and larger-scale composition structures. To work with SSP, the composer would prepare databases of time points and amplitude points and then associate these so that they could specify idiosyncratic waveforms. Thus, waveforms were typically constructed from random selections of amplitude time points, and familiar waveforms such as triangle, sine, ramp, and square waves were difficult to produce, although theoretically possible. The selection principles included randomness, groups, sequences, ratios and tendencies, and were thus closely related to Koenig's compositional practice.

This is not completely dissimilar from the SAWDUST system by Herbert Brün at the University of Illinois in the mid-1970s, which was another interactive program for manipulating parts of waveforms or amplitude points to make waveform segments. Another related development was the ASP (Automated Sound Programs) and later PILE synthesis languages by Paul Berg. These programs used instruction synthesis (sometimes called nonlinear synthesis) to create original sounds, and they ran in real time on the PDP-15 computer. Instruction synthesis does not attempt to use digital techniques to re-create something from the real world; rather it uses digital technology to explore other, usually nonlinear, methods to synthesize sounds that are idiosyncratic to the computer. Instruction synthesis can be highly efficient as well as strikingly original, creating refreshingly crunchy, noisy and idiosyncratic sounds.

All of these systems, because of their efficiency and low memory requirements, were well suited to direct, real-time synthesis on a small computer with a DAC attached. The sound materials produced by these methods are often spectrally complex, rich and unrefined, and unrelated to waveforms from the physical world. Xenakis also investigated instruction synthesis with his GENDYN (generation dynamique) program, but because it ran via the interpreted BASIC language on an early PC, it was too slow to run in real time.

In the early 1970s at Stanford University, a team of researchers received funding to build a digital synthesizer. Developed from 1975 to 1977 by Peter Samson, this became known as the Samson Box, and it was capable of real-time general synthesis using many techniques because it was fundamentally a real-time hardware version of MUSIC IV. The Samson Box was controlled from a PDP-10 mainframe, and it consisted of two full racks of digital circuitry, about the size of two large refrigerators. It was in use until 1989 and was used by many composers for performances and in films (for example, *Star Wars*).

The UPIC (Unite Polyagogique Informatique du CEMAMu) was a unique synthesis-and-control system, really a digital composition workstation, developed by Xenakis with Guy Medique throughout the 1970s and 1980s. UPIC was controlled by a large graphics tablet, which connected to a computer, and the graphical input controlled digital sound synthesis of varying types, including FM and an early dynamic stochastic synthesis. This system allowed the composer to work on the macro- and microstructure of the composition and the sound. Through several revisions, it was never quite able to be fully interactive until 1991, although a highly functional, but not real-time, version existed in 1977.

These early, noncommercial, digital sound synthesis systems have a few parallels in modern practice, but probably the most successful is the Symbolic Sound Kyma and Pacarana (previously Capybara) system. Kyma is a graphical signal flow language that performs real-time DSP synthesis and signal processing on custom DSP hardware. This was initially a plug-in hardware DSP card called the Platypus, but now it is a multi-DSP outboard box called Pacarana (previously called the Capybara). Thus, the Pacarana is a box of general DSP hardware programmed from the Kyma software. All of the sound synthesis and real-time sound processing, including live input, happens on the Pacarana, but the control is on the host computer via Kyma. Developed from the mid-1980s by Kurt Hebel and Carla Scaletti, it is a system in widespread use today, and it is prized for its stability, fine-sounding algorithms, and ease of use. These qualities have led to its use today as often in the movie industry as by composers of electronic music.

While specialized, free-standing, hardware DSP, such as the Pacarana, is becoming less necessary from the computational power point of view, it does still offer some benefits. Modern CPUs are concerned with servicing the network, disks, graphical interface, and many other tasks in addition to dealing with sound. Although modern CPUs are extremely powerful, the popular operating systems that run on them are largely ignorant of real-time operation and not really suitable for its requirements. It is only the speed of the CPUs that makes the current operating systems work at all acceptably for real-time tasks, but dedicated hardware can do much better than this and so can be more reliable. Dedicated hardware can have well-defined limits to its processing, which improves reliability, and the DACs and analog-to-digital converters (ADCs) are in an electrically less-noisy environment than inside a modern computer, which makes them operate better. External DACs and ADCs are a requirement for any professional DAW for this reason. It can be expected that external DSP hardware will decline further over the next ten years. With the increase in the power and number of general-purpose CPUs in standard PCs, there will probably be a (decreasing) niche for external DSP hardware for some time to come, and external converters will remain.

The miniaturization of digital circuits in silicone in the 1970s allowed the cost-effective development of digital hardware such as oscillators, filters, and other DSP functions. This development was quickly taken up by more commercial synthesizer manufacturers. Zinovieff was an early user of such developments as well as those already mentioned. The increasing miniaturization of digital circuits allowed two other important developments in the 1970s which led the way for later commercial digital synthesizers. In 1975, at Dartmouth College in the United States, Jon Appleton, Sydney Alonso, and Cameron Jones formed a partnership to bring an all-digital synthesizer to market that used only integrated circuits based around microprocessor control. The New England Digital Corporation was established in 1976 with a working prototype of the Synclavier. The main synthesis engine was a bank of digital hardware tone generators with 24 sine harmonics for each voice. The number of voices was 8 (in a basic system with no expansion hardware) to 32, and they were controlled from buttons on the console, thus avoiding detailed programming of the oscillators. The Synclavier was in production by the late 1970s, and while it was intended as a performance instrument, it soon had video display and disk add-ons to allow detailed programming. While very successful through the 1980s, the Synclavier was also very expensive, which made it an exclusive and quite elite instrument.

On the other side of the globe from the 1975 developments in Dartmouth, Kim Ryrie and Peter Vogel in Rushcutters Bay (New South Wales, Australia) started a project in 1975 to build a digital synthesizer based around a dual-microprocessor design by Tony Furse. Furse had earlier worked with the Canberra School of Electronic Music to build a system with many of the features that appeared later in the Fairlight, such as the light-pen interface and the graphic display. By 1976, there was a prototype, the Quasar M8, but it was bulky, took over an hour to boot from punched-paper tape, consumed 2 KW of power, and the sound quality left a lot to be desired as there was not enough processing power to suitably re-create all of the harmonics of natural sounds. The original desire was to create an all-digital synthesizer that could create sounds that were close to acoustic instruments. The disappointment with both the variety and quality of the Quasar synthesizer's sounds led the designers to consider recording real sounds. Recorded real sound had been used in musique concrète via hand-edited analog tapes and in some analog instruments that played back tapes, such as the Melotron and much earlier in Hugh Le Caine's Special Purpose Tape Recorder. Sampling, as it would come to be known, would later cause a revolution in synthesizers in the 1980s and beyond, but this was the beginning of such digital technology.

By 1979, these developments culminated in the Fairlight CMI I (Computer Musical Instrument), which gained favor with more popular musicians. The CMI I used dual Motorola 6800 CPUs, 64 KB of system RAM and 16 KB per voice for sampling, and two 8-inch floppy disks for storage. There was not much competition for the Fairlight, only the more expensive Synclavier. However, the sound quality of the original Fairlight, with 24-kHz sampling rate, also suffered somewhat, and in 1982 the CMI II was released with improved audio quality and more advanced software features. The most revolutionary of the software features was called Page R (for Rhythm sequencer), which was a real-time sequencer and editor, long before they were common in MIDI sequencers. The time-grid-based sequencer could be programmed and edited in real time using the light pen (the same as a modern-day mouse). This was so popular and revolutionary at the time that it was the prime reason for some sales. By the mid-1980s, the Fairlight had CD-quality audio, MIDI support, touch- and pressure-sensitive keyboards, and a raft of add-ons. This made the machine more capable, but the price was about the same as the Synclavier.

The popularity of the sampling techniques pioneered by the Fairlight drove the Synclavier also to adopt the technique. Shortly after, several less-expensive samplers appeared, such as the E-mu Systems Emulator keyboard in 1982 and in 1985 the generally affordable Ensoniq Mirage. However, the Mirage, an 8-bit machine, had low sound quality. Regardless, the Mirage and similarly capable add-in cards for PCs available at about the same time sounded the bell for the eventual end of the Fairlight and expensive sampling instruments. Later in the 1980s, companies like Akai entered the market with affordable samplers, and sequencers became popular on PCs such as the Macintosh, IBM PC, Atari ST, and so on. Today, sampling instruments are available as plug-ins for sequencer packages; they have many times the storage, polyphony, sound library variety, and processing power of the Fairlight at less than a hundredth of the cost.

Yamaha entered the market with two FM digital synthesizers in 1981 called the GS1 and GS2. They were innovative but very expensive and most people ignored them. In 1982 Yamaha showed an experimental FM synthesizer with "six-operator equation generators" that was never manufactured in this form, but was the forerunner of the most successful digital synthesizer. Prior to this, John Chowning had been showing off the utility and computational effectiveness of FM synthesis to anyone who would listen since the early 1970s; in 1971, Yamaha sent an engineer to examine this breakthrough. According to Chowning (Chadabe 1997, p. 117), the engineer understood it in ten minutes, and in 1974 Yamaha licensed the technology. It took until 1983 for it to appear in a successful synthesizer, but when it did it caused a revolution. The DX7 was an FM synthesizer that was polyphonic and affordable for most musicians. In addition, the sound quality for its day was outstanding. The DX7 was the first mass-market, all-digital synthesizer, and it caused a shake-up in the synthesizer world. Suddenly, this technology was affordable. It may have taken eight or nine years, but Yamaha had miniaturized about two racks full of electronics down to a couple of very large scale integrated (VLSI) chips, which made the synthesizer much smaller and cheaper.

This democratizing of the technology dramatically increased the number of people investigating how to use it. The DX7 came with 32 preset voices, and it was also very programmable, although the interface made it difficult, with a display of only two lines of text and a single set of increment and decrement buttons or a slider to change displayed values. However, this design set the standard for digital synthesizers for years to come. The quality of the factory preset voices was satisfactory for many musicians of the day, who were used to analog synthesizers. Combined with the difficulty of programming the DX7 and the nonintuitive nature of FM synthesis for most musicians, the DX7 was rarely programmed to its potential. This also started a new category on music production credits, the synthesizer programmer, who was separate from the player. There were many variants of the DX7 that Yamaha built through the 1980s, such as the DX7 II, DX9, TX7, DX100, and so on. Native Instruments now has a plug-in synthesizer, the FM8, that is a software version of the DX7.

The DX7 paved the way for a great number of other digital synthesizers, such as the Korg Wavestation, which combined sampling with digital synthesis (FM and other) and programmable mixtures of these techniques, as well as a sequencer. The combination of a sequencer built into a synthesizer was first created by Sequential Circuits with the Six-Trak, but the music workstation was significantly more than this simple combination of elements. These products allowed complete compositions to be realized in a single instrument, with all parts sequenced and different synthesis techniques combined. Many manufacturers built similar devices, such as Alesis, Yamaha, Casio, and Roland.

A class of synthesis that had been known for many years, but largely ignored because of its computational intensity, is physical modeling synthesis. This was used by Mathews, for example, in 1960 to synthesize the voice in *Daisy Bell* (also known as *Bicycle Built for Two*). Physical modeling attempts to reconstruct the sound of an instrument, or acoustical system, by mathematically approximating and modeling the sound generation mechanism of the instrument. Then, by running the calculations after excitation, sound is synthesized by the output of the process. The physical model will take into account the kind of excitation, the resonators, amplification, modification, and so on. The more detailed the model is, the more possibilities exist and the greater the potential realism.

Sometimes, astonishingly realistic sounds come from physical modeling synthesis, and it allows for significant experimentation to find new sounds. For example, how would a plucked string sound if the string was as thick as a steel cable or how would a clarinet reed exciter sound on a trumpet? The first common physical model was the Karplus-Strong plucked-string model, which produces very convincing plucked-string sounds and is quite computationally efficient. Put simply, the model generates a burst of (random) noise samples and sends them through a short delay line; the noise samples are then recycled through the delay line, and with each recycling the samples are successively averaged with the previous. This produces a strong plucked sound with a rapid decay of the harmonics, like a real string. Waveguides, which consist of an exciter (the "reed") and a resonating tube, are useful for modeling wind and brass instruments.

As DSP chips increased in power and decreased in price, physical modeling synthesis, which had been researched for some time at universities, was poised to move out of the institutions and into mainstream music. In 1993, ten years after the DX7, Yamaha introduced the VL1 and VP1 Virtual Acoustic synthesizers based on waveguides. Designed to simulate the sounds and playing characteristics of wind, string and plucked instruments, these Yamaha physical modeling synthesizers were not a great success in the marketplace for a couple of reasons: They were expensive, and most synthesizer players were primarily keyboard players, and while the Yamaha synthesizers had a keyboard, they also used a breath controller for articulation and control over the notes that was unfamiliar to keyboard players. Other manufacturers invested in physical modeling research, but they developed different instruments. Roland developed a guitar synthesizer that would take the sound of the electric guitar that was plugged into it and make it sound like whichever guitar was selected on the unit. Korg introduced a physically modeled drum synthesizer and a more general unit. Another use of physical models was to re-create the circuits of classic analog synthesizers.

As digital technology became cheaper, analog technology became less prominent and increased in price. This, combined with the market saturation of digital synthesizers, led to an expensive and elite market for analog synthesizers. The Clavia company in Sweden introduced the Nord Lead synthesizer in 1995; unlike other synthesizers of the time, it used DSP circuits to physically model the sound production techniques of analog synthesizers. The modules include the classic components of an analog synthesizer, such as oscillators, filters, envelopes, low frequency oscillators (LFOs), and so on, but also included such things as FM synthesis, sound effects such as distortion and chorus, and flexible signal routing with no restrictions on which signal can be patched into which input. The Nord Lead aspired to emulate the sounds of the analog Minimoog and the Roland TB303 drum machine synthesizers. Several companies have followed suit, and now analog modeling, or virtual analog, synthesis is a strong category with its implementation in many commercial synthesizers from Access, Alesis, Clavia, Korg, Kurzweil, Novation, Roland, and Yamaha. Indeed, there are also software synthesizer plug-ins that model Moog analog synthesizers and other analog instruments and equipment.

The advances in sound synthesis and synthesizers have closely followed the advances in microprocessors and microchip fabrication technology. As digital circuits became smaller, more powerful, and cheaper, so the synthesizer manufacturers used them to create ever-more-powerful synthesizers. Today, most of the interest is in software because general-purpose microprocessors have become so powerful that sophisticated synthesis programs can be run in a plug-in environment to replace the hardware synthesizers of even five years ago. While synthesizers are still being made for some performing musicians, as we approach the end of the first decade of the 21st century, it is clear that increasingly keyboard players will be playing with a keyboard connected to a (laptop) PC with the sounds generated in a software synthesizer. This is mainly a cost-and-flexibility issue for commercial music production, in which most commercial synthesizers find use and software synthesis has offered lower cost and improved flexibility over its hardware counterpart. There is very little advantage to hardware synthesizers in this realm of sound synthesis, with software replacing digital hardware so successfully. The only advantage that hardware might have is in reliability because hardware synthesizers are more reliable than PCs. There is still a case to be made for hardware analog synthesizers, as it is often the imperfections in their operation that are interesting, and for idiosyncratic hardware synthesis that has no counterpart in software.

5. GENERAL DIGITAL CONTROL SYSTEMS

It was clear from electronic music developments even before MUSIC-N that it was appropriate to separate the control of a system or process from the actual sound synthesis, for example, the RCA Synthesizer. These control systems are separate from, but related to, new instrument controllers (discussed below in 6. Real-Time Computer Music, Controllers, and New Instruments), and they form the basis for controlling sound synthesis systems. Control systems allow the composer or performer to approach synthesis or sound parameters as perceptually continuous functions of time and are thus separate from synthesis functions. At a higher level, control systems let the composer or performer define the musical data structures, or gestures, separately from the nitty-gritty of the synthesis functions. Control systems also typically require fewer and different resources to synthesis. Stockhausen meticulously controlled analog synthesis in several pieces, for example, *Studie II*, in which people reading a score controlled the amplitude of oscillators while recording multiple partials of a sound. MUSIC-N gave composers the ability to specify precisely the control of a process, sound, or variable parameter. With analog synthesis there was the possibility of using control voltages to change parameters over time.

In 1970, Mathews developed the GROOVE (Generated Real-time Output Operations on Voltage-controlled Equipment) system to do just that. GROOVE operated until the late 1970s, and it used a Honeywell computer connected to analog equipment as well as a two-channel DAC. Mathews envisioned this as a composition tool with real-time interaction.

As mentioned, Xenakis used digital control on the UPIC system from 1977. Initially, this was via a small minicomputer, but by 1991 it was with a PC. Xenakis also used digital means to control the performances in the *Polytope de Cluny* in 1972 and *Le Diatope* in 1978. The visuals of these works were similar, and *Le Diatope* was a large multimedia show for the inauguration of the Pompidou Centre; it had 7-channel tape playback of the spatial composition "La Legende d'Eer," four synchronized lasers, 1,680 flashes, and 400 programmable, rotating mirrors and prisms. The light program was updated 25 times a second.

At the Sonology Institute in the mid-1970s, they used a minicomputer (by then a DEC LSI-11) to control as many aspects of the analog studio as possible. There was considerable effort expended at the time achieving this as precise and repeatable digital control was deemed important.

Commercial analog synthesizers often had the possibility of external control through control voltages, but they were often difficult to make work between manufacturers. By the mid- to late 1970s, with basic microprocessors becoming smaller, cheaper, and easier to use, microprocessor control of analog synthesizers became relatively common. The digital control systems offered substantial advantages; they were stable and did not drift with time, parameters could be stored in memory and recalled later, and they allowed for repeatable results. However, there was no standard interface, so while a single manufacturer's synthesizers might interface to each other, it was not easily possible to link synthesizers from different manufacturers.

This eventually led to the development of the MIDI protocol specification through informal discussions between several American and Japanese synthesizer manufacturers from 1981 to late 1982. The Sequential Circuits company took the lead in this and drafted the first MIDI specification in consultation mostly with Oberheim and Roland Corporation. In early 1983, the first synthesizers were introduced that conformed to the MIDI protocol specification (such as the Prophet 600, DX7, and Jupiter 6), and retrofit upgrades were available for some other synthesizers, such as the Sequential Circuits Prophet 5. The use of MIDI not only opened up a new world of possibilities but also bought with it many limitations. In MIDI, there is only the most rudimentary understanding of pitch and tuning, with no allowance for microtones or different scales. Also, because of the limitations of the initial transport implementation, MIDI is a slow, low-bandwidth, 7-bit protocol, allowing only 128 values for any parameter, which is often not enough. There have been several revisions to the MIDI specification, and there is extremely limited 14-bit capability, but these fundamental limits exist to this day. The MIDI pitch bend messages needed more than the 128 values in a 7-bit data packet to bend pitches smoothly the way performers wanted, so pitch bend messages use two 7-bit data packets to allow for 14 bits of control change. This was extended to several MIDI continuous controller messages, which send a most significant byte (MSB) and least significant byte (LSB), each of 7 bits, to combine into a 14-bit value. This is very limited as it only applies to a few MIDI controller messages, and it is defined in an awkward manner with a coarse controller and a fine controller, so it is not often used or completely implemented in MIDI devices. The specification means that controller messages 0–31 are the coarse controllers, and controller messages 32–63 are for the corresponding fine controller messages; devices must be able to respond to the coarse message without the corresponding fine message following it. Perceiving little commercial need for this, much manufactured hardware only implements the minimum functionality.

However, MIDI does also offer several advantages. It cleanly separates a synthesizer's control circuitry (e.g., a keyboard) from the synthesis engine. Thus, any controller can be used to drive any kind of synthesis. The pervasive MIDI representation of musical data has led to a plethora of software, such as sequencers, score editors, algorithmic composition systems, synthesizer patch editors, and so on. MIDI is still heavily used today, but perhaps more to drive software synthesizers than the hardware variety, and it has found great utility as a control protocol for all manner of equipment, from mixing desks to effect units and lighting controllers, allowing simple automation of their functions.

All of the software systems from the 1980s onward that have been discussed have MIDI functionality: Max/MSP; Pd; Csound; sequencers such as Cubase, Logic, and Digital Performer; music notation and score editors; and more. In addition, every PC from the early 1980s has either built-in or third-party MIDI interfaces available, enabling the IBM PC, Macintosh, Amiga Atari, and BBC Micro to drive synthesizers, receive and manipulate MIDI data, edit synthesis parameters, and perform algorithmic composition functions.

The significant limitations of MIDI led to several attempts to improve the specification, but none of them were successful. The most likely replacement for MIDI is OSC, developed in 1997 at CNMAT (Center for New Music and Audio Technologies) at the University of California at Berkeley by Matt Wright and Adrian Freed. This is a relatively simple network communication protocol optimized for communication between computers, synthesizers, and media devices and is completely flexible and has high bandwidth and precise timing control. In addition, OSC is less expensive to implement than MIDI with its larger connectors and greater hardware requirements. Because OSC does not define musical constructs or pitches, the user is free to define these to suit personal needs. Thus, OSC is valuable for transmitting advanced musical concepts between software and equipment. For example, in OSC, because all messages are user defined, it is possible to define a scale as an arbitrary division of an octave (say, 31 divisions) and use that to control a sound synthesis engine to produce microtonal music. Another obvious application is with high-resolution controllers, for which OSC is not limited to 7-bit data packets and can use 16 bits to send values. Open Sound Control has been implemented in most, if not all, of the software packages mentioned and in a number of hardware interfaces from various manufacturers, for example, the Arduino, Gluion, IpSonLab, LA Kitchen Kroonde, Make Controller Kit, Monome, and Smart Controller, to name just a few. The success of OSC in replacing MIDI is evident in its uptake by the new musical instrument and new interface builders, from whom it has earned near universal acceptance. However, relatively few organizations that depend on commercial music production have embraced OSC as they have little need yet for its advanced and expanded capabilities.

6. Real-Time Computer Music, Controllers, and New Instruments

As mentioned, CSIRAC was the first computer to play music, although it was not used to expand music's horizons; rather, it was used to play a standard repertoire, although it did do it in real time. Early electronic musical instruments such as the telharmonium and theremin were similarly not used for new music but at least initially were used as instruments for established music. Percy Grainger did write new music for theremin ensembles, but it was not frequently played. Analog electronic music developed through musique concrète in France, *elektronische muzik* in Germany, and in other centers, most notably in America, Holland, Italy, and England, and it was performed as tape pieces in concert halls.

It was John Cage in America, however, with *Imaginary Landscape No. 1* (1939) for piano, Chinese cymbal, and two turntables, who first performed electronic music in the way that we understand instrumental performance. Cage did not use "electronic instruments" in his pieces, but rather normal electronic household appliances; sometimes, these were used in an unconventional manner. For example, Cage would use phonocartridges with the stylus in contact with items as a means to detect and amplify vibrations in them. He would also use contact microphones in these pieces, such as *Cartridge Music* and *Imaginary Landscapes*. Many other composers used similar techniques, usually with standard microphones, which became cheaper and more readily available. For example, Stockhausen used the technique quite early in *Mikrophonie*. This became a relatively popular way to explore the minutiae of resonances and timbre, making it available for manipulation in live electronic music.

Mathews's GROOVE system offered real-time digital control over analog synthesis. Even though it was based on a minicomputer and a large synthesis studio, it was not used for performances so much as for interactively working on compositions. The composer could define some parameters for the computer to control, leaving others under the real-time control of the composer. Laurie Spiegel spent two years from 1974 making changes to the GROOVE system so that it could be used to compose images. Spiegel's VAMPIRE (Video and Music Program for Interactive Realtime Exploration/Experimentation) allowed for real-time algorithmically generated images simultaneously with sound. The situation at the Sonology Institute with the POD, SSP, and PILE systems was similar because even though they offered real-time performance and interaction (if needed) for composition, they operated on a minicomputer attached to a studio; thus, it was not easily possible to use these systems for performance.

The performance of analog electronic music continued unabated in various guises from the 1950s through the 1970s and 1980s, and many innovative and important pieces were created. Typically, these works used various kinds of analog equipment, such as ring modulators, filters, and oscillators of various kinds as well as microphones, tape loops, and delay lines. Many performers and groups participated in live electronic music using analog techniques. As well as those already mentioned, there were many others: Robert Ashley, Gordon Muma, David Behrman, Alvin Lucier, Laetitia Sonami, Pauline Oliveros, and David Tudor, among others, and ensembles (often of American expatriates) such as Musica Elettronica Viva, Gruppo di Improvvisazione Nuova Consonanza, and Intermodulation. For many electronic musicians, the opportunity to make live electronic music for an audience was a revival of the traditional composer-performer paradigm of Western music that had largely been absent from Western practice by the end of the 19th century.

This spirit of improvisation was characteristic of America in the middle of the 20th century and later, with jazz, the Beat artists, the New York school (Cage, Tudor, Morton Feldman, Christian Wolff, and others), abstract expressionism, and free improvisation. By the late 1960s, there was a strong trend to "freedom" in social, political, and musical life. Early interactive improvising-composing instruments, or systems, were constructed by Salvatore Martirano, Behrman, Chadabe, and others, and the practice of improvisation was crucial to all of them, particularly Behrman, whose pieces were said to have the feeling of being improvised even if fully composed.

In the San Francisco Bay Area, a group called the Homebrew Computer Club was formed in 1975, and it was very influential in the development of home microcomputers and in popularizing small computers. This group encouraged the use of computers, including in the arts, and this had an influence on other local activity, for example, at Mills College.

In the late 1970s at Mills College, a group called the League of Automatic Music Composers—John Bischoff, Jim Horton, and Rich Gold (later replaced by Tim Perkis)—started making music with KIM-1 microcomputers, and they started to work out ways to interconnect them. They performed concerts from 1979 to 1983 using a network of interconnected microcomputers. The league's music was largely improvised, and this led to the development of ideas of musical interactivity in the context of a networked computer instrument environment. However, they were all still interested in this after the split in 1983, and in 1984 Bischoff and Perkins built a connecting box to interface the computers to each other. They called the box the Hub; after an initial concert in 1985, several new members joined, and the group was called The Hub. A MIDI interface system was used to organize communication between the computers and to allow some autonomy with sound synthesis and software. This group approached the networked computers as a single instrument with multiple control points and complex interactions.

Behrman was already a pioneer of electronic music improvisation when, in 1976, he used a KIM-1 microcomputer to "listen to" a bassoon and flute with a basic pitch tracking algorithm which caused the system to create sounds interactively in response to what the instruments played. George Lewis also led in this area from his time at Mills College in the 1970s, where he started using small computers (the KIM-1), to his later developments in the mid-1980s, when he developed the program Voyager. Lewis was interested in musical decision making in improvisation practice. Voyager runs on a Macintosh computer and takes MIDI data of what was played (possibly through a pitch-to-MIDI converter box), effectively listening to the performer, and makes immediate decisions on playing something appropriate. It follows the performer but still creates its own response, making decisions about melody and harmony. The output of Voyager was also MIDI information to be turned into sound by a synthesizer. While the pitch detection and classification are rudimentary (high/low, register, pitch), they were enough to make Voyager a highly successful project.

There was an obvious desire to use the flexibility, repeatability, and precision of digital synthesis and processing in real-time performance. Di Giugno's 4A, 4B, 4C, and 4X synthesizers at IRCAM were instrumental in enabling real-time digital performance possibilities. The architecture of these synthesizers allowed for the real-time update of synthesis parameters without disrupting the audio output. These synthesizers were controlled by an attached computer, either a PDP-11 or the

LSI-11 for the earlier models or a Macintosh running Puckette's Patcher software for the 4X by the late 1980s. Notable pieces using these synthesizers in real-time performance are David Wessel's *Antony* (1977) and Pierre Boulez's *Répons* (1981). At the Institute for Sonology in Utrecht during the 1970s, there was POD4, POD5, and POD6; VOSIM synthesis; PILE; and the SSP projects, all of which allowed for real-time synthesis.

Most digital synthesizers by the end of the 1970s to early 1980s were controlled with a standard, pianolike, keyboard, and this was usually tightly integrated into the architecture of the synthesizer system. Even the most expensive commercial systems, the Synclavier and the Fairlight, were exclusively keyboard driven. It was MIDI in 1983 that introduced the clean detachment of the controller from the sound-generating module. Significantly, soon after the introduction of MIDI, separate sound modules and so-called master keyboards (a MIDI-only output keyboard controller) were introduced on the market. This immediately gave people the imagination to use other controllers to generate MIDI and thus create and control sounds. Commercial manufacturers experimented with wind controllers, guitar controllers, percussion controllers, and so on so that other instrumentalists, instead of just those with keyboard skills, could use synthesizers.

In 1985, Spiegel developed a system for the Macintosh computer (and later the Atari ST and Amiga PCs) that for the first time would allow a lay user or nonmusician to control musical processes by moving the computer mouse on the screen. Music Mouse offered the user an on-screen grid to choose notes, and the computer would generate an accompaniment based on the history of selections, effectively making the computer an expert-system instrument that someone with no musical knowledge could play. This was a MIDI program that generated MIDI notes for a synthesizer to play. Intelligent Music Systems' M and Jam factory software, largely written by Zicarelli, were similar interactive automated composition software packages.

It has been the more creative and experimental musicians who have embraced the possibilities offered by the split between controlling devices and sound-generating devices. The ready availability of real-time digital synthesis (initially in hardware, but also software) with a well-defined interface has allowed the development of alternative, gestural-sensor, controllers. In 1984, Michel Waisvisz developed a controller called The Hands, which is a pair of controllers, one of which fits over each hand; and each has a selection of buttons, ultrasonic distance sensors, accelerometers and other sensors. These connect to a voltage-to-MIDI box, and the resulting MIDI information drives the sound synthesis. The Hands have been extended and rebuilt many times over the years, and while they initially drove MIDI synthesizers like the DX7, Waisvisz most effectively used them to control a live sampling software instrument, by which he could sample audio and manipulate it in real time.

The sensor interface boxes used to connect gestural-sensor controllers to a computer have changed in various ways over the last couple of decades, driven mostly by available integrated devices. STEIM's SensorLab was one of the first such devices (used initially by Sonami and many others) that allowed analog signals to be digitized and converted into MIDI data and thus transferred to a computer or synthesizer. While initial developments were built with many parts, today most use a microcontroller such as a Microchip PIC, Parallax BASIC Stamp, or Amtel AVR. These microcontrollers contain almost everything needed to make a sensor interface, including a multiplexer, DAC, CPU, ROM (read-only memory), RAM, and interfaces such as serial and USB (universal serial bus). Thus, there is usually only the need for power, a little support circuitry, and programming required to have a functioning sensor interface. Current sensor interfaces used with gestural-sensor controllers include, among others, the following: Arduino; DIEM's Digital Dance System (Denmark); Electrotap's Teabox (United States); Eowave's Sensorbox (France); Gluion (by Sukandar Kartadinata in Berlin); IpSonLab (by Lex v. d. Broek of the Sonology Institute; Holland); IRCAM's WiSe (Paris); LA Kitchen's Toaster and Kroonde Gamma (Paris); iCubeX (Canada); Make Controller Kit (United States); MIDIbox (Germany); Monome (United States); PaiA's MIDI Brain (United States); and Smart Controller (by Angelo Fraietta in Australia). Many of these work with OSC, and some are available as kits. Recent developments at CNMAT include the CNMAT Connectivity Processor; the uOSC software, which implements the complete OSC protocol on a microcontroller (PIC18F and PIC24F series); and a very-high-performance gesture-sensing controller using a VIRTIX processor.

Nicolas Collins, in 1986, created an instrument using an old trombone; a retractable dog lead; a Commodore 64 computer; a few sensors, switches, and interface electronics; and an Ursa Major DSP reverb/effects unit. The trombone acted as an interface, with electronics on it to control the DSP functions in the Ursa Major; there are switches, a breath controller, a rotary position encoder (driven by the trombone slide via the dog lead), and 21 switches. The Commodore 64 plays samples as well as controls the DSP unit, and there is stereo output from a power amplifier as well as a speaker in the bell of the trombone. Collins used this instrument in many performances and pieces, his own compositions as well as improvisations (e.g., John Zorn's *Cobra*). This is a very early example of an instrument that uses modified, or "hacked," off-the-shelf electronics to create a new instrument, a practice that has become very popular in the last ten years with hardware hacking and circuit bending performers.

Sonami is a performer who has taken the possibilities of hand controllers and extended them enormously. She has developed a succession of Lady's Gloves, a controller that is a tight-fitting glove with many sensors attached to it. The original version was finished in 1991 and was made with Paul DeMarinis. Bert Bongers made one in 1994 and another highly successful one in 2002. The current version (the fifth) has microswitches at each fingertip, bend sensors on each finger, five hall-effect sensors (used with a magnet in the thumb), pressure sensors, several accelerometers, an ultrasound sensor, and so on. This rich array of sensors is fed into a voltage-to-MIDI converter, and the MIDI information is used to control a Max/MSP patch to synthesize and play sound, and manipulate it, all in real time. As one might imagine, Sonami's musical performances are very strongly gestural.

The controls on the glove are often highly visible, with thick bundles of wires separating and fanning out to connect the various sensors.

Sensorband, formed by Edwin van der Heide, Atau Tanaka, and Zbigniew Karkowski in 1993, is a group that uses many various sensors and interfaces, from infrared beams, muscle sensors, and hand-mounted distance, pressure, and movements sensors and mercury tilt switches, as an ensemble of new electronic instrumentalists. While all of the members of Sensorband are soloists in their own right, they perform as a trio and explore gestural-sensor performance as an ensemble. Sensorband has also experimented with remote network performance in which each member performs live in a different geographical location, and they use high-speed networks and video conferencing to connect. This brings with it a new group of technical, logistic, and musical challenges.

Gestural-sensor controllers have been developed for many kinds of performances, from sensors on dancers and video tracking of dancers and performers, to brain-wave-to-MIDI controllers, extended theremin-like controllers, global positioning system (GPS)-to-MIDI controllers, and almost whatever could be imagined. There is continuing research into sensor development; for example, at CNMAT there is research into inertial sensors, resistive/conductive fibers, malleable materials, and multisensor fusion (using multiple, disparate sensors to improve gesture capture). Many people have developed sensor interfaces to somehow control sound. Buchla has also built many different kinds of controllers; Lightening and Thunder were two popular controllers in the 1990s. These are often of great interest to performing musicians because Buchla pays particular attention to the performability of his controllers, such that a genuine playing technique needs to be developed as with any other musical instrument.

Although MIDI is a universal interface, it has many limitations; in the gestural controller world, it is rapidly being replaced by the faster and more flexible OSC. The ongoing developments with controllers has led to an international conference so that those involved can share and publish their research and ideas. New Interfaces for Musical Expression (NIME; see www.nime.org) is an annual conference dedicated to new controllers and performance techniques.

Interactivity in computer music now has several decades of development behind it, and it is understood as a highly interdisciplinary activity. Of crucial interest, still, is how meaning is exchanged during real-time interaction, what form that musical information takes, and how the communication occurs. While perhaps not quite yet a mainstream activity, there is little doubt that the use of gestural-sensing controllers will develop further over the coming decades and offer greatly expanded possibilities for musical performance. Witness the success of the Nintendo Wii Remote, which is nothing more than a remote controller full of sensors, which is used for games, exercise, music, and more. So far, almost all of the musical controllers have been custom-built for a particular performer. One of the challenges will still be to develop gestural-sensing controllers to a degree at which they are no longer specific to a single performer but generalized enough to be used by anyone who is willing to practice and master them. One of the aspects to achieving this is to ignore the temptation to customize a controller constantly to suit a performer's immediate needs perfectly. To this point, recently Keith McMillan Instruments released the K-Bow sensor mechanism for a string player's bow, and StringPort, a polyphonic string-to-USB 2.0 controller interface for guitar players. The K-Bow replaces the frog on the bow and provides 3D acceleration information as well as bow pressure. This is transmitted wirelessly to a computer where it can be used to control computer processes. The StringPort similarly offers a mechanism for guitarists to control computer processes. This type of commercial sensor-gesture interfaces make it feasible for standard musicians to tap the potential of digital synthesis and DSP. In a world of constantly improving technology where it seems like there is nothing beyond our ability, there is value in the imperfections and limitations of the interface and the effort to play it, as experienced in mechanoacoustic instruments, and the struggle to overcome these limitations. Such "imperfections and limitations" could be useful for gestural-sensing controllers, and audiences engaging with performances using them, as they do not render obsolete the concept of virtuosity.

7. COMPUTER-ASSISTED COMPOSITION AND BEYOND

As mentioned briefly at the beginning of this chapter, Hiller initiated work on algorithmic composition in the mid-1950s. Despite the promise of this, with tremendous algorithmic control over compositional parameters, few composers really took to it seriously. While signal-processing systems are also part of composition, they have been covered, and this section focuses on higher-level composition systems.

Hiller investigated two approaches to algorithmic composition. The first approach was the application of music theory rules, such as harmony and counterpoint. However, after listening to the results, he was soon led to investigate other organizing principles that are more general than the rules of harmony and counterpoint. The more general organizing principle he investigated was randomness with Markov chains, which are chains of probabilities for which the probability of a next particular note depends on what the previous note or notes. Markov chains have been part of the repertoire of algorithmic composition ever since.

Regardless of Hiller's findings about the quality of the output from the application of music theory rules in algorithmic composition, this is exactly where most of the activity has been concentrated over the fifty years hence. There were, however, two composers who did practice algorithmic composition by applying more general organizing principles: Xenakis, particularly in his Free Stochastic Music (1957–1962), and Koenig with his composition projects *Project 1* and *Project 2*. Although they were aligned in that regard, Xenakis and Koenig took different paths. Koenig generalized his composition practice and expressed his composition concepts as abstractions in software. Constrained randomness was a feature of many of his abstractions, as were serial parameter organization and random choices with a repetition check. In this way, he created music that was highly original yet firmly grounded in his own compositional theories and practice. Xenakis, in contrast, invented systems with randomness and musically explored their limits. Xenakis would use probabilities to control shapes, areas and densities, cellular automata, and other techniques and apply these to musical parameters, for which stochastic methods would control numeric, and then musical, contours in a general way. By creating astoundingly original and compelling compositions, Xenakis proved the validity of his ideas and the validity of his approach.

This work, particularly Hiller's initial use of Markov chains and Koenig's algorithmic composition concepts and systems, was little recognized in its day as the achievement that it was. All of these composers have taken their particular musical position and through generalizing it they have built a powerful method of composition and expressed their musical knowledge in a way that makes it useful to others. They developed general tools that may be applied in a wide musical context. Many others worked on algorithmic composition systems, and they often came to similar conclusions (i.e., that the application of music theory rules is not as useful as generalized abstractions). They include Brün, John Myhill, and Tenney in the United States; Pierre Barbaud and Michel Phillipot in Paris; Rudolf Zaripov in Moscow; D. Campernowne and S. Gill in England; and Pietro Grossi in Italy.

As mentioned, however, most of the later research and discussion concentrated on the ideas that Hiller rejected, those concerned with applying ever more complex musical theory in an attempt to create compelling compositions. In the early 1990s, several people ran projects along these lines. David Cope developed systems to analyze and simulate musical styles of composers such as Bach, Mozart, and Brahms, and Charles Ames had a number of projects in musical intelligence in several genres, including ragtime and jazz. There are many other examples, including automated melody harmonization systems and so on. While these systems have been valuable at examining previous musical styles, understanding them, and contributing to music theory, they have not resulted in compelling compositions of contemporary music, even when the systems have had changes made to attempt this. Music theory is intrinsically averaging and concerned with previous compositions. Musical composition is inherently an expansive process that constantly extends and goes beyond theory. Although they overlap, the two domains are distinctly different, and musical composition is more than the application of music theory, or at least it is something else. While modeling musical cognition might offer some insights that may be useful for composition, it is an area that is in its infancy, and people, especially perhaps composers, perceive music differently and idiosyncratically. Such generalized cognition modeling could make generalized, perhaps averaged, results of potentially little value for composition. It would seem that "average" music is of little interest to most people, while exceptional or idiosyncratic music is of great interest, and often beautiful, to at least some people.

For the software to implement these systems, computing power has rarely been an issue, and neither has accessibility, at least since the microprocessor revolution. Early computers had severe memory limitations, and they usually had secondary-storage (i.e., tape or disk) techniques to overcome this. The same situation occurred with early microcomputers but without the secondary storage to surmount the problem. Computers have had plenty of power and memory to run such algorithms in real time since the late 1970s. Algorithmic composition systems typically manipulate numerical data that represents pitches and durations, which is at least one, two, or perhaps three orders of magnitude less intensive than manipulating and calculating multiple channels of sound samples. Innumerable Max patches have been created to implement some of these ideas, such as Markov chains, tendency masks and melody harmonization, or even Mozart's dice game. Other, purpose-built software exists also; among these are AC Toolbox by Berg; Symbolic Composer by Peter Stone; M by Zicarelli; and Open Music from IRCAM. Many of these composition environments are based on the LISP language, which is ideally suited for processing lists of data or parameters, and that is evident from the syntax required to use these systems. LISP originated in 1958 and is one of the oldest computer languages; it is still widely used today, and it was, for many years, favored by artificial intelligence researchers. Many of the software systems for algorithmic composition have existed for almost thirty years, which is a testament to its low computation requirements. It is curious that, despite massive advances in computer hardware and significant advances in software, we are mostly stuck in musical paradigms from the 1970s at best, and sometime much further back. One of the challenges facing music, and algorithmic composition, is to find new musical forms and techniques for composition that are as modern as the computers that run them.

Other systems have been used to compose music algorithmically. Fractals have been used by Charles Dodge and many others to create compositions by taking the fractal data and mapping it to musical parameters such as pitch and duration. Many other types of data have also been used to create music, for example, weather data and astronomical data. More recently, other extramusical theories have been applied to the creation of music, such as theories of genetics. Generative music has its roots in the mid-1970s, when Brian Eno first used the term and techniques in his piece *Discrete Music*. There are a number of software programs for generative music, including Karlheinz Essl's fFLOW and SEELEWASCHEN, Koan Pro by SSEYO, and the more recent noatikl, Music Genesis, and so on. The software systems developed for live coding are also used in the context of generative music, for which Impromptu, ChucK, SuperCollider, and others are of great utility and can directly create sound as well as generate and manipulate MIDI data. Some of these programs will, for example, produce MIDI data from a photograph or weather data.

The practice of generating sound, or music, from data sets is called *sonification*, and while it is arguably a peripheral activity for computer music composers, there is a crossover of activity. One of the main requirements to sonify data is to *map* it to musical or sonic parameters. Then, it can be put through a process to generate the sound or music. This mapping can be more creative or linear in its approach.

Composers such as Xenakis and Koenig typically used quite simple mappings, but with complex data sets, to achieve a suitable musical complexity. A good example of this is the pizzicato string glissandi section in Xenakis's *Pithoprakta*, where he graphed the velocity versus time of many gas particles as they underwent Brownian motion, drew lines between the time points for each particle, and then divided this graph vertically among the ranges of the string instrument family and scored the graph in musical notation. Xenakis's achievement was in making this extremely musical and appropriate within the context of the piece. With the greater flexibility of current software, more complex mappings may be attempted and often are. Those involved in sonification usually use simple mappings to "illustrate" the data. There is now an annual conference, the International Conference on Auditory Display (ICAD), where research in this field is presented.

Computers have also found unique utility in the activity of automated musical analysis. Systems for musical analysis also have found use and been extended into machine listening projects. Early systems would take information in MIDI form and make musical or analytical decisions based on what was played and when, performing an analysis either in real time or out of time. However, current research goes far beyond this. Machine listening research now attempts to model the function of the human ear-brain system so that a computer can identify features in the music. This requires sophisticated DSP that would require specialized DSP hardware only a few years ago. Machine listening has made significant advances since the late 1990s with the increase in computing power available. There are major research projects in machine listening at Stanford University, MIT, IRCAM, and other research centers. The nature of this research, for example, distinguishing a single instrumental line in an ensemble performance, means it is heavily dependent on the amount of processing power available. For this reason, it has only been since the mid- to late 1990s that significant research in the advanced machine listening area has been possible. Once machine listening systems operate well enough that they work similarly to humans, they may be integrated with music information retrieval systems and could spur other groups of applications that could have significant artistic and commercial implications. For example, there is now at least one software application for mobile phones which will "listen" to some popular music that is being played, and after extracting features will consult a database and tell the user which song is playing.

8. The Emergence of Digital Audio Workstations

A major part of the use of computers in music today is in recording and production. The advantages of digital audio techniques were obvious from the 1960s, and commercial recordings were pioneered in the early 1970s by Japanese companies such as Denon and by the BBC and Decca. Professional digital recorders from Denon used rotating head video recording technology, and this was adopted by Sony and others. As computing power increased and costs decreased, including the cost of hard disks, digital recording moved more toward computer-based hard disk recording, and it also became more mainstream. By the early to mid-1980s, digital recording was a common feature in recording studios. Sony and Philips created a task force in 1979 to develop a new digital music distribution medium. Based on Philips's optical digital video disks, the definition, or Red Book standard, was released in 1981, and the first commercial disk, an ABBA album, was released in 1982. Sony introduced the first CD player in Japan in the same year and in 1983 elsewhere. It took many years for CDs to replace vinyl records, and in a few circles they still have not. In the mid-1980s, Digidesign released a board for the Apple Macintosh computer to add DSP hardware for a synthesis program called Turbo-synth. Digidesign soon developed another use for its DSP hardware, and in 1987 Sound Tools ushered in an era of digital audio recording and editing on a Macintosh PC. Also at about this time, the first professional digital mixing consoles were introduced, but it would be the PC developments that would take over commercial music production.

As commercial musicians used MIDI and sequencers, it became increasingly obvious that the addition of digital recording to these capabilities would make a personal music production workstation possible. Slowly, as computer power increased through the late 1980s into the mid-1990s, the sequencer companies added more digital audio facilities to their sequencers, and the audio editor companies added MIDI sequencing to their software. This convergence was complete by the late 1990s, when PCs were powerful enough to record many tracks of audio through a multichannel hardware interface and work with MIDI.

This combination of hardware and software became known as a digital audio workstation (DAW). As the feature sets of the software converged and computing power increased more through the 21st century (10,000–50,000 MIPS), the surplus computing power has been taken up by sophisticated software synthesis plug-in modules that are driven by MIDI and by sophisticated audio effects, sometimes involving detailed physical modeling of analog instruments and sophisticated convolution transformation techniques.

Today, there are programs such as Garageband, which brings these commercial musical production tools to the consumer level. Garageband is not a professional tool, but it offers an extraordinary array of facilities for the average nonmusician, or nonprofessional musician, computer owner. It allows for audio recording, with sample looping and virtual (plug-in) instruments, automation, MIDI interfacing, and studio-quality audio effects such as reverberation, equalization, dynamics control, and analog modeling. Such a degree of possibilities in an easy-to-use consumer package would have been impossible to imagine just ten years ago.

While all of this commercial digital audio trickery may seem very modern, it is important to realize that the theory and techniques for this date back sometimes forty years to the fundamental research into computer music practice, and really it is usually only the packaging that is new and the fact that it can be done on an inexpensive home computer.

9. AFTERWORD

Computer music has, mostly, been intimately connected with the machines and hardware on which it has been practiced, and often advances in computing technology have enabled advances in musical possibilities, as should be clear from the chronology of computer music in the appendix to this volume. This is to be expected, of course, and the same has happened in instrumental music, but the abstract nature of the machine in the case of computer music makes the link less obvious to some. Approaching this technology with a creative mind, composers, researchers, and musicians have built an enormous number of systems and products that now touch every person's life. From the most advanced forms of contemporary music composition, sound synthesis, and performance, to the everyday consumer-oriented activities of producing mass-market music and playback systems, computers and computer music research have long been involved. Many of the initial computer music developments are still expressed today in one form or another, and in some ways they have been too successful, reducing the need to develop new processes, techniques, solutions, and algorithms. Particularly, new techniques for algorithmic composition need to be developed and new forms of music explored to overcome the limitations inherited from traditional music and to expand on the work of Hiller, Koenig, and Xenakis. The use of computers in music is possibly the most exciting and liberating development in the history of music. It is highly attractive to those creative souls who wish to explore the musical possibilities (and limits) and be as musically creative as possible.

Table 3.1 Acronyms used in this chapter

ADC	Analogue-to-digital converter.
ASP	Audio synthesis programs, a sound synthesis system using instruction synthesis developed at the institute of Sonology.
C	An early high-level computer language, noted for its efficiency and portability from one system to another.
C++	An object-oriented and more modern version of C.
CARL	Compute Audio Research Laboratory, at UCSD.
CD	Compact disk, specification was a joint venture by Philips and Sony.
CEMAMu	Centre d'Etudes de Mathématiques et Automatiques Musicales, Center for Studies in Mathematics and Automated Music.

(continued)

Table 3.1 Continued

CEMS	Coordinated Electronic Music Studio, installed at the Electronic Music Studio at the State University of New York at Albany.
CNMAT	Center for New Music and Audio Technologies at the University of California at Berkeley.
CPU	Central processing unit, of a computer.
CSIRAC	Council for Scientific and Industrial Research Automatic Computer.
CV	Control voltage.
DAC	Cigital-to-analog converter.
DAW	Cigital audio workstation, typically an audio and midi, or virtual instrument, production system.
DEC	Digital Equipment Corporation, a computer company.
DSP	Digital signal processing, the generation and manipulation of digital audio signals.
EMC	Electronic Music Centre, originally a joint venture between Columbia and Princeton universities, other institutes may also have used the acronym and name for their own electronic music centres.
FM	Frequency modulation synthesis.
FORTRAN	Formula translation, the name of an early high-level computer language.
FPU	Floating-point unit, (part of) a CPU that is hardware specialized for manipulating floating point numbers.
GENDYN	Generation dynamique, a sound synthesis program and technique using instruction synthesis developed by Xenakis at CEMAMu.
GPS	Global positioning system.
GROOVE	Generated Real-time Output Operations on Voltage-controlled Equipment, a computer-controlled analog synthesis system.
IBM	International Business Machines, a computer company.
ILLIAC	The University of Illinois automatic computer.
I/O	Input and output, of a computer system.
IRCAM	Institut de Recherche et Coordination Acoustique/Musique.
KIM-1	An early microcomputer or PC, KIM stands for keyboard input monitor.
LFO	Low frequency oscillator, usually used to modulate parameters in.
LISP	List processing, an early computer language specialized in list processing.
LOGO	An early computer language created for educational purposes and derived from LISP.
LSB	Least significant byte.

LSI	Large-scale integration, a type of integrated circuit manufacturing, also used by DEC for an integrated circuit version of their PDP class of computers, such as the LSI-11.
Max	A graphical software system for MIDI data generation and manipulation, originally developed by Miller Puckette at IRCAM.
Max/FTS	Faster than sound, an early audio DSP system for Max from IRCAM.
Max/MSP	Max signal processing, an audio DSP system for Max based on Pd.
MIDI	Musical instrument digital interface, a specification for a communication protocol through which musical instruments can communicate.
MIDI LISP	A version of the LISP computer language with integrated MIDI support.
MIDI LOGO	A version of the LOGO computer language with integrated MIDI support.
MIPS	Millions of instructions per second.
MPEG-4	Moving Picture Experts Group 4.
MSB	Most significant byte.
MUSIC-N	A set of computer languages (MUSIC I–MUSIC V) for computer music.
OSC	Open sound control, a networked communication protocol for communication between music software and hardware applications and components.
PC	Personal computer.
Pd	Pure Data, a derivative of Max that handles audio, video, and pure data equally, written by Miller Puckette at UCSD.
PDP	Programmed data processor, a name for a large family of machines at DEC, such as the PDP-11 and PDP-15.
PILE	A sound synthesis program using instruction synthesis developed at the Institute of Sonology.
PODn	A set of software systems for music composition and sound synthesis named from Poisson distribution.
RAM	Random access memory, computer storage, usually volatile (needs continuous power to maintain the information) and fast access.
RCA	Radio Corporation of America.
RISC	Reduced instruction set computer, a popular high-performance CPU architecture.
ROM	Read-only memory.
SAOL	Structured audio orchestra language, a part of the MPEG-4 specification.
SAWDUST	A sound synthesis program using instruction synthesis developed at the University of Illinois.
SCSI	Small computer system interface, usually used for disk and tape devices.
SGI	A computer manufacturer specialized in high performance UNIX workstations, originally named Silicon Graphics Inc.

(*continued*)

Table 3.1 Continued

SHARC	Super Harvard architecture single-chip computer, and the name of a family of DSP processors from Analogue Devices.
SSP	Sound synthesis program, a sound synthesis program using instruction synthesis developed at the Institute of Sonology.
SSSP	Structured sound synthesis program created by William Buxton at the University of Toronto.
STEIM	Studio for Electro-Instrumental Music.
UCSD	University of California at San Diego.
UGen	Unit generator, a functional block in the MUSIC programming language.
Unix	A computer operating system.
UPIC	Unite Polyagogique Informatique du CEMAMu, a graphical composition and sound synthesis system.
USB	Universal serial bus.
VAMPIRE	Video and Music Program for Interactive Realtime Exploration / Experimentation.
VAX	Virtual address extension, the name of computers from DEC that had extended memory capabilities from the PDP class of computers.
VLSI	Very large scale integration, a more compact and densely populated version of LSI integrated circuit manufacturing.
VM	Virtual memory, where disk or tape storage is used to simulate RAM, because RAM is expensive and tape or disk storage is cheaper and more plentiful.
VOSIM	Voice simulator, a synthesis system develop at the Institute of Sonology that was particularly useful for vocal-like sounds.
VST	Virtual studio technology, an audio plug-in specification from Steinberg GmbH.
WDR	Westdeutsche Rundfunk, West German Radio.

NOTE

1. There are various brief, anecdotal reports of computers playing music in a range of ways at about the same time as CSIRAC. These include an assortment of sound-producing mechanisms, incorporating attaching a speaker to a serial bus or part of the computer, placing radio equipment near the computer and playing sounds through the radio's speaker via radio-frequency interference, and programming computers to print on large, electromechanical, printing machines such that the printing created tones, among others. Unfortunately, there are no surviving recordings of these activities, and there is so far no surviving evidence from the time.

BIBLIOGRAPHY

Avizienis, R., A. Freed, T. Suzuki, and D. Wessel. 2000. Scalable connectivity processor for computer music performance systems. In *Proceedings of the International Computer Music Conference, Berlin*. San Francisco: International Computer Music Association, pp. 523–526.

Barlow, C. 1987. Two essays on theory. *Computer Music Journal* 11(1): 44–60.

Berg, P. 1996. Abstracting the future: The search for musical constructs. *Computer Music Journal* 20(3): pp. 24–27.

Berg, P. 2009. Composing Sound Structures with Rules. *Contemporary Music Review* 28(1): 75–87.

Berg, P., R. Rowe, and D. Theriault. 1980. SSP and sound description. *Computer Music Journal* 4(1): 25–35.

Bongers, B. 1998. An interview with Sensorband. *Computer Music Journal* 22(1): 13–24.

Chadabe, J. 1997. *Electric Sound: The Past and Promise of Electronic Music*. Upper Saddle River, NJ: Prentice Hall.

Collins, N. 1991. Low brass: The evolution of trombone-propelled electronics. *Leonardo Music Journal* 1(1): 41–44.

Collins, N. 2006. *Handmade Electronic Music: The Art of Hardware Hacking*. New York: Routledge.

Cope, D. 1991. *Computers and Musical Style*. Madison, WI: A-R Editions.

Dodge, C. 1988. Profile: A musical fractal. *Computer Music Journal* 12(3): 10–14.

Doornbusch, P. 2002a. A brief survey of mapping in algorithmic composition. In *Proceedings of the International Computer Music Conference, Gothenburg*. San Francisco: International Computer Music Association, pp. 205–210.

Doornbusch, P. 2002b. Composers' views on mapping in algorithmic composition. *Organised Sound* 7(2): 145–156.

Doornbusch, P. 2003. Instruments from now into the future: The disembodied voice. *Sounds Australian* 62: 18–21.

Doornbusch, P. 2005a. *The Music of CSIRAC: Australia's First Computer Music*. Melbourne: Common Ground.

Doornbusch, P. 2005b. Pre-composition and algorithmic composition: Reflections on disappearing lines in the sand. *Context Journal of Music Research*, Vols. 29 and 30: 47–58.

Harley, J. 2002. The electroacoustic music of Iannis Xenakis. *Computer Music Journal* 26(1): 33–57.

Hiller, L., and L. Isaacson. 1958. Musical composition with a high-speed digital computer. *Journal of the Audio Engineering Society* 6(3): 154–160.

Hiller, L., and L. Isaacson. 1959. *Experimental Music*. New York: McGraw-Hill.

Kahrs, M. 2002. Digital audio system architecture. In *Applications of Digital Signal Processing to Audio and Acoustics*, ed. M. Kahrs and K. Brandenburg. New York: Kluwer Academic, pp. 195–234.

Koenig, G. M. 1970a. *Project 1*. Electronic Music Reports 2. Sonology Institute, Royal Conservatory of Holland, The Hague, pp. 32–44.

Koenig, G. M. 1970b. *Project 2: A Programme for Musical Composition*. Electronic Music Reports 3. Sonology Institute, Royal Conservatory of Holland, The Hague, pp. 4–161.

Lewis, G. 2000. Too many notes: Computers, complexity and culture in Voyager. *Leonardo Music Journal* 10: 33–39.

Manning, P. 2004. *Electronic and Computer Music*. Oxford: Oxford University Press.

Mathews, M. 1969. *The Technology of Computer Music*. Cambridge: MIT Press.

Polansky, L., and M. McKinney. 1991. Morphological mutation functions. In *Proceedings of the International Computer Music Conference.* San Francisco: International Computer Music Association, pp. 234–241.

Roads, C. 1995. *The Computer Music Tutorial.* Cambridge: MIT Press.

Roads, C., and J. Strawn, eds. 1985. *Foundations of Computer Music.* Cambridge: MIT Press.

Rowe, R. 1993. *Interactive Music Systems.* Cambridge: MIT Press.

Smalley, D. 1986. Spectro-morphology and structuring processes. In *The Language of Electroacoustic music,* ed. S. Emmerson. London: Macmillan, pp. 61–93.

Spiegel, L. 1998. Graphical GROOVE: Memorial for the VAMPIRE, a visual music system. *Organised Sound* 3(3): 187–191.

Truax, B. 1973. *The Computer Composition—Sound Synthesis Programs POD4, POD5 and POD6.* Sonological Reports no. 2. Utrecht, The Netherlands: Institute of Sonology.

Truax, B. 1990. Chaotic non-linear systems and digital synthesis: An exploratory study. In *Proceedings of the International Computer Music Conference.* San Francisco: International Computer Music Association, pp. 100–103.

Wessel, D., R. Avizienis, A. Freed, and M. Wright. 2007. A force sensitive multi-touch array supporting multiple 2-D musical control structures. In *Proceedings of the 7th International Conference on New Interfaces for Musical Expression.* New York, pp. 41–45.

Xenakis, I. 1992. *Formalized Music.* Rev. ed. New York: Pendragon Press.

Audio Engineering Society. Audio timeline. http://www.aes.org/aeshc/docs/audio.history.timeline.html, accessed February 14, 2008.

Crab, Simon. 120 Years of Electronic Music, Electronic Musical Instrument 1870–1990. http://www.obsolete.com/120_years/machines/fairlight/index.html, accessed March 10, 2008.

Enlightened Systems. Physical Modeling Research Labs. http://www.enlightenedsystems.com/vl/research.htm, accessed March 20, 2008.

Fairlight CMI. Wikipedia. http://en.wikipedia.org/wiki/Fairlight_CMI, accessed February 27, 2008.

Fairlight US Inc. Welcome to Fairlight US. http://www.fairlightus.com/about.html, accessed February 27, 2008.

Holmes, Greg. The Holmes Page: The Fairlight CMI. http://www.ghservices.com/gregh/fairligh/, accessed February 27, 2008.

Introduction to OSC. http://opensoundcontrol.org/introduction-osc, accessed March 17, 2008.

Krazer, Stefan. Yamaha Synthesisers History. http://www.kratzer.at/DXYamahaHistory.htm, accessed March 10, 2008.

Longbottom, Roy. Computer Speeds from Instruction Mixes pre-1960 to 1971. http://freespace.virgin.net/roy.longbottom/cpumix.htm, accessed May 10, 2008.

McCallum, John C. Cost of CPU Performance through Time 1944–2003. http://www.jcmit.com/cpu-performance.htm, accessed May 10, 2008.

120 Years of Electronic Music. Computer Music: MUSIC I-V. http://www.obsolete.com/120_years/machines/software/index.html, accessed February 12, 2008.

OpenSound Control. Wikipedia. http://en.wikipedia.org/wiki/OpenSound_Control, accessed March 17, 2008.

Physical modelling synthesis. Wikipedia. http://en.wikipedia.org/wiki/Physical_modelling_synthesis, accessed March 20, 2008.

Truax, Barry. POD. http://www.sfu.ca/truax/pod.html, accessed March 5, 2008.

University of California at Santa Cruz. Short History of Computer Music. http://arts.ucsc.edu/ems/music/equipment/computers/history/history.html, accessed March 10, 2008.

Vintage Synth Explorer. Vintage Synth Explorer—Time-Line. http://www.vintagesynth.com/local/timeline.html, accessed March 15, 2008.

Yamaha DX7. Wikipedia. http://en.wikipedia.org/wiki/Yamaha_DX7, accessed March 10, 2008.

CHAPTER 4

SOUND SYNTHESIS USING COMPUTERS

PETER MANNING

THE primary focus of this chapter is the evolution of computer-based techniques of sound synthesis for composition and performance, with a particular emphasis on the development of software applications for an environment that is now increasingly based on the technology of desktop and laptop computing. The perspective that emerges necessarily intersects with other aspects of sound synthesis and signal processing, for example, the development of systems designed in the first instance for digital mixing and recording, and the musical instrument digital interface (MIDI)-based world of the commercial synthesizer and associated products that rely primarily or sometimes exclusively on the characteristics of custom-designed hardware. A useful context for the current study in the latter context has already been established in chapter 2 of this volume, and other key connections are studied later in this chapter.

Today, the possibilities of software sound synthesis are for the most part limited only by the imagination of composers and performers and their ability to articulate these ideas in ways that can be practically realized. Such favorable conditions for engaging with the medium, however, are relatively new. In the past, shortcomings in the capacity of computers to satisfy these requirements have impeded the realization of such goals, and with the passage of time the significance of these constraints is becoming increasingly obscured. Understanding these processes of evolution provides an invaluable insight not only into the history of the medium but also the important legacy features that continue to shape its further development.

1. FROM MAX MATHEWS TO CSOUND

The exploration of sound synthesis using computers can be traced back to the dawn of commercial computing in the early 1950s. Indeed, the early stages of the Australian Council for Scientific and Industrial Research Automatic Computer (CSIRAC) project discussed in chapter 3 pre-date even this distant landmark. Throughout the 1950s and 1960s, the computer industry was dominated by expensive mainframe computers, affordable only by major academic institutions and commercial enterprises. They were designed to process computing tasks using a technique known as batch processing. This involved the manual prepreparation of programs and associated data, using key punch stations to convert this information into a machine-readable format registered as digital patterns on cards or paper tape. These tasks or "jobs" were then passed to computer operators, who loaded them one by one into the computer, ready for processing via the batch stream.

To maximize the efficient use of resources, these jobs were prioritized automatically according to the expected computing demands, which had to be estimated by the user in advance. As a result, unless these priorities were altered by the direct intervention of the computer operators, more demanding tasks were invariably pushed down the queue to be run at times of low activity, more often than not overnight. Digital audio synthesis programs were to prove exceptionally computer intensive and thus almost invariably suffered such a fate. Composers faced further delays before they could audition the results since mainframe computers were not equipped with the special interfaces necessary to convert digital audio samples to equivalent voltage patterns for acoustic reproduction. It was necessary to store the generated audio data as a file of digital samples using a demountable storage medium such as magnetic tape. The associated tape reel then had to be remounted on a stand-alone digital playback unit, connected in turn to a digital-to-analog converter and an associated loudspeaker. Such equipment was not routinely manufactured at this time, and the audio quality of most early hand-built converters left a great deal to be desired.

Such working conditions are almost unimaginable today. Although by the late 1960s the introduction of time-sharing facilities made it possible for multiple users at a time to communicate directly with a mainframe computer using typewriter terminals, it was still the case that substantial computing tasks such as digital sound synthesis could only be processed in the background using the batch stream.

It is with these factors in mind that we turn to the pioneering work of Max Mathews at Bell Telephone Laboratories, New Jersey. The motivation for this initiative was based on a shared musical and technical agenda that fortuitously combined commercial objectives with those of creative intent. The research division of Bell Telephone Laboratories, seeking to increase the capacity and efficiency of their telephone communication networks, initiated a research program during the early 1950s investigating the use of digital signals as the medium of transmission. These investigations required a robust and accurate means of comparing the quality of information at both ends, and it occurred to Mathews that the reliability of these evaluations could be significantly enhanced if the associated audio test data were generated digitally to precise specifications using specially written synthesis algorithms. Moreover, if these algorithms were designed to produce music-quality rather than telephone-quality signals, the associated telecommunications networks could then be further tested regarding their suitability for high-fidelity broadcast applications.

After initial experimentation with two pilot programs, MUSIC I (1957) (which generated a simple triangle wave audio function) and MUSIC II (1958) (which permitted four functions drawn from a repertory of sixteen possible waveforms to be manipulated simultaneously), Matthews produced the first fully developed prototype MUSIC III in 1960 with assistance from Joan Miller. Although many of the key features necessary to produce a viable composing environment had by this stage been identified and partially implemented, it was a further expansion of the program, known as MUSIC IV (1962), that provided the definitive template for the important derivatives that were to follow (Mathews 1963). Although later versions of what are generically known as the MUSIC-N family of programs were to incorporate significant refinements and extensions, with just a few minor syntactical changes it is possible to execute synthesis tasks originally written for MUSIC IV using the most significant and widely used derivative in use today, Csound.

The development of Csound by Barry Vercoe illustrates the way in which the development of sound synthesis software over the years has been shaped by the functional characteristics of the associated computer technology. Mathews's generosity in making the source code of MUSIC IV available to interested researchers led quickly to the production of some important early derivatives, including MUSIC IV B, developed at Princeton by Hubert Howe and Godfrey Winham in 1964 specifically for use with the University's IBM 360 mainframe computer. Vercoe joined the staff at Princeton in 1967 to carry out research in the field of digital audio processing and took a keen interest in this program, producing his own highly optimized version, MUSIC 360, in 1968, which he distributed to the wider community free of charge. Computers such as the IBM 360, however, were still only found in larger commercial and educational institutions, and the opportunities for creative engagement were thus to remain highly constrained. By the end of the decade, however, it was becoming clear that a new generation of smaller and much cheaper minicomputers held the key to expanding general accessibility, providing at the same time a much more suitable environment for hosting specialist applications such as sound synthesis.

One minicomputer attracted particular interest in this context, the PDP-11, manufactured by the Digital Equipment Corporation (DEC). Vercoe moved to the Massachusetts Institute of Technology (MIT) in 1971 and began work on a new version of MUSIC 360 rewritten specifically for this computer. Known as MUSIC 11, this was released for wider use under license in 1978. Although this included a number of useful additions to the library of synthesis algorithms, like its predecessor it was written using low-level programming code and therefore was entirely machine specific. Whereas at the time this was a necessary expedient to optimize its speed of execution, by the early 1980s it was clear that there was a growing demand for versions that could run successfully on other machines, including newer designs that were inherently faster. The crucial breakthrough came in 1986 when Vercoe released a version of MUSIC 11 entirely rewritten using the higher-level machine-independent programming language C, now renamed Csound. Since compilers for programs written in C were by this point available for most computers, the future of the program was finally secured. Although Csound was also initially released under license, it became available as shareware, with full access to the source code, in 1992.

This extended pedigree has had a number of important consequences. First, and perhaps most significantly, it has resulted in an extremely robust and versatile open source sound synthesis program, the product of many years of painstaking research and active testing not only by Vercoe but also by the many composers and researchers who subsequently made major contributions to its continuing development. Second, Csound became an especially attractive resource for developing innovative concepts of digital synthesis, continuing pioneering research that had been carried out using earlier versions of the MUSIC-N family of programs. As a consequence, it served as the test bed for many of the audio synthesis techniques in general use today. At the same time, many of the techniques that have been developed over the years using other software environments have been rewritten as additions to the library of functions provided by Csound, thus creating a highly inclusive and exceptionally versatile synthesis resource (Boulanger 2000).

In the years leading up to the public release of Csound, it was still generally the case that significant computational delays were encountered processing the source instructions and data. The key consideration here is the threshold point at which the processing capacity of the computer is sufficient to perform all the necessary computations between one audio sample and the next. If the former exceeds the latter, then it becomes possible to synthesize the associated sounds in real time, streaming the samples directly to a digital-to-analog converter for instant reproduction. If this requirement cannot be met, the samples must instead be stored in a data file for subsequent playback when all the computations have been completed.

During the pioneering years, real-time synthesis other than in the form of directly coupled pulse trains, such as those produced by CSIRAC, was not even a remote possibility. Since tasks of even a relatively simple nature would often involve computing to actual time overheads in excess of 20 to 1, and in the case of more complex tasks overheads of perhaps 50 or 100 or more to 1, there were also finite limitations on what realistically could be considered. Mainframe computer processing time was very expensive and thus strictly rationed. Although minicomputers such as the PDP-11 were more accessible and less expensive to operate, they still lacked the processing power necessary to meet even relatively modest demands in terms of real-time audio synthesis.

The solution to this major constraint was to emerge from a technology that started to gather momentum during the early 1970s by which miniaturized arrays of logic circuits could be fabricated within a single wafer of silicon of sufficient complexity to facilitate the design of microprocessors, devices capable of performing all the functions of a conventional central processing unit (CPU) within a single computer chip. Although early microprocessors had only limited functionality, it was becoming clear by the end of the decade that the technology was not only very much cheaper but also capable of delivering superior performance. In addition, it was also possible to design special processors, specifically engineered for highly demanding applications such as digital signal processing.

The first commercial digital signal processors (DSPs) were manufactured during the early 1980s, and by the end of the decade their design had advanced to the stage at which it was possible to develop advanced workstations, optimized for intensive multimedia applications such as sound synthesis. These workstations were typically of a hybrid design, combining the resources of a conventional computer with those of a "front-end," high-speed digital synthesis system, the former handling the basic communication, control, and housekeeping operations and the latter all the processing-intensive and time-critical computations.

The resulting improvements in overall processing speed over standard computers provided by these DSP-enhanced workstations were of several orders of magnitude, sufficient to enable intensive research into the creative possibilities of software-based real-time computer synthesis. Vercoe started work on the internal modifications necessary to allow Csound to operate in real time in 1989 using a hybrid DSP system developed at MIT (Vercoe 1990). The most expedient control solution proved to be the addition of MIDI functions that could be used to regulate the processes of synthesis when it was practicable to operate in real time. Although these enhancements were included in the 1992 release of Csound, the majority of the expanded community of users only had access to conventional desktop computers. Although each processor upgrade brought a corresponding improvement in overall performance, the limitations on what could be attempted in terms of real-time synthesis in any software context were to remain significant for a number of years. Although memories fade quickly, it is worth recalling that such constraints were still to prove significant even up to a decade later.

2. THE EVOLUTION OF SOUND SYNTHESIS

Given its provenance, it is perhaps not surprising that Csound retains the hallmarks of more traditional approaches to the representation and realization of musical sounds, modeled closely in the first instance on the "note/event" descriptors associated with the preparation of conventional scores for subsequent performance via acoustic instruments. A Csound program is divided into two primary components, identified as the "orchestra" and the "score." The former is concerned with the choice and configuration of the component synthesis routines, organized within the framework of one or more contributing "instruments," and the latter with the associated control data. The original set of functions provided for the design of instruments was modeled on devices commonly found in classical analog studios of the time. These included signal generators such as oscillators and noise generators and processing devices such as filters and envelope shapers. As the years advanced, this core library steadily expanded to embrace more than 500 different functions. From MUSIC 11 onward, it also became possible to input externally generated sound material, eventually opening up the possibility of live signal processing.

One of the most distinctive features of the early MUSIC-N programs was the method used to generate periodic waves, establishing principles that have been widely adopted by software developers. This approach was stimulated by the need to reduce the computational overheads incurred in generating audio functions, whether as single frequencies or compound timbres. The processing overheads involved in repeatedly calculating each waveform sample from first principles are significant, and it occurred to Mathews that significant savings could be produced in this regard by calculating the required waveform only once and then using a suitable table lookup procedure to extract this information as the required frequency. Although it is necessary to use mathematical interpolation routines to extract accurate values from such tables, the additional overheads incurred here are far less than calculating each waveform sample directly from first principles (Mathews 1969).

This technique, known as *wavetable synthesis*, has some disadvantages since the spectral content of the resultant wave has to be fixed at the outset. Whereas the application of basic amplitude shaping to create an enveloped sound event only requires a relatively simple mathematical operation, varying the content of the timbre itself is entirely another matter. This requires much more complex processing operations on the wave, for example, using filters selectively to attenuate frequency components. Such techniques are computationally demanding, running the risk that the efficiency gains resulting from the use of wavetables will at best be reduced and in some circumstances quite the reverse.

During the pioneering years, computing overheads were so significant that options such as filters were rarely used. Instead, many composers adopted an alternative approach, known as *additive synthesis*, that involves the generation of timbres from component frequencies using a bank of oscillators and a shared wavetable consisting of a simple sine wave function. The freedom thus afforded to shape both the amplitude and the frequency of each frequency component independently and dynamically also extends to the production of both harmonic and inharmonic spectra. The significant downside to this approach is the amount of intricate and precise detail that has to be provided if the resulting timbres are to achieve the required degree of creative articulation and refinement. Indeed, there are major practical and conceptual problems here for composers in terms of the complexities of generating sounds entirely from first principles in this manner, with few models readily available to assist in this learning process.

This situation goes to the very heart of the opportunities and challenges opened up by computer-based techniques of sound production, involving a trade-off between the degree of control that may be exercised over the processes of synthesis and the need to provide compositional tools that are practicable and meaningful in creative terms. Such considerations need to be carefully borne in mind in considering the alternative methods of sound synthesis that have been developed over the years.

One of the earliest of these, FM (frequency modulation) synthesis, was pioneered by John Chowning at Stanford University during the late 1960s. The basic principle of frequency modulation involves the direct application of the periodic wave function generated by one oscillator to modulate dynamically the frequency (carrier) setting of a second oscillator. The resulting spectral transformations in the output of the latter may be analyzed in terms of three components: (1) c, the carrier (= original) frequency of the audio oscillator; (2) m, the modulating frequency of the second oscillator, which is connected to the frequency input of the first oscillator; and (3) d, the depth of modulation that results, measured in terms of the maximum frequency deviation produced either side of the carrier frequency. If the modulating frequency is about 20 Hz or less, the modulation will simply be perceived as a frequency vibrato. If it is greater, the ear detects additional frequencies as energy from the carrier frequency is stolen to produce two series of sidebands. These are located either side of the carrier frequency, drawn from the progressions $c - m, c - 2m, c - 3m \ldots$ and $c + m, c + 2m, c + 3m \ldots$, the number and relative amplitudes thereof determined by the results of complex mathematical functions, regulated in turn by the modulating index I, a value calculated by dividing the frequency of deviation by the frequency of modulation, d/m.

Chowning recognized the significance of implementing an important theoretical principle concerning the expected characteristics of sidebands that lie below 0 Hz. The ear does not recognize negative frequencies, with such components instead perceived as positive frequencies folded back into the audio spectrum. The crucial consideration here is that this fold-back should be accompanied by a change of phase, allowing the production of an enhanced repertory of timbres from the complex interactions of these interleaved frequencies and associated phases. As a consequence of extensive investigations into the characteristics of these sidebands, Chowning (1985) was able to develop and refine an extensive repertory of FM instruments that allow the simulated production of a range of musical timbres, from brass and woodwind sounds to a variety of bell and percussion sounds.

Synthesis by FM offers a number of advantages over a technique such as additive synthesis. A simple FM pair of oscillators requires just four control parameters: (1) the frequency of the control oscillator, (2) the amplitude of the control oscillator, (3) the frequency of the modulated oscillator, and (4) the overall amplitude envelope of the resulting wave function. What has proved especially appealing in this context is the extent to which suitable manipulations of these control parameters produce not only an extensive palette of distinctive timbres but also dynamic articulations thereof, in some instances creating characteristics very close in nature to those associated with acoustic instruments. It is possible, for example, to simulate an extensive repertory of brass sounds for which the brightness of the partials increases during the attack phase and falls again during the decay phase in accordance with acoustic expectations. Chowning's work attracted the attention of Yamaha, which developed a special hardware processor for their own patented versions of the FM algorithm, used in their first all-digital MIDI synthesizer, the DX7, released in 1983.

The tensions that can arise between creative accessibility and ease of use and the measure and depth of control that can thus be exercised over the synthesis process are interesting examples of FM synthesis. Although more complex FM algorithms require the use of multiple oscillators, it should be borne in mind that the underlying principles still involve only four basic parameters. Furthermore, the repertory of sounds and transformations thereof that can be generated by manipulating these variables is extensive. In terms of understanding the nature of these relationships in a musical context, however, there is no immediate sense of connectivity between the control variables and the synthesized results. Although the underlying mathematics provides an accurate analysis of the spectra resulting from different parameter values, it is quite another matter to start with the desired characteristics of a particular timbre or variation thereof and then try to work out which settings might be required to achieve them.

The desire to develop synthesis methods that correlate more closely with characteristics encountered in the natural sound world led to a number of alternative approaches that merit closer study. One family of techniques that fostered further interest in this context arose from the study of waveguides. In their simplest implementation, these consist of simple signal-processing loops in which incoming signals pass first through a digital delay line and then a low-pass filter. By applying carefully regulated feedback of the processed output signal to the input stage, it becomes possible to induce frequency-specific resonances. Such an arrangement comes very close to the behavior of naturally vibrating strings, reeds, or air columns, creating opportunities for realistic simulations of instruments that use these types of excitation. In essence, the methodology changes from one based on the production of synthetic spectra to the replication of acoustic methods of sound production, an approach known generically as *physical modeling*. Important pioneering work in the context was carried out by Lejaren Hiller and Perre Ruiz (1971a, 1971b) at the University of Illinois during the late 1960s, working with both analog and digital models of acoustic instruments. They established the mathematical principles involved in energizing their vibrations, taking into account the range of responses that could be produced within acceptable margins of stability.

Interest in these possibilities started to grow during the 1970s, and toward the end of the decade Kevin Karplus and Alex Strong carried out detailed investigations into the characteristics of plucked strings. This resulted in the Karplus-Strong algorithm, which has been developed in a number of contexts to produce a rich repertory of digital models reproducing the characteristics of stringed instruments

(Karplus and Strong 1983). There is an interesting boundary here between implementations that simply seek to limit the initial excitation of the feedback loop to a suitable impulse and those that treat waveguides more in the manner of a signal modifier or processor, where waveguide-induced resonances are added to existing audio material to create additional enhancements.

A particularly attractive feature of this technique is that whereas the underlying algorithms are necessarily complex and challenging to develop and refine, only a small number of control parameters are required to operate the resulting models. Moreover, unlike FM synthesis, there is a much clearer correlation between the control values and the possible variations thereof and the characteristics of the acoustical results. These conditions also ensure that any modifications or extensions of such models to create imaginary new acoustic instruments are predicated on principles that can be understood in musical rather than purely technical terms, allowing for a better understanding of the creative possibilities of new designs. During the 1980s, interest in physical modeling gathered pace. David Jaffe and Julius Smith at the Center for Computer Music Research in Music and Acoustics (CCRMA), Stanford, developed extensions to the Karplus-Strong algorithm in association with the original investigators, and Smith subsequently conducted further research into woodwind instrument modeling (Jaffe and Smith 1983). The further work of Smith and his associates at CCRMA led to a second collaboration with Yamaha, resulting in the VL1 "virtual acoustic" synthesizer, released commercially in 1994.

Another example that is arguably close enough to the principles of physical modeling to be regarded as an extension of it arises from the work of Xavier Rodet, Yves Potard, and Jean Baptiste Barrière at IRCAM (Institut de Recherche et Coordination Acoustique/Musique) during the early 1980s. The focus of this work was the modeling of the human voice in terms of the formants produced when the vocal chords are excited and the resulting vibrations are enhanced by our resonant cavities. Known as FOF (Fonction d' Onde Formantique), the original purpose was to reproduce the characteristics of the singing voice, initially as the basis for a software synthesis program known as CHANT (Rodet et al. 1984). It soon became clear, however, that the model could be manipulated to produce a significantly expanded range of synthesis possibilities, including realistic imitations of sounds such as bells, gongs, and other members of the percussion family.

The reworking of FOF by Michael Clarke as a function available in Csound in the mid-1980s provides an interesting example of the capacity of the latter program not only to act as a test bed for exploring new synthesis techniques but also to host adaptations of techniques originally developed in other contexts (Clarke 1996). A further example of vocal modeling, in this case based more directly on waveguide techniques, is the SPASM (Singing Physical Articulatory Synthesis Model) algorithm, developed by Perry Cook at CCRMA in 1992 (Cook 1993). One disadvantage of FOF is the significant difficulties encountered in accurately synthesizing consonants as opposed to vowels. Cook's model of the vocal tract accommodates both aspects and thus is able to synthesize speech characteristics as well as those of singing. By the end of the 1990s, the development of algorithms for physical modeling in programs had extended to the development of further specialist software applications, the most notable example being Modalys, developed by IRCAM (Vinet 2007).

Principles of analysis and resynthesis underpinned the development of another family of techniques linked by a common feature: the manipulation of audio data in the time domain, by which it becomes possible, for example, to speed up or slow down the evolution of sounds without necessarily changing the frequency characteristics of the component spectra. There are, however, some material differences in the ways in which these transformations may be achieved and the functional characteristics of the results. The first of these have their origins in the analog vocoder, a device that uses a bank of filters to measure the spectral energy of applied signals within specific frequency bands mapped across the audio-frequency range, typically three per octave. The process could then be reversed by varying the output levels of a complementary set of filters energized using either white noise to produce an approximation to the original signals or an entirely different source, resulting in a cross-synthesis by which the spectral characteristics of the original signals modify the timbres of the new material.

In a digital context, work in this area was pioneered by James Moorer at Stanford in the early 1970s and developed further by a number of other researchers, notably Paul Lansky and Charles Dodge at Princeton. The technique they developed, known as linear predictive coding or LPC, produced data in a slightly different format from that of the vocoder, but retaining a number of key features (Moorer 1979). For LPC, the initial audio data are sampled into a series of discrete snapshots or frames of data, each analyzed in terms of three primary characteristics: (1) the pitch of the sound and (2) its amplitude and (3) the spectrum of partials at that instant. A fourth characteristic, which reflects the original intention of the application as a voice analyzer and resynthesizer, is a simple flag that indicates whether the data have an identifiable pitch context or are predominantly composed of noise. The need to set such a flag as part of the analysis and resynthesis processes is not without problems in the context of generating music rather than speech, uncertainties at the boundary point creating the conditions for significant instability. Nonetheless, the technique has been successfully used in a compositional context by a number of composers, not least in the context of dynamic time stretching or compression, achieved by manipulating the timing of the component frames by means of repetition or overlap.

Although computationally more demanding, the subsequent development of the phase vocoder was ultimately to prove more popular and reliable. Here, the analysis processes are functionally simpler and much closer to those of the analog vocoder, by which a bank of filters analyzes the characteristics of audio data in terms of the amplitude and phase of the spectral energy in each band, sampled as a series of discrete frames. Ironically, whereas the phase vocoder is much more reliable than LPC for processing and manipulating pitched data, the reverse is true when handling sounds that contain significant noise components, such as speech. Pioneering work by Moorer during the late 1970s led to a number of software implementations during the 1980s and early 1990s, one of earliest and most influential versions being developed by Mark Dolson at the Computer Audio Research Laboratory (CARL), University of California at San Diego (Dolson 1986), leading to a number of important improvements and extensions from Trevor Wishart in the United Kingdom and an application-specific version known as PVOC (Phase VOCoder) (Fischman 1997). Also, IRCAM developed a special version of the phase vocoder, AudioSculpt, that allows the user to manipulate the evolution of timbre with respect to time by graphically editing associated spectrograms of the source data (Vinet 2007).

Granular synthesis, the last technique considered in this section, has an interesting provenance. The underlying mathematical principles go back to the late 1940s; Denis Gabor (1947) proposed the representation of acoustic spectra in terms of very small grains or quanta. The concept of dividing up the time domain into small intervals of sampled spectra underpinned the work of Iannis Xenakis during the 1960s, developing and applying compositional principles based on his theories of random probability. His reliance on analog technology significantly constrained the extent to which sound materials could be granulated. However, in 1974 Curtis Roads started to develop computer algorithms for granular synthesis, initially at UCSD and subsequently at MIT (Roads 1978). Almost simultaneously, Barry Truax started to develop similar algorithms, working first at Utrecht's Institute of Sonology and then at Simon Fraser University, British Columbia. Although the initial work of both pioneers was based on synthesis-only implementations, generating acoustic spectra from first principles, Truax subsequently extended the technique to embrace the analysis and resynthesis of acoustically generated sounds, thus opening up an extended range of creative possibilities. In 1988, he implemented a real-time version of his program, known as GSAMX, subsequently made available for the Apple Macintosh as MacPod.

Although other synthesis techniques can under certain conditions create granular characteristics, with a notable example the FOF algorithm, which can be programmed to generate formats as streams of discrete quanta, the full potential of this method of synthesis can only be explored in a full implementation that generates or extracts grains in an operating environment that allows significant dynamic control over key parameters such as their individual enveloping and duration, density, and crucially in a resynthesis context, the ability to vary the speed of movement through the natural time domain of the sounds selected for granulation. Whereas the last requirement makes it necessary to work with prerecorded data, the scope and extent of the live transformations that are possible outweigh the possible drawbacks when working in a live performance context. These transformations are notable for their capacity to manipulate the spectral content of sounds that in their original context might only occupy just a few seconds, or even a fraction of a second, the processes of granulation allowing the composer to extend their evolution over a significant period of time, thus creating textures that highlight inner spectral features that in a normal time domain would simply not be perceived.

3. RESOURCES FOR SOFTWARE-BASED SOUND SYNTHESIS

While recognizing that the synthesis processes described cannot embrace all of the possibilities that have emerged over the years, they are nonetheless representative of the range and diversity of techniques available to both composers and performers who wish to explore the possibilities of software sound synthesis. Whereas Csound offers many advantages, not least the ease of access to the software via the Internet for a number of modern computing platforms, including Apple Macintosh, Windows, and Linux, and the range of synthesis techniques that are supported, there are important alternatives that have yet to be considered.

Csound was not the only MUSIC-N derivative to make use of the programming language C. Two programs are of particular interest in this context, CMUSIC and Cmix. F. Richard Moore developed CMUSIC at CARL, UCSD, subsequently renamed the Center for Research in Computing and the Arts (CRCA). Like Vercoe, his engagement with the development of MUSIC-N derivatives dated to the 1970s. His starting point, however, was MUSIC V, a version developed by Mathews himself using the higher-level computer language FORTRAN. A key feature of MUSIC V was its use of simplified constructs, making it easier for composers with little or no prior experience of computers to understand, and this key characteristic was retained in the design of CMUSIC. Unlike Csound, it was designed in the first instance for use as part of a much larger suite of programs developed at CARL during the early 1980s specifically for use with UNIX-based music workstations (Moore 1982). It is also functionally less rigid in terms of the ways synthesis routines and associated data are specified, taking fuller advantage of opportunities opened up by the C programming environment to create hierarchical structures. It was also the first of the C-based MUSIC-N derivatives to be made freely available to the wider community.

Although many features are functionally similar to those generally associated with MUSIC-N programs, Cmix, developed by Lansky (1990) at Princeton University, is arguably in a class of its own. The evolutionary approach to its design, starting in the mid-1980s, reflects its intended flexibility and extensibility. Essentially, it is a library of synthesis routines written in C that can be coupled or mixed with significant freedom in organizational terms. Although from the user's point of view the learning curve is slightly more demanding than in the case of CMUSIC, the syntax is semantically more powerful, not least in terms of the resources available to assist in the development of control structures. Although initially restricted to non-real-time applications, Brad Garton subsequently developed an interactive real-time version, RTCmix, released in 1997. Like CMUSIC, Cmix was developed for the UNIX environment, and this has had implications for both programs in terms of accessibility for those using Windows-based or Mac-based computers. Although use of the C programming language facilitates portability, considerable investment of time and effort is required to adapt and suitably maintain such programs for alternative environments. An effective solution was to emerge at an early stage for CMUSIC, which in turn acted as a catalyst for some other important software developments.

The question of accessibility by the wider community underpinned the Composers Desktop Project (CDP), a U.K.-based initiative originating from a collective associated with the University of York. This enterprise has made a significant contribution to the development and creative use of the medium, not least by those not able to access institutional resources during the 1980s and 1990s. In 1986, a study was carried out to see if it might be possible to convert CMUSIC into a version that could run on an Atari microcomputer. Having established the viability of the proposal, the pioneers founded the CDP in 1987 and developed a version of the program for general distribution, supported by a special hardware unit developed specifically to allow the input and output of high-quality audio from the Atari.

Having developed this software synthesis resource, in a manner not unlike that followed by CARL, other applications were soon added. These included a set of signal-processing routines from Andrew Bentley, a drawing program for additive synthesis from Richard Orton, a graphic desktop environment from Rajmil Fischman, and an initial set of spectral manipulation programs from Wishart. In 1989, the repertory of software expanded to include a version of Csound, thus anticipating its final release as shareware by three years. By the early 1990s, it was becoming clear that the Atari had no future, and in 1994 the CDP system was rewritten for UNIX and Windows, supplemented later by a version for Macintosh. With the passage of time, the developing repertory of programs focused increasingly on the development of sound transformation software written exclusively by the CDP, with further major contributions from Wishart and Dobson (Endrich 1997).

The reference to control structures in the discussion of Cmix merits further study. So far, the primary emphasis has been on the development of different synthesis techniques and their key characteristics. The subject of composing programs is addressed elsewhere, but there are certain aspects of these that merit attention in the current context. The classic note/event approach to synthesis that underpinned the initial development of MUSIC-N programs was predicated on preconfigured synthesis instruments that respond to sequential score data commands in a manner similar to their acoustic counterparts. Although the introduction of MIDI control functions in Csound opened the possibility of interactive performance, there is a further dimension to be considered: the capacity of the composing environment to embed functions that allow internal synthesis processes to be controlled according to the current state of key values.

An illustration of the type of control structure that might be required here is the triggering of an event in response to certain conditions having been met by existing processes. An example might be an instrument that morphs between two different sounds with the transition triggered at the point at which the amplitude envelope of the first sound exceeds a specific value. A major drawback to MUSIC-N programs for many years was the absence or near absence of suitable functions for such constructs. Vercoe started to tackle this shortcoming in the design of MUSIC 11, and by the 1992 release of Csound important progress had been made in developing the repertory of supporting mathematical and logical operators, with further additions to follow. The architecture of Csound, however, limits the extent to which such context-dependent control structures can be implemented, and further progress in this regard required a radically different approach to program design, involving the use of the graphical user interface, or GUI.

This reference to the GUI focuses attention on an important development that materially transformed the entire computing industry. The ability to visualize key concepts in terms of both constructing synthesis models from component functions and then manipulating creatively facilitated important new approaches to the design of synthesis software. Crucially, it became possible to develop fully interactive control surfaces for live synthesis, for which a significant emphasis may be placed on performance actions at the point of realization.

Developments in this context date to the early 1980s, in particular the pioneering work of Miller Puckette. Although at that time software systems for real-time synthesis were still all but impracticable, the impeding development of custom-engineered digital synthesizers and audio processors raised the alternative possibility of creating a hybrid environment in which the computer could be used as a sophisticated control device. Mathews had established the viability of such an approach in this area in 1981 with a real-time scheduling program called RTSKED, and this inspired Puckette to start work at MIT on his own implementation, known initially as Music500. In 1985, he moved to IRCAM to assist Vercoe with a project known as Music Performer, which required the capture and analysis of acoustic data from a live performer to create tracking synchronization commands for a synthetically generated accompaniment part. Having developed and adapted the control structures of Music500 for IRCAM's custom-designed, real-time processing system known as the 4X, Puckette turned his attention to the development of a MIDI control program written in C for the Apple Macintosh, completing the prototype in 1988.

This new version, known as Max, was a landmark achievement in a number of respects. First, it challenged the generally dismissive attitude of research centers toward small, mass-produced computers such as the Apple Macintosh. Second, the fact that a host computer for Max was available off the shelf at a fraction of the cost of an institutional computer provided ready access to such software. The innovative internal architecture of the program and the GUI-based design of the associated user interface also opened up a powerful new vista for computer-assisted audio synthesis (Puckette 1991).

Today, the functional characteristics of the interactive graphics-based computing environment are taken for granted. In the 1980s, however, their true significance for advanced applications such as audio synthesis had yet to be fully grasped. To take full advantage of such resources, the core architecture of the associated software has to be designed from the outset to take full account of the GUI interface. Such requirements could not have been envisaged at the time the core features of MUSIC-N software were established, and it has only proved possible to make limited use of the GUI as an enhancement for Csound. While the use of graphical windows to display key features such as wave functions and the event-by-event progress of the synthesis processes was relatively easy to implement, the dynamic input of performance commands has proved much more problematic.

A key design principle of Max concerns the use of constructs associated with a technique known as object-oriented programming (OOP). Instead of using the traditional notion of an integral set of algorithms in an essentially static configuration, configured to respond to separately provided streams of control data, the two components are essentially merged as a series of processes (objects) that are networked together using direct node-to-node communication links. Here, the graphics environment comes into its own. Starting with a blank configuration area, the user assembles processes from a repertory of graphically coded library objects that are linked to create a complete process. Once assembled, the process can either be left open for further interrogation at performance time or be saved as a complete "patch" that can then be treated as an object in its own right, with only the input and output link nodes left visible to allow this special object to be linked to other processes. The freedom to develop what amount to "macro"-subroutines that function as objects in their own right creates a powerful programming environment for both composition and performance.

Max was released commercially by IRCAM in 1991, initially under license from Opcode, with further developments and improvements forthcoming from both Puckette and David Zicarelli, and in 2002 licensing and support passed to Zicarelli's own company, Cycling '74. Even before its commercial release, however, further developments were under way at IRCAM that were to achieve an even greater significance. During the late 1980s the institution started work on a custom-designed music workstation as a replacement for the aging 4X, based on a revolutionary new DSP processor manufactured by Intel. This IRCAM Signal Processing Workstation, or ISPW, also incorporated an advanced graphics interface provided by the NeXT host computer, thus opening the possibility of extending Max to create an integrated real-time synthesis system (Lindemann et al. 1991).

Since Max was written in C, porting the code to the host computer for the ISPW was a manageable proposition. Also, the necessary infrastructure was already in place to allow the introduction of an additional layer of objects concerned specifically with synthesis processes. Known as Max/FTS (Faster Than Sound), this extension was completed by Puckette in 1991. Soon, IRCAM realized the value of modifying Max/FTS for use on other high-performance music workstations and produced a portable UNIX-based version known as jmax. The ultimate key to wider accessibility, however, lay in developing an implementation that would ultimately be viable for conventional desktop computers.

In 1993, Puckette and Zicarelli began work on a synthesis extension to Max for the Apple Macintosh, known as MSP (Max Signal Processing). Although initially limited by the capabilities of the Macintosh, a preliminary version of Max/MSP was completed in 1994. In the same year, Puckette left IRCAM for UCSD and started work on a revised version of Max/FTS renamed Pd (Pure Data), an open source program first released in 1996 (Puckette 2007). Elements of Pd were subsequently incorporated in the commercial version of Max/MSP, released by Zicarelli in 1997 (Zicarelli 2002). Both programs are linked by a shared philosophy, but each offers a slightly different perspective on OOP-oriented approaches to composition and performance. The incremental increase in the processing power of desktop computers into the next decade finally allowed the real-time capabilities of the two programs to achieve their full potential, in turn inspiring the development of further extensions. Max/MSP, for example, now has a video extension known as Jitter, released in 2003. Both programs have been made available in versions for the Macintosh and Windows, with the additional option of a Linux version for Pd.

The last two synthesis programs to be considered illustrate the capacity of software-based approaches to sound synthesis to embrace an extended range of compositional and performance perspectives. In 1996, James McCartney released the first version of SuperCollider, a real-time synthesis program for the Apple Macintosh (McCartney 2002). Some similarities to MUSIC-N derivatives such as Csound can be identified in terms of the use of synthesis and signal-processing library functions, supported by a comprehensive set of arithmetic and logic functions to assist in the design of control structures. It is indeed possible to configure the program to create constructs that replicate the traditional "instrument" and preprogrammed "score" approaches to synthesis. Its structure, however, has much more in common with the GUI-based object-oriented structures of Max and its derivatives, with the user presented with a process-driven programming language that makes no material distinctions between the synthesis processes and the associated control data.

McCartney was aware of some important limitations in Max at that time at the control level. These were mainly to do with the extent to which objects could be treated dynamically as data, a feature of particular importance in live performance situations that involve improvisation and when the direct manipulation of underlying algorithms for more complex processes such as granular synthesis involve rapidly updated changes to the associated control structures. A key feature of his program is the extended range of facilities provided for the dynamic control of parameter settings, by which the conditions for change can be influenced or indeed wholly determined by the state of objects at that precise moment of activation rather than relying on externally generated data values. Subsequent versions of SuperCollider have further refined and developed these concepts, and the program became available to the community free of charge in 2002. Although the Macintosh has remained the primary host environment, a Linux version has also been developed.

In 1986, Carla Scaletti, working with Kurt Hebel, developed Kyma, an object-oriented computer language to represent music functions, initially using an Apple Macintosh computer to control external synthesis equipment. The functionality of

Kyma was extended to embrace DSP-based sound synthesis in 1987 using a special hardware system known as Platypus (Scaletti 1989). Scaletti and Hebel had their own distinctive ideas in terms of the ways in which objects could be symbolically represented and manipulated. They also envisaged a significantly expanded spectrum of applications, extending into the commercial music sector, including such activities as sound design for films and TV and the computer games industry.

These objectives were ambitious but by no means unrealistic, anticipating a time when the boundaries between these genres would become increasingly blurred, leading in turn to an increasing degree of interaction between commercial and noncommercial perspectives. As a first step, they founded the Symbolic Sound Corporation in 1989, releasing a commercial version of the Kyma software in 1991. Without the support of a commercial equivalent of the Platypus, however, the processing limitations of the conventional desktop computer during the early 1990s materially limited its functionality. This shortcoming was rectified with the release of a commercial replacement for the Platypus in 1998, known as the Capybara 320.

4. THE CHANGING ENVIRONMENT

Tensions between commercial software applications, which place a significant emphasis on proprietary characteristics, and open source programs, which provide free and unrestricted access to all aspects of the underlying synthesis processes, are by no means new, but in the current century they are taking on a new dimension in terms of their creative impact. During the early 1990s, commercial developers started to develop packages that could be sold as self-contained "plug-ins" for audio software, particular prominence accruing to Steinberg's Virtual Studio Technology (VST) system, introduced in 1996. This development was to have far-reaching implications for the future of music synthesis, which merit closer study.

In the beginning of this chapter, it was noted that the commercial development of audio software was initially associated with computer-based technologies for audio recording and editing. As the processing power of desktop computers improved during the 1990s, it became clear that their capacity to support digital signal-processing applications could extend beyond basic mixing techniques such as the regulation of amplitude and the panning of audio signals between channels to embrace treatments that hitherto had required the use of specialist auxiliary items of equipment, for example, echo and reverberation units. These processes of integration based on software components resulted in the modular and therefore extensible digital audio workstation (DAW).

The attraction of packaging such options as self-contained plug-ins that may be directly inserted in the signal paths of audio-mixing channels was further enhanced through the use of graphics-based user interfaces consisting of application-specific control panels easily accessed via the main editing window. A number of developers quickly realized that the production of plug-ins had significant earnings potential, encouraging the development of sophisticated high-end products for professional users and a complementary repertory of less-expensive plug-ins for institutions and individuals with more limited budgets. The implications of this pay-per-process strategy are further underscored when account is taken of the diversity and versatility of the commercial plug-ins that were developed, including, for example, modular simulations of hardware analog and digital synthesizers and audio processors from earlier eras and neatly packaged versions of the key algorithms that have routinely been used for techniques such as FM synthesis, granular synthesis, and physical modeling.

On the other side of the equation, it is important to recognize that the attractions of self-contained plug-ins in many situations outweigh the possible financial disincentives. Plug-ins designed to model older hardware devices, for example, will usually provide a control interface that reproduces most, if not all, of the original features, thus providing access to a rich legacy of techniques from a bygone era. It is also important to appreciate that engagement with this technology has extended into areas of creative activity not constrained by commercial imperatives, and developments in this context are gathering pace. The value of creating suitably packaged processes in a format that allows a significant degree of portability is now widely recognized by composers and performers, and this has encouraged members of both communities to develop plug-ins freely available as shareware.

In the late 1990s, IRCAM recognized the significance of the plug-in environment, starting its own investigations into protocols that could be used with a variety of host audio platforms. Although initially limited to encapsulating signal-processing functions rather than hardware-modeling applications, IRCAM's system XSPIF (released in 2003) is designed for programs such as Max/MSP, Pd, and jMax, with additional support for the generic interface protocol VST (Goudard and Muller 2003). Zicarelli and Puckette similarly recognized the value of facilitating directly the import of externally created plug-ins to Max/MSP and Pd using VST and supporting the design and export of user-designed patches as VST-encapsulated plug-ins for other platforms. In the case of Max/MSP, Zicarelli developed additional resources in the form of a competitively priced set of seventy-four plug-ins known as Pluggo, subsequently expanded to a repertory of over a hundred options. Whereas some of the implementations to emerge from the user community are of a relatively simple design, others are much more substantial, an extreme example being an application that allows the functions of Csound to be embedded within Max/MSP. Zicarelli first articulated such an ambitious proposition in 2002 (Lyon 2002), and the subsequent reality illustrates the true nature of object-oriented architectures as a powerful means of importing and exporting processes across a range of audio synthesis platforms.

In considering the creative implications of these developments, yet a further dimension has to be taken into consideration. Although the primary focus of this chapter has been the evolution of sound synthesis using computers, it is important to recognize the significance of parallel developments in the context of video applications. The evolution of commercial video-editing software during the 1990s followed a very similar path to that associated with the audio industry, and in the same way that video software has over time significantly expanded the resources that are provided for editing and manipulating soundtracks, so it is the case that recording and editing programs for DAWs incorporate increasingly sophisticated facilities for importing and editing video. Users of Max/MSP are also able to embed advanced video facilities directly via a now fully integrated extension to the programming environment known as Jitter, which extends functionality beyond simple editing functions to embrace real-time video processing and three-dimensional graphics.

This empowerment in terms of the portability of synthesis resources in an increasingly multimedia context is materially altering the ways in which performers and composers work together, extending to activities such as group improvisations both in a traditional environment performing live within the same venue and over the Internet, where the contributing musicians may be hundreds or even thousands of miles apart. Although there are some practical constraints that have yet to be fully resolved, not least the small but potentially significant time delays that occur as digital signals are transmitted over long-distance data networks, the creative possibilities of such national and international collaborations have been significantly enhanced by the use of plug-ins to share the very processes of synthesis, in essence creating communal resources for the making of music.

Such expanded perspectives of music composition and performance raise many issues and challenges that have cultural and practical dimensions extending way beyond the very private working environment that has often been associated with those engaging with the medium. This is one indeed that was omnipresent during the pioneering years of computer-based audio synthesis when pioneering composers frequently were consigned to the physically isolated and impersonal world of the card punch, mainframe computer, and audio data converter, with all the attendant delays and practical difficulties in proceeding from initial conception to perhaps just a few seconds of synthesized sound.

The jury is out on the longer-term implications of these material changes to the ways in which digital technology can be used to synthesize and disseminate music. It is, however, arguably the case that ownership of these processes is open to all via the desktop computer and the Internet and no longer is the exclusive domain of those supported by well-funded research institutions. The latter still have an important role to play in terms of supporting leading edge research, but there is now a clear and significant context for the fruits of their labors in the wider community. In terms of the underlying technology, computers are no longer subject to any significant operational constraints in terms of their capacity to meet the requirements of composers and performers. The material issue is thus the ways in which such empowerment is used to identify and fruitfully explore new horizons of creativity.

BIBLIOGRAPHY

Boulanger, R., ed. 2000. *The Csound Book*. Cambridge: MIT Press.

Chowning, J. 1985. The synthesis of complex audio spectra by means of frequency modulation. In *Foundations of Computer Music*, ed. C. Roads and J. Strawn. Cambridge: MIT Press, pp. 6–29.

Clarke, M. 1996. Composing at the intersection of time and frequency. *Organised Sound* 1(2): 107–17.

Cook, P. R. 1993. SPASM, a real-time vocal tract physical model controller; and Singer, the companion software synthesis system. *Computer Music Journal* 17(1): 30–44.

Dolson, M. 1986. The phase vocoder: A tutorial. *Computer Music Journal* 10(4): 14–27.

Endrich, A. 1997. Composers' Desktop Project: A musical imperative. *Organised Sound* 2(1): 29–33.

Fischman, R. 1997. The phase vocoder: Theory and practice. *Organised Sound* 2(2): 127–145.

Gabor, D. 1947. Acoustical quanta and the theory of hearing. *Nature* 159: 591–594.

Goudard, V., and R. Muller. 2003. XSPIF: *User Guide—A Cross Standards Plugin Framework*. IRCAM—Centre Georges Pompidou, Paris, France.

Hiller, L., and P. Ruiz. 1971a. Synthesizing music sounds by solving the wave equation for vibrating objects: Part 1. *Journal of the Audio Engineering Society* 19(6): 462–470.

Hiller, L., and P. Ruiz. 1971b. Synthesizing music sounds by solving the wave equation for vibrating objects: Part 2. *Journal of the Audio Engineering Society* 19(7): 542–550.

Jaffe, D. A., and J. O. Smith. 1983. Extensions of the Karplus-Strong plucked-string algorithm. *Computer Music Journal* 7(2): 56–69.

Karplus, K., and A. Strong. 1983. Digital synthesis of plucked-string and drum timbres. *Computer Music Journal* 7(2): 42–45.

Lansky, P. 1990. The architecture and musical logic of Cmix. In *Proceedings, International Computer Music Conference (Glasgow)*. San Francisco: Computer Music Association, pp. 91–93.

Lindemann, E., F. Dechelle, B. Smith, and M. Starkier. 1991. The architecture of the IRCAM musical workstation. *Computer Music Journal* 15(3): 41–49.

Lyon, E. 2002. Dartmouth symposium on the future of computer music software: A panel discussion. *Computer Music Journal* 26(4): 13–30.

Mathews, M. V. 1963. The digital computer as a musical instrument. *Science* 142: 553–557.

Mathews, M. V. 1969. *The Technology of Computer Music*. Cambridge: MIT Press.

McCartney, J. 2002. Rethinking the computer music language: SuperCollider. *Computer Music Journal* 26(4): 61–68.

Moore, F. R. 1982. The computer audio research laboratory at UCSD. *Computer Music Journal* 6(1): 18–29.

Moorer, J. A. 1979. The use of linear prediction of speech in computer music applications. *Journal of the Audio Engineering Society* 27(3):134–140.

Puckette, M. 1991. Combining event and signal processing in the MAX graphical programming environment. *Computer Music Journal* 15(3): 68–77.

Puckette, M. 2007. *The Theory and Technique of Electronic Music*. Singapore: World Scientific.

Roads, C. 1978. Automated granular synthesis of sound. *Computer Music Journal* 2(2): 61–62.

Rodet, X., Y. Potard, and J-B. Barrière. 1984. The CHANT project: From synthesis of the singing voice to synthesis in general. *Computer Music Journal* 8(3): 15–31.

Scaletti, C. 1989. The Kyma/Platypus computer music workstation. *Computer Music Journal* 13(2): 23–38.

Truax, B. 1988. Real-time granular synthesis with a digital signal processor. *Computer Music Journal* 12(2): 14–26.

Vercoe, B., and D. Ellis. 1990. Real-time CSOUND: software synthesis with sensing and control. In *Proceedings, International Computer Music Conference (Glasgow)*. San Francisco: Computer Music Association, pp. 209–211.

Vinet, H. 2007. Science and technology of music and sound: The IRCAM roadmap. *Journal of New Music Research* 36(3): 207–226.

Zicarelli, D. 2002. How I learned to love a program that does nothing. *Computer Music Journal* 26(4): 44–51.

PART II

THE MUSIC

COMPUTATIONAL APPROACHES TO COMPOSITION OF NOTATED INSTRUMENTAL MUSIC: XENAKIS AND THE OTHER PIONEERS

JAMES HARLEY

MUSIC has long been associated with mathematics, going all the way back to Pythagoras (6th century B.C.), who connected the two realms through the harmonic series. In the Middle Ages, according to Boethius, music was considered one of the four pillars of higher knowledge (the *quadrivium*), along with arithmetic, geometry, and astronomy.[1]

The implementation of rules for creating music began in the Middle Ages. The *canon*, derived from the Greek word for rule, is an early example of an algorithmic form for generating polyphonic music on the basis of a given melody. Beginning with *Micrologus* by Guido d'Arezzo (dating from 1050 A.D.), rule-based theories governing the practice of music have been posited by numerous writers and practitioners.

The advent of computers has enabled new approaches to music to be developed and implemented that would take advantage of the powerful computational abilities of this new technology. The first composers to engage with the possibilities that computers offered, Lejaren Hiller and Iannis Xenakis, both had scientific professional training: one as a chemist, the other as a civil engineer. Their pioneering work opened the way for others, and the field of computer-assisted composition (and analysis) has grown rapidly as the technology has become more and more powerful and accessible. The discussion here focuses in more detail on the work of Xenakis as his theoretical and creative work have so far proven to be the more influential.

1. Historical Background

As anyone who studies music knows, there are proscribed rules (or at least guidelines) for creating or analyzing music in a particular style. There are instructions for proper modal counterpoint, correct figured bass, appropriate tonal harmony, coherent musical forms, and so on. For the most part, these rules were codified by music theorists to characterize, as precisely as possible, musical practice as it was already being carried out.[2]

There are examples, however, of rules that were conceived to create new music. Mozart has been credited with putting together a "musical dice game," the *Musikalisches Würfelspiel*.[3] The game provided instructions for selecting one-measure segments of music by dice roll to generate sixteen measures of a minuet. There are eleven possible selections for each measure, aside from the eighth and sixteenth cadential measures, for which there are only two choices. The trio section is similarly generated. While the choices of succession are provided by a constrained random procedure using two dice, the coherence of the music derives from Mozart's skill in creating the source material.

A. Joseph Schillinger

Joseph Schillinger (1895–1943) was a Russian musician who ended up in New York about the same time as Leon Theremin. In fact, Schillinger collaborated with Theremin (and Henry Cowell) on the Rythmicon device, a "rhythm machine" that produced up to sixteen simultaneous pulsations, each pitched to one of the overtones of a fundamental and each layer pulsing at a rate that corresponds to the mathematical relationship of the overtone to the fundamental. This device implemented Schillinger's theory on deriving rhythms from combinations of arithmetic ratios, explained in his magnum opus, *The Schillinger System of Music*

Composition. Schillinger proposed a number of theories on the correspondences of mathematics to music (and to the arts more broadly). As Cowell stated in his "overture" to the book: "The idea behind the Schillinger System is simple and inevitable: it undertakes the application of mathematical logic to all the materials of music and to their functions, so that the student may know the unifying principles behind these functions, may grasp the method of analyzing and synthesizing any musical materials that he may find anywhere or may discover for himself, and may perceive how to develop new materials as he feels the need for them" (Schillinger 1946).

Schillinger was an influential teacher in New York during the 1930s and 1940s. His students included well-known figures in American popular music, such as George Gershwin and Benny Goodman. His influence waned as his teaching legacy died away and his books went out of print.[4] He died before having a chance to carry out any experiments with digital technology. Others have implemented parts of his system in computer algorithms for composition, notably Bruno Degazio (1988).

It is worth noting that during the same period as Cowell was collaborating with Schillinger, he was also working with the young John Cage (who went on to develop a close relationship in the 1950s with Earle Brown, who actually taught the Schillinger system after attending the Schillinger School of Music in Boston). Cage, who carried an overriding concern for rhythm and temporal structure above all, acknowledged his debt to Cowell, but the influence of Schillinger may also be possible to discern.

B. John Cage

John Cage (1912–1992) is well known for applying chance procedures to music, among many other experimental practices. He developed his method over a period of some years, leading to *Music of Changes* (1951) for solo piano. In this piece, Cage implemented a chance-based decision-making process using the *I Ching* (The Book of Changes).[5] A set of "charts," each containing sixty-four entries for sonority (notes), rhythm, and dynamics (and including silence), provided the basis for compositional decisions, along with additional rules for "replacing" the entries in the charts with new ones (or not) and determining density (number of events occurring simultaneously). The procedure Cage developed had much in common with the serialist composers associated with the Darmstadt Internationale Ferienkurse für Neue Musik around that same time, although he was not concerned with making use of tone rows or ordered parameter lists such as durations and dynamics.[6]

The rigor of Cage's approach lent itself very well to eventual implementation on the computer. Hiller worked with Cage over the period 1967–1969 on *HPSCHD*, a large-scale work for seven harpsichords, fifty-one tapes of computer-generated music, and slide projections. The programming that Hiller carried out for that work implemented Cage's compositional procedures, emulating the I Ching process using random number generation techniques. Beginning in 1982, Cage worked with an assistant, Andrew Culver, who created generalized computer algorithms for Cage's procedures that could be applied to any of his projects. Cage relied on Culver's software for the rest of his life.

2. INFORMATION THEORY

As communications systems and computing technology were being developed in the 1950s, "information theory" proved to be highly influential, not only for engineers but also for those in the field of aesthetics and, by extension, for composers. While the origins of this theory are found in modern physics—"information" being a way to measure possible alternatives in statistical formulations of, for example, entropy in the second law of thermodynamics—the interest for musicians is found in the conception of music as a communications system.

A mathematical theory of communications was put forward in 1948–1949 by Claude Shannon, a research mathematician working at Bell Laboratories, who had previously worked at the Institute for Advanced Study in Princeton with John von Neumann, among others, and had been involved in early work developing analog computing machines.[7] According to his theory, *information* is a measure of the predictability of a signal being communicated (Shannon and Weaver 1949). In a communication system, there is a source, a transmitter, a receiver, and a destination, with the message communicated subject to "noise." Information *entropy* is the measure of uncertainty in a message (the smaller the information entropy, the more predictable the message) and is characterized by means of probability theory. According to Shannon, there will always be uncertainty in a communications system because the exact nature of what is to be communicated can only be determined as an ensemble of possibilities. In a discrete system (such as a digital computer), the source makes a sequence of choices from a set of elementary symbols, the sequence forming a message. A system that produces a sequence of symbols according to certain probabilities is called a *stochastic* process (a *Markov* process would be one in which the probabilities governing one sequence of choices are dependent on previous choices).

It is significant that this important publication on information theory was brought out for the public in Urbana, Illinois (it had originally been published in-house through the *Bell System Technical Journal*), as it came to the attention of a researcher there, Lejaren Hiller. He would go on to implement the first compositional models on the computer, using principles adapted from Shannon's information theory.

Another way to view information entropy in this model of communication is as a measure of "originality" (i.e., the greater the information entropy is, the least amount of redundancy in the message). This is where communication theory can intersect with aesthetics. The other important intersection relevant for music is with perception, where the statistical model of transmission-reception can be applied to theories of how music is perceived and analyzed. Abraham Moles (1920–1992) was a French researcher who became very interested in the connections between information theory and aesthetics across many disciplines (Moles 1958). In the early years of the Groupe de Recherches Musicales (or GRM as it came to be known), Moles had a close association with work being done there and collaborated on acoustical research. His ideas influenced Iannis Xenakis, and both of them were strongly interested in applying computers to music, along with Pierre Barbaud, who in 1958 had created the Groupe de Musique Algorithmique de Paris (Barbaud 1966). Werner Meyer-Eppler (1913–1960) was a German scientist whose research interests shifted from physics to phonetics and communication research (he was a strong advocate for electronic music). His work on information theory in the area of phonology led him to coin the term *aleatoric* with reference to the statistical shaping of sounds (Meyer-Eppler 1955). Karlheinz Stockhausen (1928–2007), in particular, was strongly influenced by Meyer-Eppler's ideas, but his publications in international journals such as *Die Reihe* and *Die Gravesaner Blätter* influenced many others, including Xenakis (especially through their mutual association with Hermann Scherchen) and Gottfried-Michael Koenig.

3. Lejaren Hiller

Lejaren Hiller (1924–1994) trained as a chemist at Princeton University, but also studied music, working with both Milton Babbitt and Roger Sessions. After joining the chemistry faculty at the University of Illinois at Urbana-Champaign in 1952, he began working with digital technology for data analysis and modeling. The application of the computer to music occurred to him early on, and he worked with fellow chemist Leonard Isaacson on developing the software to produce the first computer-generated composition, *Illiac Suite* (1956–1957), for string quartet (Hiller and Isaacson 1959).[8]

Hiller was aware of Shannon's work on information theory and, indeed, was strongly influenced by the perceptual model of music related to the statistical understanding of information.[9] His view was that a musical composition could be seen as an extraction of order out of chaos or the rule-based selection of appropriate musical materials out of a random set of possibilities. The basis of Hiller and Isaacson's composition algorithms was the generation of random numbers, subject to a sequence of tests, each representing a musically relevant rule. The random numbers would be accepted or rejected at each step and a sequence of conforming data collected, to be then transcribed into music notation. Each of the four movements (called "experiments") of the *Illiac Suite* applied a different set of compositional rules. The first applied 16th-century rules of counterpoint to generate first a monodic cantus firmus, then a two-part setting, then a four-part setting. The second movement models four-part writing in a tonal style, while the third movement models serial music that includes rules for ordering rhythms, dynamics, and playing modes. The fourth movement implements low-order Markov chains to create new music guided by probabilities rather than stylistic rules. With information theory and cybernetics being written about in the press along with futuristic speculation about computers and artificial intelligence (AI), the novelty of a computer generating music stirred up a great deal of controversy. A newspaper account of the first performance of *Illiac Suite* (United Press News Release, August 10, 1956) was picked up across the country, and Hiller's article on computer music in the widely read *Scientific American* generated much feedback (Hiller 1959).

Parallel to his computer programming experiments and his ongoing work in the chemistry department, Hiller was working on his master's in music, and he transferred to the music department in 1958 on completion of his thesis (on the subject of computers and music). He was instrumental in launching the Experimental Music Studio there, and he continued to apply aspects of information theory to music, working with Robert Baker to develop the music software, MUSICOMP. A number of functions were written as subroutines, which enabled the software to be more easily adapted to different compositional aims. *Computer Cantata* was completed in 1963 (it also included computer-generated sounds along with data intended for transcription and performance by live musicians). As mentioned, one of Hiller's most ambitious projects was his collaboration with Cage on *HPSCHD* (1967–1969).

A. University of Illinois Experimental Music Studio

Hiller spent ten years building the Experimental Music Studio at Urbana-Champaign. He was joined by other composers interested in working with computers and electronic sound. One of his first students in computer music was James Tenney (1934–2006), who on graduation in 1961 went to work for three years as composer-in-residence at Bell Labs. There, he implemented compositional algorithms using Max Mathews's software that had been developed for sound synthesis. Tenney had an interest in applying stochastic procedures (based on probability functions) to music composition.

Herbert Brün (1918–2000) arrived at Urbana-Champaign in 1963, after having worked in the electronic music studio of Westdeutscher Rundfunk (WDR)-Cologne and Siemens-Munich, among other activities. He had a particular interest in using the computer to design processes that would model social systems in which the musical result would not be the goal but a by-product of the process. As Brün stated: "The programming composer composes the structures of systems in which the elements function as variables, each according to its temporary context, as potential carriers of meaning, unprejudiced by semantic or mythical traditions.

Such systems may often be analogies to present day social systems (not as they are seen, but as they are), or to a possible future social order. The musical result of structural composition would thus participate in society's self-representation: a self-critical gesture of communcation" (2004, p. 199). Brün also was strongly influenced by information theory and cybernetics, and the compositional processes he designed were used to generate scores, sounds, and even graphics.

Salvatore Martirano (1927–1995) was added to the faculty at Urbana-Champaign in 1964. He is most well known for his work in the 1970s developing the Sal-Mar Construction, a hybrid analog-digital "composing machine" that was controlled by a panel of touch-sensitive switches that generated sequences of control and performance data. The data were routed to various modular devices, and the output was sent to any of the twenty-four loudspeakers of the device. An important element of Martirano's work is that he designed this device so that the trigger switches could be operated either by a performer or by internal logic, so that the human agent may not have complete control over the device's behavior. In the 1980s, the Sal-Mar Construction work was replaced by the all-digital yahaSALma-Mac, for which the routing mechanisms of the older device were replaced by routines implemented in the Smalltalk programming language. The algorithms were intended to transform musical material according to a number of possible procedures, random processes, and Markov recursions.

The Experimental Music Studio at the University of Illinois at Urbana-Champaign has seen several generations of computer music composers come through its doors. Given the attitude of experimentation of founder Hiller and the radical approach to relating music composition to computer technology by Brün and Martirano, it is understandable that the prevailing aesthetic of the facility continues to encourage critical engagement with the tools both of music and of programming. Sever Tipei (director, Computer Music Project) states in his online biography that "the composition of music should be both an experimental and a speculative endeavor that delivers a particular world view." He regards the computer as a "collaborator whose skills and abilities complement those of the human artist."[10] Heinrich Taube developed Common Music, an object-oriented music composition environment built in the LISP programming environment (Taube 2004).

B. University of Buffalo

Hiller moved to the University of Buffalo in 1968, where he carried on his research and experimentation in music and computing until his retirement in 1989. He enjoyed fruitful collaborations with student Charles Ames, who has published a number of important articles on various aspects of algorithmic composition (cf., Ames 1987), and John Myhill (1923–1987), who was on faculty in the mathematics department but carried out research in computer algorithms applied to music (Myhill 1979).

4. IANNIS XENAKIS

Iannis Xenakis (1922–2001) began his professional career as an architectural assistant, working for Le Corbusier in Paris. According to his biographer, the environment in that studio was unusually open, with wide-ranging discussions that could include even junior engineers (Matossian 2005, p. 39). His first input into aesthetics (design) involved a new approach to prestressed concrete, the most elaborate application being the Philips Pavilion, a commission for the 1958 World Fair in Brussels. As these ideas developed, Xenakis began applying them to music as well. *Metastasis* (1954) for orchestra was his first musical application of the engineering/ design ideas he was developing for Le Corbusier, using long, interlaced string glissandi to "obtain sonic spaces of continuous evolution" (Xenakis 1992, p. 10).[11] While Xenakis was applying geometrical and architectural concepts to music, he was also criticizing serialism, the dominant musical force in European new music in the 1950s, applying his knowledge of statistics and perception (Xenakis 1955). In this article, he proposed a new form of music based on the application of statistical methods to music composition, "stochastic" music.

A. Stochastics

The first work Xenakis completed that engaged with stochastics in a profound way was *Pithoprakta* (1956) for orchestra. In this work, the global conception of musical form, allied with a statistical organization of musical texture, is fundamental. Each of the forty-six instruments of the string orchestra has its own part (the rest of the orchestra consists of two trombones, xylophone, and woodblock), each following its own rhythmic structure, melodic profile, and so on. The music is mostly quite dense, the textures evolving gradually, from the percussive knocking at the beginning to pizzicato sounds to staccato bowed notes. Xenakis had to adapt probability functions to the task of filling in the details of these global textures, acknowledging that the individual notes or details were perceptually subservient to the overall boundaries of register, timbre, and density of the orchestral sonority.

While the formal shape of *Pithoprakta* was conceived quite intuitively, Xenakis followed it with a formal model for applying stochastic functions to music. He defined what he called the "fundamental phases of a music work" (Xenakis 1992, p. 22) by way of answering the question: "What is the minimum of logical constraints necessary for the construction of a musical process?" (p. 16). These phases are as follows:

1. *Initial conceptions* (intuitions, provisional or definitive data);
2. *Definitions of the sonic entities* and of their symbolism communicable with the limits of possible means;
3. *Definitions of the transformations* that these sonic entities must undergo in the course of the composition;

4. *Microcomposition* (choice and detailed fixing of the functional or stochastic relations of the elements of phase 2);

5. *Sequential programming* of phases 3 and 4 (the schema and *pattern* of the work in its entirety);

6. *Implementation of calculations*, verifications, feedbacks, and definitive modifications of the sequential program;

7. *Final symbolic result* of the programming (notation, numerical expressions, graphs, or other means); and

8. *Sonic realization* of the program (performance, electromagnetic means, computerized construction) (adapted from Xenakis 1992, p. 22).

Achorripsis (1957), for chamber orchestra, was the first compositional result of this analytical thinking.[12] For this work, Xenakis defined the formal structure as a sequence of twenty-eight sections, each fixed at 15 s duration. He defined seven sonic entities: (1) piccolo, clarinet, bass clarinet; (2) oboe, bassoon, contrabassoon; (3) trumpets, trombone; (4) xylophone, woodblock, bass drum; (5) string pizzicato; (6) string arco; and (7) string glissandi. Each section of the piece would be defined by the presence or absence of these sonic entities and would be further defined by an overall density for each of the sonic entities present (the densities, determined by stochastic function, are classed into five levels so that they are perceptually distinct). Additional stochastic functions are implemented to select for timing, duration, register, pitch, dynamics, and so on (cf., Arsenault 2002). All of the calculations relating to stochastic functions (using Poisson, Gaussian, exponential, uniform distributions) had to be carried out by hand. However, the formalization of the compositional algorithm implemented for *Achorripsis* provided the basis for Xenakis's computer algorithm ST, which he completed in 1962 and used to generate a family of instrumental works: *ST/48-1* for orchestra, *ST/10-1* for mixed ensemble, *ST/4-1* for string quartet, *Morsima-Amorsima* for mixed quartet, and parts of *Atrées* for mixed ensemble.[13]

B. Markov Chains

Xenakis's initial attempt at setting up a composition algorithm led to further explorations of aspects of mathematics and information theory that could be applied to music. Markov chains are probability functions by which one decision exerts an influence on the next, essentially allowing for "memory" to be built into the compositional process. A first-order Markov chain would be the case if the probability of one decision acts on the next. A second-order chain would be the case if one decision acts on the next, which in turn acts on the next. The higher the order of the Markov chain, the more constrained are the decisions further along in the process. Starting from a notion of elementary "particles" or "quanta" of sound,[14] Xenakis linked "screens" (essentially, discrete frames in time that can be clearly defined in terms of events and sonic parameters) of quanta by means of transition tables that he called matrices of transition probabilities (Xenakis 1992,

p. 74). He also incorporated transitional trajectories that could range between order and disorder (entropy) in reference to specific parameters of sound and structure.

The first composition that explored Markovian probabilities was *Analogique A* (1958) for nine strings. The following year, this piece was expanded by the addition of *Analogique B* for electroacoustic sounds (an early effort at granular synthesis). Following these initial efforts, the organization of quanta into a succession of screens was broadened to include more complex sonic entities than isolated discrete sounds (short notes on the strings or electronic grains). In *Syrmos* (1959) for eighteen strings, Xenakis worked with a set of eight basic sonic entities: held bowed notes, ascending bowed glissandi, descending bowed glissandi, crossed (ascending and descending) bowed glissandi, geometric configurations of convergent or divergent glissandi, undevelopable ruled surface glissandi, "clouds" of plucked notes, and col legno struck notes with glissandi (Xenakis 1992, p. 81).

C. Games

As an extension to his work on Markov chains, Xenakis became interested in game theory or "heteronomous" music (Xenakis 1992, p. 111). A set of materials is prepared for two ensembles, each with its own conductor, and the "game" takes place as a competition between the two groups, with choices of what material to play and what to do in response to the other group being governed by a table of probabilities. The table provides "weights" for each possible choice (dependent on the previous choice of the other group), and the opponents are to strive for the highest "score" (presumably). The task of the composer is to create sets of musical materials that can function in multiple orders, and that will, as much as possible, create a successful aesthetic experience regardless of the specific choices made by the dueling conductors at any one encounter. In addition, the composer must create the probability table in such a way that it guides the players toward more successful outcomes.

Xenakis composed two works as games: *Duel* (1959) for orchestra divided into two, with six blocks of musical material (both groups use the same set of materials); and *Stratégie* (1962) for large orchestra divided into two, with six blocks of material and nineteen "tactics" (including combinations of blocks).[15]

By the late 1950s, other composers were following the lead of Cage and including chance elements in their music, including leaving the succession of sections up to the performer (such as Stockhausen's *Klavierstück XI* from 1956 or Earle Brown's *Available Forms I* from 1961). Xenakis sought to contain the possibility of "mobile form" within the theoretical framework of linked probabilities that game theory provided. While this early work of Xenakis was again carried out without the aid of a computer, this bounded approach to "interaction" has exerted influence on subsequent developers, such as Joel Chadabe and David Zicarelli with their M and Jam Factory software (Zicarelli 1987).

D. Stochastics and Boolean Logic

By 1962, Xenakis had taught himself FORTRAN and had translated his stochastics-based compositional algorithm into computer code. As he worked through this, he reformulated the details of his fundamental phases of music composition:

1. The work consists of a succession of sequences or movements each a_i seconds long;
2. Definition of the mean density of the sounds during a_i;
3. Composition Q of the orchestra during sequence a_i;
4. Definition of the moment of occurrence of the sound N within the sequence a_i;
5. Attribution to the above sound of an instrument belonging to orchestra Q, which has already been calculated;
6. Attribution of a pitch as a function of the instrument;
7. Attribution of a glissando speed if class r is characterized as a glissando;
8. Attribution of a duration x to the sounds emitted;
9. Attribution of dynamic forms to the sounds emitted;
10. The same operations are begun again for each sound of the cluster Na_i; and
11. Recalculations of the same sort for the other sequences (Xenakis 1992, pp. 134–142).

The ST program did not in fact implement much more than had already been specified for *Achorripsis*, although the stochastic functions had been extended to select durations for sections (mean durations with prior section duration as a factor in the equation) and to apply a low-level Markov process for some of the programming of details (such as pitch selection, for which the previous pitch would exert influence on the next choice).

While working on the ST programming, Xenakis was also exploring the application of Boolean logic to music (Xenakis called this "symbolic" music, by which music could symbolize or make manifest laws of mathematics or logic directly in sound). *Herma* (1961) for solo piano takes its structure from the two forms of Boolean function that exhibit the maximum number of operations for a three-variable expression (Xenakis 1992, p. 173). The three variables are represented by three large sets of pitches.[16] Stochastic functions are deployed to determine details of pitch selection from within sets (and their unions or intersections), succession, density, and so on. Dynamic markings are used to distinguish the different operations that are unfolding simultaneously (cf., Wannamaker 2001).

Xenakis applied Boolean expressions to some of the material in *Eonta* (1963) for brass and piano, but the music is not treated as symbolic of the logical functions. Rather, the techniques developed in *Herma* are used as material within a more intuitive framework. This shift between strongly formal, algorithmic conceptions and intuitive shaping of materials is a continuum Xenakis explored throughout much of his life. As the field of algorithmic composition developed, many others have worked with Boolean logic as a useful means of representing musical data in programming languages (cf., Courtot 1992).

E. Groups and Outside-Time Operations

After working out his ST composition algorithm, in which all possible elements in the process are generated by means of stochastic functions, Xenakis turned toward a more deterministic model. Part of the evolution of his thinking came from his work with logical functions and his distinguishing between relationships among sonic events and relationships between temporal units expressed by those events as they are made manifest in time. To take a simple example, the intervallic identities that characterize a particular mode (or twelve-tone set) exist no matter how the elements of the mode or set are expressed in time. This Xenakis calls *outside-time* structure. The way these elements are deployed in time generates temporal relationships to do with meter, proportion, or whatever. The deployment of these relationships is called the "temporal" structure. And, the correspondence between these two logical categories is called the *inside-time* structure (Xenakis 1992, pp. 160–161). Returning to his notion of sonic entity, as originally specified in his fundamental phases, Xenakis worked out an algebra for characterizing the basic parameters of the chosen sonic entities for a composition, usually pitch, duration, and dynamics (but there could be others, such as speed/direction of glissandi, etc.). Each of these parameters is specified according to a range of values (a parameter vector).

The outside-time structure of a composition, then, comprises a set of vector spaces around the specified sonic entities, each delineated by the relevant parameter vectors. The next step was to find a way to link these multidimensional vector spaces in a way that would allow an inside-time structure to be created. To do this, Xenakis turned to the theory of groups. According to this, a finite group of elements can be arranged in a matrix such that the pairing of one element with another will engender a transformation or link to a third element. In this way, a limited set of transformations can be derived from the elements themselves. The elements of such transformational matrices represent parameter values defined for the sonic entities being used for a particular composition. Xenakis made use of this combinatorial strategy of transformation to generate successions of elements and thus musical form (Gibson 2002).[17]

What this enabled Xenakis to do was to define the materials for a composition and the means by which those materials could be varied or transformed and then to work out the mechanisms by which the materials and their means of transformation would be expressed inside time (i.e., as a musical score). The ordering of the materials and the parameter values enabled successions and transformations of the sonic entities to be radical or gradual. The musical form, then, becomes a complex, hierarchical structure that embodies a multidimensional network of relationships.

Xenakis applied this new approach to composition first in *Nomos Alpha* (1966) for solo cello, and he analyzed his implementation of the theory to this work in detail (Xenakis 1992, pp. 218–236). He adopted this strategy to many instrumental works thereafter, often combined with other techniques, and it would become a fundamental element of his compositional style (Harley 2004, p. 44). It is interesting to note, however, that Xenakis did not implement this theory as a computer algorithm. He does not seem to have indicated the reasons for this, but he would have been hampered by a lack of access to computing facilities. And, it is likely that his attention turned elsewhere (toward digital synthesis, for one).[18]

F. Sieves

At the same time as Xenakis was implementing his theory based on vectors and groups, he developed a theory of sieves. The aim was to work out a mathematical model of scales or intervals (one might also think of it as proportions). Using the operations of logic, he was able to formalize a set of rules by which any scale (or succession of intervals/units) could be analyzed or generated. He derived his sieves from combining cycles of a pair of numbers (intervals).[19] This enabled him to create, for example, an ordered set of pitches (akin to a mode or scale) rather than select pitches from the full gamut. As with the formal organization achieved using groups, Xenakis could thereby express a richer set of relationships in the domain of pitch than he was able to before. He also implemented a method for transforming or varying the sieves, using higher-level logical operations on the generative interval pairs, which he called "metabolae." This enabled the materials to have an evolution over the course of a work.

While Xenakis used sieves in *Nomos Alpha* for the organization of pitch (the sieves were based there on the unit of a quarter tone), he foresaw that an ordered set of intervals could be applied to rhythm as well (and in fact to any elements of music that can be ordered in discrete steps). His solo percussion work, *Psappha* (1976), is a particularly strong example of sieves applied to rhythm (cf., Flint 1993). As with the compositional techniques adapted from group theory, the use of sieves was something that Xenakis continued to work with for much of the rest of his career, often exploring the "modal" characteristics of particular pitch sets, as in *Jonchaies* (1977) for orchestra or *Serment* (1981) for choir.

G. Brownian Motion and Arborescences

As noted, Xenakis put aside his computer programming after 1962, partially for lack of access to computing facilities. In 1967, however, he took up a post at Indiana University and began working toward implementing his ideas concerning digital synthesis. He was interested in exploring new sounds through stochastics, with the probability functions applied directly to the generation of sound waveforms, notably through adapting Brownian motion to amplitude fluctuations (Xenakis 1992, pp. 242–254). As he was working toward this (it took several years for him to acquire the necessary technology), it occurred to him that the technique of applying a stochastic function to generating a waveform could be applied to instrumental music, and even to multiple instrumental lines simultaneously to create a kind of polyphony he called *arborescences*. String instruments, in particular, are well suited to projecting melodic contours built from glissandi. Whereas in his earlier works the glissandi tend to be geometric (moving in one direction, creating a straight line, albeit angled away from the normal horizontal plane), stochastic contours might change direction rapidly, creating in effect a filled-in melody.

Brownian motion is a mathematical model originally developed to describe the random movement of particles suspended in a gas or liquid. To apply the model to music, one must determine the time between data points (the intervals could be regular, could be determined stochastically, or could be governed by a sieve structure) and the boundaries of the fluctuations (these could be fixed or dynamic). The particular stochastic function used to generate the contour could generate output that would vary wildly or be more controlled.

The most striking early example of stochastics applied to melodic contour is Xenakis's first work for violin solo, *Mikka* (1971). The score is a continuous line that varies from stasis (a held pitch) to rapid, wide fluctuations up and down the string. A follow-up work, *Mikka "S"* (1975), adds a second line to the first, so that the violinist, at least at times, must perform two independent glissandi simultaneously. Xenakis took up this approach, using it in many works, for solo strings, chamber formations, and orchestra, expanding from string instruments to voices, woodwinds, and brass.

As an extension to the contours generated by Brownian motion, Xenakis implemented a method for creating a more coherent polyphony on the basis of stochastic melodic contours. He used the term *arborescence* for this technique. The basic idea is that a single line would proliferate into a number of "dendrils." The generating contour might be created stochastically, or might be designed graphically. The "offshoots" again might be generated stochastically, transformed by means of functions derived from complex variables, or varied graphically by shifting the original contour around on an axis (e.g., "retrograde" transformation would be a shift of 180 degrees). Xenakis used arborescences in many works, even adapting the technique to generate material for discrete instruments such as the piano. *Erikhthon* (1974), for piano and orchestra, is entirely composed from such material, and there are even passages where the orchestral strings trace the same arborescent texture in glissando as the piano performs in notes.

In 1991, Xenakis succeeded in adapting the Brownian motion technique to a computer algorithm, GENDYN, that would generate digital waveforms on the basis of stochastic variations of waveform segments, enabling the timbre of the sounds to vary from highly unstable or noisy to stable, instrument-like tones (cf., Hoffmann 2000).

H. Cellular Automata

In the 1980s, Xenakis became interested in cellular automata as a model for generating musical material. A cellular automaton is made up of a grid of "cells," each able to present a defined number of "states" (in the simplest case, either on or off). A set of rules governs how cells interact with their neighbors, and an evaluation of their interaction produces a new generation of the grid. Cellular automata have been used to model a whole range of phenomena, from the growth of crystals to population cycles. Xenakis adopted a symbolic approach to his implementation of this model; the pitches and instruments of the orchestra would act as the cells of the automata, and the rhythmic succession of the music would represent the generations of the automaton. In *Horos* (1986) for orchestra, the pitches of a sieve are each assigned to an instrument (or group of instruments) of the orchestra so that when a particular cell of the automaton is "on" a specific sonority is sounded.

Xenakis made use of this technique in a limited way in *Horos* and similarly incorporated it in *Ata* (1987) for orchestra and *Kyania* (1991) for orchestra (Solomos 2006).

I. Influences

Xenakis implemented a large number of compositional techniques adapted from mathematics. He did not formalize them all to the extent that they could be run on a computer, but he provided enough theoretical discussion (for the most part) that others have been able to work with his tools, adapt them, and develop them further. It is not possible to trace the influence of Xenakis's work exhaustively as nearly everyone who works in the field of computational composition cites his work. It is worth noting the work of a few, at least, beyond those already cited in references. Julio Estrada, a Mexican composer, has extended Xenakis's parameter vectors and his sieves to develop his own theory of "continua" (Estrada 2002). Curtis Roads, who attended workshops in Bloomington when Xenakis was teaching there, has been instrumental in developing granular synthesis (Roads 2002). Cort Lippe, who studied with Xenakis as well as with Koenig, has expanded compositional algorithms to the domain of interactive music and real-time signal processing.[20]

5. GOTTFRIED-MICHAEL KOENIG

Gottfried-Michael Koenig, who extended the serialist approach of post–World War II Darmstadt composers to the computer, while primarily training as a musician, also studied music representation (Dannenberg 1993) and computer programming. His particular interest has been in the relationship between the objectified grammar of the computer algorithm and the subjective musical awareness of the composer: "The algorithmic description of the production process adds an objective feature. Because of it, 'form' is no longer the personal manner in which the musical material is presented or the listener's perception is guided; rather, it is the rationally discernible, reproducible effect, detached from the composer, of an organized system imposed on arbitrary material.... Form, here, is not merely a vessel, but a process that starts with the composer's inspiration and proceeds by way of design, execution, correction, and performance to the listener's ear and judgment" (Koenig 1983, p. 31). Koenig's first computer composition system was implemented in 1966 at the Institute of Sonology in the Netherlands. *Project 1* was purposefully incomplete in that the serial or random processes that the program used to act on the specified parameters of the composer might give rise to "parametric conflicts." It was up to the composer to then take the output and resolve the problems to transcribe the output into musical notation.

Project 2 was completed in 1970. A wider range of processes was implemented, including deterministic event specification and probabilistic "tendencies." In addition, the composer must specify the relevant parameters and their hierarchical relationships, along with global information affecting how the algorithm would operate. The output was complete as the composer was more interactively involved in setting up the algorithm. According to Koenig's student Otto Laske, the *Project 2* program could be extended into a knowledge-based system in which the computer "assumes some of the burden of providing analytic insights into the results computed" (Laske 1981, p. 64). Koenig also saw the potential for extending his system to add a "mentoring" element, taking the program into the realm of AI. That work, however, was never completed.

Influences

Koenig directed the Institute of Sonology for many years and so influenced numerous composers who studied there. Laske is one, already mentioned. Barry Truax is another; he went on to develop his own composition system for real-time granular synthesis. Paul Berg has developed PILE, a real-time sound synthesis program that includes higher-order processes for generating musical structures. Clarence Barlow has developed Autobusk, an algorithm that generates pitches and rhythms and implements, among other things, his theory of "harmonicity" (Barlow 1987). Finally, American composer Robert Rowe went on to develop Cypher, a composition and interactive performance system that has the ability to "listen" to incoming music, analyze it, and provide output according to a range of strategies (Rowe 2001).

6. DAVID COPE

Composer David Cope first began to develop his Experiments in Music Intelligence (EMI) in 1984. It was at first intended to be an interactive composing partner, an "analysis tool for generating extensive lists of motivic patterns" and "an imitative projector of possible next intervals of a given phrase" (Cope 1987, p. 30). Out of these beginnings, the program was developed to include functions for style dictionaries and syntax rule applications. Cope drew on a linguistic model for his system and implemented it using the LISP programming language, common in AI applications. Cope defined musical style as follows: "The identifiable characteristics of a composer's music which are recognizably similar from one work to another. These include, but are not limited to, pitch and duration, . . . timbre, dynamics, and nuance. As well, these elements together constitute grammars perceived on many levels, for instance, as melody, harmony, and counterpoint, which themselves join into introductions, motives, transitions, modulations, and cadences. Combinations of these elements constitute style when they appear repeatedly in two or more works" (Cope 1991, p. 30). The notion of a "style dictionary" is a complex one, relying on sophisticated analytical tools. Cope has implemented a hierarchical approach that adapts principles introduced by Heinrich Schenker, Leonard Meyer, Fred Lerdahl, and Ray Jackendoff, among others. Once the source material has been analyzed, it is parsed for those elements that are common, that can signify style. From there, the generative rules for creating new music conform to the analysis applied for building the dictionary/database and draw on the signature elements that define the style. To test the system, it was most effective to apply it to a known style, generally limited to a specific composer and genre.

Beginning in 1993, Cope released a series of recordings of the output of EMI, each emulating specific styles (from J. S. Bach to Wolfgang Mozart to Sergey Rachmaninoff). He has also used the software to compose a number of compositions in his own style.[21] His work has received a great deal of attention and generated controversy (cf., Cope's debate with well-known computer scientist Douglas Hofstadter in Cope 2001).

7. Composition Algorithms and Sound Synthesis

Much of the work in algorithmic composition has been oriented at least in part toward sound synthesis and playback of electronic sounds or samples. This connection dates to the MUSICOMP programming language that Hiller developed in the early 1960s and the MUSIC-N programming languages that Mathews began developing in 1957 (first used for advanced composition work by Tenney). Both Xenakis and Koenig developed sound synthesis capability for their compositional algorithms as well.

More recently, Max/MSP, the object-oriented programming language that has gained widespread use by computer music practitioners, includes many utilities for algorithmic composition but is also optimized for data manipulation relating to MIDI (musical instrument digital interface), digital audio, and image/video. The one drawback of the Max/MSP environment at the moment, however, is that algorithmic output intended for instrumental performance needs to be transcribed into notation for instrumental performance.[22] Common Music, developed by Taube, is a more complete compositional environment as it includes a music notation component along with utilities for MIDI and synthesis. OpenMusic, an object-oriented programming environment developed at l'Institut de Recherche et Coordination Acoustique/Musique (IRCAM), provides for the exporting of program output to Finale, a commercial notation editor.

There have been many efforts at developing and implementing compositional algorithms over the years, and those efforts have only increased as computing platforms and tools have become more powerful and at the same time accessible. Mention can be made here of only a few, in particular those that have been made available commercially. Symbolic Composer (www.symboliccomposer.com/), developed mainly in Italy by Peter Stone and his team at Tonality Systems beginning in the 1980s, is a full-featured environment built on LISP. It implements a hierarchical organization and provides tools for generating sounds by means of MIDI or synthesis. Composers Desktop Project (www.composersdesktop.com/), developed beginning in the 1980s by a U.K.-based collective including Richard Orton and Trevor Wishart, provides a suite of tools for signal processing and algorithmic composition. The algorithmic unit is Tabula Vigilans, and output from this script language can be imported into the Sibelius notation editor for producing scores. The Kyma system (www.symbolicsound.com/), developed by Carla Scaletti and Kurt Hebel of Symbolic Sound, is a powerful software environment for composition, synthesis, and signal processing that is linked to the Capybara "sound computation engine" (hardware). A wide range of tools is provided in the Kyma system for generating music and for processing audio in real time.

8. PROSPECTS

As computer hardware increases in processing capacity, compositional algorithms are more and more tied to real-time performance systems. Input from a variety of sources can be utilized in varying degrees to influence or control algorithms, trigger sequences of music or preproduced audio, or direct the computer output (tempo, dynamics, etc.). Composition, in this real-time environment, becomes integrally linked to performance. Composers such as Lippe (mentioned in this chapter), Philippe Manoury, or even Pierre Boulez are able to conceive ambitious compositions for instruments and voices that count on real-time computer processing not only to manipulate the amplified sounds but also to coordinate the live performance with signal processing or sequencing. The computer allows a degree of performance flexibility that was not possible when preproduced elements had to be fixed on tape or some other media. The possibilities for performer input that ventures into the territory of improvisation are also quite feasible. George Lewis is one musician who has worked many years to develop a computer system that would have the capability to listen to human musicians and not only to react but also to assert its own musicality in real time as a machine improviser (Lewis 2000).

Real-time music algorithms are able to take as input a variety of source signals. While the more common sources are MIDI and audio signals from instruments, signals can also be incorporated from video (and output from music algorithms can also be used to trigger or manipulate video material [and lighting]). One of the first people to explore the possibilities of integrating video into a music programming environment was David Rokeby, who began developing his Very Nervous System in 1986, then following up with softVNS, a set of software tools for integrating video signal into the Max/MSP software (homepage.mac.com/davidrokeby/softVNS. html). These visual-based interactive tools provide the means for integrating image and related parameters into compositional algorithms as dynamic inputs, triggers, and so on. Cycling '74, the commercial developer of Max/MSP, has since come out with the Jitter extension to this programming software, which adds more integral tools for manipulating visual data within the same environment.

The rapid development of the Internet has in part been supported by Web-optimized programming languages such as Java. Composers Phil Burk and Nick Didkovsky have developed a Java-based music programming environment, JSyn (www.softsynth.com/jsyn), which enables Web applications of a wide range, including algorithmic composition, to be implemented. Open Sound Control (http://opensoundcontrol.org/) is a protocol for network communication between devices that was developed at the Center for New Music and Audio Technology (CNMAT) at the University of California at Berkeley. This protocol can be integrated into a Max/MSP programming environment and has also been integrated in SuperCollider, a music-oriented programming language (script based) developed by James McCartney. SuperCollider is a powerful music language that is capable of implementing complex algorithms, performing real-time signal processing, generating synthesized sounds, and more. The ability to create customized graphic interfaces and to integrate the language into interactive performance contexts, including over the Web, make this a powerful platform for computer music.

While the possibility for implementing real-time compositional algorithms is now completely feasible, the issues of obtaining feedback and being able to reflect on the results remain of concern. Work on incorporating neural networks and self-modifying genetic algorithms shows potential for implementing strategies for adjusting compositional software on the basis of rule-based evaluation mechanisms. Christopher Ariza is one researcher working in this area, and his AthenaCL software incorporates a number of strategies for computer-assisted composition, including genetic algorithms (Ariza 2005a). David Birchfield has worked extensively on developing a compositional algorithm based on genetic algorithms (Birchfield 2003).

It should be noted that similar computational technology has been applied to the field of musical analysis. Indeed, this was a field in which Hiller was strongly involved early on. Empirical or computational musicology is now an accepted field of study, and insights gained through such research undoubtedly inform ongoing composition work.[23]

9. CONCLUSION

Building on the examples of computer music composition pioneers such as Hiller, Xenakis, and Koenig, there has been great deal of activity in the area of computational composition (and music analysis), even if much of the activity overlaps into the domains of synthesis, signal processing, and interactive performance. Current technology provides powerful tools for such work, and techniques and concepts adapted from domains such as mathematics, AI, systems theory, and many others provide rich soil for ongoing development of the field. Presentation venues such as the International Computer Music Conference continue annually to program current work in the field.[24]

NOTES

1. The scholar would have already mastered the lesser disciplines of rhetoric, logic, and grammar (the *Trivium*).

2. For in-depth study of the history of music theory, see Damschroder and Williams 1991 and Williams and Balensuela 2008.

3. This work was published after Mozart's death in 1793 and attributed to him. The selection table used for this musical game was first published in a journal in 1787.

4. In recent years, it has been possible to obtain these publications in reprint editions.

5. Cage outlined his chance-based compositional process in his article, "To Describe the Process of Composition Used in *Music of Changes* and *Imaginary Landscape No.4*" (Cage 1960, pp. 57–60). James Pritchett provided a comprehensive account of Cage's compositional procedure through the period when he began applying chance to music (Pritchett 1993, pp. 78–88).

6. Cage first visited Darmstadt in 1954 but had struck up a friendship with Boulez in 1949 as a result of an extended stay in Paris that year. The fascinating correspondence between Cage and Boulez, in which each discusses and debates compositional ideas and techniques, illustrates the relationship between Cage and the European serialists (Nattiez 1993).

7. While at Bell Labs, Shannon worked with John Pierce, who was instrumental, along with Mathews, in pioneering efforts in digital sound synthesis and the formulation of a computer language for music.

8. There has been some confusion regarding the date of completion of the *Illiac Suite*. The first three movements were complete by June 1956 as they were performed in a public concert at Urbana, Illinois. The fourth movement was added to the set in 1957.

9. American music theorist Leonard B. Meyer applied concepts derived from information theory to his influential model of music analysis and perception (Meyer 1956).

10. Sever Tipei, faculty biography, http://www.music.uiuc.edu/facultyBio.php?id=88, accessed March 19, 2008.

11. According to Xenakis, the innovative structural concepts introduced in *Metastasis* gave rise to the design ideas used for the Philips Pavilion (Xenakis 1992, p. 10). Le Corbusier was so impressed with Xenakis's links between music and architecture that he invited him to contribute to his book, *Modulor 2* (Le Corbusier 1955). The title, incidentally, refers to the dialectic between movement and statis, able to be interpreted on many levels (and pluralized to make that even more explicit).

12. It is interesting to note that Xenakis was thinking in terms of programmable algorithms at this stage, even though he would not gain access to a computer until 1962.

13. In these works, the sections have variable duration, determined stochastically. An additional work, *Amorsima-Morsima* for mixed ensemble (for the same instrumentation as *ST/10*) was withdrawn.

14. The concept of sonic quanta derived from a theoretical-perceptual formulation of sound by physicist Dennis Gabor and later led to the implementation of granular synthesis.

15. A third game piece, *Linaia-Agon* (1972), was composed later and scored for brass trio. This work contains programmatic elements from Greek mythology (Linos issues a challenge to the god Apollo for a contest) and combines elements of choice with scored sections that are to be performed at specific points. This work contains more "improvisation" than the earlier ones, at times providing instructions rather than scored materials (cf., Sluchin 2006).

16. These sets bear little relation to the pitch-class sets of atonal music analytical method. In the first place, Xenakis does not use pitch-class (a note in one octave is not considered as having identity with the same note in another octave), and his sets contain approximately thirty pitches each, spread across the full range of the piano.

17. In his discussion of group theory, Xenakis refers only to outside-time structures and inside-time structures. Temporal structures, defined theoretically, are not treated in detail. Rather, durations are included as one of the parameter vectors to be combined with other parameters such as pitch, dynamics, and so on (Xenakis 1992, pp. 215–217).

18. I am not aware of other computer implementations of this compositional model. However, Xenakis's work has been studied in detail nonetheless (cf., DeLio 1980, Vriend 1981).

19. Xenakis did develop an algorithm for sieves much later (Xenakis 1990). His discussion of the algorithm was added to the 1992 edition of *Formalized Music*. More recently, Ariza updated and extended the model in his own computer algorithm (Ariza 2005b).

20. For references relating to Lippe and other composers who count Xenakis as a strong influence on their work, see Harley 2006.

21. Cope has also continued to compose music on his own without the aid of EMI.

22. Keith Hamel has extended the software to enable data produced in Max/MSP to be routed into his NoteAbility Pro notation software.

23. Computational musicology is a specialization now offered at many institutions, such as the University of Limerick, Ireland, with its Center for Computational Musicology and Computer Music. The annual conference of the International Society for Music Information Retrieval is one source of current research in this domain (http://www.ismir.net/).

24. Those interested are advised to consult the annual *Proceedings of the International Computer Music Conference*, available through the International Computer Music Association (http://www.computermusic.org/).

BIBLIOGRAPHY

Ames, C. 1987. Automated composition in retrospect: 1956–1986. *Leonardo* 20(2): 169–185.

Ariza, C. 2005a. "An open design for computer-aided algorithmic music composition: athenaCL." Ph.D. dissertation, New York University. http://www.flexatone.net/caac.html, accessed April 1, 2008.

Ariza, C. 2005b. The Xenakis sieve as object: A new model and a complete implementation. *Computer Music Journal* 29(2): 40–60.

Arsenault, L. 2002. Iannis Xenakis's *Achorripsis:* The matrix game. *Computer Music Journal* 26(1): 58–72.

Barbaud, P. 1966. *Initiation à la composition musical automatique.* Paris: Edition Dunod.

Barlow, C. 1987. Two essays on theory. *Computer Music Journal* 11(4): 10–20.

Birchfield, D. 2003. Genetic algorithm for the evolution of feature trajectories in time-dependent arts. In *Proceedings 6th International Conference on Generative Art.* Milan, Italy, http://www.generativeart.com, accessed April 1, 2008.

Brün, H. 2004. . . . to hold discourse—at least—with a computer. . . . In *When Music Resists Meaning: The Major Writings of Herbert Brün,* ed. A. Chandra. Middletown, CT: Wesleyan University Press, pp. 191–200.

Cage, J. 1961. To describe the process of composition used in *Music of Changes* and *Imaginary Landscape No.4.* In *Silence: Lectures and Writings by John Cage.* Middletown, CT: Wesleyan University Press.

Cope, D. 1987. An expert system for computer-assisted composition. *Computer Music Journal* 11(4): 30–46.

Cope, D. 1991. *Computers and Musical Style.* Madison, WI: A-R Editions.

Cope, D. 2001. *Virtual Music: Computer Synthesis of Musical Style.* Cambridge: MIT Press.

Courtot, F. 1992. Logical representation and induction for computer assisted composition. In *Understanding Music with AI: Perspectives on Music Cognition,* ed. M. Balaban, K. Ebcioglu, and O. E. Laske. Cambridge: MIT Press, pp. 156–181.

Damschroder, D., and D. R. Williams. 1991. *Music Theory from Zarlino to Schenker: A Bibliography and Guide.* Hillsdale, NY: Pendragon Press.

Dannenberg, R. 1993. Music representation issues, techniques, and systems. *Computer Music Journal* 17(3): 20–30.

Degazio, B. 1988. The Schillinger system and contemporary computer music. In *Proceedings of Diffusion!* ed. J.-F. Denis. Montreal: Canadian Electroacoustic Community, pp. 125–133.

DeLio, T. 1980. The dialectics of structure and materials: Iannis Xenakis' *Nomos Alpha.* *Journal of Music Theory* 24(1): 63–96.

Estrada, J. 2002. Focusing on freedom and movement in music: Methods of transcription inside a continuum of rhythm and sound. *Perspectives of New Music* 40(1): 70–91.

Flint, E. R. 1993. Metabolae, arborescences and the reconstruction of time in Iannis Xenakis' *Psappha. Contemporary Music Review* 7/2: 221–248.

Gibson, B. 2002. Theory of groups: In search of a method to analyze group structures in the music of Xenakis. *Contemporary Music Review* 21(2–3): 45–52.

Harley, J. 2004. *Xenakis: His Life in Music.* New York: Routledge.

Harley, J. 2006. The creative compositional legacy of Iannis Xenakis. In *Definitive Proceedings of the International Symposium Iannis Xenakis (Athens, May 2005)*, ed. M. Solomos, A. Georgaki, and G. Zervos. Paris: Centre de recherché Informatique et Création Musicale. http://cicm.mshparisnord.org/ColloqueXenakis/papers/Harley. pdf, accessed April 1, 2008.

Hiller, L. 1959. Computer music. *Scientific American* 201/6 (December): 109–120 (reprinted in *Readings from Scientific American: Computer and Computation.* San Francisco: Freeeman, 1971).

Hiller, L., and L. Isaacson. 1959. *Experimental Music: Composition with an Electronic Computer.* New York: McGraw-Hill.

Hoffmann, P. 2000. The new GENDYN program. *Computer Music Journal* 24/2: 31–38.

Koenig, G.-M. 1983. Aesthetic integration of computer-composed scores. *Computer Music Journal* 7/4: 27–32.

Laske, O. 1981. Composition theory in Koenig's Project One and Project Two. *Computer Music Journal* 5/4: 54–65.

Le Corbusier. 1955. *Le Modulor 2.* Boulogne: Architecture d'Aujourd'hui, 1955 (first published in English in 1958 by Faber and Faber, London).

Lewis, G. 2000. Too many notes: Computers, complexity and culture in *Voyager*. *Leonardo Music Journal* 10: 33–39.

Matossian, N. 2005. *Xenakis.* London: Moufflon (first published in English in 1986 by Kahn and Averill, London).

Meyer, L. 1956. *Emotion and Meaning in Music.* Chicago: Chicago University Press.

Meyer-Eppler, W. 1955. Statistische und psychologische Klangprobleme. *Die Reihe* 1, 22–28. Also published in English in 1957 as Statistic and psychologic problems of sound, *Die Reihe* 1: 55–61.

Moles, A. 1958. *Théorie de l'information et perception esthétique.* Paris: Flammarion, 1958 (first published in English in 1966 by University of Illinois Press, Urbana).

Myhill, J. 1979. Controlled indeterminacy: A first step towards a semi-stochastic music language. *Computer Music Journal* 3/3: 12–14.

Nattiez, J.-J., ed. 1993. *The Boulez-Cage Correspondence.* Cambridge: Cambridge University Press.

Pritchett, J. 1993. *The Music of John Cage.* Cambridge: Cambridge University Press.

Roads, C. 2002. *Microsound.* Cambridge: MIT Press.

Rowe, R. 2001. *Machine Musicianship.* Cambridge: MIT Press.

Schillinger, J. 1946. *The Schillinger System of Musical Composition.* New York: Fischer (reprinted in 1976 by Da Capo Press, Cambridge, MA). http://www.folktronics.com/ web/node/116, accessed April 1, 2008.

Shannon, C., and W. Weaver. 1949. *The Mathematical Theory of Communication.* Urbana: University of Illinois Press.

Sluchin, B. 2006. *Linaia-Agon:* Towards an interpretation based on the theory. In *Definitive Proceedings of the International Symposium Iannis Xenakis (Athens, May 2005)*, ed. M. Solomos, A. Georgaki, and G. Zervos. Paris: Centre de recherché Informatique et Création Musicale. http://cicm.mshparisnord.org/ColloqueXenakis/papers/Sluchin. pdf, accessed April 1, 2008.

Solomos, M. 2006. Cellular automata in Xenakis' music: Theory and practice. In *Definitive Proceedings of the International Symposium Iannis Xenakis (Athens, May 2005)*, ed.

M. Solomos, A. Georgaki, and G. Zervos. Paris: Centre de recherché Informatique et Création Musicale. http://cicm.mshparisnord.org/ColloqueXenakis/papers/Solomos. pdf, accessed April 1, 2008.

Taube, H. 2004. *Notes from the Metalevel: An Introduction to Computer Composition*. New York: Routledge.

Vriend, J. 1981. "Nomos Alpha" for violoncello solo (Xenakis 1966): Analysis and comments. *Interface* 10: 15–82.

Wannamaker, R. 2001. Structure and perception in Herma by Iannis Xenakis. *Music Theory Online* 7/3, http://www.societymusictheory.org/mto/issues/mto.01.7.3/mto.01.7.3. wannamaker.html, accessed April 1, 2008.

Williams, D. R., and C. M. Balensuela. 2008. *Music Theory from Boethius to Zarlino: A Bibliography and Guide*. Hillsdale, NY: Pendragon Press.

Xenakis, I. 1955. La crise de la musique serielle. *Die Gravesaner Blätter* 1, 2–4 (reprinted in 1994 in *Kéleütha*, ed. Alain Galliari, L'Arche, Paris).

Xenakis, I. 1990. Sieves. *Perspectives of New Music* 28/1: 58–78.

Xenakis, I. 1992. *Formalized Music*. Rev. ed. Hillsdale, NY: Pendragon Press, 1992 (first published in English in 1971 by Indiana Press, Bloomington, IN).

Zicarelli, D. 1987. M and Jam Factory. *Computer Music Journal* 11/4: 13–29.

CHAPTER 6

....

ENVISAGING IMPROVISATION IN FUTURE COMPUTER MUSIC

....

ROGER T. DEAN

THIS chapter offers a fairly speculative consideration of opportunities in sonic improvisation using computers, since the field is moving rapidly. The literature mentioned and the emphases discussed are those of the period since roughly 2001, in part because in a previous book on computer improvisation (Dean 2003) I dealt in detail with much of the work up to that time. In this introduction, I summarize some core features and perennial issues involved in improvisation; in other sections, I consider specific roles of computers in improvisation, concluding with a discussion of their future, even quite long term, improvising potentials.

My topic is improvisation in which computers are involved, whether as passive mediator or by means of some more extensive "active" generation or processing of data in the computer's central processing unit (CPU). I consider the topic primarily from the perspective of sound creators and of listeners, and technical issues of software or hardware embodiment are only touched on occasionally. Similarly, I do not delve into the complexities of distinguishing improvisation from composition and from any other form of human sound generation, with or without prostheses such as instruments or computers. These activities form continua such that setting the point of distinction is necessarily somewhat arbitrary. In other earlier books (Dean 1989, 1992, Smith and Dean 1997), I discussed the nature of improvisation and its use either as primary production process or, in applied improvisation, as a step in composition. The first case is the classic image of improvisation: creating public music in real time, with or without preformed structures of conventions. The second case occurs when a series of such improvisations is used to gradually fix a work that can then be reproduced; such applied improvisation characterizes some notable theater and film, such as much of the work of Mike Leigh (Smith and Dean 1997) but is often part of the process of those composers who play conventional instruments (especially the piano) and equally of electromusicians who work within software, whether or not they have music theoretical understanding. I also previously considered culturally theorized analyses of improvisation, with particular reference to jazz and other forms of Western improvisation, but also with reference to art forms beyond music. Again, these issues are not reiterated at length (but see also Berliner 1994, Monson 1994, Fischlin and Heble 2004).

For simplicity, I continue to take improvisation in music as the process in which creation (as opposed to performative re-creation) and presentation of sonic events are simultaneous. This description is not intended to imply that the interpreter of a classical music notated score or traditional piece lacks the opportunity for creative input. My circumscription of improvisation requires in the extreme case that at any moment the next event is not fixed or reliably predictable in advance by the participants. This forms an interesting contrast to the ideas of predictability inherent in Leonard Meyer's theory of affect generation by music (Meyer 1956, 1965) and to those concerning predicting segmentation and using computers to generate music, discussed in several other chapters of this book.

If the next event cannot be reliably predicted, then it certainly cannot be the subject of what is termed *veridical* perception, which would require that preceding events indicate exactly what should follow, as judged by previous experiences of that same sequence of events. The next event could conceivably be probabilistically anticipated because of the schematic form of the piece and its observed relation to previous schema of the same improvisers or the same genre (and markedly so in John Zorn's [1985, 2000] game pieces, which have defined process rules).

It is interesting to contrast the level of reliance that a listener familiar with Western classical music hearing for the first time a Stamitz symphony, say, can place on their "sweet anticipations" (as David Huron [2006] named them) with that of a listener of free improvisation who is comparably familiar with related improvisation genres. No objective comparison seems to have been made empirically, but it seems likely to me that the precision of expectation of the free improvisation listener might need to be slighter than that of the classical listener. In a sense, they need a more large-scale "schematic" prediction framework, but one that is looser than in using schemata to anticipate Stamitz.

Underpinning this suggestion are at least three suggestions. First, the statistical complexity of free improvisation, on which precision of predictability depends, is greater than that of the classical symphony. Second, it is microstructure that eventually creates macrostructure in improvisation. And third, it is macrostructure that guides listener anticipation more than microstructure if they develop a (semiotic) field of anticipation during a particular piece. Thus, the listener may grasp the forming macrostructure when hearing improvisation and create their own schematic, whereas in the case of classical music, the process can operate almost in reverse, with the listener progressively reducing or selecting among the multiple schemata with which they are familiar in classical music progressively in favor of the scheme that they find most predictive. Among these classical schemata might be those of tonality, harmony, or repetition.

In improvisation, it is probably only once the listener has grasped some idea of macrostructure that their predictions can begin to be meaningful and successful for them, and this is thus both slower and less complete in free improvisation than in familiar classical music. These are issues yet to be approached empirically, but such work is beginning (and cf. chapter 23, this volume); related arguments underpin the discussion throughout this chapter. Broadly, one might suggest that listening to improvisation requires a fundamentally "bottom-up" approach, whereas familiar classical genres can be approached with a somewhat more "top-down" approach.

One of the more recent books on improvisation in music, David Borgo's *Sync or Swarm* (2005) is subtitled *Improvising Music in a Complex Age*, noting that a "complex age" such as the present is "one in which changes appear to be occurring at an ever-increasing rate, threatening to defy our ability to comprehend…and exerting… unpredictable influence on our personal and shared future" (p. 3). If improvisation illustrates the age, as he conceives it, then our age predicts the first two features I have just summarized. But, rather than argue that improvised music simply creates complexity, Borgo suggested that it offers "a visceral engagement with emerging scientific notions of chaos, complexity, complexity and self-organisation" (p. 9). This is perhaps a useful metaphorical statement, but I would argue, in agreement with Attali (1977), that music has prefigured such chaos and complexity theories, not just "engaged" with them. Arguably, complexity was a feature of (free) improvisation long before chaos theory in particular was popularized in the books Borgo references. Borgo discussed Evan Parker at some length and referenced his involvement with computer manipulation of sound in his electroacoustic ensemble, but seemed to view the computer as most useful in the context of acoustic structural phenomenological analysis and did not directly discuss the computer as partner in improvisation, perhaps even as an ideal vehicle for realization of chaos and complexity approaches, in spite of his title. *Swarm* is not only part of the phrase "swarm intelligence" by which he described certain patterns of animal behavior, but also a well-used series of software platforms for complexity interaction programming, important for improvisers such as Jonathan Impett and Tim Blackwell (see also Dean 2003 and chapter 18, this volume).

In most of the 20th century, it was reasonable to assert that Western music had somewhat neglected improvisation in comparison with many other cultures, but that improvisation remained statistically dominant among world musics at large, and that composition was a particularly Westernized convention (cf. Nettl 1974, Nettl and Russell 1998). Such statements and the conditions to which they pertain should continually evolve, and around a century later at least two factors have been changing rapidly in the period since the early 1990s, particularly in the 21st century. One factor is the continued decline of the traditional and indigenous musics of many cultures, especially in the sense of the frequency with which the musics are performed in situ within the cultures that generated them. Countermanding this only slightly is the increasing distribution and commercialization of so-called world music (Radano and Bohlman 2000, Bohlman 2002). Another factor is the ready availability of massive computing power and speed in laptop computers of decreasing price (cf. the discussions of hardware and CPU speed in chapter 3, this volume). This has meant that domestic, academic, and dance floor music makers all have access to powerful computation and can use it with or without extensive explicit knowledge of music theory, for example, awareness of the concept of tonality. Implicit knowledge and preference can suffice to provide the motivation for works of almost any complexity. Consequently, or at least concomitantly, laptop improvisation has become far more widespread than improvisation on the organ or the violin, for example (Cascone 2003, Collins 2003). It is difficult to compare the populations of, say, computer improvisers with those of jazz or free music improvisers who use conventional instruments, but an informal assessment in my hometown of the last two decades, Sydney, now reveals more computer improvisers than improvising violinists, or even double bass players, although the latter instrument is core to most conventional jazz groups, which I include in the improvising statistic. My criterion for this comparison is that to qualify as an improviser a performer must repeatedly perform improvisations in public, even though few people have the opportunity to do this with high frequency. I would hazard that the laptop is now among the most common improvising prostheses, a remarkable development in roughly a decade. Yet even in the 1990s, musicians rarely described themselves as playing the computer (Jordà 2007), even though some truly did play it.

At the same time, as George Lewis pointed out (2007), improvisation itself has suffered a degree of "exnomination" in that the term has been partially effaced in favor of the less-specific description (computer) "interactive performance" and related expressions for computer-mediated work. This tends to obscure what would otherwise be a very obvious and visible phenomenon of increased laptop improvisation. The coexistence of sonic computer improvisation with video-jockey (VJ) processes can also lead to an underestimation of its extent, and I return to the topic of audiovisual (AV) improvisation toward the end of this chapter. One benefit of the exnomination is that some prejudices against improvisation (as too "imperfect" a process; Gioia 1988) occasionally held by classical musicians and arts administrators are subverted.

1. What Can Computers Do in Improvisation?

A. General Features

Rather than emphasize the differences between improvisation and composition, which revolve around immediacy, intermusician interaction, flexibility, unpredictability, and the opportunity to move across the whole gamut from control to avoidance of control, I want to discuss what it is or might be that computers can uniquely permit or facilitate in improvisation.

Jeff Pressing analyzed and theorized improvisation extensively (e.g., Pressing 1988, 1998, 2002), and among his insights were those concerning motor control. One of these was that a performer (improviser, interpreter, or equally sportsperson) has to learn how to remove some rapid actions from conscious control because there are too many of them to be handled consciously. Certain musical patterns, learned in some way, are performed almost directly by the motor systems. As he noted, these probably occur in improvisation just as in performance of preformed compositions. A computer can provide myriad events in response to one motor movement of a performer. So, can the computer evade some of those limitations impelled in instrumental performance by the human motor system? Arguably yes, and an obvious example is the superhuman bass player, the contemporary speeded up version of Philip Johnson-Laird's algorithmic bass player (Johnson-Laird 1988, 1991, 2002), who not only performs a respectable jazz bass line (for example) but also can do it at any speed and can provide a multinote counterpoint at the same time. A more fundamental example is the capacity of a triggered computer-mediated event to provide several trajectories for which the physical determinants (if realized on an acoustic instrument, which traduces physical action into sound) would be mutually conflicting and often impossible.

More broadly speaking, human gesture, translated via computer, can initiate sonic events that are anywhere along a continuum of congruence to incongruence in relation to that gesture, whereas such flexibility is difficult or impossible on acoustic instruments (Pressing 1997). As also mentioned in chapter 11 of this volume, gestural possibilities with computers in composed or improvised music are substantially broader than those with acoustic instruments. While gestural activities of classical or jazz performers most probably often enhance audience interest in what they do (e.g., Dahl and Friberg 2007), sometimes they are distracting because of their irrelevance among an otherwise congruent stream and other times because they provide sonic output that is even downright distracting (e.g., for some people the "singing" of Keith Jarrett that often accompanies his exciting piano improvising). Arguably, it is rarely the case that instrumentalists' gestures influence the specific sonic information gathered by a listener as opposed to its extent. Gesture with computers can set up much more complex continua, which permit more sophisticated manipulation of directly musical features in ways that, if so desired, can support the perception by an audience member or fellow performer of what is being created sonically.

The comments so far in this section have assumed relatively "passive" roles of the computer. But, what of computers provided with generative algorithms that permit them to proceed unchallenged or to use a human control input or the musical output of a human performer on an instrument? Many precedents in this arena exist, from Fry's Computer Improviser (Fry 1980, 1989) to George Lewis's Voyager (1993, 1999, discussed extensively in Dean 2003). Lewis has provided an insightful generalization by suggesting that to be interesting as an improvising "partner" a computer system needs the capacity to act in a "dialogic" role (Lewis 2002, 2007). The Bahktinian term *dialogic* in contemporary usage has many shades, from the simple description of an interaction between two parties who are each capable of separate if not autonomous function, to a discursive mode of social development in communities that can sometimes overcome or limit polarities such as those originating from race or culture. Lewis's usage is at least as complex, and the ideal of a dialogic computer improviser as partner is an appealing one.

B. Specific Features and Potentials: The Computer as Instrument

Let us consider how we might use a computer prosthesis in an improvising context and in an ideal situation or how it might try to use us. Perhaps we prefer control, perhaps we like looser stimuli, by which the computer might help generate an unpredicted input to the process in which we engage.

If we seek control, why might we use a computer rather than a piano? Perhaps, it can allow a continuous control of timbre, tuning, spatialization. The logical implications of these suggestions are mainly transparent, but some aspects are less clear. For example, a computer interface can permit variable, whether largely predictable, unpredictable, or controlled, delays between an input and the corresponding output. For some improvising processes, this is quite a revelation. One can generate the conditions for a particular event, perhaps a change in the multiple stream structure of the ongoing improvisation yet not know when the change will happen. As I noted in earlier writing (e.g., Dean 2003), this is something very different from most improvising events experienced in small- or large-group acoustic improvising.

The unpredictability of timing can be accompanied by quantitatively predictable or unpredictable detail. For example, the computer improviser can control or extend the range of timbre generated by his or her computer. This is an ability of particular interest and one that contrasts in part with the tools available to an improviser who plays, say, the oboe. The oboist has learned his or her timbral range and may continue to extend it, but in control terms the oboist knows the range at any particular time in his or her performance experience. The oboist has established a relatively fixed "morphology" (as Trevor Wishart termed it [1985, 1994, chapter 7, this volume]) for the instrument. In contrast, the computer improviser can set up interfaces and software such that the improviser knows the range of input parameters he or she can control but without the experience of the full range of output sonorities that result: the morphology is open. As the user learns the morphology of any set of inputs, so he or she can find ways to extend the inputs and this range.

Almost conversely, the acoustic instrumentalist has difficulties with adapting to unfamiliar tuning systems. The pianist can hardly respond at all in real time; changes would involve retuning the instrument. The guitarist is limited by the frets;

the wind player cannot immediately subdivide every semitone reproducibly into arbitrarily smaller intervals on demand, and the string player could in principle, but in practice would require massive time and effort to do so. In contrast, the computer player can arbitrarily redefine the tuning system at a single key press or by having a frequency controller rather than a MIDI (musical instrument digital interface) or note activation protocol control mechanism. Furthermore, one can conceive new tuning systems that can then be readily realized by computer interfaces. As commonly happens now, the computer may simply use/manipulate frequency information from keyboard input so that the octave-rich repeating cycles of tonal music need not dominate. As discussed in chapter 11 in this volume, a particularly interesting aspect of computer mediation or control is allowing gesture to symbolize or dictate spatialization. This is another opportunity for which acoustic performers have more limited counterparts.

So, there is no denying the mutable potential of the computer as instrument in the hands of improvisers who wish to exploit it.

2. The Computer as Partner in Improvisation

This section considers how a computer can aid an improviser to develop responses and trajectory during a performance. Improvisers may choose to use more than one computer simultaneously, whether all for sound generation or for multiple components of an AV performance. But, this should not obscure the fact that anything that can be realized by using several computers at the same time can ultimately be realized on one. For other discussion of the broad issue of computer as partner, besides my own book (Dean 2003), see in particular Jordà's work (2002, 2007). Nick Collins also provides an interesting discussion of "musical robots and listening machines," which includes discussion of four interactive improvisation systems, ranging from "interactive companionship" to "novel improvisation" mechanisms (2007, p. 173). Pachet also summarized the capacities of the Korg Karma workstation (2002, 2003), based on the idea of providing responses to input in terms of "musical effect," which is "a way to integrate user input in a predefined musical style in a meaningful way" (2006a, b, p. 356). Essentially, this workstation has a repertoire of simple musical styles it can use when forewarned to support a user's input that portends to be in one of the styles and for the purpose of generating a particular "effect."

What would an improviser need in his or her performing environment and instrument to help surpass his or her present level of proficiency or even virtuosity? Broadly, this need may be characterized as "analyzing inputs" and "determining outputs" before permitting them to happen to be able to adjust the output infinitely (cf. Pachet 2006a, b, p. 359). In other words, the improviser often does not fully understand the input sonic environment and, equally, has sonic purposes in mind that are only partly fulfilled, for whatever reason. The computer instrumentalist can, if so desired, use a range of derivative analyses of the sonic inputs around to influence outputs and at least in the temporal frame of a few seconds can have greater control over the outputs. The analysis of inputs can accommodate imprecision, so that the recognition that particular criteria are fulfilled can be more relaxed in statistical terms. Some of this imprecision may be removed by "error correction" mechanisms, like those routine in CD players and other digital hardware.

More fundamentally, an improviser's computer partner may analyze many levels and many time frames of the input it receives. Given this, it can respond in ways that are statistically or eventually structurally "intelligent." In other words, it may determine statistical features and ensure that its outputs remain consistent with these, or it may recognize mechanisms at work and use these mechanisms to generate output, which clearly from time to time could be statistically novel (cf. consideration in chapter 19, this volume). Collins's discussion of William Hsu's timbral analysis and response system and of "Haile the robotic drummer" provides some examples of such systems under development (2007, pp. 175–177). The desirable nature of these "analytical" mechanisms is an issue related to how the human brain assesses and generates similar mechanisms, mechanisms that it will take us a long time to define. But, the principles behind their operation will increasingly be capable of realization.

3. The Computer as Improviser

To the degree that the computer can be imbued with the capacity to "deliberate" or to generate "qualia" (Boden 1990, 1998), so it can function as a separate or even independent agent in performance. But, there are many positions along the path toward qualia at which a computer might operate usefully. Note that it is probably a more complex task for a computer to function as a convincing improvising partner than as a convincing real-time composer functioning alone.

For example, given a model of a musical structure, a computer generative model can be made to embody it, and an improviser could activate it, while setting parameters or live coding variants. The recent work of Pachet and colleagues seems to operate in this niche (Pachet 2002, 2003, 2006a, b). A hidden Markov model is created from an incoming MIDI stream (usually from a keyboardist), and then the computer responds in a gap with material generated from it. This can be very useful educationally (cf. chapter 26, this volume) in that some of the responses will generally be outside the range otherwise anticipated by the student user. Videos on Pachet's Web site (www.csl.sony.fr/~pachet/Continuator/) demonstrate this very clearly. On the other hand, the videos of professional improvisers interacting with his system (Continuator) show it doing exactly what its name implies: continuing close to the vein of the improviser in a manner that, at least for an experienced performer, is unlikely to be challenging. Yet, clearly if a model can generate congruent material, every decision it makes can be transformed into its obverse so that it generates incongruent material. So, such approaches have the potential to provide computer responses that are anywhere along the spectrum of congruent ↔ incongruent or familiar ↔ unfamiliar, and the element of surprise that such repositioning of responses creates is one feature that makes improvisation unique and interesting.

Pachet's and to a lesser extent Lewis's software improvisers essentially can do in real time what David Cope's analyses of classical works do out of time to energize his computer models to generate genre- or composer-specific neocomposition (Cope 1991, 2001). As Wiggins et al. imply in chapter 19 of this volume, there is another approach that in the long run may be even more revealing, one in which the generative model embodies a cognitive model of improviser function. This line of research will fulfill the path envisaged by Johnson-Laird and his improvising bassist. A key precept of psychologist Johnson-Laird (1988) was that a model of a biological function, such as cognition, is not complete or even adequate unless it can be embodied in a computable algorithm. Thus, the development of computational modeling of cognition should lead to models that can appreciate music and assess its structure and emotion both in ways that musicologists do and in ways that listeners at large do (two probably very different things). But furthermore, in "run" mode such models should be able to generate their own output or responses, which would be analogs to the actions of human improvisers. Most work at present gingerly treads the boundary between structural modeling and cognitive modeling, but the future path is quite apparent. As Todd and Miranda indicated, there will be "co-evolution of composers and critics" (2006, p. 387; see also discussion in chapter 18, this volume).

4. SOME OTHER SPECIAL FEATURES OF COMPUTERS IN IMPROVISATION

Many authors have noted that performance in general, not just in music, creates multiple modes of time perception. As an obvious example, narrative film may compress years of events into a couple of hours; conversely, structural film such as Mike Snow's *Wavelength* or some of Andy Warhol's films give an impression of an abnormally (sometimes excruciatingly) slow passage of time by showing an event operating in real time. Computers provide a mechanism by which a composer or improviser can have multiple strands that operate at different rates or timescales from their own and yet can remain under their control. Conversely, as I (1989, 2003) and Pressing (1988) have discussed previously, if improvisation is a succession of states between which transitions are made as a result of musical leadership and communal following, then a computer can perhaps lead (or obstruct or follow) such transitions. Furthermore, the user can organize at the outset of the performance that the computer will make predictably or unpredictably timed interventions of such dramatic kind that they effect transitions, over any length of time. While this can also be achieved in comprovisation, in which a notated structure indicates such leaderly roles to individual improvisers and the communally responsive roles to others, it is difficult to achieve in free improvisation, in part because most such work proceeds with very dense and rapid event flux. The computer as partner can be as indifferent to such density as the user chooses and hence the source of unanticipated challenge and stimulus.

Networked improvisation provides a convenient framework for such operations and was pioneered by the League of Automatic Musicians, from which subsequently emerged in San Francisco the group named The Hub. The Hub has made many works in which the features of their network were part of the source and basis of the music. Passing control from or to another, avoiding it, allowing erratic computational responses, and so on are all among the interests in The Hub's work (cf. chapter 8, this volume). Originally, such networks needed to be local because of bandwidth limitations, but subsequently remote interactions were achieved, often with meta-data transmitted across the Internet and only rendered in sound on receipt. More complete exchange of audio data per se is now possible, but bandwidth limitations still remain. A more recent contribution to this stream of work has been from Jordà (2002, 2007), whose FMOL(Faust Music Online) interface is available on the Internet for interactive performance (http://www.iua. upf.es/~sergi/FMOL/FMOLProjectDescription98.htm), and provides a stimulating palette, and the possibility of remote collaboration.

A final feature of computers in improvisation, their uses in AV work, is only discussed briefly here. As indicated in this volume in chapter 15 on algorithmic synesthesia, computational interactions between audio and visual streams can provide performance tropes. More commonly, devices are used to ensure real-time synchrony between rhythms of audio and image, and techniques for beat tracking in music have parallels in image stream analysis and reconstruction (e.g., Collins and Olofsson 2006).

5. Some Structural and Formal Issues in Computer-Mediated Improvisation and Comprovisation

Adrian Moore discussed (2007) the temptation for the acousmatic composer to add opportunities for limited or controlled improvisation to his or her pieces, especially if he or she will perform the pieces. In part, this can be a response to the complaint that acousmatic music, with no performance action to watch, can be enlivened by the inclusion of performers. But equally, the laptop performer who does not use a Wiimote or other gestural tool may show rather little interesting physical action, so controlled improvisation within an otherwise acousmatic piece may have little impact on the visual effect. Whether this visual impact is critical is a very personal matter, and in view of the extremely limited performance actions of the soundmeister (DJ/VJ, etc.) visible on the electronica dance floor and the fact that we mostly hear instrumentalists on CD, dogmatic concern about this issue is probably a period-bound temporary factor.

But, there are other reasons for the composer to become the comproviser, and as Moore pointed out, these may be more fundamental. They range from adapting the sonic structure to the physical space and perhaps the audience, to being sure of at least some interesting components to a performance that are relatively free of risk, as well as the improvised components that inevitably constitute risks at least within the value framework of the composer. Furthermore, on a structural level, improvisation at least permits a bottom-up generation of form in which microstructure creates macrostructure, whereas composition generally is concerned with top-down-driven form in which macrostructure is embodied in microstrucure. Thus, improvisation is an important formal complement to composition. It is notable that there are many performers who use such an approach as Moore described, in which significant elements and sequences of sound are preformed and laid out ready for performance, but exactly how each element is realized is an in-performance decision. Usually, these performers are people who also produce acousmatic work; clearly, there remains a category of musicians, like the late guitar innovator Derek Bailey, who would mostly prefer not to participate in any event that has preformed structure if they can avoid it. Even such anti-idiomatic "purists" as Bailey and more overtly "flexible" free improvisers such as Evan Parker have molded to the opportunities of working within comprovised frameworks at various stages in their careers (e.g., both Bailey and Parker worked and recorded with the Ken Wheeler Big Band, a group of jazz musicians within the mainstream of contemporary jazz). Not surprisingly, computer composers are comparably pragmatic. At a 2007 sound art event organized by the University of Technology in Sydney involving nine Australian and one Japanese performers (which was certainly not preselected in relation to this issue), all but one of the performances were of this comprovisational nature, and I suspect, in agreement with Moore, that the frequency of such performance is increasing among computer composers (cf. chapter 9, this volume).

6. FUTURES: COGNITIVE MODEL IMPROVISERS AND META-IMPROVISATION

As mentioned, computational improvising agents might eventually operate on the basis of cognitive models of improvisation. Presently, our understanding of cognitive processes during improvisation is even more limited than our understanding of cognition of musical works by listeners. Leadership and communality (congruent responsiveness) are important features in group improvisation, and establishing flexible models of these functions will be complex. It could also be argued that the streaming structures of improvised music often differ from those of composition because of the real-time interaction of creators and their capacity for mutual molding. For example, I have made computer improvisation patches that generate algorithmic stream fusion and fissure, believing this to be common to improvisation and rarer in the canon of composed music (a musicological issue I am investigating). Such "rhizomatic," weblike structures as are produced seem to have relation to the processes in group improvisation, and this is under empirical study.

Johnson-Laird emphasized the importance of Turing tests for cognitive models. One variety of Turing test essentially determines whether a computational process can be distinguished by a human participant as "nonhuman." It has been extremely difficult for computer speakers, conversational agents, to pass the Turing test, in spite of a substantial cash prize being offered for many years. We know little about how computer improvisers would fare in such tests, although there are some anecdotal or observational positive reports (Pachet 2002). But, given the flexibility of improvisers and the lack of constraint of the medium, in comparison with the complex constraints of verbal conversation, they probably will do reasonably well. However, as discussed in this book in chapter 23 and elsewhere, an undesirable feature of a Turing test is that the participant is specifically primed to consider that his or her partner might be a computer, and many participants have negative images of computers, robots, and computational agents, so that cultural presumptions play a deleterious role in such tests. An alternative approach is simply to request qualitative assessments of aesthetic or structural features and of preference, comparing computational artifact with human artifact but with no reference to the existence of a computer-generated set, thus avoiding the cultural issues related to computing. If computer works attract statistically different ratings from those human works, then clearly the computer works are not fulfilling humanistic assumptions. Such empirical approaches will give us useful leads in the future toward the emancipation of computers as partners in improvisation.

So, what might a "cognitive" computational improviser do? It is probably worth considering briefly the functions of human organisms in relation to their environments to chart a simple outline of the relevant functions of such a computational improviser. As humans, we not only can sense, perceive, and analyze but also can couple these processes to action. Furthermore, the action can be adaptive (i.e., specific to the situation), and one of the key properties of organisms is that of surviving in quite a wide range of environments by changing the exploitation of their range of capacities. In the terms discussed by in chapter 18 of this volume comparing Blife (biological life as we know it) and Alife (artificial, computational "life"), the genotype (genetic makeup) of Blife commonly has a huge range of possible expression in phenotype (the proteins, structures, and their performance eventually through cognition). And, only a modest part of this phenotypic range is used (expressed) at any time and in any given environment. The range is not infinite, however, as we cannot survive permanently under water, for example. But, we can move in relation to the environment, such as to find a more conducive one, and as emphasized by a few ecological researchers (Odling-Smee et al. 2003), organisms can also to some extent modify their environment (whether by building nests or a more large-scale function). The cognitive improviser could use all of these processes, but as yet only a few are much exploited in autonomous Alife systems (cf. chapter 18, this volume).

We can also ask whether in the longer term the cognitive improviser can become what I would like to term a *meta-improviser.* Such an improviser would participate in, perhaps even generate and drive, evolving communities of improvisers, which in turn have the capacity to transform their largest-scale (computational) environment. As in Alife, that environment would contain selection pressures, but it would also emphasize the need for (genotypic and phenotypic) diversity, so that ongoing evolution has the broadest possible range of codes and agencies on which to act. Again, this need is not always expressed in communal evolutionary agent communities. The meta-improviser would then provide a virtually complete analog of human society in which diversity is maintained under a range of selection pressures toward monotonic conformity, whether they are sociocultural, economic, political, or intellectual. Improvisation remains key to the generation of creative processes and industries, and we have a unique opportunity in computer improvisation to advance them. While the term meta-improvisation has been used in a manner related to that in "meta-data," as of March 2009 Google revealed no examples of the exact term 'meta-improviser', suggesting that this arena remains to be adequately explored.

BIBLIOGRAPHY

Attali, J. 1977. *Noise: The Political Economy of Music.* Trans. B. Massumi. Repr. 1985. Manchester: Manchester University Press.

Berliner, P. F. 1994. *Thinking in Jazz. The Infinite Art of Improvisation.* Chicago: University of Chicago Press.

Boden, M. A. 1990. *The Creative Mind: Myths and Mechanisms.* New York: Basic Books.

Boden, M. A. 1998. Computing and creativity. In *The Digital Phoenix: How Computers are Changing Philosophy,* ed. T. W. Bynum and J. H. Moor. Oxford: Blackwell.

Bohlman, P. V. 2002. *World Music: A Very Short Introduction.* Oxford: Oxford University Press.

Borgo, D. 2005. *Sync or Swarm. Improvising Music in a Complex Age.* New York: Continuum.

Cascone, K. 2003. Grain, sequence, system: Three levels of reception in the performance of laptop music. *Contemporary Music Review* 22(4): 101–104.

Collins, N. 2003. Generative music and laptop performance. *Contemporary Music Review* 22 (4): 67–79.

Collins, N. 2007. Musical robots and listening machines. In *The Cambridge Companion to Electronic Music*, ed. N. Collins and J. d'Escriván. Cambridge: Cambridge University Press, pp. 171–184.

Collins, N., and F. Olofsson. 2006. klipp av: Live algorithmic splicing and audiovisual event capture. *Computer Music Journal* 30(2): 8–18.

Cope, D. 1991. *Computers and Musical Style*. Oxford: Oxford University Press.

Cope, D. 2001. *Virtual Music. Computer Synthesis of Musical Style*. Cambridge: MIT Press.

Dahl, S., and A. Friberg. 2007. Visual perception of expressiveness in musicians' body movements. *Journal of New Music Research* 29: 225–233.

Dean, R. T. 1989. *Creative Improvisation: Jazz, Contemporary Music and Beyond*. Milton Keynes, UK: Open University Press.

Dean, R. T. 1992. *New Structures in Jazz and Improvised Music since 1960*. Milton Keynes, UK: Open University Press.

Dean, R. T. 2003. *Hyperimprovisation: Computer Interactive Sound Improvisation; with CD-Rom*. Madison, WI: A-R Editions.

Fischlin, D., and A. Heble, eds. 2004. *The other side of nowhere. Jazz, Improvisation and Communities in Dialogue*. Middletown, CT: Wesleyan University Press.

Fry, C. 1980. Computer improvisation. *Computer Music Journal* 4(3): 48–58.

Fry, C. 1989. Flavor Band: A language for specifying musical style. In *The Music Machine. Selected Readings from* Computer Music Journal, ed. C. Roads. Cambridge: MIT Press, pp. 295–308. (Original copyright 1984.)

Gioia, T. 1988. *The Imperfect Art*. New York: Oxford University Press.

Huron, D. 2006. *Sweet Anticipation*. Cambridge: MIT Press.

Johnson-Laird, P. N. 1988. *The Computer and the Mind*. London: Fontana.

Johnson-Laird, P. N. 1991. Jazz improvisation—A theory at the computational level. In *Representing Musical Structure*, ed. P. Howell, R. West, and I. Cross. London: Academic Press, pp. 291–325.

Johnson-Laird, P. N. 2002. How jazz musicians improvise. *Music Perception* 19(3): 415–442.

Jordà, S. 2002. Improvising music with computers: A personal survey (1989–2001). *Journal of New Music Research* 31(1), 1–10.

Jordà, S. 2007. Interactivity and live computer music. In *The Cambridge Companion to Electronic Music*, ed. N. Collins and J. d'Escriván. Cambridge: Cambridge University Press, pp. 89–106.

Lewis, G. 1993. *Voyager*. Tokyo: Disk Union, CD AVAN 014.

Lewis, G. 1999. Interacting with latter-day musical automata. *Contemporary Music Review* 18(3): 99–112.

Lewis, G. E. 2002. Improvised music after 1950: Afrological and Eurological perspectives (With selected discography). *Black Music Research Journal* 22: 215–246.

Lewis, G. E. 2007. On creative machines. In *Cambridge Companion to Electronic Music*, ed. N. Collins and J. d'Escriván. Cambridge: Cambridge University Press. pp. 198–199.

Meyer, L. B. 1956. *Emotion and Meaning in Music*. Chicago: University of Chicago Press.

Meyer, L. B. 1965. *Music, the Arts, and Ideas*. Chicago: University of Chicago Press.

Monson, I. 1994. Doubleness and jazz improvisation: Irony, parody and ethnomusicology. *Critical Enquiry* 20: 283–313.

Moore, A. 2008. Making choices in electroacoustic music: Bringing a sense of play back into fixed media works 2007 [cited 2008]. http://www.shef.ac.uk/content/1/c6/04/14/88/3piecestex.pdf.

Nettl, B. 1974. Thoughts on improvisation: A comparative approach. *Musical Quarterly* 60: 1–19.

Nettl, B., and M. Russell, eds. 1998. *In the Course of Performance. Studies in the World of Musical Improvisation.* Chicago: University of Chicago Press.

Odling-Smee, F. J., K. N. Laland, and M. W. Feldman. 2003. *Niche Construction: The Neglected Process in Evolution.* Princeton, NJ: Princeton University Press.

Pachet, F. 2002. Playing with virtual musicians: The Continuator in practice. *IEEE Multimedia* 9(3): 77–82.

Pachet, F. 2003. Musical interaction with style. *Journal of New Music Research* 32(3): 333–341.

Pachet, F. 2006a. Creativity studies and musical interaction. In *Musical Creativity*, ed. I. Deliege and G. A. Wiggins. Hove, UK: Psychology Press, pp. 347–358.

Pachet, F. 2006b. Enhancing individual creativity with interactive musical reflexive systems. In *Musical Creativity*, ed. I. Deliege and G. A. Wiggins. Hove, UK: Psychology Press, pp. 359–375.

Pressing, J. 1988. Improvisation: Methods and models. In *Generative Processes in Music. The Psychology of Performance, Improvisation and Composition*, ed. J. Sloboda. Oxford: Clarendon Press, pp. 298–345.

Pressing, J. 1997. Some perspectives on performed sound and music in virtual environments. *Presence* 6: 1–22.

Pressing, J. 1998. Psychological constraints on improvisational expertise and communication. In *In the Course of Performance*, ed. B. Nettl and M. Russell. Chicago: University of Chicago Press, pp. 47–67.

Pressing, J. 2002. Free jazz and the avant-garde. In *The Cambridge Companion to Jazz*, ed. M. Cooke and D. Horn. Cambridge: Cambridge University Press, pp. 202–216.

Radano, R. M., and P. V. Bohlman, eds. 2000. *Music and the Racial Imagination.* Chicago: University of Chicago Press.

Smith, H., and R. T. Dean. 1997. *Improvisation, Hypermedia and the Arts since 1945.* London: Harwood Academic.

Todd, P. M., and E. R. Miranda. 2006. Putting some (artificial) life into models of musical creativity. In *Musical Creativity*, ed. I. Deliege and G. A. Wiggins. Hove, UK: Psychology Press, pp. 376–395.

Wishart, T. 1985. *On Sonic Art.* York, UK: Imagineering Press.

Wishart, T. 1994. *Audible Design. A Plain and Easy Introduction to Practical Sound Composition.* York, UK: Orpheus the Pantomime.

Zorn, J. 1985. *Cobra: Hat Art CD 2-6040.* 2 CD-ROMs.

Zorn, J., ed. 2000. *Arcana.* New York: Granary Books.

SOUNDING OUT

CHAPTER 7

COMPUTER MUSIC: SOME REFLECTIONS

TREVOR WISHART

1. MUSICAL STRUCTURE

I was initially drawn into the world of sound composition by a desire (for very personal reasons) to bring the sounds of the real world into music. Working with a cheap (analog) tape recorder, I collected the sounds of factories and power stations in the northern part of England and brought them to the analog studio at the University of York, where I had just obtained a place as a graduate. The first thing that I discovered was that my presuppositions about how musical form or structure operated, derived from the world of instrumental composition, were no longer adequate when faced with these intrinsically complex sound materials, and I spent the next four years trying to find some appropriate way to work in this new world. Finally, in the piece "Red Bird" I was drawn to the idea of sound transformation through the idea structure of that piece. "Red Bird" is a kind of contemporary "myth" in which various recognizable sound sources—birds, animals, machines, voices, a book, a fly—play out what one might describe as a structuralist narrative in an imaginary landscape, a formal idea inspired by reading Lévi-Strauss's *The Raw and the Cooked*.

A key feature in the piece is the (analog) transformation of one sound type (e.g., a human voice) into another (e.g., a bird). These transformations were extremely difficult to achieve in the analog studio—one had to use ad hoc procedures that happened to work with particular sounds, or perceptual tricks, like context cues, to achieve a plausible sound transformation. However, with the advent of digital recording and computer analysis of sounds, a more rational and highly effective approach to sound manipulation became possible, and I spent a good part of my career developing signal-processing instruments to explore every possible kind of sound transformation, from the phase vocoder-based morphing technique of Vox 5 and a host of other spectral domain processes, through time domain "waveset distortion" techniques (see section 2 in this chapter), to FOF (Fonction d' Onde Formantique) detection and manipulation and the plausible time extension of natural iterative sounds (like the rolled or guttural "rr" sounds of some languages).[1]

This work has been driven partly by a new conceptual framework for thinking about musical form. Traditionally, musical form, in Western art music, has centered on the organization of pitch and duration, abstracted properties of real events. *Timbre*, a vague term that really means those things that are not pitch and duration and that, until the late 19th century, we had no good ways to quantitatively describe, was seen more as a palette of instrumental/orchestral colors with which to "color in" a musical form provided by pitch-duration architecture.[2] During the 20th century, attempts were made to extend architectonic principles to the sphere of timbre, beginning perhaps with the "Klangfarbenmelodie" of Schoenberg's *5 Orchestral Piece*, through the serialization of choice of instrument (in particular, the Webern *Sinfonie*) to, for example, David Wessel's categorization of sounds by their spectral brightness.[3]

However, I would argue that all these approaches are an attempt to shoehorn timbre into the existing pitch-duration paradigm of musical organization, and that a more radical approach is required. There are two basic problems to be addressed. First, as I have said, timbre is merely a catch-all category to capture all those features of a sound that are neither pitch nor duration but, until recently, were not well understood quantitatively. In my book *Audible Design*, I suggested that timbre may be broken down into about twenty distinct properties; here, we might mention spectrum; spectral-envelope (e.g., the formants that generate vowels in speech); harmonicity/inharmonicity of the spectrum; noisiness (compare, e.g., voiced, unvoiced, and half-voiced speech); attack envelope; and on a larger scale, granularity; the average evolution of the loudness envelope (sustain, attack-resonance, growth, etc.); vibrato; jitter; tremolo; and so on. And, most of these characteristics can themselves vary through time in simple, complex, or subtle ways. With digital recording and computer control, we now have access to and the possibility of quantitative control of all these aspects of a sound. From a sonic perspective, pitch and duration are just two dimensions of a multidimensional space in which the real sound is located.

The second problem is more fundamental from a traditional formal point of view. The dimensions of pitch and duration have a special property—they are cyclical. By this I mean that we can move continuously (without steps) up the pitch dimension, but we eventually arrive at a place that perceptually strongly resembles our starting point, the octave above the original pitch, which we perceive as, in some sense, the *same* pitch.

Similarly, we can increase the tempo of a rhythmic passage, but we eventually arrive at a point (at double speed) at which that passage will time-lock with the original in a natural way. And, of course there are other points of correspondence in between. This cyclic property is the basis of pitch and rhythmic organization in traditional musical form.[4] Unfortunately, most of the timbral dimensions we have listed do not have this property.

The solution to this paradox I have proposed is to reintegrate all these definable properties (including pitch and duration) into the sound itself and take a holistic view of the sound. We may then make any transformation of that sound in the multidimensional space, not just along the pitch or duration axis and not just along one of the many timbral dimensions, but in any direction whatsoever, changing, for example, pitch, spectral envelope, and inharmonicity all at once. Most important, we should regard musical form as the organization of sounds through this generalized idea of transformation of sounds themselves and not simply as the organization of particular abstracted and idealized *properties* of sounds (pitch and duration). Traditional musical organization then becomes just a special case of this more general notion of musical organization. In the theoretical domain, this idea is inspired by the general historical direction of mathematical thinking, which moves from the particular (e.g., our schoolkid notion of algebra as "arithmetic with unknowns" to the generalized notion of an algebra, a system of rules for manipulating symbols, abstract algebras). In the experiential domain, the best model for this notion is that of human speech. When I speak, there are sound objects recognizable to my speech community, the syllables of a language, which are presented not only with different pitch (or pitch-motion) or durational characteristics, but also shifts of timbral characteristics—within a single speaker, voiced, unvoiced, hoarse, shouted, and so on. With a room full of English speakers for whom English is not their first language, a huge variety of variations on the formant structure of the "same" syllable is found. Nevertheless, the speech remains comprehensible; the transformations invoked by meaning context, social situation, state of health, or previous language learning environment produce outputs that we perceive as clearly audibly related. Hence, in the domain of more abstracted sound transformation, we know that listeners will be able to relate sounds with properties that have been shifted by some sonic process, provided we focus, honestly, on what we can hear. (Computers are so powerful that we can do almost anything to a signal, but there is a difference between linking the input and output of an algorithm as source and product and linking two audible entities as *perceptually* related to each other.)

The piece "Imago" is my most radical attempt to put this philosophy into practice. The 25-min work is derived entirely from the initial 0.2-s sound of two glasses touching. The piece attempts to make clear the evolution of all the sonic materials from this elementary source. The poetic of the piece is concerned with the emergence of surprising new events from the sonic materials, and the title relates to the caterpillar-pupa-butterfly sequence of metamorphosis (the butterfly is the imago stage).

The apparently simple source (a pitch with a bright attack) is developed, among other things, by

- Spectral freezing,[5] which captures the inharmonic characteristics of the attack of the sound (which, without freezing or time stretching, are heard holistically as merely a bright attack), then reimposes the attack-resonance loudness envelope on the result, producing related bell-like sonorities.
- Further extension of these by stacking tape-transposed[6] copies so that their attacks coincide to the sample. This prevents the new sound from appearing as a mere chordal superimposition of different sources and instead produces "bells" with rich internal harmonies. Stacking the sounds with attacks minutely offset produces an internal portamento to the attack, a sort of clunky formed-metal (e.g., car hubcap) sound. These are later used in the street-gamelan-like section.
- Waveset distortion (see further discussion) of various kinds, introducing spectral brightness, noise, or other (algorithmically but not perceptually predictable) transformations.
- Pitch-motion, changing the listener's intuition about the source of the sound (it moves from struck-solid-resonant to fluid and therefore possibly vocal, in this case possibly birdsong).[7]
- Texturing, especially, the "crushing" of a series of repeated events into less and less time, producing a "grating" experience and then a continuous sonority.
- Very dense textures that "white out" (to a textured noise band) and can then be manipulated by loudness envelope and filtering to suggest ocean waves.
- The "fugu" transformation and its extension.[8] This is a technique learned from Denis Smalley. An attack-resonance sound is reversed in time, then the reversed version is spliced onto the start of the original. The resulting sound increases, then decreases in both loudness and brightness. By cutting off the start of the original sound, a new fugu sound (from this edited portion) can be made. Other sounds can be made similarly by cutting off more and more of the start of the original sound. This produces a set of related sounds that increase and decrease in loudness and brightness, some a little, some a little more, and on and on. In "Imago," the initial fugu sound is developed by time extensions of the quiet skirts and by stacking of transposed copies. Ultimately, a very long sound is produced, and because of the correspondence between increase in loudness and brightness and our experience of sounds approaching us in the real world, the sound, played identically on both loudspeakers, appears to approach the listener from a distance. At the peak of maximum brightness, the two sources are time stretched for a fraction of a second, but differently, so that the succeeding sound is perceived as a stereo event, producing the perceptual effect of the sound "breaking" over one's head (complemented in the musical context by the ocean waves described—and underlined in performance by appropriate sound diffusion).
- Time stretching so that the start of the sound is smeared out, destroying its attack characteristic and generating (from several such stretched events) a layer of inharmonically colored noise texture. This is later manipulated first

by imposing a shuddering[9] envelope, then by using a pair of moving formant filters, to suggest human speech.

This spectral and textural development of the source is an integral aspect of the organization of the work, alongside traditional concerns for pitch, duration, and sectional organization.[10]

2. DEVELOPING NEW INSTRUMENTS

Throughout my compositional career, I have been fortunate (because of some background in mathematics and science) to be able to develop my own software instruments. I do not feel that this is a necessary activity for a composer, but I enjoy the possibility of discovering new ways to transform sound materials as this creates new formal possibilities for musical composition. I have also always felt that these new tools, like other musical instruments, should be as widely available to the musical community as possible so that techniques can be learned and shared. The Composers Desktop Project, founded by Andrew Bentley, Archer Endrich, Richard Orton, and myself in York in the early 1980s, has attempted to make all these tools (and tools developed by other permanent or occasional members of the group) accessible in terms of distribution, affordability, and user information and support. A private, or very expensive, composing tool is not going to contribute to the development of the musical community or to musical development in general.

While composing, I tend to divide my time between creating the music and developing new instruments. This makes for an interesting work balance as computing is characterized by difficulties related to technical competence or scientific knowledge, while composing is characterized more by psychological difficulties relating to judgment and choice. Mixing the two activities enables me to continue working when presented by temporarily insurmountable problems in one domain or the other.

The instrument I develop might be directly relevant to the work in hand (especially if I note the limitations of an existing tool and attempt to extend it) or pure speculation. Some of the latter can prove futile (the amazing new algorithm just churns out noise or does something exactly the same, perceptually, as an existing tool), but occasionally a really exciting result pops out. Time domain waveset distortion is particularly interesting in this respect. Speculating on how I might time stretch sounds in the time domain by repeating fragments of the waveform, I decide to skip the physically necessary step of trying to recognize what the moment-to-moment waveform shape was, and simply look at the shapes between three successive zero crossings, treating these as if they were true waveforms (I called these wavesets). The results of (for example) duplicating each (or each group of) these wavesets were truly remarkable and for a composer, if not a physicist, wonderfully unpredictable with the constant variability of any natural recorded input. They provided my first experience of a deterministic algorithm producing perceptually unpredictable (although always reproducible, in the non-real-time situation) results. Having developed this algorithm, I was able to explore a whole suite of new algorithmic possibilities using the waveset concept (and the same lateral expansion of an idea applies to most other tools I develop). More recently I have tried to work in a more detailed way with the special characteristics of the signal, looking for grains in grainy signals (e.g., the tongue flaps in a rolled rr) or the individual impulses (FOFs) in the vocal stream.

The Composers Desktop Project had no graphic interface for many years, and I was temperamentally opposed to the idea. So many commercial tools had wonderfully seductive graphics and woefully limited signal-processing powers, often based on the most naïve musical assumptions. In contrast, I was concerned to focus on the listening experience. Added to this, the amount of work involved in coding a graphic interface (which would add nothing to the direct musical possibilities of the instruments) did not seem worth the effort for a full-time composer and unpaid programmer. However, three factors changed my mind. The first was growing pressure from other users. The second was the advent of the Tk/Tcl language, which meant that the basic signal-processing algorithms (in C) did not need to be rewritten, the third was the support of Folkmar Hein and Berlin Technical University and a DAAD (Deutscher Akademischer Austausch Dienst) fellowship to go to Berlin. The resulting Sound Loom interface was a surprise as it enabled me to greatly extend the compositional usefulness of the existing algorithms. Such a simple feature as being able to process 100 (or 1,000) files at the press of a single button proved essential in composing "Globalalia" (made from a bank of over 8,300 source sounds), as did the development of a general sound database integrated into the graphic environment. For my current work, I have used old and new algorithms and called them from a graphic interface to clean up vocal recordings made in noisy environments. The graphic tool makes the underlying programs easy to use and to combine in rapid succession.

3. TECHNICAL DEVELOPMENT: SOME PROBLEMS

In the second half of the 20th century, the drawing together of high-level expertise in technology and the arts in such centers as Stanford, the University of California at San Diego, and IRCAM (Institut de Recherche et Coordination Acoustique/ Musique) produced a huge flowering of musical and technological innovation that I describe as the IRCAM effect simply because, living in Europe, I benefited from the most proximate of these institutions. However, the IRCAM effect also has its shadow. The resources required by these centers were extremely expensive and therefore rare; hence, access to them was heavily restricted for purely logistical reasons. Any such center of excellence working at the cutting edge with expensive equipment and know-how quickly divides the artistic world into the elect and the excluded and can harbor resentment among young, not-so-established composers, composers without the necessary technical know-how, or simply composers who failed to get invited because of the limited number of places. And, if the technical requirements of performance cannot be met easily anywhere else, there is a danger that the new approaches to music are simply ignored or bypassed by the wider musical community and hence fail to become a normal part of musical practice. Fortunately for the real IRCAM, the period of intense technical development was quickly followed by huge increases in computing power, which meant that the new tools and approaches being developed were on domestic desktops and laptops within a few years and accessible to any member of the musical community with the desire to know about them.

The current hot topic in music technology research is sound spatialization, and great advances have been made in multichannel spatialization, especially in sound field synthesis, by which a large array of loudspeakers is used to physically reproduce the sound wavefront in a space, the result being that sound localization is independent of the position of the listener—one can walk around the space while the projected sound appears to remain at a fixed location. The shadow of this work is again the specialist nature of the institutions involved in the development and the expense of the hardware involved (large arrays of high-quality loudspeakers). I would like this new technology to become as accessible as the previous wave, but we need a great leap forward in the science and technology of loudspeaker production before a 100- or 1,000-loudspeaker array can become a normal feature of everyday musical practice. Until then, sophisticated multiloudspeaker spatial projection is in danger of remaining an esoteric pursuit.

Since the days of a few large specialist institutions, there has been a large expansion in music-with-technology within music departments in universities and colleges and a vast growth in the number of students attracted to music, plus a welcome inflow of funds to those departments. However, this expansion also has its potential shadow. In many cases, the expansion has been facilitated by real or potential links with electronics, physics, or information technology departments with a science-funding basis (or with industry) and therefore access to much larger budgets than most pure music departments could ever dream. However, once these undoubtedly fruitful links are established, pressure can mount for technological or technical research outcomes, or even marketable products, at the expense of musical outputs. A new piece of marketable hardware or software can seem much more significant (especially to university or college authorities) than any new piece of music. In this context, concerts may turn out to be technical showcases in which the music becomes mere demo material for the technology. And, as the main market for technology applications for music is the film and popular music industries, pursuing innovation for the needs of art-music composers/performers is always in danger of being sidelined.

Similarly, the spread of powerful desktop and laptop computers, and access to increasingly powerful sound-manipulating tools, especially via the Web, has both positive and negative consequences. On the one hand, manipulating sound on a computer has become an almost commonplace activity. The gap that grew in the 20th century between some professional composers and a more general audience was unprecedented. In earlier epochs, it had been possible to approach the works of established composers through simpler pieces playable on domestic instruments by interested amateurs. As instrumental music became more elaborate, a gap began to open between what an amateur might be involved in and what professional composers wanted to pursue. The coming of the Society for Private Musical Performances enshrined this barrier between the amateur and the "high-art" world. The spread of the sound-making computer has suddenly negated this division. Typically, young people arrive in music technology courses having lots of experience of, at the very least, "sound play" on their domestic instrument, the computer. This, however, has created a different set of problems. It is now very easy to generate a satisfying aural landscape or scintillating sonic texture with a few mouse clicks on a free Internet download without any knowledge of what musical and signal-processing choices have been made to make this output possible. The task of unpicking this information, or learning to extend notions of musical form from the immediately satisfying to the construction of successful large-scale structure, can prove too arduous. Why bother with "music theory" if you can crank a digital handle and churn out "good sounds" (and possibly make a small fortune) without bothering with "all that." In a culture of neophilia encouraged by both constant technical innovation and the needs of the market to make past products obsolescent to open up new selling opportunities, the notion that tradition or experience might be important is hard to promote. Some inventive young composers and sound artists working in the medium are simply amazed to discover that people were making music with sounds sixty years ago.

The pace of technical development has another significant downside, particularly for works using live electronics. Constant technological obsolescence means that there is a constant danger that works fall by the wayside as the technology needed to realize them simply disappears. Some thought needs to be put into the problem of a more generalized and agreed representation of what is required in a live electronic performance, distinct from the particular patch on the particular software or hardware tool that was originally used, so that the piece can be authentically performed on whatever future platforms become available.

4. AESTHETIC ISSUES: SONIC ART AND SONIC ART

Finally, I briefly raise the issue of the "definition" of sonic art. To try to put a stamp on the new way of thinking about sound that developed first through electroacoustics and then computer music, I promoted the term *sonic art* (which I have to admit to borrowing from the Sonic Arts Union). In recent years, an interesting aesthetic issue has arisen in relation to this term as sonic art has also become a label for the work of visual artists who have begun to work with sounds, partly inspired by the later works of John Cage and partly by an aesthetic derived from the visual arts. I have enjoyed listening to insightful and witty works in which my attention is drawn to the social, political, or commercial source of the sound used, placed, as it were, in a gallery of complementary or contrasting objects evoking similar such responses. Much as I have enjoyed this work, it seems to me not to be music (and the artists involved would not necessarily claim that it was). This is no criticism of the work, simply an attempt to define categories and therefore appropriate contexts for criticism and development. For me, what makes music is a concern with both the placing of events in time and with relationships between the intrinsic properties of sounds (as opposed to the social or other contexts or memories they invoke—although this does not exclude being interested in these matters *in addition* to musical concerns, as "Red Bird" demonstrates). Cage touched the very limit of what we might regard as musical in insisting that we hear sounds for what they are, regardless of how we want to impose organization on them. The new sonic art goes beyond this, imposing a new type of organization on the sounds, but one that springs from an art aesthetic rather than a music aesthetic. Any new departure in the arts is to be welcomed, but we should recognize this development for what it is—not a challenge to music as such, but an extension of art and its various aesthetics to the world of sound.

NOTES

1. All of these tools are still available in the *Composers Desktop Project* (www.composersdesktop.com, accessed March 30, 2009).

2. This is discussed in some detail throughout my book *On Sonic Art* (1985).

3. This work was undertaken at IRCAM.

4. For a more detailed discussion of this point, see *On Sonic Art* (Wishart 1985).

5. Spectral freezing involves selecting a specific window in the sequence of spectral windows that make up the complete spectral representation of the sound and sustaining that window (or rather the sound that window represents) for a specified time before proceeding through the remainder of the sound.

6. These are transpositions created by changing the sampling rate of the source, which consequentially changes the duration of the sound. The process is exactly equivalent to slowing a tape recording of the source in an analog studio.

7. For further discussion of the implied "physicality" and "causality" of sounds, see the discussion in *On Sonic Art* (Wishart 1985) and *Audible Design* (Wishart 1994).

8. *Fugu* is the name of the fish with a poisonous liver served in specialist Japanese restaurants. The fish tastes better the nearer one cuts to the liver but is also more poisonous there. This creates a certain frisson for the macho gourmet in Japan. There is a relationship between this closeness of cutting and the sound process described.

9. *Shudder* is a stereo tremolo randomized in time and spatial position. See the *Composers Desktop Project* (www.composersdesktop.com, accessed March 30, 2009).

10. I intend to describe the structure of this (and other) works in more detail, with sound examples, in a forthcoming book.

BIBLIOGRAPHY

Lévi-Strauss, C. 1970/1992. *The Raw and the Cooked*. Trans. J. Weightman and
        D. Weightman. Harmondsworth: Penguin.
Wishart, T. 1985. *On Sonic Art*. York, UK: Imagineering Press.
Wishart, T. 1994. *Audible Design. A Plain and Easy Introduction to Practical Sound
        Composition*. York, UK: Orpheus the Pantomime.

CHAPTER 8

SOME NOTES ON MY ELECTRONIC IMPROVISATION PRACTICE

TIM PERKIS

I was asked to write a few words about my improvisational electronic performance practice. I have been doing this sort of thing for many years and have quite a few opinions about what works and what does not when playing electronic instruments in conjunction with acoustic ones. I am sure there are many other valid ways to go about this work, but what follows are things that I have learned or have come to believe, probably a blend of authentic wisdom and crackpot prejudices. Take it for what it's worth.

Most of my musical work over the years has been with live ensembles, either of all electronic/computer players (The League of Automatic Music Composers, The Hub) or in mixed improvisational electronic/acoustic ensembles. My improvisational music is in the San Francisco Bay Area tradition of improvised music, a genre with strong links to free jazz and European free improv, but with its own peculiar blend of these threads and others, from punk rock and "noise" to traditional Asian musics. For my improv performance rig—the setup I use to play in ensembles with acoustic instruments—I have changed neither the software nor the hardware for over ten years. This of course is an eternity in the world of computer technology, and I've certainly had ideas about extensions and changes I could make to my instrument. But as time has gone on, I've gotten a little stubborn about the idea of keeping it the same, and by now I've come to think of it as a long-term experiment: How long can this instrument stay interesting to myself and others? When will I stop finding new things I can do with it? Is it rich enough to be responsive to the development of my own skill and performance practice, without technical tinkering?

One thing that's wrong with much live electronic music is that the performer doesn't really know how to play his or her instrument, which he or she may just have finished building five minutes before the show. Constant technical improvement means eternal unfamiliarity with the instrument. If every time a violinist came up against some difficult musical situation he or she decided to modify the instrument—by, say, adding a new string to reach those high notes or adding a pedal-operated vibrator to improve vibrato, the violinist would be evading the development of personal musicality, the spiritual task of becoming one with and adjusting to one's means of expression.

I certainly don't claim that my instrument has the depth of possibility of a violin, but I'll never really know what it's capable of if I'm constantly changing it. As it is, after years of playing it, I'm still finding new things it can do, and I'm not at all bored with the possibilities it affords for playing with others. My years of experience with it also offer the benefit of having a pretty large repertoire of behaviors I can get to very quickly, a vocabulary that gives me a nimbleness that lets me keep up with the acoustic instrumentalists, something unusual for computer players. (Or so I'm told by the people I play with.)

Physically my instrument is not particularly novel: an '80s era MIDI (musical instrument digital interface) digital synthesizer; a laptop running MIDI processing software I've written myself; inputs from the computer keyboard and sixteen MIDI sliders; a volume pedal and a wah-wah pedal. I have experimented off and on over the years with novel controllers: infrared sensors that let you wave your hands in the air; accelerometers, multitouch pads, mice and trackballs and pressure-sensitive switches; ribbon controllers; squeezable rubber balls; and guitarlike gizmos of my own and other's devising.

None of these things have made it out of the lab and onto the stage with me. Sticking with sliders and ASCII keyboards will never win me a prize for human-computer interface innovation, but for my purposes they are hard to improve. Sliders show you at a glance their current setting and stay where you leave them. I can operate ten of them simultaneously with my fingertips if I wish, and while I don't think I ever have quite done that, I'm often moving three or four of them at once. For triggering musical events and making discrete parameter selections, single ASCII keyboard keystrokes work fine. A volume pedal is a direct and natural way to articulate phrases and control overall level, and the wah-wah pedal plays a curious and crucial role that I'll get into in detail. Nothing exotic is going on here.

Likewise, there is nothing of real interest on my computer screen. It's not necessary. Does a piano have a display? Another gripe I have with much laptop music is that the musicians are off in their own world, mesmerized by a sophisticated environment of GUI (graphical user interface) plus mouse and taken out of the shared acoustic space the rest of us in the room are inhabiting. That's fine for certain styles of preplanned and slowly changing music, but when trying to keep up with acoustic players, I want to live in the same aural-plus-kinesthetic world that they are in and not be off in the textual/visual world of the current standard GUI interface.

Besides, you would be hard-pressed to find a more awkward and unmusical controller than a computer mouse. Imagine the rich and complex control panel of an analog synthesizer, with a hundred knobs and sliders and patch cords to play with, and imagine you weren't allowed to touch them and had to poke them one at a time with a stick. That's the mouse.

My instrument grew from the idea of creating a system that was partially unpredictable and uncontrollable; something that, even when playing solo, would provide a context for me to be required to react and respond to the unexpected, just as if I were playing with other people. The instrument, originally conceived as a computer-based composition called "Touch Typing," was based on a model of the behavior of genes in biological systems. Musical improvisation can be thought of as having certain properties in common with the process of biological evolution. I've used a simplified model of sex and mutation: a string of bits defining a sound event (a "gene") is randomly mutated—one bit, selected at random, is flipped—or the entire gene is cut in half and mixed with another one. These actions are all done under the control of keys on the computer keyboard, which either play events ("express" the gene), cause a mutation to happen, or cause an event to be "bred" with another. This set of controls defines an instrument, which I freely play in the performance: I fill the role of natural selection by choosing to keep some sounds and discard others, building up a "population" of sound definitions over the course of a performance. In addition, sliders provide control over the ranges over which random variation can take place as well as direct control of certain performance parameters.

So, while all this all sounds very groovy and sophisticated (at least it seemed so fifteen years ago), another hard-won nugget of wisdom is that clever algorithms such as this really don't mean all that much musically: the algorithm doesn't define the perceptually important aspects of the music. Now, I don't wish to discount the value of this aspect of the system *too much*: these mechanisms do work and often do allow me to hit that "sweet spot" between control and randomness where all the action is. It certainly is good to be able to control the level of randomness, to be able to choose when to be surprised and when not to be surprised.

But, of far more importance are the choices made about the actual physical properties of the sound, the mapping between performance gestures and sonic qualities, and the particulars of the sounds' dynamic evolution. In trying to build a playable instrument, I'm not really attempting to simulate any real-world instrument—what would be the point of that over playing the real instrument itself?—but there does need to be an appealing kinesthetic quality, the sense that the sounds, like the sounds made by an acoustic instrument, are somehow a trace of a plausible physical process. And, I don't really think that much about this process of sound design can be automated or abstracted: it's a matter of making very particular and arbitrary decisions. There's no substitute for time and taste, in trying, listening, rejecting and accepting, following intuitions about what sounds good.

In my case, I find particularly fascinating those sounds that have fast articulation, right on the edge between what we can perceive as pitch and what we perceive as rhythm. This is the twittering realm of birdsong, a timescale that seems to live in a gap in our perceptual abilities: at these double-digit hertz rates things are happening too fast for us to parse individual events but still slow enough not to meld in our awareness to the perceptual summaries we call timbre or pitch. This is also the time rate at which the articulations of human speech stream by, as well as the upper limit of the performance abilities of virtuosic instrumentalists. For all these reasons, I think, sounds that change and move at these timescales imply a feeling of energy, skill, and intelligence just a little beyond understanding—all qualities that make for interesting music.

By working at these timescales, I can invoke a "virtual virtuosity" in my playing that provides a good match to the actual virtuosity of the players with whom I work. I noticed early on, in playing a duo with a violinist, that when a very cheesy synthesized violin sound plays in counterpoint with a real violin, it can quite convincingly seem as if two violins are playing. It's as if all the cues we use to define the reality of the violin sound—little chiffs and squeaks and timbral irregularities—don't adhere all that strongly to one pitch stream or the other. They both benefit from these features and sound real. This virtual virtuosity effect is a similar phenomenon.

What kind of roles can an electronic player take in an acoustic ensemble? Again, I speak only about my own practice—but first and foremost, I want to spend most of my time being a *player*, a single instrumental voice among others, not as an orchestral backdrop. With my particular range of sounds, I can at times be part of the wind section, be part of the percussion section, provide noise textures or quiet tones or chords that set a mood without necessarily being consciously heard. Or, sometimes I just make wild-ass electronic sounds that are frankly like nothing an acoustic player could do.

Sometimes, I think of what I do as erasing, actually thinning out or simplifying confused textures. If two players are playing things that don't really hang together very well, and I'm able to insert an electronic element that somehow melds their voices so that the three of us sound like aspects of one unified process, I've actually "erased" something, turned two voices not into three but into one.

I've never been interested in live sampling of other players and never really enjoyed playing in ensembles in which someone else is sampling me and playing back modified versions of my own voice. If I'm making a particular sound in an improv and I decide it's time for that sound to stop, I want it to stop. I suppose it's possible to make live sampling interesting, but only in very specific contexts, and most of the times I've heard it I've felt it was an obnoxious gimmick. Often, sampling not only needlessly muddies up the group sound, but seems impolite, overstepping each player's own sonic center. Just because something is technically possible doesn't mean it's a good idea.

My computer ensemble work, for example with The Hub, involves continuous mutual "sampling" of a sort, in which individual computer players are always reporting to each other information about their instantaneous state. So, this may sound like an aesthetic contradiction: to be so opposed to sampling in the acoustic ensemble context while pursuing a form of it to an extreme degree in the electronic ensembles. I can only say that the difference is context, and that in the Hub context, the very notion of individual voice identity is being questioned and examined: the whole raison d'etre of that music is the exploration of different modes of interactive influence and of new forms of social and human?machine interaction. In the acoustic ensemble work, I have a much more traditional attitude and seek to create an atmosphere that respects the "working space" of individual players.

In general, electronic music will tend to muddy up the sound—in a hall with bad acoustics, the electronic sounds lose their definition more quickly than acoustic ones, in my experience. Of course, the electronic player can overcome this effect with sheer power or by using a hyperarticulate amplification system, but this is almost invariably to the detriment of a good blended group sound. I almost always play through my own amp, which sits on the stage near me, so that my sound is localized and, again, as much like that of an acoustic player as possible.

The wah-wah pedal is a crucial part of my performance setup. It's not there for Jimi Hendrix–style psychedelia or funky "Shaft" chunka chunka riffs (although that can be fun from time to time). A wah pedal is a peaky low-pass filter, essentially a band-pass filter, that limits the acoustic energy of one's playing to a particular band. Electronic music is often a "bad neighbor" playing with acoustic players since high-quality audio systems offer flat reproduction across the entire audible spectrum. The synthesist takes up the full spectrum, leaving nothing for everyone else.

Scientists who study the acoustic ecology of natural environments have found that birds and insects modify their calls in different locations of their natural range to fit into the acoustic "landscape" of a particular location. They find a way to share the available bandwidth so that everyone can be heard. I use the wah to do something similar in an acoustic ensemble. I can always make fine adjustments to the filtering of my sound to exploit sonic peculiarities of the room, get out of the way of other players, or emphasize resonances that they are exploring. Acoustic instruments generally have distinctive formant structures, and I think families of instruments in any particular music tradition have co-evolved to share the spectrum with each other, to create a beautiful ensemble sound. The wah pedal lets me participate in this timbral harmony in a very intuitive way, making continuous adjustments to my overall instrumental formant nearly unconsciously.

Trombonist George Lewis—echoing a similar remark by Thelonious Monk—told me once that the whole point in improvising together is to make the other guy sound good. This is a beautiful philosophy of music, and I try to keep it in mind as much as possible when playing. I've evolved my ensemble instrument and practice over the years to serve this aim as well as I can.

CHAPTER 9

....

COMBINING THE ACOUSTIC AND THE DIGITAL: MUSIC FOR INSTRUMENTS AND COMPUTERS OR PRERECORDED SOUND

....

SIMON EMMERSON

UNTIL well into the 20th century, the performer of a musical instrument used some aspect of bodily muscle power to set a mechanical object in motion—a string, a membrane, a column of air, other more or less solid items (cymbals, woodblocks, and the like). Such instruments varied enormously in size (and in a usually corresponding frequency range) and loudness—the extremes of frequency need a lot of energy to produce loudly. Increasing public demand correspondingly increased concert hall size. Increasing size and mechanical resonance helped instrument builders improve sound projection to a degree, but room for maneuver was limited. Electrical amplification was introduced progressively from the 1920s, through jazz, popular music, and the demands of radio especially, but also through the increasing power of "public address" systems for political and public figures. This changed forever one aspect of this relationship: muscle power was no longer a limiting factor on loudness and hence distance of sound projection. The close and cozy relationship of human to instrument was complicated by a third party—whether considered a partner, mediator, or intruder depends on musical and social circumstance—electronic technology.

A parallel development was to combine the acoustic instrument with pre-recorded sound on a fixed medium. In Ottorino Respighi's *Pines of Rome*, composed in 1923–1924 (Respighi 1925), the composer calls for the playback of a prerecorded nightingale—at the time, from a 78-rpm preelectric gramophone disc. John Cage's *Imaginary Landscape No. 1* (1939) includes the playback of disc-recorded test tones combined with muted piano and cymbal. Daphne Oram's recently rediscovered (and unperformed) *Still Point* for orchestra, recorded sound and live electronics dating from 1948–1950, is maybe the visionary first of its kind. A better-described history begins with Pierre Schaeffer and Pierre Henry's *Orphée 51* (for voices and tape, 1951 [unpublished])—the birth of the world of "mixed music" (as the French call it) of instrument/voice and tape.

Soon after came the use of basic sound-processing equipment (and "record-playback" delay lines) to transform the sound of the instrument while performing. While the emphasis in this chapter is on the contemporary digital world, we cannot easily ignore its analog prehistory. Analog progressively gave way to digital systems in the last two decades of the 20th century. At first, the analog world was simply translated into digital terms; many of the icons used in graphical user interface (GUI) software are only visual representations of once very physical buttons, switches, potentiometers, and faders. Interfaces and controls peculiar and unique to the digital age have been slow to develop as we remain creatures of habit and history, but new ideas of control, interaction, and processing allowed by increased computation power have recently joined the field.

Of course, there are those who have abandoned the acoustic world and are developing new all-digital musical instruments, but some instrumentalists and composers refuse to give up on acoustic forces so easily and are happy not just to coexist but to develop and exploit the often difficult relationship with the technology.

The world of the acoustic instrument has changed profoundly in the wake of the onslaught of electronic sound and media. How does the instrumentalist respond—literally and musically—to this disembodied "other" (even when it is a mirror image)? It is this duality that is the focus here. Thus, completely electronically produced (or stored and performed) works—including "live" laptop performance—are not discussed (they are covered elsewhere in this book).

1. Two Paradigms

There have been many streams of development of the relationship of the live musician with the computer. Two contrasting approaches stand out, however, although there is not always a clear distinction. The first continues the very notion

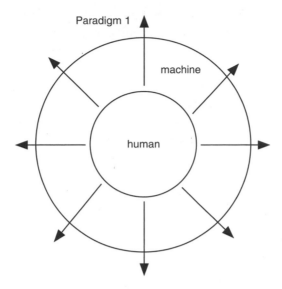

Figure 9.1 First paradigm of human/computer relationship.

of the instrument as extension of the human body (fig. 9.1); here, the computer becomes an appendage capable of transcending both the physical limitations of size and maybe soon the mental limitations of the human brain.[1] The machine seeks to extend the instrument out from its roots, possibly developing spatial timbral transformations and articulations but remaining rooted in its source. In this view, the new instrument is not considered autonomous but is integrated with the original human performance action and perception.

Contrasting with this, we can see the computer as generating *another performer* (or more than one) (fig. 9.2). This can be simply subdivided: we can generate this other performer as a (near) clone of the first—displacing timbre, time, and other

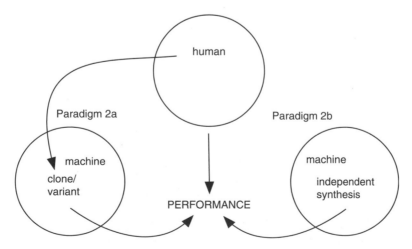

Figure 9.2 Second paradigm of human/computer relationship (two possibilities).

cues to generate a polyphony from the soloist (paradigm 2a)—or we could also consider the computer a strictly separate entity generating an independent musical stream (as in many newer interactive compositions; paradigm 2b). This added musician may progressively be gaining almost human characteristics such that the equivalent of a Turing test might be some measure of successful performance. Another musician (or more than one) emerges in our perception. One way of thinking about these systems is to ask: where is the decision making and control? The answer can be increasingly complex.

2. THREE THEMES

There are three themes that focus the discussion: *combination, transformation,* and *control* (fig. 9.3). These lie within an overall shell of *performance and composition practice*—how the music is presented (projected or diffused). These themes certainly overlap, interact, and combine but are useful starting ideas to see how the vast range of combining acoustic and digital may be comprehended:

1. *Combination:* How do the acoustic and digital sound worlds combine? Composers have exploited all the possible relationships from supportive to antagonistic, from uniform to diverse. Whether prerecorded or produced in real time, we discuss how composers have expanded our experience through this kind of extension.
2. *Transformation:* This is traditionally the domain of what is called "live electronics," but in fact is something that has changed rapidly with the

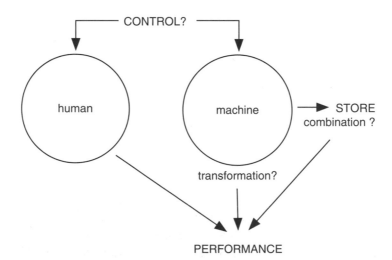

Figure 9.3 Three themes: combination, transformation, control
(for feedback and control decision paths, see figure 9.4).

development of real-time digital signal-processing (DSP) techniques. The traditional division of *time* and *frequency* domain transformations will not easily disappear. It is based on a world that tends to distinguish *events* and *signals* and was inevitably drawn from muscular energy input into acoustic instruments. An event tends to mark a point in time, whereas a signal indicates a quality over time—of course, each needs the other. The two now much more seamlessly integrate in the digital universe.

3. *Control:* In the analog (voltage-controlled) era, this was confined to switch, potentiometer, and continuous controllers (manual or pedal) supplemented by elementary sequencers (voltage memories). The former group has long been digitized and progressively extended into a vast range of sensors and interface controllers, while sequencers have developed to become powerful composition aids, with their function in live electronics replaced by an equally vast array of algorithmic and interactive machine-based functions. It is in this area that the greatest change can be perceived. We examine a wide range of options: from the computer as "real-time studio" (which is simply performing what might previously have been laboriously created in advance in a studio) to the computer as (perhaps) cocreator, decision maker, performer. It is impossible to separate this topic in its entirety, and it is interwoven into the discussion. But, it is important to address it directly; composers are often idealistic at best, at worst ambiguous about where the real control in a performance lies. This is a potential source of much frustration between performers and composers (if the two are not the same person); it is not that all performers want total responsibility for the work, but that adequate possibilities of response and control over the unfolding of the work are available to them.[2]

3. COMBINATION WITH FIXED SOUNDS

While true that the earliest dreams for electronic forms of music included what we now know as live electronics, in practice the first generation of works to bring in electroacoustic forces combined the instrumental sound with prerecorded sound (at first on analog tape). These are known in the French tradition as *mixed works* (although some are loosely bundled in the term *live electronics* in some English language discussions).

So, what has changed in the transition from analog tape to hard disc? Superficially, very little—we can, of course, simply transfer the same fixed material to the new medium. But, there was always a certain disquiet among some performers that the fixed tape part was also a straightjacket. Analog (and fixed-digital) playback systems rarely gave the performer control of one of the most precious parts of expressive musical potential: control over *time*, the speed or tempo of performance.

Triggering sound files from digital media is much easier than playing back multiple tape cues.[3] So, the flexibility of the digital medium encourages a "freeing up" of the time domain. The instrumentalist could take over as conductor of the sound—and not the reverse as previously (we return to this in section 6).

4. Types of Combination: The Musical Aims

Archetypes do not go away that easily, and many mixed electroacoustic works of the late 20th century have not developed forms and musical ideas much beyond variations of the classical and romantic concerto, at least in terms of the nature of the individual forces, call and response forms, and the like. But, in terms of approaches to materials, there has been a profound shift. In practice, the modernist idea of not repeating anything is commonly found[4] and is often articulated through moment form (sectional) structures[5] or evolutionary ("growth") forms. In addition, some works seem to be a snapshot in time of a flux of energy that *starts* and *stops* rather than having a *beginning* and an *ending*.[6] Horacio Vaggione's *Tar* (bass clarinet and tape, 1987, on Vaggione 1988) is a case in point as well as a wonderful example of an expanding granular texture centered on the soloist.

Three impulses within composition that combines the live and the acousmatic sound worlds are those of *integration* (based on attraction), *antithesis* (based on repulsion), and *co-existence*.[7] There are two approaches to integration. On the one hand, instruments can be performed in an extended manner, using playing techniques not normally associated with Western art music production, exploiting their possibilities for noise and an increased range of timbres. Amplification can aid projection of the small and usually unheard subtleties of sound production. This is, if you like, the instrument "aspiring to the condition of the acousmatic"—without visual information you might have difficulty knowing how any particular sound was produced. Trevor Wishart's *Anticredos* (amplified voices, 1980, on Wishart 1992) uses extended vocal sounds to project the "voice as synthesizer," while Denis Smalley's *Clarinet Threads* (clarinet and tape, 1985, on Smalley 1992) seamlessly expands outward the anchored clarinet sound world (see Emmerson 1998a). On the other hand, in the opposite direction, the note-dominated world of the traditionally performed instrument can invade the electroacoustic space in two ways: through literal recording or through (probably MIDI [musical instrument digital interface]-based) synthetic or sampled event-driven working (Emmerson 2007a, chapter 4). Steve Reich's *Different Trains* (for string quartet and tape, 1988, on Reich 1989) and Morton Subotnick's *Key to Songs* (ensemble and computer, 1985, on Subotnick 1986) are contrasting examples.

Repulsion and antagonism are not new drivers of musical discourse but are commonly found in avant-garde rhetoric. Luigi Nono pitted the lyrical solo soprano against factory noise and political demonstrations and slogans in *La fabbrica illuminata*[8] (solo soprano and tape, 1964, on Nono 1992). The mutual repulsion of the two worlds is there to make a political point, alienating us with its bold confrontation and gaining our attention.

In contrast, Cage's approach to such combination might be described as supremely indifferent coexistence (no judgment *a priori* regarding what should be combined and what the results might be). The combination of two of his works in performance, *Aria* (for soprano, 1958) with *Fontana Mix* (his own version for fixed sounds, 1958) is a case in point (Cage 1961). It is also possible that this kind of coexistence is done with full intention. Each of the two streams of sound inhabits its own idiosyncratic universe deliberately. In the notes to Katharine Norman's *Trying to Translate* (piano, tape and live electronics), she wrote, "I decided to explore the polarity between the instrument and the tape. . . . Piano and tape inhabit the same world but differently" (1991, p. 4). The tape contains speech (English and Gaelic) running in parallel with the piano's figurations (on Norman 2000). Both these works leave it entirely to the listener to create the meaning in the relationship between two such very different streams of sound.

5. TRANSFORMATION OF THE ACOUSTIC SOUND

At the beginning of the chapter, I suggested two paradigms for the combination of live instrumentalist and computer. The term *transformation* might more easily relate to the first—the idea of extending the instrument from its acoustic roots but retaining a sense of singularity of control. We can project the sound world into an enlarged, three-dimensional universe. But, some kinds of transformation might help us build the alternative—another apparent performer—a true polyphony. This would involve a fundamental spatial shift uprooting the sound source and throwing it elsewhere in the space. All these possibilities are articulated using acoustic sounds at the moment they are produced as sources for a range of signal-processing possibilities for projection within this vast field. Let us look at some of these.

A. Projection, Spatialization, and Separation

Our two paradigms can both be seen as products of different kinds of spatialization. In the first, we have an integrated single space—the instrument itself not substantially moving but the enlargement of the acoustic space itself (and the structural use of spatialized timbre[9])—perhaps we can think in terms of Varese's "sculpting of sound," here formed outward from the instrument, with the original acoustic sound its origin but not necessarily always its only focus. There can be motion within this, but a motion of qualitative timbral change.

In the second, we have motion or displacement. The dream of an instrument (and performer) freed of gravity is an ancient one, but our dream *is* a dream precisely because it is literally supernatural. In contrast, memory of water immersion is literal and real (the amniotic fluid of our prebirth state), but that of flying is imaginative. We see it in other species and can begin to imagine it in the echoes of modern human constructions—from cathedrals and other vast enclosed spaces,[10] to land and cityscapes. The problem is that the real instrument remains stubbornly rooted to the spot in our perception—it resists our attempts to get it to fly. Things work out better if we delay in time, but the first event will remain anchored to its original position, only then can it "take off." Psychoacoustics backs up our musical perception that sharp attacks are more clearly located—they are treated as *new origins*—but, simply transforming a continuous sound and moving it to another loudspeaker will not necessarily move the listener's perception of its origin. From whatever source, it may need a clearly separated onset to displace it successfully.

These two paradigmatic approaches to space lead to two discussions on transformation: those developing the timbral identity of the instrument itself and those focused on recognizable events displaced usually in both space and time.[11] From very different traditions, my *Sentences* (soprano and live electronics, 1991, on Emmerson 2007b), Lawrence Casserley's work with improvisers such as the Evan Parker Electro-Acoustic Ensemble (Casserley 1998, Parker et al. 1999), and Hans Tutschku's *Zellen-Linien* (piano and electronics, 2007) exploit this contrast very clearly.

B. "Events" and Time Shift

The term *event* has two overlapping meanings. The first is the idea of event as an identifiable change in a given quality, taking place at a specifiable time (with duration not considered). This need for a "time-stamp" is important; our perception notices its happening and may relate it to other such events in time. On the other hand, the term is sometimes used to mean a sonic unit, assumed to be relatively short in duration, which has a clear identity. For this use, also, the time of occurrence is usually clear and noticeable. But, there is ambiguity in both uses of the term; nothing is technically instantaneous, and "noticeable" depends on attention, learning, and cultural significance as much as acoustics.[12] In music, the MIDI specification made the idea of event explicit in its "note on/off" definitions, which are identifiable changes in pitch or velocity (effectively amplitude). The idea of event relates in classic electroacoustic terms to *gesture* (Smalley 1986), usually indicating a specific input of energy (muscular or otherwise), but can also include other changes in level, density, or timbral quality that have a time-marking function.

Software that deals with event processing and signal processing draws exact parallels with rules of *syntax* (word combination) and *phonology* (sound combination) within language. Real-time event-processing software developed rapidly on personal computers following the advent of MIDI, while signal processing required much higher computational power and moved into real-time somewhat later. The integration of—or at least the possibility of a continuity between—the two domains has now opened up.

Event processing is usually carried out over longer time spans than signal processing. The relationship of performed events to each other may be the subject of transformations following capture: rhythm, duration, and other time-point functions may be varied algorithmically, either predetermined or controlled by parameters extracted from the run-time of performance. In addition, if we see events as having duration, event processing embraces the frequency domain transformations discussed in this chapter.

It is possible, although extremely difficult, to retain a singular identity of live and time-displaced events with instrumental sound. This requires well-integrated amplification and recording and spatially "tight" mixing of the two. But, as noted, to record and displace events in time *and space* tends to create an apparently separate source of sound—another instrument. Words such as heterophony, antiphony, and polyphony (the relation of voices one to another) might become useful again to describe the various relationships of the original sound to its delays. These may of course be transformed timbrally such that the simple and predictable are avoided.

The ambiguity in the term *event* is mirrored in perception. An event is perceivable as a separate entity. But, multiplied and layered with increasing density its separateness can progressively be undermined; at the extreme, an event can become a "grain" in a swarm texture, for example, and our perception shifts up to larger-scale objects and shapes. The individual identity is subsumed in the greater whole, which takes on the role of a singular identity (no longer strictly a polyphony[13]). Thus, an instrumental event or gesture can be the origin of a texture (a larger-scale event).

C. Frequency and Timbre Domain: Into Real-Time

There is also ambiguity in the terminology here. *Frequency domain* transformation originally referred to using a set of DSP tools for spectral manipulation. Since the advent of computer applications to sound, there has been a moving boundary between techniques applicable in real-time and those available only in deferred time, the former progressively taking over with increasing computer power. We might think of successive waves of shift into the real-time, the first four (in the list that follows) coming straight from our analog world, with the others increasingly reliant on digital technology:

> Dynamic range processing: envelope shapers, gates, compressors
> Filtering
> Time and pitch transposition
> Time delay timbral effects: flanging, phasing, chorus
> Convolution
> Analysis-resynthesis and an increasing range of Fast Fourier Transform
>   (FFT)-based processes
> Microsound time domain processing (granulation, wavelet manipulation)[14]

In the earlier processes, you had to work harder if you wanted to lose the sense of source bonding to the original sound. But with the more recently available techniques, the relationship to source can become more remote; it might be better to refer to *timbre domain* as a broader embracing term, especially as microtime manipulation has become available (Roads 2001).

In the studio, we might transform an instrumental sound to something no longer recognizable, but with the live instrumental sound present, there remains a much greater possibility of an "anchoring to source" in our perception. This may be desirable or not depending on musical context—and which of our two basic paradigms is intended.

Of course, event and timbre manipulation cannot always remain clearly distinguished; in practice, we may envelope a continuous sound to create a time-stamped event, and we may time stretch an event into a slow-changing texture. From the time of Denis Gabor's earliest research into granulation (1947), there has been an uncertainty principle (the author draws an explicit equivalence to that of Werner Heisenberg in particle physics). The greater the measure of exactness of an event in time, the less exact is our knowledge of its instantaneous spectrum.

This parallels the more poetic aim of composers such as Karlheinz Stockhausen, who attempted to unify these concepts through their common axis of time, where musical form accelerates into rhythm, which in turn accelerates into timbre (Stock-hausen 1962). Curtis Roads has rationalized and extended this in a continuum from the infinitely long to the infinitely short (while pointing out that all such discussions exist in the *now* of the present and extend back into history) (Roads 2001, chapter 1). Thus, frequency becomes subsumed into the broader time domain.

This is an area of great asymmetry between our human performer and the computer partner. For the human, there are limits of event speed and duration articulation—from about twelve per second (repetitive gesture action) to limits of muscle sustain (breath and bow length, although circular breathing and bowing can result in very much longer sustains). For the computer, limits will be defined for purely musical reasons by the composer, performer and listener; they should not be described as "infinite" but as flexible.

6. Control and Decision Making

A summary of the discussion that follows is found in fig. 9.4.

A. The Score: Fixed, Flexible, Open

A score is a set of instructions; different musical cultures and genres have emphasized different functions, hence different musical parameters. Scores need not strictly be written, although the term has come to mean this. Both parties in our duo (human and computer) may be using scores in performance together—although not always the same one.

Scores may be relatively fixed, leaving very little to chance or user interpretation, although humans cannot usually fulfill the demands of scores exactly (and they usually would not wish to do so). Or, scores may be flexible, open, or improvisatory, leaving the executants—human or computer—to make decisions based on judgment of the immediate circumstances, chance or other rules.[15]

Both the human and machine executants may know of each other's score requirements (usually a single document, although not necessarily), and both may need to follow the other or a "conductor" (usually a clock). The resistance of human performers to strictly metrical clock time (which mechanical and electrical systems tend to give us) is well documented. So, if we return control over time and tempo to the human performer, we may require the computer to follow that performance (and not objective clock time) to keep track of their place in the score.

B. Score Following

Computers can easily follow scores in the sense of playing back a sequenced set of instructions (any sequencer, with or without traditional notation, is doing this).

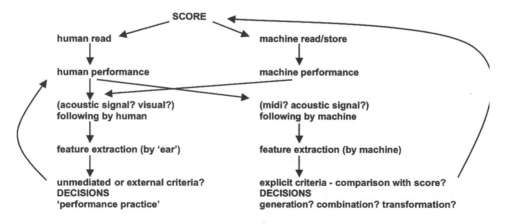

Figure 9.4 Decisions/control flow.

But, the term *score following* has come to mean something more active and engaged. It should better be called "performance following against a score." Take a work for which there is a score containing instructions both for a live performer and for a computer part to play together. The live performer plays, and the performance is analyzed as it happens. This is compared against the score of the work, which is tracked through at a rate governed by the live performer. The computer part is thus flexibly executed to follow the live performance. Earliest examples of score-following software were based on largely traditional models (even works) and were aimed to produce flexible computer-generated "accompaniments" to the live part (Dannenberg 1985). Barry Vercoe's original description of such systems as needing to listen, perform, learn (Vercoe 1985) still stands.

Even in recent developments, MIDI remains the most commonly used format for both the score and performance information (and the easiest to handle in the comparison). This presupposes a MIDI output from the performer, which limits the instrumentation or often requires a special interface or modification—and the speed of MIDI is also a severe limitation. But, relevant feature extraction from the performance *audio signals* is becoming faster and more accurate (Orio et al. 2003).

In such "compare-and-respond" systems based on fixed score traditions, the boundary between *error* and *interpretative freedom* is a fluid one, requiring a dimension of programming (and learning algorithms) that has been slow to evolve. The relationship of score to performance is, in the end, a cultural issue—Beethoven and Chopin would not recognize the modernist obsession with "accuracy" over interpretative feeling. A somewhat freer version of score following might have greater and more immediate application.

C. Fixed Sounds and Issues of Timing: Who Has Control?

In mixed music (for instruments, voices, and precomposed electroacoustic material), issues of control hit at the heart of what it is to make live music. In traditional acousmatic music, the sounds are fixed in time and performance limited to spatialization and projection. Digital systems allow and encourage a more flexible approach as I have suggested. In fact, any "fixed sound track" works especially poorly with the more strictly notated traditions of Western music.

The necessary synchronization between the two forces could only be enforced one way: the objective clock time of the prerecorded part was the inflexible conductor of the live part. There were different ways of doing this. Stockhausen's *Kontakte* has a continuous electroacoustic part to which the performers coordinate (and must synchronize frequently) through a score notated in time-space notation with "stopwatch time" marked along the top[16] (Stockhausen 1966, 1993). Javier Alvarez's *Papalotl* (piano and tape, 1987, on Alvarez 1992) has gained a reputation for perhaps the most demanding of live-to-tape synchronization, with both parts intricately and accurately notated, often demanding a hocketlike exchange between the two at shortest beat level.[17] The move of this approach to the digital domain has allowed more accurate clocks and better displays and communication, but the relationship has not fundamentally changed. Many performers hate this straightjacket on their time sense.

The options for getting around this one-way relationship are several. The first group involves "freeing up" the live performer's score. First, the composer may not intend a strict synchronization between the two streams of music. A strictly notated score can be performed against a fixed electroacoustic part without such a demand, restoring more flexible control over tempo to the performer—but this is only possible within limits. Further, the score itself can be made increasingly flexible or improvisatory. Score-following algorithms need to be adapted, and there are recent developments, for example, for open-form (but notated) works (Lawter and Moon 1998).

In a notated score, there may be events that are timed to appear "in response to" the electroacoustic part—a kind of *trompe l'oreille* for the audience. This function can clearly be delegated to the aural sense of the performer: "listen out for then respond" is a kind of instruction new to Western composition and notation but perfectly within the skills of the instrumentalist.

7. FOLLOWING THE PERFORMER: TOWARD THE INTERACTIVE

We might like to distinguish between perceptions of source and cause. A *source* would be heard as producing the sound we believe is being transformed, while a *cause* might be a trigger (an event of any kind) of a new sound element that has a separate perceptible identity. Both members of our duo, human and computer, may be both sources and causes of actions by the other—*interactivity*.

The fixed continuity of an electroacoustic part can progressively be freed up in the digital world. A performer can physically trigger sound files via a suitable switch controller (manual, pedal, breath, etc.) without the need of machine score following. This is in itself a useful and commonly used increase in flexibility. But, performers can still find this a distraction. We could, however, get the computer to do this for us by following the performance as discussed, with the score accompaniment of the earlier experiments replaced by prepared sound files; hence, the strict timekeeping of mixed music might be relaxed, placing the performer in greater control of the timeline. The degree this is literally the case is in the composer's hands; simply treating the live performer as a trigger of sounds is potentially limiting. A more flexible response may need to be enabled at the same time—to what extent the performer responds to the sound and has the space and time to do so. This also moves to more interactive modes of operation.

Score following and consequent decision mapping are underdeveloped at present. This may be due to the relative inflexibility of the MIDI specifications with respect to scoring programs and sequencers. Nontraditional ("avant-garde") notations can be both too simple (space-time, graphic, etc.) or too complex (e.g., "new complexity") for ease of MIDI translation. We require a new generation of score followers that may use visual input and an ability to read a range of symbolic notations rather than referring to a stored (probably MIDI) code.

Even this degree of freedom—multiple trigger points of relatively shorter prerecorded material—can be developed. The "grain" of the trigger tends at present to be relatively large and the sound files premixed in detail. Future systems might preserve the acousmatic intent of the electroacoustic material but *mix it live*, deriving time cues, amplitude, and spatial decisions from immediate live performance measures.[18]

This could result in anything from merely a "flexible time" version of an otherwise fixed piece to a freely mixed and mobile result. If an incoming acoustic signal is analyzed and its features extracted according to a set of criteria, then a much more open world may emerge. The computer extracts the elements of the performance and might, for example, follow "If criteria X is met, then do Y." In this case do Y is the command "play sound Y," but it could be any instruction. The criteria may be derived from a score (as discussed) and trigger a fixed sequence of sound files or might just as easily leave the order to be defined from performance data alone, freely controlled.[19] In fact, a new kind of score emerges here—one freed from the linearity of classical Western notation and based on a flexible set of "if . . . then . . . else" statements or other algorithmic "laws" (see discussion in section 11). The traditional score is dominated by pitch, whereas a flexible abstraction of features and properties from the performance sound flow might as easily be of the form "If gesture is of timbre quality A then perform sound X; if gesture is of timbre quality B then perform sound Y; else perform sound Z."[20] And (composers sometimes forget), this statement is clearly reversible—as true of the computer response to the human performer as vice versa (hence we used the term *sound* rather than *sound file*). Our performer can respond to the computer according to identical choice types.

These decisions are of first order (in Markov terms), and we may create more complex sequences of conditional and causal chains ("If A is followed by B then play X; if A is followed by D then play Y"; etc.). But here, the symmetry of human and machine breaks down in the heat of the performance: a computer can be programmed to remember perfectly such sequenced causal chains, matrices of transitions, and so on. But, while good at memorizing a fixed sequence of operations, the human performer finds it harder to memorize lists of alternative sequences and subsequent options, at least when defined *a priori* by someone else to be acted on in the flow of performance time, and a score created for the human by the computer *in real-time* from the sound flow might be an option.

8. Decisions and Choices in Real-Time

Iannis Xenakis once famously remarked that chance had to be calculated and could not be improvised (1971/1992, pp. 38–39). From a totally different viewpoint, Cage's avoidance of the term *improvisation* is related to a very similar distrust of *habit* and *memory*—important parts of an improvising musician's persona. But, others do not like the term *improvise* in any case; in the north Indian classical tradition, for example, long years of study generate a repertoire of tightly circumscribed possibilities within specific *raga* and *tala* definitions. Of course, much is then left to the ingenuity of the musician (influenced by audience participation), but the elaboration is far from totally free and open. This is true of many such traditions and cultures. For the digital musician, the term *interactive* has similar ambiguity and ambivalence.

We can appear to devalue the term by simply asserting that all the music we shall discuss is interactive. For straightforward instrument and fixed sound pieces, this interaction is very constrained, but the live musician always uniquely responds to circumstance. If the performer regains some control over timing and perhaps over other aspects of the electroacoustic sound world, this interaction—mutual influence over the unfolding of the performance—becomes greater and more meaningful. The history of this developing area suggests we are shifting away from considering interactive music as a special case in the larger sphere of live electronic music; rather, it has become the opposite: flexible and interactive systems are now the mainstream within which fixed material and unchanging relationships are the exception.[21]

What kinds of decisions may be made, and how do human and machine decisions differ?

Choice from a repertoire of recorded sound options stored in memory
Choice of sound-generative procedures (algorithms)
Choice of transformational (DSP) procedures (algorithms)
Local performance practice: temporal, dynamic, timbral, spatial choices

To describe these for the human performer is not trivial. Long years of practice in any tradition result in the sublimation of conscious choice into fast (near-autonomic) response. This may appear immediate and intuitive, but this is misleading. Larger chunk decisions may still be consciously made. Some performers prefer to try to "switch off" the conscious (self-) observer, but the trained unconscious one will remain active.

This results in two choice types—*external criteria*-based and *unmediated*. External criteria-based choices are defined clearly and explicitly stated and are then matched against the performance and a consequence is drawn; in its simplest form, "If X is the case, do Y." Unmediated choices (the word *unmediated* replaces the more common *intuitive*) are those for which the musician simply responds with the immediacy mentioned, avoiding any conscious reference to externally defined choice mechanisms.[22] This conceals, or at least brackets, the choice mechanisms, innate or learnt, behind that "rightness."[23] Chris Cutler's album *Solo* (percussion, live electronics, 2002) derives from improvised music recorded live, creating an immediacy that is palpable as a result.

Whether there is a machine equivalent for this is an interesting question. As there is no agreement on what might constitute machine consciousness, except a form of Turing test, there can be no clear notion of a corresponding unconscious. But against Turing, there is a danger of relying on procedures derived from empirical observation distilled into generative rules; these may bear no relationship to how a particular exchange was actually created in performance.[24] Learning theory might give us a better parallel. Just as many traditional musicians learn by "playing along" with mentors (real or recorded), with no explicit *a priori* rules, so we see the emergence of machine learning systems (via neural networks, for example) that do not begin from explicit rule rationalization. While the subject of a developing research culture, these are, as yet, only rarely reaching musical application.[25] Most interactive live performer plus computer music systems at present still rely on explicit rule and algorithmic definition.

9. Source/Receiver

In the human and computer duo, both are source and receiver of information. When information is acted on, it may be seen as in some sense controlling or determining a response. All such systems can be *interactive*, that is, there is a mutual and influential exchange of information.

The sense modes predominantly used in music-making by humans add to sound those of sight and touch (including breath). The human interface is highly adapted to the environment and to the information it needs and through which it affords action. There is no clear distinction of data gathering and interpretation; the two are in continuous flux.[26] Even human memory is not empty at birth. *Anticipation*—risking an estimate of a future state—is a key skill: memory is not simply a file of past acts but allows a repertoire of future-oriented options to evolve. What works is reinforced—this is one aspect of learning.

The computer may be addressed through exactly the same set of "senses," but the interface is currently crude, fragmented, and by comparison, slow and clumsy. Memory is unstructured and limited. In addition, we are only just beginning to understand and to model human processing (if that is indeed what we want—and some alternative views are emerging). A system that learns for itself has been a goal in many areas of computer science, and music applications have been a major focus of interest.

But currently, human and computer performers respond in very different ways to the mediums of sound and sight. For the human performer, the musician adapts, channels, and deepens basic skills that are inherent in the body system as it has evolved over many millions of years. The equivalent in computer terms must be taught its responses, bottom-up. It appears sometimes as if we are attempting to program the *behavioural* result of a million years of evolution without understanding the learning mechanisms from which this originates.

Touch is a special case and needs separate discussion. Musicians touch instruments that resist and respond (effectively touching back, although we do not sense a thinking being in our hands). But in ensembles, between musicians it is sight and sound that dominate. In dance, we may touch others, in music-making usually not at all. There are parallels and differences in our new relationship with technology.

Humans touch a qwerty keyboard, of course, as well as a slowly evolving set of screens, pens, and pads interfaced to the computer. Instrument controllers—whether adaptations of traditional instruments or specially constructed versions of them—respond to touch and have been joined, more recently, by controllers derived from game machines and other toys. Touch of the human by the computer is, however, a recent development. Mechanical resistance in many of the earlier interfaces is being supplemented by devices that can mimic the sensations of a range of physical substances and textures—the touch equivalent of acousmatic sound—the haptic technologies. The world of computer-controlled "feelies" is emerging and will no doubt be integrated into musical performance. Nonetheless, the situation is at present nonsymmetric: computers do not yet touch humans to any great extent. This suggests that if new two-way touch interfaces do evolve we may possibly develop relationships nearer to dance than to music as we have known it to date.

Basic MIDI data are an abstraction of touch, not of sound information.[27] MIDI originally derived from keyboard performance, that is, the opening and closing of a set of switches with the addition of velocity and (sometimes) pressure "aftertouch" (a misnomer) reinforcing the relationship.

10. FROM GESTURE TO THOUGHT: BEYOND THE MUSCLE

Just as electrical signals from the brain control muscle movements within the body, so the possibility of bypassing muscle control altogether was first suggested in the 1960s and is developing rapidly today. *Biophysical interfaces* allow us to access brain waves and other body control parameters hitherto hidden within the mechanism. The shift from relatively intrusive (contact electrode) to unintrusive (magnetic resonance scan) methods of observation may open this area up further to music in future decades, although at present these two example methods obtain very different information.

There are two ways this might be considered (corresponding to the two paradigms described at the beginning of this chapter). In a stream of thought we can trace to the earliest works of Alvin Lucier, David Rosenboom, and David Behrman (Rosenboom 1976, 1997), we can consider brain waves to be control parameters for sound creation or modification (we extend ourselves outward to become a synthesizer): the system integrates human and machine.

We can, however, conceive of future systems in which individual musicians (human or computer) might send each other signals or control data, generated or received in these internal body-signal forms.[28] While there has been no direct equivalent to this in acoustic music-making, we might see this as relating to the kind of multisensory "feel" well appreciated by improvisers who know one another well.[29] Then, there is the vaguer notion of "responding to atmosphere"—not vague, however, to DJs and improvisers, who claim it makes a critical contribution to their performance. Here, we cross the boundary to considering all those present at a performance as *participants:* from the still and silent concentration of the idealized Western concert hall to the exuberant expression at a village gamelan or rock concert, to the alternation of deep engagement and conviviality of a club environment. These in turn influence the relationships *possible* within the music (but that is outside the scope of this chapter).

11. Algorithms: Rules (Empirical and Logical), Models, and Analogies

The philosophy of science gives us two approaches to the nature of *law* or *rule.* On the one hand, we can have "empirical generalizations," derived from observation. For example, we may derive rules for improvisation within a certain tradition from observing many instances and deducing the strategies of response and gesture from which the performers typically draw. These empirical rules would need sensitive and nuanced application rather than literal interpretation, drawing on the subtleties of the immediate circumstance. The unexpected response is the source of much creativity in improvised performance.

On the other hand, we have from the hard core of physics and mathematics stricter and more "logical" rules and laws, equations and deductive systems that may with relative ease be encoded into algorithms. These include stochastics, fractals, chaos, and a host of mathematical abstractions.

An even broader picture emerges if we include the vast expanse of *models* and *analogies.* Here, the world itself becomes a source of possible generative procedures. Both aspects of law described may be at work here. Any phenomenon that is capable of abstraction into terms the computer can "understand" may be used as the source of a generative procedure for sound or sound processing. An analogy is drawn and mapped to control parameters for the performance.

The first generation of composers to use electronics drew on systems from such as language, architecture, astronomy, atomic physics, growth systems, cybernetics, and stochastics to furnish their models and analogies. Computers have allowed and encouraged a much wider range of possibilities. The Live Algorithms for Music network group describes finding *live algorithms* "in extra-musical systems that show musical characteristics or potential (e.g. that generate patterns which may be interpreted musically) [such as] evolutionary computation; artificial life; swarm intelligence; chaotic dynamics; cellular automata; neural networks; machine consciousness" (AISB Newsletter 2006). To this, we may add video and graphics as well as many different models of growth and noise. In fact, due to the increasingly integrated format and storage of all kinds of information, it becomes increasingly possible that almost *any* information can be used as a source model. Thus, showing musical characteristics or potential becomes a matter of interpretation—in computer terms mapping the variables of the model to the world of sound.[30] How relevant this might be for the poetics of the work becomes all the more important.[31]

12. CONCLUSION

Whether as extension to the human performer's mind and body or as an independent performer in its own right, the computer is helping develop new forms of music-making, but the future is never predictable: for every "hyperinstrument" (Machover and Chung 1989) there is an "infrainstrument" (Bowers and Archer 2005). Live coding (Collins et al. 2003), circuit bending, and dirty electronics (Collins 2006) have all challenged the prevailing orthodoxy of "steady improvement in technical performance." Human creativity works well with limits—a limit is not necessarily a limitation. What form self-imposed limits take will be the question.

NOTES

1. See Dean and Bailes (2007) for an interesting philosophical approach.

2. The term *adequate* is deliberately ambiguous, of course. It depends on the performance and interpretation practice of the work's genre and aesthetic approach.

3. From the earliest days of mixed music, Mario Davidovsky's *Synchronisms* series is traditionally notated and (to a degree) tries to free up the worst aspects of the relentless conductor by using multiple tape cues (Davidovsky n.d. [1965?]).

4. Possibly deriving from Arnold Schoenberg's idea of *perpetual variation*, for Stockhausen's generation repetition was anathema (although he eventually allowed "memories" and "anticipations"), and musical material was thus in a state of perpetual evolution.

5. Although unfortunately these were without the mobility or choice strategies that were one of moment form's most interesting possibilities—for example, in live works such as *Momente* (for solo soprano, four choir groups, and thirteen instrumentalists, both versions, 1965 and 1972, on Stockhausen 1992).

6. This discussion is not peculiar to mixed electroacoustic works but is true of acousmatic works in general.

7. These terms refer to the global use of the sound world; *within* each approach there can, of course, be the standard musical "arguments."

8. In other of his works, he uses political slogans, street demo recordings, references to war, and so on.

9. Timbre was always spatial from acoustic instruments—from direction-dependent changes in spectrum (Meyer 1978) to proximity sensitivity for noises, their capture, and amplification.

10. It is not chance that the hemispherical multiloudspeaker spatialization system of the Zentrum für Kunst und Medientechnologie (ZKM) in Karlsruhe is called the *Klangdom*—although it is translated officially as sound dome, in fact *Dom* also means cathedral.

11. This relates to the ideas of *local* and *field* transformations I discussed at length in Emmerson 1994b, 1998b, and 2007a. Local transformations maintain a clear link to the source instrument, while field transformations may be dislocated and distributed.

12. Ethnomusicologists know this as the "emic/etic" dilemma: we may miss significant detail listening to music from another culture just as we may also perceive differences that are not significant in that culture.

13. György Ligeti's *micropolyphony* (in some of his early instrumental works) is on the cusp of this transition between linear streams and singular blocks of sound.

14. See Roads (2001), Wishart (1994), and Truax (1994).

15. Winkler (1998) covered all these options, although inevitably from within a predominantly note-based paradigm.

16. In *Kontakte*, Stockhausen indicated the stopwatch time for significant events and section boundaries rather than a regular time grid as most other electroacoustic composers have done.

17. This requires—at least while learning—a click track.

18. In the United Kingdom, there are current developments by David Berezan (2007) and Adrian Moore (2008) that address this issue for acousmatic music composition and performance.

19. Or, it can be defined from a combination—there are many options.

20. A more detailed discussion on types and modes of control follows immediately below. See also Paine (2002) for an excellent summary and critique of the state of interactive music systems and the shift from "note"- to "sound"-based approaches.

21. That is not to imply criticism of fixed material within the work, which might be there for important poetic and aesthetic reasons.

22. This bears some relationship—not in terms of real-time performance but in terms of rule-based judgment—with the "method" of the true acousmatic composer: "It sounds right, that is all there is to it."

23. Psychologists, musicologists, and others often wish to investigate this.

24. We return to the difference between empirical rules and logical systems rules in section 11.

25. Two issues of *Computer Music Journal,* 13(3) and 13(4), were devoted to this topic as early as 1989, but this has been followed up only slowly. See Griffith and Todd (1999).

26. Following more recent writings in anthropology and evolution, this is a problem when we come to program computers as there remains a distinction of the two in almost all music systems.

27. This is also true of Western score notation that lies behind MIDI; the vast majority of the symbols describe an action of touch, not a quality of sound.

28. These forms are not only brain waves; the artist Stelarc has allowed audience members to control his limb movement through such an interface directly to muscle control points.

29. Or, this occurs when (for example) Japanese ensemble musicians synchronize perfectly after a relatively long pause without conductor or other visual cue. This is described as an example of the Japanese idea of *ma.*

30. Leigh Landy (2007) discussed the many relationships of music to its means of production, and between the composer's *intention* and the audience's *reception* in detail.

31. This chapter has not been concerned deeply with the poetics of live electronics. I discussed these at length in other works (Emmerson 1994a, 1994b, 1998a, 1998b, 2007a).

BIBLIOGRAPHY

AISB Newsletter. 2006. Live Algorithms for Music. http://www.livealgorithms.org/, accessed April 1, 2008.

Alvarez, J. 1992. *Papalotl*. CD. Saydisc: CD-SDL 390.

Berezan, D. 2007. Flux: Live-acousmatic performance and composition. In *Proceedings of the EMS-Network Conference, Leicester 2007*. EMS-Network. http://www.ems-network. org/, accessed April 1, 2008.

Bowers, J., and P. Archer. 2005. Not hyper, not meta, not cyber but infra-instruments. In *Proceedings of the 2005 International Conference on New Interfaces for Musical Expression (NIME05), Vancouver*. Singapore: National University of Singapore, pp. 5–10.

Cage, J. 1939. *Imaginary Landscape No.1*. New York: Peters Edition (EP6716).

Cage, J. 1961. *Aria* with *Fontana Mix*. LP. Time S/8003.

Casserley, L. 1998. A digital signal processing instrument for improvised music. *Journal of Electroacoustic Music* 11: 25–29. Lawrence Casserly. http://www.chiltern.demon.co.uk/ DSP_Inst.html, accessed April 1, 2008.

Collins, N. 2006. *Handmade Electronic Music: The Art of Hardware Hacking*. New York: Routledge.

Collins, N., A. McClean, J. Rohrhuber, and A. Ward. 2003. Live coding in laptop performance. *Organised Sound* 8(3): 321–330.

Cutler, C. 2002. *Solo*. CD. ReR: CC1.

Dannenberg, R. 1985. An on-line algorithm for real-time accompaniment. In *Proceedings of the International Computer Music Conference, Paris 1984*. San Francisco: Computer Music Association, pp. 193–198.

Davidovsky, M. n.d. *Three Synchronisms*. LP. CRI: SD204.

Dean, R. T., and F. Bailes. 2007. "Human understanding" in imagining and organising sound: Some implications of John Locke's Essay. *Organised Sound* 12(1): 89–95.

Emmerson, S. 1994a. "Live" versus "real-time." *Contemporary Music Review* 10(2): 95–101.

Emmerson, S. 1994b. "Local/field": Towards a typology of live electroacoustic music. In *Proceedings of the International Computer Music Conference, Aarhus 1994*. San Francisco: International Computer Music Association, pp. 31–34.

Emmerson, S. 1998a. Acoustic/electroacoustic: The relationship with instruments. *Journal of New Music Research* 27(1–2): 146–164.

Emmerson, S. 1998b. Aural landscape: Musical space. *Organised Sound* 3(2): 135–140.

Emmerson, S. 2007a. *Living Electronic Music*. Aldershot: Ashgate.

Emmerson, S. 2007b. *Sentences*. CD. Sargasso: SCD28055.

Gabor, D. (1947). Acoustical quanta and the theory of hearing. *Nature* 159: 591–594.

Griffith, N., and P. M. Todd. 1999. *Musical Networks: Parallel Distributed Perception and Performance*. Cambridge: MIT Press.

Landy, L. 2007. *Understanding the Art of Sound Organisation*. Cambridge: MIT Press.

Lawter, J., and B. Moon. 1998. Score following in open form works. In *Proceedings of the International Computer Music Conference, Ann Arbor 1998*. San Francisco: International Computer Music Association, pp. 21–24.

Machover, T., and J. Chung. 1989. Hyperinstruments: Musically intelligent and interactive performance and creativity systems. In *Proceedings of the International Computer Music Conference, Columbus 1989*. San Francisco: International Computer Music Association, pp. 186–187.

Meyer, J. 1978. *Acoustics and the Performance of Music*. Frankfurt am Main: Verlag Das Musikinstrument.

Moore, A. 2008. Fracturing the acousmatic: Merging improvisation with disassembled acousmatic music. In *Proceedings of the International Computer Music Conference, Belfast 2008*. San Francisco: International Computer Music Association. Unpaginated.

Nono, L. 1992. *La fabbrica illuminata*. CD. Wergo: WER 6038-2.

Norman, K. 1991. *Trying to Translate* [score]. London: British Music Information Centre. http://www.bmic.co.uk/collection/default.asp, accessed April 1, 2008.

Norman, K. 2000. *Trying to Translate*. CD. Metier: MSV CD92054.

Orio, N., S. Lemouton, and D. Schwartz. 2003. Score following: State of the art and new developments. In *Proceedings of the 2003 International Conference on New Interfaces for Musical Expression (NIME03), Montreal*. Singapore: National University of Singapore, pp. 36–41.

Paine, G. 2002. Interactivity, where to from here? *Organised Sound* 7(3): 295–304.

Parker, E., et al. (Evan Parker Electro-Acoustic Ensemble). 1999. *Drawn Inward*. CD. ECM Records: ECM 1693 547 209-2.

Reich, S. 1989. *Different Trains*. CD. Elektra/Nonesuch: 979 176-2.

Respighi, O. 1925. *Pines of Rome*. Milan: Ricordi.

Roads, C. 2001. *Microsound*. Cambridge: MIT Press.

Rosenboom, D., ed. 1976. *Biofeedback and the Arts: Results of early experiments*. Vancouver: ARC.

Rosenboom, D. 1997. Extended musical interface with the human nervous system. *Leonardo Monograph 1*. San Francisco: ISAST.

Smalley, D. 1986. Spectro-morphology and structuring processes. In: *The Language of Electroacoustic Music*, ed. S. Emmerson. Basingstoke, UK: Macmillan, pp. 61–93.

Smalley, D. 1992. *Clarinet Threads*. CD. Empreintes Digitales: IMED-9209-CD.

Stockhausen, K. 1962. The concept of unity in electronic music. *Perspectives of New Music* 1 (1): 39–48.

Stockhausen, K. 1966. *Kontakte*. Performance score. Vienna: Universal Edition UE14246.

Stockhausen, K. 1992. *Momente*. CD. Stockhausen Verlag: CD 7 A-B.

Stockhausen, K. 1993. *Kontakte*. CD. Stockhausen Verlag: CD 6.

Subotnick, M. 1986. *The Key to Songs*. CD. New Albion Records: NAO12 CD.

Truax, B. 1994. Discovering inner complexity: Time shifting and transposition with a real-time granulation technique. *Computer Music Journal* 18(2): 38–48.

Tutschku, H. 2007. *Zellen-Linien*. Score and recording. Hans Tutschku. http://www.tutschku.com/, accessed April 1, 2008.

Vaggione, H. 1988. *Tar*. CD. *Cultures Electroniques 3*. Le Chant du Monde: LDC 278046-47.

Vercoe, B. 1985. The synthetic performer in the context of live performance. In *Proceedings of the International Computer Music Conference, Paris 1984*. San Francisco: Computer Music Association, pp. 199–202.

Winkler, T. 1998. *Composing Interactive Music—Techniques and Ideas Using Max*. Cambridge: MIT Press.

Wishart, T. 1992. *Anticredos*. CD. October Music: Oct 001.

Wishart, T. 1994. *Audible Design*. York, UK: Orpheus the Pantomime (Trevor Wishart).

Xenakis, I. 1971/1992. *Formalized Music—Thought and Mathematics in Composition*. Bloomington: Indiana University Press (1971); Stuyvesant, NY: Pendragon Press (expanded edition 1992).

PART III

CREATIVE AND PERFORMANCE MODES

CHAPTER 10

DANCING THE MUSIC: INTERACTIVE DANCE AND MUSIC

WAYNE SIEGEL

DANCE and music are commonly considered independent art forms. Yet, the relationship between them is as intimate as it is intricate. In many cultures, the two are so intertwined that they are inseparable. The origins of this relationship go back beyond recorded human history to the dawn of humanity itself. In Western music, dance forms such as the minuet and the waltz have developed into abstract musical forms. In jazz and popular music, terms such as *salza, samba, jive,* and *tango* refer to dance forms as well as musical forms. On the experimental pop music scene, musical genre terms such as *breakbeat* and *electronic dance music* reveal an intimate relationship to dance. In many such cases, dance steps imply a well-defined framework for musical parameters such as tempo, meter, rhythm, melody, harmony, and musical form.

In contemporary Western culture, the most common dance performance situation involves dancers performing live to music played back from a fixed medium such as a CD or hard disk. Dancers follow the music, taking their cues from a predetermined, fixed sound world. What if the dancers could influence control or even "play" the music while dancing? What if the dancers could "dance the music" rather than "dance to the music"?

Dancing and playing music as a single integrated process is not new; it is something human beings have done since time immemorial. Today, technology offers new forms of interaction between dance and other art forms. Motion-tracking technology can endow dancers with the ability to control sound, lighting, graphics, robotics, and other aspects of a live performance. This chapter focuses on the use of motion-tracking technology to allow dancers to interact with music, a topic I call *interactive dance.*

1. DEFINITION

Interaction can be defined as "the combined or reciprocal action of two or more things that have an effect on each other and work together" (*Encarta World English Dictionary* 2007). In interactive dance, the physical movement of a dancer has an effect on the music, and the music has an effect on the dancer. In a given artistic situation, the nature of this relationship may range from banal simplicity to unfathomable complexity. Although it may be useful to distinguish between various categories of interaction, it should be kept in mind that the gamut from the simplest to the most complex form of interaction is actually an unbroken continuum.

It may be safely said that dance is primarily a visual medium, whereas music is primarily an auditory medium. Nevertheless, the term *primarily* bears a considerable burden in this statement. If I attend a concert performance of Tchaikovsky's *Swan Lake,* there is, of course, a visual component to the performance. I see the string players drawing their bows, the timpanist swinging the mallets, the clarinetist rocking to and fro, the conductor waving the baton. If I am culturally attuned to this situation, I will know that the primary function of all these physical gestures is to make the music sound exactly the way it should. The purpose of the gestures is to create music. The visual experience may add to or detract from the musical experience; it is in any case secondary. If I attend a performance of the ballet *Swan Lake,* the situation is quite different. The orchestra is hidden away in an orchestral pit. The dancers are in focus. Every step, every gesture made by the dancers is made in the service of visual expression. The music is an important component of the whole experience, but the dance performance unfolding on the stage is unmistakably a visual art form.

I make this distinction to stress the difference between interactive dance and gestural control of musical instruments. Whether new or old, electronic or acoustic, nearly all musical instruments translate human movement into sound. If an instrumentalist, whether a violinist, a rock guitarist, or a theremin player, makes a strange or awkward gesture during a performance, the audience will accept this as a necessary means to a noble end: producing the proper sound. Interactive dance places quite different demands on the dancers than the demands placed on the instrumentalist simply because dance is a primarily visual medium. If a dancer performing a work for interactive dance is forced to make an awkward gesture foreign to the performance, it will detract from the visual focus and disturb the visual expression. Nevertheless, the relationship between visual and musical performance is far from simple. Anyone attending a live rock concert may wonder which of the many gestures made by the musicians are made to create sounds and which are made for their purely visual content. Is the musical performance primary and the visual performance secondary? Or, is it the other way around?

Michel Chion (1990) argued that audio content and visual content in multimedia cannot be broken down into two independent elements. He stated that an immediate and necessary relationship arises between what one sees and what one hears. Chion termed this phenomenon *synchresis*. In its extreme case, we sometimes think we have seen what we have actually only heard or vice versa. In dance, this perceptual entanglement is important because what we hear in the music will influence what we see in the dance performance, and what we see in the dance performance will influence what we hear in the music. This cross influence will occur even if there is no intentional relationship between music and dance. Again, this is nothing new. What is new in the case of interactive dance is that the dancers are able to have a direct effect on the music during a performance.

2. WHY INTERACTIVE DANCE?

This brings us to the provocative question, Why? Why would one want a dancer to influence the music during a performance? The most obvious reason would be to allow synchronization between dance and music. But, synchronization between dance and music is commonplace. A well-rehearsed dance performance may be perfectly synchronized with music played back from a fixed medium. Synchronization does not require sophisticated technology—not as long as it takes place within the constraints of linear time.

Linear time is a major feature of our Western cultural worldview, made manifest by Newton in the late 17th century. It portrays time as an absolute physical reality and says that the passage of time is independent of consciousness. Linear time flows like a conveyor belt that moves horizontally from past to present to future at the same unchangeable speed for all of us (Hall 1983). Many other conceptions about time have been suggested before and after Newton. For Aristotle time *was* motion. His studies of the motion of bodies led him to appreciate the fundamental importance of time. At the onset of the 20th century, Einstein introduced the theory that time is relative to position and speed. According to Einstein's theory, which is now widely accepted among scientists, time is no longer universally fixed but flexible and variable depending on where and at what speed it is measured (Davies 1995).

Having influence on or being in control of our immediate surroundings is, for most of us, highly attractive. It gives us a sense of (although not necessarily proof of) having a free will. In the linear view, time seems out of our control. Freedom from linear time in a performance situation can be exhilarating not only for the performer but also for the audience. It is an essential part of what makes live performance exciting. Interactive dance allows for precise synchronization between dance and music in combination with temporal freedom. The relationship between physical gesture and music in a dance performance may be direct and highly synchronized or indirect, asynchronous, random, or even nonexistent. However, I would argue that pursuing interactive dance will probably not be very fruitful if one's interests lie in the last of these. Giving the dancer a feeling of being free in time or even free from time is in my view the single most important motivation for working with interactive dance.

3. Motion-Tracking Technologies

To work with interactive dance, some sort of interface is needed to detect the dancer's movements. Many different technologies have been used for tracking human movement. For convenience, we can adopt Alex Mulder's taxonomy (1994) and divide human movement-tracking technologies into three primary groups: "inside-in" systems, "inside-out" systems, and "outside-in" systems.

A. Inside-in Systems

Inside-in systems utilize sensors placed on the body to track body movement. They are especially suitable for tracking fine motor movement. They do not require that the performer move in reference to a fixed point on the stage, but they do not necessarily provide information about position on the stage. They can also restrict movement and are sometimes aesthetically obtrusive since they have to be worn by the performer.

Inside-in systems developed for dance in the 1980s and 1990s include Mark Coniglio's MidiDancer (n.d.), the Yamaha Miburi, and the DIEM (Danish Institute of Electronic Music) Digital Dance System (Siegel 1998). These systems use flex sensors to measure angles of body joints. A wireless transmitter and receiver are used to transfer motion-tracking data to a computer. Several general-purpose wireless sensor systems not specifically designed for dance have been used for interactive dance. The advantage of these systems is that they can be configured with various types of sensors. The user usually needs to make some modifications to the system, however, if it is to stand up to the wear and tear of a dance performance. Sensors useful for motion tracking include flex sensors; accelerometers, which measure acceleration and tilt; and piezoelectric sensors and contact pressure sensors, which can, for example, be attached to a dancer's shoe to register steps. General-purpose systems include the Kroonde manufactured by La Kitchen (no longer in production), the I-Cube developed by Mulder (n.d.), and the MidiTron developed by Eric Singer (n.d.).

B. Inside-out Systems

Inside-out systems employ sensors, such as a compass or camera, on the body to sense external sources. These systems generally provide information about the performer's position in the room in reference to a fixed point. A common example of an inside-out system is the Nintendo Wii Remote. With over 20 million units sold within the first year of its release in September 2006 (Wikipedia 2008), the Wii Remote illustrates the increasing availability of motion-tracking technology. The Wii Remote uses infrared detection to sense its position in three-dimensional (3-D) space when pointed at the light-emitting diodes (LEDs) within the stationary sensor bar (usually placed above the video monitor). The Wii Remote also contains an accelerometer and is designed to allow users to control a computer game using physical gestures as well as traditional button presses. The controller connects wirelessly to the console using Bluetooth and features rumble as well as an internal speaker for user feedback.

C. Outside-in Systems

Outside-in systems use external sensors that sense sources or markers on the body. These include cameras and infrared sensors used to monitor a dancer on a stage. Outside-in systems generally suffer from occlusion, making them less suitable for tracking small body parts or multiple dancers in a dance performance. They do not have to be worn by the performer (unless markers are used) and are generally good at determining the position of a single performer on a stage, but they demand that the performer move in reference to a fixed point (e.g., a camera).

Numerous outside-in systems utilizing ultrasonic or infrared sensors have also been used for motion tracking. Touch-sensitive dance floors also fall into this category, such as the MIDI Dance Floor (Pinkston et al. 1995) and the Magic Carpet (Paradiso et al. 1997).

D. Hybrid Systems

Not all motion-tracking systems can be clearly categorized. For example, accelerometers, which have in fact been used for dance performance, might be considered a hybrid. They measure rotation in reference to gravitational pull, placing them in the inside-out category; they also measure relative acceleration, placing them in the inside-in category as well. Combining more than one system to improve motion-tracking precision is of course also possible.

E. Mocap

The use of *motion capture* or *mocap* is widespread in the production of animated films. This technique involves using sensors to acquire data representing the position of an actor's body or face, data that are fed into a computer and used to animate a digital character model in 3-D animation. Three basic types of motion-tracking systems are used to transfer human or animal movement to animated characters: optical, magnetic, and electromechanical.

Optical (outside-in) systems typically use six to twenty-four video cameras arranged in a circle around the performer. The performer wears reflective markers, allowing the cameras to precisely track these points on the body in three dimensions. Magnetic (inside-out) systems calculate position and orientation by the relative magnetic flux of three magnetic coils on both the transmitter and each receiver. The relative intensity of the voltage or current of the three coils allows these systems to calculate both range and orientation by meticulously mapping the tracking volume. Fewer markers are required than with optical systems. The markers are not occluded by nonmetallic objects but are susceptible to magnetic and electrical interference from metal objects in the environment. Mechanical (inside-in) systems directly track body joint angles. A performer attaches a skeletal-like structure to his or her body, and as the performer moves so do the articulated mechanical parts, measuring the performer's relative motion.

Motion capture systems used in the film and entertainment industry are generally very expensive and not well suited to interaction since they are often cumbersome and rarely wireless. Many of them are designed to capture motion data for off-line rendering.

The actual visual appearance of an actor or dancer during a motion capture session is of no importance when the purpose of the performance is to transfer natural motion to an animated figure in a film. As the technology develops, these systems are becoming faster, less cumbersome, less expensive, and more common.

F. Computer Vision

Camera-based motion-tracking systems are becoming increasingly widespread and affordable as research progresses in the field of *computer vision*, the science of machines that see. Many of the methods employed are computationally demanding and still in the state of basic research, but the field has developed greatly since the 1980s in parallel with increasing computational power and speed of computers. Methods of computer vision have found their way into a wide range of commercial products, ranging from medical scanning to control of industrial processes (Wikipedia 2008). The development of programming tools for computer vision in combination with the rapid growth of code-sharing communities has generated extensive artistic experimentation with computer vision.

Camera-based video-tracking systems have been used for interactive dance performance since the 1980s. These include the Very Nervous System developed by

David Rokeby (2007); Big Eye, developed at STEIM (Studio for Electro-instrumental Music, Amsterdam); EyesWeb, developed at the University of Genoa (Camurri et al. 2000); and Eyecon, developed for Palindrome Dance Company by Frieder Weiss (n.d.).

Several software tool kits for computer vision have been developed for Max/MSP (Max Signal Processing)/Jitter, a programming environment used extensively by electronic musicians and video jockeys (VJs). Max/MSP/Jitter offers powerful control of and connectivity between MIDI (musical instrument digital interface), audio signal processing, synthesis and analysis, OpenGL-based 3-D graphics, video filtering, network communications, and serial control of hardware devices (Cycling74). Computer vision object libraries for Max/MSP/Jitter include Rokeby's SoftVNS, Singer's Cyclops, and Jean-Marc Pelletier's cv.jit. The last is the most sophisticated of the three and also the only one that is freeware (for Max/MSP/Jitter owners). The cv.jit object library includes tools to assist users in tasks such as image segmentation, shape and gesture recognition, and motion tracking and educational tools that outline the basics of computer vision techniques (Pelletier n.d.).

4. CHOICE OF INTERFACE

The choice of interface will depend on artistic needs as well as more mundane factors such as availability, cost, and dependability. If a dance interface in itself requires highly specific movements on the part of the performer, it will greatly restrict the dancer's freedom of movement within the context of a performance. An artist may accept such restrictions as a freely chosen artistic framework, but the technical and aesthetic advantages and limitations of an interface should be considered before making such choices. A highly specialized musical interface often requires months or years of training for sophisticated use. Dancers are often skilled performers who have meticulously mastered countless performance techniques. A motion-tracking interface for dance should allow the dancer to use these previously acquired performance skills. An interface that demands new and specialized skills will also demand extensive training time and, when it comes down to it, devotion to such an endeavor.

The interactive environments discussed here are not limited to use by dancers. Two closely related areas that employ this technology are musical interface design and adaptive music. In the case of musical interface design, motion-tracking technology can allow a musician to control all or part of a musical performance through physical motion. Having a trained musician control musical parameters has its obvious advantages. It also opens quite a different realm of design problems, the most challenging being the absence of a physical musical instrument to provide tactile feedback. *Adaptive music* is computer-generated music that can be controlled, advertently or inadvertently, by an individual listener or audience, for example, within the context of a public sound installation. Presenting nonexpert and perhaps even unsuspecting "users" with interactive musical systems based on motion tracking has been employed in various contexts. The real challenge in adaptive music is making the interaction natural and intuitive enough for participants both to understand what is going on and to feel that they are somehow in control of the resulting sound. Although related, these topics are both beyond the scope of this chapter.

In any case, it would be an oversimplification to categorize a motion-tracking system used for interactive dance as a musical instrument. As mentioned in the beginning of the chapter, dance is a visual medium, placing different demands on the dancers than those placed on the instrumentalist. A dancer performing a completely fixed choreographic sequence may not necessarily pass through exactly the same physical space from performance to performance. A dance interface should be able to deal with relative movement gestures.

Tactile feedback, or the lack thereof, is an important consideration in designing electronic musical instrument interfaces based on motion tracking. A lack of physical contact with an actual object can present substantial problems in terms of control and expression. Without physical resistance, the instrument can be difficult to learn to play.

The problem is quite different in the case of a dance interface. Many of the movements employed in dance require in themselves enormous strength and energy. Dancers are trained to control their movements in an empty space as well as in relation to other dancers or objects on the stage. Gravity and inertia provide the resistance that necessitates effort on the part of the dancer.

Response time and transmission bandwidth are also important factors. If a dance interface is sluggish in tracking movement, there will be an inherent and perhaps unpredictable delay between action and reaction. The amount of lag that can be tolerated will depend on the type of gesture and the type of correspondence between gesture and sound used. For example, if a slow, sweeping movement is used to evoke a crescendo, a lag time of over 1 s might be imperceptible. However, if a sudden and precise gesture like the striking of a fist on a table is to evoke a sound with a sharp attack, a delay of 50 ms will be much too long.

The interface chosen will inevitably influence the interaction and artistic content of a work. In some cases, the interface literally defines the work. *Very Nervous System*, besides being the name of video tracking system, is also the title of an interactive installation by Rokeby that was premiered at the Venice Biennale in 1986. The work uses video cameras, computers, and synthesizers to create an interactive space in which body movements are translated into music. The technology developed for this work was eventually developed and marketed as a combined hardware and software system (VNS). Later, as computers became faster and more powerful, VNS developed into a software application that could be used with a standard video camera. About the work entitled *Very Nervous System*, Rokeby stated: "The installation could be described as a sort of instrument that you play with your body but that implies a level of control which I am not particularly interested in. I am interested in creating a complex and resonant relationship between the interactor and the system" (2007). The performer (in this case, an individual audience participant) waves his or her arms and hands to control the musical performance. The visual content of the performance is clearly secondary in relation to the music being controlled. In this sense, the system resembles a musical instrument, but for Rokeby the focus is more on social interaction rather than instrumental performance or dance.

5. MAPPING MOTION TO MUSIC

Another important point to be considered is that of mapping. How are a dancer's physical movements to be translated into sound? The relationship between input (the dancer's movement) and output (the resulting sound) might be very simple or direct. A simple mapping implies a one-to-one correspondence between motion and sound. Mappings might also be very complex, involving complicated schemes or complex algorithms for translating movement into sound. Generally, extremely simple mappings tend to be immediately understood by the observer but trivial, whereas the apparent relationship between movement and sound is lost when complex mappings are used. Yet, simple mappings do not necessarily induce perceptible links between motion and sound. For example, the fast and high kick of a leg might result in (1) the triggering of loud percussive sound or (2) the sudden reduction of volume of an ongoing audio sequence. The former would probably be more perceptible than the latter since the gesture "implies" something being kicked, yet both cases are examples of simple mappings. It is important to consider whether a mapping is natural or unnatural, that is, whether it complies with our common experience of the real world. An artistically viable balance must be found if interactive dance is to be employed in a meaningful way (Winkler 1995).

The Nürnberg-based Palindrome Dance Company has worked extensively with interactive dance. Choreographer and dancer Robert Wechsler has collaborated with composers Butch Rovan and Dan Hosken and technical designer Frieder Weiss in creating a series of groundbreaking interactive works involving various types of technology (Wechsler n.d.). Wechsler's observations about mapping position on stage to musical parameters are of interest here:

> Position tracking appears to be weak for a variety of reasons: It lacks immediacy, it is not palpable or tactile and finally, location, as a parameter of movement, is simply of little interest to us compared to, say, body height, shape or movement dynamic. Let us look at these points separately. A human body cannot immediately change its position on stage. It takes time, and this time frame defeats a convincing interactive effect. During the time it takes to change position, a musician or theatre technician might easily have simply moved a slider. Or, easier still, the performer could be following a cue in the music, what is utterly normal and expected on a stage. Thus, since the experience might have been created

another way, the observer simply has no sense that anything special has taken place. (Wechsler 2006, pp. 70–71)

Wechsler's comments tie in with another point to be considered: audience expectations. In a conventional concert performance, mapping between motion and music is taken for granted. We believe that the pianist is playing all the notes we hear during a performance, even if we cannot actually see the performer's fingers. One might call this a "pact" between performer and audience. This pact may be disrupted if the listener begins to suspect that a singer on stage is not really singing. But, even in such cases the listener might accept this behavior within a particular cultural context as "part of the show."

A pact between performer and audience cannot be taken for granted when working with technology and techniques that are new or not widely in use. There is no standard solution to this problem. Some artists take great pains to explain the relationship to the audience. Others simply do not believe that the audience need be aware of such mappings to appreciate the performance. Both positions can have artistic worth. In extreme (worst) cases, a performance might, on the one hand, be reduced to a demonstration of a certain technology with no artistic weight. Or, on the other hand, a performance might reveal a totally inappropriate use of technological tools within a worthy artistic context. A certain amount of artistry can be observed in most musical performances. The border between virtuosity and gimmickry is a matter of convention and taste. In the best cases, artistry and art fuse into an inseparable whole.

6. Gesture Recognition

Human movement can be interpreted on different levels. Movements of the hands, face, and body as a whole can be interpreted as gestures and as such constitute sophisticated forms of communication. High-level interpretation of human movement requires specialized tools for gesture recognition and analysis. Researchers at the University of Genoa described the expressive content of human movement as follows:

> Expressive content concerns aspects related to feeling, mood, affect, intensity of emotional experience. For example, the same action can be performed in several ways, by stressing different qualities of movement: it is possible to recognize a person from the way he/she walks, but it is also possible to get information about the emotional state of a person by looking at his/her gait, e.g., if he/she is angry, sad, happy. In the case of gait analysis, we can therefore distinguish among several objectives and layers of analysis: a first one aiming at describing the physical features of movement, for example in order to classify it, a second one aiming at extracting the expressive content gait coveys, e.g., in terms of information about the emotional state the walker communicates through his/her way of walking.

> From this point of view, walking can be considered as an expressive gesture: even if no denotative meaning is associated with it, it still communicates information about the emotional state of the walker, i.e., it conveys a specific expressive content. (Camurri et al. 2004, p. 16)

Antonio Camurri and his colleagues (2004) described four levels of motion tracking: (1) sensor data; (2) low-level interpretation of sensor data, such as speed, acceleration of body parts, or amount of body contraction/expansion; (3) segmentation of the input stream into expressive features associated with gestures, such as trajectories; and (4) analysis and extraction of high-level expressive information, such as gestures or groups of gestures implying emotions such as fear, anger, and joy or more structural descriptions such as "pushing" or "gliding."

The prospect of translating expressive content of human movement into musical expression is indeed fascinating. Yet, there are certain hurdles to be overcome. Interpreting gestures or gesture groups as described takes time since the gesture must be completed before it is possible to determine what the expressive content might be. A similar problem arises in creating interaction based on analysis of musical phrases. The system must wait until the gesture or phrase is completed before reacting: it will always be "one step" behind. This presents a problem if gestures are used to directly control musical parameters. Yet, gesture analysis can be used effectively to influence parameters that are less time critical. The use of sophisticated gesture analysis might even allow a system to anticipate the next gesture.

7. Case Study: The DIEM Digital Dance Project

The Digital Dance project (Siegel 1998) was a research project conducted at DIEM, Denmark's national center of electronic music, between 1995 and 1999. The project involved hardware and software development as well as the creation and performance of works for interactive dance. The goal of the project was to create a computer music composition that allowed a dancer to directly influence musical processes in a meaningful way. Our work included (1) developing an interface for detecting a dancer's movements, (2) mapping these movements to musical parameters, (3) defining the roles of the artists involved, and (4) creating a software composition for interactive dance.

A. DIEM Digital Dance Interface

Our motivation for developing a new hardware interface was quite simply that no wireless inside-in hardware system was commercially available when we began working with interactive dance. We chose an inside-in system based on flex sensors, concentrating our efforts on minimizing the obvious drawbacks of this type of system. We formulated the following list of requirements: (1) the interface must directly measure angles of body limb joints; (2) response must be fast and accurate (repeatable); (3) the interface must be durable and reliable for stage use; (4) the interface must be easily mountable on any dancer; (5) the interface must be unobtrusive; (6) the interface must not restrict the dancer's movement; (7) data transmission between the interface and the computer must be wireless; (8) simultaneous use of multiple systems must be possible; (9) use with any computer or software environment must be possible; and (10) the system must be based on inexpensive technology. Several types of sensors were considered, including potentiometers, strain gauges, silicone-carbon resistors, conductive foam, conductive coating, piezoelectric elements, magnetic induction, hydraulic pressure, and optical fiber. We decided to develop our own flex sensor based on strain gauge technology. Later, the system was adapted to use standard, inexpensive, commercially available flex sensors based on conductive coating. These were less stable but more durable than the sensors we constructed (fig. 10.1).

The original prototype was conceived as a bodysuit. This idea was eventually abandoned for two reasons: (1) the sensors tended to shift slightly in relation to the dancer's limbs, making measurements inaccurate; and (2) a custom-fitted suit could only be used by one dancer. Our next solution was to tape the sensors to the dancer's body. This worked fairly well but was a bit awkward and time consuming. In the finished version, the sensors are mounted on individual elastic sleeves for the elbows and knees. Small pockets for the sensors are sewn onto elastic supports used for sports injuries and such. A similar ankle support with an open heel is used for the ankles. These remain in place quite well and are a fairly comfortable solution for the dancers, who need only wear the number of sensors necessary for a particular performance. These sensor-sleeves can be easily hidden by tricot or a costume during performance. A number of design problems remain unsolved. Simple flex sensors are not well suited for measuring complex joints such as the neck, hips, or shoulders. The knees also present a challenge. The kneecap creates a flat area when fully bent, causing the flex sensors placed on the knee to

Figure 10.1 The DIEM Digital Dance interface.

straighten out slightly in this position, thus causing the sensors to register a decrease in bend rather than an increase.

Up to fourteen flex sensors are connected to a self-contained, wireless transmitter unit. A stationary receiver unit converts sensor data to MIDI. Controller values between 0 and 127 for all fourteen sensors are sent out the MIDI port of the receiver unit about thirty-two times per second.

B. Two Compositions

Two of my compositions for interactive dance are discussed: *Movement Study* for one dancer and computer music system and *Sisters* for two dancers and computer music system. I present these descriptions in hope that my personal experience might benefit others working with interactive dance. In both works, I constructed the musical form and structure that was the basis for a composition. The choreographer established the form and structure of movement. The dancer was responsible for realizing the choreographer's visual ideas as well as the composer's musical ideas.

These two works have certain aspects in common. Both works utilize the same technology: the DIEM Digital Dance System based on bending sensors worn by the dancer to measure angles of the dancer's limbs as described in the preceding section. Software for both works was created using the Max/MSP programming environment. In both cases, the software interprets the incoming data to allow the dancer's movements to control and influence the music. Both works have developed and changed over the years in working with many different choreographers and dancers. Here, the similarity ends.

The musical ideas and working processes used in the two works are quite different. The first piece, *Movement Study*, was created as a rule-based composition first. This software composition was then interpreted by various choreographers in different ways in compliance with a few very general ideas about how the music should sound in various sections. These ground rules provided a framework for the choreographic interpretation without limiting the choreographer to specific choreographic ideas. In fact, the various choreographic interpretations were all quite different. The music varies with respect to specific choreographic interpretations and to specific performances of the same choreographic interpretation. In all cases, compositional structure and musical identity are easily recognizable from performance to performance (fig. 10.2).

In the case of *Sisters*, the situation was reversed. Here, the choreographer was asked to create a work without taking the music composition or dance interface into consideration. An initial choreographic sketch was created and rehearsed by the dancers before they began working with the Digital Dance interfaces. A software composition was created to accompany the choreography.

In both works, the choreography as well as the music were altered and adapted during the rehearsal process in an effort to create an integrated work. It was

Figure 10.2 Pernille Fynne performing with the DIEM Digital Dance interface.

apparent in this process that the dancer takes on a unique role in performing a work for interactive dance since the realization of both the composition and choreography depend on the same performer.

Movement Study

The first sketch of *Movement Study* was composed in collaboration with the choreographer Warren Spears (1955–2005) and presented at a workshop organized by DIEM and the Danish Dance Theatre in Copenhagen in 1996. A new version was developed with dancer/choreographer Helen Saunders. This work was further developed by dancer Pernille Fynne and performed in Thessaloniki with subsequent performances by Mata Sakka at the Cunningham Dance Studio in New York; by Saunders in Denmark, Finland, and Iceland; and by Ma Bo of the Beijing Modern Dance Company. The composition software uses the sensor data to generate MIDI notes, patch changes, and controller values to control two outboard synthesizers: Proteus and Morpheus (both manufactured by E-MU systems).

The work falls into four sections that are performed without break. In the first section, changes in angles of the ankles, knees, elbows, and index fingers are mapped directly to amplitude and spectrum of eight independent long-drone notes, one for each of the eight limbs. When an elbow, for example, is bent to its minimum angle or "closed," no tone is heard. As it is opened (angle increased), the tone becomes louder and brighter and then softer and darker as it is closed again. If a limb is closed completely, a new note event is triggered, and a new pitch and timbre are chosen by the computer program the next time the limb is opened.

The harmonic structure is determined by a set of compositional rules. There are seven subsections consisting of seven different harmonic structures or chords. In any one subsection, each voice has a limited number of possible pitches that might be chosen in that subsection according to a set of predefined probabilities for each of these pitches occurring. The choices made by the composition software are tightly controlled random choices. On the one hand, no one can predict exactly which pitches will be played at any given moment within a particular subsection; on the other hand, it is certain that the pitches chosen will lie within the harmonic structure for that subsection.

These seven harmonic structures cannot be influenced by the dancer. The dancer, however, can influence the speed at which the piece progresses through the seven subsections before finally reaching the second section. Movement from one subsection to the next is based on the number of new note events triggered by the dancer. The more often the dancer's limbs are placed in the closed position, the faster the program moves to the next subsection. If limbs are never completely closed, the program will remain within the current subsection, allowing the dancer to manipulate volume and brightness only of pitches contained in this subsection. It is, for example, possible for the voice associated with the right index finger to remain in subsection 1 while the left knee is in subsection 2 and the right ankle is in subsection 5. This would mean that the pitches chosen by these various voices would not lie within a single harmonic structure. This "incongruity" might be corrected by software in the course of the performance. If the limb of a voice that has fallen behind is finally closed, the software will skip to the highest section currently used by any other voice. Or, in the example, the next time the right index finger is closed, it will skip ahead to section 5, the section that the right ankle has already reached.

The first section of *Movement Study* gives the dancer direct control of two very perceptible parameters: amplitude (volume) and spectrum (brightness). But, the dancer does not make choices related to melody, harmony, or rhythm. This allows for a certain degree of expressive control of the music without restricting the performer's freedom of movement or demanding excessive concentration on instrumental performance.

In the second section, the angular velocity of knees, elbows, and index fingers is mapped to activity of eight voices in a contrapuntal texture of plucklike sounds. Limb position is sampled every 80 ms. The greater the difference between the present angle and the previous angle, the greater the activity. The computer generates random rhythms in which the number of notes played by each of the eight voices is directly related to the activity of the associated limb. The choice of harmonic material is related to the technique used in the first section. This section serves as a transition between the first and third sections.

In the third section, activity of knees, elbows, and index fingers is mapped to activity in a pulse-based six-voice contrapuntal texture. Six polyphonic percussive voices are controlled by the knees, elbows, and index fingers (angles of ankles are not used for this section). A fixed, regular pulse is set by the computer, and the six voices are always rhythmically synchronized. A 10/8 meter is implied in the software, with pitch probabilities for all voices defined for each of the 10 beats as well as pitch probabilities for sixteenth notes that can occur between the 8 note beats. Pitch choices are made on the fly by the computer program according to the composition algorithm.

The dancer controls only the activity of each of the six voices, not the musical material to be played. The more the dancer moves, the more notes will be filled into the implied sixteenth-note matrix. If the dancer stops moving, probabilities drop to zero, and no notes are played: the music stops immediately. The tempo is fixed but can be influenced slightly by the dancer: increased overall activity (average activity of all six limbs) increases the tempo slightly.

The fourth section is similar in construction to the first section, although the tonal material used in the two sections is different. The other main difference is that in some of the subsections of this section the angles of each joint controls pitch bend as well as volume and brightness for the associated drone. This allows the intonation to change for each voice separately (plus or minus a quarter tone).

The transition between the first slow section and the second random rhythmic section consists of an overlap. The eight separate voices change sections independently so that the left elbow might start section 2 while the right elbow is still in section 1. A fade function is built into the software so that all of the drone voices of section 1 finally fade out slowly once section 2 is under way. The transition from section 2 to section 3 is similarly an overlap, while the transition from section 3 to section 4 is abrupt. When the dancer moves into a certain position on the stage, section 3 stops with a loud gonglike sound, and section 4 fades in. This is the only event triggered by a computer operator in the work. All other processes are initiated by the software as a result of the dancer's movement.

An essential idea in *Movement Study* is that the dancer is able to influence musical processes and not simply trigger sequences and events. Since the compositional program and Digital Dance System were developed first, the task of the choreographer was to experiment with the hardware and software to get acquainted with the system and then begin to develop a choreographic idea that could integrate an artistically viable choreography with the movements necessary to control the music. The dancer must also be given a certain amount of freedom to be able to react to the music and directly influence it. Although the system has been used by choreographer/dancer teams, it seems that the best results can be achieved when the dancer and choreographer are the same person. This allows the choreographer to try out the system in a "hands on" situation to gain a better understanding of how various movements influence the music. Through the process of direct experimentation, either a fixed choreographic structure or an improvisational strategy could be developed. The choreographer created a choreographic study within the framework of movement dictated by the hardware and software. The dancer is placed in an entirely new situation, with the responsibility of interpreting both musical and choreographic ideas and integrating them into a single work.

Sisters

The choreography for *Sisters* was created first by Marie Brolin-Tani. I then created the music to fit the choreography. The work was premiered at an open house presented by the Marie Brolin-Tani Dance Theatre in November 1998. The dancers were Pernille Fynne and Sophie Konning (fig. 10.3). Various versions have since been performed by several different dancers in Denmark; Bourges, France; and Miami, Florida. Brolin-Tani's idea for the choreography was a work based on the life of the Mexican artist Frida Kahlo. The two dancers represent two aspects of the artist, which might be described as the contrast between the masculine and the feminine or between physical beauty and a sick and fragile body dependent on "machines" to keep it alive. One of the costumes is inspired by the corset worn by Kahlo, and the wires of the interface are exaggerated and made visible to the audience. The other costume is more feminine, and the interface is hidden. The composer's task was to create software that would produce sounds to accompany the choreography. When rehearsals began, both the music and the choreography were gradually developed and changed.

The music composition was created for two dancers and an interactive computer music system. Both dancers wear a DIEM Digital Dance interface with bending sensors on their elbows and knees. The technical setup consists of a Macintosh computer with an audio interface. Software was designed by the composer using the Max/MSP programming environment. About fifty sound files are loaded into in the computer's random-access memory (RAM), and these sound files are played back in various ways and altered in real time using comb filter and resonance filter algorithms. The dancers control playback and filter parameters in various ways during the course of the piece, but there are no prerecorded sequences or tracks. All of the sounds heard in the piece are produced as a direct reaction to the dancer's movements.

Each dancer controls four different sounds with her elbows and knees at any given time. In some cases, the samples are looped, and the angular velocity (activity levels) of the elbows and knees is mapped to the volumes of the sounds: the more the dancer moves, the more sound is heard. In other cases, the elbows and knees are

Figure 10.3 Pernille Fynne and Sophie Konning performing *Sisters.*

used to control "scrub" functions in much the same way that a tape can be slowly scrubbed forward and backward over a tape head to create fast and slow playback both forward and backward. For example, when a dancer moves her arm from straight to bent, a short sample will be played. When the dancer moves the same elbow from the bent position to straight, the same sound will be played backward.

Since the music for *Sisters* had to be adapted to the dancers' movements, it was important that the composition software could be easily changed. Which sounds will be controlled by the dancers' elbows and knees and how they are controlled change during the course of the piece. In addition, the sounds are processed in real time by the computer to create tonal material out of recorded noiselike sounds such as those of water, fire, and wind; breaking stones and wood; scraping gravel; and so on. The work consists of twenty-eight sections that are changed manually by a computer operator. Automation of section changes was not used because the specific breakup into sections was not decided until after rehearsals had begun. Each section contains information regarding which sound is to be controlled by each of the eight sensors as well as information regarding the cutoff frequency and Q of the comb filters and resonant filters for each voice. These parameters can be easily changed for the various sections in a kind of score, which includes information about all these parameters for all of the sections. In this way, a new version of the work using different combinations of sounds and filter parameters can be easily created, and various versions of the composition can be tested quickly and easily.

The Pandora Project

The Pandora Project was started in 2008 as a continuation of previous work we have done with interactive dance. The project involves experimenting with current motion-tracking technology for interactive dance. Several software composition environments were created, and experiments were made in collaboration with choreographer Brolin-Tani and several dancers using two different hardware systems: (1) an I-Cube Wi-micro System with four accelerometers attached to a dancer's arms and feet and (2) the cv.jit (Pelletier n.d.) software library to extract motion data from the input from a digital camera connected to a computer. We have focused on using the same software composition environments with these two very different types of hardware interfaces to reveal their inherent differences, advantages, and drawbacks.

The goal of the Pandora Project was to examine and develop technologies for working with interactive sound in contemporary dance and to test these technologies in an artistic collaboration between composer, choreographer, and dancers. Two intensive workshops were held in Aarhus, Denmark, during the summer of 2008, where the composer, the choreographer, and three dancers experimented with interactive dance.

The first workshop was held June 16–20, 2008. Three preliminary experiments were conducted. Each experiment consisted of two parts, one using computer vision (CV) and the other using accelerometers (AC). The two parts of each experiment were otherwise identical. For each experiment a solo dancer was asked to improvise in dialogue with the choreographer and the composer.

Both systems were configured to detect motion. For the CV system, a camera was placed in the center of the room facing the stage. The camera image received by the computer was divided into six image zones. The object *cv.jit.framesub* (Pelletier n.d.) was used to report changes between consecutive frames in each image zone. Data from this object was used as a simple motion detector: the greater the change between consecutive frames, the greater the activity level of the dancer in that particular image zone.

For the AC system, hardware accelerometers worn by a dancer were connected to an I-Cube system configured to transmit values representing the average difference in acceleration values over a period of 2 ms. This data was similarly used for simple motion detection: the greater the difference between acceleration values, the greater the activity level of the dancer in relation to that particular sensor or limb.

The first experiment involved dynamic control of sounds similar to the techniques employed in "Sisters." The dancer controlled the amplitude and timbre of six sounds. Mapping was simple: increased movement produced greater volume and brighter timbre dynamically.

The second experiment involved control of a composition algorithm designed to generate rhythm and contrapuntal melodies similar to the techniques employed in the third section of "Movement Study." Increased movement produced increased rhythmic activity and melodic activity as well as increased tempo.

In the third experiment a motion threshold was defined to trigger drum-like sounds. In the CV controlled experiment, any motion in an image zone that exceeded the threshold would trigger a sound. In the AC controlled experiment, sensor data from any of the accelerometers that exceeded the threshold would trigger a sound. In both cases these triggered events were performed with a computer-generated rhythmic accompaniment.

The latency of the two systems was similar. The AC system appeared to respond slightly faster than the CV system, but no precise benchmarking was carried out. It was apparent that adjusting and fine-tuning hardware and software is extremely important regardless of which type of technology is being employed: the similarity of the audio results for the same mapping using these two very different hardware systems was striking when the hardware and software was properly adjusted. Problems with occlusion generally found in camera-based systems were not immediately apparent because image processing was used for simple motion detection. Only the first two of Camurri's four levels of motion tracking were employed: (1) sensor data, and (2) low-level interpretation of sensor data (Camurri et al. 2004). The drawback of having to wear a sensor system was minimal with the AC system because of the small size of the system.

An informal discussion between the dancer, the choreographer, the composer, and other workshop participants was held following the three experiments, focusing on how the dancer and observers experienced each experiment. In general, both dancer and observers found the first experiment to be the most successful. The relation between movement and sound was intuitive and expressive. The dancer had more precise control over the sounds when using the AC system, but the CV system provided a more obvious relationship between visual and audio elements. Despite these differences, both parts of the experiment were found to be technically and artistically viable.

It was generally agreed that the second experiment was less successful, mainly because mapping between motion and compositional parameters was less obvious. The third experiment was more problematic. With the AC system the triggering of drum-like sounds quickly became tedious, especially for the dancer. The mapping tended to inhibit the dancer's freedom of movement, since movement always triggered a sound. With the CV system the interaction was less sensitive, allowing for greater freedom of movement but less direct control.

After the discussion some new experiments were conducted, including the use of both systems simultaneously with one dancer and with two dancers. Subsequently, the composer and the choreographer discussed the three experiments and worked out a set of four choreographic sketches with interactive sound using some of the techniques that had been explored. A new workshop was held July 30–31, during which the choreographer and composer worked with three dancers on four choreographic sketches with interactive sound (inspired by the myth of Pandora). These four sketches were finally performed for video documentation in a theater with a lighting rig. Focus was on interaction between movement and sound, but interactive computer graphics projected on the dancers were also incorporated with the assistance of Tobias Ebsen.

In the first sketch, *Water*, CV was used with a single camera front stage and the image divided into twelve zones, each associated with a particular (water-related) sound and tonality. The dancers controlled the amplitude and timbre of these sounds, and the composer changed the sounds and tonalities during performance. In the second section, *Who*, the audio composition was closely related to that of the first sketch. The AC system was active. The choreography was fixed. Only one dancer was wearing the system controlling the sound and computer graphics; however, all three dancers moved in synchronization so that they all appeared to be controlling the sound, as in the first sketch, until the solo dancer began moving independently of the others and the "secret" was revealed.

The third sketch, *The Box*, used the CV system with a single camera mounted above the stage and the image divided into twelve zones. A specially focused red light illuminated one of the twelve image zones near center stage so that it stood out clearly as a bright red square representing Pandora's box. The mapping between movement and sound was similar to the first sketch. However, the mapping was much more sensitive for the illuminated zone than for other zones. A loud, violent reaction occurred when a dancer moved into Pandora's box. Three dancers improvised with the basic rule that they all start in the same image zone stage left and gradually begin to move toward and explore Pandora's box. The final section, *Fire*, used the same techniques as the first section but with the camera mounted above the stage, and with sounds evoking images of fire. The fixed choreography depicted a wild dance of fire.

At writing, the Pandora Project is still under way. The composer, choreographer, and dancers have all found the results encouraging. A full-length dance performance is being developed using both types of technology mentioned.

8. CONCLUSION

Let us examine the artistic roles of the choreographer, dancer, and composer in creating a work for interactive dance. The choreographer establishes the form and structure of movement. If a motion detection system is to be used to control musical processes, the number of movements that can control these processes will be further limited to the number of body movements detectable by hardware and software. The composer's ideas also limit the number of possibilities, as do the choreographer's aesthetic choices regarding which types of body movements are to be used for a particular work. Within this framework, the dancer must be given a certain amount of freedom of movement to control and interact with the music.

The composer constructs the musical form and structure that is to be the basis for a composition. The musical processes that are to be controlled by the dancer during performance must be defined, as must the rules for which body movements will affect the music and how these movements will affect the music. Compositional processes and interpretation of the dancer's movements can change within the course of a single work.

The dancer takes responsibility for realizing the choreographer's ideas. This is a traditional artistic division of labor. But, the dancer must also take responsibility for realizing the composer's musical ideas and must train with the system to become proficient in its use. This is a new and uncharted area for most dancers; it will require an understanding of the hardware system used as well as the musical ideas, explicit and implied, represented in the composition software. The compositional and choreographic ideas must obviously not conflict, but in any case uniting these two elements into a series of effortless and natural dance movements presents a great challenge for the dancer.

The reactions of the dancers I have worked with have been overwhelmingly positive. In discussions with the dancers, the words *freedom* and *control* seem to reoccur. They felt a great amount of freedom in the direct relationship between movement and music and were very enthusiastic about working with the interface and performance software. In addition to being given control of the musical performance, some of the dancers found that working with the system heightened their own consciousness of how they move when they dance. In a television interview prior to the first performance of *Movement Study*, Saunders stated: "What I really like about it is that you can use the computer as an instrument and for the first time the dancer is in charge. As a choreographer this is really interesting because you no longer have to scream at your dancers 'two steps to the right!' You can just be there and do it yourself as you feel it at that time. It gives you a new kind of freedom" (quoted in Siegel 1998, p. 41).

Giving a dancer control of various aspects of musical performance opens new possibilities for precise synchronization between dance and music outside the framework of linear time. Interactive dance can also increase the potential for performer interpretation or improvisation and serve as a source of inspiration for the dancer during performance. Transferring the paradigm of the musical instrument to a dance interface is problematic. The dancer's role in a performance situation differs greatly from the traditional role of the instrumental performer. Dancers are usually not musicians with specialized training in performing or interpreting a musical work. Also, the visual appearance of the dancer's movements on stage is of primary importance, whereas the visual appearance of an instrumentalist's movements is generally of secondary concern. If a dancer is asked to perform as an instrumentalist in the context of a dance performance, then the effort required to control the music might make it difficult or impossible for the dancer to concentrate on dancing.

Clearly, certain types of dance interfaces cater to certain types of choreographic and compositional ideas. But, if a dance interface is to be used by more than a handful of performers, then it must be capable of interpreting dance gestures without severely limiting the types of gestures that can be employed by the dancer or demanding that the dancer master difficult instrumental techniques.

Specialized programming environments such as Max/MSP have shifted attention from hardware-mapping or rigid software-mapping solutions to more flexible forms of mapping allowing very different structural models from composer to composer, from composition to composition, and within the context of a single composition since any control data can be easily mapped to any synthesis parameter or algorithmic function. The artistic success of a composition for interactive dance will to a large degree depend on the ability of the artists involved to find suitable models of mapping gesture to sound and on their ability to integrate music and choreography into a single coherent work.

Interactive dance is no longer restricted to use by a technological elite. The widespread use of sensing devices, wireless personal communication, and computer vision is quickly making interactive dance an accessible medium for composers, choreographers, and dancers. However, a standardized interface device or system has yet to be adopted, indicating that the field is still in an experimental phase. This is perhaps related less to a lack of suitable technology than to a lack of artistic experience in the field. Clearly, there is still much room for experimentation. I believe that the artistic benefits are well worth exploring.

BIBLIOGRAPHY

A few short passages in the chapter are direct quotations from my earlier publication, *The Challenges of Interactive Dance* (Siegel and Jacobsen 1998).

Camurri, A., S. Hashimoto, M. Ricchetti, R. Trocca, K. Suzuki, and G. Volpe. 2000. EyesWeb—Toward gesture and affect recognition in interactive dance and music systems. *Computer Music Journal* 24(1): 57–69.

Camurri, A., G. Volpe, S. Menocci, E. Rocca, and I. Vallone. 2004. Expressive gesture and multimodal interactive systems. In *Proceedings of AISB 2004 Convention: Motion, Emotion and Cognition*. Leeds: AISB, pp. 15–21.

Chion, M. 1990. *Audio-Vision*. New York: Columbia University Press.

Computer vision. 2008. Wikipedia article. http://en.wikipedia.org/wiki/Computer_vision, accessed March 15, 2008.

Coniglio, M. n.d. MIDI-Dancer. Troika Ranch. http://www.troikaranch.org/mididancer.html.

Cycling74. n.d. http://www.cycling74.com/.

Davies, P. 1995. *About Time*. New York: Simon and Schuster

Encarta World English Dictionary. 2007. Microsoft Corporation. http://encarta.msn.com/dictionary_/interaction.html.

Hall, E. T. 1983. *The Dance of Life*. New York: Doubleday.

Mulder, A. 1994. Human movement tracking technology. In *Hand Centered Studies of Human Movement*. Vancouver: Simon Fraser University. http://www.xspasm.com/x/sfu/vmi/HMTT.pub.html, accessed March 1, 2008.

Mulder, A. n.d. I-Cube X. Infusion Systems. http://infusionsystems.com.

Paradiso, J., C. Abler, K. Hsiao, and M. Reynolds. 1997. The magic carpet: Physical sensing for immersive environments. In *CHI '97 Extended Abstracts on Human Factors in Computing Systems: Looking to the Future*. Atlanta: ACM. http://www.sigchi.org/chi97/proceedings/, pp. 277–278.

Pelletier, M. J. n.d. International Academy of Media Arts and Sciences. http://www.iamas.ac.jp/~jovano2/cv/.

Pinkston, R., J. Kerkhoff, and M. McQuilken. 1995. A touch sensitive dance floor/MIDI controller. In *Proceedings of the 1995 International Computer Music Conference*. San Francisco: International Computer Music Association, pp. 224–225.

Rokeby, D. 2007. http://homepage.mac.com/davidrokeby/home.html.

Siegel, W., and J. Jacobsen. 1998. The challenges of interactive dance, Cambridge MA. *Computer Music Journal* 22(4): 29–43.

Singer, E. n.d. http://www.ericsinger.com.

Wechsler, R. 2006. Artistic considerations in the use of motion tracking with live performers: A practical guide. In *Performance and Technology: Practices of Virtual Embodiment and Interactivity*. Houndmills, UK: Palgrave Macmillan, pp. 60–77.

Wechsler, R. n.d. Palindrome. http://www.palindrome.de/.

Weiss, F. n.d. Palindrome. http://eyecon.palindrome.de.

Wikipedia. 2008. http://en.wikipedia.org/wiki/Wii#Name.

Winkler, T. Making motion musical: Gesture mapping strategies for interactive computer music. In *Proceedings of the 1995 International Computer Music Conference*. San Francisco: International Computer Music Association, pp. 261–264.

CHAPTER 11

GESTURE AND MORPHOLOGY IN LAPTOP MUSIC PERFORMANCE

GARTH PAINE

1. INSTRUMENT OR INTERFACE

This chapter discusses the design and development of new interfaces for electronic music performance for which the affordances inherent in the acoustic instrument move into the virtual. It gives particular attention to the way in which performative gestures are linked to principal control components used to shape the resultant sound properties in musical performance and outlines issues to do with authenticity and a perception of counterfeit musical performances using laptop computers. It seeks to draw the research into approaches to mapping together with a consideration of phenomenology to better understand the conscious and unconscious nature of the engagement between a musician and the musician's instrument.

A. Gesture

Relationships to sound are in part physical: musical instruments generally require us to blow, pluck, strum, squeeze, stroke, hit, and bow. The acoustic instrument vibrates in a manner determined by the energy transmitted into it. The physical gesture determines the amplitude, pitch, and timbre of each event.

Within this context, a proprioceptive relationship is established, that is, a largely unconscious perception of movement and stimuli arising within the body from the relationship between the human body and the instrument during performance; a direct relationship is established between the physical gesture, the nature of the stimuli, and the perceived outcome. The resulting awareness is multifaceted and has been at the core of musical performance for centuries. I would argue that these levels of engagement extend to distributed cognition, a product of the whole body and not simply the brain, and as such allow musicians to enjoy an embodied relationship (by which the instrument and performer may appear to dissolve into one entity) with their instrument, a relationship that is often communicated to the audience through their performance gestures. Computer-based music, however, heralded the dislocation of the excitation, sonification mechanism, dissolving the embodied relationship the musician previously enjoyed with the instrument while simultaneously introducing a broad range of possibilities that defy the limits of the human body, raising questions about the role of gesture in musical performance and the value of haptics in successful musical instruments.

B. Interface

Playing a musical instrument causes the transfer of spatial (pitch) and temporal (duration/rhythm) information from the conscious and subconscious systems of the body to the apparatus that physically produces the sound. Any such information transfer operates from within complex traditions of culture, musical design, and performance technique and is shaped by human cognitive and motor capacities (e.g., the event speed and complex polyrhythms in the compositions of Colon Nancarrow;[1] Carlsen 1988, Gann 1995, Duckworth 1999) as well as personal experiences (Pressing 1990).

The mechanization of musical instruments has a long history. Mechanical automation has surfaced in the music boxes of Europe, hand-cranked street organs, through to the theatrical extravagance of the Wurlitzer organ and the player piano. A brief overview of mechanized musical instruments would include Salomon de Caus's pegged organ (1644), Johann Maelzel's (inventor of the metronome) forty-two robot musicians for which Beethoven composed the *Wellington Victory March,* music boxes, and musical clocks.

Electrical automation also has a long history, dating to the late 18th century with Cahill's telharmonium,[2] a vast electromechanical synthesizer that occupied five train carriages when touring. Developments proceeded through various machinations to purely electronic instrument such as Friedrich Adolf Trautwein's trautonium, on which Oskar Sala was a virtuoso, and the Ondes Martenot to the theremin, made famous by the virtuosic performances of Clara Rockmore (Chadabe 1997) and perhaps the most famous electronic instrument for which gesture is critical in its performance. Each of these instruments retains a limited and clearly defined timbral range, a fixed morphology (Wishart 1996) for which even for the theremin a clear relationship between gesture and musical outcomes was evident. The performance of the theremin traditionally allocates the left hand to the control of amplitude and the right to the control of pitch. Some timbral variation can be associated with changes in pitch through modifying the shape of the right hand, but the synthesis engine remains unchanged, so while pitch is characteristically fluid on the instrument, the timbre, or in Wishart's sense, the morphology (the relationship among pitch, timbre, and time) remains fixed.

C. The Computer as Instrument

By contrast, the computer is a utilitarian child of science and commerce, a chameleon with no inherent property other than acting as an interface to desired functionality. Kittler's notion of *construction by process* (Kittler and Johnston 1997) neatly summarizes the computer as having a context generated by its momentary context. Elsewhere (Kittler 1999), he referenced the typewriter, pointing out that the letters of the typewriter are dissociated from the communicative act with which it is commonly associated. When we examine the computer, this dissociation is magnified many times. Each key on a typewriter has a single associated function, whereas a computer keyboard is amorphous, adapted to the programmer's desire as an interface to a communication framework, a controller for a game, or a function key changing the sound volume or display brightness.

When the computer is used as a musical instrument, this disjunction between interface and function is a dramatic diversion from the fixed morphology of traditional instruments for which each element of the interface (the keys on a wind instrument for instance) has affordances for a limited set of clearly understood/defined functions, and the gestures evoked through engaging with the interface have a functional musical association that may also be communicated to and understood by an audience (for instance, the quality of finger movement, bow movement, or the force of a percussive attack).

The computer as musical instrument offers the possibility for interactive music systems (Paine 2002), which, if they utilize real-time synthesis, are one of the few possible dynamic authoring systems available for which the nuance, temporal form, and micro- or macrostructures can be produced, selected, and developed in real time. In that sense, it is the iconic instrument of our time, eschewing the traditional composer/performer model for a real-time authoring environment. Such a claim cannot be supported when addressing the DJ/VJ (video jockey) model as performative outcomes are sculpted from prerecorded material (which through the process of recording is archived with a fixed morphology) and collaged into new soundscapes (in which the potentials are fundamentally preestablished by the material). By contrast, real-time synthesis on a laptop computer offers an almost-infinite aesthetic scope, posing the challenge of how to constrain the system in such a way it provides a virtuosic performance of a recognizable musical work— in other words, all possibilities are not contained in all works—a situation that in theory would produce a superwork that contained all possible works, clearly an untenable and undesirable effect.

Perhaps the notion of control is passé? Perhaps the laptop musician is not so much "in control" as he or she is navigating the potentials inherent in the work? If this is so, then performance gestures take on a very different function; their designation moves from an event-based classification to encompass the notion of gesture as form and timbre as interrelationships, influencing orchestration, focus, or structural evolution as the performance/musical work evolves. Many approaches have been taken to this problem (Mulder 1994, Mulder and Fels 1998, Bongers 2000, Hunt and Kirk 2000, Cook 2001, Wanderley 2001, Wessel and Wright 2002), which commands an annual international conference, the International Conference on New Interfaces for Musical Expression.[3]

2. WHY ARE GESTURE AND MORPHOLOGY IMPORTANT?

The conception of computer-based instruments is still often established on precepts of acoustic instruments. They often exhibit the following, among other features:

a. Limited and fixed timbral characteristics, which operate on
b. Excitation-sonification models (attack, sustain, decay envelopes, as well as timbral structure, i.e., noise in the attack stage, etc.) derived from existing acoustic instruments

In other words, they are derived from prior experience, from history and tradition. Ought these precepts remain true in all cases for computer-based performance instruments? It is in fact meaningless to argue so, for as Kittler (1999) pointed out, the computer does not act as a signifier for any one approach to communication, let alone musical performance. Its amorphous nature lends itself to a remarkably wide range of real-time music-making possibilities, from interactive installation works utilizing video tracking or biological or environmental sensing to a synthesis engine addressed from an interface of knobs and sliders to an entity in a collaborative networked ensemble such as The Hub.[4] Indeed, the software tools artists exploit in these varying applications are just as diverse in their approach to control. Ableton Live[5] focuses on the triggering of sample files or the sequencing of effects, with the gestural input addressing events (start/stop) and variation of defined variables (volume, pan, effect mix, effect parameters, etc). On the other hand, tools such as Max/MSP [Max Signaling Processing]/Jitter[6] from Cycling74 strive to be a blank canvas to avoid imposing a musical ideology. A more extreme case is the live coding, or real-time scripting movement, using open source software languages such as SuperCollider,[7] Impromptu,[8] and ChucK,[9] to create performances consisting of musicians writing and executing the software to generate the sounds in front of the audience. Such an approach forces reflection on the fact that if the instrument has changed so fundamentally, then so can the performance practice (Borgo 2005).

Kim Cascone, a recognized exponent of laptop music performance, commented that "if computers are simply the repositories of intellectual property, then musical composition and its performance are now also located in this virtual space. The composer transfers his or her mental work into the computer, and it is brought to life by interacting with it through the interface of a software application" (2000, p. 95). For Cascone and others, a laptop music performance presents a dichotomy by which the virtualization of the sonification-excitation mechanism and the subsequent dissolution of the embodied relationship acoustic musicians enjoy with their instruments deprives the audience of a conduit to engagement because if the audience is unable to identify the role the performer is playing in the production of the music they hear, the authenticity of the action is questioned:

> Spectacle is the guarantor of presence and authenticity, whereas laptop
> performance represents artifice and absence, the alienation and deferment of
> presence. . . . Laptop music adopts the quality of having been broadcast from an
> absent space-time rather than a displaced one.
>   The laptop musician broadcasts sounds from a virtual non-place; the
> performance feigns the effect of presence and authenticity where none really exists.
> The cultural artifact produced by the laptop musician is then misread as
> "counterfeit," leaving the audience unable to attach value to the experience.
> The laptop performer, perhaps unknowingly, has appropriated the practice of
> acousmatic music and transplanted its issues. (Cascone 2000, p. 95)

This alienation has attracted a wide variety of solutions; some performers destroy or hack objects during their performances, an action that may or may not have anything to do with sound production, while others project imagery, seeking to avoid a sense of "artifice and absence, the alienation and deferment of presence" (Cascone 2000, p. 95).

Some argue that the focus has moved from the visual, the excitement of watching the flamboyant performer (Nigel Kennedy, for instance), to the audible, a deep listening experience in which the intricacy of the sonic event is primary. "Digital performance is totally referential as a performative process. Therefore, when considering its cultural implications, it is perhaps more productive to consider it as a form of aesthetic regurgitation rather than altering old notions of performativity. The upside to this is that it means we have over a century and a half of critical materials developed in critical response to such approaches. The downside is that most of those critical materials ultimately secretly reaffirm the object they wish to critique" (Cascone 2000). Many laptop music performers, however, do see the need to inject a sense of the now, an engagement with audience, in an effort to reclaim the authenticity associated with "live" performance. Music performances on acoustic instruments illustrate relationships common to all acoustic phenomena by which the source of the sound is readily identifiable. The acoustic model established our precepts of "liveness." The performance gesture on an acoustic instrument is inherently associated with musical sonification. When this is not the case, a gestural paradigm needs to be invented, composed, and rationalized; it could be anything, a point illustrated by the fact that real-time music systems are used in sound installations (Paine 2001, 2006, 2007), with dancers, acrobats, to sonify data associated with factory operations, pilot systems in aircraft, and weather states (Paine 2003), to mention but a few.

Cascone essentially suggested that we need to rethink the paradigm of musical performance, which he would argue has been largely in the domain of entertainment, a spectacle of virtuosity, of expression, of passion and angst, expressed through a music using instruments that encourage theatricalized gesturing. Stanley Godlovitch discusses the act of musical performance in detail in his book *Musical Performance: A Philosophical Study* (1998) and points out that it is far more than purely entertainment; it is a ritualized form of collective conscience, a rare opportunity within modern Western society for communal catharsis. Music plays an important role in the emotional state of the society from which it emerges, and the performance practice of the time is in part a critique of the fashion (manners, customs, and clothing) of the time.

I posit therefore that the physicality of musical performance remains a critical and inherently valuable characteristic of live music. The laptop computer may circumvent the need for gestural input in and of itself; however, a number of interfaces for musical performance encourage gesturing, be it moving sliders, turning knobs, shaking, rotating, or the like, and here lies the real problem: what characteristics of human movement are meaningful when controlling or creating live electronic music on a laptop computer?

Inventing a gestural language without inherent intent leaves the computer musician open again to charges of counterfeit. The question of designing interfaces that address authenticity, that illustrate a link between action and result is therefore of paramount importance.

The flaw in this argument may be that musicians continually adapted existing technologies for music-making (the turntable, the mixing desk, etc.), seeking instruments that express the evolving cultural climate even though they were never designed for that purpose. Genres evolve in accordance with these creative redeployments of technology and the resulting remediation of the concept of musical performance. Until recently, DJs far outnumbered laptop musicians. Nevertheless, they are never understood to be making the musical material in the moment, but to be navigating a pathway through current musical artifacts, drawing links, and opening communication channels and new perspectives on music composed by others. The DJ is to some extent the live exponent of the remix, and the DJ's act is often highly gestural, ranging from accentuated swaying to the beats of the music to spinning on the turntable itself, horizontally suspended from one hand on the platter. What I believe this tells us is that the need for showmanship, for performance (Godlovitch 1998), is far from obsolete, that communal catharsis is just as current and critical to today's society as it has always been.

It is critical that new instruments be developed that facilitate and nurture this expression, musical instruments that facilitate subtlety and nuanced expressivity of the same granularity as traditional acoustic musical instruments.

As outlined, unlike acoustic instruments, the performer's physical gestures are decoupled from the sound-generating mechanism in electronic musical instruments. A crucial step in the development of new musical interfaces, therefore, is the design of the relationship between the performer's physical gestures and the parameters that control the generation of the instrument's sound (Cook 2001, Wessel and Wright 2002). This process is known in the computer science and engineering worlds as *control mapping* (Wessel 1991, Rowe 1993, Mulder 1994, Winkler 1995, Roads 1996, Mulder et al. 1997, Rovan et al. 1997, Chadabe 2002); however, the musician perceives it as a more homogeneous engagement in which agency is decisive.

The issue of embodied knowledge is vital in both the learning and the teaching of musical performance skills and the relationship the musician has to his or her instrument. Don Ihde's phenomenological explorations of music and sound (1990) refer to "embodiment relations," a relationship with an instrument by which the instrument "disappears" in use to become a conduit for expression rather than an object in its own right.

In their article "Corporeal Virtuality: The Impossibility of a Fleshless Ontology," Ingrid Richardson and Carly Harper (2001) extended Ihde's approach (itself drawn from Merleau-Ponty 1962), interlinking epistemology, phenomenology, and notions of experience in a framework for the consideration of experiential engagement:

> Phenomenology, via both Merleau-Ponty and Heidegger, not only prioritises the body as . . . [a] condition of knowledge, but can also situate technics or equipmentality in primary relation with that body, as mutually imbricated in the processes of knowing and perception. Both Heidegger and Merleau-Ponty develop a latent "phenomenology of instrumentation" ((Ihde 1990): 40) and thus lay the potential groundwork for a promising reconfiguration of agency in relation to high technology.
>
> Merleau-Ponty, in particular, challenges dominant neo-Cartesian models of subjectivity, by highlighting the a priori coincidence of consciousness and the body i.e. abandoning the mind/body dualism in favour of the notion of a "body-subject."

Richardson and Harper were seeking to address interaction in virtual environments through a materialist, somatic approach to existence and the production of knowledge. I believe this approach is equally valid in electronic musical instruments. Phenomenology (after Idhe and Merleau-Ponty) provides a framework for the consideration of experiential engagement, or "embodiment relations," which as Ihde commented, is the state of interaction a highly trained musician develops with the dynamical system that is his or her instrument. The musician does not consciously consider every action he or she executes in performance; it is a trained, subliminal process that utilizes principal components to shape the sound properties. Ihde referred to this as Lifeword perception, citing Merleau-Ponty as follows: "What counts for the orientation of the spectacle is not my body as it in fact is, as a thing of object space, but as a system of possible actions, a virtual body with its phenomenal 'place' defined by its task and situation. My body is wherever there is something to be done" (Merleau-Ponty 1962, from Ihde 1990, p. 39).

To summarize, I propose that one of the reasons for the perseverance of acoustic musical instruments is that their design and construction provide a set of affordances that have facilitated modes of engagement that extend to profound "embodiment relations" (Ihde 1990, p. 39) that encourage expression on a highly abstract but simultaneously visceral and rewarding basis.

The Thummer Mapping Project (ThuMP) project sought to understand the way in which these phenomenological approaches might yield information about the epistemic condition of knowledge, that is, the subconscious body of knowledge associated with "embodiment relations" (after Idhe) that could guide electronic instrument/interface design in such a manner that the gestural language used to engage with the instrument would exhibit affordances sufficiently convincing to overcome any concern about authenticity in performance.

3. THE THUMP PROJECT

Although a considerable body of literature exists discussing models of mapping, one to many, many to many (Hunt and Kirk 2000, Hunt et al. 2000, Hunt and Wanderley 2002), the literature is largely devoid of discussion regarding underlying musical intentionality associated with the control mechanisms outlined.

In 2005–2006, in an effort to develop a model of musical intentionality I established the Thummer Mapping Project (ThuMP) (Paine et al. 2007) at the University of Western Sydney with colleague Ian Stevenson and industry partner Thumtronics[10] P/L. Rather than analyzing the mapping strategies displayed in existing electronic music interface paradigms, ThuMP sought to develop a generic model of successful and enduring acoustic musical instruments, with the selection constrained by the specification that all instruments should be able to produce a continuous tone that could be varied throughout. The ThuMP project interviewed wind, brass, string, and piano accordion performers, asking each musician to reflect on personal practice and to specify the control parameters he or she brought to bear in playing the instrument, seeking to prioritize the parameters and understand their inherent interrelationships.

Each interview was analyzed by a researcher skilled in qualitative data analysis yet a layperson regarding musicianship. This was done to reduce bias in the analysis that may have been introduced as a result of training within a particular musical paradigm. The musical parameters each interviewee discussed included pitch;

dynamics; articulation (attack, release, sustain); and vibrato. Through further content analysis, based solely on the logic outlined in each discourse, the physical controls (speed, direction, force, etc.) that each musician utilized to affect these control parameters were also noted. In addition, the interconnections between these controls and the overall effect on the sound of the instrument were distinguished. The analysis was then represented diagrammatically, noting these connections and interrelatedness of the physical controls, the control parameters, and their effect on the overall sound of the instrument (see fig. 11.1).

Using the NVivo[11] qualitative data analysis program, each of the pathways outlined diagrammatically was then supported with transcript data. For example, fig. 11.2 indicates that pathway 6 concerns the embouchure and its affect on the dynamics of the flute. As stated by the participant:

> I personally believe that you should have it as wide as possible, not to the point where it's really windy sounding, but you want to have all those extra harmonics and the richness of the sound. So you would use the smaller embouchure, the smaller circle, when you're playing softer because when you're playing softly the air has to come out faster, has to still come out fast, I shouldn't say it has to come out faster.
>
> To play softly you can't just stop blowing because it doesn't work, so it's like; you know if you put your thumb over the end of the hose and the water comes out faster because you've made a smaller hole, kind of the same thing when you're playing softer.
>
> For loud, more air. That's qualified by; the embouchure has to get larger to allow that air to come out.... That's where the angle of the air comes in as well, you've got to aim the air, angle the air downwards.
>
> For softer, smaller embouchure. Less air than is required for the loud playing but still enough air so that the note works. Also, the angle of the air generally angles upwards.

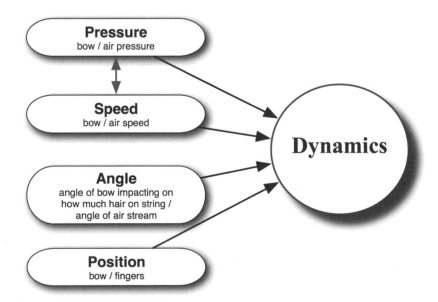

Figure 11.1 Common underlying physicality involved in controlling sound dynamics.

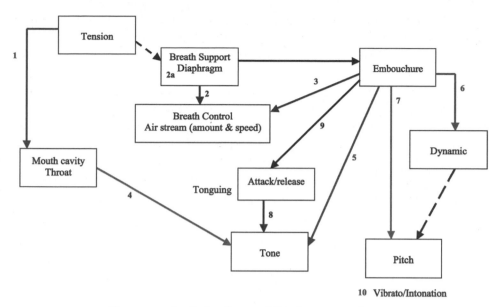

Figure 11.2 Analysis of control for the concert flute.

The transcribed discourse was then subject to a summary analysis, so that each pathway was succinctly represented. For example, pathway 6 was summarized to include the following:

> A smaller embouchure is used to play softly—because the air still has to come out fast. There is less air than when playing loud, but still enough to make the note work. The air is angled upwards.
>
> To play loudly, more air is required, that is, the embouchure gets larger to allow more air and the air is angled downwards.

A second round of interviews was conducted with the instrumentalists to clarify the relationships between the physical controls of the instrument, the defined principal control parameters (dynamics, pitch, vibrato, articulation, release, attack), and the tone color as outlined in fig. 11.3.

The principal aim of this phase was to identify the commonalities among the interviews regarding controllable sound properties and the physical controls that are exercised in the manipulation of these properties. Four parameters, pressure, speed, angle, and position, were consistently noted across all the interviews (see fig. 11.1). A robust generic model representing these physical controls was developed for: dynamics, pitch, vibrato, and articulation, including attack, release, and sustain, represented in the model in figure 11.3.

With regard to the physical controls that are exercised in the manipulation of these properties, a number of commonalities were identified. However, given the variance evident in the physical manipulation of the instruments included in the study (e.g., the flute and the double bass), the commonalities identified were based

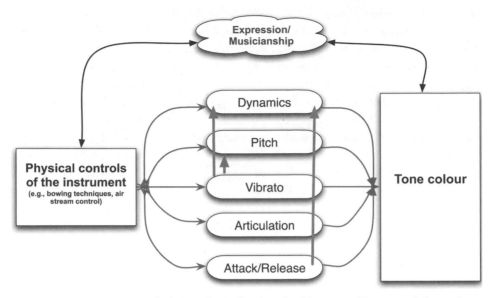

Figure 11.3 Common underlying physicality involved in controlling sound dynamics.

on similarities in the underlying physicality of the process involved. To illustrate, in controlling the sound dynamics, double bass players vary the amount of bow hair used to impact the string by varying the angle of the bow (relative to the string) and increasing the pressure between the bow and string; flute players vary the angle of the airstream and the amount of air moving through the instrument, which is in turn a product of embouchure size and diaphragmatic support. The underlying physical process across these two manipulations can then be identified as a variance of angle and pressure. This type of analysis was repeated for each of the four control parameters outlined and was again represented diagrammatically.

In summary, fig. 11.3 represents a generalized model of the control parameters identified in the interviews using the NVivo qualitative data analysis approach, all of which depend on the pragmatics of the instrument in question (i.e., bowing technique and airstream control) but that determine the most critical musical attribute, the overall tone color. The principal controls are dynamics, pitch, vibrato, articulation, and attack and release.

It should be noted that tone color is seen here not simply as a variable but as the principal objective of all control, with musical concepts such as dynamics and volume, expression, duration, and intonation falling under more general concepts, such as pitch, dynamics, and articulation.

Interrelationships exist within even the most generalized model, and in asking musicians to identify the interrelationships of the myriad specialist control parameters relating to their instrument, they often commented that they were all interrelated—that very little could be done by isolating a single parameter.

The Thummer Mapping Project produced a generic model that illustrated the relationships between musical characteristics and human control gestures within a context that ensured the gestures were meaningful. It is suggested that the model can be translated into a gestural language for controlling/creating live electronic music on a laptop computer. It is further suggested that control mechanisms should be developed from a consideration of the outlined gestural model rather than the reverse, which has previously been the norm in electronic interface design, that is, that the gestures are developed to make the most efficient use of a preexisting, or already designed and manufactured, musical interface. The ThuMP approach made the musical context paramount, shifting the principal consideration from electrical engineering, ergonomics (most acoustic musical instruments are not considered ergonomically sound), and computer science considerations to a basis that provided an inherently musical framework for the development of a gestural control paradigm for musical performance using electronic musical interfaces, and as such at least partly addressing the issues of authenticity outlined.

4. Composition in the Timbre Domain

A possible criticism of the model derived from ThuMP is that it is based on a consideration of musical instruments developed and utilized for chromatic/tonal music, a musical paradigm built on the musical note, and as such is an event-based paradigm. Wishart (1996) outlined the dramatic shift that occurred in electroacoustic composition as well as some late 20th century acoustic music (Varèse, Xenakis, etc.) by which the morphology of the harmonic material became a paramount compositional consideration. This movement from an event-based, note-driven compositional approach (lattice-based composition) to a temporal, timbral, morphological approach also has profound implications for instrument design and hence for approaches to electronic music performance interfaces and the associated design of control mechanisms, physical and virtual (software). This movement toward timbral composition introduces the possibility of gestural control having a direct relationship to musical content.

In approaching such a task, one must also consider the act of musical performance. I cited both Cascone and Godlovitch's considerations of this and outlined notions of body knowledge and somatic engagement with a musical instrument. Richardson and Harper pointed to Heidegger and Merleau-Ponty's notions of phenomenology of instrumentation. It stands to reason that musical practice evolves in accordance with these perceptual changes and that the nature of performative gesture and control also transforms. Richardson and Harper discussed the associated transformation of corporeal possibilities with reference to the human-technology relationship:

This provides an important and highly relevant theorisation of corporeal transformation, an idea that becomes central in the context of human-technology relations ((Weiss 1999): 10). Knowledge of our bodies is technologically mediated and our perception is instrumentally embodied, both in the sense that tools assimilate and materially impinge upon our field of perception, and in the sense that as environmental probes, sensory tools become virtually inseparable from what we would discern as our own perceptual and sensorial boundaries.... [E]mphasising the corporeal-instrumental embodiment of knowledge becomes particularly imperative when critiquing technologies of virtuality. (Richardson and Harper 2001)

5. GESTURE AND SPATIALIZATION

Gestures, regardless of size, reflect a spatial characteristic. A gesture is always in reference to another point and contains morphology, direction, energy, and intent. There is a history of sound diffusion, dating from the antiphony of biblical times to the complexity of modern-day movie theater surround-sound systems and acousmatic diffusion systems such as those of the Birmingham ElectroAcoustic Sound Theatre (BEAST), Le Groupe de Recherches Musicales (GRM), Zentrum für Kunst und Medientechnologie (ZKM), Karlsruhe, Groupe de Musique Experimentale de Bourges (GMEB), and the Gmebaphone (Bourges), and other institutions with an interest in acousmatic music. Denis Smalley referred to the practice of sound diffusion as "'sonorizing' of the acoustic space and the enhancing of sound-shapes and structures in order to create a rewarding listening experience" (Austin 2000, p. 10).

The more abstract electronic music becomes, the more important it is for many listeners to identify and localize a source for heard events to make meaning from the musical activity in front of them. Dan Trueman and Perry Cook took a novel approach to this issue when they designed the Bowed-Sensor-Speaker-Array (BoSSA) (Trueman and Cook 2000). They made reference to the violin's "spatial filtering audio diffuser":

> Traditional musical instruments provide compelling metaphors for human-computer interfacing, both in terms of input (physical, gestural performance activities) and output (sound diffusion). The violin, one of the most refined and expressive of traditional instruments, combines a peculiar physical interface with a rich acoustic diffuser. We have built a new instrument that includes elements of both the violin's physical performance interface and its spatial filtering audio diffuser, yet eliminates both the resonating body and the strings. The instrument, BoSSA (Bowed-Sensor-Speaker-Array), is an amalgamation and extension of our previous work with violin interfaces, physical models, and directional tonal radiation studies.
>
> The BoSSA instrument utilises geosonic loudspeakers, which they argue has allowed them to "substantially reinvent their approach to the performance of live interactive computer music." (Trueman et al. 2000, p. 38)

> Through the design and construction of unique sound diffusion structures, the nature of electronic sound can be reinvented. When allied with new sensor technologies, these structures offer alternative modes of interaction with techniques of sonic computation. This paper describes several recent applications of Geosonic Speakers (multichannel, outward-radiating geodesic speaker arrays) and Sensor-Speaker-Arrays (SenSAs: combinations of various sensor devices with outward-radiating multichannel speaker arrays). Geosonic Speakers, building on previous studies of the directivity of acoustic instruments (the NBody Project),[12] attempt to reproduce some of the diffusion characteristics of conventional acoustic instruments; they engage the reverberant qualities of performance spaces, and allow electronic and acoustic instruments to blend more readily. (Trueman et al. 2000, p. 38)

In addition to the work by Trueman et al. (2000), Simon Emmerson outlined the perceptual issues relating to the "local-field" confusion (Emmerson 1990, 1996, 1998, 2000, 2001). Local-field refers to the expansion of a sound source brought about by amplifying and diffusing the sound of an acoustic instrument, which in normal use constitutes a point source location. When acoustic instruments are used in electroacoustic music performances, amplification of the acoustic sources brings the electronic or recorded sounds and the acoustic sources into the same sonic space, situating the acoustic instrument within the broader sonic experience, while simultaneously alerting us to the fact that the presence of an acoustic instrument on stage does not necessarily obviate these issues of perceptible sound source (Riikonen 2004).

The diffusion of sound sources, however, can add substantially to the performance of electroacoustic and acousmatic music. Once individual sonic elements are treated independently in terms of diffusion, they are perceived as individual entities within the broader architecture of the music. This provides a compositional tool by which sonic elements can be characterized as having some autonomy, a collaborator rather than simply a subservient part of the overall composition, a cincture at the base of a much larger and consuming structure (Paine 2005). New interfaces can offer a truly new opportunity for the musician to take control of spatialization during performance. As the sound source is not located at the interface but diffused through an array of loudspeakers, gestural performance can meaningfully extend to the spatialization of individual elements of the composition. To some extent, it can be argued that such an application of gesture through new interfaces for electronic music performance may assist in overcoming the local-field confusion discussed and distinct from the point source approach displayed in the development of the geosonic loudspeaker (Trueman et al. 2000).

Such an application of performance gesture would need careful consideration to address the possible confusions between performance, as in the excitation and creation of the events being heard in real time, and control, as in the triggering, mixing, or in this case spatialization of events previously generated or recorded. It may be that a control-create confusion would replace the local-field dilemma if this issue is not properly addressed.

I have used this technique in interactive responsive sound environment installations:

> As I step over the threshold, through the open door into the room, the resonant singing dissipates as if the attention of the room has been interrupted. As it turns its attention to me, I am greeted by a multitude of small, intimate trickling bubble-like sounds, moving from the far corner around the room to greet me, to investigate my appearance and in that instance to make me aware of my presence, my immediate and total presence within the system. No longer an observer, but an integral part of the whole, I move another step, and sense a whoosh of small watery sounds moving away from me as if in fright, dancing to-and-fro, at once intimate and curious, wrapping around me and then dashing away as if to get a bigger-picture view—acting as an observer as the dynamic of my movement increases rather than immersing me. I am aware of the space as alive, dynamically filling itself with sonic invitations to engage with it in a dance, enquiring as to my intentions, which I seek to make clearer through my gestures and behavioural responses, exploring the terrain, I find myself embraced in a kind of sonic womb. (Paine 2007, p. 348)

I have experienced this same sense of intimacy in a BEAST concert in Birmingham in 2003. The 2020 Re:Vision concert,[13] featured over one hundred loudspeakers[14] mounted in a full three-dimensional array around the audience (front, sides, back, above, and below and many points in between), a setup also mirrored now in a number of research institutions. The experience of being immersed in the sound is qualitatively and perceptually distinct from that of listening to music presented as a stereo image (as per a proscenium arch theater) by which the audience is always and necessarily separate from the activity to which they can only relate as spectators.

Sound diffusion is practiced with both multichannel source material and stereo source material that is diffused (dynamically spatialized) through multiple loudspeakers. Stereo diffusion presents a number of issues regarding the maintenance of a coherent sonic image, which can easily become unintelligible when spread over physical and sonic distances not experienced during composition. A good deal of research pertaining to spectral or dynamic separation of sounds has taken place, but discussion is beyond the scope of this chapter.

In summary, music that is designed for loudspeaker presentation has the ability to utilize a number of strategies for the diffusion of that musical material over many loudspeakers to engage the architectural space and to present sonic elements as individual and intimate. Spatialization of sonic entities may assist in communicating the "embodiment relations" (Ihde 1990) musicians experience. I propose that both traditional and digital instruments allow embodiment relations, but the special spatialization potential afforded by gestures enacted on digital interfaces may provide a rich and rewarding avenue for development of the way in which abstract music engages an audience.

6. CONCLUSION

Cascone (2000, p. 95) stated that "laptop performance represents artifice and absence, the alienation and deferment of presence." This chapter specifically focused on addressing these issues through notions of somatalogical and epistemic affordances, Ihde's embodiment relations (1990), within the context of developing performance interfaces that provide sufficiently convincing gestural control affordances to overcome any concern about authenticity in performance while providing the potential for highly nuanced, expressive, embodied music performances.

The discussion of ThuMP gave a brief outline of a new approach to these issues, presenting a model for musical control developed from a musician's perspective. This model permits the design of computer music performance interfaces, derived from a musical rather than an engineering or computer science perspective as has been the norm in the past, that utilize a gestural language for controlling/creating live electronic music on a laptop computer.

The identified interrelationship of all musical parameters exemplifies a dynamical system. The relationship between the complexity of control parameters and the evolving nature of musical practice has also been discussed with specific reference to the notion of dynamic morphology (Wishart 1996), addressing both musical material and the notion of morphology of gesture in musical control.

The adoption of interface technologies such as the WiiMote[15] and the Wacom[16] graphics tablet for laptop music performance makes the consideration of morphological approaches to musical interfaces an imperative. The extraordinarily swift adoption of these interfaces for laptop music performance is a clear indication that gestural control is seen as important to both musicians and audiences alike and remains one of the most intricate and complex areas of development in laptop music performance tools.

Acknowledgments: I would like to thank the MARCS Auditory labs and colleagues Ian Stevenson from the School of Communication Arts and Angela Pearce from the School of Psychology at the University of Western Sydney for their assistance during ThuMP.

NOTES

1. See "Conlon Nancarrow," Wikipedia, http://en.wikipedia.org/wiki/Conlon_Nancarrow, accessed February 2, 2008.

2. See Jay Williston, "Thaddeus Cahill's Teleharmonium," *Synthmuseum.com*, http://www.synthmuseum.com/magazine/0102jw.html, accessed February 2, 2008.

3. See the NIME Web site, http://www.nime.org/, accessed June 3, 2008.

4. See the official Web site of the "original computer network band," The HUB, http://hub.artifact.com/, accessed June 3, 2008.

5. See the development company's official Web site, http://www.ableton.com/, accessed June 3, 2008.

6. See the development company's official Web site, http://www.cycling74.com/, accessed June 3, 2008.

7. See the official repository and development community for the Supercollider synthesis software, http://supercollider.sourceforge.net/, accessed June 3, 2008.

8. See the official repository and development community for the impromtu software environment, http://impromptu.moso.com.au/, accessed June 3, 2008.

9. See the official download and information page for the musical programming language Chuck, http://chuck.cs.princeton.edu/, accessed June 3, 2008.

10. See the official Web site for Thumtronics Ltd., http://www.thumtronics.com, accessed December 3, 2008.

11. See the official Web site for QSR International, the developer of the qualitative analysis software Nvivo, http://www.qsrinternational.com/, accessed December 3, 2008.

12. See "N-Body: Spatializing electric and virtual instruments," http://www.music. princeton.edu/~dan/nbody/, accessed July 5, 2008.

13. See "Previous Events," Electroacoustic Music Studios/Beast, http://www.beast. bham.ac.uk/about/pastevents.shtml, accessed July 5, 2008.

14. Loudspeaker specifications can be found at "About BEAST," Electroacoustic Music Studios/Beast, http://www.beast.bham.ac.uk/about/index.shtml, accessed March 21, 2009.

15. See the official Nintendo P/L Web site for the Wii gaming console and accessories, http://www.nintendo.com/wii/what/accessories, accessed December 3, 2008.

16. See the official Wacom P/L Web site, http://www.wacom.com, accessed December 3, 2008, which provides information on the Wacom Tablet products.

BIBLIOGRAPHY

Austin, L. 2000. Sound diffusion in composition and performance: An interview with Denis Smalley. *Computer Music Journal* 24(2): 10–21.

Bongers, B. 2000. Physical interfaces in the electronic arts—interaction theory and interfacing techniques for real-time performance. In *Trends in Gestural Control of Music*, ed. M. M. Wanderley and M. Battier. Paris: IRCAM-Centre Pompidou, pp. 41–70.

Borgo, D. 2005. *Sync or Swarm: Improvising Music in a Complex Age.* New York: Continuum.

Carlsen, P. 1988. *The Player-Piano Music of Conlon Nancarrow: An Analysis of Selected Studies.* Vol. 1. SAM monographs, no. 26. Brooklyn: Institute for Studies in American Music, Conservatory of Music, Brooklyn College of the City University of New York.

Cascone, K. 2000. Comatonse recordings: Articles and reviews. *Computer Music Journal* 24 (4): 91–94.

Chadabe, J. 1997. *Electric Sound: The Past and Promise of Electronic Music.* Upper Saddle River, NJ: Prentice Hall.

Chadabe, J. 2002. The Limitations of Mapping as a Structural Descriptive in Electronic Music. Paper presented at the NIME 2002, Dublin.

Cook, P. 2001. Principles for designing computer music controllers. In *Proceedings of the NIME-01 New Interfaces for Musical Expression in Proceedings of CHI 2001, Seattle.* http://www.nime.org/2001/papers/cook.pdf, accessed February 6, 2008.

Duckworth, W. 1999. *Talking Music: Conversations with John Cage, Philip Glass, Laurie Anderson, and Five Generations of American Experimental Composers.* New York: Da Capo Press.

Emmerson, S. 1990. Computers and live electronic music: Some solutions, many problems. In *Proceedings of the International Computer Music Conference, Glasgow, Scotland.* http://www.omf.paris4.sorbonne.fr/EARS-MINT/PERIODIC01_MINT/icmc90–94. htm, accessed February 6, 2008.

Emmerson, S. 1996. Local/field: Towards a typology of live electronic music. *Journal of Electroacoustic Music* 9: 10–12.

Emmerson, S. 1998. Acoustic/electroacoustic: The relationship with instruments. *Journal of New Music Research* 27(1–2): 146–164.

Emmerson, S. 2000. "Losing Touch?" The human performer and electronics. In *Music, Electronic Media and Culture*, ed. S. Emmerson. Aldershot, UK: Ashgate, pp. 194–216.

Emmerson, S. 2001. New spaces/new places: A sound house for the performance of electroacoustic music and sonic art. *Organised Sound* 6(2): 103–105.

Gann, K. 1995. *The Music of Conlon Nancarrow.* Music in the Twentieth Century. Cambridge: Cambridge University Press.

Godlovitch, S. 1998. *Musical Performance: A Philosophical Study.* London: Routledge.

Hunt, A., and R. Kirk. 2000. Mapping strategies for musical performance. In *Trends in Gestural Control of Music*, ed. M. Wanderley and M. Battier. Paris: IRCAM—Centre Pompidou, pp. 231–258.

Hunt, A., M. Wanderley, and R. Kirk. 2000. Towards a model for instrumental mapping in expert musical interaction. In *Proceedings of the International Computer Music Conference, Berlin.* http://recherche.ircam.fr/equipes/analyse-synthese/wanderle/ Gestes/Externe/Hunt_Towards.pdf, accessed February 6, 2008, pp. 209–211.

Hunt, A., and M. M. Wanderley. 2002. Mapping performer parameters to synthesis engines. *Organised Sound* 7(2): 97–108.

Ihde, D. 1990. *Technology and the Lifeworld : From Garden to Earth.* Indiana Series in the Philosophy of Technology. Bloomington: Indiana University Press.

Kittler, F. A. 1999. *Gramophone, Film, Typewriter.* Writing Science. Stanford, CA: Stanford University Press.

Kittler, F. A., and J. Johnston. 1997. *Literature, Media, Information Systems: Essays.* Critical Voices in Art, Theory and Culture. Amsterdam: GB Arts International.

Merleau-Ponty, M. 1962. *Phenomenology of Perception.* New York: Humanities Press.

Mulder, A. 1994. Virtual musical instruments: Accessing the sound synthesis universe as a performer. In *Proceedings of the First Brazilian Symposium on Computer Music, Caxambu, Minas Gerais, Brazil.* http://xspasm.com/x/sfu/vmi/BSCM1.pdf, accessed February 6, 2008, pp. 2–4.

Mulder, A., S. Fels, and K. Mase. 1997. Mapping virtual object manipulation to sound variation. *IPSJ SIG Notes* 97(122): 63–68.

Mulder, A., and S. Fels. 1998. Sound sculpting: Performing with virtual musical instruments. In *Proceedings of the 5th Brazilian Symposium on Computer Music, Belo Horizonte, Minas Gerais, Brazil.* http://hct.ece.ubc.ca/publications/pdf/mulder-fels-1998b.pdf, accessed February 6, 2008, pp. 3–5.

Paine, G. 2001. "Gestation." Exhibition catalogue. http://www.activatedspace.com/ Installations/Gestation/Gestation.html, accessed February 6, 2008.

Paine, G. 2002. Interactivity, where to from here? *Organised Sound* 7(3): 295–304.

Paine, G. 2003. Reeds, a responsive environmental sound installation. *Organised Sound* 8(2): 139–150.

Paine, G. 2005. Sonic immersion: Interactive engagement in realtime responsive environments. In *Proceedings of the e-Performance and Plugins, Sydney*. http://www.scan.net.au/scan/journal/display.php/journal_id=90, accessed February 6, 2008.

Paine, G. 2006. Interactive, responsive environments: A broader artistic context. In *Engineering Nature: Art and Consciousness in the Post-Biological Era*. Chicago: University of Chicago Press, Intellect, pp. 312–334.

Paine, G. 2007. Hearing places: Sound, place, time and culture. In *Hearing Places*, ed. R. Bandt, M. Duffy, and D. MacKinnon. Newcastle, UK: Cambridge Scholars Press, pp. 348–368.

Paine, G., I. Stevenson, and A. Pearce. 2007. The Thummer Mapping Project (ThuMP). In *Proceedings of the International Conference on New Interfaces for Musical Expression (NIME07), New York City, NY*. http://itp.nyu.edu/nime/2007/proc/nime2007_070.pdf, accessed February 6, 2008, pp. 70–77.

Pressing, J. 1990. Cybernetic issues in interactive performance systems. *Computer Music Journal* 14(1): 12–25.

Richardson, I., and C. Harper. 2001. Corporeal virtuality: The impossibility of a fleshless ontology. *Body, Space and Technology Journal* 2(2). http://people.brunel.ac.uk/bst/vol0202/index.html.

Riikonen, T. 2004. Shared sounds in detached movements: Flautist identities inside the "local-field" spaces. *Organised Sound* 9(3): 233–242.

Roads, C. (ed.). 1996. *The Computer Music Tutorial*. 2nd ed. Massachusetts: MIT Press.

Rovan, J., M. Wanderley, S. Dubnov, and P. Depalle. 1997. Mapping Strategies as Expressive Determinants in Computer Music Performance. Paper presented at the AIMI International Workshop Kansei, The Technology of Emotion, Genoa, Italy.

Rowe, R. 1993. Interactive Music Systems. Massachusetts: MIT Press.

Trueman, D., C. Bahn, and P. Cook. 2000. Alternative voices for electronic sound. *Journal of the Acoustical Society of America* 108(5): 25–38.

Trueman, D., and P. Cook. 2000. Bossa: The deconstructed violin reconstructed. *Journal of New Music Research* 29(2): 121–130.

Wanderley, M. 2001. Gestural control of music. In *Proceedings of the International Workshop on Human Supervision and Control in Engineering and Music, Kassel Germany*. http://recherche.ircam.fr/equipes/analyse-synthese/wanderle/Gestes/Externe/kassel.pdf, accessed February 6, 2008.

Weiss, G. 1999. *Body Images: Embodiment as Intercorporeality*. New York: Routledge.

Wessel, D. L. 1991. Instruments that learn, refined controllers, and source model loudspeakers. *Computer Music Journal* 15(4): 82–86.

Wessel, D., and M. Wright. 2002. Problems and prospects for intimate control of computers. *Computer Music Journal* 26(3): 11–22.

Winkler, T. (1995). Making Motion Musical: Gestural Mapping Strategies for Interactive Computer Music. Paper presented at the 1995 International Computer Music Conference, San Francisco.

Wishart, T. 1996. *On Sonic Art*, ed. S. Emmerson. Philadelphia: Harwood.

CHAPTER 12

SENSOR-BASED MUSICAL INSTRUMENTS AND INTERACTIVE MUSIC

ATAU TANAKA

MUSICIANS, composers, and instrument builders have been fascinated by the expressive potential of electrical and electronic technologies since the advent of electricity itself. Musical applications have accompanied, and often driven, developments in magnetic and electrical field effects, the transistor revolution, digital representation, and more recently advanced sensing and mobile technologies. Scientific progress has given rise to entire movements and styles in music—magnetic recording giving birth to musique concrète and electroacoustic music, radio broadcast technology inspiring the field of radio art and *hörspiel*, and the transistor being the key component in synthesizers that catalyzed the birth of electronic music. These developments are considered in a chronology in the appendix to this volume. The synthesizer, followed by the digital sampler, gave rise to a new family of musical instruments. Early experiments to validate these inventions as true musical instruments consisted of testing their ability to imitate the timbral richness of acoustic instruments. Ironically, while the expressive fidelity of electronic imitations continued to be criticized, their convenience often resulted in these new instruments replacing traditional orchestral instrument performers in commercial recordings. At the same time, electrical and electronics technologies were applied to enhance, then extend, traditional instruments. The emblematic example of this is the electric guitar. Magnetic coil transducer technology was applied first to amplify an acoustic guitar. The arrival with Leo Fender of the solid-body electric guitar gave rise to a guitar with little acoustical properties, its sound being uniquely identified by associated amplification technology. A technology of extension resulted in the creation of an entirely new instrument, spurring on the development of major movements in popular music.

This chapter pinpoints a specific movement within this broad spectrum of music technology to identify a musical and instrument-building tradition concerned with gesture. This area of research and creative practice, often labeled NIME after the international conference series New Interfaces for Musical Expression, goes beyond enhancing traditional instrument performance practice to looking at new paradigms for instrumental performance. At the same time, the focus remains on establishing the notion of an instrument and applying the metaphor to new technologies. In this way, NIME does not consider the sociological impact of technology on musical authorship, distribution, and consumption. There is also a wealth of etudes and sketches that look at musical instruments from an industrial design perspective, which falls beyond the scope of this chapter.

This text instead focuses on musically driven efforts to exploit analog and digital technologies to capture musical gesture and afford new forms of sonic articulation and musical expression. These new instruments permit the live performance of electronic and digital music by capturing different kinds of performer gesture, be they free-space movement, action on an interface, or geographical displacement. From a musical point of view, the field draws on traditions of instrument design, instrument building, and subsequent composition/improvisation for and performance on the instrument. From a research perspective, it is a domain informed by related fields of real-time technologies and human-computer interaction. Not surprisingly, the NIME conference, as the leading professional meeting in the field, historically arose out of the more generalist conference on Computer Human Interaction (CHI), a special interest group of the Association for Computing Machinery (ACM).

The founding of NIME in 2001 represented the historical culmination of what until that point was a disparate field of practice. This text retraces the history of music technology in the 20th century that led up to the founding of NIME and introduces composers and performers who have established a performance practice on interactive, sensor-based musical instruments. The chapter finishes by indicating current directions in the field, including the musical exploitation of biometric signals and location-tracking technologies.

1. HISTORICAL MOVEMENTS

The advent of electricity had a profound impact on the imagination of musicians. This was due in no small part to the fact that sound played such an integral part in these early developments. The telegraph used a series of audible pulses to communicate text. Later, the telephone carried audio directly from one location to another. Radio allowed sound to be transmitted over wireless links, and wire recording captured and stored audio for later playback. Each of these inventions operated on the notion of *transduction*—the process of converting a physical phenomenon to and from an electrical signal, allowing physical variations to traverse different media and span distance and time. It would only be later that image could be manipulated electrically in this way. Photography is the chemical impregnation of image, and even film only uses electricity indirectly to illuminate a series of photographic images. Sound, on the other hand, accompanied electricity as the first medium to be transduced and transmitted on electrical wires.

This close coupling between audio and electricity gave rise to new forms of creative musical expression, including radio art and electronic music. In the spirit of the time were a group of engineers and musicians worldwide who imagined new musical instruments that leveraged the power of electricity to permit gestural instrumental performance of electronic musical sounds.

The most famous of these instruments was the theremin, invented in 1919 by the Russian engineer and amateur musician Leon Theremin. The theremin consisted of electrical circuitry powering two antennas in an orthogonal arrangement. The antennas generated and detected perturbations in the electrostatic field around the instrument. By moving one's hands in the zone around the antennas, the performer affected the electrostatic fields, changing the sound produced by the instrument. The theremin's circuitry was configured so that the horizontal antenna affected the amplitude of the resulting sound, and the vertical antenna affected the frequency, or pitch, of the sound. The timbre was a fixed periodic waveform that could be adjusted by auxiliary controls. In this way, the theremin used the metaphor of a traditional musical instrument like the violin, with one gesture controlling the pitch and another articulating the volume of sound. Like the violin, the tonal range was continuous in that there were no indicators (or frets) quantizing the frequency output to specific notes of the musical scale. While on the violin there was contact with physical materials—bowing of the string and pressing of the string on the fingerboard, gestures on the theremin took place in free space in front of the instrument.

The theremin was not the only instrument produced in this early era of electrical exploration. In France, the Ondes Martenot was invented in 1928 by Maurice Martenot and was successfully integrated in orchestral ensembles of the time, with works by composers such as Arthur Honegger, Olivier Messiaen, and Edgard Varèse. Aided by a traditional musical keyboard for pitch selection, articulating sound took place by moving a ring connected to a string in three-dimensional space over the keyboard. In Germany, the trautonium was created in 1929 and functioned on a resistive wire in contact with a metal plate. Invented by Friedrich Trautwein, it was developed by and performed on by Oskar Sala, with compositions by Paul Hindemith. In Canada, the inventor Hugh Le Caine created a series of instruments, the best known being the Electronic Sackbut of 1945, recognized as the first voltage-controlled synthesizer. Control of volume, pitch, and timbre was realized in three dimensions by means of pressure sensors.

Electronic musical instrument building met the digital era with the work of Max Mathews. Credited as the inventor of digital audio, the process by which analog audio signals are coded as a series of binary numbers, Mathews worked as an engineer and researcher at Bell Laboratories in the 1960s. Alongside his seminal work of that time, notably on the MUSIC family of computer sound synthesis and composition programming languages, Mathews created an instrument called GROOVE (Generated Real-Time Output Operations on Voltage-Controlled Equipment), a hybrid analog-digital system in which a two-dimensional joystick controller modulated electronically generated sound output. The instrument was designed and built in collaboration with the composer and developer, Laurie Spiegel, who would continue the approach with Music Mouse, an early example of Macintosh music software in the 1980s.

2. Defining the Instrument

The focus of the systems described here is the notion of an instrument. As there can be many assumptions on what constitutes a musical instrument, it is useful here to try to define the makeup of a musical instrument and in what ways new technologies and new musical movements extend and challenge these established notions.

Today, the most common definition of a musical instrument is of an acoustical instrument that is a member of the classical orchestra. These instruments can be categorized in instrument families (stringed instruments, woodwind instruments, brass instruments, percussion instruments) and within each family can be subdivided into instruments based on note range and articulatory means.

This definition of musical instrument goes beyond the classical orchestra to include instruments used in popular and ethnic musics and more recently non-acoustical instruments such as the synthesizer. In all cases, it is implied that the musical instrument is a self-contained and autonomous sound-producing object that enables a musician to perform in a live situation.

Developments in musical style have extended the use of the word *instrument* to include new musical devices, at times challenging the very nature of the word. Musique concrète is a studio-based art by which sound is constructed in a painterly way. What was afforded by editing sound as recorded on tape through electronic treatments was to free the composer from the abstraction and detachment of composing on paper and transmitting the work to an instrumentalist. This direct manipulation of the medium was heralded as a revolution in Pierre Schaeffer's manifesto for the field, liberating the composer from the musician. This touches on the politics of creativity that are beyond the scope of this chapter and have been discussed elsewhere in this and other volumes. What is relevant to the present discussion is the fact that even in this nonperformative extreme, the term instrument has been used—it has been said that with musique concrète the studio became the *instrument* of the composer.

In other developments of musical style, the evolution of disc jockey (DJ) from a radio broadcast role to a performer in hip-hop and techno musics has brought with it the development of DJ culture in which the vinyl record turntable has become a musical instrument in its own right. The development of *turntablism* extends the traditional notion of musical instrument—the turntable is indeed autonomous and self-contained and, in those styles of music, is used to perform in live concert situations. At the same time, the turntable challenges traditional definitions of musical instrument as it relies on prerecorded materials to make sound. It can be argued that in the late 20th century musicians began to work with sound at a higher level of abstraction than that of individual notes and timbres. This coincides with postmodernist notions of appropriation, reproduction, and simulation. What is relevant here is that musicians, regardless of the level of abstraction, seek to be expressive and performative with sound and, to facilitate this musical urge, invent musical instruments.

Beyond the conceptual considerations of turntable-as-musical-instrument, this serves as an illustrative example of the *scope* of the musical instrument. The turntable is autonomous and self-contained in a way similar to a traditional instrument. However, as an electronic instrument, it needs a speaker system to produce sound. In this way, it is similar to the electric guitar—an electric guitar is incomplete without a guitar amplifier. The choice of amplifier and associated circuitry (be it tube or solid state) and the quality and size of the speakers have an enormous effect on the final sound and ultimately the expressivity of the instrument. The question then arises whether the instrument definition in the case of the electric guitar stops at the guitar itself or expands to include the amplifier and the effects pedals in between?

The turntable adds to this its dependence on vinyl records as source material. While the turntable itself is self-contained, it is ultimately an open-ended system that depends on *content* played on it. The performance of a DJ depends as much on his choice of records as it does on his performance technique. The very same turntable can be used in a noninstrumental way by a radio DJ or purely for music listening by a consumer in a home hi-fi system. The instrument then depends not only on content, but also on *context*. Finally, there is the question of *configuration*, as many turntablists perform with two or even three turntables connected by an audio DJ mixer. The number of turntables used changes the nature of the instrument, as can the choice of DJ mixer, the characteristics of its equalizers and cross-fade slider. This raises the question of the scope of the instrument as embracing content, context, and configuration—is the musical instrument in question the turntable itself or the system of turntables, record collection, DJ mixer, and ultimately sound system chosen by the performer?

3. OPEN-ENDED SYSTEMS

The view of a musical instrument as an open-ended system comprised of multiple components can be applied to digital technology and becomes a musical perspective from which to broach questions of the "instrumentality" of hardware/software architectures of live computer music performance systems.

Such a system typically consists of the following components:

- Input device—often a sensor and data acquisition subsystem to capture performer gestures
- Mapping algorithms—software subsystem to translate gestural data into musical information
- Sound synthesis engine—real-time audio generation in which sound synthesis parameters are modulated by live input
- Compositional structure—a structural layer defining the musical sections or progression of the work
- Output system—audio output subsystem consisting of output channel configuration and digital-to-analog converters (DAC)

Typical questions that arise include the following: Is the instrument just the sensor hardware, or does it include software components like the mapping and sound synthesis software subsystems? Where does the instrument end and the composition begin? Is the entire system specific for one musical work, or can parts of it (e.g., the synthesis or compositional components) be altered or generalized to create different works for the same instrument? What happens to the boundaries distinguishing traditional roles of instrument builder, composer, and performer?

Confronting these questions from an engineering perspective are rhetorical concerns defining open-ended or closed systems. A musical point of view differentiates the way these questions are confronted. This distinguishes sensor-based musical instrument design as a creative musical pursuit distinct from a purely technical engineering pursuit. In this way, the notion of musical instrument as instrument is distinct from that of a tool.

The term *tool* implies that an apparatus takes on a specific task, utilitarian in nature, carried out in an efficient manner. A tool can be improved to be more efficient, can take on new features to help realize its task, and can even take on other, new tasks not part of the original design specification. In the ideal case, a tool expands the limits of what it can do. It should be easy to use and be accessible to a wide range of naïve users. Limitations or defaults are seen as aspects that can be improved.

A musical instrument's raison d'etre, on the other hand, is not at all utilitarian. It is not meant to carry out a single defined task as a tool is. Instead, a musical instrument often changes context, withstanding changes of musical style played on it while maintaining its identity. A tool gets better as it attains perfection in realizing its tasks. The evolution of an instrument is less driven by practical concerns and is motivated instead by the quality of sound the instrument produces. In this regard, it is not so necessary for an instrument to be perfect as much as it is important for it to display distinguishing characteristics, or "personality." What might be considered imperfections or limitations from the perspective of tool design often contribute to the personality of a musical instrument.

Computers are generalist machines with which software tools are programmed. By itself, a computer is a tabula rasa, full of potential but without specific inherent orientation. Software applications endow the computer with specific capabilities. It is with such a machine that we seek to create instruments with which we can establish a profound musical rapport.

The input device is the gateway through which the user accesses the computer software's functionality. As a generalist device, generalized input devices like the keyboard or mouse allow the manipulation of a variety of different software tools. Music software can be written to give musically specific capabilities to the computer. Input devices can be built to exploit the specific capabilities of this software. On this generalized platform, then, we begin to build a specialized system, each component becoming part of the total instrument description.

In instrumental writing, composing with musical specificity for a target instrument is called *idiomatic writing*. A music written for a certain instrument should in principle respect and abide by the qualities of that instrument. These qualities include tonal range, techniques of articulation, and facility of performer execution. It is for considerations of idiomatic writing that music for violin differs from music for flute, even if the two instruments share similar tonal ranges. Good instrumental writing should make an instrument "speak" by highlighting its capabilities as well as its limitations. This implies not only staying within the bounds of an instrument, but also pushing the envelope and testing the limits and breaking point of conventional technique.

4. CONTROLLERS

Interactive musical instrument development in the 1980s focused on novel controllers. In computing science, this was the era when input devices such as the mouse, trackpad, and tablet became commercially viable. The research in the field of human-computer interaction (HCI) that led up to these developments dealt with enhanced task performance afforded by novel input devices. Input devices such as mice, coupled to advanced graphical user interfaces (GUIs) extended the forms of interaction a computer user could have beyond the classical typewriter keyboard. In a similar way, computer music and electronic music, which had until then relied on the metaphor of the classical piano keyboard as a live input device, sought to leverage the interactive possibilities of new input devices as controllers to allow new forms of musical interaction.

At the same time, commonly available computing power was still insufficient in the mid-1980s to allow sound synthesis in software on personal desktop computer systems in real time. Digital sound synthesis took place through offline calculations using synthesis and composition languages such as MUSIC V, Csound, and Cmix. Live computer music performance took place on special-purpose synthesis hardware popularized by synthesizers such as the Yamaha DX7 and samplers like the E-mu Emulator II. The arrival of the musical instrument digital interface (MIDI) standard in 1983 allowed the possibility of interoperability across systems—for one keyboard to control another or for a computer-based sequencer to orchestrate a number of synthesizers. This generalized interface bus for interoperation and control became the ideal communications bus for a family of alternate controllers to be developed, both commercially and in the research field.

This spawned a series of electronic musical instrument products that sought to extend the reach of synthesizer performance to nonkeyboard players. Manufacturers such as Yamaha, Akai, and Casio commercialized MIDI controllers based on metaphors of woodwind and brass instruments, using breath pressure sensors and key systems based on wind instrument fingerings that output MIDI note and control data. Guitar-based interfaces were also invented, with hexaphonic pickups detecting the vibration of individual strings on a traditional guitar in the case of the Roland family of guitar synthesizers or using the form factor and physiognomy of a guitar in a completely virtual setup as in the case of the Stepp, SynthAxe, and Yamaha systems.

Some systems went beyond the traditional musical instrument metaphor to imagine new forms of gestural interaction with synthesized sound. The D-beam used infrared distance sensing to capture hand gesture in front of an instrument to create MIDI continuous control data output. The system was later licensed by Roland and integrated as an auxiliary control on synthesizers, much in the way that Moog had in the analog era integrated continuous ribbon controllers above its keyboards. The Sound-beam system continues to be used as a dedicated controller for music therapy applications, and the technique of distance sensing has been generalized and is a common component in instrument systems described in this chapter.

Musicians were captivated by the expressive possibilities of novel interfaces and created custom MIDI controllers. Jean Michel Jarre used Bernard Szajner's Laserharp was a system that used a series of light beams in a vertical array; interruption of the beams by the performer's hands triggered sounds. Serge de Laubier and Remy Dury created the Meta-Instrument, a seated elbow and lower arm prosthesis that used multidimensional joints to translate limb articulation with fifty-four degrees of freedom to control sound synthesis parameters. De Laubier has continued development of the Meta-instrument to be a standing system controlling real-time software sound synthesis and computer graphics. Dury has adapted some of the input technology from the Meta-instrument to an advanced woodwind controller, the KRL.

Mathews continued the research questions he started with GROOVE in creating the Radio Baton, a multidimensional percussion surface. The system consists of two batons and a rectangular surface. The batons are wired to microradio transmitters, each transmitting on a separate frequency. The percussion surface serves as matrix antenna, defining zones that could report the x, y, and z coordinates of baton position. The MIDI output from the hardware was coupled to step sequencer software, allowing different musical compositions to be performed from the Radio Baton. Typical mappings included tempo beating on one baton stepping through the notes of the composition, and x–y and z position of the two batons modulating expressive sound synthesis parameters. For Mathews, the Radio Baton as musical instrument consisted of the hardware and composition playback software. Other musicians, notably Andrew Schloss and Richard Boulanger, took the hardware as instrument and programmed their own software programs to create different musical compositions.

5. HYPERINSTRUMENTS

While inventing new instruments is the primary pursuit of interactive music, traditional instruments remain an important foundation and serve as springboards for ideas. Established performance practice on existing instruments serves as an important point of reference and source of metaphors for many sensor instruments. Meanwhile, the accumulated history of performance technique on existing instruments gives a richness of musical interaction that serves as a gold standard for evaluating new instruments developed with interactive technologies. History provides a temporal dimension to the tradition of musical instrument development that is not typically associated with the accelerated nature of technology development. Musical instruments evolve out of a synergistic relationship between developments in musical style and material craftsmanship. Digital media, on the other hand, evolve based on engineering advances, an unstoppable technological progress independent of whether the end user has demonstrated a need, with the next level of advancement in format or capacity coming before the previous has been fully explored or assimilated. In music, this means that hardware and software are updated before the musician has had time to create profound musical relationships with a stable system.

Extensions to existing instruments have been a rich area for the musical application of sensor technology. The term *hyperinstrument* was used by American composer Tod Machover as follows:

> The hyperinstrument project was started in 1986 with the goal of designing expanded musical instruments, using technology to give extra power and finesse to virtuosic performers. Such hyperinstruments were designed to augment guitars and keyboards, percussion and strings, and even conducting. . . . The research focus of all this work is on designing computer systems (sensors, signal processing, and software) that measure and interpret human expression and feeling, as well as on exploring the appropriate modalities and innovative content. (http://opera. media.mit.edu/projects/hyperinstruments.html)

At IRCAM (Institut de Recherche et Coordination Acoustique/Musique), the MIDI Flute was created for use in Boulez's Explosante-Fixe. Alongside the large research-lab-driven efforts are equally important musician-oriented projects in which a composer or a performer develops a single instrument in a highly personal evolution. Frances-Marie Uitti is a virtuoso cellist who has concentrated on contemporary music and has developed extended technique on the violoncello, notably with the use of two bows simultaneously. Part of her innovations in cello performance has been the development of a hypercello, a traditional cello extended with sensors. The instrument was developed in a long collaboration with the Studio for Electro-Instrumental Music (STEIM) in Amsterdam and with musicians and composers, including Joel Ryan. She continues development of the instrument, creating a six-stringed electric cello with interactive electronics in collaboration with David Wessel and Adrian Freed at the Center for New Music and Audio Technologies (CNMAT) of the University of California at Berkeley.

Sarah Nicolls similarly explores extensions to the modern piano. She has commissioned a series of works from composers, including Richard Barrett and Michael Edwards, for piano extended by electronics, and from this has distilled a kind of musical technical specification for a sensor-based piano with which she can perform a body of work. She has built a standing grand piano that allows her to perform prepared piano articulations inside from an upright standing position. Sensors on the pianist's body activate motors and actuators on the piano. In her case, sensing electronics are placed not only on the piano itself but also on the performer's limbs—shoulders, arms, and hands. Here, limits of the instrument go beyond the physical instrument to include electronics on the performer's body.

Nicolas Collins is a composer who has taken the tinkering and hacking aesthetic of the do-it-yourself (DIY) school to create a series of idiosyncratic musical devices. One of his long-standing projects has been an instrument based on a traditional trombone, the "trombone-propelled electronics." The traditional instrument is used as a platform for creating an entirely new instrument—Collins, unlike Nicolls and Uitti, is not a virtuoso on his instrument, and his instrument does not extend traditional performance practice on the instrument. Instead, it uses articulations from trombone performance—breath pressure, slide manipulation—to modulate electronic processes on an outboard signal processor.

6. STUDIO FOR ELECTRO-INSTRUMENTAL MUSIC

Studios for electroacoustic music composition and production have often played pivotal roles in the development of technology-based music. This rich tradition includes the Köln studio, IRCAM (Institut de Recherche et Coordination Acoustique/Musique), EMS (Electronic Music Studios), and CCRMA (Center for Computer Research in Music and the Arts). In the area of sensors and music, the studio that has been the leading center in the field is STEIM in Amsterdam. It was founded in 1968 by a collective of composers, including Misha Mengelberg, Louis Andriessen, and Dick Raaijmakers. It was with the arrival of the late Michel

Waisvisz in 1973 that STEIM took on an instrument-building workshop approach, first producing the Cracklebox, an instrument by which the performer becomes part of the electrical circuitry of the instrument through touch and human conductivity.

The output of the STEIM workshop includes hardware interfaces, programming languages for interaction mapping, and real-time sound and image manipulation software. With these systems, instrument builders have built a family of instruments and artists have realized a diverse range of projects. The Sensorlab was a high-quality sensor interface designed and built by Peter Cost in the mid-1980s. Spider was a programming language by Tom Demeyer with which mapping algorithms were deployed on the Sensorlab hardware. Johan den Biggelaar and Bert Bongers built The Hands, for which Frank Balde programmed performance software. This became the instrument used by Waisvisz for over two decades.

These instruments were at once idiosyncratic instruments highly personalized to a particular artist's needs and at the same time general platforms for groups of artists to explore and extend. Edwin van der Heide took the MIDI Controller, an early version of The Hands, and adapted it for his own solo performances, duos with instrumentalists, and ensemble work with Sensorband. Other configurations of sensors connected to the Sensorlab gave rise to different instruments. A series of stretch sensors connecting strings resembling a spider's web became The Web.

In 1994, Laetitia Sonami worked with Bongers to extend a series of glove interfaces she had previously produced to create an instrument called the Lady's Glove. Bend sensors, Hall effect proximity sensors, and force-sensing resistors (FSRs) were sewn on a Lycra glove and connected to a Sensorlab. With this, Sonami created a musical instrument that allowed movement without spatial reference and with an embodied approach to computer music.

7. Sensor Interfaces

The period in the late 1980s and 1990s represented a rich period in gestural computer music. Real-time systems began to be portable. Advances in the MIDI specification brought forth the aforementioned alternate controllers by commercial instrument companies. Advances in microelectronics democratized sensor interface device production. Originally, such interfaces, which converted analog control voltage output of sensors to digital data, were the fruit of specialized design efforts at early studios dedicated to the field, such as STEIM or the Institute of Sonology. Even after the popularization of interactive music, input devices were expensive exotic devices, as evidenced by IRCAM's AtomicPro. By the early 2000s, however, PIC (programmable integrated circuit) and FGPA (field-programmable gate array) technology allowed inexpensive, one-chip solutions to multichannel data acquisition. This resulted in low-cost artist systems such as Infusion Systems'

I-Cube, Making Things, and Phidgets, ultimately leading to grassroots open source hardware plans for kits exemplified by the Arduino and Mu-IO. Sensors followed a similar path, integrating sensing and signal preprocessing into single-chip solutions that output preconditioned calibrated voltages from acceleration, magnetic fields, gyroscopic rotation, temperature, and other physical effects. This has led ultimately to the introduction of mass-market consumer devices that incorporate sensors such as ultrasound, and accelerometers.

In the research arena, these developments of increasingly convenient sensing and faster computer processing speeds resulted in systems combining musical modalities. SenSAs and Bubbas, produced at Princeton University by Dan Truman and Perry Cook combined spherical speaker systems with sensor input to create self-contained electronic instruments with sound radiation properties allowing better integration in ensembles with acoustical instruments. CNMAT created the Rimas box as a sensor interface sampling at audio sampling rates, allowing gestural control to be treated in the same signal-processing chains as the audio synthesis. At Newcastle University's Culture Lab, Kazuhiro Jo has created low-cost DIY circuitry to preprocess sensor signals to be able to use audio analog-to-digital convertors (ADC) as data input channels in the Inaudible Computing project.

8. AUDIO AS SENSOR

While sensors can be used to capture performer gesture to extend an instrument's musical palette, the actual sound output of an instrument can be a rich source of information about performer expressivity. The sound of an acoustical instrument, then, can be thought of as data to be "sensed" and analyzed. In this light, a microphone becomes sensor. This builds on the rich traditions of electroacoustic music created for instrument and electronics, making audio itself as the source of interaction. Sophisticated audio effects and signal processing, commonly used in all styles of music, consists for the most part of electronic sonic treatments. With audio sensing, information about musical gesture is extracted from the signal and mapped to sound synthesis parameters. The use of microphone as sensor creates a closed feedback loop and holistic interactive control dynamic. The application of mapping techniques distinguishes the use of microphone as interactive sensor from simple effects.

This approach has been used widely at IRCAM by composers Philippe Manoury and Kaija Saariaho, paralleling and mutually influencing the development of the Max/MSP (Max Signal Processing) software. Fundamental to the development of this now industry standard system, composers Cort Lippe and Zack Settel were fundamentally involved in the development of Max/MSP, creating signal analysis/resynthesis modules specifically for a body of instrumental compositions. Lippe's "Music for Clarinet and ISPW," and Settel's "Hok Pwah" for voice and percussion and "Taudrium" for contrabass are emblematic of this microphone-as-sensor approach.

Ryan has created a veritable musical instrument that is a sophisticated signal-processing network for acoustical instruments. Performing with virtuosos like saxophonist Evan Parker, the musical instrument definition in this case spans performers and systems, becoming an instrument as ensemble, as meta-system. Ryan takes the microphone-as-sensor instrument notion to its logical extreme by taking the stage and performing alongside the musician whose sound he is treating, creating a duo of instrument and extension of instrument. He has proven the richness of his instrument by using it in a multitude of different musical contexts, styles, and situations.

9. VIRTUAL REALITY SYSTEMS

The development of glove-based instruments paralleled developments in the late 1980s and early 1990s of VR technology. The VR systems brought novel input and display systems such as glove interfaces, bodysuits, and head-mounted stereoscopic video displays (HMDs) to create immersive audiovisual environments. This sparked the imagination of artists to create artistic work with these technologies. It also triggered the democratization of sensor technologies in consumer products such as video game controllers. The Nintendo Power Glove, introduced in 1989, while not a commercial success, became a cult device for hacking among artists, who would extend and dismantle it to recover the bend sensors embedded within.

Suguru Goto is a Japanese composer based in France who has worked with VR devices. His "o.m.2-g.i.-p.p." was a sound/image composition for the Body Suit, an instrument that is a full bodysuit armed with sensors, and HMD. The American Joseph Butch Rovan's work with glove controllers includes "Collide," for which subtle finger gestures control sound synthesis and navigation through a series of film noir images.

10. TABLETOP AND SURFACE INSTRUMENTS

Developments in the early 2000s in areas of computer science research such as Computer Supported Cooperative Work (CSCW) and social computing focused on multiuser systems. Tabletop interfaces with multitouch technology allow the tracking of multiple gestures simultaneously on a common surface. Jeff Han's multitouch tabletop created at New York University is one such device. Proximal interaction techniques and electronically tagged objects are another way to track simultaneous objects for musical control. James Patten's AudioPad, developed at

the Massachusetts Institute of Technology (MIT) Media Labs is a musical composition and performance interface based on this approach. Computer vision-based
tracking of multiple objects and their orientations is another approach to control
multiple sound synthesis parameters. The ReacTable, developed by Sergi Jordà and
his team at the Music Technology Group in Barcelona is an instrument comprised
of several modules. A computer vision system called reacTIVision developed by
Martin Kaltenbrunner is a software framework for tracking fiducial markers and
for multitouch finger tracking. Modular software synthesis allows live repatching
of sound based on object manipulation. Finally, physical objects visually tagged
with the markers are placed on a computer camera/projection surface to complete
the instrument.

Synthesizer designer and instrument builder Don Buchla used a series of 36
FSRs in a single-user instrument approach to multitouch sensing with Thunder.
The instrument in effect creates a span of ribbon controllers on a circular surface in
front of the musician. A mapping program interface (STORM) allows any combi-
nation of sensor input to create specific MIDI output. Composer and performer
Wessel of CNMAT has performed extensively with this tactile instrument.

11. FREE-SPACE GESTURE

Buchla continued with his exploration of MIDI instruments to capture performer
gesture with Lightning. Operating on principles of triangulation of infrared beams,
the system consists of two smart wands not dissimilar to those of Mathews' Radio
Baton. Here, the wands are equipped with infrared transmitters, and the performer
waves them in free space in front of a base unit receiver. The horizontal and vertical
movements of the wands are captured independently across a series of zones set by
the receiver. Some distance/depth effects are also possible. Firmware in the Lightning allows the musician to determine how sound is articulated as each wand
moves within a zone and from zone to zone. Improvising sampling musician Bob
Ostertag has performed extensively with Lightning, using it to trigger and modulate samples without a traditional keyboard.

The use of infrared light beams restricts the instrumentalist to a line-of-sight
relationship with the base unit, and a coordinate system is anchored to the device.
To create a nonreferential spatial system in the way that Sonami conceived, accelerometers offer a more generalized solution. Without an absolute reference, however, accumulated error of successive delta values limits the usefulness of
accelerometers in calculating position. Instead, selective filtering of accelerometer
data allow its use in calculating tilt and detecting dynamic motion.

Much in the way that the Power Glove in the 1980s democratized access to VR
technology, the Nintendo Wii Remote's arrival in 2006 made free-space sensing
available to a wide range of artists in an affordable package. The Wii Remote

contains a 2-D accelerometer and connects to a host over Bluetooth. Music software on the computer would then receive a stream of serial data representing the motion of the device in three dimensions. This essentially replicates and generalizes specialist systems that had been created by Sonami and others over the years.

12. BIOSIGNAL INSTRUMENTS

The idea to interface the intention of the musician, be it physical gesture or musical thought, directly to sound output has fascinated composers for decades. To do so entails creating a musical system based on human physiology. Biofeedback systems have traditionally been the means to look at evoked response. Since then, the notion of biocontrol has been developed. Recently, the area of brain-computer interface has received much attention and has potential in musical applications.

Analog biofeedback systems have been employed in music since the 1960s. David Tudor, composer and collaborator of John Cage, used biofeedback in his signal paths that directly manipulated audio. Alvin Lucier's "Music for Solo Performer" is the seminal work in this area. Lucier wrote: "I realized the value of the EEG [electroencephalogram] situation as a theater element. . . . I was also touched by the image of the immobile if not paralyzed human being who, by merely changing states of visual attention, can activate . . . a large battery of percussion instruments" (Lucier 1995).

David Rosenboom created a family of mixed media biofeedback works and defined the field as follows: "The term 'biofeedback' will be used herein to refer to the presentation to an organism, through sensory input channels, of information about the state and/or course of change of a biological process in that organism, for the purpose of achieving some measure of regulation or performance control over that process, or simply for the purpose of internal exploration and enhanced self-awareness" (Rosenboom 1976).

The use of EEGs, or the recording of brainwave signals, has fascinated numerous artists and musicians. Since Lucier and Rosenboom's time, advanced multi-channel electrode systems allow more detailed monitoring of human brain activity. Meanwhile, low-cost electronics have made notions of biofeedback accessible to a wider range of artists. Interfaces such as the Interactive Brainwave Visual Analyzer (IBVA) of Masahiro Kahata have been used by New York musician Miya Masaoka to extend her instrumental performance practice. As a low-amplitude, high-noise signal, however, extracting meaningful signals from the brain remains a challenge. The use of medical electrode systems has allowed rigorous study of musical intent as expressed in the EEG. The Dutch scientist Peter Desain has studied evoked response in EEG to rhythmic stimuli, examining the possibility of detecting through EEG a subject imagining a rhythm by matching EEG output to recorded traces while listening to that rhythm. Developments in the area of brain-computer interfaces (BCIs) have been extended to musical interaction. The Brazilian composer Eduardo Miranda proposes brain-computer music interfaces (BCMIs) in which continuous EEG readings activate generative music algorithms and biosignal complexity modulate musical dynamics. Andrew Brouse has created meditative installation/performances using this technology.

The advent of digital signal-processing techniques in the 1980s made reproducible control of interaction elements more reliable than with analog techniques. With this came the fundamental shift from artistic use of biofeedback to introducing the notion of *biocontrol*. While biofeedback allows the physiological state to be monitored and to be translated to other media by means of visualization or sonification, biocontrol seeks to create reproducible volitional interaction using physiological biosignals. Performance artists such as Laurie Anderson and Pamela Z have used the BodySynth of Chris van Raalte and Ed Severinghaus to capture theatrical movement to trigger musical accompaniment to their actions. The BioMuse by R. Benjamin Knapp and Hugh Lusted allowed continuous tracking of brainwaves (EEG), eye movement (electro-oculogram, EOG), and muscle tension (EEG) signals to shape and modulate sound synthesis parameters and musical flow. I have created a body of work and performed extensively with the BioMuse system in solo and group concert settings. Teresa Marrin Nakra of the MIT Media Lab has used Delsys active dry electrode systems in a bodysuit for electromyographic (EMG) tracking of gesture of an orchestral conductor. Yoichi Nagashima has created homemade circuitry pre-dating the DIY movement to replicate EMG-based musical interaction. More recently, Miguel Ortiz Pérez, working at the Sonic Arts Research Centre (SARC) in Belfast with BioMuse inventor Knapp, has used a commercial version of the BioMuse (BioFlex) to analyze muscular gestures in musical performance.

13. ENSEMBLES

Ensemble performance is an essential component of musical practice and often creates compelling musical contexts to uncover musical qualities of an instrument. Music, from this point of view, is an inherently social activity—communication dynamics exist between performer and audience, and an interaction dynamic exists between a performer and his or her instrument. Ensemble performance adds a sophistication and complexity to these flows by intermixing human interaction among performers with instrumental interaction of each performer with the performer's instrument. This results in streams of nonverbal communication that are at the heart of musical interaction. Individual human-machine interaction creates a musical whole by becoming the conduit of a collective communicative space. Ensemble situations in this way create critical test cases for the immediate expressivity and context-switching capabilities of an instrument. A successful ensemble can also be thought to become a sort of meta-level instrument comprising multiple actors.

Acoustical instruments display a musical flexibility that allows them to traverse a variety of musical contexts and styles. From solo to ensemble, in groups of differing scales from chamber music to bands to orchestras, and for musical styles that may see a single instrument performing folk, popular, symphonic, or avant-garde musics, instruments in the traditional acoustical musical instrument family have developed over the history of music an extraordinary capacity to adapt to different musical contexts.

Do interactive, technology-based musical instruments exhibit a similar level of adaptability? Much in the way that we sought to identify the articulatory potential of an instrument that defined its musical richness, a corollary to this is the ability of an instrument to change musical contexts, to play among other instruments and musically contribute to the whole yet maintain its own sonic identity. Traditional instruments and ensembles have developed this over the course of musical history. To what extent can technology instruments begin to attain this level of complexity and adaptability?

Group performance has been a part of interactive instrument history since the early instruments were introduced. The theremin and Ondes Martenot have figured in symphony orchestras not only as soloists but also as integral parts of the orchestra, motivated in part by the desire to prove their musical adaptability and in a hope to integrate electronic instruments into orchestral tradition. Ensembles consisting only of electronic instruments have also existed, notably a chamber ensemble of Ondes Martenots.

In 1966, the American composer Cage created *Variations V* for a group of theremin-like antennas. Rather than investigate the expressive depth of chamber music performance, here a 1960s ethos in "happenings" brought about creating a unique event to see the ways that technology could extend music to occupy space. This aesthetic pioneered by Cage and Tudor, of a group of musicians channeling chance and complexity through live performance, was taken up in the 1980s by The Hub, a computer network band composed of San Francisco musicians John Bischoff, Tim Perkis, Chris Brown, Scot Gresham-Lancaster, Mark Trayle, and Phil Stone. The work of The Hub is presented in depth elsewhere in this volume. As their name implies, they made use of, at first, homemade network interconnection technology to create a digital music ensemble. In this light, they are the precursors in the field of network music, a field of musical research unto itself described by Álvaro Barbosa and others. For the themes of instrumental performance central to this chapter, it can be said that The Hub created a collective musical instrument out of the very technologies that facilitate being an ensemble.

By the early 1990s, sensor-instrument performance had become active, particularly in the Netherlands, with projects from the Institute of Sonology at the Royal Conservatory of the Hague and at STEIM. From this active scene of experimentation, instrument building, and performance, three musicians, Edwin van der Heide, Zbigniew Karkowski, and I, formed Sensorband, a trio of sensor-based instrumentalists. Van der Heide performed on the MIDI Conductor, an early version of what was later to become The Hands used by Waisvisz. Karkowski performed on a scaffolding cage armed with a series of infrared beams, and I performed on the BioMuse EMG interface. This grouping of distinct instruments united by the theme of gestural interaction in a musical group applied the notion of a chamber music ensemble made up of a single instrument family, in this case the family of sensor instruments. Sensorband toured extensively for ten years before disbanding in 2003. I went on to form another trio, Sensors_Sonics_Sights with Laurent Dailleau and Cécile Babiole. Alongside the BioMuse were ultrasound rangers used by Babiole and Dailleau's theremin. This second-generation band is notable for its juxtaposition of historical instruments like the theremin alongside modern biosignal interfaces and the integration of live image manipulation into the instrumental ensemble.

The Hub and Sensorband were early examples of network ensembles and sensor-instrument groups, respectively. They inspired a series of groups, including the German group Tryonis and the Australian group Metraform. However, the number of ensembles dedicated to computer-based instruments remains small. Ensemble performance of interactive instruments with acoustic instruments is more common. Wessel of CNMAT performed throughout the 1990s with the Buchla Thunder controller in various improvised music contexts, including with trombonist George Lewis and Pakistani vocalist Shafqat Ali Khan. Ryan of STEIM tours extensively with the saxophone virtuoso Parker. The improvised music scene in general assimilated performers on keyboard samplers. From this practice, Ostertag extended this tradition to perform in ensembles with Fred Frith and other notable improvising musicians, using the Buchla Lightning infrared wand controller to articulate and sculpt output from a sampler.

Meanwhile, the rapid miniaturization of computing power that allowed real-time computer music to run on laptop computers created an artists' scene unto itself of laptop music. While other writings comprehensively cover this musical movement, it is interesting to note that ensemble formation also took place in this scene—that is, sensor instruments and gestural articulation were ultimately not a prerequisite for the computer music "band." The Princeton group created the Princeton Laptop Orchestra (Plork). Underground artists in the laptop music scene created all-star lineups, including the laptop orchestra constituted by Mego label manager and musician Pita Rehberg in the early 2000s. More stable ensembles emerged from the Japanese scene, including the laptop orchestra organized by Philippe Chatelain and the Sine Wave Orchestra organized by Jo Kazuhiro and colleagues.

If performing on laptop computers facilitated computer use in a musical ensemble, this was taken even further by projects that treated acts of computer programming or electronic circuit building as musical acts that could be set in a group context. Ge Wang created a live performable computer music programming language, ChucK, and with Perry Cook made duo performances of "Co-Audicle" in which the two performers coded from scratch directly onstage, projecting their code onstage in a live setting. Masayuki Akamatsu and students at the International

Academy of Media Arts and Sciences (IAMAS) created and performed with the Breadboard Band, a musical ensemble that constructed sound-producing electronics circuits on prototyping boards live.

14. NETWORK MUSIC

Following the seminal work of The Hub, by the early 2000s, network-based music applications became a fertile area for exploration of ensemble performance. Most projects looked at the network as a conduit by which to facilitate remote performance of traditional music. Musicians and researchers Chafe, Settel, and Rowe at CCRMA (Stanford), McGill University, and New York University, respectively, used ultra-high-bandwidth Internet2 infrastructure to demonstrate low-latency ensemble performance of jazz. Elaine Chew has conducted rigorous study of distributed chamber music rehearsal. Recently, remote orchestra conducting has become a practical reality. Synchronization of loop-based systems in commercial sequencer software appeared in the late 1990s with the ResRocket system, while research systems like PeerSynth and SoundWire have integrated network latency in sound synthesis.

Networks have also become an integral part of the computer music instrument, with remote ensemble performance becoming not a replacement for single-site performance but a distinct mode of play that took on its own musical properties, notably in Jordà's FMOL (Faust Music On Line). The accessible and democratized nature of the Internet resulted in musicians and researchers creating public participation systems that incorporated elements of networked ensemble play in musical activities aimed at the layperson. This resulted in attempts to create commercial software and in public exhibition installation works such as Barbosa's "Public Sound Objects."

15. MOBILE AND GPS-BASED INSTRUMENTS

As musicians looked toward advances in new sensor systems, location tracking in outdoor space by means of the global positioning system (GPS) entered the instrumentarium of composers and artists. While GPS had been available to civilians since the late 1980s, military scrambling of the signal via selective availability (SA) deliberately reduced distance resolution, making it unuseful for artistic purposes. The opening up of direct non-SA satellite signals to the general populace in the Clinton administration of the late 1990s spawned the boom of consumer satellite navigation systems. This was seized on by artists, who founded the

Locative Media art movement in the early 2000s; direct high-resolution tracing of the geography of human movement became the material of mixed-media artworks. In the music realm, this has borne a family of location-based musical works. The specific temporal requirements of music place advanced demands on GPS technology. This has been articulated through either artistic use of errors in the signal or research efforts that have made contributions to development in technical fields.

While location-tracking techniques such as GPS have inspired and facilitated artists' works, the relationship between urban space and sound pre-dates the arrival of digital technologies. Artists such as Janet Cardiff created the notion of sound walks; a prescribed path through urban space was accompanied by soundscape and narrative. This has spawned a series of commercial applications in the area of audio guides, and the increasing memory capacity of personal music players, networked capabilities of mobile telephones, in conjunction with the location awareness afforded by GPS allowed such systems, artistic or commercial, to become at once increasingly sophisticated and part of public consciousness.

While these early works relied on prerecorded audio content, the potential of topological movement-generating music became of interest to composers. I worked with Ali Momeni and visual artist Petra Gemeinboeck in 2006 to translate notions from locative media to create a musical work, Net_Dérive, that used mobile digital devices to realize a gamelike exploration of the city in a fashion inspired by the Dérive of the radical 1960s art movement, the Situationist International. In Net_Dérive, a scarflike wearable computing harness houses two mobile phones and a GPS unit— one phone acting as a sound/image capture device and the other a mobile network connected rendering device. An abstract soundscape is generated serverside based on latitude/longitude data from the location of a group of users. A constant polyrhythm shifts based on the relative proximity of the different participants, while specific coordinates are programmed to trigger voice commands instructing the person to move in certain directions. This generated soundscape is streamed over mobile broadband Universal Mobile Telecommunications System (UMTS, or 3G) networks back to each of the participant's rendering device and is heard over headphones, accompanying the person's meandering walk through a city neighborhood.

Yolande Harris, in her series of GPS music pieces, questions the assumptions of locative media, notably those of permanent movement, networked connectivity, and participative collective action. In "Taking Soundings," she challenges the notion of stasis by placing a GPS unit in a fixed place. Noise in the GPS signal creates a jittery trace that is far from stationary. Harris sonifies this unstable information, poetically creating the sound of a single location on earth. "Sun Run Sun" is for single users walking with a purpose-built single-board computer with sound synthesis and location-tracking capabilities. A fixed point version of the Pure Data graphical music programming environment runs a generative sine wave patch on a single-board computer system, Satellite Sounders, built by Sukandar Kartadinata. Parsing of GPS data creates parameters mapped to synthesis parameters. This creates a direct yet complex relationship between location and the resulting sound, by which returning to a prior location may drive synthesis parameters similarly but does not necessarily reproduce the exact same sound.

Art Clay in "China Gates" uses secondary information in the GPS format, that of the synch pulse, to drive the timing of a distributed percussion performance. The GPS pulse becomes a metronome and conductor, creating a flashing pulse that directs percussionists to hit a gong they are carrying outdoors. A score directs their position, which in turn modulates the pulsing frequency, creating a slowly shifting acoustic ostinato of an ensemble of percussionists outside of visual contact in outdoor space.

Despite the relatively high accuracy of non-SA GPS, the temporal resolution (or sampling period) of commercial GPS units at the time of writing was about 0.5 s, making it a relatively coarse musical control signal. Research projects of Settel at the Société des Arts Technologiques (SAT) and McGill University in Montreal have used the recent arrival of ultra-high-resolution GPS devices to create responsive instruments that have the temporal resolution more commonly associated with sensor-based instruments and reactivity necessary for gestural music performance. Better location resolution and higher sampling rates allow subtle movements orientation, and small bodily variation in place to be detected to modulate musical processes, including the Audioscape virtual soundscape software.

Finally, exploiting mobile telephone's speakerphone capabilities without location sensing, two composers have created forms of acoustical ensemble for mobile phones. Greg Schiemer in his work "Mandala" arranges three performers in resonant outdoor spaces swinging mobile phones around on a string. Each phone emits a series of sine tones, and the swinging causes Doppler effects, creating shifting frequency sweeps among the three phones. Wang similarly fashioned a mobile phone orchestra, creating a conducted score in which simultaneous sounding of a group of mobile phones create cancellation and reinforcement effects, resulting in an acoustic dynamic beyond the capabilities of any single phone's speaker. Careful tuning of frequencies creates sum and difference tones that extend the frequency range of the resulting music beyond the range of the small speakers by the effect of implied fundamental.

16. CONCLUSION

Since the advent of electricity, musicians, composers, and artists have sought to tap the creative musical potential of new technologies. Inspired by the communicative possibilities afforded first by electromagnetic waves and analog circuitry and later by digital systems and networks, they seized the power of electrical, electronic, and computer technology to create expressive systems that could be considered musical instruments. The rich tradition and articulative depth of acoustical instruments set a high standard to try to match. In this way, musicians bring with them high expectations in the musical exploitation of any given technology. The responsiveness, resolution, and finesse of a technology translate to the often-elusive musical "feel" that is central to the successful deployment of an instrument in a performative context. This places demands on technology systems that, if solved, often contribute to engineering advances. In this way, music remains, as it always has been, the field of creative practice that directly addresses technique—whether the acoustical phenomenon of the natural overtone series or of network transmission latency.

The notion of the musical instrument, then, is a useful metaphor that defines creative contexts for technology, delineates demanding usage scenarios, and ties innovation to artistic tradition. This metaphor is not a comparative abstraction but a working model with which musicians have created functional systems and produced lasting artworks. Early in the 20th century, electrostatic and electromagnetic field perturbations captured performer gesture with the theremin and related instruments. Electrical systems could be used to extend existing instruments, in the 1950s with the electric guitar and in the 1990s with hyperinstruments.

Musicians have the uncanny ability to appropriate and repurpose machinery and technology for expressive musical ends. This could mean taking an apparatus destined for playing back recorded music, such as the turntable, and making it an expressive instrument. This also meant taking fundamental nonmusical technologies, such as VR systems, to create live, performable instruments. From electrostatic fields to infrared beams, ultrasound sensors to bend and pressure sensors, any sensing device that could translate real-world phenomena into electrical signals was ripe material for musical instrument building in the NIME tradition. Sensing could be extremely intimate, looking at physiological effects of the performer's own body such as with bioelectrical sensors, or it could be completely external to the performer, such as with GPS signals, and still be compellingly musical and ultimately social.

With the advancement of technology come not only an extension of musical tradition, but also a questioning of it. While this chapter does not cover phenomena such as the electroacoustic studio or file-sharing technologies that have the disruptive power to put in question traditional musical roles of authorship and performance, it does look at the ways in which sensors, open-ended architectures, and programmable systems have extended the notion and very definition of the term *instrument*. An instrument could be a piece of hardware or a software program but could also be a reconfigurable hardware/software system. The composition could be specifically built into a system as much as a single instrument could execute a family of works. By questioning and extending traditions of the instrument, some of the basic tenets of musical instrumentality come to light—the ability for an instrument to enter into different contexts and retain its musical identity.

One of the clearest ways in which musical instruments change contexts is in different ensemble frameworks. Moving from a solo situation through chamber ensembles to orchestras places different performative and stylistic demands on an instrument. The performer's ability to navigate these different contexts with a given instrument is a testament to that instrument's richness. Technology musicians have taken up this call with their electronic and digital instruments, creating different groups, bands, and ensembles. This has taken on different forms—be it the integration of an instrument like the Ondes Martenot into the classical orchestra or Sensorband creating a sensor-instrument family of instruments on the chamber music model. Notions of interaction and collaborative systems from research fields like HCI have informed the conception and realization of shared instruments like the reacTable and other instruments using the tabletop metaphor. And, high-speed computer networks have been used not only to study ensemble performance at a distance but also to create entirely new shared musical experiences.

Music has always been a technical art, and electronic and computer music are no exception. While paradigm shifts that accompany new technologies create frontiers that redefine the artistic process, musical traditions are useful points of departure that help us to question assumptions, extend practice, and push the envelope of what is musically possible with technology. The instrument and the ensemble are two such extensible traditions. They not only extend romantic notions of the virtuoso to contemporary technological contexts but also extend musical contexts of performance to include participation and collective public action. In this way, musicians have always brought insight into the artistic application of electrical, electronics, and communications technologies. This tradition will continue to give rise to new musical instruments and musical styles.

BIBLIOGRAPHY

Attali, J. 1985. *Noise: The Political Economy of Music*, trans. Brian Massumi. Minneapolis: University of Minnesota Press.

Bailey, D. 1993 (originally published in 1980). *Improvisation: Its Nature and Practice in Music*. New York: Da Capo Press.

Barbosa, A. 2008. *Displaced Soundscapes*. Saarbrücken: VDM Verlag Dr. Müller.

Baudrillard, J. 1983. *Simulations (Foreign Agents)*. New York: Semiotext(e).

Chadabe, J. 1996. *Electric Sound: The Past and Promise of Electronic Music*. Upper Saddle River, NJ: Prentice Hall.

Chafe, C., and M. Gurevich. 2004. Network time delay and ensemble accuracy: effects of latency, asymmetry. In *Proceedings of the AES 117th Conference*. San Francisco: AES.

Clay, A. 2008. Inventing malleable scores: From paper to screen based scores. In *Transdisciplinary Digital Art: Sound, Vision and the New Screen*, ed. R. Adams, S. Gibson, and S. M. Arisona. New York: Springer.

Collins, N. 2006. *Handmade Electronic Music: The Art of Hardware Hacking*. New York: Routledge. http://www.nicolascollins.com/trombone_propelled_electronics.htm, accessed August 8, 2008.

de Laubier, S. 1998. The meta-instrument. *Computer Music Journal* 22(1): 25–29.

Desain, P., A. M. G. Hupse, M. G. J. Kallenberg, B. J. de Kruif, and R. S. Schaefer. 2006. Brain-computer interfacing using frequency tagged stimuli. In *Proceedings of the 3rd*

International Brain-Computer Interface Workshop and Training Course 2006, ed.
   G. R. Müller-Putz, C. Brunner, R. Leeb, R. Scherer, A. Schlögl, S. Wriessnegger, and
   G. Pfurtscheller. Graz, Austria: Verlag der TU Graz.
Freed, A., R. Avizienis, and M. Wright. Beyond 0-5V: Expanding Sensor Integration
   Architectures. In *Conference on New Interfaces for Musical Expression (NIME-06)*. Paris.
Glinsky, A. 2000. *Theremin: Ether Music and Espionage*. Chicago: University of Illinois Press.
Harris, Y. 2007. Taking soundings: Investigating coastal navigations and orientations in
   sound. In *Proceedings of the 4th Mobile Music Workshop*. Amsterdam.
Jordà, S. 2002. FMOL: Toward user-friendly, sophisticated new musical instruments.
   Computer Music Journal 26(3): 23–39.
Jordà, S., G. Geiger, M. Alonso, and M. Kaltenbrunner. 2007. The reacTable: Exploring the
   synergy between live music performance and tabletop tangible interfaces. In
   *Proceedings of the 1st International Conference on Tangible and Embedded Interaction
   2007*, pp. 139–146.
Kahn, D. 2001. *Noise, Water, Meat: A History of Sound in the Arts*. Cambridge: MIT Press.
Kahn, D., and G. Whitehead, eds. 1994. *Wireless Imagination: Sound, Radio, and the
   Avant-Garde*. Cambridge: MIT Press.
Kartadinata, S. 2006. The gluion: Advantages of an FPGA-based sensor interface. In
   Conference on New Interfaces for Musical Expression (NIME-06). Paris: NIME.
Kirisits, N., F. Behrendt, L. Gaye, and A. Tanaka. 2008. *Creative Interactions: The Mobile
   Music Workshops 2004–2008*. Di'Angewandte, Vienna.
Knapp, R. B., and H. Lusted. 1996. Controlling computers with neural signals. *Scientific
   American* 275(4): 82–87.
Lucier, A. 1995. *Reflections: Interviews, Scores, Writings*. Köln, Germany: MusikTexte.
Machover, T. "Hyperinstruments." http://opera.media.mit.edu/projects/hyperinstruments.
   html, accessed March 30, 2009.
Manning, P. 2004. *Electronic and Computer Music*. Oxford: Oxford University Press.
Miranda, E. R. 2006. Brain-computer music interface for composition and performance.
   International Journal on Disability and Human Development 5(2): 119–125.
Nakra, T. M. 2000. "Inside the conductor's jacket, analysis interpretation and musical
   synthesis of expressive gesture." Ph.D. thesis, MIT. http://hdl.handle.net/1721.1/9165,
   accessed March 30, 2009.
New Interfaces for Musical Expression (NIME). http://www.nime.org, accessed March 30,
   2009.
Rosenboom, D. 1976. *Biofeedback and the Arts: Results of Early Experiments*. Vancouver:
   Aesthetic Research Centre of Canada.
Rowe, R. 2004. *Machine Musicianship*. Cambridge: MIT Press.
Rowe, R. 2005. Real time and unreal time: Expression in distributed performance. *Journal of
   New Music Research* 34(1): 87–96.
Schaeffer, P. 2002. *Traité des objets musicaux*. Paris: Seuil Editions.
Schiemer, G. 2007. Pocket Gamelan: playing Mandala 6: a demonstration. In *Proceedings of
   the 9th International Conference on Human Computer Interaction with Mobile Devices
   and Services: MOBILEHCI 07*. New York: ACM, pp. 231–232.
Smith, H., and R. T. Dean 1997. *Improvisation, Hypermedia and the Arts since 1945*.
   Amsterdam: Harwood Academic.
Stelkens, J. 2003. peerSynth—A P2P multi-user software synthesizer with new techniques
   for integrating latency in real time collaboration. In *Proceedings of the ICMC Singapore*.
   USA: International Computer Music Association.

Tanaka, A. 2000. Musical performance practice on sensor-based instruments. In *Trends in Gestural Control of Music*, ed. M. Wanderley and M. Battier. Paris: IRCAM, pp. 389–405.

Tanaka, A. 2004. Von Telepräsenz zu Co-Erfahrung: Ein Jahrzehnt Netzwerkmusik (From telepresence to co-experience: A decade of network music). In *Neue Zeitschrift für Musik*, ed. G. Föllmer. Mainz: Schott Musik International.

Tanaka, A. 2008. Visceral mobile music systems. In *Transdisciplinary Digital Art: Sound, Vision and the New Screen*, ed. R. Adams, S. Gibson, and M. S. Arisona. New York: Springer.

Tanaka, A., and P. Gemeinboeck. 2008. "Net_Dérive: Conceiving and producing a locative media artwork." In *Mobile Technologies: From Telecommunications to Media*, ed. G. Goggin and L. Hjorth. New York: Routledge.

Xu, A., W. Woszczyk, Z. Settel, B. Pennycook, R. Rowe, P. Galanter, J. Bary, G. Martin, J. Corey, and J. R. Cooperstock. 2000. Real-time streaming of multichannel audio data over Internet. *Journal of the Audio Engineering Society* 48: 1–22.

Wang, G., G. Essland, and H. Pentinnen. 2008 MoPhO: Do mobile phones dreams of electric orchestras? In *Proceedings of the International Computer Music Conference*. Belfast.

Winkler, T. 1998. *Composing Interactive Music: Techniques and Ideas Using Max*. Cambridge: MIT Press.

Wozniewski, M., N. Bouillot, Z. Settel, and J. R. Cooperstock. 2008. An augmented reality framework for wireless mobile performance. In *Proceedings of the 5th Mobile Music Workshop, May 13–15*. Vienna, Austria.

Zimmermann, R., E. Chew, S. A. Ay, and M. Pawar. Forthcoming. Distributed musical performances: Architecture and stream management. *ACM Transactions on Multimedia Computing Communications and Applications*.

CHAPTER 13

SPATIALIZATION AND COMPUTER MUSIC

PETER LENNOX

THIS chapter is about the possibility of a new kind of music; computer-managed signal processing offers unprecedented possibilities in the control of sound fields, and the promise of three-dimensional music is on the horizon. A paradigm shift is under way; as technological constraints are rolled back, so must conceptual constraints be reevaluated. Some of these are concerned with what spatiality actually *is*. Although we think of three-dimensional Euclidean space, it is by no means clear that this is anything other than a conceptual latecomer (however useful). In a similar vein, our thinking may well be colored by visual metaphors; we speak of auditory images having apparent source width and focus. Consider: if we had evolved without vision, would we *ever* have developed concepts of perfect forms such as triangles, exact circles, precise shapes, and completely straight lines? Auditory spatial perception tends to suffer in direct comparison with vision, but it may be that we are comparing apples and oranges, and that spatiality in audition is fundamentally different in several important respects. New musical metaphors can illuminate these, and the control possibilities offered by digital audio are at the forefront of these experiments.

> Spatial audio and especially spatial audio for electroacoustic music is a domain inspired by but not limited to experiences in the natural world. Then too, electroacoustic music'capacity to manipulate audio signals creates a context in which there can be uniquely complex interactions between spatial hearing and other domains of perception and cognition. This is especially true when

electroacoustic composers play with the fundamentals of spatial organization in music by manipulating perceptual grouping and violating spatial schemata. Spatial audio, and especially spatial audio for electroacoustic music, is an artistic domain that often throws the spatial conventions of the natural world into relief by distorting or violating them. In order to appreciate the crisscrossing of boundaries and conventions in this artistic interplay, our concepts and terminology should be in good alignment with the listener'perceptual and cognitive processes. (Kendall and Ardila 2008, p. 126)

1. SPATIAL PERCEPTION OF REAL AND ARTIFICIAL SOUND

Information resides in structure, in this case, *audible* structure. The question is whether finer control of the structure that appeals to auditory spatial perception can be used in conjunction with the structural parameters of music: is spatial music likely to be more meaningful? We know from experience that perception is finely attuned to audible spatial structure. We can hear nuances that inform us of room height, size, emptiness or cluttered-ness, smooth-and-hardness or soft-and-irregular-ness. We can hear whether a space is fully enclosed, has *some* openings into an adjacent space (windows or doorways), or is just partially enclosed (between two buildings, for instance). We can (roughly) tell where we are in the space—in the middle, at the edge, entering or leaving. We can hear about the objects in our space—some because they are large enough to reflect, absorb, or occlude sound and some because they are actual sound sources. In the last case, we hear something of what *kind* of object: large or small, heavy or light, some details of structure (i.e., material consistency such as steel or wood, hollowness, and so on). We hear about the processes involved in their production of sound: bouncing, scraping, breaking (see Warren and Verbrugge 1984). We even perceive whether a source is *inanimate*, simply moved by external forces such as wind, *mechanical* (moved by internal forces but automatically), or *animate* It is probably important to distinguish these rapidly. We also hear where sources *are*and their movement through the shared space toward or away from us, along with interactions such as passing behind an obstacle, close to an opening or large reflective wall. From all these items, we gain sophisticated knowledge of the world, circumnavigating pitfalls and obstacles, finding opportunities and estimating the intentions of others.

How accurately we hear all these items is not clear since hearing in real environments is normally accompanied by other senses; perception is inherently multimodal. Likewise, *how* we make sense of audible information is a matter of scientific conjecture, and *perception* refers to the most sophisticated information processing known. But, the acoustic structure of the world about us is presented in the structure of the sound fields present at our two-eared hearing *system*, with pickups (eardrums) that are separated by an obstacle (the head) and a distance of approximately 170 mm. These two facts taken together mean that the wavefronts from a source that is not equidistant from the ears (i.e., not directly in front, behind, above, or below) are differentially affected by the system (because path length from source to each ear differs very slightly), so that the signals at the eardrums are similar but not identical. These *interaural differences* provide the basis for spatial sound systems.

In the laboratory, it is convention to refer to azimuth and elevation when speaking of spatial hearing. These terms are head-centric, and if the head is held level, so that the ears are equal distance from the ground and the person is facing the horizon, the *azimuth* exactly coincides with "horizontal"—the plane perpendicular to gravity. *Elevation*, in the same case, describes the variation away from that plane. Hence, 0 degrees azimuth and elevation would be a point exactly ahead of the person'nose. If elevation was +45 degrees elevation, the target would be up, forward and if −45 degrees, down, forward.

Different spatial hearing mechanisms are involved for azimuth and elevation; in the example, there are no interaural differences that could distinguish the three target positions described. Elevation perception is instead largely due to the pinnae (the external parts of the ear, which produce a direction-dependent filtering consisting of peaks and troughs imposed on the frequency envelope of the incoming signal) effects, which are primarily operant on high frequencies from about 1.5 kHz (rather weakly) up to about 16 kHz. It is often thought that perception in elevation is less robust than in azimuth, but this would only be true if we could not tilt our heads; in the real world, we actually rarely listen with our azimuth exactly coincident with the external horizontal plane. So, although elevation perception in the laboratory is solely due to the pinnae, perception in the vertical plane in the real world can utilize interaural differences. In addition, head movement and perceiver movement can improve the robustness of spatial hearing.

2. The Possibility of a Kind of Music That One Could Actually Be Inside

One can listen to an excellent mono recording and hear a great deal of spatiality in it, but it is like listening through a window: you do not feel quite immersed in the recorded environment. In this sense, the recording is not your whole environment; it is an item *in* my environment.

One could take a piece of music and arrange it, spatially, with the listener surrounded by the musical elements. Instead of the convention of the listener sitting passively facing a sound stage, one would have music that a listener could *get inside*, even explore, be an active participant rather than recipient.

The key difference, though, is that early acoustic music may well have been spatially complex due to the stochastic nature of the intricate room reflections, but its spatiality was not particularly controllable. It is precisely this aspect that computer music *should* be able to address; however, there is a trade-off between complexity and control—increased control generally means curtailed complexity (and vice versa).

From a composer'viewpoint, it would seem obvious that a prerequisite for imagining and constructing spatial music would be the ability to place any sound source in a precise location. It follows that precise control of trajectories would be the next step, perhaps followed by control of the size (and shape?) of the virtual space depicted by our artificial sound field.

To have precise control of a given listening environment, one would have to treat each point in that space as an addressable "sound pixel"; by specifying the contents of each pixel, we could build up complex sound imagery (whether literal or impressionistic). However, controlling hundreds of thousands of loudspeakers using analog methods was impractical. Fortunately, the principle of "phantom imaging," the perceptual illusion of one or more sources in the space between two loudspeakers (the basis of stereophonic sound) can efficiently reduce the numbers used. Careful control of the relative amplitudes of the loudspeaker signal feeds can be equivalent to control of the position of an interspeaker phantom image, achieved because the interaural differences are similar (not identical) to those that would be occasioned by a real source.

In addition to physical constraints, there are the conceptual ones, inherited from previous situations. Music is what it *is* partly because of what it *was*; it is not *very* spatial because it could not be in the past (many acoustic instruments are cumbersome, and musicians had to hear each other to play together, so a static ensemble was convenient). Likewise, engineering methods and tools reflect inherited musical traditions. Conventional musical notation systems describe notes, sequences, amplitudes, durations, rhythms, speed, but not *spatiality*. Traditionally, spatiality has played a minor role in musical thinking, and concepts of musical spatiality are rudimentary.

3. Spatiality: Compositional Parameter or Engineering Concern?

Can spatiality be added on, or should it be intrinsic? Is spatiality simply titillation for the senses but without deep compositional meaning? Or, can it be a fundamental musical parameter? Obviously, in real environments, for something to *be* a "thing," it must be *somewhere*, and it must have *extensity*—there are no point sources in nature and no free-field conditions; these are merely convenient engineering concepts: "Extensity, being an entirely peculiar kind of feeling inde-scribable except in terms of itself, and inseparable in actual experience from some sensational quality which it must accompany, can itself receive no other name than that of *sensational element*" (James 1890b). We can see how this kind of music leads to the early spatial sound system: stereo. The phantom image is only properly displayed when the listener sits in the correct spot, equidistant from the speakers and facing them. This is very like the concert hall situation; indeed, we refer to the "stereo soundstage."

This brings us back to the kinds of concepts of "space" that can be incorporated into the inherited music-listening paradigm. If the listener is static and passive, then of course spatiality means the way we can arrange sources around that listener—in what *direction* and at what *distance*. This is why "surround sound" is often thought synonymous with "spatial sound" or even "3-D (three-dimensional) sound." I call this the "direction-is-space fallacy" simply to highlight that we can have more spatiality if we reconsider how spatial perception might have evolved in real environments rather than abstract spaces.

Rather than simply distributing musical sources in a circle around the listener (a job for straightforward engineering controls), composers could now incorporate spatial meaning into the lexicon of musical meanings they have traditionally employed. The pressing questions are, What *are* these "spatial meanings"? and How can we control them? As Kendall and Ardila (2008) implied, we do not want to simply copy the real world; we want to build on it. But, we do want to use everything we can of what we know about human spatial perception, how it works in different contexts, why it works, and so on. It is certainly about a great deal more than the receipt of signals.

A. Spatial Meaning and Auditory Displays: The Encode-Decode Chain

It is useful to consider the problems of maintaining veridicality in spatial audio production in terms of encoding and decoding through successive systemic stages. The composer tries to inject meaning at one end of the chain, hoping that enough of it will survive the successive steps for the perceiver to "get it." More layers produce more opportunities for *meanings* to be scrambled (fig. 13.1).

Although engineers traditionally concern themselves with signal qualities, what they are conveying are *patterns*; they are de facto responsible for capturing, storing, and transmitting *meanings*.

Domestic Stereo: Spatial Meanings in Terms of Perceptual Separability by Direction Distance and Size

The most familiar spatial sound system is two-speaker stereo. This does not model the acoustic fields of a whole environment but the effects such an environment would have on the ear signals of a listener in a known position; it is a point rather

"Meanings"

encode

Spatial audio capture and/or synthesis system

encode

Multi-channel storage and transmission system

decode

N-speaker sound field projection system

encode

Spatial audio sensory apparatus

Perception

Figure 13.1 From meanings to perception: the encode-decode chain in spatialized audio.

than a volume solution. The aim of any panning method is to coherently and predictably control perception of (phantom) source direction though interaural differences.

Stereo does not convey the entire spatial characteristics of whole environments but a limited range of items (musical or other) depicted as "audio images" across a bounded soundstage. So, items could be perceived as *separate*, which might be musically useful. For instance, several singers could (using pan-pot techniques to cause specific sets of interaural differences for each) be spatially distinguished by their left-right separation. This *separateness* reinforces the impression that they are "real" objects (which naturally cannot spatially coincide).

To a lesser extent, the perceptual impression of *range* (distance between source image and listener; distinct from *distance* between items in the environment) can be manipulated by altering the dry-reverb (or direct-to-indirect signal) *ratio* or *balance* using artificial reverberation. So, some images can appear to be beyond the line between the two speakers, adding the illusion of depth of field; Rumsey (2002) called this *ensemble depth* This can be metaphorically mapped to foreground-background separation so that (for instance) some voices can be "lead" and some "backing." In popular music engineering, this is further emphasized by using *aural excitation* (the addition of high-frequency harmonics) on foreground items and dynamic range compression on backing items, mimicking and exaggerating the physics of real audible environments. This "nearer than/further than" axis is at least as impressive as the left-right axis.

Using dynamic combinations of panning, alteration of dry-reverb balance, change in amplitude, and filtering, one can give the impression that some items in the soundstage are moving and others not. So, additional layers of meaning can be supported; some items can "bounce" across the stage ("ping-pong effects"), others can come from *over there* to *here*, and some can *depart*.

Implicit in producing a soundstage that contains separate images is the fact that we have produced a slightly simplified environment that is rather like the proscenium arch presentation of the theater. The stage depth is, admittedly, illusory and rather vague. It does not really have heterogeneous height, and its strong point—the left-right axis—is limited to the 60-degree (subtended angle at the listener position) presentation. Nevertheless, using artificial reverberation, it is possible to give the impression of listening into a large or small, enclosed or open space containing several spatially separated images that can interact with each other and with the background place. This is a remarkable range of spatial parameters that can be combined in various ways to bring structural characteristics similar to those in real environments into music—all using just two loudspeakers.

Surround Sound Display Technologies

Although the real world audibly surrounds one, this is not to say that surrounding the listener with sound is the *same* as real spatiality. A blanket multichannel of mono sound is spatially homogeneous and uninformative; a heterogeneous but random sound field is barely more informative.

Without wishing to perpetuate the direction-is-space fallacy, it seems reasonable (given our music heritage) that the principle of stereo can be extended to surround the notional listener.

This flaw has been carried over into Dolby 5.1; although now no longer a square layout, and the stereo stage at the front has been corrected, imagery elsewhere is vague. Strictly, this is hardly a fair criticism; the system is not supposed to have similar directional resolution in every direction. Basically, it should be thought of as a stereo system plus a center, dialogue channel, plus two ambience channels (left surround and right surround). Looked at that way, it does also bring a pair of extra image positions—at the surround speakers—and can depict a sense of rapid movement of images from the front stage to one side or the other. But, it was designed simply to add a little bit of immersiveness to an audiovisual experience in which the visual element is very strictly limited to the same kind of proscenium arch presentation on which stereo was predicated. Nevertheless, the system'ubiquity means that composers and engineers will naturally try to push the technological boundaries.

Legacy Metaphors: Pan Pots, Reverbs, and Surround Sound

Since these are early days for what could be described as *deliberately* spatial music, it is hardly surprising that tools are underdeveloped. There is a veritable "chicken-and-egg" problem here. Equipment designers and engineers are hardly likely to produce spatial manipulators that are not asked for by composers and musicians. Composers are not likely to compose pieces that cannot be performed and heard. The public is highly unlikely to clamor for a musical form that they have never heard.

Consequently, progress relies on the misuse of preexisting devices and metaphors. Chiefly, this means the ubiquitous panning methods that have worked well in the stereo paradigm; however, simply surrounding the listener with stereo fields and addressing them through panning techniques works less well perceptually (as in the discussion on image separation above). More robust panning laws utilize more speakers simultaneously, and digital techniques can utilize phase and amplitude in frequency-dependent ways; nevertheless, panning simulates direction only. Using it to simulate movement results in objects moving in circles around the listener, as though on the end of virtual string. A trajectory control for surround listening should do more; bodies should be able to move in straight lines, for instance.

Another missing ingredient is that when a corporeal object-as-sound-source moves in the real world, it does more than alter direction in relation to the listener; it *interacts* with the local physical features. This means the sounds of locomotion, coming into direct contact with other material objects and surfaces. It also means approaching and passing surfaces, resulting in audible structure; I call this *ambience labeling information* (which simply means the effect of an environment on the signal content from a sound source). In other words, one does not just hear a source; one hears its spatial relationships with environmental features around it. I can hear a motorbike passing a fence, through a tunnel, behind a large building, and out into the open even when I do not know exactly *where* it is. I can tell roughly how fast it is traveling, but not from the change in perceived direction (from me). Conventional position controls do not manage this useful information, which might be why composers are sometimes frustrated that they have planned an elegant and complex spatial trajectory for a virtual sound object, yet the results sound slightly vague. In the real world, sounds do not move, physical objects do. We do not have to be too literal about this, trying to replicate the complexity of these interactions. Rather, *some* salient cues can be selected to make position and movement slightly more apprehensible. The architect and composer Jan Jacob Hoffman (whose compositions sound like imaginary material structures, creaking and under tension) does this. Entirely constructed in Csound, his objects are given some almost tangibility by varying the quality of a halo of early reflections that cluster round them. His periphonic Ambisonic (discussed in greater detail in the section on new encoding strategies, technologies, and computer music) synthesized places have a real feel to them (see Hoffman 2001).

To cope with this poor signal-to-noise ratio, complex perceptual mechanisms have evolved, referred to collectively as *precedence effects* (for a review, see Litovsky et al. 1999) These vital cognitive mechanisms can separate *most* direct from *less*-direct signals, detect the directional differences, partially suppress the perceived level and directionality of the indirect (or less-direct) ones, and so improve signal detection (including direction and distance detection). All these remarkable feats are achieved in real time, and no one has (so far) succeeded in approaching similar performance algorithmically. Natural reverberation is informative about environment characteristics, and it tells us how near/far a source of interest is, sometimes how near the source is to the boundaries, even whether that source has turned to face us or away from us. Conversations with visually impaired but auditorily proficient individuals revealed that reflected audible energy offers a great deal of information that can be used in navigation. Clearly, artificial reverberation is not nearly so informative and subtle; use of artificial reverberation evolved within the stereo paradigm, and competent surround reverbs are rare. Since very few spatial sound systems use height information, reverbs featuring the vertical dimension are exceedingly rare.

Indeed, the "up-down" dimension has been significantly neglected in artificial spatial sound for various reasons. One reason for ignoring the up-down dimension could be that we simply do not perceive as well in this axis; there is no reason to assume that our spatial perceptual abilities are similar in every direction. Perhaps acuity in the horizontal is more important because most threats occur at ground level? I think we can discount this simply because of the observation that we can tilt our heads; if an interesting target source attracts attention, we can face upward. It could just be that there is actually less information to be had in the vertical dimension, so that the sound field in this region tends to be less structured; there are, after all, fewer occluding objects, surfaces, early reflections in this direction—perhaps there is less for the hearing system to use?

To Sum Up Legacy Issues

Conceptual constraints affect existing technologies: distribution formats, domestic equipment, conservative layouts. What composers would *like* to be able to do with spatial sound is limited by how it will be presented to the listener. At the moment, distribution formats are the domain of interested distributors. It is only recently that software such as QuickTime and Windows Media Player has been adapted to allow online distribution of multichannel material, and many more channels will be needed to encapsulate the kinds of spatiality envisaged here. As the distribution model of the music industry evolves, the pace of change of distribution of spatial music is likely to quicken. Multichannel support in many professional audio systems is limited—sometimes to working with stereo pairs, at best to 5.1 surround. It is especially significant that encoding spatiality is directly tied to the audio display characteristics; in other words, a composer must directly manage loud-speaker signal feeds, an archaic limitation that is beginning to change (see next section).

We have as our concepts for musical spatiality some notions of "sources-in-positions" (or at least, of directionalizing sources with a bit of reverb to simulate distance) and some notions of background "sound-of-place." We have a few rather basic controls aimed at manipulating these and rudimentary "surround sound systems" that can display the results.

We do *not* have control (or the capacity to display, yet) of attributes such as virtual objects' sizes, orientation, and precise position within a virtual location. We also do not have particularly good audible depiction of virtual places—with a wall over there, a door opening here, the ceiling so high, the floor cluttered with furniture, and so on. These attributes are all audible in the real world, and we should be able to have them in our artificial one.

Finally, the kind of *ambulant, active* listening that we can do in the real world, where we can *investigate* an interesting item by moving toward and around it, is not facilitated by domestic surround sound. It is a reasonable argument that this kind of listening is perhaps inappropriate for any music for which the listener should be a passive receiver. It remains to be discovered whether anyone would actually want "explorable music."

B. New Encoding Strategies, Technologies, and Computer Music: Controllability and New Metaphors

Domestic-size spatial sounds really "scale up" to large listening spaces, so there is traditionally less reliance on consumer formats for concert situations. Diffusion methods (albeit often using stereo source material) aimed at live control of multi-speaker setups have been usual in electroacoustic circles for some years. However, the systems used are installation specific, and the composer is still managing speaker feeds. Importantly, this music often has little emphasis on providing images of *real* objects, so the need for accurate control of the perceptible attributes of phantom images is lessened. It would be nice to retain the option of "image management," however.

Ironically, it may be domestic technologies that come to the rescue. Jean-Marc Jot of Creative Audio proposed the principle of "speaker layout agnosticism" (2008) by which management of the *specific* speaker layout is dealt with invisibly by the sound card. This would allow sound designers, without knowing the details of the actual target system, to define spatial concerns. These will be translated at the point of performance by the local machine that *does* "know" what layout is available. A complex composition could automatically be downmixed to a domestic system, yet still contain complex spatiality when listened to on a large array.

Jot predicted that loudspeaker layout agnosticism will eventually be achieved via scene description methods, which makes good sense. Instead of using many full audio-bandwidth channels to code spatiality (for which interchannel relationships must be very carefully treated), signal content and spatial designation data can be stored and transmitted separately and the sound field reconstituted at the point of listening.

It is important to realize that the B-format signals are *not* loudspeaker feeds; these must be supplied by a loudspeaker decoder that takes in the spatial representation signals and is programmed (or constructed, in analog terms) to supply the desired number of loudspeaker feeds. It is useful that Ambisonics is hierarchical, so high-order material can be listened to on a low-order decoder and vice versa, although always the spatial resolution is of the lower order employed. Similarly, if one has material that is periphonically encoded, this can still be listened to in a horizontal-only setup but simply with the loss of elevation information.

The really interesting point is that the number of channels used to carry the directional information determines a *minimum* but not a *maximum* number of loudspeakers. So, for very large listening areas, the four-channel B-format feeds a decoder that can be designed to supply signals for a large number of individually driven loudspeakers, say thirty-two (although not simply randomly placed). If second-order decoder and signals were to be used in the same layout, then the directionality is sharper, especially for off-center listeners. A similar increment is to be had by going up to third order. A particular advantage is that, with suitable equipment, orders can be combined. This means that the particularly impressive whole-ambience recordings captured by the aforementioned first-order B-format microphones can be combined with the much more directionally precise (if not quite as realistic) sources that are feasible through synthesis of higher-order encodings. This can engender perceptions of background and foreground, making the synthesized material more corporeal.

Ambisonics can be thought of as using *pixels*, so that a given audio image is produced by many loudspeakers in concert, with their combined wavefronts resembling those that would be generated by a real source in the desired direction. Consequently, the system has the advantage of not sounding "speakerish," and images do seem to float in midair. It is still a point source solution (i.e., predicated on a sweet spot in the center), and off-center listeners do not quite receive the full spatial impression, but progressively higher orders deliver progressively improved results to larger numbers of off-center listeners.

Today, of course, many of these obstacles have simply evaporated, and Ambisonics is comparatively easy to manage using domestic equipment; it may be an idea whose time has come. An upcoming generation of engineers, musicians, and composers is more comfortable with computers and different ways of working; *better* surround sound is an attainable goal.

Many low-cost solutions, such as Reaper and AudioMulch, are innovative with respect to multichannel support. As they will host Steinberg'Virtual Studio Technology (VST) effects plug-ins (many of which are freely downloadable), spatial audio experimentation is accelerating.[1]

There are quite a few examples of "Ambisonics inside," for which the consumer does not know the internal workings are Ambisonic. Some 5.1 surround music releases consist of Ambisonics decoded to the familiar 5.1 layout (e.g., surround releases by Dallas Masters, 2001). The recent release for the Sony PS3 games console of the rally game Colin McRae DiRT by Codemasters renders complex spatial sound scenes using Ambisonics inside. The obvious advantage in both these cases is the fact that very little work needs to be done as consumers migrate to 6.1 and 7.1 layouts. The Codemasters example shows that real-time scene description can be done via Ambisonics.

There remains the problem that it does not matter how pinpoint focused images are; what has been described so far is still surround sound, rather than properly spatial. One cannot walk toward, past, or between images; there is no parallax. To this extent, items in the sound field do not quite have corporeal existence. There is a technology that addresses some of these issues. Wave field synthesis (WFS; now commercially available as IOSONO), instead of being predicated on reassembling the sound field at a particular point, models the wavefronts in a given bounded volume of space. In any given point within that volume, the field is no more impressive (and possibly slightly less so) than any of the other technologies discussed. However, having no sweet spot, it is accessible for all listeners, and for the moving listener it is profoundly impressive. Images remain solidly *out there*, externally real and not egocentrically referenced as in phantom-imaging systems. Images can even be generated inside the listening volume, so that one can walk past and around them (there are some limitations to this as one passes between the speaker array and the image). However, the system uses hundreds of adjacent loudspeakers, precisely controlled by digital signal processing (DSP) and requires extensive listening room treatment; in addition, it does not currently depict elevation information (although conceivably this could be supplemented in a hybrid using Ambisonics). Consequently, although the approach shows great promise for 3-D sound in large areas, installation is expensive and, presumably, permanent.

An alternative approach, given that there is no off-the-shelf technology that can capture and depict a very large audio environment in a similarly large setting (which I think of as *one-to-one spatial mapping*), is to construct a cellular representation. Here, a large sound field is dissected into smaller cells using multiple SoundField microphones, whose signals can be used to drive multiple surround-sound cells. This has been successfully trialed at Derby University using three cells. Three microphones were used to capture a scene (a choir in the cathedral). The microphones were in a line with 25-meter separation between each—one in the congregation position, one in the center of the choir, and one beyond that, at the altar. The result was replayed in a volume of equivalent size, with similar spacing between the centers of the fields; each field had a 10-meter radius and for the demonstration was horizontal only. Visitors, including the choir, were invited to walk through the "virtual audio environment." Proper psychophysical tests could not, unfortunately, be accommodated, but the results were perceptually impressive. Imagery was still not quite as solid as in WFS, but the effect of being able to walk toward the choir, pass through the middle, and sense being surrounded by the choristers, then out toward the altar was particularly effective, and the field was *navigable*; blindfolded volunteers could tell where they were and find particular destinations (approximately). What was shown was that the approach is upwardly scalable; that is, the same approach could be used to capture an even larger place (a village?), that a similar conceptual approach can be used for synthesis (large soundscape composition), and that, of course, the resultant could be *virtually* toured via computer. Naturally, hybrids of captured and synthesized materials are feasible. We have here a development route toward a "musical garden." It is already theoretically feasible, using a program like Reaper in master/slave configuration, to manage very large fields using a network, where audio signals do not need to be passed around the network, merely control-and-clocking signals. Hence, again, domestic technology (with a few additions) and freely available plug-ins can be utilized.

The navigable sound field might be of interest to the visually impaired, for utility or entertainment, and indeed for museums (what would it sound like to be in ancient Rome?). Several composers have expressed keen interest, and their aesthetic explorations would be invaluable.

It is clear in this section that many of the technological constraints on spatial sound experiments are simply falling away, driving conceptual development. Jot'concepts of speaker layout agnosticism using audio scene description are almost on us. Why stop at scene descriptions of directional vectors? Why not have object size and orientation described in an *absolute* position (not referenced from a particular listener position)?

C. New Spatial Metaphors

These technological constraints are all fairly prosaic; more interesting is the combinatorial aspect of bringing these under the heading of "music" Tying *tonal, rhythmic,* and *spatial* progression together is one family of examples. Again, this can be quite simplistic—a simple tone that rises as it rises, so to speak, a galloping rhythm that departs and returns, and so on. This can lead to experiments with the spatial dissolution of a chord structure and its reassembly in some other position.

Some of the effects that evolved in former technologies can be effective here, such as the sweepable high-pass filter combined with simple panning or pitch shifting with directional changes. But, there are more abstract families of treatments that might be interesting: the metamorphosis from pinpoint foreground "object" to overarching background "place," from spacious to claustrophobic, or from "in the head" to "out there"; these can be effectively combined with musical transitions. Having tried some of these combinations, I am struck by the fact that it is not simple to anticipate which will be perceptually effective, and that none are *automatically* so.

Naturally, not all composers want the same thing; for some, music is a way of understanding human perception, while for others it is the other way round—and the two approaches are not mutually exclusive.

D. Just Over the Horizon

The discussion of embodied spatial cognition in an environment and compositional tools raises another important topic: the compositional environment. Environments affect how perceivers think. Rather than thinking of spatial planning as essentially an exercise in cartography, we should admit that we are really hoping to plan an environment to be occupied by humans, admitting that *spatial* perception is actually *place* perception. So, it behooves us to try to construct a compositional environment that can accommodate a real, flesh-and-blood composer. Such an environment should be "friendly" to composers—it is no coincidence that "user friendly" is a common term.

Electronics (and the descendant, computer signal processing) currently offer too much and too little control. For example, in Ambisonics, it is mathematically trivial to invert or spin an entire sound field but the result can sound disappointing, not at all as though the world turned upside down or spun around, simply peculiar.

Composing with tools that are mathematically elegant might provide intellectual appeal, but there is no *feel* for the eventual perceptual result. Composing abstract Euclidean space can produce results that are perfect, yet arid. This might be suitable for some pieces, but one should not be forced to work that way, and many listeners will not respond in an embodied way. Computers can too easily be opaque and "once removed," removing the visceral aesthetics from the equation. A composer should be able (if he or she so wishes) to use spatial sound as a raw material, like a sculptor carving meaning out of a block.

In recent experiments with DJs, Caryl Jones used a simple MIDI (musical instrument digital interface) control surface coupled to VST plug-ins for panning and reverb. She found that the method of controlling the plug-in was crucial as DJs work very rapidly and intuitively. Most of her test subjects found simply circular panning musically uninteresting, but the capacity to tap a button, causing 45-degree "jumps" in time to the rhythm did seem creatively worthwhile. The DJs were also surprisingly enamored with the ability to place the stereo soundstage to one end of the room while casting large Ambisonic spatial reverbs in other directions, simulating variations in venue size; it was especially important to be able to vary this in real time according to musical content. In a continuation of this work, Matt Trevor and Brad Porter coupled Wii controllers to various plug-ins hosted within AudioMulch, giving real-time control of panning, variable high-pass filtering, "bit crunching," pitch shifting, multitap delays, and so on. The aesthetically interesting results came out of the ways these could be *combined*, thus granting real-time exploration of metaphorical associations between signal content and spatial treatments. A parallel exploration by James Miles into playable spatial drum effects used foot switches and MIDI drum pads to actuate panning, reverb, and "call-and-response sampling" (the drummer produces a phrase that is then controllably repeated and spatially routed, so the drummer than subsequently interacts with it). The principle underlying all these experiments was that of "embodied musical composition"—physical exploration of what is perceptually effective. Musicians often refer to this as "jamming," so these were examples of "spatial jamming."

4. CONCLUSION

Just occasionally, when one listens to the real world, it *is* almost musical; certainly, it is potentially an aesthetic experience, good or bad. When we close our ears to this (as many of us do much of the time), our perception is simply *lessened*. If we turn to artificial soundscapes, they do not yet feature the subtle detail that real ones do; greater understanding and finer control of spatial structure are needed. An artificial soundscape that mimics a real one is just one goal; artificial soundscapes that do *not* mimic real ones, yet sound perceptually plausible, constitute something quite different. A spatially *extended* type of music could offer new musical dimensions. Certainly, an aesthetic input to the design of the compositional environment will probably produce something that cannot be logically anticipated.

NOTE

1. For details of freely available plug-ins, B-format recordings and Ambisonic compositions, see www.ambisonia.com for decoders, 3-D reverbs, and panners and see Bruce Wiggins's page at http://www.derby.ac.uk/staff-search/dr-bruce-wiggins. For a fuller explanation of Ambisonics, see http://www.ambisonic.net. For general surround sound discussions, see http://mail.music.vt.edu/mailman/listinfo/sursound.

BIBLIOGRAPHY

Blauert, J. 1997. *Spatial Hearing: The Psychophysics of Human Sound Localization.* Revised ed. Cambridge: MIT Press.

Dibben, N. 2001. What do we hear when we hear music? Music perception and musical material. *Musicae Scientiae* 5(2): 161–194.

Elen, R. 1998. Ambisonic.net. http://www.ambisonic.net, accessed March 30, 2009.

Gaver, W. W. 1993a. What in the world do we hear? An ecological approach to auditory source perception. *Ecological Psychology* 5: 1–29.

Gaver, W. W. 1993b. How do we hear in the world? Explorations in ecological acoustics. *Ecological Psychology* 5: 285–313.

Guastavino, C., and B. Katz. 2004. Perceptual evaluation of multi-dimensional spatial audio reproduction. *Journal of the Acoustical Society of America* 116: 1105.

Hoffmann, J. J. 2001. Sonic Architecture. http://www.sonicarchitecture.de, accessed March 30, 2009.

James, W. 1890a. The perception of space: The feeling of crude extensity. In *Principles of Psychology.* New York: Holt, chap. 20. Published in *Classics in the History of Psychology,* an Internet resource developed by Christopher D. Green (2004). http://psychclassics.asu.edu/James/Principles/prin20.htm, accessed June 2008.

James, W. 1890b. The perception of "things." In *Principles of Psychology.* New York: Holt, chap. 19. Published in *Classics in the History of Psychology,* an Internet resource developed by Christopher D. Green (2004). http://psychclassics.asu.edu/James/Principles/prin19.htm, accessed June 2008.

Jot, J-M. 2008. Keynote speech delivered at the International Spatial Audio Workshop at University of York, UK.

Kahneman, D. 2002. "Maps of Bounded Rationality." Nobel Prize lecture. nobelprize.org/nobel_prizes/economics/laureates/2002/kahnemann-lecture.pdf, accessed March 30, 2009.

Kendall, G. S., and M. Ardila. 2008. The artistic play of spatial organization: Spatial attributes, scene analysis and auditory spatial schemata. In *CMMR 2007, Lecture Notes in Computer Science 4969*, ed. R. Kronland-Martinet, S. Ystad, and K. Jensen. Berlin: Springer-Verlag, pp. 125–138.

Lennox, P. P., T. Myatt, and J. M. Vaughan. 2001. 3D audio as an information-environment: manipulating perceptual significance for differentiation and pre-selection. In *Proceedings of the 2001 International Conference on Auditory Display, Espoo, Finland*. International Community for Auditory Display. www.icad.org, accessed March 30, 2009.

Litovsky, R. Y., H. S. Colburn, W. A. Yost, and S. J. Guzman. 1999. The precedence effect. http://www.waisman.wisc.edu/~litovsky/papers/1999-3.pdf, accessed June 2008.

Rumsey, F. 2002. Spatial quality evaluation for reproduced sound: Terminology, meaning, and a scene-based paradigm. *Journal of the Audio Engineering Society*, 50(9): 651–666.

Warren, W. H., and R. R. Verbrugge. 1984. Auditory perception of breaking and bouncing events: A case study in ecological acoustics. *Journal of Experimental Psychology: Human Perception and Performance* 10: 704–712.

CHAPTER 14

THE VOICE IN COMPUTER MUSIC AND ITS RELATIONSHIP TO PLACE, IDENTITY, AND COMMUNITY

HAZEL SMITH

In Computer Music the voice has been used to explore and problematize concepts of place, identity, and community. While the exploration of subjective and social experience through verbal content is often not as intensive in computer music as it is in song-setting or poetry, the transformation and contextualization of the voice is much more radical and multidimensional. In computer music, techniques such as sampling, granular synthesis, filtering, morphing, and panning across the spatial spectrum provide the means for extensive exploration of the relationship of the voice to the environment, the voice as a marker of identity, and the role of voices in forging or eroding community. Computer music also exploits the range of the voice from speaking to singing—including breathing, mouth, and throat sounds—and this makes it easier to introduce a wider range of identities and contexts than in singing alone.

The chapter concerns the spoken voice rather than singing, and its emphasis is cultural, interpretative, and highly selective rather than technical, taxonomic, comprehensive, or historical; an analysis of different verbal/vocal techniques in computer music has already been effectively carried out by Cathy Lane (2006). I consider place, identity, and community separately, but inevitably these are all interwoven and interdependent. Electroacoustic sounds often function as multiple metaphors: a piece can seem to be about nature, for example, but also be interpretable as a psychological landscape. In addition, many of the works function on a meta-level (a piece that challenges us with two simultaneous sonic environments may also be about the difficulties and attractions of trying to listen to two different sound sources at once).

1. THE VOICE AND ITS RELATIONSHIP TO THE ENVIRONMENT

Postmodern geographers such as Steve Pile, David Harvey, and Doreen Massey have suggested place is not bounded or fixed, but fluid and dynamic—culturally, politically, and economically. Any place is traversed by shifting economic and social relationships and has links to other places (Smith 2000). In computer music, the fluid relationship of the voice to the environment is projected in a multilayered and changing way by means of a "voicescape" that challenges the idea of place as static, unidimensional, bounded, or natural. The voicescape consists of multidimensional and multidirectional projections of the voice into space (Smith and Dean 2003). In the voicescape, there is a plurality of voices, and at least some are digitally manipulated: identities are merged, multiplied and denaturalized through technological interventions. Voicescapes may create a strong connection between voice and place, but they also undo any such relationship: a voice may seem to emanate from several places at once, morph through different contexts, or reside in a space that is abstract.

The voicescape in computer music features the voice in a range of environments from urban to rural, everyday to surreal, domestic to public, Western to non-Western, and some pieces move between multiple environments and between specific and nonspecific spaces. These voices may be "found" voices that arise in "sound walks," voices that emerge as part of quasi-documentary interviews, or voices and environments that are constructed in the studio. Sometimes, there may be a strong sense of a particular place; at other times, the space into which the voice is projected is more abstracted. The environments are not necessarily discrete—they are often superimposed, juxtaposed, or morph into each other. The voice may be foregrounded or backgrounded with regard to the environment, detached from or integrated into it, commensurate with or antithetical to it, creating various kinds of "landscape morphology" (Field 2000): the relationship between voice and space is also always constantly changing and "becoming," so that a voice may be foregrounded at one point of the piece and backgrounded at another. This range of techniques and approaches allows the composer to exploit the voice and its digital manipulation to evoke ideas not only about ecology, industrialization, gender, and ethnicity, but also about displacement, marginalization, and alienation.

In some pieces, voice and environment are molded together to produce what I have elsewhere called a "hyperscape" in which both body and environment are dismantled and then put together in continuously changing ways that challenge the unity and stability of each (Smith 2000). Trevor Wishart's explosive and dense *Vox 5* (1990) is one of the most powerful examples of this. Wishart achieved these effects by employing computer programs he wrote to manipulate sound analysis data obtained from Mark Dolson's Phase Vocoder program. In his sleeve notes, he documents how the programs "permitted the spectra of vocal sounds to be stretched (making them bell-like) or interpolated with the spectra of natural events"(Wishart 1990, program notes).

In *Vox 5*, chest and throat sounds are superimposed onto, juxtaposed with, and morphed into, environmental sounds. There is sometimes a strong sense of a particular environment—such as when seagull and sea sounds are coordinated near the beginning—but there is often considerable ambiguity about some of the sounds that are a mixture of the bodily and environmental (as well as those that are more strongly instrumental). At times, sounds cross generic boundaries, for example, the human sounds seem like animal sounds, and there is a continuum among human, animal, environmental, and climate sounds. Moreover, the landscape and impression of the climate is constantly changing and unstable: At one point (ca. 0 min 32 s), we hear bird and simulated sea sounds; at another point (ca. 2 min 23 s), the throat sounds morph into bee sounds, and toward the end of the piece (ca. 4 min 32 s) there is a thunderstorm.

The voice in *Vox 5* emanates not from the head but from the chest and throat, suggesting the deeply grounded home of the voice in the entire body. The vocal aspect of the piece projects the effort of coming into being: it struggles to articulate itself, and at one point (ca. 3 min 44 s) we hear the edges of words, the beginnings of language. Wishart has said that the piece contains "poetic images of the creation and destruction of the world contained within one all-enveloping vocal utterance (the 'Voice of Shiva')"(1990, sleeve notes); the elemental power of the piece seems to make it computer music's answer to Stravinsky's *Rite of Spring*. But, the unstable merging of the human and environmental mean that *Vox 5* is widely interpretable; it could also be understood as an evocation of birth and the acquisition of language or the birth of language itself. Alternatively, the piece could be interpreted psychoanalytically as playing out the primal desires of the unconscious or as a glimpse of the Lacanian "real": the prelinguistic realm that precedes the child's entry into language (Lacan 1977).

Other computer music pieces negotiate the relationship between the voice and different kinds of cultural space. Paul Lansky's *Stroll* (1994), which the composer refers to as a short "reality play," projects the impression of two spaces that are both conflicting and complementary: that of a concert or studio space where a chamber music ensemble plays tonal, bright, and somewhat jazzy music and that of a crowd in an urban shopping mall (although the instrumentalists might also be playing in the mall). The voices in the shopping mall are initially more distinct—we can hear the voices of children—and are accompanied by other noises, such as the clatter of shopping carts. However, they become progressively more filtered and less individuated (although individual voices occasionally obtrude, and the sounds oscillate between voicelike and noiselike).

The piece reflects the heterogeneity of urban life: sometimes the two environments seem in conflict, at other times they appear to be interwoven, reciprocal, and reflective of each other. This ambivalent relationship between the two spaces also gives us a new slant on musical concordance and discordance. As the piece progresses, the crowd voices become more integrated with the chamber music, while the chatter from the shopping mall becomes inflected by rhythm and pitch and is more teleologically structured. Important here are the demands on our attention: the shopping mall crowd sounds and the chamber music seem to require different modes of listening that can only be resolved when they are fused. The piece consequently achieves a meta-level that raises questions about the act of listening itself. It becomes about our attempts to resolve the two modes of listening recorded—sometimes concentrating on one sound source more than the other—with our absorption greatest when the two are meshed together.[1]

The effect is at times reminiscent of weddings where people play to the chatter of voices and the tinkle of teacups and where musical space and social space are subject to continuous interruption. But, the piece also suggests that our lives have to adapt to a multiplicity of stimuli and social registers simultaneously, and that the urban is sonically heterogeneous. With one foot firmly rooted in the everyday and another in the making of music, the piece oscillates between integrating and separating the worlds of popular culture and high art.

Hildegard Westerkamp's *A Walk Through the City* (1996) is also an "urban environmental composition" (program notes) based on sound bites from Vancouver's skid row. However, it is concerned with interweaving real-world space and a studio-based, poetic space. It juxtaposes, but also intertwines, a soundscape of the city (including incidental voices and studio transformation of some of the sounds) with a performance of a poem that can be interpreted as commenting on, and relating to, the soundscape. The simultaneous separation and merging of spaces reflects the double face of the city, its dynamism but also its brutality; *A Walk Through the City* is the sonic equivalent of de Certeau's "long poem of walking" (1984, p. 101), which mobilizes resistant meanings beneath the city's surface. Walking is a way of unpicking what de Certeau calls "the city-concept," the powerful, hierarchical, and sanitized city that "must repress all the physical, mental and political pollutions that would compromise it" (p. 63).

The cityscape is presented through synecdochal fragments (that is, parts substitute for the whole); it is also partially abstracted—so the opening helicopter sounds turn into sustained dronelike sounds with slowly sliding pitches that nevertheless retain something of their aerodynamic quality. This morphing

between the concrete and the abstract creates "a continuous flux...between...
real and imaginary soundscapes, between recognisable and transformed places,
between reality and composition" (Westerkamp 1996, program notes). The more
abstracted sounds are broken at about 3 min 29 s by the loud and intrusive
screeching of car brakes, car horns, ambulance sirens, and the swish of traffic,
although the drone sounds still fade in and out. The voice of the poet enters at
about 4 min 54 s but is increasingly counterpointed with "unscripted" voices from
the city: the looped, ethereal voices of children singing and speaking, human chesty
sounds, and the words of street people and immigrants. We hear the voice of one
drunk, who keeps asking why he has to be in this condition, "Tell me, just one
thing, why do I have to get drunk, why, you tell me that?" (Westerkamp 1996). The
voices not only are indices of the colorfulness of the city, but also convey its
economic deprivations and underlying brutality in the form of noise pollution,
the plight of the disadvantaged, the vulnerability of children. Similarly nonverbal
sounds continue throughout the piece, conveying both the negative and positive
faces of the city—at about 8 min 0 s onward they become, for a short period, highly
rhythmic and dynamic.

The poem is performed by its author, Norbert Ruebsaat, whose voice sometimes seems to be projected naturalistically and at other times—including the first
time it appears—is treated in such a way as to seem "boxed in." The words are
delivered at varying dynamic levels and toward the end (after a short monologue by
the vagrant) transform into multiple whispers. The poem is not read in an entirely
linear fashion; some sections of it are repeated, and sometimes the author's voice is
multitracked, with different versions of the voice competing with each other. The
words strongly reinforce the soundscape and speak of the violence, loneliness,
deprivation, and alienation experienced in the city, for example, in phrases such
as "somewhere a man/is carving himself/to death/for food" and "day like an open
wound." The poem both stands apart from the soundscape and is integrated into it,
with some illustrative effects, for example, after the words "cymbal crash" there is a
literal crash.

Katharine Norman's *In Her Own Time* (1996) negotiates not only different
spaces but also different time frames. Here, the telling of stories interweaves
personal and cultural memory through shifts between a past and present sense of
a particular place. As Fran Tonkiss suggests, sound may be the most dominant
aspect of memory: "Hearing ... involves a special relationship to remembering. It
might, as Benjamin says, *be* the sense of memory. The past comes to us in its most
unbidden, immediate and sensuous forms not in the artifice of the travel photograph, but in the accident of sounds half-remembered" (2003, p. 307).

Relevant to the piece is also the Freudian concept of *Nachträglichkeit* or after-
wardness. This has been adapted by contemporary commentators to explore the
act of remembering not simply as the uncovering or restoration of a buried past but
as a reenactment or reinvention of the past in the present (King 2000, p. 12). This
reworking of Nachträglichkeit has often pivoted around the idea that the past is not
a recording that can be played back word for word but is "an intricate and ever

shifting net of firing neurons . . . the twistings and turnings of which rearrange themselves completely each time something is recalled" (Grant quoted in King 2000, p. 15). This is particularly relevant to Katharine Norman's attempt to catch her mother's act of remembering in real-time sound and by means of a quasi-documentary style that has an unedited and naturalistic feel to it, so that it incorporates voices in a way that Norman herself calls "unclean" (2004). The piece is less a voicescape than an interruptive monologue. Norman's mother relates stories about bombing in London during World War II, accompanied by musical sounds and punctuated by occasional prompts from the interviewer (who is Norman). The mother's voice appears throughout in stereo and is at times processed, if somewhat minimally. The accompanying drone sounds sometimes suggest overflying airplanes, but at other moments have a more abstract connection with the text.

In Her Own Time (Norman 1996) evokes a domestic environment (at one point, the phone rings). Within this, however, we are displaced into a previous era as Norman's mother tells us that the prospect of war seemed exciting when they were children. Now, however, her adult view of the severity of war is superimposed on this. The piece also "travels," and at one point we are transported—seemingly in a car—to the location at which an uncle who was killed by a bomb used to live. There is a stark contrast between the domestic warmth of the present, which is reinforced by the mother's unpretentious, light-handed storytelling, and the grim history of war. It evokes the ever-present tension between the freedoms of everyday life and the sometimes-horrific memories, both personal and cultural, that human beings repress.

Most of the pieces we have considered so far involve Western environments, but computer music composers have also negotiated the voice in relation to non-Western spaces. Pamela Z's *Gaijin* (2001a) is about how Z, an African American, responds to living in Japan. Z is a composer, performer, and multimedia artist who uses electronic processing and sampled sounds and whose oeuvre is a mixture of singing, speaking, and multimedia elements. These sounds are often triggered via custom MIDI (musical instrument digital interface) controllers such as BodySynth or Light SensePod, both of which allow her to manipulate sound with physical gestures.

Her work *Gaijin*, which arose out of her residency in Japan in 1999, is a multimedia work: it involves both live performance and electronic processing and combines spoken text, music, and butoh performance (Z 2001a, 2001b). In *Gaijin*, a sense of place is intertwined with feelings of displacement: it explores the experience of being foreign in Japan. The piece probes "the idea of foreignness—whether that means visiting a country that you're not used to, or feeling like a foreigner in the place where you live, or all kinds of other ways that a person could feel foreign" (Z 2000) and the word *gaijin* means foreigner. Z has said, "One of the things I learned in Japan is that if you're not Japanese, if you don't look Japanese, if you don't speak Japanese, then you will always be a gaijin. It was a real lesson to me because I began to be aware of what people who live in my own country must feel like when they're never allowed to feel that they belong, because other people don't allow them to or because they just don't feel like they do" (Z 2000). As George Lewis points out, this experience is intensified "when the subject singing of her Japanese experience is an African American woman who . . . sits as a group near the bottom of the US social hierarchy" (2007, p. 67).

Although Z refers to her adoption of "character" in such works (Z 2000), the notion of character is somewhat different from that in more conventional narrative because of its propensity for transformation rather than development or consistency. The excerpts from *Gaijin* on Z's Web site include multiple layers of sonic, verbal, and visual material; readings from a book about how to fit into Japanese culture; a polyphonic rendering of the word *other*; a performance of immigration requirements by Z, who puts herself in the visa document as its official voice and yet is clearly an addressee of it; Z singing in Japanese enka-style crooning (Lewis 2007, p. 68); and visual and sonic renditions of the Japanese alphabet. There are video images of butoh movement, whose minimalism and slowness is often in strong contrast to the polyphonic "Pamela" soundtrack and live performance, and Z herself is sometimes dressed in traditional Japanese style.

Finally, my collaboration with Roger Dean, *The Erotics of Gossip* (Smith and Dean 2008), is based on a particularly flexible relationship between voice and place that is sometimes realist, sometimes not. The piece is one of a series of sound technodramas by us that combine words and sound (and technological manipulation of words and sound). In the piece, the environments slide between locatable sites of power such as the courtroom, pulpit, and classroom and ambiguous, imagined, and futuristic spaces (Smith and Dean 2003). For example, at one point a churchlike environment produced by organ effects accompanies a monologue by a pompous clergyman. However, this fit between voice and place is seriously disrupted by atonal sliding sounds. In other places, sound and voice combine to evoke an unreal or imagined space. For example, there is a passage that begins, "For many months I observed the orders not to talk," which is about a futuristic authoritarian regime where talk is prohibited, but two women develop an intimate relationship with each other through "a dialogue made of hands" (Smith and Dean 2008). The accompanying sound, which circles around a few notes initially but becomes progressively denser, reinforces the threatening scenario evoked by the words, but together they create an allegorical and futuristic space rather than a realistic one.

The relationship between voice and place is also complex and transformative in another of our sound technodramas *Nuraghic Echoes* (Smith and Dean 1996). Inspired by the Nuraghi, the stone towers that arose out of Nuraghic civilization in 1500 BC, the work consists of three textual/voice strands that relate to the past, present, and future and three sonic strands that are in both conjunctive and disjunctive relationship to the textual/voice strands. Through these shifting relationships the work both suggests a sense of place and yet dissolves it into "in-between and non places" (discussed in Bailes et al. 2007).

2. Human to Nonhuman Identities

So far, the focus has been primarily on the relationship of voice to place but less on the identities that the voices project. However, in the voicescape the voice is no longer a fixed marker of identity: identities are merged, multiplied, and denaturalized through technological interventions. These include overlaying and multiplication of voices, exploitation of the spatial spectrum so that voices are projected from different positions in audio space, the use of reverberation to change the quality of the voice, and other forms of digital manipulation such as filtering and granular synthesis. Sometimes, the voice has a cyborg quality to it as in Charles Dodge's early speech songs (1992), and even when the voice is used naturalistically—as in Norman's *In Her Own Time* (1996)—it may be subject to some processing.

Computer music composers seem to play more with social identity and less with the direct expression of subjective experience that is central to much traditional poetry (although usually deconstructed in experimental poetry). If there is an emphasis on subjective experience, composers project fluid and transformative subjectivities. On the other hand, as noted, some works could be interpreted psychoanalytically as projecting unconscious experience or what Lacan calls "the real": the prelinguistic realm in which the child exists before he or she enters language and that the adult always wishes to recapture but cannot. Wishart's *Vox 5* (1990) for example, in its emphasis on prelinguistic utterance—and its merging of the body and environment—could be interpreted as a journey into the unconscious. Music is intrinsically stronger than poetry in its capacity to project the real because it is relatively unencumbered by semantic meaning. Due to its greater degree of abstraction, music also has an even greater capacity than poetry to project metaphors that have multiple meanings.

Sometimes, computer music composers manipulate the voice for the purposes of political intervention. Wishart's *Voiceprints* (2000c), for example, processes well-known voices, resulting in a comment about the commodification of identity, and has a strong satirical aspect. The sleeve has a made-up dictionary definition on the cover: "1. n. by analogy with 'fingerprints'—sound recordings of individual persons' voices used for the identification or assessment. 2. vb. to make a 'voiceprint'" (Wishart 2000c, sleeve notes). However, the word *voiceprints* also suggests footprints, which are more ambiguous as markers of identity. Footprints show that someone has been present and suggest the gender of that person, but do not identify exactly who (they also tend to reveal the imprint of the shoe rather than the foot). "Two Women" (Wishart 2000b) is divided into four sections in which the voice is subjected to extreme variations of speed and pitch. There is considerable fragmentation, looping, and repetition of the words that are integrated into sweeping musical textures; these are alternately forceful and delicate, dense and sparse. "Siren" treats the voice of Margaret Thatcher quoting St. Francis of Assisi, "Where there is discord, may we bring harmony" (program notes). The word *harmony* is stretched and emphasized, although some of the other words are speeded up: the voice is accompanied by train and other cataclysmic electroacoustic sounds. "Facets" treats the voice of Princess Diana talking about press photographers, "There was a relationship which worked before, but now I can't tolerate it because it has become abusive, and it's harassment" (program notes). It begins in a hesitant, fragmented way that captures a whining whimsicality; it then becomes much more dense as the talk turns into fast babble, accompanied by sustained electronic sounds that unwind toward the end. "Stentor" treats the voice of Ian Paisley, who says in a kind of reverse-prayer, "Oh God, defeat all our enemies . . . we hand this woman, Margaret Thatcher, over to the devil, that she might learn not to blaspheme. And Oh God in wrath, take vengeance upon this wicked, treacherous, lying woman. . . . Take vengeance upon her O Lord!" (program notes). The extreme elongation on "Oh God" sounds like a brutal clarion call, and there are accompanying thunderclaps and other elemental sounds. "Angelus" again processes Princess Diana's voice commenting on the "fairy story" in which she was a principal actor and saying she wants to be "the queen of people's hearts"; it transposes recognizable words to babble and then to pure pitch, after which Diana's voice returns again in recognizable but fragmented form. Each voice conjures up iconic moments in recent British history: Paisley's is inseparable from the divisive history of Northern Ireland, Diana's from the perturbation to the monarchy. There is also plenty of irony: Thatcherism could hardly be said to bring harmony, at least not in the sense of social cohesion. Again, identity is interwoven with place and movement between places, and the pieces are framed by train station voices announcing departures and arrivals—perhaps interpretable as a comment on shifting identities.

In *Voiceprints* (Wishart 2000c), the emphasis is on mediation: all the comments have been communicated via the media and are now processed again by Wishart. We are used to visual artists satirizing commodification (e.g., Warhol in his silk screens of Jackie Onassis and Marilyn Monroe), but these pieces engage with a similar phenomenon in sonic terms. Like Warhol's images, which often seem to combine the projection of a mediatized image with a certain affection—even reverence—for their subjects, these portraits are also highly ambiguous. Wishart depoliticizes the extracts of Diana's voice by calling them personal portraits, but they can be read, nevertheless, as combining satire and pathos. These processed voices also raise the question of how far a voice retains its own identity when it is digitally manipulated: the voices range from recognizable Diana and Thatcher to moments when we would not know who was speaking. Perhaps the pieces suggest the fragility of political power and celebrity (and more broadly speaking of any concept of identity or personality). Of these pieces, "American Tryptich" (Wishart 2000) seems to be particularly successful with its iconic blend of the voices of Martin Luther King, Neil Armstrong, and Elvis Presley—sometimes combined in ways that are highly polyphonic and rhythmic, but also employing environmental sounds such as crackly radio sonics from outer space.

Voiceprints (Wishart 2000c) plays with particular identities, but Lansky's pieces often call into question what constitutes an identity. Lanksy's "smalltalk" and "Late

August" on his CD *smalltalk* (1990) take up the idea of identity in compelling ways; here, identity becomes the contours and rhythms of speech:

> Sometimes when at the edge of consciousness, perhaps just falling asleep or day dreaming, sounds that are familiar will lose their usual ring and take on new meaning. Conversation in particular has this ability to change its nature when one no longer concentrates on the meanings of the words. I remember when I was a child falling asleep in the back of a car as my parents chatted up front. I no longer noticed what they were saying but rather heard only the intonations, rhythms and contours of their speech. The "music" of their talk was familiar and comforting, and as I drifted off it blended in with the noise of the road. (program notes)

This effect is achieved through a filtering process: "The music was created by processing a conversation between Lansky and Hannah MacKay (his wife) through a series of plucked-string filters tuned to various diatonic harmonies. The resulting sound is like a magic zither, where each string yields a fragment of speech" (Garton 1991, p. 116).

The conversation is recognizable as conversation (one can even recognize the genders of the speakers), but the words are not distinguishable. Lansky, who sometimes sees himself as the musical equivalent of a photographer, compares the process "to blowing up the pixels of a colour photograph so that familiar shapes become abstract squares." Lansky then added "a soft, sustained chorus" (1990, program notes).

Although Lansky sees the chorus as "a place to let your ears rest when listening to the music of conversation or attempting to hear the words behind it" (1990, program notes), I agree with Brad Garton that it is the chorus that underpins the whole work:

> To me . . . these subtle harmonies embody the meaning of the piece. The chords, outlined by the choral sounds, define different harmonic regions as the piece progresses. I can easily imagine these harmonic regions shadowing the flux of context and meaning in the real conversation, or that the flow of harmony represents some deeper continuity which underlies even the most innocuous conversations we have with our family and friends. In any case, it is by pushing my concentration through the words to the longer tones that I become fully enveloped in the music. Some of the most gorgeous moments occur when there is a temporary lull in the conversation, and this harmonic substrate is allowed to exist briefly by itself. (Garton 1991, p. 116)

According to Lansky, *smalltalk* tries to capture the spirit, emotions, and music behind and within our conversation (1990, program notes). This turns into an experiment in cultural identity when Lansky applies the same process to Chinese speakers in another piece, "Late August." Although the pieces sound quite similar, Garton points out that "Late August" is "much more animated, the harmonic rhythm of the piece moving along at a faster rate" (1991, p. 116). This may be because Chinese is a tonal language, and the Chinese use pitch to discriminate between words that look the same when written. Consequently, the piece is culturally resonant but in ways that are quite indirect.

Other works investigate identity from the point of view of ethnicity, although this may occur as part of a broader probing of identity. In Z's work, exploration of identity takes the form of an eclectic attitude toward different traditions—including opera, electroacoustic music, and sound poetry—which she moves between or superimposes. *Bone Music* (Z 2004a), for example, emphasizes a solo singing line (with rhythmic accompaniment) that seems to emanate from a mixture of Western and non-western musical traditions—there could be a hint of eastern European and Indian music—but then explodes into a babble of electroacoustically generated voices that grow to considerable intensity. Sometimes Z's works consist of a solo singing line, sometimes she duets with herself—singing or speaking through the use of a delay system or multitracking. In this way, she often creates several layers of utterance; sometimes, this becomes a dense polyphony of voices.

Lewis points to the transformation, multiplication, and layering of the voice in Z's work. Referring to Z's music as "post-genre (and post-racial) experimentalism," he suggested that such multiple identities are commensurate with fluid and polyphonic notions of African American identity (2007, p. 65). Certainly, Z's work is interpretable from a number of different points of view, opening up many questions about cross-cultural relationships, articulation, and language—questions that embrace racial identity but are not limited to it.

In Z's work, identity is about her relation to others. Her text-based works are often interrogative, addressing ambiguously either another person or the audience at large. "Pop Titles 'You'" (Z 2004c) takes one of the most interesting devices in poetry (the use of the second person and the ambiguity it creates about the addressee) and makes rhythmic and musical effects out of it. The "you" could be a lover, a relation, the general public, Westerners, and so on. "Questions" (Z 2004d) combines a track in which numerous questions are asked with another track that features expressive singing.

Lewis draws attention to the way in which black musicians have often been stereotyped as nontechnological or black culture as incompatible with technology, but nevertheless point to the fluidity of Z's thinking:

> Certainly, artists such as Pamela Z reject the notion that electronics could be rigidly raced, and that any entry into the medium by African Americans necessarily constituted inferior imitation of white culture, economic opportunism, and/or general racial inauthenticity. Moreover, in Z's post-genre (and post-racial) experimentalism, we find a twinned practice of cultural mobility with self-determination that authorizes her to draw from any source, to deny any limitation whatsoever. This assertion of methodological and aesthetic mobility may be viewed as an integral aspect of the heterophonic (rather than simply hybrid) notion of identity found in her work. (2007, p. 65)

Lewis also discusses how Z draws on the operatic tradition without resorting to the stereotypical roles which women often take in opera: "Pamela Z takes on many dramatis personae, but two that practically never appear in her work are the hysterical victim and the Medea figure so beloved by European opera. In general,

Z's stage personae represent women in full control and authority—never confrontational, but powerful and confident. For Z, opera (and its bel canto evocation and extension in her work) does not lead inevitably, following Catherine Clément, to the 'undoing of women'" (2007, p. 69).

Gender identity is in fact an important issue in electroacoustic music because there is a predominance of male composers. Bosma argues that there is much stereotyping of the roles of men and women in this music, particularly with regard to singing: "A musical partnership of a male composer and a female vocalist is typical of electroacoustic music. This stereotype relates woman to body, performance, tradition, non-verbal sound and singing, and man to electronic music technology, innovation, language and authority. It resonates with the tendency in contemporary Western culture to associate singing with women, not men, . . . while technology is seen as a man's world. . . . More generally, it reflects the dualistic opposition of masculinity versus femininity and mind versus body that is so prevalent in our culture" (Bosma 2003, p. 12).

However, she argues that this stereotyping is somewhat deflected by recording: "The gender distribution of . . . pre-recorded voices in much more equal compared to the use of live voices, and the use of pre-recorded voices is much more varied than the use of live voices in this genre. Moreover, pre-recorded voices are often manipulated, sometimes dissolving or bending the gender of the voice" (2003, p. 12).

Donna Hewitt is an Australian composer-performer who has developed the eMic (Extended Microphone Interface Controller) and employs it to challenge male constructions of female identity:

> The eMic is based on a sensor-enhanced microphone stand and I use this in combination with AudioMulch and Pure Data software. The interface, which is intended to capture standard popular music and microphone gestures, challenges the passive stereotype of the female singer (with their voice controlled by a male front-of-house mix engineer), in that it enables the performer to take charge of their own signal processing. The eMic project has helped me establish a unique creative space where I can comment on, and subvert, existing stereotypical male constructions of the female vocal performer. (2007, p. 186).

"Geekspeak" (Z 2004b), on the other hand, is a humorous exploration of masculinity. Masculinity was once stereotypically defined through heroism, virility, and rationality, but as David Buchbinder has pointed out (1994), the traditional models of masculinity have been dying since the end of World War II. It is arguable, however, that these defining markers of masculinity have been replaced, at least partly, by technological ability and know-how. "Geekspeak" satirizes the effect of technology on men and the degree to which they start to identify themselves through that technology; it is also about how we put labels on people, whether those labels have any validity, and whether they might also apply to ourselves (Z 2004). To make the piece, Z sampled the voices of a number of researchers and programmers who she met during an artist-in-residency at Xerox PARC (the Palo Alto Research Center) in Palo Alto, California (program notes). The piece is a mixture of genres: similar to sound poetry in its loops, multiple voices, collage, and overlays (but nevertheless arguably a parody of sound poetry in the kind of technical material it chooses to make into musical motives, such as a loop of the word *backslash*). Nevertheless, it also has elements of the documentary or radio show with much background noise—someone flicking the pages of the dictionary, the sound of a computer keyboard as one of the interviewees looks up the word *geek* on the Internet. The male voices struggle with definitions of what a nerd or geek might be while not ever admitting to being one.

Of course, whether the interviewees are nerds or geeks depends on what the definition of a nerd or geek is: different definitions vie with each other during the piece, some more pejorative than others, some eliding the notion of nerd and geek. Nobody raises the issue of whether a geek or nerd could be female, and all the voices are male. Certainly, the interviewees show characteristics that might be seen as geeky or nerdy (the final speaker says, "Why would I spend money on clothes when I could buy an external hard drive?"), and all of them are geeks in the sense of being computer geeks who rhapsodize about hardware/software. The phrase spoken by one of the men, "I find it difficult to articulate it" is also mischievously repeated (sometimes in truncated form), thereby hinting that the wordiness and self-confidence of some of the interviewees might just be top show. It is ironic that the piece is about technophilia but written by someone who is a technophile herself, and if it is partly satirical, it is also sympathetic. Is the implication that women who are technophiles actually manage to avoid being geeks, or does the composer actually implicate herself in geekiness?

Processing of the voice can also undermine gender stereotypes. For example, it can provoke ideas about the instability of gender and sexual ambiguity through "sonic cross-dressing," or gender morphing, with the gender of the voice transmuted through pitch and timbre changes, or the continuum between male and female extensively activated (Smith 1999). (Such manipulation of the voice could have interesting applications with regard to ethnic identity, although seemingly this is a less-explored area.) Gender morphing is a prominent feature of my collaborations with Roger Dean. In *The Space of History* (Smith et al. 2006), for example, a putative female "terrorist" meditates on what the reactions of the audience would be if she locked them in the concert hall. However, later in the piece, after she has left the performance space, her voice is manipulated in ways that problematize her identity: her voice sounds sometimes like a child, sometimes like a man, and sometimes cyborglike and appears at many different points along the continuum between male and female. This challenges stereotypical images of terrorists in terms of gender, age, and behavior.

Such explorations can probe the norms of both gender and sexuality. Barry Truax (2003) has drawn attention to the lack of homoerotic content in electro-acoustic music; his own work, however, has tried to overcome this by blurring gender distinctions, sometimes through manipulation of the voice:

My first work based on the granulation of sampled sound was *The Wings of Nike* (1987) whose sole source material for three movements was two phonemes, one male, the other female. They were used with high densities of grains, including transpositions up and down an octave, thereby sometimes blurring the distinction in gender. A more extensive use of gendered text was involved in *Song of Songs* (1992) where a decision has to be made how to use the original *Song of Solomon* text which includes lines that are conventionally ascribed to the characters of Solomon and Shulamith, his beloved. The simple solution was to have both the male and female readers of the text record it without changing any pronouns. When these versions are combined, the listener hears both the male and female voice extolling the lover's beauty. (p. 119)

In Truax's music-theatre piece/opera "Powers of Two: The Artist" (1995), he brings together two high-pitched male voices. He suggests that "the intertwining of two high-pitched male voices creates a potentially homoerotic sound that, it seems, most heterosexual composers have avoided" (Truax 2003). Truax points out that gender is inescapable in opera, and that while heterosexuality has been the predominant norm, there has also been a tradition of partially concealed homosexual themes that have been apparent to the homosexual community. It is this tradition to which he gives a new twist with his own electroacoustic operas.

3. The Voice, Computer Music, and Community

Voicescapes tend to embody ideas about social interactions and their role in community. Sometimes, the words are blurred or incomplete, conveying only the contours of speech but nevertheless suggesting the dynamics of social exchange, the ambience of talk and gossip, and the shifting balance between talking and listening. Different pieces engage with different kinds of community, from the family to the shopping mall, and often explore ideas around communication and the degree to which we are listening, or not listening, to each other.

Community does not necessarily mean knowing other people in depth. Rather, Iris Marion Young suggests that community can be defined as "a being together of strangers" and is the embrace of difference expressed in the overlapping and intermingling of different social groups. This brings about a form of public life in which "differences remain unassimilated, but each participating group acknowledges and is open to listening to the others. The public is heterogenous, plural, and playful, a place where people witness and appreciate diverse cultural expressions that they do not share and do not fully understand" (1990, p. 241).

Lansky's "Idle Chatter" could be interpreted as such a being together of strangers. A very animated and rhythmic piece made out of the sounds of talking—treated in such a way that they sound almost like bee sounds—accompanied by sustained singing, it suggests a community of chatterers. Nevertheless, we cannot hear the content of the talk or identify individual speakers; the piece challenges the dividing line between speech and noise and is what Dean calls NoiseSpeech (Dean 2005, Dean and Bailes 2006): "NoiseSpeech . . . refers to a range of sounds close to the maximal complexity of noise but which seem to be derived from speech though lacking any detectable words or phonemes. NoiseSpeech can be made by digital manipulation of speech sounds, such that words and phonemes are no longer intelligible, or by superimposing the formant structure (spectral content) or prosodic pitch and dynamic features of speech onto other sounds, both noise, and environmental and instrumental sound" (Dean and Bailes 2006, p. 85).

Lansky describes his methods, intentions, and techniques in making the piece in the program notes to the CD: "Idle Chatter" is an eloquent attempt to say nothing without taking a breath . . . . The sounds in "Idle Chatter" were all created using linear prediction and a massive amount of sound mixing. Rhythmic templates and masks were used to scatter arbitrary vowel and consonant sounds in relatively even distributions throughout the piece. An underlying idea was to create an elusive illusion of regularity and coherence. The choral sounds were similarly created but without the use of rhythmic masks, and with much more intense distributions. A great deal of the piece was written with computer aided algorithms" (1987).[2]

Similarly, although with different intentions and effects, in "The Erotics of Gossip" (Smith and Dean 2008) an interactive Max patch is used to convey the impression of gossiping voices. The process is described as follows:

> An interactive MAX patch was . . . used to create a varied multiplicity of overlapping spoken texts, notably in the passage about 2′ into the piece. Here the algorithm allows the random and controlled fragmentation of the individual recorded verbal phrases, and their overlapping in time and across the sonic space. One impact of this approach is to blur the identities of the individual speakers, and to merge their phrases into each others' as well as to disintegrate and reassemble them. At the moments where the greatest density of phrase overlap occurs, an impression is created of a speaking crowd, rather than a group of speaking individuals: this is another way in which the voicescape decentres voices. At other places in the piece, such a crowd voice is used as a lower dynamic sonic background; raising the question whether gossip can be music (or vice versa). In a notable passage after 9′20″, such a complex multiple and delocalised voicescape, seeming to include both real and unreal voices, crowds and individuals, transforms into a purely sonic (and apparently non-verbal) soundscape. (Smith and Dean 2003, p. 121)

Gossip is sometimes conceptualized as destructive and unethical, but it can also be seen to be subversive, creative, and a means of creating community. Through the use of Max patches in the piece, we were able to show these two different sides of gossip in passages that involved two women gossiping, two men gossiping, and a man and a woman gossiping.

Some pieces address the histories of particular types of community. Wende Bartley's "Rising Tides of Generations Lost" (1994) is a feminist piece about women's histories. Bartley says of the piece: "The ancient art of storytelling, always present among us, preserves what we cannot afford to lose, reminds us of what we have forgotten, highlights that which is collectively experienced, and points to new possibilities. *Rising Tides of Generations Lost* is one attempt to retell a small portion of the story of woman. Our collective foremothers issue forth a clear call to give voice to the rising energy centuries of common experience has created" (program notes).

In "Rising Tides of Generations Lost" (Bartley 1994), the sampled voices move from whispered vowel consonants and syllables to spoken syllables, words, and phrases accompanied by sustained electroacoustic sounds. The piece represents a coming into language, recapturing the historical and continuing need for women to find their own voices and language. The piece is at once both a historical remembering and a call to action and captures the way that women have been vilified and repressed throughout history. In the middle of the piece (ca. 11 min 30 s), one voice—overlaid with others that echo and intersect it—intones: "I compel you to see and feel. . . .To have the courage and the conscience to speak and act for your own freedom though you may face the scorn and the contempt of the world for doing so" (Bartley 1994). The multiple voices do not represent different aspects of the self, but more the collective sufferings and courage of women. The piece ends with some everyday conversation at about 12 min 45 s. One voice hints at loneliness and betrayal, "I don't have anybody," but then the voices split into numerous renderings of "I," some flattened and truncated to sound like "a." During the piece, the musical sounds move from drone to fire sounds and then into more tonal and instrumental music. The fire sounds recall the burning of women as witches, while the tonal and instrumental music might refer to musical histories that have both included and excluded women.

The piece alludes to the hidden aspects of women's experience, a theme that is also taken up in Lane's "Hidden Lives" (1999). In this piece, women speakers read from *The Book of Hints and Wrinkles* (1939); Lane characterizes this as "a small piece of social history from the 1930s which describes how women should manage both their houses and themselves" (2006, p. 7). In "Hidden Lives," the whispers and stutters of women gradually grow into fragments of "advice" taken from the book; this is the kind of domestic dogma that the history of female emancipation has tried to rebut and that suggests a crippling timetable of wifely duty and servitude. Here again, the treatment of the voice is closely tied to notions of place and begins with "outside" city crowd sounds and a loud shutting sound at about 40 s (if this is the door of a house, it sounds fittingly like the closing of a prison gate). After a series of voice sounds that are at the edges of words, but not actual words, there is a another door sound followed by breathy voice sounds. This gives an overall impression that is windlike, perhaps suggesting that women's voices can be blown to pieces. After that, the voices build up in restless stuttering and whispered patterns that evoke hidden secrets, repressed longings, underlying distress. Then, the words become clearer but gradually build up into a babble of phrases to do with housework and child care in which one kind of duty and obligation competes with another.

Toward the end of the piece, it sounds as if the women are literally blown away, and "Hidden Lives" finishes with reentry into the outside world. Lane says that she has "attempted to reinforce the sense of the words, or rather the world that they are describing, by structuring them as if moving through a series of rooms in a house, and the spatial claustrophobia of the work serves to emphasize the meaning and context" (2006, p. 8). Norman suggests that the voices themselves evoke domestic routines, "flurries of vocal fragments . . . gradually build into swishing, repetitive surges before subsiding again. These repetitive rhythmic waves are too fast to be soothing, and have a sense of industry that is perhaps reminiscent of sweeping, scrubbing or polishing" (2004, p. 111). "Hidden Lives" is, however, open to a variety of interpretations and is another example of a work that can be interpreted psychoanalytically, as I suggested. The prelinguistic babble at the beginning suggests the work of Julia Kristeva and her concept of the semiotic: a concept closely related to the Lacanian "real" but used by Julia Kristeva and other feminist writers to delineate certain aspects of female experience and expression (Kristeva 1986).

4. CONCLUSION

As discussed, the voice in computer music illuminates and problematizes place, identity, and community, and these different concepts are interwoven in the voicescape, which is based on the idea of multiple projections of the voice into space. The voice presents or simulates urban and rural spaces, non-Western spaces, and historical spaces, but it also juxtaposes, breaks up, and morphs them. The voice creates and deconstructs political, gendered, and ethnic identities, while assemblages of voices sometimes evoke particular types of communities and their histories. However, the exploration of place, identity, and community with regard to voice in computer music is very different from that in poetry, in which the semantic import of the words may be greater but the range and manipulation of the voice less. While computer music is not so likely to use the voice as a conveyor of subjective experience, many of the pieces can be interpreted psychoanalytically. Given that writers and musicians tend to approach words and voice differently, it is in many ways surprising that it has not been more common for writers and musicians to work together, drawing on expertise from both areas. However, it is clear that computer music is loosely connected to multimedia endeavors that combine image, voice, and text, and that this might be one of the directions in which the computerized voice becomes more omnipresent in the future.

NOTES

1. An important early precursor to this kind of meta-piece is Alvin Lucier's "I Am Sitting in a Room" (1969), made with a tape recorder rather than a computer. In this piece, the voice is recorded, played back, and rerecorded until the words become unintelligible and dissolve into the "sound" of the room. The voice narrates a text that is about this process.

2. Pieces such as "Idle Chatter" manipulate the formants of speech. Formants are "regions of the sound frequency spectrum in which energy is particularly concentrated, and are found also in instrumental sounds . . . .Whether a human voice is soprano, or baritone, there are generally and characteristically five formants, and this has been the basis for a large body of research on digital speech synthesis. . . . Linear Predictive Coding (LPC) is an early digital technique which analyses a speech utterance into a simplified data set that includes representation of the characteristic formants. This data set is then used to resynthesise a version of the utterance and, in the resynthesis step, modifications can be introduced. For example, speech can be transformed into song, and words can be lengthened or shortened in time, with or without pitch change" (Smith and Dean 2003, p. 114).

BIBLIOGRAPHY

Bailes, F., H. Smith, and R. T. Dean. 2007. Hearing and imaging place in sound: A program to interrelate the cognitive, cultural and creative. In *Hearing Places: Sound, Place, Time and Culture*, ed. R. Bandt, M. Duffy, and D. MacKinnon. Newcastle, UK: Cambridge Scholars, pp. 126–142.

Bartley, W. 1994. Rising tides of generations lost (1985–93). In *Claire-voie*. Montreal: empreintes DIGITALes. IMED-9414-CD.

Bosma, H. 2003. Bodies of evidence: Singing cyborgs and other gender issues in electrovocal music. *Organised Sound: An International Journal of Music Technology* 8(1): 5–17.

Buchbinder, D. 1994. *Masculinities and Identities*. Melbourne: Melbourne University Press.

Dean, R. T. 2005. NoiseSpeech, a noise of living bodies: Towards Attali's "Composition." *nmediac: The Journal of New Media and Culture* 3(1). http://www.ibiblio.org/nmediac/winter2004/NoiseSpc.htm, accessed April 7, 2008.

Dean, R. T., and F. Bailes. 2006. NoiseSpeech. *Performance Research. A Performance Research Lexicon* 11(3): 85–86.

de Certeau, M. 1984. *The Practice of Everyday Life*. Trans. S. Rendall. Berkeley: University of California Press.

Dodge, C. 1992. Speech songs. In *Any Resemblance Is Purely Coincidental*. San Francisco: New Albion Records. NA 043 CD. Originally realized in 1972.

Field, A. 2000. Simulation and reality: The new sonic objects. In *Music, Electronic Media and Culture*, ed. S. Emmerson. Aldershot, UK: Ashgate, pp. 36–55.

Garton, B. 1991. Paul Lansky: smalltalk. *Computer Music Journal* 15(3): 115–117.

Hewitt, D. 2007. Artists' statements 11. In *The Cambridge Companion to Electronic Music*, ed. N. Collins and J. d'Escriván. Cambridge: Cambridge University Press, p. 186.

King, N. 2000. *Memory, Narrative, Identity: Remembering the Self*. Edinburgh: Edinburgh University Press.

Kristeva, J. 1986. *The Kristeva Reader*. Ed. T. Moi. Oxford: Blackwell.

Lacan, J. 1977. *Écrits: A Selection*. Trans. A. Sheridan. New York: Norton.

Lane, C. 1999. Hidden lives. Unreleased recording. Extract on accompanying CD to *Organised Sound: An International Journal of Music Technology* 11(1): 3–11.

Lane, C. 2006. Voices from the past: Compositional approaches to using recorded speech. *Organised Sound: An International Journal of Music Technology* 11(1): 3–11.

Lansky, P. 1987. Idle chatter. In *New Computer Music: Barlow, Dashow, Kaske, Lansky, Roads, Waisvisz*. Mainz: Wergo Computer Music. WER 2010-50. Originally releazed in 1985.

Lansky, P. 1990. *smalltalk*. San Francisco: New Albion Records. NA030CD DDD.

Lansky, P. 1994. Stroll for chamber group and chamber music on tape. In *CDCM Computer Music Series Volume 18. The Composer in the Computer Age—111*. Los Angeles: Centaur Records. CRC 2213. Originally realized in 1988.

Lewis, G. E. 2007. The virtual discourses of Pamela Z. *Journal of the Society for American Music* 1(1): 57–77.

Lucier, A. 1969. I am sitting in a room. http://www.ubu.com/sound/lucier.html, accessed May 9, 2008.

Norman, K. 1996. In her own time. In *London*. London: Sonic Arts Network. NMC DO34.

Norman, K. 2004. *Sounding Art: Eight Literary Excursions Through Electronic Music*. Aldershot, UK: Ashgate.

Smith, H. 1999. Sonic writing and sonic cross-dressing: gender, language, voice and technology. In *Musics and Feminisms*, ed. S. Macarthur and C. Poynton. Sydney: Australian Music Centre, pp. 129–134.

Smith, H. 2000. *Hyperscapes in the Poetry of Frank O'Hara: Difference, Homosexuality, Topography*. Liverpool: Liverpool University Press.

Smith, H., and R. Dean. 1996. *Nuraghic Echoes*. Sydney: Rufus. CD RF025.

Smith, H., and R. T. Dean. 2003. Voicescapes and sonic structures in the creation of sound technodrama. *Performance Research* 8(1): 112–123.

Smith, H., and R. Dean. 2008. The erotics of gossip. In *The Erotics of Geography*. Book and CD-ROM. Kane'ohe, Hawaii: Tinfish Press.

Smith, H., R. Dean, and G. White. 2006. *The Space of History*. PennSound. http://writing. upenn.edu/singles/index.php, accessed April 7, 2008. Also available in H. Smith, 2008, *The Erotics of Geography*, book and CD-ROM, Tinfish Press,Kane'ohe, Hawaii.

Tonkiss, F. 2003. Aural postcards: Sound, memory and the city. In *The Auditory Culture Reader*, ed. M. Bull and L. Back. Oxford: Berg, pp. 303–310.

Truax, B. 1995. Extracts from powers of two: The artist. http://www.sfu.ca/sonic-studio/ excerpts/excerpts.html, accessed April 7, 2008.

Truax, B. 2003. Homoeroticism and electroacoustic music: Absence and personal voice. *Organised Sound* 8(1): 117–124.

Westerkamp, H. 1996. A walk through the city. Norbert Ruebsaat, poetry and reading. In *Transformations*. Montreal: empreintes DIGITALes. IMED. 9631. Originally realized in 1981.

Wishart, T. 1990. Vox 5. In *Vox*. London: Virgin Classics. VC 7 91108-2.

Wishart, T. 2000a. American triptych. In *Voiceprints*. New York: Electronic Music Foundation. EMF CD 029.

Wishart, T. 2000b. Two women. In *Voiceprints*. New York: Electronic Music Foundation. EMF CD 029.

Wishart, T. 2000c. *Voiceprints*. New York: Electronic Music Foundation. EMF CD 020.

Young, I. M. 1990. *Justice and the Politics of Difference*. Princeton, NJ: Princeton University Press.

Z, P. 2000. Parts of speech. Interview by Tom Sellar. http://www.pamelaz.com/theater.html, accessed April 7, 2008.

Z, P. 2001a. Excerpts from *Gaijin*. http://www.pamelaz.com/video.html, accessed April 7, 2008.

Z, P. 2001b. *Nihongo de Hanasoo* (from *Gaijin*). http://www.pamelaz.com/video.html, accessed April 7, 2008.

Z, P. 2004a. Bone music. In *A Delay Is Better*. Boulder, CO: Starkland. ST-213.

Z, P. 2004b. Geekspeak. In *A Delay Is Better*. Boulder, CO: Starkland. ST-213.

Z, P. 2004c. Pop titles "You." In *A Delay Is Better*. Boulder, CO: Starkland. ST-213.

Z, P. 2004d. Questions. In *A Delay Is Better*. Boulder, CO: Starkland. ST-213.

CHAPTER 15

ALGORITHMIC SYNESTHESIA

NOAM SAGIV, ROGER T. DEAN, AND FREYA BAILES

WE often think about our senses as separate and independent of each other. However, there are at least four problems with this naïve view. First, our experience of the world around us is a rich multisensory one. Under normal conditions, our senses are constantly flooded with information. Even when we are sitting quietly at home and reading this book, we not only see the text, but also hear the pages flipping, experience the smell of the book, and feel the smooth texture of the pages. Likewise, while drinking from a cup of tea, we would notice its smell and color in addition to the liquid's taste, temperature, and texture or viscosity. Although we can try to focus our attention on some things and ignore others, it would be safe to say that our sensory experience is rarely limited to one modality even if we try very hard.[1]

Second, our sensations do seem to come together somehow into a unified experience. The sights and sounds of most events we witness do not appear to be two independent streams of information; in fact, they seem inseparable. A third problem is that the senses do not merely converge somewhere; they also influence each other. As discussed here, visual inputs can influence auditory perception and vice versa.

The fourth reason to doubt the independence of the senses is that, for some individuals, stimulation in one sensory modality may actually give rise to perceptual experience in more than one modality. This remarkable form of perception is labeled *synesthesia*, and we distinguish here, before drawing some parallels between the two, between the involuntary psychological phenomenon and synesthesia in art involving intentional intermedia experimentation.

Bill Viola (1995, p. 152) stated: "Western science has decided it is desirable to isolate the senses in order to study them, but much of my work has been aimed at putting it back together." Scientists no longer limit themselves to studying the senses in isolation, and hundreds of recent studies have now examined cross-modal interactions and multisensory perception. However, it would be fair to say that artists were ahead of scientists on this front. Some notable examples include composers Richard Wagner and Alexander Scriabin and painters James McNeill Whistler and Wassily Kandinsky.

Wagner (1849) advocated a concept of a unified art work (*gesamtkunstwerk*, encompassing music, theater, and visual arts), which he was able to realize supervising closely the set design and writing librettos for his own operas. Scriabin was particularly preoccupied by the relationship of music and color (Galayev 1998), including a light organ in his orchestral work "Prometheus: Poem of Fire." He died before completing his "Mysterium," which was meant to include dancers and scents also.

Whistler's search for parallels between music and painting is evident in the musical titles of some of his paintings (e.g., *Nocturne* or *Symphony*; see Lochnan 2004). Likewise, Kandinsky's work was inspired by music (Betancourt 2007) (and he is in fact thought to have been a synesthete; Ione and Tyler 2003).

No doubt, technology has made it easier to create multimedia today (e.g., the simple visualization one encounters using a media player), but the central question is not how to implement it but what to implement. We soon discuss different approaches to real-time algorithmic synesthesia, in particular sharing features between simultaneously produced sound and image. We begin with the "genuine" synesthetic experience naturally occurring in a minority of individuals.

Synesthesia is usually defined as a condition in which stimulation in one sensory modality also gives rise to a perceptual experience in other modalities (Sagiv 2005). For example, for some synesthetes, music may evoke vivid visual imagery (e.g., colors, shapes, and textures; Steen 2001). Others may experience different sensory combinations, such as colored smell, taste, or pain (Day 2005); experience taste while listening to spoken words (Ward and Simner 2003); or have tactile experiences induced by smell (Cytowic 2002), to name a few examples. Although synesthesia covers a whole range of cross-sensory phenomena, it is often induced by lexical and conceptual inducers (e.g., letters and numbers; Simner 2007). What is common to these is that the synesthetic imagery is induced reliably, automatically, and involuntarily, and that they involve an actual perceptual experience rather than a mere association or metaphoric description (e.g., Baron-Cohen et al. 1987, Martino and Marks 2001). Although different synesthetes generally disagree on particular correspondence (e.g., B-flat may be pink for one synesthete but green for another), the mapping is consistent over long periods of time for each synesthete. This consistency is one of the hallmarks of synesthesia and often is utilized to verify the genuineness of the subjective reports of synesthetes (Hubbard and Ramachandran 2005, Rich et al. 2005).[2] Recently, psychophysical measures such as reaction times and stimulus detection rates have been used to establish consistency (e.g., Sagiv et al. 2006). Many of the experimental studies were based on congruency paradigms by which synesthetes were required to respond to stimuli colored either congruently or incongruently with their synesthetic experience (e.g., Ward and Sagiv 2007). Faster responses expected in the congruent condition were taken as corroborating evidence for synesthetes' subjective reports, although admittedly such simple behavioral measures alone may not suffice to verify the rich phenomenological descriptions provided by synesthetes.

Much of the recent literature on synesthesia has focused on the developmental form of the condition, that is, healthy individuals who have had these experiences for as long as they can remember. Nevertheless, it is possible to acquire synesthesia either temporarily (with hallucinogenic drugs or during other altered states of consciousness) or more permanently following sense organ, nerve, or brain injury (for more detailed overviews of cognitive and neural mechanisms, see, e.g., Hubbard and Ramachandran 2005, Robertson and Sagiv 2005, Sagiv and Ward 2006).

Recent studies suggested that the condition may be more common than previously thought—about 4% of the general population may experience one form or another (Simner et al. 2006). The most common inducers appear to be ordinal sequences such as letters or numbers or the days of the week. The most common resultant synesthetic experience is a color experience. Curiously enough, these forms of synesthesia do not fall within the boundaries of the common narrow definition as the inducer and concurrent percept may both belong to the same modality (e.g., a visually presented letter or word evokes a color experience). Furthermore, in some cases, thinking about the inducer may suffice to elicit the synesthetic experience (e.g., the concept of Monday evoking the color red). Nevertheless, there is a general agreement among researchers that these forms should be considered types of synesthesia in their own right (while the inclusion of other synesthesia-like variants is still debatable; Sagiv 2005).

Synesthesia was once considered a rare abnormality at best. Scientists would often dismiss odd subjective reports made by synesthetes, but attitudes are changing. We now aim to explain synesthesia rather than dismiss it. Furthermore, synesthesia can be utilized as a test case for theories of perception (surely, a good theory must be able to explain not only how a system usually works but also how it deviates from "normal" function). The remainder of our discussion of the psychological phenomenon of synesthetic perception focuses predominantly on auditory-visual interactions. Let us now introduce algorithmic synesthesia. We hope to convince you that the psychological and artistic explorations of synesthetic perception are complementary. *Algorithmic synesthesia* is a term we introduced (Dean et al. 2006) to describe multimedia works in which sound or image share either computational process or data source. For example, a single algorithmic process, whether running freely or under the control of a performer, may generate both sonic and visual streams, ab initio or by transformation of preexistent sound and image. Alternatively, a common data set or data stream might be the source for different algorithmic processes that generate, respectively, sound and image. The core idea is that such relationships might encourage an audiovisual perceptual or cognitive interaction with some interesting features in common with synesthesia itself. There is no claim that algorithmic synesthesia necessarily involves all or even any of the specifics of synesthetic perception just summarized. However, in common with synesthetic perception, the association between audition and vision is more than metaphorical, involving shared material or algorithmic processing (see Seitz 2005 for discussion of synesthesia in relation to metaphor). It is worth noting that the sharing of underlying structure also binds a musical score (visual) to its sonic realizations (albeit with considerable imprecision), while the piano roll or its contemporary equivalent, the MIDI (musical instrument digital interface) sequence file, also binds a preconceived graphic form to a more precise sonic realization. However, unlike the situation of algorithmic synesthesia, audiences are generally not exposed to both streams of data but rather only to the sound.

Relatively few creative artists have overtly attempted algorithmic synesthesia as yet, but it has become more common (at least implicitly) because of its increasing accessibility through laptop performance. There are as yet no empirical studies of its impacts as far as we can determine (indeed, at the time of writing, Google Scholar still only referenced our work in response to a search for the term), and it has been argued more broadly that "a central concern of any new workable theory of electronically mediated meaning must be to understand the implications of multimodality" (Nelson 2006, p. 56).

1. THE COGNITIVE BASIS OF AUDITORY-VISUAL CROSS-MODAL INTERACTIONS

The significance of examining cross-modal interaction from both creative and scientific angles becomes apparent when bearing in mind that we can appreciate art, communicate about it and through it, owing to the fact that art can effectively engage perceptual and cognitive brain mechanisms common to us all (Zeki 1999). Artists are somewhat like scientists in the laboratory in that they try to probe these mechanisms and discover what drives them. Therefore, before proceeding to explore further creative aspects of algorithmic synesthesia, we review some cognitive perspectives on auditory-visual interaction.

A. Cross-Modal Convergence

As noted in the beginning of the chapter, even in the most ordinary situation, our experience of the world around us is inherently multimodal. We use information acquired by different sense organs to learn about objects and events around us. These objects and events produce familiar and sometimes less-familiar sensory signals. Our brains in turn try to make sense of these signals, identify sources, and more broadly, find meaning. This is by no means an easy task. Sensory information varies widely with context. For example, under different lighting conditions objects may reflect different wavelengths; retinal size and shape vary with distance and viewing angle; salience varies with the background and masking by other objects. Similarly, we are able to recognize invariant sound sources and patterns despite ever-changing source distance, speed, direction of motion, acoustics of the environment, and a whole range of other factors influencing the sound spectrum. Speech recognition provides a striking demonstration of our ability to extract information despite changes in identity of the speaker, accent, pitch, speed, presence of noise, and spectral distortions introduced by devices (e.g., mobile phones or poor-quality speakers).

Under normal conditions, auditory and visual information converge to facilitate perception. For example, both faces and voices can provide clues to recognizing people. When one source of information is of poor quality, the combination may be essential. Furthermore, lip reading enhances speech perception (in individuals with normal hearing, particularly in noisy environments).

Binding together visual and auditory information (e.g., in the sense of attributing them to the same source) is but one of several binding problems that our brains must solve to combine the various features we perceive into objects and make sense of a deluge of sensory data (e.g., Treisman 1996). Attentional mechanisms are thought to be essential for this process.

B. Cross-Modal Interactions

It is clear that input in one sensory modality does not merely enhance or complement perception in other modalities; it can also alter what is being perceived. For example, listening to one syllable (ba) repeatedly while seeing a person uttering a different syllable (ga) results in hearing da rather ba (McGurk and MacDonald 1976). Visual information can also override auditory information in localization tasks. The ventriloquist effect demonstrates this well: when watching a movie, you perceive speech as coming from the actor's mouth rather than the speakers to the right and left of the screen.

While vision often overrides auditory information in case of discrepancies, it is more difficult to find examples in which audition overrides vision. Shams and colleagues showed that the number of flashes of light one perceives may correspond to the number of beeps you hear during the same time window rather than the actual number of flashes displayed (Shams et al. 2000, 2002), and in recent preliminary work we have shown that the superimposition of rhythmic patterns, by means of pitch differences or to a lesser extent spatialization differences, can enhance such illusions (Wilkie et al. forthcoming). Interestingly, the ventriloquist effect can be reversed when the image becomes very blurry. Under such conditions, localizing by sound may indeed seem like an optimal choice (Alais and Burr 2004).

Such interactions suggest that multimodal information processing involves more than convergence of otherwise independent streams of information. Indeed, at the neural level, we find that activity in brain areas thought to be unimodal can be modulated by information coming from other senses (for a review, see Macaluso and Driver 2005). For example, Calvert et al. (1997) found that silent lip reading activates the auditory cortex, while Sadato et al. (Sadato et al. 1996) found that Braille reading in blind individuals is associated with primary visual cortex activation.

C. Matching and Mismatching Information

How does one determine that there is a match between auditory and visual signals? What do they have in common, and how can we compare these radically different inputs? We are looking for covariance or coupling of the signals along any two dimensions. Common onset and offset times, or generally speaking, synchronized dynamics, may imply a common source object or causal relationship. Synchrony is indeed a very powerful cue to causality or unity (even when it is improbable given physical location). The rubber hand illusion demonstrates this in the visuotactile domain (Botvinick and Cohen 1998). This illusion arises when the same tactile stimulus is simultaneously applied to the hand when it is hidden from view and to a visible rubber hand placed in an anatomically plausible position in front of participants. Under these conditions, they are likely to feel that the rubber hand is their own (i.e., visuotactile synchrony influences perceived hand position and limb ownership).

In the auditory-visual domain, the ventriloquist effect represents another illusion of unity mediated by synchrony. While the brain may tolerate a short lag,[3] the illusion breaks down at larger ones (evident in occasional broadcasts in which such a lag is present for some reason or another). Interestingly, apparent synchrony depends not only on the timing of the auditory and visual events but also on the distance of the source. For example, Alais and Carlile (2005) showed that we can tolerate and in fact expect larger lags for more distant sources, compensating for the later arrival of sound waves relative to light waves. This would relate well to the fact that film sound designers routinely use such timing differences in the belief that they accentuate the impression of reality (sounds of doors opening, etc.).

It is important to remember that while in the laboratory or studio we can create and combine auditory and visual streams to create illusions of unity, the reason that these illusions work is that in everyday life synchrony is indeed a reliable cue to a common source. Indeed, perfect synchrony is unlikely to occur by chance and is difficult to fake (although recall the Marx Brothers mirror scene in *Duck Soup*). While onset and offset are perhaps the most salient manifestations of synchronized dynamics, we are likely to notice a whole range of other correlations (e.g., pitch-space on the piano keyboard or a correlation between the size of a spider and the loudness of the spectator's scream) as well as make assumptions about likely correlations based on prior experience (large objects resonate at lower frequencies). Some auditory-visual associations we encounter are more arbitrary than others. For example, the visual appearance of the doorbell has very little predictive value concerning the sound heard when it is pressed. In novel situations, synchrony or co-localization alone may enable us to recognize a relationship (or perceive an illusory one).

One of the approaches to algorithmic synesthesia—simultaneous visualization and sonification of the same data set—does guarantee the presence of correlations that we are likely to encounter when sound and vision emanate from one source. How transparent or cognitively accessible the relationship will be is a different question, and we elaborate on this in the third part of this chapter.

D. Arbitrary Associations or Common Trends?

One of the puzzling features of synesthesia (the psychological phenomenon or condition) is the seemingly arbitrary nature of synesthetic correspondences. Synesthetes rarely agree about the specific colors they may associate with, for example, the letter *H*, Wednesday, middle C on the piano, or the taste of pistachio ice cream. Obviously, once a certain correspondence has been learned, it is no longer arbitrary for the person who has acquired it. Indeed, synesthetes are consistent in the cross-modal correspondences they experience across very long time periods (Sagiv 2005). Consequently, for a given individual, the feeling of seeing, for example, the color purple may have as much explanatory power about the timbre they hear (e.g., a trumpet) as the experience of the sound itself. The visual aspects become a part of the auditory experience. Shanon (2003) took this one step further and claimed that synesthesia entails more than cross-activation of different senses—it actually involves a relaxation of the boundaries between them.[4]

Interestingly, we find that once an association has been formed, we may also find evidence for bidirectional interaction even though the phenomenology is usually unidirectional. For example, synesthetes commonly report seeing numbers in color, but they do not "see" numbers when viewing a colorful display. Nevertheless, we see that given a numerical task, performance (reaction time) can be influenced by stimulus color (Cohen Kadosh et al. 2005). This effect can be present in addition to the more common finding that numbers may interfere with color judgments (number stimuli may slow color-naming time if the synesthetic color they evoke is incongruent with the presented target color).

Synesthetic correspondences are not completely idiosyncratic. In fact, in recent years we find that some trends seen in synesthetes are also found in nonsynesthetes. Such common inclinations are more consistent with the idea that synesthesia utilizes universal mechanisms rather and possibly represent an exaggeration of normal function rather than a gross abnormality (Sagiv and Ward 2006).

E. Common Auditory-Visual Associations in Synesthetes and Nonsynesthete Observers

Many synesthetes experience synesthesia in response to an auditory stimulus. Quite commonly, this is due to the linguistic aspects of a stimulus (Day 2005, Simner 2007). Still, some individuals automatically visualize colors when they listen to music or, in some instances, when exposed to a wide range of environmental sounds. Anecdotal reports suggested that for such synesthetes, experiences may depend on different factors—pitch, timbre, loudness, intervals, and chords. When synesthetes are asked to match colors to sound, they tend to choose brighter color with higher-pitch sounds (Marks 1975). Interestingly, this trend is also seen in nonsynesthetes (Marks 1974, 1987, Hubbard and Ramachandran 2005). A recent study by Ward et al. (2006) demonstrated this in a group of ten synesthetes and ten nonsynesthete controls using the same stimuli and methodology. They used seventy tones with varying pitch and timbre and asked participants to choose the color that went best with the presented tone. The procedure was repeated on a different occasion to establish consistency. While synesthetes were much more consistent in their responses than the nonsynesthete group, both showed essentially similar patterns. Regardless of timbre, all subjects associated brighter colors with higher pitch. However, more saturated colors were chosen at around middle C. Furthermore, timbre influenced saturation, regardless of pitch—pure tones were typically associated with less-saturated colors (low chromaticity). Although only synesthetes automatically visualized colors when presented with the sounds, the fact that nonsynesthetes made similar choices when required to match colors with tones is consistent with the idea that synesthetes utilize universal mechanisms. Still, we need to explain why some individuals have full-fledged synesthetic experiences while in most of us synesthetic associations remain below the threshold of conscious perception, manifesting only in behavioral measures and similarity judgments.[5]

Mondloch and Maurer (2004) showed that associations between pitch and brightness and between pitch and object size are present in preschool children (30–36 months old). Like adults, they associated higher pitch with brighter, smaller visual stimuli, although the association with size was weaker than the association with brightness. The fact that such associations are present very early in life is consistent with the neonatal synesthesia hypothesis (for a review, see Maurer and Mondloch 2005).[6] Marks (1975) also described a relationship between loudness of sounds and the size of the photism (louder sounds are associated with larger visual images).

F. Shared Meaning, Synesthesia, Language, and Gestures

We are able to share meaning through both a symbolic verbal system and nonverbal means. Some neuroscientists believe that we developed this capability using the "mirror neuron system" (e.g., Rizzolatti and Arbib 1998). Mirror neurons were first identified in the monkey premotor cortex (including an area homologous to the human language area). These neurons fire both when the monkeys perform a specific action or when they watch others perform it, thus creating a link between observer and the observed, enabling us to share meaning (at the very least, intentions) by simulating others' behavior. Ramachandran and Hubbard (2001) further suggested that certain common cross-modal associations may have facilitated the evolution of language, with natural constraints in the mapping of sound into objects providing the basis for a protolanguage.

Auditory and visual signals coming from a variety of sources (not necessarily human) can communicate meaningful information about their provenance. Some of these signals give rise to learned auditory-visual associations. More abstract stimuli produced (e.g., by musicians) can convey meaning when the listener appreciates the physical effort required to produce that sound, even when the gesture is not visible (Smalley 1992). Furthermore, when a gesture is present, it does have an impact on the experience of the listener (Dahl and Friberg 2007); for example, perceived sound duration can be influenced by the performer's gestures (Schutz and Lipscomb 2007). For the performer, the body also becomes synesthetically/kinesthetically linked to the auditory and visual aspects of the performance. For the audience, a body frame of reference becomes more important when the spatial extent of the stimuli varies or in interactive multimedia (e.g., Ben-Tal 2008). We return to the issue of spatial extent, and it is discussed from a different bodily perspective in chapter 11, this volume.

2. COGNITIVE/ALGORITHMIC UNDERPINNINGS

We noted that perception and cognition not only align visual and sonic information but also tolerate or gain from their asynchrony. Such effects are well known in film; the sound designer in particular spends much effort on using quite unrealistic sonic action to amplify a realistic impression, and the sound may involve disparate noises as well as phase-shifted temporal associations (Chion 1994, van Leeuwen 1999). Thus, algorithmic control can vary the extent of perceptual association between sonic and visual events. It is interesting that in the creative arts it is common to anticipate multiplicity of interpretation on the part of vusers (viewerlisteners). The disparities between synesthetes in the nature of the reproducible synesthetic associations they experience potentially offers routes by which algorithmic synesthesia could amplify such multiplicity of all vusers' interpretations: the cognitive and affective responses of a person for whom the algorithmic alignment is consistent with their (synesthetic or merely preferential) associations will probably be rather differently influenced from a person whose associations are distinct.

Conversely, in the field of sonification, which seeks to make large quantities or rapid streams of data cognizable by representing them in sound, so-called zero-order transcoding involves complete synchrony between what is being represented and its sonic output. But, just as stock marketeers follow moving averages, representing blocks of data rather than individual events, so a range of sonification mechanisms perturbs this temporal relationship (see final section of this chapter).

It is often argued (see chapter 23, this volume) that humans can engage in several different modes of listening. In some, the emphasis is on everyday detection of events for the purpose of interpreting them in terms of their origins in some physical gesture. In others, so-called musical listening, sound is assessed for its intrinsic character with little reference to whether any natural object or event could generate such a sound. In computer music, commonly the sounds are such as can only be made by digital sound processing, techniques invented by humans. So, for sonification, the key question is to what degree the sound-generating algorithm is transparent, that is, permits the listener to understand the nature of the data being sonified. By extension, in algorithmic synesthesia, multimedia artists have the opportunity to place their processes anywhere along a spectrum of transparency of relationship between sound and image (and performer/creator) and to lead the vuser to establish personal understanding of such consistencies in this relationship as the artist builds in. All of this has to be taken in the context that with artistic multimedia, just as with physical environmental inputs, we discriminate in attention and importance between different signals, and just as we stop attending to the air-conditioning noise, so we may perhaps treat some components of a multimedia event. We may even be exposed to an excess of incoming information, beyond our capacity to handle.

Nevertheless, it is important to consider that while listening and viewing or while walking around the physical environment, we may also be generating our own distinct internal data streams, some of which may be imagined. Mental imagery for music is very often multimodal (see Bailes 2007). For instance, when we imagine a favorite piece of music, we may experience a mix of auditory, visual, and even kinesthetic mental representations. The multimodal nature of mental imagery is of considerable interest with respect to synesthesia, again underlining our propensity for cross-modal cognition. We might ask whether synesthetes experience cross-modal impressions when imagining sound or imagining vision. Very little is known beyond anecdotal report. While truly synesthetic experience may be idiosyncratic (although consistent), it seems likely that the triggering of a visual image by sound or a sonic image by vision for nonsynesthetes is largely contingent on the learned associations between sound and vision encountered through perceptual experience (or conditioning; see Cook 1998, p. 36). Eitan and Granot (2006) asked experiment participants to imagine the motions of a human character in response to simple melodic stimuli that were either an intensification or an abatement of a particular parameter such as dynamics, pitch contour, and pitch interval. They found significant relationships between certain musical parameters (such as pitch contour) and the imagined motion described by the presumably nonsynesthete respondents, and not all the relationships were as one might predict.

Ward (2004) argued that there is evidence of emotionally mediated synesthesia, describing the case of a synesthete for whom emotionally charged names of familiar people and other word categories were associated with a higher incidence of synesthetic color than emotionally neutral names and words. Perhaps emotion, familiarity, and attention play a similar role in the strength of cross-modal associations by nonsynesthetes. Some researchers have focused on suggested links between cross-modal perception, the perception of affect and artistic creativity (Dailey et al. 1997): participants who were classified as the most creative reported stronger associations between colors, pure tones, vowels, and emotional terms.

Should findings from the psychology of cross-modal perception and synesthesia guide us in the creative processes of algorithmic synesthesia? It is inevitable that artists will take into consideration some cognitive and perceptual constraints on the listeners and viewers, but the degree to which one seeks to mimic or recreate a genuine synesthetic experience is a matter of taste. Either way, there is always room for creativity, even when adopting a set rules or constraints and the results may or may not be interesting in either framework. The substantial variability in the phenomenology of genuine synesthetic perception demonstrates this and in fact guarantees that the artist retains considerable levels of freedom. Ultimately, even the attempts of a synesthete to convey his or her particular experience to others using sound, image, or both must involve some choices regarding which aspects of an incredibly rich personal experience to represent digitally. The difficulty may be due to the sheer complexity or due to attentional limits of the synesthete as an introspective observer (during the course of our work with synesthetes, we have often heard individuals complaining that they do not have time to observe all the synesthetic properties they perceive).

The observation that synesthetes often find their synesthetic experience pleasurable and aesthetically pleasing suggests that re-creating it does have an aesthetic potential. However, we must keep in mind that some aspects of synesthetic imagery may be very predictable and unremarkable; for synesthetic imagery to be interesting, the inducing stimulus may itself need to be interesting or novel. One factor with algorithmic synesthesia, as implied here, is that synesthetes in the audience may feel unease if their own synesthetic experience disagrees with choices made by the artists (e.g., "The colors are all wrong!"), but of course they must be used to such experiences in their day-to-day environments.

Let us now summarize potential strategies for algorithmic synesthesia based on the principles of naturally occurring auditory-visual synesthetic perception and some of the issues that they raise.

- *Synchrony:* Synchronized temporal patterns may be the most powerful cue for unity at a basic perceptual level. Once achieved, this unity can alter perception and so permit certain cross-modal interactions (keeping in mind that unity may be achieved with some small temporal misalignment). This is in contrast to nonsynchronous synesthesia, which may be linked to the evoking stimulus semantically, whether thematically or though learned associations. Having said that, some synesthetic imagery may be linked to more global parameters of a piece and not be temporally aligned.

- *Onset times* are not the only parameters we could manipulate. Direction of motion and location in space could also be used. We could covary pitch, loudness, and timbre with size, shape, hue, saturation, and lightness. It may prove particularly useful to use mappings found in both synesthetes and nonsynesthetes, such as pitch-lightness, pitch-size, loudness-size, timbre-chromaticity.
- *Different variants of color music synesthesia* include colored pitch, colored timbre, colored intervals, colored chords, or more global parameters (tonality of a piece). It is conceivable that color schemes based on any of these parameters could prove interesting (albeit disconcerting for some genuine synesthetes).
- *Similarly, language-based synesthesia could occur at different levels*—letter (grapheme), phoneme, whole words, or concepts. These may become useful when text or speech are included. More generally, this suggests the possibility of synesthetic streams arising simultaneously at different levels of processing of the same stimulus, modulated by selective attention to one level or another. In turn, we could potentially manipulate the audience's attention to different levels (or streams) by specifically choosing to visualize or sonify these rather than others.
- *Familiarity and consistency:* True synesthetes are very sensitive to deviations from their synesthetic correspondences, which may remain constant for years. It is unlikely that such fixity of correspondence could be achieved with a nonsynesthetic audience, even if considerable time is provided to allow them to learn associations. Thus, for the general audience, a deliberate change of mapping between sounds and image could still possibly serve creative aspects of algorithmic synesthesia.
- *Familiarity and meaning:* Synesthetic experience is sometimes weak for highly unfamiliar stimuli. It "grows" as the potential inducers acquire meaning. Using abstract, unfamiliar material may make it harder to form cross-modal associations on one hand, but on the other hand easier to accept a given scheme.
- *Finally, we need to beware of sensory overload.* This often occurs for genuine synesthetes and may be a concern in algorithmic synesthesia as well.

3. ALGORITHMIC SYNESTHESIA AS A CREATIVE POSSIBILITY

Through metaphor and synesthesia (cross-modal thinking and the unity of the senses), we acquire the means of enriching our experience of the symbolic codes of specific art forms by engaging with subsidiary meaning through other modes of perception (Cunliffe 1994, p. 163). The previous sections make quite clear, in agreement with Cunliffe (1994), that by sharing computational process or data, one may be able to establish creative exchanges between different modalities, and these may be cognitively and emotively interesting. In this final section, we briefly discuss some of the generic creative possibilities just listed, noting that such work is now widespread (cf. Whitelaw 2004, Dean et al. 2006), but little is systematic, and none has been subjected to empirical study, so we are at the beginning of our potential application of this mode of creative work.

For creative and algorithmic processes in particular, it is useful to envisage a continuum (or several) in which one can operate. There is probably only one way to conceptualize a single continuum between the visual and the sonic stimuli that encompasses all the materials relevant to algorithmic synesthesia: visual ↔ text-image ↔ speech ↔ music ↔ sound. We note that other aspects of synesthesia, such as those involving gustation, would require different treatment and are not addressed here. We note again that graphemic stimuli seem to be the most commonly potent. Moving and colored images of words or letters are now quite often used in creative writing for intermedia (see, e.g., Smith 2005). However, it is not clear that anyone has tried to use these relationships in the systematic manner that might challenge synesthetes, and more pertinently, relatively few have tried to use them in the potential manner of systematic algorithmic synesthesia. The opportunity is obvious.

Some software already encourages sound creation originating in image. For example, MetaSynth is a program that permits the conversion of image to sound (e.g., color to spatialization or intensity) and to a more limited extent the converse process, and it is now widely used by composers, particularly in the creation of materials with which they will later work more intensively during an acousmatic composition. Conversely, many programs provide a continuous representation of a sound flux, mapped in simple or complex ways. As discussed, color and sound have strong relationships, and a long artistic history of artistic works, including Messiaen's *Chronochromie*, has sought to exploit them.

We have created subcontinua, for example between noise and speech, as have many composers (see chapter 14, this volume, on speech in computer music). The issues of synchronicity and relative speed of change in sound and image streams are already important in intermedia work and most highly formalized in film sound design. As mentioned, a perceived unity between sound and image (which may require some precise temporal misalignment) can create desirable versimilitude, which can eventually create cross-modal interactions by which one component becomes an index for the other. However, such synchronies are also the source of potential flexibility for composition developing and exploiting intermedia synesthesia, as in the case of the influence of multiple rapid aural events on the perception of the number of visual events they accompany (Shams et al. 2000, 2002, Wilkie et al. forthcoming). As suggested, a range of mappings of sound and image (e.g., pitch and darkness of color, etc.) deserve systematic attention. We have begun the empirical counterpart to such creative investigations by showing that rhythmic parameters of repetition of a sound (creating metrical patterns, for example), or to a lesser degree spatial parameters (alternating sidedness of the sound field), do have an influence on viewer perception of flashes. Thus, such approaches may be powerful in creative intermedia with complex sound and image.

It is particularly interesting to consider the future issue of three-dimensional (3-D) synesthesia and its possible algorithmic counterpart. A synesthete may project color onto the evoking stimulus, his or her immediate peripersonal space (which is within reach), and only rarely onto more distant space. It may be imaged on some internal mental screen, not clearly localized in space, or onto a bodily reference frame (such as the hand, or a screen "inside" the forehead). It will be difficult but fascinating to establish and control counterparts of these different processes in algorithmic synesthesia. Perhaps the most feasible opportunity is that of creating algorithmic synesthesia in the immediate peripersonal space of the vuser. This effect might coexist with their ability to move around a 3-D sonic field (the future traversable "sonic garden" that is open to investigation, as discussed in chapter 13, this volume). In such a future environment, the vuser could move both to and from sonic components and bring with them components of their own peripersonal sonic and visual image.

We have discussed (Dean et al. 2006) some examples of computer sonic works that at least engage the field of algorithmic synesthesia, such as from Robin Fox, Nick Collins, David Worrall and Stuart Ramsden, PanSonic, Andrew Gadow, and ourselves. But, essentially these use various forms of transcoding of sound into image or vice versa without as yet deeply assessing their potential for algorithmic synesthesia. Thus, in conclusion we note that the composer of a new work in a relatively unfamiliar idiom, such as many within acousmatic music, always has to deal with the need for new listeners to construct their own associations as the piece develops. Music, more than many arts because of its abstraction and limited external referentiality, provides special opportunities for interpretive multiplicity on the part of listeners. Algorithmic synesthesia foregrounds the corresponding issue in multimedia creative work, amplifies this multiplicity of interpretive possibility, and offers bold opportunities for contemporary intermedia.

Acknowledgments: We thank Oded Ben-Tal for helpful discussions and comments on the manuscript.

NOTES

1. Even under conditions of sensory deprivation (i.e., complete removal of sensory input), we may begin hallucinating before long (see, e.g., Merabet et al. 2004).
2. Consistency is rather easy to test for some types of synesthetic experiences (e.g., colors) by requesting synesthetes to choose a color from a given set or simply naming it. Other aspects may be more challenging to measure or quantify. Note, however, that there is no a priori reason to believe that a synesthetic correspondence must be consistent. While

consistency is well established in most recent reports of (developmental) synesthesia, it not clear that this is the case in drug-induced synesthesia.

3. For examples of illusory synchrony, see Nicholas Cook's discussion of "The Rite of Spring" sequence from *Fantasia* (Cook 1998, chap. 5).

4. Werner (1930, cited in Merleau-Ponty 1962/2002, p. 266) has noted this earlier: "For the subject does not say only that he has the sensation both of a sound and a color; it is the sound itself that he sees where colors are formed." Admittedly, for a nonsynesthete it is very difficult to understand what this means. It is not clear to us either, although we accept that a genuine synesthetic experience (whether naturally occurring or chemically induced) can be quite profound and perhaps qualitatively different from artificial multimedia.

5. We only have tentative answers to this question, and debates concerning the cognitive, neural, and genetic factors are ongoing. While this is outside the scope of this chapter, for further discussion see Merleau-Ponty (1962), van Campen (2008), and Ward (2008).

6. According to the neonatal synesthesia hypothesis, all newborns experience synesthesia (or at the very least cross-sensory confusion) until about 4 months of age. Indeed, electroencephalographic studies in infants and animal studies showed cross-activation of sensory areas, suggestive of higher connectivity within the brain. Some of these connections are pruned during development, but synesthetes may retain a higher proportion. Preliminary brain imaging studies suggest that this could indeed be the case (Rouw and Scholte 2007). Nevertheless, disinhibition or unmasking of existing connections has been suggested as a possible mechanism for acquired synesthesia associated with visual loss (Jacobs et al. 1981, Armel and Ramachandran 1999).

BIBLIOGRAPHY

Alais, D., and D. Burr. 2004. The ventriloquist effect results from near-optimal bimodal integration. *Current Biology: CB* 14(3): 257–262.

Alais, D., and S. Carlile. 2005. Synchronizing to real events: Subjective audiovisual alignment scales with perceived auditory depth and speed of sound. *Proceedings of the National Academy of Sciences of the United States of America* 102(6): 2244–2247.

Armel, K. C., and V. S. Ramachandran. 1999. Acquired synesthesia in retinitis pigmentosa. *Neurocase* 5(4): 293–296.

Bailes, F. 2007. The prevalence and nature of imagined music in the everyday lives of music students. *Psychology of Music* 35(4): 555–570.

Baron-Cohen, S., M. A. Wyke, and C. Binnie. 1987. Hearing words and seeing colours: An experimental investigation of a case of synaesthesia. *Perception* 16(6): 761–767.

Ben-Tal, O. 2008. "Musical Toys: Interactive Audio for Non-Musicians." Paper presented at Proceedings of the 6th Linux Audio Conference, Feb 28–March 2, 2008, Cologne, Germany.

Betancourt. 2007. A taxonomy of abstract form using studies of synesthesia and hallucinations. *Leonardo* 40(1): 59–65.

Botvinick, M., and J. Cohen. 1998. Rubber hands "feel" touch that eyes see. *Nature* 391(6669): 756.

Calvert, G. A., E. T. Bullmore, M. J. Brammer, R. Campbell, S. C. Williams, P. K. McGuire, P. W. Woodruff, S. D. Iversen, and A. S. David. 1997. Activation of auditory cortex during silent lipreading. *Science (New York, N.Y.)* 276(5312): 593–596.

Chion, M. 1994. *Audio Vision.* New York: Columbia University Press.

Cohen Kadosh, R., N. Sagiv, D. E. Linden, L. C. Robertson, G. Elinger, and A. Henik. 2005. When blue is larger than red: Colors influence numerical cognition in synesthesia. *Journal of Cognitive Neuroscience* 17(11): 1766–1773.

Cook, N. 1998. *Analysing Musical Multimedia.* Oxford: Clarendon Press.

Cunliffe, L. 1994. Synaesthesia, arts education as cross-modal relationships rooted in cognitive repertoires. *Journal of Art and Design Education* 13(2): 163–172.

Cytowic, R. E. 2002. *Synaesthesia: A Union of the Senses.* 2nd ed. Cambridge: MIT Press.

Dahl, S., and A. Friberg. 2007. Visual perception of expressiveness in musicians' body movements. *Journal of New Music Research* 29: 225–233.

Dailey, A., C. Martindale, and J. Borkum. 1997. Creativity, synaesthesia, and physiognomic perception. *Creativity Research Journal* 10(1): 1–8.

Day, S. 2005. Some demographic and socio-cultural aspects of synesthesia. In *Synesthesia: Perspectives from Cognitive Neuroscience*, ed. L. C. Robertson and N. Sagiv. New York: Oxford University Press, pp. 11–33.

Dean, R. T., M. Whitelaw, H. Smith, and D. Worrall. 2006. The mirage of algorithmic synaesthesia: Some compositional mechanisms and research agendas in computer music and sonification. *Contemporary Music Review* 25(4): 311–327.

Eitan, Z., and R. Y. Granot. 2006. How music moves: Musical parameters and listeners' images of motion. *Music Perception* 23:221–247.

Galeyev, B. M. 1988. The Fire of "Prometheus": Music-kinetic art experiments in the USSR. *Leonardo* 21(4): 383–396.

Hubbard, E. M., and V. S. Ramachandran. 2005. Neurocognitive mechanisms of synesthesia. *Neuron* 48(3): 509–520.

Ione, A., and C. Tyler. 2003. Neurohistory and the arts. Was Kandinsky a synesthete? *Journal of the History of the Neurosciences* 12(2): 223–226.

Jacobs, L., A. Karpik, D. Bozian, and S. Gothgen. 1981. Auditory-visual synesthesia: Sound-induced photisms. *Archives of Neurology* 38(4): 211–216.

Lochnan, K. A. 2004. *Turner Whistler Monet.* London: Tate Gallery Publishing.

Macaluso, E., and J. Driver. 2005. Multisensory spatial interactions: A window onto functional integration in the human brain. *Trends in Neurosciences* 28(5): 264–271.

Marks, L. E. 1974. On associations of light and sound: The mediation of brightness, pitch, and loudness. *American Journal of Psychology* 87(1–2): 173–188.

Marks, L. E. 1975. On colored-hearing synesthesia: Cross-modal translations of sensory dimensions. *Psychological Bulletin* 82(3): 303–331.

Marks, L. E. 1987. On cross-modal similarity: Auditory—visual interactions in speeded discrimination. *Journal of Experimental Psychology: Human Perception and Performance* 13(3): 384–394.

Martino, G., and L. E. Marks. 2001. Synesthesia: Strong and weak. *Current Directions in Psychological Science* 10: 61–65.

Maurer, D., and C. J. Mondloch. 2005. Neonatal synesthesia: A re-evaluation. In *Synesthesia: Perspectives from Cognitive Neuroscience*, ed. L. C. Robertson and N. Sagiv. New York: Oxford University Press, pp. 193–213.

McGurk, H., and J. MacDonald. 1976. Hearing lips and seeing voices. *Nature* 264(5588): 746–748.

Merabet, L. B., D. Maguire, A. Warde, K. Alterescu, R. Stickgold, and A. Pascual-Leone. 2004. Visual hallucinations during prolonged blindfolding in sighted subjects. *Journal of Neuro-ophthalmology: The Official Journal of the North American Neuro-ophthalmology Society* 24(2): 109–113.

Merleau-Ponty, Maurice. 1962. *Phenomenology of Perception.* New York: Routledge and Kegan Paul. Repr. London: Routledge, 2002.

Mondloch, C. J., and D. Maurer. 2004. Do small white balls squeak? Pitch-object correspondences in young children. *Cognitive, Affective and Behavioral Neuroscience* 4(2): 133–136.

Nelson, M. E. 2006. Mode, meaning, and synaesthesia in multimedia L2 writing. *Language Learning and Technology* 10(2): 56–76.

Ramachandran, V. S., and E. M. Hubbard. 2001. Synaesthesia—A window into perception, thought and language. *Journal of Consciousness Studies* 8: 3–34.

Rich, A. N., J. L. Bradshaw, and J. B. Mattingley. 2005. A systematic, large-scale study of synaesthesia: Implications for the role of early experience in lexical-colour associations. *Cognition* 98(1): 53–84.

Rizzolatti, G., and M. A. Arbib. 1998. Language within our grasp. *Trends in Neurosciences* 21(5): 188–194.

Robertson, L. C., and N. Sagiv. 2005. *Synesthesia: Perspectives from Cognitive Neuroscience.* New York: Oxford University Press.

Rouw, R., and H. S. Scholte. 2007. Increased structural connectivity in grapheme-color synesthesia. *Nature Neuroscience* 10(6): 792–797.

Sadato, N., A. Pascual-Leone, J. Grafman, V. Ibanez, M. P. Deiber, G. Dold, and M. Hallett. 1996. Activation of the primary visual cortex by Braille reading in blind subjects. *Nature* 380(6574): 526–528.

Sagiv, N. 2005. Synesthesia in perspective. In *Synesthesia: Perspectives from Cognitive Neuroscience,* ed. L. C. Robertson and N. Sagiv. New York: Oxford University Press, pp. 3–10.

Sagiv, N., J. Heer, and L. Robertson. 2006. Does binding of synesthetic color to the evoking grapheme require attention? *Cortex; a Journal Devoted to the Study of the Nervous System and Behavior* 42(2): 232–242.

Sagiv, N., and J. Ward. 2006. Crossmodal interactions: Lessons from synesthesia. *Progress in Brain Research* 155: 259–271.

Schutz, M., and S. Lipscomb. 2007. Hearing gestures, seeing music: Vision influences perceived tone duration. *Perception* 36(6): 888–897.

Seitz, J. A. 2005. The neural, evolutionary, developmental, and bodily basis of metaphor. *New Ideas in Psychology* 23(2): 74–95.

Shams, L., Y. Kamitani, and S. Shimojo. 2000. What you see is what you hear. *Nature* 408: 788.

Shams, L., Y. Kamitani, and S. Shimojo. 2002. Visual illusion induced by sound. *Brain Research. Cognitive Brain Research* 14(1): 147–152.

Shanon, B. 2003. Three stories concerning synaesthesia—A commentary on Ramachandran and Hubbard. *Journal of Consciousness Studies* 10: 69–74.

Simner, J. 2007. Beyond perception: Synaesthesia as a psycholinguistic phenomenon. *Trends in Cognitive Sciences* 11(1): 23–29.

Simner, J., C. Mulvenna, N. Sagiv, E. Tsakanikos, S. A. Witherby, C. Fraser, K. Scott, and J. Ward. 2006. Synaesthesia: The prevalence of atypical cross-modal experiences. *Perception* 35(8): 1024–1033.

Smalley, D. 1992. The listening imagination: Listening in the electroacoustic era. In *Companion to Contemporary Musical Thought: Volume 1*, ed. J. Paynter, T. Howell, R. Orton, and P. Seymour. London: Routledge, pp. 514–554.

Smith, H. 2005. *The Writing Experiment: Strategies for Innovative Creative Writing*. Sydney: Allen and Unwin.

Steen, C. J. 2001. Visions shared: A firsthand look into synesthesia and art. *Leonardo* 34: 203–208.

Treisman, A. 1996. The binding problem. *Current Opinion in Neurobiology* 6(2): 171–178.

van Campen, C. 2008. *The Hidden Sense. Synesthesia in Art and Science, Leonardo*. Cambridge: MIT Press.

van Leeuwen, T. 1999. *Speech, Music, Sound*. London: Macmillan.

Viola, B. 1995. *Reasons for Knocking at an Empty House: Writings 1973–1994*. London: Thames and Hudson.

Wagner, R. 1849. *Das Kunstwerk der Zukunft*. Leipzig: Otto Wigand.

Ward, J. 2004. Emotionally mediated synaesthesia. *Cognitive Neuropsychology* 21(7): 761–772.

Ward, J. 2008. *The Frog Who Croaked Blue*. Oxford: Routledge.

Ward, J., B. Huckstep, and E. Tsakanikos. 2006. Sound-colour synaesthesia: To what extent does it use cross-modal mechanisms common to us all? *Cortex; a Journal Devoted to the Study of the Nervous System and Behavior* 42(2): 264–280.

Ward, J., and N. Sagiv. 2007. Synaesthesia for finger counting and dice patterns: a case of higher synaesthesia? *Neurocase: Case Studies in Neuropsychology, Neuropsychiatry, and Behavioural Neurology* 13(2): 86–93.

Ward, J., and J. Simner. 2003. Lexical-gustatory synaesthesia: Linguistic and conceptual factors. *Cognition* 89(3): 237–261.

Whitelaw, M., *Metacreation: Art and Artificial Life*. 2004. Cambridge, Mass.: MIT Press.

Wilkie, S., C. Stevens, and R. T. Dean. 2008. Psycho-acoustic manipulation of the sound-induced illusory flash. In *Lecture Notes in Computer Science*. Berlin: Springer, pp. 223–234.

Zeki, S. 1999. Art and the brain. *Journal of Consciousness Studies* 6(6–7): 76–96.

CHAPTER 16

AN INTRODUCTION TO DATA SONIFICATION

DAVID WORRALL

THE aim of this pragmatic introduction to data sonification is to provide an understanding of the origins and conceptual issues involved in this young, inter-disciplinary, and quickly evolving discipline. It begins by summarizing different ways sonification has been defined, the types and classifications of data that it attempts to represent with sound, and how these representations perform under the pressure of real-world usage. The need for better tools for data sonification is raised and leads to discussion of the value of collaborative research and a reflection on the relationship between music sound and science.

1. DEFINING AND CLASSIFYING SONIFICATION

The nonmedical[1] definition of the term *sonification* has evolved since 1994 as its use in auditory displays has developed. For the purpose of discussing multivariate data mappings, Bly (1994, p. 406) described sonification as "audio representation of multivariate data." The sonification of univariate data is also possible, and thus Scaletti (1994, p. 224) proposed a more formal working definition for her investi-gation of auditory data representation: "a mapping of numerically represented relations in some domain under study to relations in an acoustic domain for the purposes of interpreting, understanding, or communicating relations in the domain under study." To differentiate sonification from other uses of sound, Scaletti explicitly drew attention to two parts of her definition: a *technique* (mapping numerical data to sound) and an *intent* (to understand or communicate something about the world). Barrass (1997, pp. 29–30), reworking Scaletti's definition, en route to a definition of *auditory information design* (the design of sounds to support an information processing activity), emphasized the idea of information (the content) over data (the medium): "a mapping of information to perceptual relations in the acoustic domain to meet the information requirements of an information processing activity."

Both Scaletti's and Barrass's definitions can be read to mean both the process of representing and the resulting sonic object. The *Sonification Report* (Kramer et al. 1999) was a major effort at summarizing the field to date. Its focus was on sonification as a process: "The use of non-speech audio to convey information. More specifically, sonification is the transformation of data relations into perceived relations in an acoustic signal for the purposes of facilitating communication or interpretation." The first sentence of this 1999 definition appears to be the most widely used. The exclusion of speech audio is to discriminate sonification from speech-related interfaces such as text-to-speech software. While speech research is an extensive research field in and of itself, there is no reason why speech audio should *necessarily* be excluded from the definition. As Hermann argued, speech does have attributes that, if data driven, could be useful for sonification purposes (2002, p. 23), and some research suggested speech-audio displays could be used to convey nonverbal information on which people could make useful decisions (Nesbitt and Barrass 2002).

While speech and nonspeech sounds share such identifiable auditory characteristics as pitch, rhythm, articulation, and rugosity, as well as some larger gestalts such as phrase and prosody, the ability to simultaneously listen to music and talk or read without confusion is easily demonstrated. This is supported by cognition research that finds that the auditory cortices in the two hemispheres of the brain are relatively specialized enough to be able to exploit the temporal and spectral differences between speech and musical sounds (Zatorre et al. 2002). The more recent finding that speech that is temporally compressed until incomprehensible as speech could significantly improve menu navigation in personal digital assistant (PDA) devices (Walker et al. 2006), further emphasizes the importance of not excluding speechlike sounds from the definition of sonification.

While the "representation of data relations in sound relations" (Anderson et al. 2002) is likely the most succinct, it avoids the intent referenced in the 1999 definition: "for the purposes of facilitating communication or interpretation." It also does not quite capture distinctions between, for example, data sonification and data-driven music composition. While a purpose of music is the expression of musical and broader cultural considerations, whatever they may be, among composers, performers, and listeners, the purpose of sonification is to represent data in sound in such ways that structural characteristics of the data become apparent to a listener. I use the following definition to clarify the object of the action and to lift the "nonspeech audio" restriction: "Sonification is the acoustic representation of data for relational interpretation by listeners, for the purpose of increasing their knowledge of the source from which the data was acquired." In the early literature (Kramer 1994), *sonification* is used as a shortened form of *data sonification* as a subcategory of *auditory display*, but the distinction seems to have subsequently disappeared. All three terms are now used both nominally and verbally, as are the expressions *to sonify* and, although less common, *to audify*. Terminology such as this, as *auditory display* and *sonification* and even *data* and *information*, should be considered descriptions rather than definitions, for, as in other fields, their meanings, driven by the need for finer distinctions and qualifications, have too great an inertia to be arrested by any current desires for semantic tidiness.

There can be numerous reasons why sound might be the preferred representational medium for certain types of data in particular circumstances, including the known superiority of the hearing sense to discriminate certain kinds of structures. Some examples of such situations are referenced in this chapter; however, a detailed comparison with other sense-mode representations is beyond this current discussion.

2. CLASSIFYING SONIFICATIONS

There are a number of ways in which sonifications can be classified: distribution technology (medical, public arena, interactive); intended audience (anesthetists, stock brokers, the visually impaired); data source (electrocardiogram, stock market, hearing aids); data type (analog, digital, real time, spatial, temporal); and so on. Twenty or so years since concerted research began, data sources and target applications for sonification have now become too numerous to review in this context. They are also the easiest to locate using on the World Wide Web.[2] For the current purpose, I partially follow Kramer (1994, pp. 21–29) in using a description of the type of representation that is used to present information to the auditory system.

There are two broad distinctions at either end of a representational continuum: analogic and symbolic. *Analogy*[3] is a high-level cognitive process of transferring information from a particular subject (the analog or source) to another particular subject (the target) or of establishing the relation between the source and the target. The purpose of analogic representation is to make the structure of the information better suited or simpler for the target than it was in its original form. Analogic representation is more connotative than denotative. A good example of analogic sonification is a Geiger counter that produces clicks in a loudspeaker at a rate proportional to the strength of radiation in its vicinity.

By contrast, a *symbolic*[4] representation is a categorical sign for what is being represented. It is more denotative than connotative and thus more abstracted from the source than an analogic representation. In symbolic representation, source data are aggregated and "assigned" to the elements of a schema (symbols) according to a set of rules that, as a result, implicitly makes the distinction between data and information. These symbols are then displayed to the target, who processes them according to his or her knowledge of the schema used. By illustration, consider a stream of noise emanating from a source. On listening to the stream, a target recognizes that some segments of it are symbols in one known schema; other sounds are symbols in another known schema, and there are still other sounds for which he or she does not have a schema (other than the "everything I do not have another schema for" schema). An example would be a sound stream of English speech spoken by someone with influenza, who at some point says something to a dog in a language that the target does not recognize. The semantic meaning of the English is understood by the target, as are the influenza symptoms, but the dog-directed sound contains no recognizable information: it is just data. Two important features of this symbolic process are that (1) a variety of display schemata can be used to represent symbolically the same information or different information by different discrete-element aggregation of the data and (2) the relationships between the symbols themselves do not reflect relationships between what is being represented. For example, there is no relationship between the ideas represented by the words *loss*, *boss*, and *lass* (or the number 1055) even though the structure of the symbols is similar.

In data sonification, for which the source is data and the target is listeners, the type of representations a sonifier might employ is a function of the structure of the data, the kind of information needing to be extracted from it, and how easily (easily, efficiently, and effectively) that information can be processed by the listeners' hearing systems: physiological, perceptual, cognitive, and memoric. Apart from the data-processing skills necessary, sonifiers need a thorough working knowledge of the ways hearing systems organize acoustic waves into events using processes known as *auditory stream segregation* and *auditory stream integration* (Bregman 1990); ongoing research in the field is directed at the empirical investigation of these processes under various real-world conditions.

3. TYPES OF DATA REPRESENTATION

The data representation types described here, loosely based on Campo's groupings (2007), are discrete, continuous, and interactive. These types can be located at different points on the analogic-symbolic continuum discussed as follows: discrete representations mostly function symbolically, continuous representations mostly analogically, and interactive representations mostly analogically but in a discontinuous manner. In practice, a particular sonification may use one or more of them, even simultaneously, to satisfy the needs of the specific application.

A. Discrete Data Representations

Discrete data representations (DDRs) are representations in which every data point (datum) is sonified with an individual auditory event. The DDRs are strongly symbolic and can be used if there is no single preferred ordering of the datum. User-defined subsets of the data can be formed at will and randomly recalled, much as a visual scene can be scanned in whatever way the viewer chooses. This flexibility of access to the data assists the user to build up a mental representation of the data space and the position of each data point in it.

Auditory Warnings: Alarms and Alerts

Many animals use sounds of various kinds to warn those in their vicinity to the presence of others. *Alarm signals,* known in animal communication sciences as *antipredator adaptations,* can be species specific and are particularly effective when imminent danger is sensed. Boisterous alarms tend to provoke a "fright-or-flight" response; in ongoing monitoring situations, such sonifications is perhaps not subtle enough: the ensuing panic is more likely to lead to a silencing of the alarm or, when that is not possible, adaptation by cognitive filtering.

The term *alert* indicates the possibility of a more considered, attentive approach, but the distinction is by no means common practice. Patterson (1982, 1989) experimented on alerts for aircraft navigation and produced a set of guidelines covering all aspects of warning design. The warning signals he suggested are meant to be recognizable instantly by listeners and use quite low-level intensities and slower onset/offset times to avoid startling the pilot, a balance being needed between an auditory warning needing to impress itself on the consciousness of the operator and one that is not so insistent that it dominates cognitive function. Patterson categorized warning signals into three priority levels: emergency, abnormal, and advisory.

Extant guidelines for ergonomic and public safety applications of auditory warnings (McCormick and Sanders 1984) can be adapted for both general sonification purposes (Warin 2002) and more specific human-computer interaction (HCI) tasks, the initial purpose for which purpose research into auditory icons and earcons was undertaken.

Auditory Icons

The first detailed studies of the use of the sound capabilities of the newly emerged personal computers in the 1980s was as interface tools to operations of the machine itself. The desktop metaphor, first commercialized on the 1984-released Macintosh computers, was recognized as a paradigm shift and quickly adopted by all personal computer manufacturers. In summarizing his work going back to 1988, Gaver

(1994) outlined how sounds that were modeled after real-world acoustics and mapped to computer events could be used to enhance this desktop metaphor. He called these sounds *auditory icons* for conceptual compatibility with Apple's computer Desktop Icon and Finder metaphors (folders, trash can, menus, etc.). Gaver's reasons for using real-world sounds were based on an interpretation of James (J. J.) Gibson's theories of direct perception in which information about events in the world is perceived directly through patterns of energy, and understood innately, rather than through inferential representational structures in the mind (1966).

Building on the earlier work, Gaver developed, with others, various Finder-related tools: SonicFinder, Alternative Reality Kits (ARKs), and Environmental Audio Reminders (EARs). They extended Auditory Icons from sampled recordings of everyday sounds to synthesized abstract models of them that could more easily be manipulated (by pitch change, filtering, etc.) to represent qualitative aspects of the objects represented. He also suggested extending the range of applicability to remote machines, such as to indicate whether a printer in another room is functioning and the frequency of the page output.

For blind users, Mynatt developed a library of Auditory Icons, called Mercator, to complement the existing widget hierarchy of an existing graphical user interface (1994). She reasoned that auditory icons offer the most promise for producing discriminable, intuitive mappings on the same "direct perception" basis as Gaver and thus argued that "[w]hat this realization means to an interface designer is that we can use sounds to remind the user of an object or concept from the user's everyday world" (p. 543).

Real-world sounds easily convey simple messages that are cognitively processed without much learning if the sounds are easy to identify. Yet, sound in the interface that seems cute or clever at first may grow tiresome after a few exposures. (Gaver and Smith 1990). In evaluating Mercator, Mynatt also observed a number of limitations, including the difficulty users had in identifying cues, especially those of short duration; the need for high (spectral) quality of sound; and the need to evaluate Icons in a complete set for maximum dissimilarity while maintaining ease of identity. Both Gaver and Mynatt raised the question of whether the concept of Auditory Icons breaks down with virtual objects that do not have a clear counterpoint in the everyday world. Mynatt concluded, at the same time as cautioning that the participant sample size was too small for formal statistical analysis, that while nonsighted users could successfully navigate the system, the overall test results indicated that the goal of designing intuitive auditory icons was not satisfied in the prototype interface. There were suggestions (Blattner et al. 1989) that problems of memorizing a large number of such icons were caused by the lack of structural links between them. In addition, auditory icons can be homonymic—different physical events give rise to similar sounds. Later research (Sikora et al. 1995, Roberts and Sikora 1997, Bussemakers and de Haan 2000) showed that test participants found auditory icons were the least pleasant and least appropriate for use in computer interfaces.

Earcons

One alternative to using real-world sounds to reflect various computer activities is to use structured sequences of synthetic tones called *earcons*, which are nonverbal audio messages that are used in the computer/user interface to provide information to the user about some computer object, operation, or interaction (Blattner et al. 1989). Earcons are made by transforming tone parameters (pitch, loudness, duration, and timbre) into structured, nonverbal "message" combinations. Blattner et al. found the use of musical timbres proved more effective than simple tones, with gross differences needed for effective distinction to occur.

Brewster et al. (1994) undertook a number of experiments investigating the comprehensibility of earcons under various parametric transformations. They created motifs for a set of simple operations, such as "open," "close," "file," and "program." A compound earcon was then created that gave a sound for "open file" or "close program" by simply concatenating the two motives. They experimentally tested the recall and recognition of different types of earcons and reported that 80% recall accuracy could be achieved with careful design of the sounds and that earcons "are better for presenting information than unstructured bursts of sound . . . " and "high levels of recognition can be achieved by careful use of pitch, rhythm and timbre" (p. 496).

One of the most powerful features of earcons is that they can be combined to produce compound messages, so symbolic sound elements (motives) and their transformations can be used hierarchically to represent events or objects. A drawback, however, is that the deeper the structural hierarchy being represented, the longer a sequentially structured earcon takes to play, thus interfering with the speed at which a user can interact with the computer. Playing earcons more rapidly would be to risk recognition errors, although this could presumably be controlled. Brewster et al. (1993) experimented with a different approach, namely, to play the earcons at the same rate but present the information in parallel, taking the time of only a single earcon to do so. Their results indicated that parallel and serial earcons were recognized equally as well. In both cases, recognition rates improved with repeated usage, which is the case in most HCI applications. Interestingly, more "training" produced greater improvements for parallel earcons than serial ones, with 90% recognition rates easily achieved. Furthermore, given that their symbolic structures are similar to the semantic aspects of music, the hypothesis that musicians would perform better than nonmusicians was not verified: there were no differences in performance between the two groups except that some of the nonmusicians took slightly longer to learn the system. Results from several experimenters had confirmed that correct identification of earcons decreased markedly if they occurred concurrently.

McGookin (2004) undertook a detailed investigation of this phenomenon and produced a set of design principles, including using spatial separation and a 300-ms time offset. His findings indicated that, even when using these guidelines, the accuracy of concurrent earcon identification still decreased from 90% to 30%

when the number of earcons increased from one to four. However, these guidelines did improve the accuracy with which individual earcons were identified.

Overall, earcon studies indicated that they can be an effective means of communicating hierarchical structures, but that the number of them concurrently usefully identifiable is quite limited.

Speech Noises

NoiseSpeech is made by digitally processing sounds so that they have some of the acoustic properties of speech (Dean 2005). It is made either by applying the formant structures of speech to noise or other sounds or by distorting speech sounds such that they no longer form identifiable phoneme sequences. The "hybrid" sounds that result from this process encapsulate some of the affective qualities of human speech while removing the semantic content. Experimental evidence suggested that most listeners cluster the sonic characteristics of Noise-Speech with speech rather than those musical instrument or environmental sounds (Dean and Bailes 2006).

Less abstracted than NoiseSpeech, spearcons (speech earcons) are spoken phrases that have been time compressed until they are not recognizable as speech (Walker et al. 2006). They were designed to enhance hierarchical menu navigation for mobile and screen-limited devices, in which they can be created automatically by converting menu item text (e.g., Export File) to synthetic speech via text-to-speech (TTS) software. Keeping pitch invariant, this synthetic speech is then time compressed, rendering it incomprehensible. While each spearcon in an application is unique, phonetic similarity is maintained. For example, the initial phonemes are invariant in Open File, Open Location . . . , and Open Address Book, as are the endings of Open File, Export File. The relative lengths of the text strings are maintained by their spearcons, and this assists the listener to learn and identify the mappings.

Discrete Data Representations Compared

The postulation that, because of the connection to fundamental percepts, auditory icons should be easier to learn than earcons was questioned by Lucas (1994), who found it took significantly less time to learn spoken messages than it did to learn either earcons or auditory icons, and unlike earcons and auditory icons, these spoken messages were consistently interpreted error free. Further, he found no significant differences in the amount of time needed to learn the meanings associated with earcons or auditory icons. This result is at odds with ecological theory, and Ballas (1994) suggested that the activity of listening contains intermediate mental processes that take account of a listener's expectations and experience and the context in which the auditing occurs. One could speculate that, because the listener is also immersed in a real auditory scene as well as the computer's virtual one, a differentiation between virtual and real elements requires greater cognitive processing than if the two scenes were not superimposed. Bussemakers and de Haan (2000) undertook a comparative study of earcons and auditory icons in a multimedia environment and found that having sound with a visual task does not always lead to faster reaction times. Although reaction times were slower in the experiment with earcons, it seemed that users were able to extract information from these sounds and use it. Furthermore, users found real-life sounds annoying when they heard them frequently.

Earcons are constructed from lexical elements that are ordered categorical symbols. So while, like musical themes, their meaning is multiplicative under symmetry group transformation (transposition, retrogradation, inversion, etc.), the information needs to go through a decoding phase. As there is no standard syntax or lexicon, their meanings have to be learned (Blattner et al. 1989), requiring an initial high cognitive load. Moreover, without absolute standardization across all software and hardware, disarray rather than greater clarity seems the more likely outcome.

Palladino and Walker (2007) conducted a study comparing menu navigation performance with earcons, auditory icons, and spearcons. Their results indicate that faster and more accurate menu navigation was achieved with spearcons than with speech-only, hierarchical earcons and auditory icons (the slowest). They suggest that one reason for the speed and accuracy of spearcons is that, because they retain the relative lengths of their sources, these different lengths provide a "guide to the ear" while scanning down through a menu, just as the ragged right edge of items in a visual menu aids in visual searching. Because spearcons can be created and stored as part of a software upgrade or initialization process, access times would be no longer than earcons and auditory icons. Furthermore, language- or dialect-specific issues can be managed by the operating system's standard internationalization procedures.

Since the mapping between spearcons and their menu item is nonarbitrary, there is less learning required than would be the case for a purely arbitrary mapping. Unlike earcon menus, spearcon menus can be rearranged, sorted, and have items inserted or deleted without changing the mapping of the various sounds to menu items. Spearcons may not be as effective at communicating their menu location as hierarchical earcons. However, spearcons would still provide more direct mappings between sound and menu item than earcons and cover more content domains, more flexibly, than auditory icons.

While auditory icons and earcons clearly have lexical properties (pitch, duration, etc.), they are used as auditory cues or messages, as signifiers of stable gestalts (i.e., as clear denoters of the presence of known, separable, or discrete information states). The design of sets of auditory icons, earcons, spearcons, and so on is concerned with finding ways to indicate these states effectively under auditory segregation pressure, that is, the ability with which they remain immutable to the human auditory system in the presence of each other and the perceptual environment in which they exist. These audio cues (or messages) function semantically in that they convey information about the state of the system of which they are a part and so can be used to reduce visual workload or function as a way of monitoring the system when visual or other means are not available or appropriate.

B. Continuous Data Representations

Continuous data representations (CDRs) treat data as analogically continuous. They rely on two preconditions: an equally spaced metric in at least one dimension and sufficient data to afford a high enough sampling rate for aural interpolation between data points. Most commonly, CDRs are used for exploring data to learn more about the system that produced it. Their applications range from monitoring the real-time operation of machines, stock markets, the environment, and government policy to discover new regularities, to helping visually impaired students gain access to information normally presented graphically. Their advantages include low cognitive load (due to direct perception), which is excellent for large data sets and time series. There are two types, which I label *audification* and *processed audification.*

Audification

Audification is a technique for translating data directly into sound. Kramer (1994, p. 186) described it as a "direct translation of a data waveform to the audible domain." Audification may be applicable as a sonification technique to many data sets that have an equally spaced metric in at least one dimension. It is most easily applied to those that exhibit oscillatory time series characteristics, although this is not a requirement. Because of the integrative capabilities of the ear, audification is useful as a technique for very large numerical data sets with datum that can be logically arranged as a time sequence of audio samples. These samples can be either stored in an audio file for delayed audition or played directly through the computer's audio hardware in real time. On playback, any number of standard audio signal-processing techniques such as filtering, compression, and frequency shifting can be applied under user control to enhance information detection.

Audification has been shown to be effective when the data are voluminous, such as when produced by monitoring physical systems such as seismology. Speeth (1961), for example, audified seismic data for the 90% successful differentiation of events caused by bomb blasts from those caused by earthquakes. Speeth's experimental results were remarkable because the task is apparently very difficult to achieve using visual plots of the data (Frysinger 2005), and by time compressing the signals to bring them into audio range analysts could review twenty-fours hours of data in a few minutes. Hayward (1994), in describing the use of audification techniques on seismic data, found the technique useful but stressed that proper evaluation and comparisons with visual methods are needed. In summarizing a body of work on earthquake data, Dombois (2002) remarked that "eyes and ears give access to different aspects of the phenomenon of earthquakes. Free oscillations are relatively easy to recognize as the ear is all too familiar with many kinds of resonance. On the other hand synthetic seismograms, which are calculated for fitting as good as possible the curve of a measured seismogram, show low significance in the auditory display. This is less astonishing if one remembers that the power of calculation routines has been judged only by the visual correspondence of measured and synthetic seismogram." In monitoring the operation of a complex machine, Pauletto and Hunt (2005) determined that a key set of attributes (noise, repetitive elements, regular oscillations, discontinuities, and signal power) in helicopter flight data was equally discernable via an audification or a visual spectrogram. Krishnan et al. (2001) undertook a comparative study of audification and other sonification techniques to represent data related to the rubbing of knee-joint surfaces and did not find that audification was the best technique for displaying the difference between normal and abnormal signals.

In summary, audification with variable sample rate playback can be useful for data "dredging" large data sets at high speed, for bringing subaudio information into an audible range, and for real-time monitoring by allowing buffered time-lapse playback of the most recent data.

Processed Audification

To provide feature amplification to audification data, signal-processing techniques may be applied. This is a relatively unexplored territory, but initial results (Worrall 2004, Campo 2007) are encouraging: when audification may be an appropriate technique, but the data needs to be "massaged" beforehand, or when there are not enough data to sustain it, for example, it is possible to apply signal-processing techniques such as granulated time stretching (vocoding), pitch shifting while keeping time invariant, using the data to amplitude or frequency modulate a carrier signals, to name a few. Campo also suggested modulating frequencies of an array of sines for detection of polarity and time alignments in multiple channels of electroencephalographic (EEG) data.

Parametric Mapping

Parameter mapping is the most widely used sonification technique for representing high-dimensional data as sound. Parameter-mapping sonifications are sometimes referred to as sonic scatter plots or nth-order parameter mappings. Typically, data dimensions are mapped to sound parameters, which can be physical (frequency, amplitude); psychophysical (pitch, loudness); or perceptually coherent complexes (timbre, rhythm). Parameter-mapping sonifications can have both analogical and symbolic components. Analogic variations in the sound can result when mapping from a large data domain into a small perceptual range or when data are specifically mapped to acoustic modifiers such as frequency or amplitude modulators.

This technique has a number of positive aspects. Many data dimensions can be listened to simultaneously. It is very flexible, and the mappings can be easily changed, allowing different aural perspectives of the same data. In addition, acoustic production can be assigned to sophisticated tools developed for computer music. These are readily available and permit many quite sophisticated parameter mappings to be synthesized in real time.

The main limitation of the technique is the lack of orthogonality in the psychophysical parameter space; loudness can affect pitch perception, for example. Although conceptually simple, in practice parameter mapping requires a working knowledge of how the parameters interact with each other perceptually. Linear changes in one domain produce nonlinear auditory effects, and the range of the variation can differ considerably with different parameters and synthesis techniques. These perceptual interactions, caused by coupled perceptual parameters, can obscure data relations and confuse the listener. Flowers, an experienced multivariate data sonifier, observed that while "the claim that submitting the entire contents of 'dense and complex' datasets to sonification will lead to the 'emergence' of critical relationships continues to be made, I have yet to see it 'work'" (2005). However, although a truly balanced multivariate auditory display may not be possible in practice (Kramer 1994), given powerful enough tools it may be possible to heuristically test mappings to within acceptable limits for any given application.

Frysinger (2005) provided a useful overview of the history of the technique, and Flowers (2005) highlighted some of its pitfalls and possible future directions.

C. Interactive Data Representations

Sound Graphs

The term *auditory graph* is used in a variety of ways, often simply meaning the output of a multivariate data sonification. To provide a restricted meaning, I use the term *sound graph*, after Stockman (2005) and others, to refer to a sonic representation of a visual graph. Other names by which it is known are *tone graph, auditory graph, tree-graph*, and *auditory box plot*. Its function is to provide a sonified interface to a discrete (buffered) data set so that the relationships between the data points can be interactively investigated asynchronously. The addition of auditory tick marks, axes, and labels to add context is not uncommon (Stockman et al. 2005).

Although the original impetus for the sound graph was to provide the visually impaired with access to line graphs and spreadsheets, it clearly has wider application, including as a design space for parameter mappings. A slightly different interpretation was provided by Vickers (2005), whose CAITLIN (Computer Audio Interface to Locate Incorrect Nonsense), based on design principles similar to auditory icons, is used to aurally identify and locate bugs in computer programs.

Model-Based Sonifications

Model-based sonification is a relatively new technique in which parameters of a virtual physical model function in same way as the coordinates of a visual display. The number of representational dimensions is not limited to those of a simple sonification parameter map, and they are able to maintain a greater consistency of dimensional orthogonality.

Digitally modeling the resonating components of a musical instrument (called physical modeling) is a relatively common practice in computer music. For such dynamic models, the temporal behavior of the components of the model are determined ahead of time by detailing their resonant properties and the way they are connected to form a single resonator. The instrument is then excited with virtual bows, drumsticks, scrapers, and so on, and the virtual contact microphones placed at strategic places on the "body" of the instrument capture its resonance (Pearson 1996).

In model-based sonification (Hermann and Ritter 1999, Hermann 2002), a variable of the data set to be sonified is assigned to some structural properties of a component (elasticity, hardness, etc.) of the model. A user interacting with this model via "messages" (virtual beaters, scrapers, etc.) causes it to resonate. The resulting sound is thus determined by the way the data integrate through the model. By virtually beating, plucking, blowing, and scraping the model, the characteristics of the data set are available to the listener in the same way that the material and structural characteristics of a physical object are available to a listener who beats, plucks, blows, or scrapes it.

Model-based sound synthesis has proved remarkably effective in producing complex, "natural"-sounding acoustic events. While the building of such models requires considerable skill, this would not be a barrier for their use in data sonification if templates were to become readily available. And, although they can be computationally expensive, given the facilities, such models tend to lend themselves to parallel computing. The technique is new, and results of empirical testing against other sonification methods will, in time, determine the degree to which it becomes generally accepted as a technique for data exploration.

4. THE NEED FOR BETTER TOOLS

The *Sonification Report* considered the field of sonification research to consist of three principal components: (1) research in perception and cognition, (2) development of research and application tools, and (3) design and applications using the sonification techniques. To use these components in consort requires the integration of concepts from human perception, acoustics, design, the arts, and engineering (Kramer et al. 1999). Hermann amplified this by considering knowledge of data availability and meaning as well as domain-specific dependencies to be sufficient for simple-purpose sonifications such as for auditory alarms and the enhancement of graphic user interfaces. However, in sonifications of higher-dimensional data, he considered expertise in other techniques is also necessary: statistics and data mining, human computer interaction, computer science, acoustics, sound engineering, physiology and neurobiology, psychology, psychoacoustics, musicology, and cognition (Hermann 2002, pp. 24–25).

The need for better software tools, including some general proposals for adapting sound synthesis software to the needs of sonification research, has been a constant theme among auditory display researchers and was highlighted in the *Sonification Report* (Kramer et al. 1999). Now, a decade later, it is evident that the need is as strong as ever. Several attempts to provide generic tools are either in hibernation or extinct, others not (Campo et al. 2004, Worrall et al. 2007). As exploratory research continues, and software development iterates, it becomes clearer that the tools needed are not simple adaptations to existing sound synthesis software, fine though much of it is, but more robust models that can better integrate current expertise and the software expression of it from the variety of fields, which need to meet to advance the research into how data might be better displayed to our auditory systems.

5. SOUND, SCIENCE, AND SONG

In everyday life, sounds are produced when physical objects touch or have an impact on each other. It takes no special training to be able to infer certain material qualities from the sound of impacting objects: their density, hardness, and perhaps shape for example, as well as the manner of impact (collision and recoil, scraping, plucking, blowing, etc.). All this information is available and perceived by us almost instantaneously and effortlessly millions of times every day, even when we are not looking at the objects and often even when asleep. Not having earlids, our hearing constantly monitors the world around us and, in doing so, directs our visual and kinesthetic attention. The observation that our hearing leads our vision in making sense of the world is amply demonstrated by the importance of Foley (sound effects) in film; the imitation of the sound of a horse's hooves, over stones, through mud, and so on by knocking coconut halves together is much more convincing than an unenhanced recording of the sound of the hooves themselves. An important aspect of Foley is that its effectiveness is in remaining hidden, that is, it functions not to distinguish itself but to enhance the realism of the audiovisual scene as a whole.

A. Acoustic Generation

The ability for digital computers to generate, transform, and present sound to users in a timely manner is fundamental to sonification research. The vast majority of the tools and techniques used for the computer synthesis of sound have been developed by composers and engineers engaged in the task of making new music, leading John Chowning to remark: "With the use of computers and digital devices, the processes of music composition and its production have become intertwined with the scientific and technical resources of society to greater extent than ever before." Because, as he went on to say, "a loudspeaker controlled by a computer is the most general synthesis medium in existence (Chowning in Roads 1996, p. ix), these researchers were quick to begin exploring adaptations and eventually alternatives to the static models of musical instrument tones as described in the then-current literature (Olson 1967, pp. 201–241), an experience which analog synthesis had already revealed to be deficient of the lively qualities of the sounds of acoustic instruments.

The original periodic synthesis techniques include additive, subtractive, and modulation models (Mathews 1969), which were augmented by dynamic (nonperiodic) techniques such as microphone-sampled waveforms, stochastic function, and granular synthesis-generated timbres (Xenakis 1971, pp. 242–254, Truax 1988, Roads 2004). As computing hardware became faster and object-oriented software tools became more prevalent, the development of software models of physical resonance systems ranged from difference equations, mass-spring, modal, nonlinear excitation, waveguide, and formant (after speech) synthesis to the highly individual Karplus-Strong techniques for plucked-string and drumlike sounds. Roads provided a brief introduction to these techniques (1996, pp. 261–315), most of which are still under active development. Their usefulness to sonification is that they provide appropriate coupling mechanisms between data structures and the synthesis models used to express them. As Hermann concluded (2002), apart from the often considerable time involved in setting up such systems, their major disadvantages are the time and expertise needed to set up the models and the computing resources necessary to implement them. As experience grows and computation speeds increase, neither of these impediments is likely to prove permanent. Computing science and software engineering continue to play important roles in the development of the theoretical models and efficient algorithmic processes within which these sound synthesis techniques can be implemented.

B. Sonification Research

The systematic study of using computers to "display" information to the human auditory system is a relatively young discipline. The first International Conference on Auditory Display (ICAD) was held in 1992, and Kramer's extensive introductions in the proceedings (Kramer 1994) provide an overview of interesting precedents, the then-current state of the field as well as some possible futures. Before the computing resources with which to process large amounts of data were readily available, sonification was restricted to relatively simple tasks, such as increasing the frequency of a metal detector's audio oscillator in proportion its proximity to metals and the timely production of attention-capturing beeps and blurps. As size and availability of data sets have grown and the complexity of communication tasks increased, so have the expectations of sonification, requiring sonifiers to draw on skills and research knowledge from a variety of disciplines.

In such interdisciplinary inquiries, researchers from various fields come together to share and integrate their discipline-specific knowledge and in doing so reinvigorate themselves with new questions and new methods. For example, when introducing the concept of intelligent help using knowledge-based systems,

Pilkington (1992, p. vii) noted that different disciplines often adopt different forms of evidence. While psychologists prefer experiments, computer scientists prefer programs, composers prefer cultural activities, and linguists prefer rules, for example, this can lead to communication failures when they try framing a theory that will satisfy each discipline's criteria of proof. Moore observed that in interdisciplinary research the challenge is to do justice to several points of view simultaneously because "[a]n awareness of [a variety of] points of view is important not so much because ignorance of any one of them makes it impossible to do anything but because what may be done will eventually be limited by that lack of awareness" (1990, p. 23). As experience continually reaffirms, knowledge is not value free, so when these differing points of view come from disciplines with divergent aims, a lack of such awareness may not be obvious. The opportunities to examine more closely disciplinary assumptions that collaborative work provides to researchers can lead through apparent impasses and strengthen the foundations of domain knowledge.

In the current context, it may be worthwhile to speculate on the kinds of knowledge and experience a cultural activity such as music composition can bring to the data sonification process and, inversely, of what use are the results of experimental psychology to music composition. As numerous historical examples from the ancient Greeks, who believed in a direct relation between the laws of nature and the harmony of musical sounds through the numerical symbolism of the Middle Ages[5] and beyond, attest, musicians were sonifying numerical data millennia before computers and multivariate data sets occupied the Western mind. While their approaches were perhaps more heuristic and teleological, surviving artifacts from past eras are more likely than not to have been either workable solutions to practical problems or sufficiently novel to have induced a new way of thinking music. However, no sound recordings, except of the very recent past, are extant, and the function of the musical score as something more than an aide-mémoire is only a relatively recent one.

So, although musicologists have described many of the unnotated performance practice and "style" characteristics of the music from then-contemporary nonmusical sources, such descriptions are rarely couched in the phenomenal language of modern science. From the contemporary design perspective, the appropriation of scripted musical gestures of the historical past, together with some ahistorical harmony book's "rules of composition" that omit reference to the pitch or temperament system employed or the timbral distinctiveness of the instruments of the period, fails to grasp the cultural imperative: music is not science, and its aims are not always for clarity of line or purpose. The sounds of music are social sounds, and as society changes so the ways its components interact are determined as much by cultural forces as by psychoacoustics (Attali 1985, pp. 46–86).

The parametric analysis of tone according to physical characteristics (frequency, loudness, etc.) and the availability of tools for additive synthesis from these parameters belies the psychoacoustics evidence that, for all but the simplest sonifications, the results of design by simply assigning data dimensions to such physical parameters quickly leads to unsegregated, difficult-to-interpret clumping. Whether stream segregation is maintained during a temporal simultaneity of two or more separate spectra as components of textures or "chords" or whether integration, occlusion, or emergence results (Bregman 1990, pp. 456–528) is dependent on a combination of characteristics, including the system of tuning in use, the spectral density profiles (timbres) involved, the duration of the simultaneity, the previous and following directional profiles of the spectral contributors, their relative amplitudes, and so on. Furthermore, hearing is very sensitive to spectral congruence. Sequences of spectral events that are highly congruent, such as occurs when using general MIDI (musical instrument digital interface) instruments or auditory icons, for example, quickly pall on the ear. The extra cognitive load needed to work within such soundscapes is not insignificant and possibly contributes to the annoyance commonly reported by listeners when using such sonifications for extended periods of time. There are ways out of this impasse, as illustrated by the introduction to sound synthesis techniques in common use in computer music, such as physical modeling (including voice), granulation, and stochastics, as well as careful attention to second-order features such as reverberation and spatialization.

Flowers (2005) commented that most of the problems that arise in data sonification stem from lack of adequate understanding about key properties of auditory perception and attention and from inappropriate generalizations of existing data visualization practices. Such generalizations arise more as a result of the overwhelming dominance of vision over audition in the perceptual psychology literature than experimental evidence (Bregman 1990, pp. 1–3) and can be overcome with more sustained applied research in auditory perception, including the role which silence plays in auditory perception and a deeper understanding of the relationship between speech and nonspeech auditory processing (Slevc et al. 2008). For sonification design to advance as a practice, sonification designing needs to be practiced and critiqued and its designs interpreted, not just listened to as "furniture music" (*musique d'ameublement*, after Satie). To that end, task and data analysis of information requirements (Barrass 1997, pp. 35–45) together with generally available data sets and interesting mapping templates in software environments that combine sonic complexity with experimentation flexibility will encourage the much-needed communitywide sharing of examples toward a catalogue of best practice.

C. Data Music

The advent of the Internet and the percolation of computing devices into ordinary, everyday objects and activities means that most of us exist in an increasingly datarized ether. One characteristic of music is that it is continually being recontextualized, both technically and culturally, as it is influenced by, and influences, the fluctuating zeitgeist. So, from a cultural, experimental composition perspective, data sonification is of significant interest.

Computer-based composition tools have their origins in the desire to explore and express algorithmically generated structures at both micro- (sound synthesis) and macro- (gestural) compositional levels. As a cultural activity, making new music is not only about exploring new ways to put new noises together but also about providing others with the opportunities to engage both actively and passively in that exploration. Once digital musical instruments became available, MIDI was quickly adopted as a computer protocol suitable for capturing and transmitting data from human performance gesture and for coordination with other technologies, such as lighting controllers. However, not all interesting sources of data have MIDI interfaces or are related to human corporeality and proprioception. So, at a time in human history when there is an imperative for us to take responsibility for our relationships with both natural and human-made environments, the extension of sound synthesis software to explore such datascapes aurally opens the possibility of compositional access to, and thus cultural dialogue about, a broader spectrum of phenomena: interspecies, planetary, and interstellar.

One way of classifying data music (data sonification music) is according to where it can be placed on a perceptual continuum, with works using representational data mapping on one end and those using free data transformation on the other. Closer to the "free data" end would be data music that uses arbitrarily formatted digital documents as control data for some sound synthesis routines as arbitrarily determined by the sonifier (Whitelaw 2004). In such circumstances, it is likely that the (possibly imagined) content of the documents would play a role in culturally contextualizing the resulting soundscape, in keeping with postmodernist or other mannerist aesthetics.

At the representational end is data music that employs the techniques used in pragmatic information interpretation for decision making, system regulation, vision substitution, and so on, techniques that are derived from a developing knowledge of psychoacoustics and the cognitive sciences more generally. For composers who are interested in engaging with listeners as interpreters rather than the struggling receivers of obscure messages, this research offers a stronger technical basis for their practice, not necessarily for overtly programmatic narratives but to control better the overall dramaturgy of a composition (Landy 2007, pp. 36–38). For example, although the techniques for making adherent tone complexes has formed the basis of studies in orchestration for at least two centuries, to discover how to disassemble the ensemble, to compose coherent sounds that maintain their perceptual segmentation, what is needed is "unorchestration" studies that include psychoacoustic techniques for producing disaggregated complex sounds in situational environments (Bregman 1990, p. 458) and a developing understanding of auditory cognition.

Notwithstanding the particular application, whether for cultural spectacles or for more pragmatic reasons, there is a general need for a new generation of software, tools that integrate flexible sound synthesis engines with those for data acquisition, analysis, and manipulation in ways that afford both experiments in cognition and lucid, interpretive auditory displays.

NOTES

1. In chemistry, the term simply means "the production of sound waves." The term is used in relation to a technique known as *sonication*, in which "a suspension of cells is exposed to the disruptive effect of the energy of high-frequency sound waves" (Online Medical Dictionary 1997, *sonification*, and Biology Online 2001, *sonication*); or in chemistry, where it refers to "the use of (often ultra)sound waves to increase the rate of a reaction or to prepare vesicles in mixtures of surfactants and water" (ChemiCool 2008, *sonication*).

2. For example, in June 2008, an Internet google of the phrase *stockmarket sonification* revealed over 6,000 links (cf., 50 million for *stockmarket*).

3. This is from the Greek *analogia* for proportion, from *ana-* for upon, according to, plus *logos* for ratio, also "word, speech, reckoning" (Online Etymology Dictionary 2001).

4. This is from the Greek *symbolon* syn- (together) plus stem of *ballein* for to throw, evolved from the "throwing things together" to "contrasting" to "comparing" to "token used in comparisons to determine if something is genuine." Hence, it is an "outward sign" of something (Online Etymology Dictionary).

5. Dufay's 1436 motet *Nuper rosarum flores*, which is based on the proportions of the Florence Cathedral for whose consecration it was composed, is but one example.

BIBLIOGRAPHY

Anderson, J., P. Sanderson, and M. Norris, M. 2002. The role of auditory attention and auditory perception in the design of real-time sonification of anaesthesia variables. In *Proceedings of HF2002 Human Factors Conference*, November 25–27, Melbourne, Australia.

Attali, J. 1985. *Noise. The Political Economy of Music*. English trans. Minneapolis: University of Minnesota Press.

Biology Online. 2001. A part of the Scientific American Partner Network. http://www.biology-online.org/dictionary/.

Ballas, J. A. 1994. Delivery of information through sound. In *Auditory Display, Vol. 18, Santa Fe Institute, Studies in the Sciences of Complexity Proceedings*, ed. G. Kramer. Reading, MA: Addison-Wesley, pp. 79–94.

Barrass, S. 1997. "Auditory information design." Ph.D. thesis, Australian National University. http://thesis.anu.edu.au/public/adt-ANU20010702.150218, accessed May 13, 2008.

Blattner M., D. Sumikawa, and R. Greenberg. 1989. Earcons and icons: Their structure and common design principles. *Human Computer Interaction* 4(1): 11–44.

Bly, S. 1994. Multivariate data mappings. In *Auditory Display, Vol. 18, Santa Fe Institute, Studies in the Sciences of Complexity Proceedings*, ed. G. Kramer. Reading, MA: Addison-Wesley, pp. 405–416.

Bregman, A. 1990. *Auditory Scene Analysis: The Perceptual Organization of Sound*. Cambridge: MIT Press.

Brewster, S. A., P. C. Wright, and A. D. N. Edwards. 1993. Parallel earcons: Reducing the length of audio messages. http://citeseer.ist.psu.edu/154731.html, accessed June 5, 2008.

Brewster, S. A., P. C. Wright, and A. D. N. Edwards. 1994. A detailed investigation into the effectiveness of earcons. In *Auditory Display, Vol. 18, Santa Fe Institute, Studies in the Sciences of Complexity Proceedings*, ed. G. Kramer. Reading, MA: Addison-Wesley, pp. 471–498.

Bussemakers, M. P., and A. de Haan. 2000. When it sounds like a duck and it looks like a dog... auditory icons vs. earcons in multimedia environments. In *Proceedings of the 10th International Conference on Auditory Display*. Georgia Institute of Technology, Atlanta, pp. 184–189.

Campo, A. de. 2007. Toward a data sonification design map. In *Proceedings of the 13th International Conference on Auditory Display*, Montréal, Canada, June 26–29, pp. 342–347.

Campo, A. de., C. Frauenberger, and R. Höldrich. 2004. Designing a generalized sonification environment. In *Proceedings of the 10th International Conference on Auditory Display*, Sydney. http://sonenvir.at/, accessed August 7, 2007.

ChemiCool. 2008. A part of the Scientific American Partner Network. http://www.chemicool.com/dictionary.html.

Dean, R. T. 2005. NoiseSpeech, a noise of living bodies: Towards Attali's "composition." *Journal of New Media and Culture* 3(1). http://www.ibiblio.org/nmediac/winter2004/NoiseSpc.htm, accessed June 12, 2008.

Dean, R. T., and F. Bailes. 2006. NoiseSpeech. *Performance Research* 11(3): 85–86.

Dombois, F. 2002, Auditory seismology on free oscillations, focal mechanisms, explosions and synthetic seismograms. In *Proceedings of the 2002 International Conference on Auditory Display*, Kyoto, Japan, July 2–5.

Flowers, J. H. 2005. Thirteen years of reflection on auditory graphing: Promises, pitfalls, and potential new directions. In *First Symposium on Auditory Graphs*, Limerick, Ireland, July 10, 2005.

Frauenberger, C. 2007. Analysing time series data. In *Proceedings of the 13th International Conference on Auditory Display*, Montréal, Canada, June 26–29.

Frysinger, S. P. 2005. A brief history of auditory data representation to the 1980s. In *First Symposium on Auditory Graphs*, Limerick, Ireland, July 10.

Gaver, W. W. 1994. Using and creating auditory icons. In *Auditory Display, Vol. 18, Santa Fe Institute, Studies in the Sciences of Complexity Proceedings*, ed. G. Kramer. Reading, MA: Addison-Wesley, pp. 417–446.

Gaver, W. W., and R. B. Smith. 1990. Auditory icons in large-scale collaborative environments. In *Proceedings of Human-Computer Interaction: Interact '90*, ed. G. Cockton, D. Gilmore, B. Shackel, and D. Diaper. Cambridge, UK, pp. 735–740.

Gibson, J. J. 1966. *The Senses Considered as Perceptual Systems*. Boston: Houghton Mifflin.

Hayward C. 1994. Listening to the Earth sing. In *Auditory Display: Sonification, Audification, and Auditory Interfaces*, ed. G. Kramer. Reading, MA: Addison-Wesley, pp. 369–404.

Hermann, T. 2002. "Sonification for exploratory data analysis." Ph.D. thesis, Bielefeld University, Bielefeld, Germany.

Hermann, T., and H. Ritter. 1999. Listen to your data: Model-based sonification for data analysis. In *Advances in Intelligent Computing and Multimedia Systems*, ed. G. E. Lasker. Baden-Baden, Germany: International Institute for Advanced Studies in System Research and Cybernetics, pp. 189–194.

Kramer, G. 1994. Some organizing principles for representing data with sound. In *Auditory Display: Sonification, Audification, and Auditory Interface, Vol. 18, Santa Fe Institute, Studies in the Sciences of Complexity Proceedings*, ed. G. Kramer. Reading, MA: Addison-Wesley, pp. 185–221.

Kramer, G., B. Walker, B. T. Bonebright, P. Cook, J. Flowers, P. N. Miner, and J. Neuhoff. 1999. *Sonification Report: Status of the Field and Research Agenda*. Technical report,

International Community for Auditory Display. http://www.icad.org/websiteV2o/
    References/nsf.html, accessed February 29, 2008.

Krishnan S., R. M. Rangayyan, G. D. Bell, and C. B. Frank. 2001. Auditory display of knee-
    joint vibration signals. *Journal of the Acoustical Society of America* 110(6): 3292–3304.

Landy, L. 2007. *Understanding the Art of Sound Organization.* Cambridge: MIT Press.

Lucas, P. A. 2004. An evaluation of the communicative ability of auditory icons and
    earcons. In *Auditory Display, Vol. 18, Santa Fe Institute, Studies in the Sciences of
    Complexity Proceedings,* ed. G. Kramer. Reading, MA: Addison-Wesley, pp. 79–94.

Mathews, M. V. 1969. *The Technology of Computer Music.* Cambridge: MIT Press.

McCormick, E. J., and N. Sanders. 1984. *Human Factors in Engineering and Design.*
    International student ed. New York: McGraw-Hill.

McGookin, D. K. 2004. "Understanding and improving the identification of concurrently
    presented earcons." Ph.D. thesis, University of Glasgow. http://theses.gla.ac.uk/14/01/
    mcgookin.pdf, accessed June 20, 2008.

Moore, F. R. 1990. *Elements of Computer Music.* Englewood Cliffs, NJ: Prentice Hall.

Mynatt, E. D. 1994. Auditory presentation of graphical user interfaces. In *Auditory Display:
    Sonification, Audification, and Auditory Interface, Vol. 18, Santa Fe Institute, Studies in
    the Sciences of Complexity Proceedings,* ed. G. Kramer. Reading, MA: Addison-Wesley,
    pp. 533–556.

Nesbitt, K. V., and S. Barrass. 2002. Evaluation of a multimodal sonification and
    visualisation of depth of market stock data. In *Proceedings of the 2002 International
    Conference on Auditory Display,* Kyoto, Japan, July 2–5.

Olson, H. F. 1967. *Music, Physics and Engineering.* New York: Dover.

Online Etymology Dictionary. 2001. Ed. D. Harper. http://www.etymonline.com/

Online Medical Dictionary. 1997. http://cancerweb.ncl.ac.uk/omd/index.html. Newcastle:
    Department of Medical Oncology, University of Newcastle upon Tyne.

Palladino, D. K., and B. N. Walker. 2007. Learning rates for auditory menus enhanced with
    spearcons versus earcons. In *Proceedings of the 13th International Conference on
    Auditory Display,* Montréal, Canada, June 26–29.

Patterson, R. D. 1982. *Guidelines for Auditory Warning Systems on Civil Aircraft.* Paper
    no. 82017, Civil Aviation Authority, London.

Patterson, R. D. 1989. Guidelines for the design of auditory warning sounds. *Proceeding of
    the Institute of Acoustics* 11(5): 17–24.

Pauletto, S., and A. Hunt. 2005. A comparison of audio and visual analysis of complex time-
    series data sets. In *Proceedings of ICAD 05-Eleventh Meeting of the International
    Conference on Auditory Display,* Limerick, Ireland, July 6–9.

Pearson, M. 1996. TAO: A physical modelling system and related issues. In *Organised Sound.*
    Vol. 1. Ed. L. Landy. Cambridge: Cambridge University Press, pp. 43–50.

Pilkington, R. M. 1992. *Intelligent Help. Communicating with Knowledge-Based Systems.*
    New York: Oxford University Press.

Roads, C. 1996. *The Computer Music Tutorial.* Cambridge: MIT Press.

Roads, C. 2004. *Microsound.* Cambridge: MIT Press.

Roberts, L. A., and C. A. Sikora. 1997. Optimising feedback signals for multimedia devices:
    Earcons vs. auditory icons vs. speech. In *Proceedings of the International Ergonomics
    Association Congress,* Tampere, Finland, pp. 224–226.

Scaletti, C. 1994. Sound synthesis algorithms for auditory data representations. In *Auditory
    Display, Vol. 18, Santa Fe Institute, Studies in the Sciences of Complexity Proceedings,* ed.
    G. Kramer. Reading, MA: Addison-Wesley, pp. 223–251.

Sikora, C. A., L. A. Roberts, and L. Murray. 1995. Musical vs. real world feedback signals. In *Proceedings of the ACM SIGCHI Conference on Human Factors in Computing Systems*. New York: Association for Computing Machinery, pp. 220–221.

Slevc, L. R, J. C. Rosenberg, and A. D. Patel. 2008. Language, music, and modularity: Evidence for shared processing of linguistic and musical syntax. In *Proceedings of the 10th International Conference on Music Perception and Cognition (ICMPC10)*, ed. M. Adachi et al. Sapporo, Japan, August.

Speeth, S. D. 1961. Seismometer sounds. *Journal of the Acoustic Society of America* 33: 909–916.

Stockman, T., L. V. Nickerson, and G. Hind. 2005. Auditory graphs: A summary of current experience and towards a research agenda. In *Proceedings of First Symposium on Auditory Graphs*, Limerick, Ireland, July 10.

Truax, B. 1988. Real-time granular synthesis with a digital signal processing computer. *Computer Music Journal* 12(2): 14–26.

Vickers, P. 2004. External auditory representations of programs: Past, present, and future—An aesthetic perspective. In *Proceedings of ICAD 04-Tenth Meeting of the International Conference on Auditory Display*, Sydney, July 6–9.

Vickers, P. 2005. Whither and wherefore the auditory graph? Abstractions and aesthetics in auditory and sonified graphs. In *First Symposium on Auditory Graphs*, Limerick, Ireland, July 10.

Walker, B. N., A. Nance, and J. Lindsay. 2006. Spearcons: Speech-based earcons improve navigation performance in auditory menus. In *Proceedings of the 12th International Conference on Auditory Display*, London, June 20–23.

Warin, C. 2002. "Sound as means for data representation for data mining." Master's degree thesis, Facultés Universitaires Notre-Dame de la Paix, Namur.

Whitelaw, M. 2004. Hearing pure data: Aesthetics and ideals of data-sound. In *Unsorted: Thoughts on the Information Arts: An A to Z for Sonic Acts X*, ed. A. Altena. Amsterdam: Sonic Acts/De Balie, pp. 45–54.

Worrall, D. 1996. Studies in metamusical methods for sound and image composition. *Organised Sound* 1(3): 20–26.

Worrall, D. 2004. *Auditory Display as a Tool for Exploring Emergent Forms in Exchange-Trading Data*. Research Report, December, Sonic Communications Research Group, University of Canberra.

Worrall, D., M. Bylstra, S. Barrass, and R. T. Dean. 2007. *SoniPy*: The design of an extendable software framework for sonification research and auditory display. In *Proceedings of the 13th International Conference on Auditory Display*, Montréal, Canada, June 26–29.

Xenakis, I. 1971. *Formalized Music: Thought and Mathematics in Music*. Bloomington: Indiana University Press.

Zatorre, R. J., P. Belin, and V. B. Penhune. 2002. Structure and function of auditory cortex: music and speech. *Trends in Cognitive Sciences* 6(1): 37–46.

CHAPTER 17

ELECTRONICA

NICK COLLINS

The human construct that we call our music is merely a
convention—something we have all evolved together, and
that rests on no final or ultimate laws.

—Reich 2002, p. 131

There are as many histories of electronic music as historians. Each electroscribe
dwells on certain events that reflect their biases and theories, possibly magnifying
the role of certain characters with each iteration through the standard sources (Lev
Termen, Karlheinz Stockhausen, Aphex Twin . . . let's get them out of the way).
Each exposition is doomed to establish certain categorizations, for the sake of
manageable theorizing and readability, although it is often helpful to focus on
central exemplars of particular concepts and allow for fluid and fuzzy borders
(Lakoff 1987). For instance, it is hard to engage with the musics I describe without a
host of genre labels and stylistic terms jumping forward—jumbling historical
order, for example, electro, glitch, 2 step, grime, minimal techno, Detroit techno,
industrial, circuit bending—any of which may fail to be well defined,[1] although we
try our best to corral them. Such resistance to conclusive delineation is inevitable
regardless of disclaimers and protestations of continuity appearing in first para-
graphs like this one. Just as sampling and generativity are rife in the audio cultures
I describe, I imagine that you will find your own ways to explore these circuits,
but I do hope I can nudge you in a few unexpected directions.

Although this book tackles most closely the home computer age and the role of
computers in music, I have decided in this chapter to acknowledge the necessity of
a broader survey. This resolve is a desire to engage not only with digital culture in
general but also with its necessarily analog roots[2] and the continued existence

of hybrid signal chains. Analog is still with us in electronic music practice, from the 5-volt laying-on-hands antics of circuit bending, through the brave persistence of vinyl even in the face of CD, DVD, and hard-drive disk jockeying, to the impossibility of sidestepping microphones and speakers as interfaces to the real world (the network live coding ensemble PowerBooks UnPlugged comes to mind as an example; they scatter themselves around the performance space and use their built-in laptop speakers for spatialization).

Further, computers are not always the primary tools, although other hardware devices employed may utilize digital integrated circuits. Roland xoxs are the sought-after basis of so much electronic dance music (EDM) production; much interesting audio art is made by wounding CDs or CD players; John Oswald conjures plunderphonics from a hardware sampler; a hardware sequencer was used by Squarepusher for much of his early work in the 1990s. Yet, it is very difficult to deny the pervasive influence of digital audio and the new music representations underlying hardware and software interfaces; digital technology's cheapness and engineering convenience inevitably trumped analog. Roland 909s play back some samples even if 808s are fully analog. Most guitarists do not realize that their cheap multifx pedals are really digital signal-processing units. All but the merest trifle of contemporary recording involves a computer, even for a string quartet (arguably more essentially still here, given the classical recording industry's predilection to edit to within a byte of perfection).

One term used to capture the state of transduction between mediums, pressure waves in air and electrical signals, is *electroacoustic*.[3] Unfortunately, this term is most associated with certain art musics that followed the 1950s experiments of musique concrète and *elektronische musik*, and some of its practitioners have separated themselves from much of the electronica described in this chapter.[4] *Electronica* as a term appeared in the later 1990s as a descriptor for divergent EDMs and their abstractions. Used in North America less broadly than Europe, it has been charged by some as a deliberate marketing term for popular electronic music, a catchall label that could keep up with the broadly diffusing styles that followed the rave era of EDM. Confusingly, in the United States it might simply denote EDM and in Europe electronic music outside the core EDM territory. This Latinate tag does not connote music so much as technology itself, and an observer of the experimental arts scene might link electronica to the first Ars Electronica festival of 1979 or to the improvising collective Musica Elettronica Viva formed in 1966. But, it will do as a tool for our purposes to give some of the character and flavor of the era described; as you may surmise, there is no perfect term that could possibly keep up with the wild cultural memetics of music and technology (see Landy 2007 for more on the categorization debate).[5]

My remit is to concentrate on the age from the founding of the MIDI standard (1983), and this coincides with the proliferation of digital equipment, the rise of EDM, and then its multiply fractured and fast breeding offshoots. There are also parallel adventures in digital art, noise music, video jockeying (VJing), live electronics, and a host of other movements touching on the electric and the programmable. While the precedents are many and varied—voltage-controlled synths in popular music from Wendy/Walter Carlos through Kraftwerk to postpunk synth pop, dub sound systems, Bronx block parties and hip-hop, Raymond Scott,[6] the sci-fi otherworldiness that became quickly tied to the new alien sounds from speakers, the Kim-1 Bay scene as an early home computer enthusiasts' network—the very real rise of the adaptable home computer helped bring an age of mass producer and consumer electronic music into being, particularly from around 1995 with the ascension of the Internet.

While a central thesis of this chapter is that we are in a mass participation era, it would be naïve to assert equality of opportunity. Human society is not built that way in practice, even if the liberal ideal is to seek uniform access. Indeed, many authors have argued that we need difference, inequality, and aspirations to allow a dynamic engine of culture (Reynolds 2007); I do not delve further into issues of race, gender, and locality, although these are central topics in the sociology of popular music in particular, and inevitable in human dealings, if to be minimized as factors of discrimination. I simply note that since aesthetics are up for debate, a meritocracy in art is a difficult proposition. Any one style itself is not necessarily wildly popular or mainstream or cannot hold majority opinion for long. Much of the technology itself is available to all, however, and many electronic musics have crossed over into mass appeal, from EDM to the more abstract electronica freely employed in technology commercials.

Thus, provisos and preamble now disposed, let the survey begin.

1. ELECTRONIC DANCE MUSIC AND ITS ABSTRACTIONS

Who requires ineradicable ostinatos?

—Boulez 1955

A dance-tune plopped out... a combo of abstract tape-noises with a slow gut-shaking beat deep beneath.

—Burgess 1962, reprinted 1994, p. 40

The label *electronic dance music* or *EDM* has the virtue of foregrounding one of the music's prime functions and its favored timbres. It has often been denigrated by critics for simplicity of musical construction and artistic scope, although these critics are sometimes only familiar with a caricature of one or two scenes within a turbulent culture. Yet, if we avoid characterizing it by stereotypes of four-to-the-floor kick and throwaway production (as if all tracks were really composed in less time than the sequencer takes to play through them), we must recognize a broad field of intensive investigation containing many tribes and practices and extending away from club-only music to listening and abstract functions, even if a central point of reference remains the club (Thornton 1995, Redhead 1997, Butler 2006, Brewster and Broughton 2006, Reynolds 2008).

Simon Reynolds characterized thirteen essential attributes of EDM worth paraphrasing here: (1) machine music, technology obsessive; (2) texture/rhythm versus melody/harmony; (3) promoting physical responses; (4) mass communion; (5) pleasures on the surface; (6) drugs; (7) primacy of sound over visuals and crowd over artist; (8) facelessness, antipersonality cult; (9) collective, generic, democratic; (10) cultural taxonomists impatient for the next scene; (11) valuing the underground; (12) site specific (particular clubs); and (13) mixed crowds and mashed-up tracks (Reynolds 2007, pp. 312–329). While the entries in this list overlap somewhat, Reynolds used them as the basis for an entertaining tribute to dance culture (particularly 1988–1998) and was quick to acknowledge "a partial blueprint: culture is always messy, evading our attempts at definition" (ibid., p. 218) and the fecundity of the scenes themselves, which sidestepping commercial imperatives in popular music can supply "avant-garde ideas working in a popular context" (ibid., p. 328). The facelessness of individual artists, whose single releases are mixed and matched by DJs over long-controlled sets, is an interesting dynamic in the culture (Brewster and Broughton 2006); the DJs themselves have often stolen much of the credit and in turn become producers themselves.

Counterexamples to any of the thirteen attributes can occur; for example, Daft Punk touring definitely contravenes attribute 8, and political authorities usually do their best to stamp out attribute 6. Most of Reynolds's inquiry is sociological, although to be fair the simple musical recipe of attribute 2 is complicated further elsewhere in his writings—the "great divide: songs versus 'tracks,' melody versus rhythm 'n' FX" (Reynolds 2007, p. 218), the attitude to vocals in particular subgenres from full diva presence (U.S. garage), the "vocal science" of sampling and processing (U.K. garage/2 step), through live vocals over instrumentals (toasting over dub, MCing over grime), to the purely instrumental track (techno, techstep). A more analytical approach to the music itself is presented by Mark Butler (2006) or algorithmic investigations employing analysis by synthesis (Collins 2001, Mesker 2007).

Just as Wagner saw Beethoven as the "apotheosis of the dance," EDM was always to be a fertile ground for those who sought its abstraction and extrapolation. From ambient music in the chill-out rooms of clubs (ca. 1990) to Warp Record's *Artificial Intelligence* compilation of 1992, the noncontradiction of electronic listening music founded in dance music styles emerged: for living rooms, postclub comedowns, everyday listening; for the reinvigoration of much electronic music on the back of the rave boom. Awkward descriptions such as "intelligent dance music" (IDM) or the more amusing "braindance" subsequently appeared, and eventually the electronica category, forcefully expanding to keep up with experiments. While connections to the ambient music movement may be traced (Prendergast 2003), there is no restriction on abstract EDM to seek peace and furniture musicality; indeed, the fiercer currents of dance music, from hard core (ca. 1990) into jungle (ca. 1992) and beyond, always fuel athletic experimentation teetering on the borders of the danceable. Yet, the rich tapestry of EDM remains an important point of reference, often at the exclusion of much wider electronic music history.[7]

To momentarily trace dance music's origins, if a year had to be chosen as the starting point, we might indicate 1973, by the close of which DJ Kool Herc was first crudely looping the most danceable drum breaks in records at Bronx parties using two copies and two turntables, or Kraftwerk were feeling their way into electronic automation. By 1983, the Belleville Three in Detroit, the Warehouse club in Chicago, the New York/Jersey clubs with their postdisco hi-NRG, eclectic playlists, and soulful garage were preparing groundwork for the late 1980s rave explosion (ca. 1988, the so-called second summer of love, where clubbers particularly loved MDMA [methylene dimethamphetamine, Ecstasy]), but it was hip-hop and synth pop that broke first into the popular imagination.

Since the explosion of popularity also caused an explosion of styles and voices, we could let ourselves be carried away with a discussion of the many genre labels and their obsessive manipulation by promoters and fans. This is a war of description that can never be won for the act of categorizing always loses us information. New styles are being incarnated as I write, and I am doomed to fail to cover them adequately. Current fads are always at the mercy of the next media headline, so while we might spare a thought for *grime* (gritty post-U.K. garage nurtured on the pirate radio scene, cast through a wringer of 1990s RnB production fads and with prominent London MCs) and *dubstep* (heavy bass and delay/filter-obsessed post-U.K. garage emanating from Croydon), these are already faded/fading and difficult enough to describe in singular musical terms. I doubt there will ever be an exhaustive musicological study of all EDM, as it would be simply too exhausting!

It is perhaps more productive to trace the technology to afford a glimpse of what went on in countless bedroom studios. Some of the trends were mentioned in the discussion of analog and digital hardware (as opposed to software) synths and sequencers. Also worth mentioning are the tracker programs appearing in the 1980s, the late 1980s appearance of Cubase on the Atari ST with its innovative graphical tracks and timeline interface, and the subsequent rise of software sequencers for both MIDI and audio. Feeding off the dirty power supplies in the British raves around 1990 were the Amigas and Atari STs running early sequencer/tracker and VJ software. From 1995, computer software sequencing and synthesis and the Internet would come to dominate both electronic music production and distribution. Yet, many electronica artists have found certain early interfaces extremely productive (witness Bogdan Raczynski, Venetian Snares, or the 8-bit scene's use of tracker programs). Many an hour has been spent by musicians poring over the minutiae of manual cut and splice in Cubase or Logic or their ilk, chaining together intensive breakbeat manipulations by hand. Manual work is still far more prevalent than might be expected, so even though algorithms are a natural candidate for generative dance music (Collins 2001), the production of fixed tracks with obsessive attention to detail is a more natural mode for the recording-fixated, DJ set feeding majority of bedroom producers.

As a case study in more abstract, art-conscious EDM, of musics that require an electronica superset rather than just straightforward electronic music for dancing, we might look to a Sheffield record label, Warp Records (Young 2005, Reynolds 2008) and, more particularly, to the duo Autechre (Mesker 2007). Rob Brown and Sean Booth provide some of the most obvious examples of warped dance music, abstract enough in many places to leave any dance function far behind. For example, by manipulating the tempo and timing of events on multiple layers, they effect a looped transition between two metrical levels on *Fold 4, Wrap 5* (1998), with a nod to Jean-Claude Risset's experiments in continuous ritardando. They have explored the use of generative algorithms, run live to produce particular recorded tracks (e.g., on the album *Confield* from 2001)[8] but hold allegiance to no one piece of equipment, experimenting with all manner of hardware and software in the pursuit of new sonic worlds. While they may not have had traditional tutoring in electroacoustic music or awareness of the grand heritage of electronic music, like many new media artists, they learned as they went and should not be disparaged for this; it can be a strength to work outward from a different tradition, to pick things up through wholly practical means, to rediscover, but also inevitably to introduce variation.

Musicians on the fringes of dance music soon enough looked backward to discover the great history of experimental electronic music and automatically merged to become part of that progression (even had they not looked, they could not have helped the latter). While human creativity has been theorized in myriad ways, the essential component of trial and error, of human inquisitiveness probing to the heart of machines and musics, seems highly pertinent to the billions of personal investigations empowered. As Drew McDermott wrote, "each occurrence of creativity is unique" (McDermott 2001, p. 89), and I have no wish to denigrate the fascinating music that has arisen from EDM as much as to denigrate the currents of electroacoustic music with which EDM's abstractions now interact.

2. MUSICIANS' RELATIONSHIP WITH TECHNOLOGY

If this chapter has something of the taste of a catalogue, it is because there is no one central trend to cover but a variety of approaches to electronic music over time. This section, however, tackles two currents in electronic music in which technology has played a primary role in influencing the musical outcomes: (1) sampling and copyright and (2) glitch and microsound.

A. Sampling and Copyright

> Appropriate that the sampling aesthetic (taking liberties with other people's musical property) should have fallen into the light-fingered hands of delinquents.
>
> —Reynolds 2007, p. 146

The technique of collage is innate to treating recording technology seriously as a source of materials and a basis for constructing new works. The line from Pierre Schaeffer to John Oswald is not too far, and while Schaeffer pressed records (in 1948 for the first studies) then spliced magnetic tape (from 1951), and the latter most famously used a hardware sampler in the 1980s, their music has certain affinities; compare, for example, the classical music remixing of Schaeffer's *Courante-Roucante* to Oswald's *7th*. In between the two fall many unpoliced examples, James Tenney's *Collage #1 (Blue Suede)* (1961) presenting an early example of explicit plundering and manipulation of licensed music, Stockhausen's *Telemusik* (1966) ring modulating recordings from a number of countries, and Bernard Parmegiani's *Pop'eclectic* (1969) and *Du pop à l'âne* (1969) citing extensively from both classical and rock; even if all of these remained below the popular radar, Goodman and Buchanan's sampladelic *The Flying Saucer* (1956) and the Beatles's *Revolution 9* (1968) certainly did not.

The Jamaican studio dubs prepared for live sound system combat (Brewster and Broughton 2006, Reynolds 2007, pp. 248–263) have been credited with foregrounding notions of remixing and reuse in popular music. Alongside King Tubby and his peers, New York DJs in the early days of disco and rap music were exploring the possibilities of new combinations for records in DJ mixes and mash-ups (Brewster and Broughton 2006). Early hip-hop remained a Bronx secret until the Sugarhill Gang's 1979 hit *Rapper's Delight* made appropriation highly visible by using (even if replayed by session musicians) a loop from Chic's *Good Times* of the same year. In the 1980s, popular music artists, particularly in hip-hop, quickly took up the cut-and-paste aesthetic to their own ends, from novelty records produced with sampling keyboards to more considered montages. Work might be created live by careful multideck record mixing to showcase newly developed turntable skills (such as on 1981's *Adventures of Grandmaster Flash on the Wheels of Steel*) or piece by piece in the studio using both analog and digital tools. Brian Eno and David Bryne's *My Life in the Bush of Ghosts* (1981), Afrika Bambaataa and the Soul Sonic Force's electro anthem *Planet Rock* (1982), the Fairlight digital treatments on Kate Bush's *The Dreaming* (1982), the sampling and scratching on Herbie Hancock's *Rockit* (1983), or the highly influential but underground remix competition winner, DD and Steinski's *Lesson 1* (1983) could all be feted from this period.

Implicit in the manipulation of recordings is the ownership of recordings, and a series of high-profile lawsuits at the close of the 1980s soon suppressed some of the wilder (and highly creative) abuses of hip-hop artists in particular. Yet, sampling can never stop for no recording can be preserved untouched forever—witness officially sanctioned remix culture and unofficial mash-ups or the cult status of plunderphonic works (Cox and Warner 2004). The latter have been preserved from harm even in the face of court orders requiring the destruction of every copy (a fate leveled at Oswald's freely distributed *Plunderphonics* EP in 1989, yet which can now be downloaded from his Web site). A chief rule of evading copyright lawyers is not to stick your head so far above the parapet that you make enough money to afford their fees. It is easy to burn with ire at the commercial forces restricting human creativity and hustle, but the legal issues and copyright debate continues at the time of writing in a world of prolific downloading and audio watermarking, even if the imposition of digital rights management has been (temporarily?) relaxed.

The meta-musical materials implicit in utilizing recording technology and sound studio as remix laboratory have thus had a strong impact across the musical spectrum. In part, this only reflects the natural magpie tendencies of composers as styles evolve; the history of music is just material for more mashing, recycling, and repackaging.

B. Glitch (Only Mistakes Are Original) and Microsound (Lost in Close-up)

> With samplers I never read the instructions. I like to learn from my mistakes and incorporate blunders.
>
> —Kurtis Mantronik 1987, interviewed in Reynolds 2007, p. 40

The close relationship of musicians to technology allowed them to critique it as much as they adored it, and the cracks in software and idiosyncrasies of machines they played with every day, in short, the *glitch*, soon became a subject for art conscious of its own technological backbone and fallibilities. Such a movement might be seen as seizing on technological failure perhaps as revenge for the crashing of computers at important stages of a mix.[9] Various alternative names and associated crosscurrents include clicks and cuts (named after an influential compilation series on the Mille Plateaux label), click hop, microhouse (both crossing back into EDM), and microsound (the name of a mailing list as well as a book on granular synthesis by Curtis Roads). The click and the glitch evoke short impulses, momentary breaks in audio fidelity, microscopic tears. The building of larger clouds of sound out of tiny source granules and the technological facility of obsessively sifting in digital audio editors to the highest zoom factors (fig. 17.1) underlie the microsound aesthetic (Thomson 2004). It would therefore seem possible to separate glitch (malfunctions in equipment, dropouts, and other errors in the digital audio stream) from a constructive process of microsound feeding up to the macrolevel.

Glitch has been theorized as "postdigital" (Cascone 2000). To my taste, post-digital is a rather awkward term, just as fallible as postmodern, and while having no technological basis (it is hard to escape the tyranny of 1's and 0's if you want to use most contemporary equipment) also says very little about escaping perfection. Digital is an approximation to start with, albeit an arbitrarily good one, and the clean digital luster is really just a timbral choice; some artists seem to miss their old tape recorders and crackling vinyl enough simply to sample back on the vinyl glow (as became prevalent in 1990s trip-hop, for example).

Forcing error correction in CD hardware is hardly going beyond the digital; it is simply the deliberate mucking up of the machine. Artists often misunderstand and glorify the mundane purposes of much digital signal processing, injecting surefire humanity, although sometimes obfuscating the raw reality of the

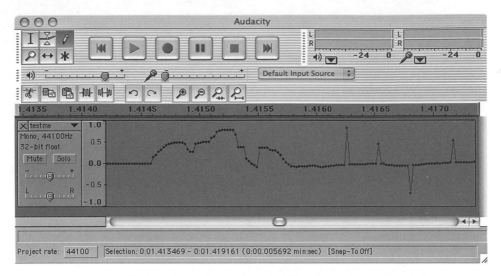

Figure 17.1 At a high zoom in the Audacity audio editor, drawing tools become
available to tweak individual digital samples.

engineered tool. Undoubtedly, the original engineer's intentions are not the only
intentions at play in culture, and I do not wish to give the impression that
fascinating music has not arisen from such movements.

Although artists such as Oval, Fennesz, General Magic, and Pita have been
promoted as the modern prophets of the movement (Young 2002), a history of
(digital) glitch would usually begin with Yasunao Tone wounding CDs to force
them to skip in CD players (1984–1985) (Stuart 2003). But, he is certainly not
the first to air the possibility of the deliberate misuse of technology. An interview
with Holgar Czukay and Irmin Schmidt of early 1970s krautrock fame revealed
the motto "the most inventive way to use a synthesiser is to misuse it" (Shapiro
2000, p. 36). Further examples are plentiful, indeed, intimately linked to the
controlled trial and error of creativity, and some artists may seek circumstances
that promote such possibilities, as revealed by the quotation at the beginning
of this section. The misuse of the TB-303 in the creation of Phuture's *Acid
Tracks* (1985, released 1987; see Butler 2006, p. 68) is well known. Operator instructions on mixing desks do not tell you to connect the output directly back to
the input, but this has not prevented a half century or more of exploration of
feedback.

Roads's microsound book (2001) is an adaptation of his doctoral thesis,
completed in Paris, and reflecting his interest in granular processes since the
1970s. The canon of granulation might cite Denis Gabor, Iannis Xenakis, Karlheinz
Stockhausen, Barry Truax, and Curtis Roads, although many others have dabbled.
Indeed, granular synthesis is often touted as the defining sound of much recent
electroacoustic music, probably because it is relatively straightforward to get
promising sound transformations. The same utility has endeared it to all producers, not just those located on some conservatory trajectory, and the connection

with the glitch is a paean to the small scale and even the mythical quanta, conceptualized to within a microsecond of their life.

We might be a little cautious, though, around fine details at microtimescales; there is only one perceptual timescale for the playback of audio, the environmental rate of the brain's processing. A preoccupation with leaving marks deep in audio might lead us back to audio watermarking as momentarily dropped into the previous section or to an encounter with Richard D. James's face and Aaron Funk's cats embedded via the granular spectral painting package MetaSynth (http://www.bastwood.com/aphex.php). But such trickery, even if extramusically fun, can also have an air of falsity about it as minute adjustments with a pen tool at some high zoom factor may only provide tweaks of distortion.

Nevertheless, such currents in electronic music, often taking place as they do outside traditional electroacoustic schools and exploiting the Internet for discussion and distribution, prove the existence of radical new work in experimental electronic music that nevertheless sidesteps the landscapes and spatial perfections of many acousmatic concerts. Even if the reader is not convinced by the abstractions surrounding EDM, sampling and glitch in particular may convince one of the alternative splendors born outside the institutional laboratory. But, it must be admitted that artists can themselves slide between these categories; Autechre, for example, have produced tracks associated with glitch and have an electro heritage (itself related to hip-hop and sampling). The microhouse genre shows how quickly these currents cross fertilize; as analysts, we may often choose features of musics we wish to use to promote a coherent whole when these features are really just a convenient talking point for gathering the illusion of an unambiguous trend.

3. From Sound Art to Digital Art

[There is] no such thing as an unmusical sound object.

—Wishart 1985, p. 6

Yet no-one has thought of numbering the makers of Aeolian harps among the great composers.

—Berlioz 1970, p. 220

It is clear that whenever the experimental is invoked, wherever the vanguard of ideas and technology leads, the cultural negotiation and commodity consensus that is fine art is not far away. If it is a truism to state that art is simply a human social fabrication, a layer of additional theorizing imposed on craft, it is nevertheless a very real force buffeting many careers.

To some artists, *music* is a dirty word or at least a territory they do not wish to inhabit in their practice, having defined it perhaps in opposition to their own working spaces. Nevertheless, they might still go around organizing sounds. While Trevor Wishart coined the term *sonic art* in an attempt to broaden the basis of music (1985), sonic arts in some circles[10] has become a shelter for fine artists employing the auditory modality in their work who may wish to distance themselves from the traditional social roles of music and particularly the conservatory attitudes of classical music tradition that seem so far from experimental art. If the latter attitude, it may often reflect an ignorance of how truly experimental music actually became in the 20th century, and the clean break of redefining the term rings a little false. It is also a little ignorant of how electronic music has moved on from the traditional ivory tower (helped by the healthy interactions with popular music described here, for example). But, the former attitude, of new social roles, of new spaces for sound, has some legitimacy, particularly in the site-specific encounters of installations and new communication routes.[11]

Sound artists would probably best meet experimental musicians, perhaps, through John Cage, and the image of Cage playing Duchamps at electrochess is one that might unify the conceptual and musically practicable. Sound artists can also draw on much work in media and theatre, leading us back to consider futurism, dada, radiophonics, currents in sound poetry, happenings, and the like (Kahn 1999, LaBelle 2007). Gallery presentation probably most embodies sound art's essential role, although the virtual gallery is a more contemporary spin on this location.

Much sound art often engages with fundamental physical properties of electricity and sound and psychoacoustics. Alvin Lucier's work has been observed as engaging with principles from acoustics to neuroscience (LaBelle 2007), and the same investigative spirit might summarize Maryanne Amacher. Ryoji Ikeda's $+/-$ (1997) audio CD employs the acoustic of whichever room it is played back in to allow the unique navigation of interference patterns. Bill Viola's *Hallway Nodes* (1973) sets up physically palpable low-frequency standing waves (Hegarty 2007, p. 175). La Monte Young's *Dream House* has been permanently outputting some high overtones on the harmonic series since 1993, give or take a powercut. Christina Kubisch's *because tomorrow comes #2* (2000), presented at the Hayward Gallery as part of the Sonic Boom exhibition, allowed visitors to wander an outdoor space receiving the soundscape via headphones and electromagnetic induction.

My reason for raising sound art is not to dwell on it at length, although of course you may find all sorts of interesting crossovers and possibilities there. It is to bring us to consider digital art, the nexus of so much current art practice, and another grand site of interaction between fields. Much experimental electronic music (if you will grant me leave to call it that for convenience) is now diffused within a context of digital arts festivals (the aforementioned Ars Electronica, Transmediale, Inter-Society for the Electronic Arts festivals). Just as sound artists may become musicians (Alva Noto, also known as Carsten Nicolai, comes to mind), musicians also become sound artists, producing their own installations. They might also go into audiovisuals (as partially discussed in this chapter) or explore the computational and conceptual at greater depth through software art, through generative music; inter- and cross-media work has become a way of vaunting new skill sets and mind-sets. Networking itself is another glorious territory of much relevance to contemporary practice (well, not free wine-splashed gallery openings, but the possibilities of network infrastructure and multilocation connectivity through telecommunications). Suffice to say that in a world so dependent on the Internet, artists would find many things to reflect on, even if latencies are a hindrance to real-time musical interaction (Rohrhuber 2007). Drawing on both acoustics and networks, [The User]'s Silophone project (since 2001; http://www.silophone.net/) allows a remote user to utilize a chamber in Montreal as a reverberator, submitting samples to be processed.

Ultimately, the computers took over. We play computer games and write game music. We write our own programs and defer composition to them. The chatter of our e-mails can form the source data for sonification. We are besieged by the digital and by digital art. And, speaking of this density of information . . .

4. OVERLOAD

No more sonatas, no more cantatas. Is not the music of this world.
I give myself to overload.

—Silverberg 1989, p. 166

Robert Silverberg, an author often preoccupied by paradoxes raised by the possibility of time travel, imagines Giovanni Battista Pergolesi (1710–1736) being transported to the present just before death. Although he is first recuperated by modern medicine, rather than composing the new antique works his time-meddling rescuers hoped for, he falls into the drug and extreme noise culture of *overload* and quickly dies again. While Silverberg invented the name for this genre, he was writing in 1984, well after the rise of industrial music and the noise movement in the 1970s, a movement far more extreme than the pub rock with spitting of much punk music. His short story can be viewed neatly as an allegory of changing musical styles over time.

Noise music (Cox and Warner 2004, Hegarty 2007, Landy 2007, pp. 126–129), as a deliberate practice of extremes of sound, bridges sound art and electronic music, although by the various definitions of noise I review, it might equally bridge between acoustic folk and hyperamplified medical auscultation. The link to electronics is unsurprising, not just because of the ready availability of technology. Just as synthesizers were quickly associated with the high technologies and alien cultures of science fiction, their otherwordly aspects have been of great use in disturbing convention. Amplification is also a key tool, often wielded in the face of sound-level legislation.

A history of noise in music might explore reception and innovation across the whole of music history and the continual renegotiation of music within society's current mores and needs. When engaging with society, extramusical statements often intrude through visuals or performance art. For our purposes, the era from Throbbing Gristle, the highly theatrical early industrial band (1975) is most pertinent. In the subsequent decades, noise has been a site of free expression, but also of the exploration of many darker sides of the human psyche. Merzbow (Masami Akita), prolifically releasing work since 1979, a doyen of the Japanese noise scene, has a febrile fascination with sadomasochism.

There are various primary aspects that might be drawn out in theorizing noise, and I present a personal selection here:

1. Psychoacoustic aspects: loudness, sensory dissonance[12]
2. The contrary: accepting what is not currently considered music, exploring your antiaesthetic (patterns you dislike), going where others will not tread
3. The physical, the sensationalist; seeking raw stimuli, powerful forces
4. The oppositional: political and antisocial acts (although these are often extramusical)
5. Too much information: inability to parse the totality of data may lead to a sense of noise

In finding examples to convey some of these trends I could respectively mention the following: (1) Russolo, Merzbow, and many other artists' exploration of the timbral resources of machinery and distortion; (2) Cage; (3) the high volume levels (up to or beyond the 120-dB SPL threshold of pain) of sound systems used by MEGO record label artists that have a sadistic disregard for human hearing, but also the rich physical sensations conveyed by bass first pushed to the limits in Jamaican sound system culture; (4) Atari Teenage Riot, a highly politicized ensemble whose 1990s digital hard-core music anticipates what later became break-core (extremely frenetic hyper-speed gabba-jungle) and illustrates another connection within this chapter, of extreme dance musics to noise; and (5) Farmers Manual, who have often explored the overload of data in the digital world. Point 1, as opposed to the rest, outlines the classic nature-versus-nurture debate. We have certain physiological limits (so the 120-dB sound system will cause hearing damage) but also an upbringing within a vibrant and fast-paced culture that desensitizes us to some sounds or makes us prone to others.

You may productively consider many more attributes of noise, and the references given will lead to some alternative theories and descriptors. R. Murray Schafer has simply written "Noise is any undesired sound" (Schafer 1986, p. 110).

In this 21st-century era, we are also often faced with a sense of having pushed already to the furthest reaches of art in the 20th century (what to do after Cage, what to do after the postmodern) and now are hammering inside the cage of human perceptual and cognitive limits. As Paul Hegarty (2007) noted, the transgressions implicit in extreme music are difficult for any one anarchic noise ensemble to keep making. And, if certain ethics remain staunch boundaries of taste, eternal rebellion is a rather tiresome position. Instead, more limited reactions against the particularities of each era's society and technology would seem a more likely future trend.

Much noise music has been played live, spurred by the sense of losing oneself in real-time action. I now turn to a more general discussion of live electronic music beyond the various currents already explored.

5. Live Electronica

With all this technological engagement and future-oriented posturing, the traditional performing musician has been usurped by sequenced playback, by prerecorded tracks mixed by a trusted selector, by algorithmic splendor. Yet, the compulsion to play live, even among the digital hinterland, is a strong human impulse to social contact. One much-discussed consequence of this desire is the phenomenon of the almost immobile laptop artist, coaxing rumbles from minute manipulation of a trackpad as if sheer bloody-minded attention must automatically lead to fulsome experience. Where briefly laptop music was a buzzword, it is now an acknowledged and unremarkable phenomenon; the acousmatic state of electroacoustic music concerts has become an obvious point of reference to such practice (Cascone 2003). Playing from behind the curtain has been explicitly adopted by electronica acts; not caring about the evidence of vision regarding physical concrete action, Autechre often perform with the lights out. Some DJs employ a range of live fx beyond the basic manipulation of track playback and often do so while hidden in a DJ booth. It should be noted that there is nothing a priori wrong with simply listening or dancing. Contemplation can be a dignified and vital concert mode, just as uninhibited dancing regardless of any further human spectacle.

Nevertheless, perhaps this scene is typified by a software like Ableton Live, used by both laptopists and DJs, if the distinction is even useful anymore given that the vast majority of DJs now carry a laptop containing their record collections. Ableton, the company, produces a live sequencer that can be operated on the fly with dynamic loading of tracks, further enabling radical effects to be indiscriminately employed. Many a laptop set is now driven by this engine, and some decry this ubiquity of approach as hardly "live" to begin with; such a dissenting view usually puts a premium on well-understood and visually obvious musicianship of proven heritage and prosthetic reality.

As if to enrage the physicalists further, a significant trend in live performance is the combination of audio and visuals (indeed, Ableton now also allows for this option, as do hardware DVD decks for [D+V]Js). Visual action is imposed as more exciting than human bodies on stage, for jump cuts and the impossibilities possible with SFX could fling myriad human motion across a screen; yet more typically, abstract two- and three-dimensional forms and stuttering and effects-laden video blaze their trail. The division of attention between modalities in such circumstances is a rather important question and an open problem in theory. Some issues might be briefly summarized; both audio and visuals distract from true appreciation of either one alone, and while it is easy to achieve various lazy correlations, taking advantage of the brain's own predilection to seek meaning, a continuum from controlled synchronization to abstract opposition is much harder to effect. Such multimodal territory is of great interest to explore but also invokes a fight for primacy between the so-called first and second senses. As audio and visual may remain equally virtual in scope, audiovisuals can also distract from issues of physical engagement and do not solve the quandary raised by acousmatic music except to shine some light in the darkness (for more on audiovisual practice and history, see Alexander and Collins 2007).

One policy for laptop artists that confronts some of the issues is to "reveal the whole interface" (www.toplap.org), that is, to project laptop screens. Projecting to reveal Ableton Live would play into the hands of criticism, so instead: *live coding* (Collins et al. 2003, Ward et al. 2004), focused on the new ubiquity of arts programming and the joy of algorithms. Live coding's counterculture is a precarious deal with formalism and the most abstract of human actions, far distant from the evident physicalities of guitar playing or bashing rocks together. Live coding is a paradigmatic cerebral activity, which has itself been satirized by Amy Alexander in her VJ Übergeek persona, dancing while strapped to an ASCII keyboard.

Whether the computer—such a general and customizable device—could ever take on the authenticity of traditional musical instruments is debatable (such authenticity in respect of guitar and TR808 is discussed in Théberge 2001; of course, laptops are such a common sight on stage these days that they may already be accepted). In some quarters, arguments rage over embodiment as an essential attribute of cognition, of true music-making. Yet, the very existence of controversy often makes us aware of new musical schisms, and there is nothing a priori to stop a rise in live coding.

Live coding is another musical interaction with the computer indicative of the digital age. The inclinations in generative music alluded to in the previous section are amenable and adaptable to live music; we must simply choose where to place hooks for interaction. While live coding manipulates running algorithms, generative music programs set the algorithms in advance to delimit the space of possible action. Live engagement with such programs is to enter a particular predefined interaction space. The potential complexity of such systems here is a function of the availability of artificial intelligence (AI) research to the construction of musical machines. Interactive music systems in software, and even musical robots in hardware, present the algorithmic interlocutors of contemporary discourse and are an active area of current research (Rowe 2001, Collins 2007). With the availability of machine listening algorithms in audio programming environments, the role of AI in live music-making is ever increasing.

It does not just have to be computers, of course. Well, first, it does not have to be the latest machines; substantial retro movements idolize older models and processing limitations, for example, in the 8-bit scene, which harks back to the original 1980s demo scene and tracker programs.

I stated in the beginning of the chapter that I could not in fairness restrict this survey to just computers, just digital. The circuit benders and hardware hackers are crawling in the innards of electronics, from toys to newly designed circuits. They may be preparing hacks for live use or even constructing circuits live in a sense analogous to some live coding displays. Alternative interfaces are also popular, from the more easily adaptable game controllers, to custom-built kit (Kanta Horio's amplified paper clips on a magnet board [fig. 17.2], Kristin Erickson's recent experiments with tap dancers triggering sounds via contact microphones

Figure 17.2 In Kanta Horio's *particle*, paper clips are placed on a board of computer-controlled electromagnets. Live video of the system in action is broadcast in the venue for an audience, who also hear the movement of the clips amplified by contact microphones. (Courtesy of Kanta Horio.)

and onset detection). Physical computing allows many artists to approach alternative interfaces via programmable boards (Arduino, Wiring et al.) and a wide choice of sensors. There is simply not room to pursue every variant and practice.

6. CONCLUSION

> The search for truth in art becomes a travesty in which each era's practice only parodies its predecessor's prejudice.
>
> —Minsky 1981

It is clear that any new technology is employed by many musicians as soon as they can get their hands on it, and computers are just another tool in a long line of high technology for music-making. Technology is always in popular music's armory as much as a lure for experimentalism, and indeed, the commercial and "fine" art are often hard to tease apart.

While there will always be reactionary elements who hold limpetlike at a certain arbitrary point—the voice, mechanical-acoustic prosthetics, electrical instruments before the triode, valve-based systems, transistor-based systems, and so forth—the tide of technology is not about to abate, and a musician can always ride on the crest of the waveform. Indeed, with the speeding up of accessibility, of time to market, of affordability, there are precious few differences between the opportunities for research (academic) and commercial (mass consumption) sectors, and electronic music has become a mass pursuit rather than a rarefied world of privileged studios and electroacoustic composers, regardless of the strictures on dissemination still posed by pyramidical capitalism and not-having-enough-time-in-the-day-to-hear-it-all.[13]

Download culture keeps trying to run wild, and schemes are always being put in place to temper the piratical inclination. While it would be wonderful if every artist who chose to release an MP3 could be rewarded, you cannot beat the middlemen. Recent frenzied publicity around Radiohead's free download album *In Rainbows* (2007) had not accompanied the various prior releases by less-well-known bands that employed the same "pay what you like" tactics; Radiohead's prior fanbase was built by traditional A&R. Professional publicists may continue to cling to the ediface of music, just as the most experimental composers often cling to academic sinecures, sometimes using their position of privilege to disparage more popular and commercial culture.

Meanwhile, no one can keep up with every artist, and there is no shame in not knowing a name when someone drops an allusion to a band. I think it is generally a good thing that you cannot keep up with the permutations and fertilizations of electronic music in a world of a trillion Web pages. We are past the myth of genius, but I fear there are some necessary limits on consumption meaning the promotion of only a few at epic scales in capitalist society; yet, this should be no bar on our own local communities and significant interactions.

The many labels, styles, and genres broached in this chapter have been handled throughout with a sense that these very categories are often awkward, often incomplete. An exhaustive musical analysis and an exhaustive sociology would not agree, for society and music interact in rather splendid ways, and individual artists are never guaranteed to hold the same musical theories as each other. No one artist likes to be pigeonholed, and these times of plenty allow plenty of genre jumping and self-reinvention. Electronica is an insufficient term, just a temporary wrapper for this discussion of contemporary electronic musics.

To close with some polemic: we should not be ashamed of trial and error because that may be all that leads to creativity. Crossover is everywhere, not all ostinati are harmful, electroacoustic composition has nothing to fear. There is great difficulty in separating out musical ideas, technological opportunities, and socio-political and aesthetic nuances, but this also beckons great adventure.

NOTES

1. These well-defined terms might be suspect both because music has not been categorized with respect to essential music analytic traits or with respect to sociological currents. For example, defining hard house as against Chicago house, deep house, handbag house, electro house, or bassline house might require the analysis of cultural movements outside music as much as specifics of the music itself.

2. Digital is an arbitrarily good approximation to analog given fine-enough sampling in time and amplitude to forestall any arguments about the perceptual quality.

3. Analogously, to bridge analog and digital forms, we might talk of "digitanalog."

4. Electronica often connects with the popular domain, always a suspicious connection for the supposedly uncompromised visionary idling through life on a university subsidy or starving to depth in a garret studio.

5. Even *electronic music* or *electric music* themselves can be inadequate descriptors. They might be both too broad to focus on any one time or style and give a false impression of the primacy of the electronics above human biology and sound's transmitting air particle collisions. Leigh Landy suggested the novel "sound-based music" in reviewing the mass of descriptive terms on offer (Landy 2007). Yet, many of the musics in this chapter are arguably electronic "note-based music," and there is a musicological and psychological debate to be had about the continuum from discrete notes to continuous sound transformation; his suggestion is not pursued further here.

6. Raymond Scott's advertising work foreshadows the adoption of such acts as Autechre and Oval by technology companies to promote their products.

7. For instance, while respecting some of the earlier pioneers, the Modulations film and book project's primary focus is on EDM (Shapiro 2000).

8. See also the Sound on Sound interview at http://www.soundonsound.com/sos/apr04/articles/autechre.htm.

9. I am reminded of the cautionary tale of New Order losing the first mix of *Blue Monday* (1983) because someone accidentally kicked the computer on which they had been programming.

10. There is a further terminological division of 'sound art' from 'sonic arts' that is not explored here; see Landy (2007) for more on current categorization in the field.

11. I have demoted to this endnote the connection to the site specificity of dance music claimed by Simon Reynolds (2007).

12. Many authors seem to discount sensory dissonance (see the references on noise in Cox and Warner 2004, for instance) and rarely manage to make the key step of dissociating sensory dissonance from functional dissonance (human auditory limits vs. cultural factors) that analysts such as James Tenney and William Sethares have more thoroughly made explicit.

13. Much as I would like to, I certainly do not have a spare thousand years to hear every moment of Jem Finer's *Longplayer*.

BIBLIOGRAPHY

Alexander, A., and N. Collins. 2007. Live audiovisual performance. In *The Cambridge Companion to Electronic Music*, ed. N. Collins and J. d'Escrivan. Cambridge: Cambridge University Press, pp. 126–139.

Berlioz, H. 1970. *Memoirs*. Trans. D. Cairns 1969. Freymore, UK: Panther Books/Granada

Boulez, P. 1955. At the end of fruitful land. In *Die Reihe*, ed. H. Eimert. Vienna: Universal Edition, U.E.A.G., pp. 19–29 UE26101e. English trans. Bryn Mawr, PA: Presser, 1958.

Brewster, B., and F. Broughton. 2006. *Last Night a DJ Saved My Life*. London: Headline Book.

Burgess, A. 1994. *The Wanting Seed*. London: Vintage.

Butler, M. J. 2006. *Unlocking the Groove*. Bloomington: Indiana University Press.

Cascone, K. 2000. The aesthetics of failure: "Post-digital" tendencies in computer music. *Computer Music Journal* 24(4): 12–18.

Cascone, K., ed. 2003. The laptop and electronic music. *Contemporary Music Review* 22(4).

Collins, N. 2001. Algorithmic composition methods for breakbeat science. In *Proceedings of Music without Walls*, De Montfort University, June 21–23, Leicester, UK.

Collins, N. 2007. Musical robots and listening machines. In *The Cambridge Companion to Electronic Music*, ed. N. Collins and J. d'Escrivan. Cambridge: Cambridge University Press, pp. 126–139.

Collins, N., A. McLean, J. Rohrhuber, and A. Ward. 2003. Live coding techniques for laptop performance. *Organised Sound* 8(3): 321–330.

Cox, C., and D. Warner, eds. 2004. *Audio Culture: Readings in Modern Music*. New York: Continuum.

Flür, W. 2003. *I Was a Robot*. 2nd ed. London: Sanctuary.

Hegarty, P. 2007. *Noise/Music: A History*. New York: Continuum.

Kahn, D. 1999. *Noise, Water, Meat: A History of Sound in the Arts*. Cambridge: MIT Press.

LaBelle, B. 2007. *Background Noise: Perspectives on Sound Art*. New York: Continuum.

Lakoff, G. 1987. *Women, Fire, and Dangerous Things*. Chicago: University of Chicago Press.

Landy, L. 2007. *Understanding the Art of Sound Organization*. Cambridge: MIT Press.

McDermott, D. V. 2001. *Mind and Mechanism*. Cambridge: MIT Press.

Mesker, A. N. 2007. "Analysis and recreation of key features in selected Autechre tracks from 1998–2005." Master in arts (research) dissertation, Macquarie University, Sydney.

Minsky, M. 1981. Music, mind and meaning. *Computer Music Journal* 5(3): 28–44.

Prendergast, M. 2003. *The Ambient Century*. London: Bloomsbury.

Redhead, S., ed. 1997. *The Clubcultures Reader*. Oxford: Blackwell.

Reich, S. 2002. *Writings on Music 1965–2000*, ed. P. Hillier. New York: Oxford University Press.

Reynolds, S. 2007. *Bring the Noise: 20 Years of Writing About Hip Rock and Hip Hop*. London: Faber and Faber.

Reynolds, S. 2008. *Energy Flash: A Journey through Rave Music and Dance Culture*. 2nd ed. London: Picador.

Roads, C. 2001. *Microsound*. Cambridge: MIT Press.

Rohrhuber, J. 2007. Network music. In *The Cambridge Companion to Electronic Music*, ed. N. Collins and J. d'Escrivan. Cambridge: Cambridge University Press, pp. 140–155.

Rowe, R. 2001. *Machine Musicianship*. Cambridge: MIT Press.

Schafer, L. M. 1986. *The Thinking Ear*. Toronto: Arcana Editions.

Shapiro, P., ed. 2000. *Modulations. A History of Electronic Music: Throbbing Words on Sound*. New York: Caipirinha Productions/Distributed Art.

Silverberg, R. 1989. Gianni. In *The Conglomeroid Cocktail Party*. London: VGSF, pp. 152–170.

Stuart, C. 2003. Damaged sound: Glitching and skipping compact discs in the audio of Yasunao Tone, Nicolas Collins and Oval. *Leonardo Music Journal* 13: 47–52.

Théberge, P. 2001. "Plugged in": Technology and popular music. In *The Cambridge Companion to Pop and Rock*, ed. S. Frith, W. Straw, and J. Street. Cambridge: Cambridge University Press, pp. 3–25.

Thomson, P. 2004. Atoms and errors: Towards a history and aesthetics of microsound. *Organised Sound* 9(2): 207–218.

Thornton, S. 1995. *Club Cultures: Music, Media and Subcultural Capital*. Cambridge: Polity Press.

Ward, A. J. Rohrhuber, F. Olofsson, A. McLean, D. Griffiths, N. Collins, and A. Alexander. 2004. Live algorithm programming and a temporary organisation for its promotion. In

Proceedings of the README Software Art Conference, Aarhus, Denmark. http://www.
  toplap.org/index.php/Read_me_paper, accessed March 23, 2009.

Wishart, T. 1985. *On Sonic Art.* York: Imagineering Press.

Young, R. 2002. Worship the glitch. In *Undercurrents: The Hidden Wiring of Modern Music,*
  ed. R. Young. London: Continuum, pp. 45–55.

Young, R. 2005. *Warp: Labels Unlimited.* London: Black Dog.

CHAPTER 18

GENERATIVE ALGORITHMS FOR MAKING MUSIC: EMERGENCE, EVOLUTION, AND ECOSYSTEMS

JON MCCORMACK, ALICE ELDRIDGE, ALAN DORIN, AND PETER MCILWAIN

We confront a natural world that allows great liberty in selecting, emphasizing, and grouping, and ... *we* therefore must compose it in order to appropriately aesthetically experience it—[this] holds out an invitation not simply to find the natural world beautiful, but also to appreciate its true nature.

—Carlson 2008, p. 168

For the first time in our history, computer processes give us the ability to compose autonomous artificial universes that can *generate* original aesthetic experiences.

These experiences invoke, at their best, the sensation of a new kind of sublime: opening a window through which we glimpse the true nature of both the natural world and computation. One becomes immersed in a kind of generative aesthetic where the dynamics and real-time sensation of a computational process become something more than the blooming, buzzing confusion of a billion bits flipping in invisible memory. Software magically elevates the invisible and the unimaginable to the *real*. Computation is the medium for exploring these new realities and expressing an original kind of modality.

Music is often seen as a very direct form of human expression—with personal creativity as the conceptual omphalos and primary origin of the compositional process. However, another mode exists within which compositions generate and self-organize, shifting and oscillating, adapting, developing, and becoming whole: *like an organism*. The artist works in a symbiotic tandem with the machine, creating and interacting with processes that seek an expression of autonomy. Our interest is in using the computer as an expressive, collaborative partner, one that answers back, interacts, and responds intelligently. This contrasts with many existing computer-based music tools that aim to automate, digitize, or replicate existing practice.

In this chapter, we examine special kinds of processes that give rise to outcomes beyond those that would appear possible from the individual parts that define them. We look at processes inspired by nature and how they can be transformed to offer the musician or sound artist both new compositional tools and a foundational philosophy for understanding creative practice. Our approach comes largely from the systems sciences of general systems theory (Bertalanffy 1968), cybernetics (e.g., Ashby 1956, Wiener 1961), and most recently artificial life (Alife) (Langton 1995). These disciplines have sought to understand the world in ways that favor process dynamics over the static, structural relations of objects, leading to a perspective defined by mechanisms rather than materials.

These ideas have been recognized in contemporary computer music; composers and performers have begun to explore concepts and techniques from disciplines such as Alife as a means of developing software for composition and performance. Alife itself may be seen as an expression of a deep and ancient drive to animate the inanimate, to imitate and comprehend nature and life itself. In its strongest form, it aims to synthesize living forms in nonbiological media: to create "life-as-it-could-be." This agenda is predicated on the assumption that the biological life forms that we know (and often love or destroy) are only one instance of a wider phenomenon of life. "Weak" Alife is purely epistemic and aims to replicate lifelike phenomena *in simulation* to understand the key organizing principles of living systems. As a research program, this is grounded in the abstraction of life's processes as code.

Extending this idea, we might describe our interest as one of making "art-as-it-could-be." By this we imply a desire to extend current musical practice, to explore new and interesting ways of creating art or musical idioms, rather than completely replicating or automating any existing human practice. We are primarily concerned with engaging human audiences rather than investigating musical creativity in artificial societies (Saunders and Gero 2001, McCormack 2005) or modeling traditional compositional techniques or extant styles (an agenda of classic artificial intelligence).

Artists and musicians have always been inspired by nature and often describe their work with recourse to biological or natural metaphors. For example, Steve Reich described *Music for 18 Musicians* in these terms: "Sometimes everything just comes together and suddenly you've created this wonderful organism" (Reich 1997). We are similarly inspired by biological metaphors. However, rather than replicating the visible forms of nature directly, we aim to capture the processes that generated them, such that the mechanisms themselves become the object of appreciation as much as the forms they generate. Due to its flexibility and programmability, digital technology is an obvious and suitable medium to explore this methodology fully.

The descriptions that follow shift over a number of levels, from the broad issues of generative aesthetics, to the finer-grained detail of specific systems and the algorithms that enable them. We stress that this is not a comprehensive survey or definitive guide. Our aim is to provide an inspirational sample of the approaches with which we are familiar and the conceptual, practical and aesthetic questions they raise.

1. GENERATIVE ART

Generative art[1] is characterized by its approach to art making rather than by any particular media, content or motivation. The generative artist creates a system, or process, that is subsequently set in motion and runs with some degree of autonomy. The enaction of this process constitutes or creates the work (McCormack and Dorin 2001).

Whether the generative system is digital, physical, social, or chemical, its key elements and their roles can be understood using metaphors from evolutionary biology. We employ the terms *genotype, substrate*, and *phenotype* for this purpose. The genotype is the data specification of the process (verbal or written instructions, software rules, etc.). The genotype is enacted by a *mechanism* (performer, machine, software), which acts on a material substrate, changing its structure. The substrate is the material that physically or symbolically maintains the current system state (acoustic environment, physical configuration, set of variables). The enaction of the genotype on the substrate creates the phenotype—the work experienced by the audience. These key elements are illustrated in fig. 18.1.

Typically, the generative process is designed so that it exhibits a range of behaviors within constraints arising from the underlying, artist-devised mechanisms. Each incarnation of a specific digital generative system may exhibit variation due to the indeterminacy of many generative processes.[2] Indeed, for many practitioners, the unpredictability of generative processes is of major appeal.

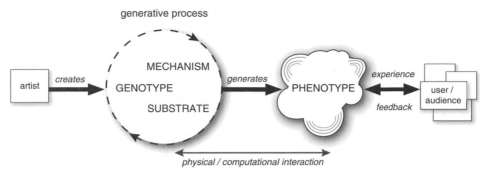

Figure 18.1 Overview of the generative process.

It is not the indeterminacy that is of central importance here, but that the end product is something *more* than is specified in the instruction set. A form of amplification occurs (often referred to as *database amplification* in computer science literature; Smith 1984) as the processes give rise to outcomes that "outperform the designer's specification" (Ashby 1952). When achieved, the results embody a sense of autonomy and intention beyond those of the composer. These characteristics can be enhanced by including feedback through which the genotype is modified by the phenotype. We consider digital and acoustic ways of implementing feedback in this chapter.

The use of indeterminate processes is of course nothing new and was perhaps most infamously espoused by John Cage and his contemporaries. Although their motivations varied and few used digital machines, the various forms of compositional process they explored share conceptual similarities with computational generative approaches.

Cage's interest in these ideas, wrote Dick Higgins, lay in placing the "material at one remove from the composer by allowing it to be determined by a system he determined. And the real innovation lies in the emphasis on the creation of a system" (Nyman 1999, p. 6).

Many works of the American experimentalist and minimalist movement can be understood as systems that are defined and then left to be enacted by human or physical mechanisms. Any ambiguity in the instructions, or their interpretation by performers, brings about an assortment of possible outcomes. The performance score for La Monte Young's *Composition No. 10*, 1960 ("Draw a line and follow it") leaves much to interpretation. Terry Riley's *In C* consists of 53 score fragments through which performers are free to move at their own speed. This defines a more constrained performance space than La Monte Young's *No. 10*. No two performances will be the same, but any particular performance remains a performance of *In C*. In these instances, the amplification from sparse instruction set to an engaging performance comes courtesy of the performers' musical intuitions.

In other instances, if the performer's role is minimal, acoustic feedback in physical space supports the autonomy of the work and acts, quite literally, to amplify the instruction set. The score of Reich's *Pendulum Music* (1968) defines a physical performance system (a number of suspended microphone-amplifier-speaker circuits) and a performance instruction (release the microphones in unison). The piece is played out by gravity, coming to an end when the microphones stop swinging and the performers break the circuit by pulling the leads from the amps. Alvin Lucier's *I am Sitting in a Room* (1970) uses a process of physical feedback more directly. A sentence is recorded and then rerecorded as it is played back through speakers in the same room. The process is repeated until the details of the spoken voice dissolve, leaving only the resonant frequencies of the room. This feedback between the procedure and environment is central to cybernetic art and the ecosystemic approach discussed in this chapter.

In contemporary digital generative art, the process is similarly primary, but computer simulation allows a type of control different from that possible in the physical realm. The speed and dexterity of modern computers permits a new form of creative freedom for any artist working with generative systems. However, a machine specification is far more definite than a performer's interpretations—how then do we get any variation or creativity from this deterministic machine, so often thought of as incapable of "originating anything" (Menabrea 1842)? The answer lies in the strange and unusual properties of many generative systems, which include autonomous action, the ability to adapt and self-modify, to evolve and change, and to originate new configurations and sequences, independently or in synergistic tandem with the composer.

We begin our tour of generative systems by demonstrating how the mathematical concept of the *graph* or *network* can be used as the basis for a creative, generative composition system.

2. MUSICAL NETWORKS

Networks are found throughout natural and constructed environments. From neurons in the human brain to the abstract social interactions of organisms, these structures consistently exhibit complex and interesting properties. The mathematical concept of a graph—a set of *nodes* connected by *edges*—has been studied for centuries. The graph is known as a *network* when its edges and nodes are paths for dynamical processes or connections describing them.

Networks have been used to analyze and synthesize music (e.g., Gjerdingen 1989), but here we discuss their application as a representational and compositional method. Music generating networks enable composers to readily create nonlinear, cyclic, or cascading musical structures.

Nodal[3] is a software composition environment that generates music in this way (McIlwain and McCormack 2005). A composer manually constructs a network of nodes connected by edges. These nodes represent musical events, such as notes. Network edges are traversed in real time by any number of software "players" who interpret the network layout and translate it into music. Edge length between nodes represents interonset time: the longer the edge, the greater the time between events. This establishes a visual relationship between geometric space and metrical structure and between network topology and musical structure. The network generates compositions with complex sequences from comparatively simple topologies (fig. 18.2). Networks with feedback (outputs connected to inputs in a cycle, capable of dynamically spawning new players) are especially rich. Although deterministic, feedback networks are capable of generating highly intricate musical outcomes even from simple topologies, highlighting the generative power of this representation scheme.

Nodal is an example of an environment specifically designed for generative music composition, with networks providing the generative notational system. Each network created by the composer represents a different composition. This methodology permits compositional flexibility within the fixed constraints of a network topology, geometry, and traversal. An alternative approach is to design

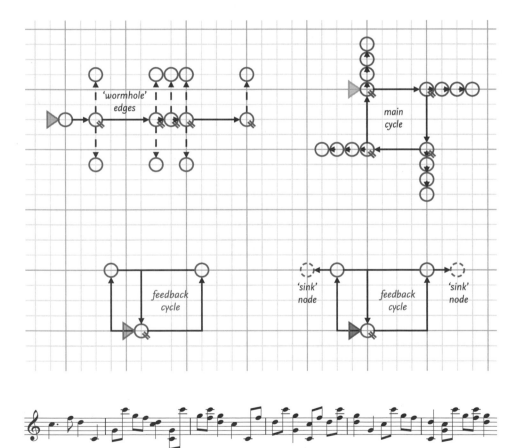

Figure 18.2 Nodal networks. *Clockwise from top left:* linear sequences, rhythmic loop, three-node feedback network, and three-node feedback network with sinks. The first few bars output from the final feedback network are shown at the bottom of the figure.

complete generative systems for specific compositions or performances. We now describe a particular class of algorithm, the *cellular automata* (CA), a simple, archetypal example that illustrates many of the strange and interesting properties of generative systems.

3. CELLULAR AUTOMATA

Cellular automata (CA) originated in the 1950s following a discussion between John von Neumann and the mathematician Stanislaw Ulam about how to specify the architecture of a self-reproducing machine (Burks 1970). A CA is an abstract machine that at any time is in one of a number of possible *states*. For instance, a binary automaton may be in either of the two states: *on* or *off*. The machine is located in a grid cell among a number of identical neighbors. Often, the cells are arranged into a two-dimensional grid, but arrangements are possible in any number of dimensions.

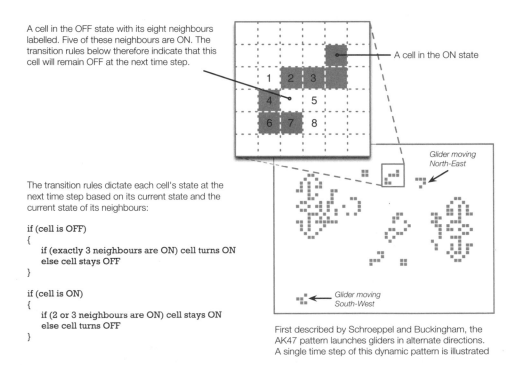

A cell in the OFF state with its eight neighbours labelled. Five of these neighbours are ON. The transition rules below therefore indicate that this cell will remain OFF at the next time step.

A cell in the ON state

The transition rules dictate each cell's state at the next time step based on its current state and the current state of its neighbours:

```
if (cell is OFF)
{
    if (exactly 3 neighbours are ON) cell turns ON
    else cell stays OFF
}

if (cell is ON)
{
    if (2 or 3 neighbours are ON) cell stays ON
    else cell turns OFF
}
```

Glider moving North-East

Glider moving South-West

First described by Schroeppel and Buckingham, the AK47 pattern launches gliders in alternate directions. A single time step of this dynamic pattern is illustrated

Figure 18.3 The Game of Life binary cellular automata.

The state of every automaton in the grid is updated simultaneously in discrete time steps. The future state of a single automaton is governed by its own current state, the current state of all its neighbors, and a set of transition rules. For instance, the rules might specify that if a cell is on and two or three of its neighbors are also on, then at the next time step the automaton will remain on; otherwise, it will turn off. At each time step, every automaton is tested in this way to determine its next state.

The entire grid of CA is initiated randomly or sometimes from a pre-determined pattern of states. The system is then automatically updated step by step, ad infinitum as defined by the transition rules. The state of each cell in the grid is usually depicted visually to allow the perception of patterns formed by the various states of the machine (see fig. 18.3).

Since von Neumann's CA, researchers have experimented with different transition rules. These efforts attempt to define a CA grid capable of generating and sustaining large-scale, persistent, dynamic spatial patterns, purely as the result of spatially and temporally localized, decentralized interactions between individual automata. One particularly successful rule set, dubbed the *Game of Life*, was discovered by mathematician John Conway and popularized by Martin Gardner in *Scientific American* in the 1970s. The rule set for this CA is given in fig. 18.3. This CA has generated a great amount of interest due in part to the wide range of patterns it produces. These have been imaginatively named after things in the real world ("boats" and "toads") or worlds of science fiction ("lightweight space ships," "glider guns," and "gliders"; fig. 18.4). The patterns documented include static forms and coherent patterns that move across the grid as the individual automata states are updated by the transition rules.

Under different rule sets or initial conditions, a CA may settle into one of a handful of qualitatively different states (Wolfram 1984): ordered or repetitive states; chaotic patterns with no obvious repetition or order; and complex behaviors that reside somewhere between order and chaos. It is this last behavior that is most reminiscent of natural phenomena.

Perceived similarities between these dynamics and those of natural, biological and musical phenomena, have prompted musicians to use CAs as a means of

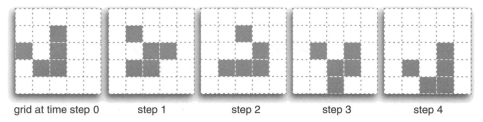

grid at time step 0   step 1   step 2   step 3   step 4

Figure 18.4 Game of Life cellular automata glider pattern. The figure shows the four-time-step cycle of cell updates that leads to the reappearance of the original pattern offset on the grid; hence, the pattern appears to "glide" through space.

generating sonic forms (see, e.g., Miranda 1993, Bilotta and Pantano 2002, and Burraston et al. 2004 for a comprehensive overview of the use of CAs in MIDI [musical instrument digital interface]-based music). Ironically, the CA rules that reliably generate complexity (instead of falling into a short loop or stasis) are relatively scarce. It is also notoriously difficult to discover new interesting rule sets (Sims 1991), so composers have often tended to reuse rule sets known to give rise to complexity.

One of the pioneers of CA music was Iannis Xenakis, who utilized a CA to develop the scores for his works *Horos* (1986) and *Ata* (1987) (see also chapter 5, this volume). Xenakis's interest in the CA rule set stemmed from its ability to capture the nature of fluid dynamics, as well as its generative efficiency: "I was also attracted by the simplicity of it: it is a repetitious, a dynamic procedure which can create a very wealthy output" (Hoffman 2002, p. 131).

Others have adopted CAs on the basis of more specific homologies between their dynamics and some natural process. The granular synthesis engine *Chaos-Synth* (Miranda 1995) is driven by a CA rule set that models the pattern formation seen in some chemical reactions. The CA progresses from an initially random state to produce spatial oscillations. This progression bears strong morphological resemblance to the spectral evolution of wind instruments (or voice) by which partials converge from an initially noisy, random distribution to harmonic oscillations.

Cell states in *ChaosSynth* are used to parameterize a granular synthesis engine. This consists of a bank of oscillators, each of which is associated with specific groups of cells. The duration and frequency of each oscillator is determined by the arithmetic mean of the associated cell group. This direct mapping preserves the structural evolution of the CA, creating convincing vocal sounds.

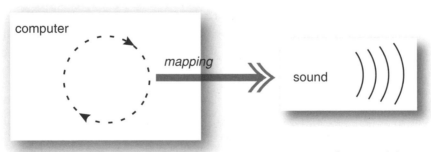

simulation runs inside computer

outputs from model are mapped to DSP synthesis parameters

Figure 18.5 Schematic overview of the standard design of a generative music system. A model is run in software (typically iteratively). The numerical outputs of this model are transformed into sound by defining a mapping between simulation variables and the parameters of a DSP algorithm. The generative process (*dotted loop*) is purely digital, existing inside the computer.

Miranda's synth exemplifies the most common approach to designing and implementing a generative system based on appropriated models. The model is implemented in software, and its numerical outputs are mapped onto musical (MIDI) events or digital signal-processing (DSP) parameters. An overview of this approach is given in fig. 18.5.

4. Emergence

The jump from static discrete states to dynamic patterns in the CA suggests a similar phenomenon to that described by Reich. He described phase-shifting rhythms as a "wonderful organism": from the combination of small, static interacting parts emerges a coherent dynamic form that takes on a life of its own. The fascination with the emergence of life from nonliving components, whether metaphorically or biologically, unites many scientists, philosophers, and musicians. Somehow, from the interactions between collections of atoms, molecules, organelles, cells, and organs we emerge as sentient beings. This is perhaps the ultimate form of emergence, the significance of which is instinctively appreciated. But, the term itself is nebulous and means many things to many people working in different disciplines (see, e.g., Bedau 1997 for a list of classifications).

In a creative context, emergence is associated with novelty, surprise, spontaneity, agency—even creativity (McDonough 2002). Emergent phenomena are characterized by the appearance of order, structure, or behavior at a hierarchical level above that specified in the underlying system and invariably demand a new level of language to describe them. In the *Game of Life* presented in the preceding section, the rules describe what happens in each static cell and are applied from a single time step to the next. Despite this temporal and spatial locality, the glider, the glider gun, and the hosts of other patterns that appear, can most sensibly be described as entities that move *across* cells and *through* time. These forms and behaviors are not specified anywhere in the CA algorithm but arise as a result of the interactions between static cells.

The one-bit animation of the CA grid may seem a far cry from the enigmatic phenomena of life, but this simple system provides an explanatory mechanism demonstrating the emergence of form and behavior from the dynamic interaction of primitive components. Observations like those made about the *Game of Life* motivate Alife researchers to examine the organizing principles of life using abstract software models of biological phenomena. Many generative artists also try to replicate the emergence observed in complex systems to create artworks with a degree of autonomy: artworks that surprise, exceeding their creator's expectations, and revealing a little about the workings of the world.

Formally, there are different kinds of emergence, and the term is often understood differently across many domains. We find it useful to distinguish emergent phenomena from gestalt processes—colloquially described as situations in which "the whole is greater than the sum of its parts." Perceptually, a chord *could* be considered emergent; after all, harmony is a property of the relations between notes and cannot be ascribed to the constituent tones of a chord. However, this simple gestalt is significantly different from the harmonic structure that emerges in process-based compositions such as Cornelius Cardew's *The Great Learning, Paragraph 7* (1968).

The score of this work consists of a set of ordered musical phrases and verbal directions. A group of singers (human musical automata) are all given this same set of instructions (just as the rules for each CA cell are the same). Each singer starts on a self-selected note and sings the fragment a specified number of times at his or her natural breath rate before moving on to the next phrase. Each time a singer moves on to a new phrase, the starting pitch must be selected from the notes that are currently being sung by neighboring singers. This process acts to carve out a coherent harmonic path from an initial cacophony.

The trend to organization in *The Great Learning* is dependent on two notable features: each singer carries out the same instruction; and each actively responds to the current activity of neighboring singers. Through the interactions of distributed active parts, the inherent order of the system increases without external guidance. The work self-organizes, the entire process revealing how emergent phenomena can arise.

Examples of self-organization abound in nature. The emergence of coordinated behavior in groups of animals such as flocking birds, swarming insects, or schooling fish, appears to be a finely orchestrated act. But, such coordinated activity can arise without external control. If individual birds attempt to fly close to other birds, whilst avoiding collisions and maintaining the same general speed and direction as their neighbors, a dynamic, cohesive flock is formed. A systemic (rather than perceptual) property that distinguishes gestalt from emergent phenomena is the *active* nature of the component parts, which allows for internally generated (rather than externally imposed) organization. Self-organization occurs at every level in the biological world, from chemical interactions to social systems.

Digital computers are simulation machines *par excellence*, ideally suited to exploring the innovative systems-theoretic idea that processes can be generalized through *abstraction*, decoupled from their material origins, yet retain the essential dynamic properties that make them interesting. If flocks can self-organize, then why not sonic structure?

These concepts and techniques drive a 21st-century approach to musical automata. The prospect of developing software with a degree of autonomy motivates an increasing number of musicians, particularly those working in electroacoustic improvisation. The active nature of the computational medium allows musicians to conceive and build instruments that they can play, and that can play with them, provoking a rethinking of the relationship between human and machinic agency (Bowers 2002, Eldridge 2007).

Drawing a parallel between the self-organization of swarming creatures and the spontaneous emergence of structure in a group of improvising musicians, Tim Blackwell has developed a series of Swarm Music systems (e.g., Blackwell 2003), based on similar principles to the flocking bird model described previously. Rather than flying around in a spatially explicit three-dimensional model of the real world, particles swarm in a multidimensional abstract space that is mapped to musically meaningful parameters of a granular synthesis engine. This allows the human and the virtual swarm to interact in a shared environment where the actions of the performer influence the activity of the swarm.

Similar models have been used recently by Adam Green (Waters 2007a) and explored extensively by Jonathon Impett (2001). These musicians' approach differs from the simple one-way mapping described in fig. 18.5. A generative model is still implemented in digital simulation and the outputs used to organize musical parameters. However, in these cases the simulation also *responds* to the performer's gestures. The generative system escapes the confines of the digital symbolic and is influenced by its external environment (fig. 18.6).

The adaptive self-organization harnessed by these musicians is one form of emergence. These models "work" because they mimic the finely tuned interactions of biological creatures. But, how did these specific characteristics arise? How might artists design their own algorithms to allow creative exploration rather than commandeering those already developed by scientists?

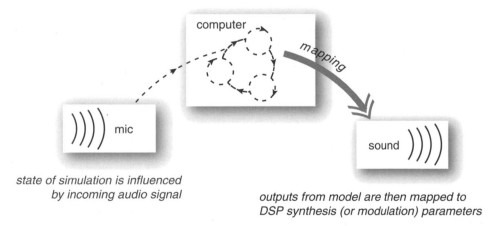

Figure 18.6 Schematic of a design commonly used in interactive generative music.
As in fig. 18.5, the simulation model outputs are mapped to DSP parameters.
In addition, features of an external audio signal are defined as inputs into the model,
affecting its future state. The generative process is digital but is influenced by the
external acoustic environment.

5. Evolution

Evolution is *the* central idea in modern biology. It describes how, over time, one species can change and give rise to another. The mechanism of natural selection, proposed by Charles Darwin and Alfred Russell Wallace in 1858, explains how evolution occurs. It can be summarized by three simple operational principles. Evolution occurs when:

1. There is a population of individuals that can copy themselves;
2. The copying process is imperfect, leading to variation;
3. Variation in the copying process leads to differences in the ability of offspring to survive and copy themselves.

The process of evolution by natural selection explains how species change and adapt without explicit teleological goals or outside help. It shows how complexity and suitability can arise without a designer.

It is possible to think of evolution as a creative process because it has the explanatory power to account for the diversity of life on Earth from prokaryotic cells to linguistic *Homo sapiens*. While evolution may seem vastly different from human creativity, it is a process eminently capable of discovering novel and appropriate adaptations. Importantly, evolutionary mechanisms are far better understood than human creative processes. The challenge for us is to understand how a process that is successful in one domain (biology) can be transformed to be useful in another (artistic creativity).

How can evolution be used for creative discovery? The standard computer science approach, *evolutionary computing*, includes techniques such as genetic algorithms, evolutionary strategies, and genetic programming (Eiben and Smith 2003).

Evolutionary computing systems operate on a population of candidate solutions that are evaluated according to a fitness measure (fig. 18.7). Each solution is encoded as a symbolic string, or digital genotype. From this string, a phenotype (the candidate solution) is created, and the fitness measure judges its value. The most successful phenotypes are selected and subject to modification by either random mutation or crossover by breeding with other successful solutions (see fig. 18.8). These offspring form the next generation, and the process is applied repeatedly until a successful solution is found or some resource constraints are exceeded (e.g., running out of time).

Evolutionary computing methods have been applied to creative tasks, including music composition and sound synthesis (see, e.g., Miranda 2007). However, a problem with simple evolutionary methods, such as genetic algorithms, is that they require a *machine-representable* fitness measure. In biology, fitness is determined by an organism's ability to pass on its genes to its offspring. In simulation, we need a comparable way of assigning a value to the success of a phenotype, similar to judges giving a numerical score to a performance in a competition (fig. 18.8).

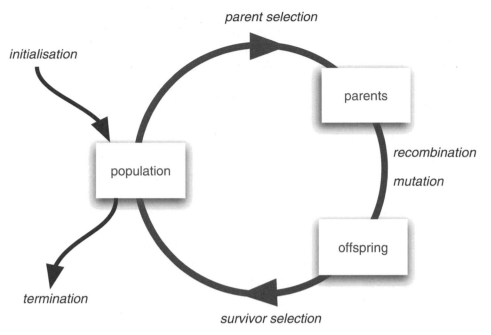

Figure 18.7 Overview of an evolutionary algorithm.

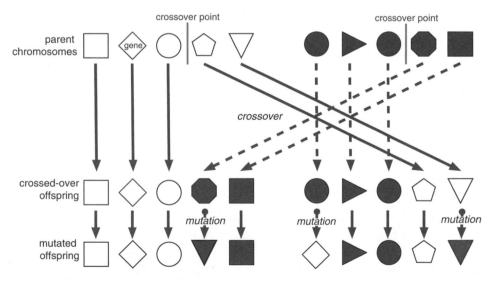

Figure 18.8 Evolutionary computing concepts of crossover (recombination) and mutation in a digital genotype. A crossover point is randomly selected at a location in the parent's genotypes. Combining sections from each parent generates two offspring. Each gene is then subject to the possibility of random mutation. The probability of mutation is usually set so that on average only one gene in each chromosome is mutated.

Some of the most successful musical applications harness the power of evolutionary computing to modify or create variations on existing musical fragments. The pioneering work of Andrew Horner and David Goldberg used a genetic algorithm for automated thematic bridging (1991). Early versions of Al Biles's well-known GenJam (Biles 1994) used genetic algorithms to evolve an artificial jazz improviser capable of jamming in real time within a traditional jazz idiom.

Research into evolutionary methods for composition and sound design is ongoing, but the need for an explicit, formal measure of musical fitness limits the usefulness of simple genetic algorithms. For well-defined tasks, such as tuning the parameters of a modular synth to match the spectral evolution of a target sound, a fitness function can be defined relatively easily. However, many musical activities cannot be sensibly conceived within this optimization framework.

A number of methods have been proposed to circumvent the need for an explicit fitness measure. A popular technique (that borrows from biology) employs *coevolution*, evolutionary change due to competition between two species. A common example is the evolutionary relationship between predator and prey: predators evolve to catch prey, forcing the prey to evolve strategies of evasion. This leads to an escalating competitive cycle, an "arms race" of ongoing evolutionary change.

In a musical context, coevolution is often framed as a battle between a population of male "composer" agents who compete against each other to compose good compositions and female "critic" agents who critique and rank the compositions they hear (Todd and Werner 1998). Fitness of the composers is implicitly determined by how well they please their critics. The fitness of the critics is based on their ability to make correct predictions about the composers' behavior. The initial populations are seeded with simple composition algorithms and methods for critically evaluating them. The aim is to spark an arms race between critics and composers leading to an increase in compositional and critical sophistication. In one experiment, females also preferred a certain amount of "surprise" in the composition, a feature that was added to avoid composers and critics converging to stale solutions.

David Casal and Davide Morreli use a similar coevolutionary mechanism in their *Frank* system. Casal's motivation was "to have someone I'd enjoy playing with, who wouldn't get tired of me and vice versa." Frank uses MPEG7 (Moving Pictures Experts Group 7) feature extraction techniques and a database of acoustic lexemes to analyze an audio repository built from analysis of live sound input or existing audio files. Critics are coevolved with potential outputs to generate sonic responses to Casal's live instrumental input. The genetic algorithm is also used to enhance continuities and create variation, avoiding gestural tedium (Plans-Casal and Morelli 2007).

Coevolution's success relies on imbuing the critics with a means of improving musical judgment and the composers with a means to improve based on this judgment. In Todd and Werner's system (1998), female critics were initialized with a probabilistic model based on simple folk-tune melodies. Under evolutionary pressure, the system quickly diverged, and the critics' judgment lost any resemblance to human criticism. The artificial composers and critics do not have the material experience, understanding, or foundational primitives to comprehend music the way that human composers or critics do. This is an endemic problem: it is difficult to judge how well the critics are really doing using human criteria as the basis for aesthetic judgment in an artificial system.

An alternative approach that removes the need for a formal assessment procedure is to have a human evaluate the fitness of each member of the population (fig. 18.9). This method, known as *aesthetic evolution* or the *interactive genetic algorithm*, was first described by the zoologist Richard Dawkins in his book, *The Blind Watchmaker* (1986). Dawkins interactively evolved a population of simple line drawings. The software displays fifteen phenotypes (the drawings), created by mutating the genotype (numbers coding the characteristics of the drawings) of a single parent. The user selects the most aesthetically interesting phenotype to become the parent of the next generation. The system then displays a new population of mutated offspring—drawings with slight variation from the parent—for selection, and the entire process is then repeated. Ideally, at each generation the drawings become more interesting as the phenotype space is explored aesthetically.

Aesthetic evolution has been successfully used to evolve images, shapes, sounds, and music (Bentley and Corne 2002, Machado and Romero 2007). A major concern in the sonic domain is the difficulty in judging a large number

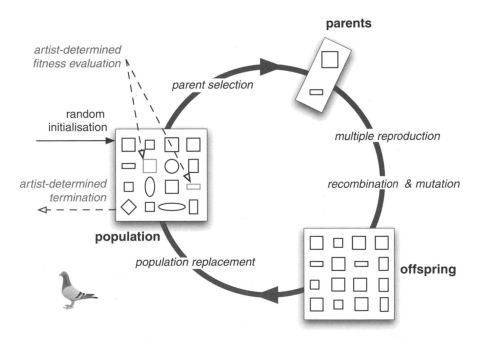

Figure 18.9 Aesthetic evolution utilizes human evaluation of fitness ranking in a population.

of phenotypes subjectively if each must be heard individually. Fine-grained fitness ranking is also difficult for people to perform concisely (Dorin 2001).

In summary, evolution is a powerful metaphor that has inspired many new forms of music and art. However, despite these achievements, the algorithms and methods discussed so far still seem to fall short of what we might expect from a system that has given rise to AIDS, orchids, platypus, and language. In our opinion, a more systemic approach is required, one that considers the dialectic of composition as a system of interacting components, rather than as a problem to be solved or function to be optimized. Hence, we consider the concept of ecosystems, as it provides a rich set of inspirational metaphors for generative art.

6. ECOSYSTEMS

Natural ecosystems have inspired much art and composition—who has not wondered at the richness of sound apparent in the dawn chorus of the bush, the croaks of numerous cohabiting frog species, or the diverse buzzes, chirps, and flutters of insects in a tropical forest? These spectacular sonic proceedings are the direct result of ecosystems in action. In a popular context, the term *ecosystem* has become synonymous with the idea of a network of dynamically interacting components, with multiple feedback loops, in some "stable" or "harmonious" configuration. Cynically, one might view this as glib lip service to a modern environmentalism.

In biology, the ecosystem is a concept used to describe the diverse and heterogeneous interactions of organisms with one another and their environment. This perspective contrasts with the myopic view of evolution as "survival of the fittest" or one that considers it only in terms of "selfish genes." A variety of heterogeneous conditions and resources generated within the ecosystem allow species to specialize and coexist within particular habitats. Ecosystems tell of multiple specializations coexisting, the maintenance of diversity, of adaptive, self-modifying configurations: ideas that can motivate and inspire new kinds of sonic (eco)systems.

As discussed, the standard evolutionary approach focuses on interspecies competition or on the optimization of a population to an explicit or artist-determined fitness function. In contrast, the ecosystemic approach involves the instantiation of an autonomous dynamical system of components interacting with and via a shared environment. The entire system is then allowed to run its course. Unlike evolutionary optimization, fitness is an implicit side effect of components striving to maintain viability in a dynamically changing environment. How they achieve this is determined by the rules of the system. If coupled to the real world, the digital and physical components interact and may affect one another directly, leading to an informationally open set of possibilities.

A simulated ecosystem derived from Alife science, typically contains individual agents that represent organisms. These inhabit a virtual space that is organized according to simulated physical and chemical laws. Interactions between species and their abiotic environment provide a changing landscape for evolutionary adaptation to occur, leading to the emergence of complex feedback loops. This is a necessary precursor to the novelty and dynamism emergent from real ecosystems.

No explicit fitness function is required to guide the evolution of individuals in a population. Instead, rules dictate the kinds of relationships that act *between* individuals in the software, and each is permitted to manipulate the virtual environment to gain resources required for reproduction. If an agent fails to gain sufficient resources, it will be unable to reproduce and will eventually die from starvation or old age. This ensures that the fitness measure of an agent's success is implicit: only agents able to locate a mate and acquire sufficient resources for survival and reproduction will be deemed fit.

Interactions between individuals in a standard evolutionary algorithm are often restricted to competition, whereas in a simulated ecosystem organisms may engage in symbiosis, mutualism, parasitism, predator-prey relationships, competition, and so on. This wide gamut of potential interactions increases the scope for the emergence of complex agent behavior and structure. The artist working in this fashion must compose the environment and internally coherent rules of interaction. For instance, for ecosystemic interactions to emerge automatically, energy must not be available to virtual organisms for free; costs are associated with actions such as growth, movement, sensing (e.g., listening), acting (e.g., singing), metabolizing, and so on. The ecosystem moves through a trajectory of states that constitute the artwork.

In the audiovisual ecosystem *Eden*, virtual organisms compete with one another for resources and mates as they roam a two-dimensional world (McCormack 2001). Organisms may create and detect sonic structures in the virtual world. The organism-specific meanings of these sonic emissions emerge during the evolution of the system, often constituting warning calls, mating cries, or indications of the presence of food. The movement of human visitors around the artwork (fig. 18.10) is detected and fed back into the virtual ecosystem to govern the availability of resources—if humans like what they see and hear, the virtual organisms are rewarded with increased availability of food, thereby influencing their viability and the likelihood that they will produce offspring that the visitors will also find interesting.

Organisms in the virtual world of composer Palle Dahlstedt's *Living Melodies*, coevolve musical communication strategies (Dahlstedt and Nordahl 1999). The sounds they produce are used to generate "listening pleasure" in other organisms that has an impact on the ability of the agent listeners to reproduce. This musical material is also intended for human listening, forming an ever changing musical composition.

Rodney Berry explored the idea of virtual ecosystems in his early work with Dahlstedt and Catherine Haw, *Gakkimon Planet*, as well as in an interactive sonic

Figure 18.10 Eden, an evolutionary sonic and visual ecosystem.

ecosystem built with Alan Dorin and Wasinee Rungsarityotin, *Listening Sky* (Berry et al. 2001). These are agent-based virtual ecosystems in which agents' genotypes encode song patterns to be played in the world and a preference for hearing specific patterns. Evolution creates a range of agent behaviors in response to musical phrases heard. For instance, agents may flee from songs they "dislike" or eat creatures that sing "liked" musical phrases. These autonomous, self-contained worlds may be navigated by a human avatar, which can explore the sonically heterogeneous environments interactively.

The term *performance ecosystem* has recently been used to describe the works of various electroacoustic improvisers (Waters 2007a). It is adopted in part for its sociocultural implications and also to signify the interactions between the commonly distinct concepts of instrument, performer, and environment. Although the aesthetics and practical approaches of implicated musicians differ, their work is more or less unified by an interest and instantiation of *feedback*—a key ecosystemic process that in this context blurs the distinctions between these concepts.

Lucier's *I Am Sitting in a Room* is perhaps the simplest of feedback systems. The combination of microphone, speakers, physical space, and spoken voice are at once composition and instrument. The spoken voice sets in motion a process that is sculpted passively by the acoustics of the room. Various contemporary musicians explore similar feedback systems with more responsive mechanisms. Works such as

Nic Collins' *Pea Soup* (1974 and 2000), the *Virtual/Physical Feedback Instrument* projects of Simon Waters (Waters 2007b) and John Bowers, and the *Audible Eco-Systemic Interface* project of Augustino Di Scipio, all incorporate active mechanisms in feedback processes that couple distributed elements into a unified performance system (Di Scipio 2003).

Di Scipio's *Audible Eco-Systemic Interface* project lies close to the concept of ecosystemics that we promote here. He explores a form of interaction that draws heavily from biological and cybernetic principles and differs significantly from the simple one-way reactivity common in computer music: "The notion that a computer reacts to a performer's action is replaced with a permanent contact, in sound, between computer and the environment (room or else). The computer acts upon the environment, observes the latter's response, and adapts itself, re-orienting the sequence of its internal states based on the data collected" (Di Scipio 2003, p. 275). Superficially, the works are similar to Collins's *Pea Soup* in their incorporation of computers, microphones, loudspeakers, and rooms (Waters 2007a). Di Scipio, however, uses feature extraction to generate low-rate control signals that modulate sound material. The system has a sense of history in that cross-comparisons are

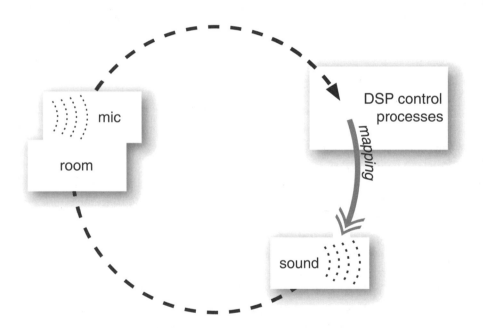

There is no model independent of sound itself. Digital control processes are driven by sonic features and modify DSP parameters

Figure 18.11 Schematic of the design of works in Di Scipio's Audible Eco-Systemic Interface project. The generative process is distributed across the conjunction of computer, microphones, and room. Sound is the medium as well as the (by-)product of a set of distributed interactions.

made between microphone input and digital output, generating difference signals that are fed back into the system as controls.

Di Scipio's approach shares a core organizing principle with Alife agent-based simulations—a "network of interdependencies among system components" (Di Scipio 2003, p. 269). However the design and realization of his work are quite distinct from the simulation-mapping paradigm described previously.

Rather than implementing a model in software and mapping the numerical outputs to synthesis parameters to create sound (as in figs. 18.5 and 18.6), Di Scipio's generative system is implemented as a set of interactions between distinct physical and digital components (fig. 18.11). Digital processes actively monitor, generate, and modify acoustic events, but sound itself, not computation, is the medium.

7. GENERATIVE AESTHETICS

We now consider the aesthetic nature of generative systems, with a view to more fully understanding and critiquing generative artworks. Generative aesthetics provides an important contribution to art theory, particularly that based around process art and software art systems.

A technical procedure alone is normally insufficient to form the basis of a creative work or practice. For a generative system to be useful in a creative practice, there must be additional considerations beyond technical mimicry. The aesthetic qualities of the work and the mechanisms used to produce it are of great importance in their evaluation. Clearly, the generative artist engages in *meta-creation* (Whitelaw 2004)—designing processes that generate artifacts or outcomes rather than directing the design of these explicitly.

It is beneficial if the system possesses some coherent basis or narrative that may act as both an explanatory and conceptual device, articulating the choice of interacting components and their internal rules. This does not preclude the possibility of a radically different "strange ontology" as the basis for this narrative (Whitelaw et al. 2009), or multiple, abstract, even absurd interpretations of the system description (within the limits of what can be computationally realized in the case of software). Indeed, as we have discussed, some of the most successful systems abandon any conceptual requirement for dependence on relations from the physical sciences because, unlike science, art has no requirement of verification or validation in these terms.

Many artists prefer to avoid articulating any kind of narrative explanation of their compositional systems, often because they simply do not conceptualize composition in those terms. Nonetheless, a narrative may be implicit. For example, Cardew's *The Great Learning, Paragraph 7* has a coherent narrative and musical ontology embedded in the score; obviating the need for a narrative explanation from the composer.[4]

A narrative about the system and its rules allows the composer and audience to appreciate qualities that may not be apparent when listening to the music alone. A coherent story does not necessarily impose creative limitations. A liberating property of generative systems is that a formal description, along with a coherent and complete set of rules, are capable of generating novel and surprising outcomes.

Most of the generative systems described in this chapter originated in other disciplines. How successful is the direct creative appropriation of models from the computing, life, or physical sciences? This remains a central and vexed question. Clearly, many scientific processes may be rich, beautiful, and profound as they stand, but may not remain so when reappropriated as generative artworks. A cellular automata grid running the *Game of Life* exhibits emergent properties when visualized, but are these properties as visceral when sonified?

In general, adapting or deriving a process-based composition or sonic artwork from an existing process in a scientific domain can be conceptually difficult. A challenge for artists working in this area is to create mappings that are meaningful in relation to the process itself, in addition to the goal of revealing the process in a new way. Arbitrary mappings of system dynamics to obvious musical properties, such as pitch or timbre, rarely succeed in conveying deep musical ideas.

At the opposite extreme, designing a creative generative model or system from scratch, while challenging and often difficult, can be aesthetically rewarding. However, establishing a dichotomy between original and borrowed processes is probably simplistic. The most successful creative systems often begin with an established generative method but invariably end up in a very different place.

A major issue for the design of emergent generative processes is that of *control*. The capabilities of an interesting emergent system must surprise its designer. Unlike conventional software, the responses and outputs of the system cannot be completely *known*. For example, when we type a particular key on the keyboard we expect the letter corresponding to that key to appear at the current cursor position. A good generative system offers no such guarantees. It must have a degree of unpredictability to be interesting. This unpredictability must be *appropriate* in the creative context of the system language, not simply random variation within a fixed set of parameters (a common fallback strategy if all else fails). Crafting a system that demonstrates this "appropriateness" remains one of the grand design challenges for creative generative systems (McCormack 2005).

Since a good generative system is unpredictable and capable of generating appropriate novelty, controlling it raises many issues. In an interactive or improvisational context, the performer or user needs an intuitive sense of the system's autonomy to understand *how* to engage with it. In an off-line compositional system, the user needs a sense of how parameter adjustment affects system response in relation to the creative goals of the composer. To date, most software systems are designed as tools: the user does something and the system responds in a predictable way. This is unsurprising because tool-making is an instinctive and prehistorical idea that has provided for much of our success as a species. However, it is possible to conceive of a generative software system in other ways (McCormack 2004), as an organism, for example, by which the human and machine engage in a (nonverbal) dialogue, informing and responding to each other synergistically (Eldridge 2005).

An ecosystemic metaphor considers components and their interaction in a potentially noisy environment. Ecosystems generally establish a network of tightly coupled positive and negative feedback loops. The system must organize to offer viable configurations, otherwise it breaks down and ceases to exist. In a well-designed system, viable dynamic configurations are explored and exploited. The system flips between stable states, each of which represents a different aesthetic possibility. The appropriateness of these possibilities is a side effect of a well-designed system. Hence, the creative ability of the artist is reflected in their design of system components and interactions—the narrative of its generative aesthetic.

Generative aesthetics requires an understanding of the *aesthetics of process*. For many artists and composers, this is difficult to achieve as most of our knowledge of complex process design comes from other disciplines. Computer science specializes in understanding algorithmic processes, but normally limits aesthetic consideration of an algorithm to its efficiency, utility, or beauty—concepts long abandoned or reappropriated in contemporary art.

Process aesthetics are not often taught in music conservatories or fine art colleges, so artists frequently must discover what works through a process of play and experimentation. While experiment and play may be productive ways of working, it is commonly observed that this mode of discovery results in lots of wheel reinventing. Our hope for this chapter is that it seeds some ideas about the role of generative systems in contemporary composition, improvisation, and performance. As the field matures, we expect to see a growing shared vocabulary and a wider recognition of the inspirational qualities of process philosophies.

Acknowledgment: This research was supported by an Australian Research Council "Discovery Projects" grant, DP0772667.

NOTES

1. Within the computer music community, *generative* is sometimes used synonymously with *algorithmic*—we consider generative music to be a subset of algorithmic music and draw a distinction in terms of the primacy of the process over the outcome.

2. Indeterminacy arises from the fact that many generative systems (even those that are fully deterministic) are highly sensitive to initial or environmental conditions, quickly diverging on each successive run. This indeterminacy is different from the randomness of stochastic processes (which nonetheless may form part of a generative system).

3. Nodal is free software available from http://www.csse.monash.edu.au/~cema/nodal/.

4. Cardew did articulate many aspects of his compositional process, but whether he conceptualized in those terms is not relevant to the point we are making here.

BIBLIOGRAPHY

Ashby, W. R. 1952. *Design for a Brain: The Origin of Adaptive Behaviour.* London: Chapman and Hall.

Ashby, W. R. 1956. *An Introduction to Cybernetics.* London: Chapman and Hall.

Bedau, M. A. 1997. Weak emergence. In *Philosophical Perspectives: Mind, Causation, and World,* ed. J. Tomberlin. Oxford: Blackwell.

Bentley, P. J., and D. W. Corne, eds. 2002. *Creative Evolutionary Systems.* London: Academic Press.

Berry, R., W. Rungsarityotin, A. Dorin, P. Dahlstedt, and C. Haw. 2001. "Unfinished Symphonies—Songs of 3 1/2 Worlds." Paper presented at the Workshop on Artificial Life Models for Musical Applications, Sixth European Conference on Artificial Life, September 9, Prague, Czech Republic: Editoriale Bios.

Bertalanffy, L. v. 1968. *General System Theory: Foundations, Development, Applications.* Rev. ed. International Library of Systems Theory and Philosophy. New York: Braziller.

Biles, J. A. 1994. "GenJam: A Genetic Algorithm for Generating Jazz Solos." Paper presented at Proceedings of the 1994 International Computer Music Conference, September 12–17, San Francisco.

Bilotta, E., and P. Pantano. 2002. Synthetic harmonies: An approach to musical semiosis by means of cellular automata. *Leonardo* 35(2): 153–159.

Blackwell, T. M. 2003. "Swarm Music: Improvised Music with Multi-Swarms." Paper presented at the AISB Symposium on Artificial Intelligence and Creativity in Arts and Science, April 7–11, Aberystwyth, Wales.

Bowers, J. 2002. *Improvising Machines: Ethnographically Informed Design for Improvised Electro-Acoustic Music.* Norwich, UK: University of East Anglia.

Burks, A. W. 1970. Essay 1—Von Neumann's self-reproducing automata. In *Essays on Cellular Automata,* ed. A. W. Burks. Chicago: University of Illinois.

Burraston, D., E. Edmonds, D. Livingstone, and E. Miranda. 2004. "Cellular Automata in MIDI Based Computer Music." Paper presented at the 2004 International Computer Music Conference, November 1–6, Miami, FL.

Carlson, A. 2008. Aesthetic appreciation of the natural environment. In *Arguing about Art: Contemporary Philosophical Debates,* Third Edition, ed. A. Neill and A. Ridley. London: Routledge, pp. 157–171.

Dahlstedt, P., and M. G. Nordahl. 1999. "Living Melodies: Coevolution of Sonic Communication." Paper presented at First Iteration: A Conference on Generative Systems in the Electronic Arts, December 1–3, Melbourne, Australia.

Dawkins, R. 1986. *The Blind Watchmaker.* Essex, UK: Longman Scientific and Technical.

Di Scipio, A. 2003. "Sound is the interface": From interactive to ecosystemic signal processing. *Organised Sound* 8(3): 269–277.

Dorin, A. 2001. "Aesthetic Fitness and Artificial Evolution for the Selection of Imagery from The Mythical Infinite Library." Paper presented at Advances in Artificial Life, Proceedings of the 6th European Conference on Artificial Life, September 10–14, Prague.

Eiben, A. E., and J. E. Smith. 2003. *Introduction to Evolutionary Computing,* Natural Computing Series. New York: Springer.

Eldridge, A. C. 2005. "Cyborg Dancing: Generative Systems for Man-Machine Musical Improvisation." Paper presented at Third Iteration, November 30–December 2. Melbourne: CEMA.

Eldridge, A. C. 2007. "Collaborating with the behaving machine: Simple adaptive
    dynamical systems for generative and interactive music." D.Phil. dissertation, COGS,
    University of Sussex, Brighton.
Gjerdingen, R. 1989. Using connectionist models to explore complex musical patterns.
    Computer Music Journal 13(3): 67–75.
Hoffman, P. 2002. Towards an "automated art": Algorithmic processes in Xenakis'
    compositions. *Contemporary Music Review* 21(2/3): 121–131.
Horner, A., and D. E. Goldberg. 1991. *Genetic Algorithms and Computer-Assisted Music
    Composition.* Chicago: University of Illinois.
Impett, J. 2001. "Interaction, Simulation and Invention: A Model for Interactive Music."
    Paper presented at the Workshop on Artificial Life Models for Musical Applications,
    Sixth European Conference on Artificial Life, September 9, Prague, Czech Republic:
    Editoriale Bios.
Langton, C. G. 1995. *Artificial Life: An Overview, Complex Adaptive Systems.* Cambridge,
    Mass.: MIT Press.
Machado, P., and J. Romero, eds. 2007. *The Art of Artificial Evolution: A Handbook on
    Evolutionary Art and Music.* Springer Natural Computing Series. Berlin: Springer.
McCormack, J. 2001. "Eden: An Evolutionary Sonic Ecosystem." Paper presented at
    Advances in Artificial Life, 6th European Conference, ECAL 2001, September 10–14,
    Prague, Czech Republic.
McCormack, J. 2004. *Impossible Nature: The Art of Jon McCormack.* Melbourne: Australian
    Centre for the Moving Image.
McCormack, J. 2005. Open problems in evolutionary music and art. In *EvoWorkshops 2005,*
    ed. F. Rothlauf. LNCS 3449, Berlin: Springer-Verlag, pp. 428–436.
McCormack, J., and A. Dorin. 2001. "Art, Emergence and the Computational Sublime."
    Paper presented at Second Iteration: A Conference on Generative Systems in the
    Electronic Arts, December 5–7, Melbourne, Australia.
McDonough, R. 2002. Emergence and creativity: Five degrees of freedom. In *Creativity,
    Cognition, and Knowledge,* ed. T. Dartnall. Westport, CT: Praeger.
McIlwain, P., and J. McCormack. 2005. "Design Issues in Musical Composition Networks."
    Paper presented at Proceedings of the Australiasian Computer Music Conference, July
    12–14, Brisbane, Australia.
Menabrea, L. F. 1842. "Sketch of the analytical engine invented by Charles Babbage."
    Bibliothèque Universelle de Genève.
Miranda, E., and J. A. Biles, eds. 2007. *Evolutionary Computer Music.* London: Springer.
Miranda, E. R. 1993. Cellular automata music: An interdisciplinary project. *Interface:
    Journal of New Music Research* 22(1): 3–21.
Miranda, E. R. 1995. Granular synthesis of sounds by means of a cellular automata.
    Leonardo 28(4): 297–300.
Nyman, M. 1999. *Experimental Music—Cage and Beyond,* ed. A. Whittall. 2nd ed. Music in
    the 20th Century. Cambridge: Cambridge University Press. Original edition Schirmer
    Books, New York, 1974.
Plans-Casal, D., and D. Morelli. 2007. "Remembering the Future: An Overview of
    Co-evolution in Musical Improvisation." Paper presented at the 2007 International
    Computer Music Conference, August 27–31, Copenhagen, Denmark.
Reich, S. 1997. *Music for 18 Musicians* (CD liner notes), New York: Nonesuch Records.
Saunders, R., and J. S. Gero. 2001. Artificial creativity: A synthetic approach to the study of
    creative behaviour. In *Proceedings of the Fifth Conference on Computational and*

Cognitive Models of Creative Design, ed. J. S. Gero. Sydney: Key Centre for Design Computing and Cognition, pp. 113–139.

Sims, K. 1991. "Interactive Evolution of Dynamical Systems." Paper presented at First European Conference on Artificial Life, December 1991, Paris, France.

Smith, A. R. 1984. Plants, fractals and formal languages. In *Computer Graphics*, ed. H. Christiansen. New York: ACM SIGGRAPH. Original edition *Proceedings of SIGGRAPH '84*, Minneapolis, MN, July 22–27.

Todd, P. M., and G. M. Werner. 1998. Frankensteinian methods for evolutionary music composition. In *Musical Networks: Parallel Distributed Perception and Performance*, ed. N. Griffith and P. M. Todd. Cambridge: MIT Press/Bradford Books.

Waters, S. 2007a. "Performance Ecosystems: Ecological Approaches to Musical Interaction." Paper presented at the Electroacoustic Music Studies Network, The 'languages' of electroacoustic music, EMS07, June 12–15, Leicester, UK.

Waters, S. 2007b. The VPFI (Virtual/Physical Feedback Instrument) Flute: A Performance Ecosystem. http://musariada.mus.uea.ac.uk/~simon/performance-ecosystem/, accessed March 18, 2009.

Whitelaw, M. 2004. *Metacreation: Art and Artificial Life*. Cambridge: MIT Press.

Whitelaw, M., M. Guglielmetti, and T. Innocent. 2009. Strange ontologies in digital culture. *ACM Computers in Entertainment* 7(1): Article 4.

Wiener, N. 1961. *Cybernetics: Or Control and Communication in the Animal and the Machine*. 2nd ed. Cambridge: MIT Press.

Wolfram, S. 1984. Universality and complexity in cellular automata. *Physica 10D*: 1–35.

PART IV

COGNITION AND COMPUTATION OF COMPUTER MUSIC

CHAPTER 19

COMPUTATIONAL MODELING OF MUSIC COGNITION AND MUSICAL CREATIVITY

GERAINT A. WIGGINS,
MARCUS T. PEARCE,
AND DANIEL MÜLLENSIEFEN

THIS chapter is about computational modeling of the process of musical composition based on a cognitive model of human behavior. The idea is to study not only the requirements for a computer system capable of musical composition but also to relate it to human behavior during the same process so that it may, perhaps, work in the same way as a human composer, but also so that it may, more likely, help us understand how human composers work. Pearce et al. (2002) gave a fuller discussion of the motivations behind this endeavor.

We take a purist approach to our modeling: we are aiming, ultimately, at a computer system that we can claim to be creative. Therefore, we must address in advance the criticism that usually arises in these circumstances: a computer cannot be creative because it can only do what it has explicitly been programmed to do. This argument does not hold because, with the advent of machine learning, it is no longer true that a computer is limited to what its programmer explicitly tells it, especially in a relatively unsupervised learning task like composition (as compared with the usually supervised task of learning, say, the piano). Thus, a creative system based on machine learning can, in principle, be given credit for creative output, much as Wolfgang Amadeus Mozart is deemed the creator of the *Magic Flute* and not Leopold Mozart, Wolfgang's father, teacher and de facto agent.

Because music is a very complex phenomenon, we focus on a relatively[1] simple aspect that is relatively easy to isolate from the many other aspects of music: tonal melody. To compose music, one normally needs to learn about it by hearing it, so we begin with a perceptual model that has proven capable of simulating relevant aspects of human listening behavior better than any other in the literature. We also consider the application of this model to a different task, musical phrase segmentation, because doing so adds weight to its status as a good, if preliminary, model of human cognition. We then consider using the model to generate tonal melodies and show how one might go about evaluating the resulting model of composition scientifically. Before we can begin this discussion, we need to cover some background material and introduce some descriptive tools, the subjects of the next section.

1. BACKGROUND

In this section, we explain the basis of our approach to the cognitive modeling of musical creativity and supply background material to the various detailed sections to follow. We begin by motivating cognitive modeling itself, and then argue why doing so is relevant to the study of musical behavior. We make a distinction between different kinds of cognitive model that serve different purposes in the context of research. Next, we outline an approach to modeling creative behavior, within which we frame our discussion. Finally, we briefly survey the literature in modeling of music cognition and musical composition, and in the evaluation of creative behavior, to supply background for the presentation.

A. Methodology

Our Starting Point: Cognitive Modeling

Cognitive science as a research field dates to the 1950s and 1960s. It arises from a view of the brain as an information-processing machine and the mind as an epiphenomenon arising in turn from that processing. The aim is to understand the operation of the mind and brain at various interconnected levels of abstraction in the expectation that, ultimately, cognitive scientists will be able to explain the operation of both mind and brain, from the level of physical neurons up to the level of consciousness. There is an important distinction between the study of the operation of the mind in general and the resulting emergent behavior of particular minds or groups of minds; the former is our focus here. This cognitive focus follows, in the current context, from a view of music not as a Romantic, quasi-platonic and transcendent entity with an absolute definition in the external world, but as a fundamentally social phenomenon, driven by and formed from the human urge to communicate. Only thus can we account for the multifarious musics of the human world and the way they change over time, given the lack of any strong evidence for the existence of innate specifically musical abilities shaped directly by evolution (Justus and Hutsler 2005). Necessarily, therefore, we look for the source of music in humanity and in individual (but not particular) humans, the latter being our main interest here.

The difficulty with studying minds and brains is that they are difficult to measure. The only way one can measure a mind is by recording its effect on the world; therefore, one can only infer the causes of one's results. Brains are a little more accessible, but ethical issues restrict the extent to which we can do controlled experiments with them[2]; anyway, they are so complicated that we lack the technology to study them in the detail we really need. To overcome these problems, cognitive scientists have tended to focus on particular aspects of measurable behavior, in an abstract way, ignoring surrounding detail, in the hope of understanding them in isolation before moving on to more inclusive theories. The choice of abstraction is crucial because, done wrongly, it can obscure parts of the phenomenon studied or blur the distinctions between different effects.

Computational Cognitive Models

With the advent of computers, cognitive scientists were able to take their models of the mind to new levels of precision. Previously, they were able to describe what effects arose from which stimulus, but it was impossible to give a mechanistic theory from which predictions could be made because doing so would have been an intractable pen-and-paper exercise, enormously time-consuming and error prone. However, with fast computers and access to large, high-quality databases of stimuli, it is now possible to embody a cognitive theory as a computer program and thus apply it to large amounts of data and to test its consequences exhaustively—thus, importantly, generating new hypotheses for testing against human behavior from these predictions. In a cyclic way, we can then refine our theory to account for incorrect predictions and try again. In addition to goodness of fit to the observed data and behaviors, we prefer simpler models over more complex ones, models that selectively predict just the observed data and, finally, models that generate surprising, but true, predictions (Cutting et al. 1992, Honing 2006).

As well as supplying a way forward, computational modeling gives cognitive scientists a new and useful challenge: to define their working abstraction and their theory precisely enough that it can be given an operational interpretation as a computer program. Much research in computer representation of music is also engaged in this challenge (e.g., Wiggins et al. 1993, Marsden 2000).

Another issue that is brought into sharp focus is the distinction between modeling what a phenomenon *does*, and modeling *how* it does it, which have been labeled *descriptive* and *explanatory* modeling, respectively (Wiggins 2007); Marr (1982) and McClamrock (1991) also discussed these and related issues. To understand this distinction, an analogy is helpful. Consider models of the weather. Such a model could be made by taking a barometer, correlating atmospheric pressure with the weather and the wind direction, and writing down whether it was raining or not at the time. Given enough data, this simple lookup table will probably predict the weather correctly much of the time. However, it only computes its predictions in terms of observed correlated connections: it encodes nothing of the mechanisms by which the weather operates and therefore cannot explain how the weather works or account for conditions it has not met before unless by some naïve generalization such as interpolation. If it is indeed reasonably accurate, the model can nevertheless be a useful predictor of the weather, so we might say it *describes* the weather to some degree.

Now, imagine a different, supercomputer-based weather model which not only has detailed information about the same empirical data but also encodes knowledge of physics (e.g., of the process whereby liquid water will precipitate from humid air as temperature drops). This physical model need only be in terms of mathematical equations such as Boyle's law and not, for example, in terms of the movement of individual molecules of gas, but it nevertheless captures a different *kind* of detail from the descriptive one—and we can ask it, Why? So, this *explanatory* model gives an account of the weather by saying (at another level of abstraction) *how* the effects described by both models actually arise. Like the descriptive model, we can test it by giving it conditions that we have newly experienced for the first time and checking its predictions against reality; if they turn out to be wrong, one source of potential error is now the mechanism itself.

A final useful concept here is that of the *meta-model*, named from the Greek μετα, meaning after or beyond, as in "metaphysics". We employ this to refer to the use of a model, intended for and validated with respect to a particular (cognitive) phenomenon, (directly or indirectly) to predict the behavior of another related but different phenomenon for which it was neither intended nor designed. It is useful to make this distinction because this capacity adds considerable weight to the argument that the model is in some sense a *good* model in general terms (Honing 2006) and can also support a case that it is an explanatory one. We give an example of such a model and a meta-model derived from it in the next section.

Computational Cognitive Modeling of Creative Behavior

Since the point of this chapter is to consider creative applications of cognitive models, we need a framework within which to do so. Boden (1990) proposed a model of creative behavior which revolves around the notion of a *conceptual space* and its exploration by creative agents. The conceptual space is a set of concepts which are deemed to be acceptable as examples of whatever is being created. Implicitly, the conceptual space may also include partially defined concepts. *Exploratory creativity* is the process of exploring a given conceptual space; *transformational creativity* is the process of changing the rules that delimit the conceptual space. Boden (1998) also made an important distinction between mere membership of a conceptual space and the *value* of a member of the space, which is extrinsically defined but not precisely. Various other models of creativity exist (e.g., Wallas 1926, Koestler 1964), but are not sufficiently detailed for implementation; Ritchie (2007) gave an alternative view of ways to study creative systems, but it does not suit our purposes here.

Boden's model, however, is amenable to implementation. Wiggins (2006a, 2006b) provided one possible formalization, a creative systems framework (CSF), which may be directly constructed or used to identify aspects of creative systems and compare them with each other and with human behavior. There is not enough space to present the full framework here; it suffices to echo Boden's idea of a conceptual space, defined by a mutable rule set R and a further mutable set of rules E, according to which the quality of the items created can be evaluated. This dichotomy is important—for example, it is possible to recognize a joke without thinking it to be a good one—so it is necessary to separate these things. An explicit component of Wiggins's formalism which is only implicit in Boden's original thought experiment is the idea of a *traversal strategy T*, which is used by a creative agent to explore the conceptual space—in other words, while it is actually doing the creative stuff. This is necessary not only for a computer system (otherwise nothing will happen) but also for an explicit model of a specific creative agent. The difference, for example, between a first-year music student and an experienced professional organist harmonizing a chorale melody lies not only in the quality of the output produced but also in the encoding of the strategies used; the unexceptional student is likely to use trial and error to some extent, whereas the organist can intuitively "see" the right harmonization.

Throughout the rest of this chapter, we use all three of the concepts behind these abstract rule sets, referring to them as R, T, and E, to identify as precisely as we can which aspect of a creative system we are discussing.

B. "Noncognitive" Musical Composition Systems

For completeness, we must acknowledge the existence of a substantial body of work in autonomous systems for musical composition that is not directly related to music cognition and therefore not directly related to this chapter. The earliest such system of which we are aware is that of Hiller and Isaacson (1959), in which a stochastic model was used to generate a musical score, which was subsequently performed by human musicians. Since the 1950s, various attempts have been made at creating music without explicit reference to the processes humans use in doing so. In many of these attempts, the emphasis is on reproducing the style of existing (or formerly existing) composers. In context of the CSF, the focus is then primarily on *R* and *E*; *T* is usually treated mainly as an implementation detail, without regard to simulation of human behavior. A particularly good example of this approach is CHORAL (Ebcioğlu 1988), a rule-based expert system implemented in a specially written backtracking specification language (BSL) and used for the harmonization of chorale melodies in the style of J. S. Bach. Here, *R* and *E* are intertwined in the code of the program, and it is not clear how to decide which is which (although there is an excellent specification of several hundred Bach-harmonic rules in Ebcioğlu's thesis, which may well be a good approximation to *R*); *T* is entirely implicit and is obscured to most readers because it is encoded in Ebcioğlu's backtracking strategy.

Other systems make more of an explicit attempt to model evaluation on the basis of musical attributes perceived by a hypothetical listener. For example, Robertson et al. (1998) presented HERMAN, a system capable of generating continuous music, whose emotional property can be varied from neutral to "scary." Rutherford and Wiggins (2002) demonstrated empirically that human responses do to an extent match the intention of the program's operator. The focus here was again on *R* and *E*, although the difference between them was made more explicit by the use of specific heuristics; *T* was again relegated to a matter of implementation.

It is important to understand that both CHORAL and HERMAN, and many other systems like them, rely on music theory for the basis of their operation and, as such, encode those aspects of music cognition that are implicit in music theory (which, we suggest, are many). However, it is difficult to argue that such knowledge-based systems actually model human creative behavior because they are programmed entities and merely do what their programmers have made them do: in the terms outlined, they are descriptive, and not explanatory, models. We suggest that, for an autonomous composition system to be considered genuinely "creative," it is necessary (although not sufficient) that the system include a significant element of *autonomous learning*. Then, while the *urge* to create may well be instilled by a programmer, the products of creativity are not.

No review of this field would be complete without mention of the work of David Cope (2005). Cope's *Experiments in Musical Intelligence* program has long standing in computer music research as the standard of stylistic recomposition. Regrettably, however, the publications do not tell us how it works; therefore, it is impossible to discuss its behavior in detail.

C. Noncomputational Models of Music Cognition

There is a long history of efforts to develop models of listening-related music cognition that are both formal (although not specifically computational) and general. From the point of view of the CSF, we view all these theories as contributing primarily to *R*, in a hypothetical creative system, although *E* is presumably also affected since these theories are not about creating music but listening to it.

The earliest attempt of which we are aware was that of Simon and Sumner (1968), who assumed that music cognition involves pattern induction and attempted to define a formal language for describing the patterns perceived and used by humans in processing musical sequences. They began with the notion of an *alphabet*, an ordered set of symbols, for representing the range of possible values for a particular musical dimension (e.g., melody, harmony, rhythm, and form; using alphabets for diatonic notes, triads, duration, stress, and formal structure). Simon and Sumner defined three kinds of operation. First, subset operations may be defined to derive more abstract alphabets from existing ones. Second, sequences of symbols may be described by patterns of operations that relate a symbol to its predecessor (e.g., *same* or *next*). Finally, a pattern of operations may be replaced by an abstract symbol. According to this model, when we listen to music, we first induce an alphabet, initial symbol and pattern consistent with what we hear, and then use that pattern to extrapolate the sequence.

Deutsch and Feroe (1981) extended the pattern language of Simon and Sumner and fleshed out its formal specification. They used it to define various common collections of notes (such as scales, triads, and chords) through the recursive application of different operators to an alphabet based on the chromatic scale. Arguing that patterns are learned through long-term exposure to a particular music style, they motivated their approach by appealing to parsimony of encoding (reduced representational redundancy) and constraints on memory and processing (through chunking). However, experiments have yielded mixed support for the predictions of the model (Deutsch 1980, Boltz and Jones 1986).

The generative theory of tonal music (GTTM) of Lerdahl and Jackendoff (1983) is probably the best-known effort to develop a comprehensive method for the structural description of tonal music. Inspired by the use of Chomskian grammars to describe language, the theory is intended to yield a hierarchical, structural description of any piece of Western tonal music, corresponding to the final cognitive state of an experienced listener to that composition.

According to GTTM, a listener unconsciously infers four types of hierarchical structure in a musical surface: *grouping structure*, the segmentation of the musical surface into units (e.g., motives, phrases); *metrical structure*, the pattern of periodically recurring strong and weak beats; *time-span reduction*, the relative structural importance of pitch events within contextually established rhythmic units; and *prolongational reduction*, patterns of tension and relaxation among pitch events at various levels of structure. According to the theory, grouping and metrical structure are largely derived directly from the musical surface, and these structures are used in generating a time-span reduction that is in turn used in generating a prolongational reduction. Each of the four domains of organization is subject to *well-formedness rules* that specify which hierarchical structures are permissible and which themselves may be modified in limited ways by *transformational rules*. While these rules are abstract in that they define only formal possibilities, *preference rules* select which well-formed or transformed structures actually apply to particular aspects of the musical surface. Time-span and prolongational reduction also depend on tonal-harmonic *stability conditions*, which are internal schemata induced from previously heard musical surfaces.

When individual preference rules reinforce one another, the analysis is stable, and the passage is regarded as stereotypical; conflicting preference rules lead to an unstable analysis, causing the passage to be perceived as ambiguous and vague. Thus, according to GTTM, the listener unconsciously attempts to arrive at the most stable overall structural description of the musical surface. Experimental studies of human listeners have found support for some of the preliminary components of the theory, including the grouping structure (Deliège 1987) and the metrical structure (Palmer and Krumhansl 1990).

Narmour (1990) presented the implication-realization (IR) theory of music cognition which, like GTTM, is intended to be general (although the initial presentation was restricted to melody) but which, in contrast to GTTM's static approach, starts with the dynamic processes involved in perceiving music in time. The theory posits two distinct perceptual systems: the *bottom-up* system is held to be hard-wired, innate, and universal, while the *top-down system* is held to be learned through musical experience. The two systems may conflict, and in any given situation, one may override the implications generated by the other.

In the bottom-up system, sequences of melodic intervals vary in the degree of closure that they convey. Strong closure signifies the termination of ongoing melodic structure; an interval that is unclosed is said to be an *implicative interval* and generates expectations for the following interval, termed the *realized interval*. The expectations generated by implicative intervals for realized intervals were described by Narmour (1990) in terms of several principles of continuation which are influenced by the Gestalt principles of proximity, similarity, and good continuation. The IR model also specifies how the basic melodic structures combine to form longer and more complex structural patterns of melodic implication within the IR theory. In particular, structures associated with weak closure may be *chained* to subsequent structures. In addition, structural tones (those beginning or ending a melodic structure, combination, or chain) that are emphasized by strong closure at one level are said to *transform* to the higher level.

The IR theory has inspired many quantitative implementations of its principles and a large body of experimental research testing its predictions as a theory of melodic expectation (Cuddy and Lunny 1995, Krumhansl 1995a, 1995b, Schellenberg 1996, 1997, Thompson et al. 1997, Krumhansl et al. 2000), which we may interpret as supportive. Our experiments seem to add further support, but with the proviso that our system is (in Narmour's terms) top-down only (Pearce and Wiggins 2006).

D. Computational Models of Music Cognition

Given that we wish to base our autonomous creative system on behavior that is learned, rather than programmed, we need to identify a starting point from which the learned behavior can arise. In humans, this starting point seems to be the ability to hear music and perceive its internal structure; it is hard to imagine how musically creative behavior could arise otherwise unless it is an intrinsic property of human brains. There is no evidence for this claim, but there is evidence that music is learned: without learning, it is very hard to account for the ubiquity of music in human society while still explaining the variety of musics in different cultures and subcultures. Various authors (e.g., Justus and Hutsler 2005, Mithen 2006, Cross 2007, Bown and Wiggins 2009) have studied these questions; the consensus seems to be that music cognition and music creation coevolve—indeed, we arguably see the cultural aspects of this process continuing in the present day, not only in (pre)history.

There are not very many computational models of music cognition in the literature, and those that do exist span a wide range of musical dimensions—music cognition is too complicated a phenomenon to be modeled directly all in one go. Aspects of the general frameworks described have been implemented piecemeal. The approach usually taken is the standard scientific reductionist approach: attempt to understand each aspect of the problem while holding the others fixed, then try to understand their interactions, and only subsequently put all the understanding together. Again, a general distinction can be made between programmed-rule-based and machine learning approaches. It is worth mentioning that this distinction is independent of the structural divisions of the CSF: each of the three rule sets, R, T, and E, may be either human programmed or learned as long as there is a context in which they can interact. However, there is a difference in relation to the descriptive/exploratory distinction: a preprogrammed rule-based system (of which our simple weather predictor was an extreme example), is less likely to be an explanatory model than a descriptive one because, by definition, it does not give any account of how the rules arise in context of their eventual usage.

On the machine learning side, Bharucha (1987) developed a connectionist model of harmony based on a sequential feed-forward neural network. The model accurately predicts a range of experimental findings, including memory confusions for target chords following a context chord (Bharucha 1987) and facilitation in priming studies (Bharucha and Stoeckig 1986, 1987). In addition, the network model learned the regularities of typical Western chord progressions through exposure, and the representation of chord proximity in the circle of fifths arose as an emergent property of the interaction of the network with its environment. Large et al. (1995) examined the ability of another neural network architecture, RAAM (Pollack 1990), to acquire reduced representations of Western children's melodies represented as tree structures according to music-theoretic predictions (Lerdahl and Jackendoff 1983). The trained models acquired compressed representations of the melodies in which structurally salient events were represented more efficiently (and reproduced more accurately) than other events. Furthermore, the certainty with which the trained network reconstructed events correlated well with cognitive representations of structural importance as assessed by empirical data on the events retained by trained pianists across improvised variations on the melodies.

Perhaps the most complete computational theory to date is that of Temperley (2001), which is inspired to an extent by GTTM. Temperley proposed preference rule models of a range of fundamental processes in music cognition which include meter recognition, melodic segmentation, voice separation in polyphonic music, pitch spelling, chord analysis, and key identification. The rule models reflect sophisticated knowledge from music theory and are implemented in a suite of analysis tools named Melisma, whose source code is publicly available. When applied to real-world analysis problems, the Melisma tools generally exhibit reasonable performance (see discussion regarding melodic segmentation or Meredith, 2006, regarding pitch spelling) and in some areas have become a standard for rule-based music analysis algorithms. Most of the algorithmic models bear little underlying conceptual coherence and make strong use of domain-specific knowledge, as reflected by the respective rules and their combination. Temperley (2007) aimed at a reformulation of some of these rule-based models in the general probabilistic framework of Bayesian statistics. He derived a so-called pitch and a rhythm model based on frequency counts in different music corpora and applied them to several musical processes, such as meter determination, key finding, and melodic error detection.

As the Bayesian models do not always outperform the rule-based algorithms, the value of the Bayesian reformulation seems to lie rather in the more coherent underlying theory, although a more comprehensive and rigorous evaluation is still required (Pearce et al. 2007).

E. Computational Cognitive Models of Musical Composition

By comparison with cognitive-scientific research on musical listening, cognitive processes in composition remain largely unexamined (Sloboda 1985, Baroni 1999). This section reviews research on the cognitive modeling of music composition with an emphasis on computational approaches; Deliège and Wiggins (2006) presented a range of work in the noncomputational context.

Johnson-Laird (1991) argued that it is fundamental to understand what the mind has to compute to generate an acceptable jazz improvisation before examining the precise nature of the algorithms by which it does so.[3] To study the intrinsic constraints of the task, Johnson-Laird applied grammars of different expressive powers to different subcomponents of the problem. His results suggested that, while a finite-state grammar is capable of computing the melodic contour, onset and duration of the next note in a jazz improvisation, its pitch must be determined by constraints derived from a model of harmonic movement that requires a context-free grammar.

Lerdahl (1988) explored the relationship between listening and composition and outlined some cognitive constraints that it places on the cognitive processes of composition. He framed his arguments within a context in which a *compositional grammar* generates both a structural description of a composition and, together with intuitive perceptual constraints, its realization as a concrete sequence of discrete events which is consumed by a *listening grammar*, which in turn yields a structural description of the composition as perceived. A further distinction is made between *natural* and *artificial* compositional grammars: the former arise spontaneously within a culture and are based on the listening grammar; the latter are consciously developed by individuals or groups and may be influenced by any number of concerns. Noting that the two kinds of grammar coexist fruitfully in most complex and mature musical cultures, Lerdahl argued that when the artificial influences of a compositional grammar carry it too far from the listening grammar, the intended structural organization can bear little relation to the perceived structural organization of a composition. He outlined some constraints, largely based on the preference rules and stability conditions of GTTM, placed on compositional grammars by this need to recover the intended structural organization from the musical surface by the listening grammar.

Temperley (2003) expanded the proposal that composition is constrained by a mutual understanding between composers and listeners of the relationships between structural descriptions and the musical surface into a theory of *communicative pressure* on the development of musical styles. Various phenomena are discussed, including the relationship between the traditional rules of voice leading and principles of auditory perception (Huron 2001) and trade-off between syncopation and rubato in a range of musical styles.

Baroni (1999) discussed grammars for modeling the cognitive processes involved in musical listening and composition, basing his arguments on his own grammars for the structural analysis of a number of musical repertoires (Baroni et al. 1992). He characterized a listening grammar as a collection of morphological categories that define sets of discrete musical structures at varying levels of description and a collection of syntactical rules for combining morphological units. He argued that such a grammar is based on a stylistic mental prototype acquired through extensive exposure to a given musical style. While the listening grammar is largely implicit, according to Baroni, the complex nature of composition requires the acquisition of explicit grammatical knowledge through systematic, analytic study of the repertoire. However, he stated that the compositional and listening grammars share the same fundamental morphology and syntax. The distinguishing characteristics of the two cognitive activities lie in the technical procedures underlying the effective application of the syntactical rules. As an example, he examined hierarchical structure in the listening and compositional grammars: for the former, the problem lies in picking up cues for the application of grammatical rules and anticipating their subsequent confirmation or violation in a sequential manner; for the latter, the structural description of a composition may be generated top-down.

Perhaps surprisingly, given that we are now considering composition, in terms of the CSF the emphasis is, again, on R and maybe E: the method of traversal T being treated almost as a given.

Turning now to machine-learning approaches, Conklin (2003) examined four methods of generating high-probability music according to a statistical model. The simplest is sequential random sampling: an event is sampled from the estimated event distribution at each sequential position up to a given length. Events are generated in a random walk, so there is a danger of straying into local minima in the space of possible compositions. Even so, most statistical generation of music uses this method.

The hidden Markov model (HMM) addresses these problems; it generates observed events from hidden states (Rabiner 1989). An HMM is trained by adjusting the probabilities conditioning the initial hidden state, the transitions between hidden states, and the emission of observed events from hidden states to maximize the probability of a training set of observed sequences. A trained HMM can be used to estimate the probability of an observed sequence of events and to find the most probable sequence of hidden states given an observed sequence of events. This can be achieved efficiently for a first-order HMM using the Viterbi algorithm; a similar algorithm exists for first-order (visible) Markov models. However, Viterbi's running time increases exponentially in the context length of the underlying Markov model (Conklin 2003), which means that it is not good for practical use. However, there do exist tractable methods for sampling from complex statistical models (such as those presented here) that address the limitations of random sampling (Conklin 2003). We return to this in the section titled "A Simple Model of Musical Creativity."

Notwithstanding the problems of complexity, Conklin made a real attempt to address the question of what a traversal strategy *T* might be, as well as considering *R* carefully. In our work, we follow his statistical approach, but note that something more semantically sensitive will be appropriate in future work.

F. Evaluation of Creative Behavior

The evaluation of creative behavior, either within a creative system or from outside it, is very difficult because of the subjectivity involved and because individual outputs cannot necessarily be said to be representative of the system's capability.

On the computational side, *analysis by synthesis* has been used to evaluate computational models of composition by generating pieces and evaluating them with respect to the objectives of the implemented model. The method has a long history; Ames and Domino (1992) argued that a primary advantage of computational analysis of musical style is the ability to evaluate new pieces generated from an implemented theory. However, evaluation of the generated music raises methodological issues which have typically compromised the potential benefits thus afforded (Pearce et al. 2002). Often, compositions are evaluated with a single subjective comment, for example: "[the compositions] are realistic enough that an unknowing listener cannot discern their artificial origin" (Ames and Domino 1992, p. 186). This lack of precision makes it hard to compare theories intersubjectively.

Other research has used expert stylistic analyses to evaluate computer compositions. This is possible when a computational model is developed to account for some reasonably well-defined stylistic competence or according to criteria derived from music theory or music psychology. For example, Ponsford et al. (1999) gave an informal stylistic appraisal of the harmonic progressions generated by their *n*-gram models.

However, even when stylistic analyses are undertaken by groups of experts, the results obtained are typically still qualitative. For fully intersubjective analysis by synthesis, the evaluation of the generated compositions must be empirical. One could use an adaptation of the Turing test, in which subjects are presented with pairs of compositions (one computer generated, the other human composed) and asked which they believe to be the computer-generated one (Marsden 2000). Musical Turing tests yield empirical, quantitative results which may be appraised intersubjectively and have demonstrated the inability of subjects to distinguish reliably between computer- and human-composed music. But the method suffers from three major difficulties: it can be biased by preconceptions about computer music; it allows ill-informed judgments; and it fails to examine the criteria used to judge the compositions.

Assessing human creativity is no easier, but at least one technique has been proposed that seems promising. Amabile (1996) proposed a conceptual definition of creativity in terms of processes resulting in novel, appropriate solutions to heuristic, open-ended, or ill-defined tasks. However, while agreeing that creativity can only be assessed through subjective assessments of products, she criticized the use of a priori theoretical definitions of creativity in rating schemes and failure to distinguish creativity from other constructs. While a conceptual definition is important for guiding empirical research, a clear operational definition is necessary for the development of useful empirical methods of assessment. Accordingly, she presented a consensual definition of creativity in which a product is deemed creative to the extent that observers who are familiar with the relevant domain independently agree that it is creative. To the extent that this construct is internally consistent (independent judges agree in their ratings of creativity), one can empirically examine the objective or subjective features of creative products that contribute to their perceived creativity.

Amabile used this operational definition to develop the consensual assessment technique (CAT), an empirical method for evaluating creativity. Its requirements are that the task be open ended enough to permit considerable flexibility and novelty in the response, which must be an observable product that can be rated by judges. Regarding the procedure, the judges must

1. Be experienced in the relevant domain;
2. Make independent assessments;
3. Assess other aspects of the products such as technical accomplishment, aesthetic appeal, or originality;
4. Make relative judgments of each product in relation to the rest of the stimuli;
5. Be presented with stimuli and provide ratings in orders randomized differently for each judge.

Most important, in analyzing the collected data, the interjudge reliability of the subjective rating scales must be determined. If—and only if—reliability is high, we may correlate creativity ratings with other objective or subjective features of creative products.

Numerous studies of verbal, artistic, and problem-solving creativity have demonstrated the ability of the CAT to obtain reliable subjective assessments of creativity in a range of domains (Amabile 1996, chap. 3, gives a review).

The CAT overcomes the limitations of the Turing test in evaluating computational models of musical composition. First, it requires the use of human judges expert in the task domain. Second, since it has been developed for research on human creativity, no mention is made of the computational origins of the stimuli; this avoids bias due to preconceptions. Third, and most important, the methodology allows more detailed examination of the objective and subjective dimensions of the creative products. Crucially, the objective attributes of the products may include features of the generative models (corresponding with cognitive or stylistic hypotheses) that produced them. Thus, we can empirically compare different musicological theories of a given style or hypotheses about the cognitive processes involved in composing in that style.

We propose to use the CAT in evaluating creative computer systems as well as human ones.

2. Toward a Computational Model of Music Cognition

Having laid out the background of our approach and supplied a context of extant research, we now present our model of melody cognition (the information dynamics of music or IDyOM model). We describe it in three parts: first the computational model itself, second its application to melodic pitch expectation, and third the extension of the same model to melodic grouping (which we then call a meta-model of music cognition). As with the other cognitive models described, we view the expectation model as supplying R, and perhaps some of E, in our creative system. For want of literature on the subject, we begin with a naïve statistical T.

The following discussion is a brief summary; detailed presentations of the model are available elsewhere (Pearce and Wiggins 2004, Pearce 2005, Pearce et al. 2005).

A. The Computational Model

The Representation Scheme

We use a *multiple-viewpoint system* (Conklin and Witten 1995) as the basis of our representation scheme. The scheme takes as its *musical surface* (Jackendoff 1987) sequences of note events, representing the instantiation of a finite number of discrete features or attributes. An *event* consists of a number of *basic features* representing its onset time, duration, pitch, and so on. Basic features are associated with an alphabet: a finite set of symbols determines the possible instantiations of that feature in a concrete note.

The representation scheme also allows for the construction of *derived features* which can be computed from the values of one or more basic features (e.g., interonset interval, pitch interval, contour, and scale degree). In some locations in a melody, a given derived feature may be undefined. Furthermore, it is possible to define derived features that represent attributes of nonadjacent notes, and compound features may be defined to represent interactions between primitive features.

To ensure that our results pertain to real-world musical phenomena and to ensure ecological validity, we use music data from existing repertoires of music. Here, we use data derived from scores, but the representation scheme is rather flexible and could be extended to represent expressive aspects of music performance (e.g., dynamics, expressive timing). Although we focus on melody, and not all musics have an equivalent analog of the Western notion, stream segregation (Bregman 1990) appears to be a basic perceptual process. Furthermore, the multiple-viewpoints framework has been extended to accommodate the representation of homophonic and polyphonic music (Conklin 2002).

The Modeling Strategy

The basis of IDyOM is n-gram models commonly used in statistical language modeling (Manning and Schütze 1999). An n-gram is a sequence of n symbols, and an n-gram model is simply a collection of such sequences, each associated with a frequency count. During the *training* of the statistical model, these counts are acquired through an analysis of some corpus of sequences (the training set) in the target domain. When the trained model is exposed to a sequence drawn from the target domain, it uses the frequency counts associated with n-grams to estimate a probability distribution governing the identity of the next symbol in the sequence given the $n - 1$ preceding symbols. The quantity $n - 1$ is known as the *order* of the model and represents the number of symbols making up the context within which a prediction is made.

The modeling process begins by choosing a set of basic features that we are interested in predicting. As these basic features are treated as independent attributes, their probabilities are computed separately; in turn, and the probability of a note is simply the product of the probabilities of its attributes. Here, we consider the example of predicting pitch alone.

The most elementary n-gram model of melodic pitch structure (a monogram model where $n=1$) simply tabulates the frequency of occurrence for each chromatic pitch encountered in a traversal of each melody in the training set. During prediction, the expectations of the model are governed by a zeroth-order pitch distribution derived from the frequency counts and do not depend on the preceding context of the melody. In a digram model (where $n=2$), however, frequency counts are maintained for sequences of two pitch symbols, and predictions are governed by a first-order pitch distribution derived from the frequency counts associated with only those digrams whose initial pitch symbol matches the final pitch symbol in the melodic context.

Fixed-order models such as these suffer from a number of problems. Low-order models (such as the monogram model discussed) clearly fail to provide an adequate account of the structural influence of the context on expectations. However, increasing the order can prevent the model from capturing much of the statistical regularity present in the training set. An extreme case occurs when the model encounters an n-gram that does not appear in the training set, in which case it returns an estimated probability of zero. To address these problems, the

IDyOM model maintains frequency counts during training for *n*-grams of all possible values of *n* in any given context. During prediction, distributions are estimated using a weighted sum of all models below a variable order bound. This bound is determined in each predictive context using simple heuristics designed to minimize uncertainty. The combination is designed such that higher-order predictions (which are more specific to the context) receive greater weighting than lower-order predictions (which are more general). In a given melodic context, therefore, the predictions of the combined model may reflect the influence of both the digram model and (to a lesser extent) the monogram model. In addition to the general, low-order statistical regularities captured by these two models, the predictions of the IDyOM model can also reflect higher-order regularities which are even more specific to the current melodic context (to the extent that these exist in the training set).

Inference over Multiple Features

One final issue to be covered regards the manner in which IDyOM exploits the representation of multiple features of the musical surface described. The modeling process begins with the selection, by hand, of a set of features of interest and the training of distinct *n*-gram models for each of these features. For each note in a melody, each feature is predicted using two models: first the *long-term* model that was trained over the entire training set in the previous step; and second a *short-term* model trained incrementally for each individual melody being predicted. Figure 19.1 illustrates this (and other aspects of the model of pitch expectation and the meta-model of melodic segmentation discussed in a separate section).

The task of combining the predictions from all these models is achieved in two stages, both of which use a weighted multiplicative combination scheme in which greater weights are assigned to models whose predictions are associated with lower entropy (or uncertainty) at that point in the melody. In this scheme, a combined distribution is achieved by taking the product of the weighted probability estimates returned by each model for each possible value of the pitch of the next note and

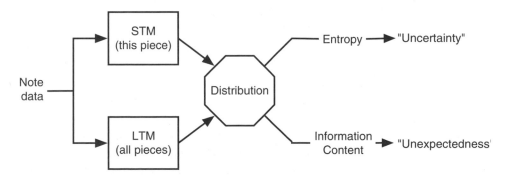

Figure 19.1 Our development of Pearce's (2005) cognitive model. The central distribution gives the model of pitch expectation; the entropy and information content outputs, coupled with some peak picking, constitute the meta-model of melodic segmentation.

then normalizing such that the combined estimates sum to unity over the pitch alphabet. The entropy-based weighting method and the use of a multiplicative as opposed to an additive combination scheme both improve the performance of the model in predicting the pitches of unseen melodies (Pearce and Wiggins 2004, Pearce et al. 2005).

In the first stage of model combination, the predictions of models for different features are combined for the long-term and short-term models separately. Distributions from models of derived features are first converted into distributions over the alphabet of the basic feature from which they are derived (e.g., to combine a distribution over pitch contours with one over scale degrees, first we need to convert both into distributions over chromatic pitch). If any feature (derived or otherwise) is undefined at a given location in a melody, a model of that feature will not contribute to the predictions of the overall system at that location. In the second stage, the two combined distributions (long term and short term) resulting from the first step are combined into a single distribution which represents the overall system's final expectations regarding the pitch of the next note in the melody. The use of long- and short-term models is intended to reflect the influences on expectation of both existing extraopus and incrementally increasing intraopus knowledge, while the use of multiple features is intended to reflect the influence of regularities in many dimensions of the musical surface.

B. Modeling Melodic Pitch Expectancy

The conditional probabilities output by IDyOM in a given melodic context may be interpreted as contextual expectations about the nature of the forthcoming note. Pearce and Wiggins (2006) compared the melodic pitch expectations of the model with those of listeners in the context of single intervals (Cuddy and Lunny 1995), at particular points in British folk songs (Schellenberg 1996), and throughout two chorale melodies (Manzara et al. 1992). The results demonstrated that the statistical system predicts the expectations of listeners as least as well as the two-factor model of Schellenberg (1997) and significantly better in the case of more complex melodic contexts.

C. Modeling Melodic Segmentation

Musical segmentation is a fundamental process in music-cognitive theory and simulation (e.g., Jackendoff 1983, Cambouropoulos 1996, Lerdahl and Potter et al. 2007, Wiggins 2007). In this section, we show how our model of pitch expectation can be used to predict human judgments of melodic segment boundaries. Inevitably, this meta-model (see the "Background" section) is not superior to all existing segmentation models from the literature because it includes no direct encoding of many of the musical features that we know determine segmentation: metrical structure, harmony, and so on. However, it performs surprisingly well in comparison with other descriptive, programmed models. Our model can predict both large-scale and small-scale boundaries in music.

From a musicological perspective, it has been proposed that perceptual groups are associated with points of closure at which the ongoing cognitive process of expectation is disrupted either because the context fails to stimulate strong expectations for any particular continuation or because the actual continuation is unexpected (Meyer 1957, Narmour 1990). In addition, empirical psychological research has demonstrated that infants and adults use the implicitly learned statistical properties of pitch (Saffran et al. 1990), pitch interval (Saffran and Griepentrog 2001), and scale degree (Saffran 2003) sequences to identify segment boundaries on the basis of higher digram ($n = 2$) transition probabilities within than between groups. Finally, in machine learning and computational linguistics, algorithms based on the idea of segmenting before unexpected events perform reasonably well in identifying word boundaries in infant-directed speech (Elman 1990, Brent 1999, Cohen et al. 2007). There is some evidence that high predictive uncertainty is also associated with word boundaries (Cohen et al. 2007).

Drawing on this background, we achieve our meta-model by applying information-theoretic principles (Shannon 1948) to the distributions produced by the statistical model of melodic expectation. In particular, we represent unexpectedness of a note by its *information content* (the negative log of its conditional probability), and we represent uncertainty about the identity of the next note by the *entropy* (the average information content) of the distribution governing the note's identity computed from both the short-term and the long-term model. Our prediction of large-scale structure works by looking for relatively large, simultaneous, positive change points in the entropy and information content of the music at each note as it proceeds (Potter et al. 2007), essentially implementing Narmour's (1990) proposal. Entropy measures uncertainty, so a downward trend followed by a sudden increase corresponds with closure at the end of a phrase and then the relative uncertainty generated by not knowing what comes next. Unexpectedness measures something related (although of course the beginning of each new phrase need not necessarily be very unexpected in absolute terms).

Here, we focus on the effects of unexpectedness (modeled by information content) on low-level melodic segmentation, leaving the role of entropy for future research. Using a model of both pitch and rhythmic structure (interonset interval and rests), we derive an information-content profile for the notes in a melody, from which we identify segment boundaries by picking peaks at points where the note-by-note information content is high *relative to the local context* (see Müllensiefen et al. 2008 for further details).

The performance of our model was evaluated in two studies in which we compared its prediction accuracy to the performance of several other models specifically designed for melodic segmentation, such as *Grouper* (Temperley 2001), the *Local Boundary Detection Model* (*LBDM*) (Cambouropoulos 2001), and three of the *Grouping Preference Rules* (*GPRs*) from GTTM (Lerdahl and Jackendoff 1983).

The data for the first evaluation study were collected from twenty-five expert judges in an experimental setting. Their task was to indicate phrase endings within each of fifteen popular melodies on a score through repeated listenings to each melody. For all the 1,250 note events in this data set, we computed the F score, a widely used evaluation measure in information retrieval (see, e.g., Jurafsky and Martin 2000), to indicate the correspondence between the algorithmic segmentation solutions and the boundaries selected by at least 50% of the experimental participants; this is merely a majority vote—more principled approaches will be applied in future work. The F score can vary between 0, when there is no correspondence, and 1, indicating perfect agreement between model and ground truth data.

The second evaluation study used 1,705 German folk songs from the Essen collection (Schaffrath 1995) as ground truth data. This data set comprised 78,995 notes at an average of about forty-six events per melody, and overall about 12% of notes fall before boundaries. Phrase boundaries were annotated by the musicologist who encoded the data, and the F scores on this data set reflect the degree to which the boundaries predicted by a given model correspond to those annotated in the scores.

As can be seen from table 19.1, the IDyOM model reaches a performance comparable to the three best-performing segmentation models, namely, Grouper, LBDM, and the GPR2a rule from GTTM. An acceptable melodic segmentation can be obtained by picking the peaks in the information content profile produced by the general-purpose learning model, suggesting that unexpectedness (as measured by information content) is very strongly related to boundary detection in melodies.

Table 19.1 Segmentation model performances (F score) on the Essen folk song data and data from an experimental study

Model	F (Essen data)	F (experimental data)
Grouper	0.65	0.76
LBDM	0.62	0.71
GPR2a	0.60	0.76
IDyOM	0.58	0.77
GPR2b	0.38	0.16
GPR3a	0.34	0.22
GPR3d	0.29	0.08
Always	0.22	0.14
Never	0.00	0.00

D. Discussion

We have described in outline the IDyOM model of music cognition, which has been developed over several years and is still developing. While this model is still in its infancy, it has demonstrated a capacity to perform reasonably reliably and to a reasonable level of competence on certain well-defined, restricted, appropriate tasks. What is more, the model is able to describe two distinct (although not separate) phenomena, pitch expectation and phrase segmentation; we believe this property is methodologically important enough to deserve a name, so we call the phrase segmentation model, which is derived from the pitch expectation model without changing it, a *meta-model* (because it is a model *beyond* the original model using the same process). Finally, the IDyOM model provides a mechanism learned from, but independent from any prior knowledge of, the data over which it operates and is therefore a candidate explanatory model of why the corresponding observed human behavior is as it is at this level of abstraction. Thus, IDyOM provides supporting evidence for the hypothesis that, at some level of abstraction, this kind of music-cognitive processing is effectively modeled by statistics and probability (Huron 2006, Temperley 2007).

How, then, does this model relate to the generation of music? In terms of the CSF, we can use IDyOM to estimate the probability of an entire melodic composition, giving us R, and choose a threshold below which any composition will be deemed "not a melody." So much is easy; defining T and E, however, is less so. First, what makes a "good" melody? Ponsford et al. (1999) initially hypothesized that music with high probability would be good, but this was quickly shown not to be the case; rather, very highly probable pieces tend to be syntactically correct but musically dull. We suggest, in fact, that one way to characterize E would be to look at dynamic changes in the information-theoretic measures introduced as they vary with time. However, before we can properly consider trying to find *good* solutions, we need to be able to find any solution that conforms to R to any reasonable level. Minimally, this is what T is for. In the next section, we present the first stages of development on a potential creative system based on the cognitive model described that works by applying a standard method of string generation to the production of melodies from its learned Markov model.

Of course, the model we have presented here leaves a lot to be desired in terms of general musical properties, such as those in harmony, rhythm, meter, or musical contexts in which these notions do not hold sway or are, at least, different. This is the way of the reductionist scientific method: one must delay gratification for quite a long time when modeling complex phenomena.

However, we believe that our approach is applicable in these above, either in addition to or instead of the existing data and representation: our underlying learning model is amenable to study in any musical context representable by discrete symbols. In principle, those symbols can denote anything from complex polyphony to harmonic labels, to sophisticated representations of timbre and sound spectra. Even in continuous contexts, there are related models that may apply, although there are open questions regarding how to combine them with the discrete ones. Since human perception tends to be categorical, we may even hypothesize that the continuous models are more than we need—at least until we have empirical evidence otherwise.

The immediate focus required, therefore, to expand this thinking to other styles and kinds of music, is on representations at an appropriate level of abstraction of the percepts generated by our senses, which can then be used in supporting or falsifying our learning model. Evidently, there is a rich vein of work to be mined here, and some of it will be future work for us.

3. A Simple Computational Model of Musical Creativity

We now describe our experimental exploration of the generative capacity of our perceptual model. Following Johnson-Laird (1991), we analyze the computational constraints of the melody composition task in two ways: first, examining whether our learned finite context grammars can compose stylistically successful melodies or whether more expressive grammars are needed; and second, determining which representational structures are needed for the composition of successful melodies.

Our experiment is designed to test the hypothesis that our statistical models are capable of generating melodies that are deemed stylistically successful in the context of a specified tradition. Three multiple-feature systems (Pearce 2005) were trained on a data set of chorale melodies and were then used to generate melodies which were empirically evaluated. As described next, the three IDyOM systems are equivalent except for the sets of derived features they use to generate their pitch predictions.

Our work differs in several ways from extant statistical modeling for music generation, particularly no symbolic constraints were imposed on the generation process—it was based entirely on the learned models. This focuses the analysis more sharply on the inherent capacities of statistical finite-context grammars since our goal was to examine the synthetic capabilities of purely statistical, data-driven models of melodic structure. While most previous approaches used sequential random sampling to generate music from statistical models, to generate our output we used the Metropolis-Hastings algorithm, a Markov Chain Monte Carlo (MCMC) sampling method (MacKay 1998). The following description applies it within our generation framework. Given a trained multiple-feature model m for some basic feature τ_b, to sample from the target distribution $p_m(s \in [\tau_b]^*)$, the algorithm constructs a Markov chain in the space of possible feature sequences $[\tau_b]^*$ as follows (notation: $\leftarrow$ denotes assignment; $++$ denotes incrementation; "an event" means a musical note, which is a collection of features, in the terms used):

1. Number of iterations $N \leftarrow$ a large value; iteration number $k \leftarrow 0$; initial state s_0 some feature sequence $t^j_1 \in [\tau_b]^*$ of length j;

2. Select event index $1 \leq i \leq j$ at random or based on some ordering of the indices;

3. Let s'_k be the sequence obtained by replacing event t_i at index i of s_k with a new event t'_k sampled from a distribution q that may depend on the current state s_k—in the present context, an obvious choice for q would be $\{p_m(t|t_1^{i-1})\}_{t \in [\tau b]}$;

4. Accept the proposed sequence with probability

$$\min\left[1, \ \frac{P_m(S'_k) \cdot q(t_i)}{P_m(S_k) \cdot q(t'_i)}\right]$$

5. If accepted, $s_{k+1} \leftarrow s'_k$, else $s_{k+1} \leftarrow s_k$;

6. If $k < N$, $k{+}{+}$ and iterate from 2, else return s_k.

If N is large enough, the resulting event sequence s_{N-1} is guaranteed to be an unbiased sample from the target distribution $p_m[\tau_b]^*$. However, there is no method of assessing the convergence of MCMCs or of estimating the number of iterations required to obtain an unbiased sample (MacKay 1998). Because these sampling algorithms explore the state space using a random walk, they can still be trapped in local minima. However, we expect that this method will be better than sequential random sampling at generating melodies that faithfully represent the inherent capacities of the four systems.[4]

Finally, to evaluate the systems as computational models of melodic composition, we developed a method based on the CAT. The method, described fully by Pearce (2005), obtains ratings by expert judges of the stylistic success of computer-generated compositions and existing compositions in the target genre. The empirical nature of this method makes it preferable to the exclusively qualitative analyses typically adopted, and we expect it to yield more revealing results than the Turing test methodology used in previous research (Hall and Smith 1996, Triviño-Rodriguez and Morales-Bueno 2001).

A. Hypotheses

We used three different systems to examine which representational structures were needed for competent melody generation. Our null hypotheses were that each system could generate melodies rated as equally stylistically successful in the target style as existing, human-composed melodies.

System A is a single-feature system that generates predictions based on chromatic pitch alone. We expected the null hypothesis for the simplistic system A to be refuted. System B is a multiple-feature system whose feature set was optimized through forward, stepwise feature selection to provide the closest fit to human expectancy judgments in chorale melodies (Manzara et al. 1992). The set of three features selected included features related to tonality and melodic structure with an influence of both rhythmic structure and phrase structure. For this system, Baroni's (1999) proposal that composition and listening involve equivalent grammatical structures is relevant. If the representational structures underlying listening to and composition of music are similar, we would expect grammars that model perceptual processes well to generate satisfactory compositions. Since system B represents a satisfactory model of the cognition of pitch structure in the chorale genre, we expected to retain the null hypothesis for this system.

System C is a multiple-feature system whose feature set was optimized through forward, stepwise feature selection to yield the best pitch prediction performance over the entire chorale data set. The selected set of nine features included features related to pitch, melodic structure, and tonal structure with strong interactions with rhythmic, metric, and phrase structure. In terms of model selection for music generation, highly predictive theories of a musical style, as measured by information content, should generate original and acceptable works in the style (Conklin and Witten 1995). Systems A, B, and C in turn exhibit increasing accuracy in predicting unseen melodies from the data set. On this basis, we expected to retain the null hypothesis for system C.

B. Method

Our judges were sixteen music researchers or students at City University, London; Goldsmiths, University of London; and the Royal College of Music. Seven judges reported high familiarity with the chorale genre, and nine were moderately familiar.

Our data set was a subset of the chorale melodies placed in the soprano voice and harmonized in four parts by Bach. These melodies are characterized by stepwise patterns of conjunct intervallic motion and simple, uniform rhythmic and metric structure. Phrase structure is explicitly notated. Most phrases begin on the tonic, mediant, or dominant and end on the tonic or dominant; the final phrase almost always ends with a cadence to the tonic. Our stimuli were as follows: Seven existing *base* melodies were randomly selected from the set of chorales in the midrange of the distribution of average information content (cross-entropy) values computed by system A. All seven were in common time; six were in major keys, and one was minor; they were 8–14 bars (mean 11.14) and 33–57 events (mean 43.43) long. The base melodies were removed from the training data set. Seven novel melodies were generated by each system via 5,000 iterations of Metropolis sampling using the seven base chorales as initial states. Only pitch was sampled; time and key signatures and rhythmic and phrase structure were left unchanged. Figure 19.2 shows one base chorale melody and the three melodies generated using it; Pearce (2005) gave further examples.

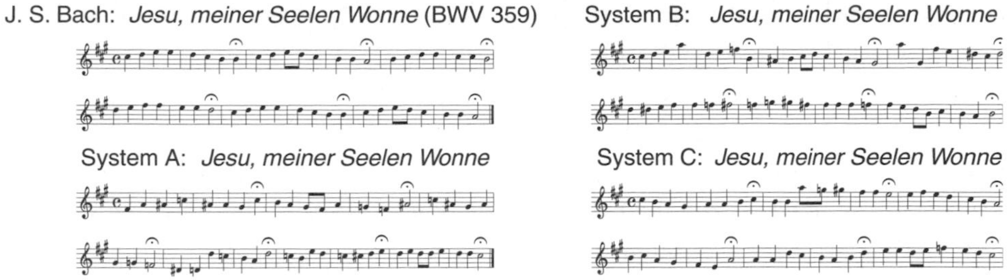

J. S. Bach: *Jesu, meiner Seelen Wonne* (BWV 359)   System B: *Jesu, meiner Seelen Wonne*

System A: *Jesu, meiner Seelen Wonne*   System C: *Jesu, meiner Seelen Wonne*

Figure 19.2 An example of one base chorale melody and the three melodies generated using it.

Our judges supplied their responses individually and received instructions verbally and in writing. We told them they would hear a series of chorale melodies in the style of Lutheran hymns and asked them to listen to each entire melody before answering two questions about it by placing circles on discrete scales in the response booklet. The first question was, "How successful is the composition as a chorale melody?" Judges were advised that their answers should reflect such factors as conformity to important stylistic features, tonal organization, melodic shape and interval structure, and melodic form. Answers to this question were given on a seven-point numerical scale, 1–7, with anchors marked low (1), medium (4), and high (7). To promote an analytic approach to the task, judges were asked to briefly justify their responses to the first question. The second question was, "Do you recognize the melody?" Judges were advised to answer "yes" only if they could specifically identify the composition as one with which they were familiar.

The experiment began with a practice session during which judges heard two human-composed melodies from the same original genre (but not one of those in the test set). These practice trials were intended to set a judgmental standard for the subsequent test session. This departs from the CAT, which encourages judges to rate each stimulus in relation to the others by experiencing all stimuli before making their ratings. However, here, we intended the judges to use their expertise to rate the stimuli against an absolute standard: the body of existing chorale melodies. Judges responded as described for both of the items in the practice block. The experimenter remained in the room for the duration of the practice session, after which the judges were given an opportunity to ask any further questions; the experimenter then left the room before the start of the test session.

In the test session, the twenty-eight melodies were presented to the judges, who responded to the questions. The melodies were presented in random order subject to the constraints that no melodies generated by the same system or based on the same chorale were presented sequentially. A reverse counterbalanced design was used, with eight of the judges listening to the melodies in one such order and the other eight listening to them in the reverse order.

C. Results

We report analyses of the twenty-eight melodies from our test session; we discarded the data from the practice block.

Interjudge Consistency

All but 2 of the 120 pairwise correlations between judges were significant at p 0.05, with a mean coefficient of $r(26) = 65$ $(p < .01)$. Since there was no apparent reason to reject the judges involved in the two nonsignificant correlations, we did not do so. This high consistency warrants averaging the ratings for each stimulus across individual judges in subsequent analyses.

Presentation Order and Prior Familiarity

Two factors that might influence the judges' ratings are the order of presentation of the stimuli and prior familiarity. The correlation between the mean success ratings for judges in the two groups was $r(26) = 91$, $p < .01$, indicating a high degree of consistency across the two orders of presentation and warranting the averaging of responses across the two groups; although the mean success ratings tended to be slightly higher when judges recognized the stimulus, a paired t test revealed no significant difference: $t(6) = 2.07$, $p = .08$.

Influence of Generative System and Base Chorale

Now, we examine the primary question: what is the influence of generative system on the ratings of stylistic success? The mean success ratings for each stimulus, shown in table 19.2, suggest that the original chorale melodies were rated higher

Table 19.2 The mean success ratings for each stimulus and means aggregated by generative system and base chorale

Base	A	B	C	Original	Mean
249	2.56	2.44	5.00	6.44	4.11
238	3.31	2.94	3.19	5.31	3.69
365	2.69	1.69	2.50	6.25	3.28
264	1.75	2.00	2.38	6.00	3.03
44	4.25	4.38	4.00	6.12	4.69
141	3.38	2.12	3.19	5.50	3.55
147	2.38	1.88	1.94	6.50	3.17
Mean	2.90	2.49	3.17	6.02	3.65

Table 19.3 The median, quartiles, and interquartile range (IQR) of the mean success ratings for each generative system

Statistic	A	B	C	Original
Median	2.86	2.57	3.07	5.93
Q1	2.68	2.25	2.68	5.86
Q3	3.29	2.75	3.61	6.29
IQR	0.61	0.50	0.93	0.43

than the computer-generated melodies, while the ratings for the latter showed an influence of base chorale but not of generative system. Melody C249 is an exception, attracting high average ratings of success. We analyzed the data with Friedman's rank sum tests, using within-subject factors for generative system with four levels (original by J. S. Bach and systems A, B, C) and base chorale with seven levels (249, 238, 365, 264, 44, 153, and 147).

We examined the influence of generative system in an unreplicated complete block design using the mean success ratings aggregated for each subject and generative system across the individual base chorales. Summary statistics for these data are shown in table 19.3. The Friedman test revealed a significant within-subject effect of generative system on the mean success ratings: $\chi^2(3) = 33.4$, $p < .01$. We compared the factor levels pairwise using Wilcoxon rank sum tests with Holm's Bonferroni correction for multiple comparisons: the ratings for the original chorale melodies differed significantly from the ratings of melodies generated by all three computational systems ($p < .01$). Furthermore, the mean success ratings for the melodies generated by system B were significantly different from those of the melodies generated by systems A and C ($p < .03$). These results suggest that none of the systems is capable of consistently generating chorale melodies that are rated as equally stylistically successful as those in the data set, and that system B performed especially poorly.

D. Learning from Qualitative Feedback

Objective Features of the Chorales

Next, we aimed to identify how the systems lack compositionally by examining which objective musical features of the stimuli the judges used in making their ratings of stylistic success. To achieve this, we analyzed the stimuli qualitatively and developed a set of corresponding objective descriptors, which we then applied in a series of multiple regression analyses using the rating scheme, averaged across stimuli, as a dependent variable. We now present the descriptive variables, their quantitative coding, and the analysis results.

The chorales generated by our systems are mostly not very stylistically characteristic of the data set, especially in higher-level form. From the judges' qualitative

comments, we identified stylistic constraints describing the stimuli and distinguishing the original melodies. We grouped them into five categories—pitch range,
melodic structure, tonal structure, phrase structure, and rhythmic structure—each
covered by one or more predictor variables.

Pitch Range

The data set melodies span a pitch range of about an octave above and below C,
favoring the center of this range. The generated melodies are constrained to this
range, but some tend toward extreme tessitura. We developed a predictor variable
pitch center to capture this difference, reflecting the absolute distance, in semitones,
of the mean pitch of a melody from the mean pitch of the data set (von Hippel
2000). Another issue is the overall pitch range of the generated chorales. The data
set melodies span an average range of 11.8 semitones. By contrast, several of the
generated melodies span pitch ranges of 16 or 17 semitones, with a mean pitch
range of 13.9 semitones; others have a rather narrow pitch range. We captured these
qualitative considerations in a quantitative predictor variable *pitch range*, representing the absolute distance, in semitones, of the pitch range of a melody from the
mean pitch range of the data set.

Melodic Structure

There are several ways in which the generated melodies did not consistently
reproduce salient melodic features of the original chorales. The most obvious
was a failure to maintain a stepwise pattern of movement. While some generated
melodies were relatively coherent, others contained stylistically uncharacteristic
leaps of an octave or more. Of 9,042 intervals in the data set melodies, only 57
exceed a perfect fifth, and none exceeds an octave. To capture these deviations, we
created a quantitative predictor variable called *interval size*, representing the
number of intervals greater than a perfect octave in a melody. The generated
chorales also contain uncharacteristic discords such as tritones or sevenths. Only
8 of the 9,042 intervals in the data set are tritones or sevenths (or their enharmonic
equivalents). To capture these deviations, we created a quantitative predictor
variable *interval dissonance*, representing the number of dissonant intervals greater
than a perfect fourth in a melody.

Tonal Structure

Since system A operates exclusively over representations of pitch, it is not
surprising that most of its melodies fail to establish a key note and exhibit little
tonal structure. However, we might expect systems B and C to do better. While the
comments of the judges suggest otherwise, they may have arrived at a tonal
interpretation at odds with the intended key of the base chorale. To independently
estimate the perceived tonality of the test melodies, Krumhansl's (1990) key-finding
algorithm, using the revised key profiles of Temperley (1999) was applied to each of
the stimuli. The algorithm assigns the correct keys to all seven original chorale
melodies. While the suggested keys of the melodies generated by system A confirm

that it did not consider tonal constraints, the melodies generated by systems B and C retained the key of their base chorale in two and five cases, respectively. Furthermore, especially in the case of system C, deviations from the base chorale key tended to be to related keys (either in the circle of fifths or through relative and parallel major/minor relationships). This suggests some success on the part of the more sophisticated systems in retaining the tonal characteristics of the base chorales.

Nonetheless, the generated melodies were often unacceptably chromatic, which obscures the tonality. Therefore, we developed a quantitative predictor called *chromaticism*, representing the number of chromatic tones in the algorithm's suggested key.

Phrase Structure

The generated chorales typically failed to reproduce the implied harmonic rhythm of the originals and its characteristically strong relationship to phrase structure. In particular, while some of the generated melodies closed on the tonic, many failed to imply stylistically satisfactory harmonic closure. To capture such effects, we created a variable called *harmonic closure*, which is zero if a melody closes on the tonic of the key assigned by the algorithm and one otherwise. Second, the generated melodies frequently failed to respect thematic repetition and development of melodic material embedded in the phrase structure of the chorales. However, these kinds of repetition and development of melodic material are not represented in the present model. Instead, as a simple indicator of complexity in phrase structure, we created a variable *phrase length*, which is zero if all phrases are of equal length and one otherwise.

Rhythmic Structure

Although the chorale melodies in the data set tend to be rhythmically simple, the judges' comments revealed that they were taking account of rhythmic structure. Therefore, we adapted three further quantitative predictors modeling rhythmic features from Eerola and North's (2000) expectancy-based model of melodic complexity. *Rhythmic density* is the mean number of events per tactus beat. *Rhythmic variability* is the degree of change in note duration (i.e., the standard deviation of the log of the event durations) in a melody. *Syncopation* estimates the degree of syncopation by assigning notes a strength in a metric hierarchy and averaging the strengths of all the notes in a melody; pulses are coded such that lower values are assigned to tones on metrically stronger beats. All three quantities increase the difficulty of perceiving or producing melodies (Eerola and North 2000).

The mean success ratings for each stimulus were regressed on the predictor variables in a multiple regression analysis. Due to significant collinearity between the predictors, in each analysis redundant predictors were removed through

Table 19.4 Multiple regression results for the mean success ratings of each test melody

Predictor	β	Standard error	t	p
(Intercept)	6.4239	0.3912	16.42	.0000
Pitch range	−0.29	0.08	−3.57	<.01
Pitch center	−0.21	0.10	−2.01	<.1
Interval dissonance	−0.70	0.28	−2.54	<.05
Chromaticism	−0.27	0.03	−8.09	<.01
Phrase length	−0.53	0.28	−1.91	<.1

Overall model: $R = .92$, $R_{adj}^2 = .81$, $F(5, 22) = 25.04$, $p < .01$

backward stepwise elimination using the Akaike Information Criterion (Venables and Ripley 2002).

More positive values of the predictors indicate greater deviation from the standards of the data set (for pitch range and center) or increased melodic complexity (for the remaining predictors), so we expected each predictor to show a negative relationship with the success ratings. The results of the multiple regression analysis with the mean success ratings as the dependent variable are shown in table 19.4. The overall model accounts for approximately 85% of the variance in the mean success ratings. Apart from rhythmic structure, at least one predictor from each category made at least a marginally significant contribution to the fit of the model. Coefficients of all the selected predictors are negative, as predicted. Overall, the model indicated that the judged success of a stimulus decreases as its pitch range and center depart from the mean range and center of the data set, with increasing numbers of dissonant intervals and chromatic tones and if it has unequal phrase lengths.

E. Improving the Computational Systems

The constraints identified mainly concern pitch range, intervallic structure, and tonal structure. To examine whether the systems could be improved to respect such constraints, we added several viewpoints to those used in selecting system C, and the resulting models were analyzed in the context of prediction performance.

Regarding tonal structure, it seems likely that the confusion of relative minor and major modes is due to the failure of any of the systems to represent mode, so we added appropriate features to examine this hypothesis. We also hypothesized that the skewed distribution of pitch classes at phrase beginnings and endings could be better modeled by linked features representing scale degrees at phrase beginnings and endings. Finally, on the hypothesis that intervallic structure is constrained by tonal structure, we included a further feature representing an interaction between pitch interval and scale degree.

To examine whether the systems could be improved to respect such constraints, we added the four selected features to the feature selection set used for system C. We ran the same feature selection algorithm over this extended feature space to select feature subsets that improved prediction performance; the results were given by Pearce and Wiggins (2007). In general, the resulting multiple-feature system D showed a great deal of overlap with system C: just three of the nine features present in system C were not selected for inclusion in system D. However, three of the four new features were selected for inclusion in system D. Ultimately, system D exhibited a lower average information content ($H=1.91$) than system C ($H=1.95$) in predicting unseen compositions in the data set. The significance of this difference was confirmed by paired t tests over all 185 chorale melodies: $t(184)=6.00$, $p<.01$.

F. A Melody Generated by System D

We now present preliminary results on system D's capacity to generate stylistically successful chorale melodies. We used it to generate several melodies, as described, with the same base melodies.

Figure 19.3 shows system D's most successful melody, based on chorale 365. Its tonal and melodic structure are much more coherent than system C's melodies. Our multiple regression model, developed to account for the judges' ratings of stylistic success, predicted that this melody would receive a rating of 6.4 on a 7-point scale of success as a chorale melody. While this result is positive, other melodies were less successful; system D must be analyzed using our method to examine its ability to compose stylistically successful melodies *consistently*.

G. Discussion and Conclusions of the Experiment

Our statistical finite-context grammars did not meet the computational demands of chorale melody composition, regardless of the representational primitives used. Since we attempted to address the limitations of previous context-modeling approaches to generating music, we might conclude that more powerful grammars are needed for this task. However, other approaches are

System D: *Jesu, meiner Seelen Wonne*

Figure 19.3 Melody generated by system D based on the same chorale as fig. 19.2.

possible. Further analysis of the capacities of finite-context modeling systems may prove fruitful; future research should use the methodology developed here to analyze system D and identify and correct its weaknesses. The MCMC generation algorithm may be responsible for failure rather than the limitation of the models to finite-context representations of melodic structure; more structured generation strategies, such as pattern-based sampling techniques, may be able to conserve phrase-level regularity and repetition in ways that our systems were not.

Our evaluation method also warrants discussion. The adapted CAT yielded insightful results for ratings of stylistic success even though the judges were encouraged to rate the stimuli according to an absolute standard (cf. Amabile 1996). However, the results suggest possible improvements: first, avoid any possibility of method artifacts by randomizing the presentation order of both test and practice items for each judge and the order in which rating scales are presented; second, the judges' comments sometimes reflected aesthetic judgments, so they should also give ratings of aesthetic appeal to delineate subjective dimensions of the product domain in the assessment (Amabile 1996); and third, although influence of prior familiarity with the test items was ambiguous, bias resulting from recognition should be avoided.

Our results suggest that the task of composing a stylistically successful chorale melody presents significant challenges as a first step in modeling cognitive processes in composition. Nonetheless, our evaluation method proved fruitful in examining the generated melodies in the context of existing pieces in the style. It facilitated empirical examination of specific hypotheses about the models through detailed comparison of the generated and original melodies on several dimensions. It also permitted examination of objective features of the melodies that influenced the ratings and subsequent identification of weaknesses in the systems and directions for improving them. This practically demonstrates the utility of analysis by synthesis for evaluating cognitive models of composition—if it is combined with an empirical methodology for evaluation such as that developed here.

4. CONCLUSION

In this chapter, our aim has been to connect music cognition and creativity conceptually and computationally by covering the issues that arise when we try to model human cognition and behavior in these domains. We reviewed the literature on cognitive modeling and paid special attention to existing computational cognitive models of perception and composition. We also summarized an evaluation methodology (CAT) for systems that perform creative tasks. This methodology chimes well with the CSF, which distinguishes a set of rules R according to which a creative product can be constructed, a rule set E which is used for evaluation of creative output, and a set of rules T which can be used to traverse R.

The computational cognitive model that we have examined in some detail is based on an unsupervised machine-learning paradigm and was originally constructed as a general model of human melodic learning. When applied to the prediction of melodic expectation, the basic model showed performance superior to other models specifically designed to predict melodic expectation. When extended to the further task of melody segmentation, the resulting meta-model's performance was comparable with specialist segmentation models. These results point to the fact that the model seemed to capture a more general, underlying perceptual mechanism; we suggest, therefore, and because it is based on unsupervised machine learning, that it may be an explanatory model for both these cognitive phenomena at this level of abstract representation.

Finally, we applied the pitch expectation model to the creative task of melody composition and evaluated the generated melodies in a user study applying a variant of the CAT evaluation methodology. Despite its failure to compose melodies indistinguishable from original melodies of the target style consistently, the system produced a number of acceptable melodies. We argue that the percentage of "good melodies" among its output is less important than the fact that any acceptable melodies were produced by an unsupervised learning model that lacked any predefined knowledge of musical structure but gained its knowledge exclusively through unsupervised learning on a training set. This means that we cannot be accused of showing the model how to appear to be creative and makes it applicable to any musical style or corpus.

We believe this to be the first time that an empirically validated computational cognitive model based on unsupervised machine learning has been used as the defining context (R) for a creative system, and it is therefore satisfactory that we have any good results at all, especially given that we have made no attempt to model T or E in a realistic way. This work is only a beginning, but taken together, the results of the perceptual modeling and the melody production task suggest that the methods and approach presented here constitute a productive, general framework for the study of computational creativity. It provides clear directions for the future, which we expect to generate interesting empirical and theoretical developments in our ongoing research.

NOTES

1. And, we do mean "relatively"—it is absolutely clear that this is an oversimplification. However, one has to start somewhere.

2. Often, therefore, we are able to learn more about brain operation from pathological cases (e.g., brain-damaged patients) than from normal ones.

3. Improvisation may be seen as a special case of composition in which the composer is the performer and is subject to extra constraints of immediacy and fluency (Sloboda 1985).

4. We do not propose Metropolis sampling as a cognitive model of melodic comparison but use it merely as a means of generating melodies that reflect the internal state of knowledge and capacities of the trained model.

BIBLIOGRAPHY

Amabile, T. M. 1996. *Creativity in Context.* Boulder, CO: Westview Press.

Ames, C., and M. Domino. 1992. Cybernetic Composer: An overview. In *Understanding Music with AI: Perspectives on Music Cognition,* ed. M. Balaban, K. Ebcioğlu and O. Laske. Cambridge: MIT Press, pp. 186–205.

Baroni, M. 1999. Musical grammar and the cognitive processes of composition. *Musicæ Scientiæ* 3(1): 3–19.

Baroni, M., R. Dalmonte, and C. Jacoboni. 1992. Theory and analysis of European melody. In *Computer Representations and Models in Music,* ed. A. Marsden and A. Pople. London: Academic Press, pp. 187–206.

Bharucha, J. J. 1987. Music cognition and perceptual facilitation: A connectionist framework. *Music Perception* 5(1): 1–30.

Bharucha, J. J., and K. Stoeckig. 1986. Reaction time and musical expectancy: Priming of chords. *Journal of Experimental Psychology: Human Perception and Performance* 12(4): 403–410.

Bharucha, J. J., and K. Stoeckig. 1987. Priming of chords: Spreading activation or overlapping frequency spectra? *Perception and Psychophysics* 41(6): 519–524.

Boden, M. 1998. Creativity and artificial intelligence. *Journal of Artificial Intelligence* 103(2): 347–356.

Boden, M. 2003. *The Creative Mind: Myths and Mechanisms.* London: Routledge.

Boltz, M. G., and M. R. Jones. 1986. Does rule recursion make melodies easier to reproduce? If not, what does? *Cognitive Psychology* 18(4): 389–431.

Bown, O., and G. A. Wiggins. 2009. From maladaptation to competition to cooperation in the evolution of musical behaviour. *Musicae Scientiae.* Special issue on evolution of music.

Bregman, A. S. 1990. *Auditory Scene Analysis.* Cambridge: MIT Press.

Brent, M. R. 1999. An efficient, probabilistically sound algorithm for segmentation and word discovery. *Machine Learning* 34(1–3): 71–105.

Cambouropoulos, E. 1996. A formal theory for the discovery of local boundaries in a melodic surface. In *Proceedings of the III Journées d'Informatique Musicale,* Caen, France.

Cambouropoulos, E. 2001. The local boundary detection model (LBDM) and its application in the study of expressive timing. In *Proceedings of the International Computer Music Conference.* San Francisco: ICMA, pp. 17–22.

Cohen, P. R., N. Adams, and B. Heeringa. 2007. Voting experts: An unsupervised algorithm for segmenting sequences. *Intelligent Data Analysis* 11(6): 607–625.

Conklin, D. 2002. Representation and discovery of vertical patterns in music. In *Proceedings of the Second International Conference of Music and Artificial Intelligence, Vol. 2445,*

Lecture Notes in Computer Science, ed. C. Anagnostopoulou, M. Ferrand, and A. Smaill. Berlin: Springer, pp. 32–42.

Conklin, D. 2003. Music generation from statistical models. In *Proceedings of the AISB 2003 Symposium on Artificial Intelligence and Creativity in the Arts and Sciences*, Brighton, UK: SSAISB, pp. 30–35.

Conklin, D., and I. H. Witten. 1995. Multiple viewpoint systems for music prediction. *Journal of New Music Research*, 24: 51–73.

Cope, D. 2005. *Computer Models of Musical Creativity*. Cambridge: MIT Press.

Cross, I. 2007. Music and cognitive evolution. In *Handbook of Evolutionary Psychology*, ed. R. Dunbar and L. Barrett. Oxford: Oxford University Press, pp. 649–667.

Cuddy, L. L., and C. A. Lunny. 1995. Expectancies generated by melodic intervals: Perceptual judgements of continuity. *Perception and Psychophysics* 57: 451–462.

Cutting, J. E., N. Bruno, N. P. Brady, and C. Moore. 1992. Selectivity, scope, and simplicity of models: A lesson from fitting judgements of perceived depth. *Journal of Experimental Psychology: General* 121(3): 364–381.

Deliège, I. 1987. Grouping conditions in listening to music: An approach to Lerdahl and Jackendoff's grouping preference rules. *Music Perception* 4(4): 325–360.

Deliège, I., and G. A. Wiggins. 2006. *Musical Creativity: Current Research in Theory and Practice*. Hove, UK: Psychology Press.

Deutsch, D. 1980. The processing of structured and unstructured tonal sequences. *Perception and Psychophysics* 28(5): 381–389.

Deutsch, D., and J. Feroe. 1981. The internal representation of pitch sequences in tonal music. *Psychological Review* 88(6): 503–522.

Ebcioğlu, K. 1988. An expert system for harmonizing four-part chorales. *Computer Music Journal* 12(3): 43–51.

Eerola, T., and A. C. North. 2000. Expectancy-based model of melodic complexity. In *Proceedings of the Sixth International Conference on Music Perception and Cognition*, ed. C. Woods, G. Luck, R. Brochard, F. Seddon, and J. A. Sloboda. Keele, UK: Keele University.

Elman, J. L. 1990. Finding structure in time. *Cognitive Science* 14: 179–211.

Hall, M., and L. Smith. 1996. A computer model of blues music and its evaluation. *Journal of the Acoustical Society of America*, 100(2): 1163–1167.

Hiller, L., and L. Isaacson. 1959. *Experimental Music*. New York: McGraw-Hill.

Honing, H. 2006. Computational modeling of music cognition: A case study on model selection. *Music Perception* 23(5): 365–376.

Huron, D. 2001. Tone and voice: A derivation of the rules of voice-leading from perceptual principles. *Music Perception* 19(1): 1–64.

Huron, D. 2006. *Sweet Anticipation: Music and the Psychology of Expectation*. Cambridge: Bradford Books/MIT Press.

Jackendoff, R. 1987. *Consciousness and the Computational Mind*. Cambridge: MIT Press.

Johnson-Laird, P. N. 1991. Jazz improvisation: A theory at the computational level. In *Representing Musical Structure*, ed. P. Howell, R. West, and I. Cross. London: Academic Press, pp. 291–325.

Jurafsky, D., and J. H. Martin. 2000. *Speech and Language Processing: An Introduction to Natural Language Processing, Computational Linguistics, and Speech Recognition*. Upper Saddle River, NJ: Prentice Hall.

Justus, T., and J. J. Hutsler. 2005. Fundamental issues in the evolutionary psychology of music: Assessing innateness and domain specificity. *Music Perception* 23(1): 1–27.

Koestler, A. 1964. *The Act of Creation*. London: Hutchinson.

Krumhansl, C. L. 1990. *Cognitive Foundations of Musical Pitch*. Oxford: Oxford University Press.

Krumhansl, C. L. 1995a. Effects of musical context on similarity and expectancy. *Systematische Musikwissenschaft* 3(2): 211–250.

Krumhansl, C. L. 1995b. Music psychology and music theory: Problems and prospects. *Music Theory Spectrum* 17: 53–90.

Krumhansl, C. L., P. Toiviainen, T. Eerola, T. Järvinen, and J. Louhivuori. 2000. Cross-cultural music cognition: Cognitive methodology applied to North Sami yoiks. *Cognition* 76(1): 13–58.

Large, E. W., C. Palmer, and J. B. Pollack. 1995. Reduced memory representations for music. *Cognitive Science* 19(1): 53–96.

Lerdahl, F. 1988. Cognitive constraints on compositional systems. In *Generative Processes in Music: The Psychology of Performance, Improvisation and Composition*, ed. J. A. Sloboda. Oxford: Clarendon Press, pp. 231–259.

Lerdahl, F., and R. Jackendoff. 1983. *A Generative Theory of Tonal Music*. Cambridge: MIT Press.

MacKay, D. J. C. 1998. Introduction to Monte Carlo methods. In *Learning in Graphical Models*, NATO Science Series, ed. M. I. Jordan. Dordrecht, the Netherlands: Kluwer Academic Press, pp. 175–204.

Manning, C. D., and H. Schütze. 1999. *Foundations of Statistical Natural Language Processing*. Cambridge: MIT Press.

Manzara, L. C., I. H. Witten, and M. James. 1992. On the entropy of music: An experiment with Bach chorale melodies. *Leonardo* 2(1): 81–88.

Marr, D. 1982. *Vision*. San Francisco: Freeman.

Marsden, A. 2000. *Representing Musical Time: A Temporal-Logic Approach*. Lisse: Swets and Zeitlinger.

McClamrock, R. 1991. Marr's three levels: A re-evaluation. *Minds and Machines* 1: 185–196.

Meredith, D. 2006. The ps13 pitch spelling algorithm. *Journal of New Music Research* 35(2): 121–159.

Meyer, L. B. 1957. Meaning in music and information theory. *Journal of Aesthetics and Art Criticism* 15(4): 412–424.

Mithen, S. J. 2006. *The Singing Neanderthals: The Origins of Music, Language, Mind, and Body*. Cambridge: Harvard University Press.

Müllensiefen, D., M. T. Pearce, and G. A. Wiggins. 2008. Melodic segmentation: A new method and a framework for model comparison. In *Proceedings of ISMIR 2008*. http://www.ismir.net, accessed March 17, 2009.

Narmour, E. 1990. *The Analysis and Cognition of Basic Melodic Structures: The Implication-Realisation Model*. Chicago: University of Chicago Press.

Narmour, E. 1992. *The Analysis and Cognition of Melodic Complexity*. Chicago: University of Chicago Press.

Palmer, C., and C. L. Krumhansl. 1990. Mental representations for musical metre. *Journal of Experimental Psychology: Human Perception and Performance* 16(4): 728–741.

Pearce, M. T. 2005. "The construction and evaluation of statistical models of melodic structure in music perception and composition." Ph.D. thesis, City University, London.

Pearce, M. T., D. Conklin, and G. A. Wiggins. 2005. Methods for combining statistical models of music. In *Computer Music Modelling and Retrieval*, ed. U. K. Wiil. Heidelberg: Springer-Verlag, pp. 295–312.

Pearce, M. T., D. Meredith, and G. A. Wiggins. 2002. Motivations and methodologies for automation of the compositional process. *Musicae Scientiae* 6(2): 119–147.

Pearce, M. T., D. Müllensiefen, D. Lewis, and C. S. Rhodes. 2007. *David Temperley, Music and Probability*. Cambridge: MIT Press. *Empirical Musicology Review* 2(4): 155–163.

Pearce, M. T., and G. A. Wiggins. 2004. Improved methods for statistical modelling of monophonic music. *Journal of New Music Research* 33(4): 367–385.

Pearce, M. T., and G. A. Wiggins. 2006. Expectation in melody: The influence of context and learning. *Music Perception* 23(5): 377–406.

Pearce, M. T., and G. A. Wiggins. 2007. Evaluating cognitive models of musical composition. In *Proceedings of the 4th International Joint Workshop on Computational Creativity*, ed. A. Cardoso and G. A. Wiggins. http://www.doc.gold.ac.uk/~mas02gw/isms/CC07/, accessed March 17, 2009.

Pollack, J. B. 1990. Recursive distributed representations. *Artificial Intelligence* 46(1): 77–105.

Ponsford, D., G. A. Wiggins, and C. S. Mellish. 1999. Statistical learning of harmonic movement. *Journal of New Music Research* 28(2): 150–177.

Potter, K., G. A. Wiggins, and M. T. Pearce. 2007. Towards greater objectivity in music theory: Information-dynamic analysis of minimalist music. *Musicae Scientiae* 11(2): 295–324.

Rabiner, L. R. 1989. A tutorial on Hidden Markov Models and selected applications in speech recognition. *Proceedings of the IEEE* 77(2): 257–285.

Ritchie, G. 2007. Some empirical criteria for attributing creativity to a computer program. *Minds and Machines* 17(1): 67–99.

Robertson, J., A. de Quincey, T. Stapleford, and G. A. Wiggins. 1998. Real-time music generation for a virtual environment. In *Proceedings of the ECAI'98 Workshop on AI/Alife and Entertainment*, ed. F. Nack. Brighton, UK.

Rutherford, J., and G. A. Wiggins. 2002. An experiment in the automatic creation of music which has specific emotional content. In *Proceedings of the 2002 International Conference on Music Perception and Cognition*. AMPS and Causal Productions, Sydney, Australia.

Saffran, J. R. 2003. Absolute pitch in infancy and adulthood: The role of tonal structure. *Developmental Science* 6(1): 37–49.

Saffran, J. R., and G. J. Griepentrog. 2001. Absolute pitch in infant auditory learning: Evidence for developmental reorganization. *Developmental Psychology* 37(1): 74–85.

Saffran, J. R., E. K. Johnson, R. N. Aslin, and E. L. Newport. 1990. Statistical learning of tone sequences by human infants and adults. *Cognition* 70: 27–52.

Schaffrath, H. 1995. The Essen folksong collection. Database containing 6,255 folksong transcriptions in the Kern format and a 34-page research guide [computer database], ed. D. Huron. Menlo Park, CA: CCARH.

Schellenberg, E. G. 1996. Expectancy in melody: Tests of the implication-realisation model. *Cognition* 58(1): 75–125.

Schellenberg, E. G. 1997. Simplifying the implication-realisation model of melodic expectancy. *Music Perception* 14(3): 295–318.

Shannon, C. E. 1948. A mathematical theory of communication. *Bell System Technical Journal* 27(3): 379–423, 623–656.

Simon, H. A., and R. K. Sumner. 1968. Pattern in music. In *Formal Representation of Human Judgement*, ed. B. Kleinmuntz. New York: Wiley, pp. 219–250.

Sloboda, J. 1985. *The Musical Mind: The Cognitive Psychology of Music*. Oxford: Oxford Science Press.

Temperley, D. 1999. What's key for key? The Krumhansl-Schmuckler key-finding algorithm reconsidered. *Music Perception* 17(1): 65–100.

Temperley, D. 2001. *The Cognition of Basic Musical Structures*. Cambridge: MIT Press.

Temperley, D. 2003. Communicative pressure and the evolution of musical styles. *Music Perception* 21(3): 313–337.

Temperley, D. 2007. *Music and Probability.* Cambridge: MIT Press.

Thompson, W. F., L. L. Cuddy, and C. Plaus. 1997. Expectancies generated by melodic intervals: Evaluation of principles of melodic implication in a melody-completion task. *Perception and Psychophysics* 59(7): 1069–1076.

Triviño-Rodriguez, J. L., and R. Morales-Bueno. 2001. Using multi-attribute prediction suffix graphs to predict and generate music. *Computer Music Journal* 25(3): 62–79.

Venables, W. N., and B. D. Ripley. 2002. *Modern Applied Statistics with S.* New York: Springer.

von Hippel, P. T. 2000. Redefining pitch proximity: Tessitura and mobility as constraints on melodic intervals. *Music Perception* 17(3): 315–327.

Wallas, G. 1926. *The Art of Thought.* New York: Harcourt Brace.

Wiggins, G. A. 2006a. A preliminary framework for description, analysis and comparison of creative systems. *Journal of Knowledge Based Systems* 19(7): 449–458.

Wiggins, G. A. 2006b. Searching for computational creativity. *New Generation Computing* 24(3): 209–222.

Wiggins, G. A. 2007. Models of musical similarity. *Musicae Scientiae, Discussion Forum 4a,* pp. 315–337.

Wiggins, G. A., E. Miranda, A. Smaill, and M. Harris. 1993. A framework for the evaluation of music representation systems. *Computer Music Journal* 17(3): 31–42. Machine Tongues series no. 17; also Edinburgh, DAI Research Paper no. 658.

CHAPTER 20

....

SOUNDSPOTTING: A NEW KIND OF PROCESS?

....

MICHAEL CASEY

SOUNDSPOTTING is a new approach to creating musical streams by selecting and concatenating source segments from a large audio database using methods from music information retrieval. The soundspotting process computes a similarity score between a target audio segment and all the available segments in the source database and selects the closest-matching source to concatenate to the audio output stream forming a real-time response to the target. Examples of target signals are solo instruments, a synthetic signal generated by an algorithm such as frequency modulation (FM), or a previous output of the soundspotting process, thus yielding an audio information feedback circuit. Soundspotting enhances the techniques of sampling, plunderphonics, remixing, and mashups by adding automatic audio organization and an external driving target signal. In addition, soundspotting opens up new possibilities for experimental music processes extending the gradual processes of Steve Reich and others by admitting control from external audio sources and deterministic ordering and selection criteria. In this chapter, we explore the techniques, technologies, and musical possibilities for soundspotting and show how it extends the canon of existing computer music methods.

Figure 20.1 outlines the main components of a soundspotting system. The first step is for the user to select a database of source audio material. The system extracts musical features from the source audio database, and these features are stored in a second memory buffer. The user then introduces a target signal, and the soundspotting system extracts musical features from the target and matches these

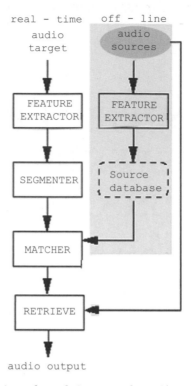

Figure 20.1 Overview of a real-time soundspotting system. The system preanalyzes a set of audio sources, extracting musical features; the features are stored in a source database. At performance time, a live audio target signal has the same musical features extracted; they are segmented into musical events that are matched against the source database. The closest-matching source audio is retrieved and concatenated to an audio output stream.

features against the memory buffer of musical features extracted from the source database. The matching process computes a distance score from the target features to each segment of database features. The system then selects the closest-matching segment, retrieves the corresponding source audio from the source memory buffer, and concatenates it to the output stream. A real-time soundspotting system repeats this matching process continuously and thus forms an output stream of source audio material organized by its proximity to the target audio signal.

The challenge in designing a soundspotting system is selecting a matching algorithm that computes similarity such that the result is meaningful to human hearing; that is, the algorithm must compute *perceptual similarity*. Consider, for example, a process for which the matching criterion is not based on perceptual similarity but instead counts the number of times the digit 3 occurs in the signal's digital waveform representation. Finding source segments whose 3 count is closest to the target will be perceptually indistinguishable from a process that uses random selection. Using suitable perceptual criteria for matching is therefore essential for achieving a musically meaningful output from the soundspotting process.

A good soundspotting system matches the musical content of the target, such as the melody line, chords, rhythm, or timbre, while preserving the acoustic identity, or recognizability, of the source, such as "Abba" or "Beethoven's *Fifth*" or "the voice of Marilyn Monroe." This goal of dual identity does not come about easily; it requires musical sensitivity to the sonic materials and to the perceptual parameters of soundspotting. These constraints describe a *well-formed* soundspotting system; the musical identity of the target signal and the acoustic identity of the source signal are preserved. Not all soundspotting systems are well formed, and they sometimes produce results that are perceptually meaningless or seemingly random despite the best efforts of the programmer.

One of the most important perceptual criteria is the size of audio segment or event granularity that a soundspotting system uses for matching and concatenation. The segments should be of sufficient length that they preserve the acoustic identity of the source while matching the musical identity of the target. Consider, for example, a system that matches snippets of an audio waveform in 0.01-s units; there is not enough information in the audio grain of this length to recognize the source audio as coming from a specific source. At this scale, soundspotting simply *reconstructs* the target signal by splicing small pieces of waveforms together. The shorter the grains, the more exact the reconstruction of the target waveform and the less the identity of the source perceived. Given enough source material to draw from, the process will succeed in very closely approximating the target waveform, possibly exactly; in doing so, it achieves effectively nothing by a circuitous route. To facilitate recognition of the identity of the source, it must be segmented into sufficient length, say 0.25 s or greater. However, longer segments reduce the probability of a close musical match to the target signal due to the increased degrees of freedom. Conversely, employing larger source databases increases the probability of good matches; greater segment choice yields more close matches. Soundspotting therefore works best when the source database is large, consisting of many hundreds of thousands of segments that are each at least a quarter second long.

A final important feature of successful soundspotting is that, for a given source and target, the result is deterministic, hence predictable. That is, the system behaves in predictable ways vis-à-vis human hearing. Soundspotting therefore yields a musical instrument, the control of which can be learned by a musician through practice. It is our contention that these criteria of human perceptual sensitivity and determinism are essential for building successful computer music instruments.

1. A Brief History of Soundspotting

The first systems that organized sound segments by relating them to a target signal were the non-real-time systems Caterpillar, Musaicing, and the first SoundSpotter system. The Caterpillar system (Schwarz 2000) is based on pitch-synchronous overlap-add (PSOLA) speech synthesis that concatenates prerecorded speech phonemes, with units selected by constraint satisfaction for both spectral match quality using audio features and for temporal well-formedness of the selected units. Also known as *concatenative speech synthesis*, the goal in PSOLA is to synthesize natural-sounding speech from prerecorded phonetic units given a target of, say, a voice sample or a text string. Caterpillar, then, is a musical version of PSOLA: here, the source database consists of a segmented collection of musical instrument notes sampled over a range of timbres, pitches, and intensities. The system is driven by a set of symbols (notes) or an artificial audio source, say a melody line performed on a standard wavetable music synthesizer. Caterpillar assembles melodic sequences using the well-formedness constraints of concatenative synthesis. The usual application for such systems is to improve the quality of musical instrument synthesis over that of standard wavetable techniques such as those described in the work of Mathews et al. (1969) that are currently widely deployed for music synthesis.

Musaicing (Zils and Pachet 2001) performed audio matching on databases of audio, again using a target signal. The matching was performed off-line due to the large amount of computation required for the algorithms employed. The idea behind the system was to produce the audio analog to the photo mosaic phenomenon that was prevalent as a form of visual collage in the 1990s and was seen in many corporate advertising campaigns (Silvers and Hawley 1997). Unlike Caterpillar, Musaicing did not employ temporal constraints; therefore, the well-formedness of the sequence of matched outputs was left somewhat to chance. MatConcat (Sturm 2004) was a similar off-line system for constructing an audio mosaic by globally constraining the quality of the matching. In this case, the system used global constraints to choose the best path through the source material.

SoundSpotter (Casey 2002) was developed at Mitsubishi Electric Research Laboratories (MERL) in 2001 as a system for fast retrieval of audio segments by similarity using the MPEG7 (Moving Pictures Experts Group 7) audio descriptor set that was then in development by an international team of researchers (Peeters 2000, Casey 2001, Quackenbush and Lindsay 2002). The MPEG7 international standard developed numerous content-based descriptors for audio, images, and video to support multimedia search applications. The first SoundSpotter system, like Musaicing and Caterpillar, was a non-real-time system; instead, it used an OpenGL graphical user interface that supported user selection of musical segments and sported a search button to retrieve lists of closest-matching segments in order of similarity to the user's query. MERL's SoundSpotter system was the first to employ matching on sequences of audio features. This ensured that matched segments were well formed as coherent temporal musical event sequences, and that the matching was temporally sensitive to the specific rhythmic and gestural content of the query. In the early versions of SoundSpotter, this was achieved by converting audio features to strings of discrete state symbols using a hidden Markov model (Casey 2001, 2002, 2005). However, by 2003, SoundSpotter's search button and user query selection of musical segments had been replaced by a live audio input that was matched continuously and in real time, and the sequence-based matching was performed directly on the audio features themselves rather than employing a hidden Markov model to generate discrete state symbols. This was one of the first real-time soundspotting systems, and it was made an open source software project in 2004 to encourage development among a community of musicians and computer music software experts. Sound-Spotter is currently available via SourceForge (http://sourceforge.net/) open source software repository (Casey 2004).

A number of other real-time systems appeared in the years 2002 and 2003 in the research literature for music information retrieval and computer music performance systems. These included MoSievius (Lazier and Cook 2003), which performed matching on individual spectral frames; a similar system was employed for the French performance *La Légende des siècles* by Olivier Pasquet (Schwarz 2006), also performing matching directly on spectral frames using a fast Fourier transform (FFT). These systems employed individual frame matching and had no mechanism for constrained matching in time; therefore, the matching is based only on the instantaneous similarity between each target frame and a frame in the source database. There are two musical problems with instantaneous matching; the first is that the *grain* size of matched segment has to be small to produce close matches, therefore reducing the *identity* of the source. Second, there is no concatenation quality; grains from different sources are assembled consecutively because of their instantaneous closeness to the target, but their juxtaposition does not offer a coherent-sounding result because of the dislocation from their source sequence.

Granuloop (Xiang 2002) was a percussive soundspotting system for applications to rhythm tracks that worked by beat tracking the source database and target signal and matching the interbeat intervals on beat boundaries. Beat replacement was also presented by Casey (2003) as a studio-based application for SoundSpotter, enabling a rhythm track to be reorchestrated by matching an existing target rhythm track to a database of percussion sounds.

Three similar systems—ScrambledHackz (Koenig 2006), Remix-TV (Casey and Grierson 2007), and AudioVisual Matching (Collins 2007)—extended the application of soundspotting to the video domain. In the first two systems, the source material for soundspotting is the audio track extracted from video; either a collection of films, as in the case of Remix-TV, or a collection of talking head videos such as interviews with Michael Jackson, as in the case of ScrambledHackz. The earlier work of John Oswald, *Plunderphonics*, which uses snippets from a decade of pop songs, selected and assembled by hand, also featured the visual image of Michael Jackson, but in this case it was his head superimposed on the image of a naked woman as the cover art for the album. The image brought notoriety to the *Plunderphonic* project when a cease-and-desist order was issued by Jackson's label, Sony Music (Oswald 1985). The third system uses combined audiovisual features to perform the matching (Smaragdis and Casey 2003); here, the matching is both visually and acoustically constrained so that the input must contain features from both modalities. The addition of constraints from the visual domain makes it harder to generate acoustic matches, so may limit the purely musical effectiveness of soundspotting.

Relationship to Process Music

Soundspotting affords a space of musical possibilities by varying the constituent audio sources, target signals, and soundspotting parameters. The canonical sound-spotting scenario is to employ a fixed set of audio materials, such as a collection of archival recordings, and to enlist a musician to perform a score, or to improvise, yielding the target signal; the musical feedback between the performer's live input and the instantaneous response from matching to the source material creates the soundspotting counterpoint. A different process is created when the source materials consist of the target signal itself, say a live performance of a fixed score, which is accumulated into a source memory buffer. Here, the target signal is matched to its own history, thus creating an *associative memory canon*. It is clear that the method of feeding the target through a self-referencing memory process produces a deterministic output, and it is this process that generates the ensuing canon without further intervention from a composer. Careful composition or selection of target materials leads to the construction of a counterpoint that is relational at each time instant to the history of a performance. A third example of a soundspotting process scans the source memory in order of similarity, or dissimilarity, from an initial target segment, thus creating a *musical sort*—an example of which is sorting the thematic material of Beethoven's *Fifth Symphony* in order of dissimilarity from the opening motif.

Such musical sorting describes a new type of musical process, one that is defined by a perceptual similarity algorithm. The process is deterministic and governed by choice of initial target segment. Let us compare this type of musical process to the early minimalist experimental works of Steve Reich and Terry Riley. In his early works, Reich created music as an emergent property of a deterministic process: "Come Out" (1964), "It's Gonna Rain" (1965), "Piano Phase" (1965), and "Violin Phase" (1965) consisted of a priori source material to which a process was applied to generate a deterministic "temporal object" (Nyman 1974). Processes were chosen specific to the source materials so that they extracted the latent musicality of the source. The combination of process and source generated, autonomously, the musical work. As Reich stated: "Once the process is set up and loaded it runs by itself" (1968). These works required a source memory, either encoded in score form for a musician to play or as sounds on magnetic tape, and a process such as two or more instrumentalists performing a score at slightly different speeds or two tape machines playing the same tape at slightly different speeds. Reich explored a range of processes that were concerned with accessing a fixed-source memory according to different rules, with the process itself both defining and becoming a part of the music. In soundspotting, the addition of an external musical source as a target, coupled with audio matching, results in a new class of musical process: a *deterministic associative memory process*.

Similarly, Riley's "In C" describes a nondeterministic process that results in a recognizable work but with musicians making choices in performance. The work is, in this respect, malleable, offering a great many possible outcomes from a single score. "In C" consists of a sequence of musical cells that are repeated by each performer at their preference. While the succession of cells is deterministic, the number of repetitions per cell is left for the performer to choose. Thus, when performed by an ensemble, the work forms a pyramid structure as the parallel cells multiply until the performers finally converge on the last cell to end the performance. An alternate version of "In C" is a soundspotting process that we can call "In Sort Order" (Casey 2003); here, we take the cells as performed by a group of musicians, and we order them according to their similarity or dissimilarity to the initial cell. The sorting of a performance of "In C" creates a meta-process that produces an entirely different musical structure out of the work's acoustic materials.

For the contemporary computer musician critically assessing the impact of these early works, the question arises regarding whether this music bears any relation to the computational practices that are prevalent in the 21st century. It can be argued that, for all the complexity of object-oriented code, real-time graphical programming languages, real-time signal-processing software, direct manipulation interface technologies, and ever-decreasing hardware size, there are inherited legacies contained in our approaches to computer musics. One of the most commonly used legacies is variable-rate digital audio wavetable playback. This is the digital equivalent of speeding up or slowing down the tape transport on a reel-to-reel player. So, in Reich's early experiments, the tape was doing nothing less than the most common of computational transforms used in today's computer music: wavetable playback via band-limited resampling (Mathews et al. 1969).

It is convenient for the purposes of creating a lineage of process music to define the early process musics of Reich, Riley, and others as deterministic memory processes. The materials for the music consist of a sequence of memory that can be played in serial fashion. In Reich's work "Come Out," the memory was accessed both serially and concurrently by a number of different voices, forming a *Canon* (Reich 1968), with each voice accessing the memory at a different speed. By allowing the operation of splicing, the memory is made randomly accessible; this was the process employed in "It's Gonna Rain," in which short sections of the memory were looped, but the overall memory process was accessed serially by splicing into the tape at progressively increasing lengths. In these works, the source material is locked into a piece of tape or as a sequence of pitches to be performed. The operation of the process is sequential, acting on the source material to generate the audible result; the process itself is completely in control of the result.

The deterministic nature of the processes makes these works conceptual time objects from which all performances of the works are instances that bring variation and nuance. Such nondeterministic aspects of the realization of a process create a musical tension between the objective nature of a process and the subjective experience of a performance. The impact of Reich's early works can be felt in the music of today, especially in the lingering tail of the ambient music movement that started with the "Discrete Music" of Brian Eno, whose experiences of Reich's early works were a direct influence on his own deterministic musical processes (Eno 1975, 1999).

The analogy between tape manipulations and computation can be taken further to the point at which the modern computer *is itself* a manifestation of a tape transform; a program is a series of instructions on the tape to be read, along with data, from specific locations on the tape; and information written back to the tape after a simple operation is applied to the data by controlling a tape transport to seek to a specified location. This set of operations is the basis of the *Turing Machine*, which is the origin of modern computation (Turing 1936). Thus, process music on tape is in the direct lineage to process music involving computers; there are no substantial differences in these underlying processes, and the early works mentioned are as much examples of computational processes as they are of tape music processes.

There are many possible arrangements of the constituents of soundspotting; it is hoped that the following sections provide an insight into the potentialities, and that they encourage further exploration. In the remainder of this chapter, we first describe a number of soundspotting systems that have been developed over the last few years. This is followed by a detailed description of one open source software system called SoundSpotter, giving details of its use and its implementation. Finally, we describe a series of recent works and performances by composers, instrumentalists, and video artists that have used SoundSpotter for new music works.

2. SoundSpotter: A Soundspotting Implementation

SoundSpotter is an open source software system for soundspotting first developed in 2003 and steadily enhanced by the contributions and suggestions of a community of composers, musicians, and software developers engaged in its use. The system was designed to meet a set of requirements for real-time audio matching: given an input segment, the time to perform the necessary computation for matching cannot exceed 10 ms, that is, a perceptible delay, so efficient algorithms and implementations are required, especially for matching to large source audio databases. Due to the low latency requirement, a musical feedback loop is admitted between the performer and the process so that the performer becomes, seamlessly, part of the process; as such, the system design and the employment of efficient algorithms for feature extraction and audio sequence matching make SoundSpotter a musical instrument.

SoundSpotter implements real-time targeted matching of its audio input to a source audio memory using audio feature extraction and sequence matching, and it outputs concatenated matching audio segments using overlap-add buffering. Among its novel features are real-time controls offering on-the-fly parameter exploration of musically important components of the process. These parameters are variable segmentation of the input audio, feature selection, variable match distance, matching without replacement, and source memory location and range; each of these controls is described here. In its current implementation (as of August 2008), SoundSpotter is capable of real-time matching more than two hours of audio source material on current-generation hardware. Ongoing research and development already have yielded new algorithms that perform more efficiently with shorter match times for larger source audio databases. Once these new algorithms are incorporated into the implementation, future versions will be able to perform matching in thousands of hours of audio in real time (Casey et al. 2008, Slaney and Casey 2008).

SoundSpotter is implemented in C++ and has been tested on multiple platforms and operating systems, including PC Windows, PC Linux, and Mac (PPC and Intel) running the OSX operating system. The programming interface separates the host environment, such as Max/MSP (Max Signal Processing) or Pure Data, from the core computation engine and the process state. This enables easy integration with different computer music environments; current development includes versions for SuperCollider and a stand-alone version using native host platform graphical interfaces. The advantage with implementing SoundSpotter as an external object to be used within an existing computer music environment is that a large number of analysis and synthesis tools are then available to interoperate with it, such as onset detectors, beat trackers, phase vocoders, and cross-synthesis and video tools.

SoundSpotter was designed primarily as a computer music instrument implementing a deterministic associative memory process. As such, the development was undertaken to meet the following design objectives:

- The process is driven by a live audio target (possibly streamed from disk).
- The source database is a single large audio buffer.
- Perceptual features of the target and source audio are used for matching.
- For a given target, source, and parameter set, the output is deterministic.
- The user has real-time control over the matching process.
- The response to audio input is instantaneous.

SoundSpotter extends the previous work in soundspotting discussed in several important respects. The first is that it is a dedicated real-time system designed for use in musical performance by musicians without the need for a computer operator. Second, as mentioned, SoundSpotter uses sequence matching directly on the temporal patterns in the audio feature space; this provides a well-formed sequence as output; thus, it is a form of concatenative quality constraint as found in the Catepillar system, but it operates in real time and on polyphonic target and source materials.

Third, variable-length segmentation is employed so that the sequence size can be changed on the fly during a performance; this is important so that the matching can be adapted to the musical context, with longer windows used for matching slow sections of music and shorter windows employed for musical passages with greater note densities; this implements *gestural* control.

Fourth, real-time feature selection changes the feature space used for matching without requiring reextraction of features from the source database. This enables the soundspotting process to be steered toward the musically most relevant features for the current musical context, such as matching pitch versus timbre. As such, SoundSpotter is timbre, time, and pitch sensitive with complete control given to the user in real time. Furthermore, real-time control over match distance is implemented, which admits the full range of similarity to dissimilarity in the matching process; it is not necessarily the closest match that will provide the musically most interesting result. Often, it is the furthest match that provides the most interesting contrast to the current target signal while retaining a deterministic relationship to it. Beyond this, matching without replacement is implemented by efficient table lookup so that, once matched, a source segment can be removed from future searches for a given amount of time. This allows the full range of source material to be matched even when the target signal is held in a steady state, for example, thereby increasing the cycle length of any looping sequences that may occur in the output.

Finally, SoundSpotter employs a LIVESPOT function that performs matching to an accumulating real-time source buffer that is fed from the target signal; this operation implements a self-referential process with the current target signal input matched to the recent history of the same signal, say from the beginning of a performance to the instant before the current input.

SoundSpotter Design and Implementation

Audio Features

Content-based music information retrieval systems work by extracting musically relevant feature vectors that represent points in a multidimensional feature space (Casey et al. 2008). To use SoundSpotter, such features must be extracted from the source audio material as well as from the live target. Some early soundspotting systems were proposed that attempted to match the audio waveform directly or the audio spectrum directly. These systems were not able to produce musically interesting matches because they were too sensitive to the minute numerical details of these signal representations. What is required for musical matching is to reduce audio signals to a representation that preserves only those aspects of the audio that we wish to be sensitive to and discards extraneous information that is not important to human hearing and musical listening.

There are many differences between waveform and spectrum representations of sound and those aspects of a sound that are most salient to human hearing. First, a time domain audio waveform contains all the phase information of a sound, but it was discovered by Georg Ohm in 1843 that the ear is, essentially, phase deaf (Helmholtz 1865). This phenomenon is known as *Ohm's law*. The problem with a waveform representation is that two sounds that sound similar to the human ear but have different relative phases of their frequency components would not appear the same to an algorithm using waveform representations for matching.

The phase information can be suppressed by computing a Fourier transform of the waveform and converting the resulting complex numbers into polar form. This operation separates the magnitude information for each frequency component from the phase information. Taking only the magnitude part of the spectrum yields a representation that is agnostic to phase, closer to the human ear's sensitivity to the spectrum under most listening circumstances. However, the Fourier transform divides the frequency spectrum evenly into linear frequency bands, and the human ear is sensitive to frequency on a logarithmic scale. This means that humans hear frequency components more densely at lower frequencies than high frequencies,and the effect is gradual across the audible frequency range. An algorithm that performs matching in linear frequency is therefore sensitive to the numerical details of higher-frequency components that human hearing is not. So, two spectra that are heard as the same by human hearing will appear different and be computed as different in the linear frequency representation.

What is required is a method to reduce the complexity of audio signals into meaningful musical units but not discrete classical Western music units such as note, key, or instrument; rather, we require continuous numerical features that represent the right kind of information about a sound so that we can perform meaningful comparisons between sounds. Our chosen features are called *cepstral coefficients*, and they have been widely used in speech recognition and music information retrieval systems. The most common type of cepstral coefficients used are Mel frequency cepstral coefficients (MFCCs), employing a linear log frequency scale to model the decreasing-frequency resolution of the human ear in increasing-frequency bands. SoundSpotter currently employs cepstral coefficients derived from a strictly logarithmic frequency scale, so they are log frequency cepstral coefficients. The differences between Mel scale and log scale are slight and have no impact on the musical result in our experience; logarithmic in frequency is analogous to an equal-temperament scale like the pitch classes arranged across a piano keyboard.

Figure 20.2 is a schematic diagram of the extraction of MFCC features in SoundSpotter. We assume a sample rate of 44.1 kHz, a hop size of 2,048, and window length of 2,048 samples (46.44 ms). Each block of 2,048 samples is hamming windowed, and a 16,384-point FFT is computed. The result is a spectrum consisting of real coefficients representing the magnitudes of 8,193 evenly spaced frequency samples of the spectrum. The spacing of the frequency samples is therefore $44,100/16,384 = 2.69$ Hz. The window length, and hence frequency spacing, is chosen to convert the linear frequency samples into *musical* frequency samples organized on a logarithmic frequency scale corresponding to equal-temperament twelve-tone pitch classes spanning Co (65.4 Hz) to D7 (7,902.1 Hz) by summing the powers (magnitudes squared) in the linear frequency (FFT) bands that fall between the low edge and high edge of each logarithmic band. The low

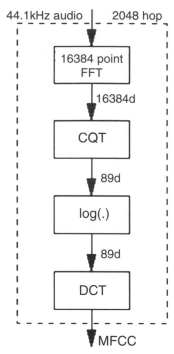

44.1kHz audio | 2048 hop

16384 point
FFT

16384d

CQT

89d

log(.)

89d

DCT

MFCC

Figure 20.2 Melfrequency cepstral coefficient feature extraction. Audio sources and input streams are analyzed using the fast Fourier transform (FFT). A constant-Q transform and log-amplitude step are applied, creating an auditory representation that is more like human hearing than the FFT. This auditory transform is decorrelated using a discrete cosine transform (DCT). The output is a set of eighty-nine vectors that represent the timbre and pitch components of the input audio signal.

edge and high edge are defined to be a quarter tone below and above the center frequency of each equal temperament pitch class, respectively. The transformation of the FFT power spectrum into a logarithmic frequency power spectrum is a constant Q transform (CQT); the Q of a frequency band is the ratio between its frequency and its bandwidth. The Q is constant because the bandwidth is always one semitone wide but centered on each equal-temperament pitch class, so the Q is $2^{-1/12} = 0.94387$.

After the equal-temperament pitch class power spectrum is computed, the base 10 logarithm is taken and a discrete cosine transform (DCT) applied. The operation of taking the logarithm of the magnitude spectrum converts multiplicative components of the spectrum (which are convolutive in the time domain) to additive components. Additive components are easy to decorrelate, meaning they can be separated from each other. The additive components are decorrelated by the DCT, which is an efficient version of the inverse FFT for signals that are real and positive.

This method, of taking the log of the magnitude spectrum and performing the inverse Fourier transform, produces the *cepstrum*, named by (Bogert et al. 1963) as a way to distinguish it from the *spectrum*. As well as naming the transformed spectrum the *cepstrum*, Bogert also named the transformed frequency domain the *quefrency* domain to distinguish it from frequency. Instead of being measured in hertz, the quefrency domain is measured in milliseconds, reflecting its relationship to the time domain due to the inverse FFT, or DCT, operation. Increasing positions in quefrency correspond to components with increasing period in time, which is the decreasing frequency.

The main advantage of using the cepstrum as representation for audio is that it separates out components of the spectrum that are due to periodic signals (such as the glottal impulse signal in speech) from the wideband filtering of the spectrum by formants (such as the vocal tract response in speech). In musical terms, the cepstrum separates the harmonic pitch content, represented by periodic components in the spectrum, from timbral components due to formants, for example, which are represented by the broad spectral envelope in the spectrum. In the cepstrum, these elements appear in different locations, with the broad-spectrum envelope components being lower quefrency. The net effect for the purposes of soundspotting is that the musician has control over the musical sense of the matching algorithm, that is, that pitch can be matched independently of timbre, and conversely, timbre can be matched independently of pitch. By changing the location within the cepstrum that matching is performed, the soundspotting algorithm is steered toward the musical intentions of the musician controlling the system.

Feature extraction for the database of audio sources can either be precomputed, as they are in SPOT mode, or extracted in real time as an accumulating resource during a performance, as is the case in LIVESPOT mode. The computation time needed to preextract features from a source audio buffer is many hundreds of times faster than real time, with the complexity primarily determined by the FFT algorithm.

Segmentation

One of the principal differences between the way SoundSpotter and other soundspotting systems work is in the use of temporal features. The motivation for temporal features stems from musical gesture occurring as a change over time. By matching changes over time in the cepstral features, SoundSpotter matches not just the instantaneous timbre and pitch content of the live audio input, but also how they change over time as a coherent sequence.

Temporal features are distinct from features that are computed from a spectrum using longer windows, therefore using a greater duration of information. This is because a spectrum, or cepstrum, computed over a longer time interval provides *less* information about changes over time than multiple spectra computed over shorter intervals. Conversely, the spectrum computed over a longer interval contains more information about frequency (if the information exists in the signal) by providing a denser sampling of the frequency information and by extending the range of the spectrum to lower frequencies. The spectrum length and temporal hop size essentially trade off density of spectral information against resolution in time;

SoundSpotter provides default settings for these parameters that mediate this trade-off for musical applications.

Temporal features are obtained by sequencing feature vectors into a series of vectors according to a segmentation method. The type of segmentation that is appropriate to a given musical application is dependent in large part on the type of audio that is used. For example, audio sources that primarily consist of onsets and beats can be segmented on beat boundaries so that musical matching can occur on the beats, whereas audio sources that consist of texture, such as scrunching leaves, crowd noise, or the granules of a rainstick, cannot meaningfully be divided into beats or onsets. The choice of how to perform segmentation is therefore a musical choice that is left to the musician using the system.

The simplest and most general segmentation in SoundSpotter is to use periodic windowing employing a sequence length that is fixed unless changed by the performer. The sequence length determines the number of feature vectors that are taken together to be matched against the source material in segments consisting of the same number of vectors as the input. If the sequence length parameter is constant, then the segments are fixed length. If the sequence length parameter is varied, then the segments are nonuniform. Here, matching is unconstrained by content-based boundaries, such as beats. For musical performance, sometimes it is desirable to have parameters adapt to the musical context. For example, when a performer is playing long sustained notes on an instrument, the matching should also use long sequences so that the result is a sustained coherent matching segment. But, when the performer plays rapidly changing pitches and timbres, tending toward the frantic, the sequence length should be kept short so that the matching can respond in short segments that mirror the gestural material of the input. Therefore, it is sometimes musically preferable to control windowing automatically by measuring some feature of the input, such as onset density, and setting the length of the window algorithmically using the numerical value of the onset density feature.

A second type of segmentation is to divide the features into sequences by interonset interval. In this scenario, matching is triggered at event boundaries that can be detected as onsets. A variety of onset detection methods can be employed, such as Pure Data's bonk~ object, which is also available in other computer music environments. In this scenario, SoundSpotter triggers matching at onset boundaries under the control of an onset detector rather than at regular intervals determined by a fixed window length as in the first segmentation scenario. The length of the match sequence is always the last interonset interval, and if onset detection was applied to the source features, the matching is aligned to onsets in the source audio buffer. This segmentation method has the desirable side effect of reducing the number of sequence comparisons that need to be made during matching. This is because onsets sparsely populate the source database compared with the totality of all feature vectors. By constraining the matching to occur only at onset boundaries, a large proportion of the database is eliminated; thus, fewer computations are required, and hence the matching is faster. This allows more source audio to be used in the matching because there is more time available to perform the matching. To perform matching by onset detection, the frame indexes of onsets are stored in a lookup table that is separate from the audio features. This allows fast retrieval by traversing only the list of known onsets in the match algorithm.

A third type of segment is beat, or tactus, intervals, which are determined by a common metrical pulse that tracks tempo in the target and source audio. The principals of this segmentation scenario are similar to those of the second; that is, segmentation occurs at event boundaries that are determined by the musical content of the target and source audio buffers. The major difference is that the additional parameter, tempo, is present as a musical feature. New potentialities in matching are afforded by the tempo feature. Matching is no longer constrained to fixed-length (or fixed-tempo) sequences; instead, we may find that the best-matching material to the target signal is material that occurs at a different tempo but over the *same number of beats*. In this case, the current tempo of the target signal and the tempo of the matched source segment are known; therefore, a timescale modification can be applied to bring the source material to the same tempo as the target signal. Given the ratio of tempos between target and source, there are many timescale modification algorithms that can bring them to the same tempo. The choice of algorithm depends primarily on the availability of implementations within the host environment, but a popular choice is to use a phase vocoder to perform the timescale modification (Portnoff 1976, Dolson 1986). As in the second segmentation scenario, using onsets only, there is a significant reduction in computation time when using beats for matching over exhaustive subsequence searching using fixed-length windows. Therefore, when possible, onset detection, tempo, and beat tracking should be employed if the target and source materials are of a rhythmic nature.

Figure 20.3 shows the BeatRoot onset detection and beat-tracking tool (Dixon 2001), which can be used to perform beat tracking on source material prior to loading into SoundSpotter. The output of the BeatRoot tool is a series of time locations and instantaneous tempi for each beat location. SoundSpotter can read this file and label the corresponding cepstral features with their tempo and beat locations. At SPOT time, the tempo and beats are also extracted from the target signal, using, for example, Pure Data's bonk~ object (Puckette 1997), and Sound-Spotter performs a beat-constrained search over the source audio using the beat time point information provided by BeatRoot.

One effect of using beats is that slower-tempi target signals produce fewer beats per unit time and therefore have longer intervals before matching. At down-tempo speeds, this is manifest as a clear delay between the target signal and the resulting matched beats. Even at higher tempi, the matching is always at least one beat behind because the information about the beat location needs to be collected before the matched information for that beat duration can be output. To synchronize the response of SoundSpotter to the musical phrase information in the work, predictive (noncausal) methods need to be employed. One such method is to have

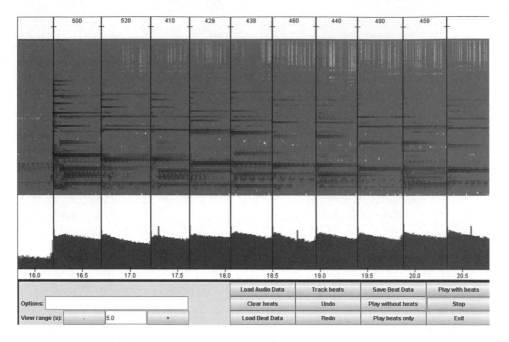

Figure 20.3 BeatRoot is a free software tool that analyzes audio and places beat markers where it estimates a metric pulse is heard. The numbers across the top are the interbeat intervals in milliseconds; the instantaneous tempo is inversely proportional to this value. Such tempo tracking can be used to segment audio into musically salient segments for soundspotting.

a stored performance of the work that can be used to take a sneak peak at what is coming next so that matching can be performed in time to synchronize output with the current target input. However, this look-ahead procedure takes us away from the realm of soundspotting and into a domain known as *score following* (Dannenberg 1984, Vercoe 1984, Raphael 1999, 2001); it is a topic of further research to determine the relationships between these two domains of computer music performance system.

Sequence Matching

A *sequence matching algorithm* operates on the sequence of the audio features of the target signal and all subsequences of the same length as the target in the source audio memory. Depending on the type of segmentation employed (i.e., window, onset, and beat), subsequences consisting of the same number of vectors do not necessarily represent audio of the same duration. It is only in the case of fixed-length windows that the sequences represent the same audio duration; when using onsets and beats, the interonset intervals and the tempi, respectively, determine the duration of the segments. However, this complexity is eliminated in the matching algorithm, which is agnostic to the segmentation method employed. It simply receives a sequence of features and matches them to sequences of the same length in the source memory.

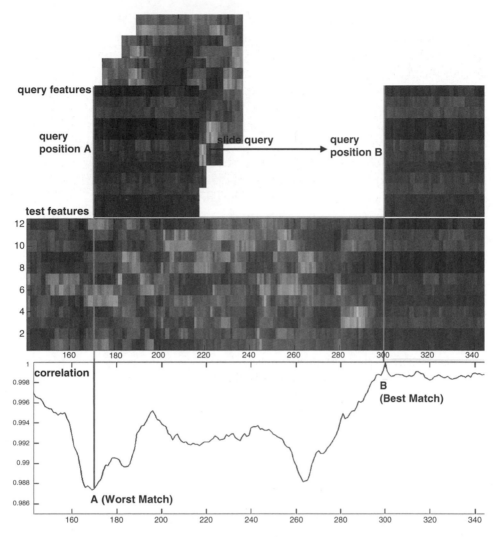

Figure 20.4 Matching by cross correlation. The target audio segment (query features) slides across the source database (test features), and a correlation value between the two is computed at every time point in the database. The point of maximum correlation is the minimum distance, or closest match, between the target signal and source database.

SoundSpotter uses a technique called *matched filtering* to find a match. Figure 20.4 illustrates the process of matched filtering for sequences of MFCC features. A sequence of feature vectors representing the target segment is first positioned over the first subsequence of the source features with the same length; a measure of the similarity between the two sequences is obtained by multiplying and accumulating the corresponding intersequence vector elements. The result is a single number representing the correlation of the two sequences; the trace of this number is shown in the lower graph of fig. 20.4.

The correlation coefficient's range depends on the numeric range of the vector elements and their cardinality. However, this makes the matching dependent on the total power of the audio segment and the length of the audio segment. Intuitively, soundspotting should be able to match sequences that contain the same musical information but are at different volumes; also, we want a distance measure that produces the same range of values regardless of the length of the sequences. We achieve this by first normalizing the sequences of vectors, of both the target and the source, so that each sequence has unit norm. This means that if we take the sum of squares of all the vector elements in a sequence, they add to 1. For sequences that are unit norm, the range of possible values for the correlation is $[-2, 2]$. By subtracting the correlation value from 2, the squared Euclidean distance is obtained, yielding values in the range $[0, 4]$, with 0 meaning the most similar possible sequence (the identity) and 4 corresponding with the most dissimilar possible sequence.

Figure 20.5 shows a schematic diagram of the matched filter algorithm, also shown in fig. 20.4, for a target sequence matched against a longer source sequence. The feature dimensionality is d, sequence length is w, and the source buffer length is n. The correlation is computed by aligning the target sequence over a

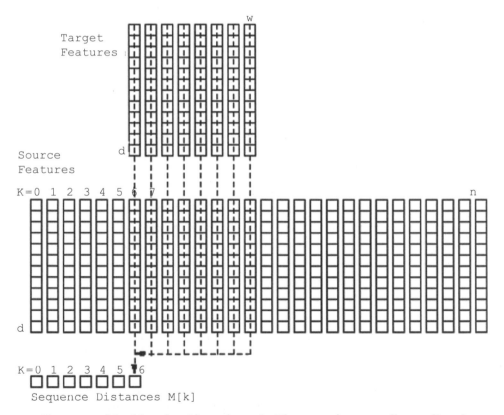

Figure 20.5 Matching algorithm schematic. The target features cells are aligned with each time point in the source database and a correlation value computed. The resulting correlation signal is a measure of the intersequence distance.

subsequence of the source buffer, cross multiplying the corresponding vector elements, and summing them to give the result. A correlation is computed for each time location in the source audio buffer. Higher values mean higher correlation and therefore greater similarity; the time index of the maximum value of the correlation is the index of the closest-matching audio segment in the source database.

Efficiency of the match algorithm is essential to performance; the algorithm, as stated, has a complexity that depends on the dimensionality of the features, the sequence length, and the size of the source memory buffer. This dependence is linear, which means that if we increase any of these values by a factor of, say, two, then it will take twice as long to compute the result. This complexity is over and above the computation required for feature extraction, which depends only on the FFT size and hop size, which remain fixed in SoundSpotter, and is small compared to the dependency on the source memory size.

In the description given of the matching algorithm, a sequence of such vectors must be collected before matching can take place. In fact, this type of processing creates a periodic bottleneck of computation that depends on the target sequence length. To limit the effect of the complexity due to the sequence length, the real-time nature of soundspotting processes can be fruitfully exploited. Each new feature vector in the target sequence arrives after a fixed time period of, say, 2,048 samples, so we can *incrementally* compute the partial correlation of each target feature vector, when it arrives, with the source features. Once the entire sequence of target vectors is collected, the partial correlations are summed, thus yielding the sequence correlation result. This technique is efficient because the computation load of the matching algorithm is spread out evenly in time, across feature vectors (frames), thereby reducing the peak computation requirement.

With a good understanding of the computation requirement of the Sound-Spotter algorithm, an accurate estimate can be made regarding the maximum amount of source material that can be matched for a given sequence length and feature dimensionality. Most current hardware operates on the order of 2 GHz or so. Features arrive every 46.44 ms, thus creating a 21.53-Hz frame rate. We divide 2 GHz by 21.53 to get the number of floating-point operations available at each incremental matching step: 92.88 million. For 50-dimensional feature vectors, the number of multiply and add floating-point operations is equivalent to 550 (a multiply operation takes ten times longer than an add operation); this yields 168,870 possible sequences matches. At the given frame rate (21.53 Hz), this is a total duration of 7,801.9 s, which is a little over 2 h of audio.

SoundSpotter Interface

Figure 20.6 shows an interface to SoundSpotter in the Pure Data computer music environment. The upper part of the interface performs the operations necessary to define a source memory buffer. The user triggers a new source memory by pressing the button called SOURCE and selects a sound file. The system then performs feature extraction on the sound file, and the features and the audio source are

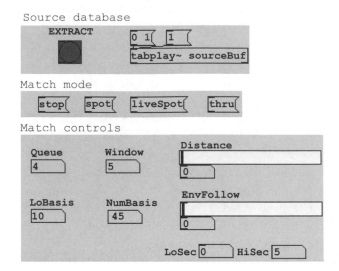

Figure 20.6 SoundSpotter interface. SoundSpotter's controls consist of source database selection via an extract button and a match mode panel for selecting different matching behaviors and control over the matching algorithm via real-time parameter changes.

stored in the core memory of the computer. The user may listen to the source buffer directly using the tabplay~ object shown in the interface. To employ many sound files in the source memory, they must first be concatenated into a single long sound file prior to source selection in SoundSpotter. Once features are extracted, the other necessary controls to begin soundspotting are to press the SPOT mode button, which initiates soundspotting from the source memory, and to turn the LiveInput gain up to a suitable level, say 75 dB. Once these actions are performed, SoundSpotter will respond to any audio input above the automatic silence detection threshold.

SoundSpotter Mode Control

The middle section of the interface determines the behavior of SoundSpotter. The modes of operation are STOP for no response, SPOT for soundspotting to a fixed-source audio buffer, LIVESPOT for soundspotting to an accumulating memory buffer gathered from the live audio input, and THRU to pass the input directly to the output.

In SPOT mode, SoundSpotter performs matching to an extant memory source; this is the canonical form of soundspotting. Here, the source memory and the target signal are from different sources, so soundspotting in this context performs intersource matching.

Accumulating (Dynamic) Source Memory

In LIVESPOT mode, SoundSpotter performs matching to an accumulating memory of target signal input. Here, the source memory and the target signal are from the same source, so soundspotting performs intrasource matching. Changing these relationships creates different musical processes.

Sequence Length (Window)

Segmentation is controlled, in real time, by a parameter that controls the length of the sequence to match. A *sequence* is a temporal series of audio features taken together as a unit. This can be controlled directly either by the user or by an automatic segmenter that sets the Window at each onset point to be the last interonset interval. Therefore, the previous Window block of feature vectors of the input stream is used for matching.

The granularity of SoundSpotter is controlled by changing the Window parameter. Short windows create a very choppy match process in which it is hard to discern the identity of the source frames but the identity of the target is maximally preserved. By contrast, longer windows create a more temporally coherent output that preserves the identity of the source, but as the windows get longer, the identity of the target signal diminishes. Segmentation is one of the most important parameters for controlling the relationship between the identity of the target signal and the identity of the source in the matching process.

Match Control (Distance)

Real-time control over search radius sets the euclidean distance for matching. For example, when the search radius is zero, the segment that is closest to zero distance is selected for output. If the radius is set to 0.4, then the segment closest to a distance of 0.4 from the input sequence is selected. The Distance parameter range is between 0 (most similar) and 4 (most dissimilar) by normalizing features to unit norm in the match function.

Feature Selection (loBasis, basisRange)

The real-time controls include feature selection using an element range for vector features. Low element a and high element b control the range of values accessed by the matching algorithm. By selecting ranges of coefficients, the matching can be made sensitive to different audio properties such as timbre or pitch. In a typical audio application, the first twelve cepstral coefficients are used to characterize wideband, or timbral, spectral information only. In Sound-Spotter, the remaining seventy-seven coefficients are used to match increasingly narrowband, or higher-frequency, components of the spectrum. Range selection over the MFCC feature allows matching to be steered toward timbral features, pitch features, or both. The matching algorithm is able to work on time-varying feature selection because the range of features defines a complete metric subspace for the matching algorithm. The loBasis and basisRange parameters are illustrated in fig. 20.7.

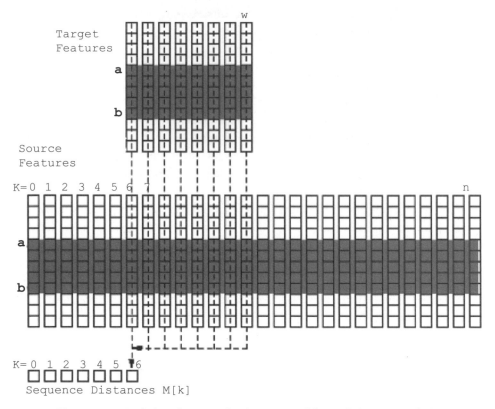

Figure 20.7 Real-time feature selection. One of the real-time controls in
SoundSpotter is the position and range of features to use for matching. The MFCC
features at the lower end of the feature range select for timbre, whereas those at the
higher end of the range select for pitch.

Forgetting: Long-Term Memory Loss (LoSec), Short-Term Memory Loss (HiSec)

It is often desirable to control the range of source memory that is accessible to
matching. For example, in LIVESPOT mode it is desirable to have a short-term
memory loss function so that matching does not include target signal material that
recently entered the source memory (thereby creating a short-term *echoic* memory
process instead of a long-term associative memory process). To do this, we set the
end point of the source memory for matching purposes to be a given number of
seconds, HiSec, before the *actual* current end point in the accumulating source
memory. When the source memory is restricted in this way in LIVESPOT model,
this is called *short-term memory loss*. In SPOT mode, HiSec simply changes the end
point of the extant source material that is accessible to matching. The LoSec
parameter alters the start point of the extant memory source. In LIVESPOT
mode, this can be interpreted as long-term memory loss. Unlike the start point
of the source, memory does not change as the source buffer accumulates, so the

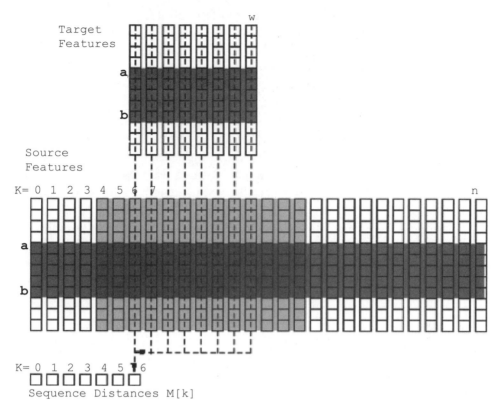

Figure 20.8 Real-time source database selection. The parameters loSec and hiSec select the low and high end points of the source database, respectively, with loSec specifying seconds from the beginning and hiSec specifying seconds from the end of the source database. This parameterization is designed to enable online resizing of databases while persisting the relative selection range.

LoSec parameter offers a method to increment the most distant memory of the target signal over time so that there is long-term memory loss. In SPOT mode, the LoSec parameter simply changes the start time of the source memory that is accessible to the matching process. The action of the HiSec and LoSec parameters is illustrated in fig. 20.8.

Matching without Replacement (frameQueue)

As with memory loss parameters, the frameQueue parameter also removes part of the source memory from the matching process. In this case, source memory segments that have already been matched are removed from matching for a specified number of match cycles. This has the effect of forcing new segments to be matched if the target signal is held steady or simply repeats the same short-term pattern. Without the frameQueue parameter, this steady-state input would generate a repetitive steady-state output segment, sounding as a repeated audio sample. By increasing the frameQueue, we suppress repeated sequences. The next-closest available match is output instead of the absolute closest; this often has the effect of forcing SoundSpotter to traverse a sequence of similar segments that are connected in time (such as a long-held note on an instrument), which creates a well-formed sustain, with no literal repetition, in the output audio sequence.

Feedback Matching

A final parameter that can be controlled in the SoundSpotter interface is the level of feedback sent to the matching process. SoundSpotter feedback takes the current matched output and inserts it as the next target input segment to generate a self-similar matching process. Used in conjunction with a frameQueue set to remove previously matched frames for long periods (say, the length of the source buffer), this creates a complex traversal of the source memory in a similarity chain. For example, segment A matches segment F, which then matches segment D and so on. Mixing a live target input with feedback matching can engender a complex behavior between the target and matched source, leading to a process with characteristics of a chaotic system but still deterministic.

3. A SoundSpotter Repertoire

In the following section, three works are described, in order of their first performances, that have the common trait of combining instruments and electronics using SoundSpotter. As stated, it was one of the design goals of the system to enable operation by a musician with acoustic input as the primary control mechanism. In the works described here, some are controlled purely by the acoustic input of an instrumental performer; others require the performer to control some of the soundspotting parameters during a performance, making musical decisions about the way that the program responds to their input, and others require a separate computer operator to carry out a series of more complex manipulations of the soundspotting system. In the latter case, the computer and the acoustic instrument are performed in equal measure; thus, these works are computer music duets for instrument and computer. The three works listed here start with the historically earliest real-time performance of a work using the SoundSpotter system in a public concert.

Departure on the Chao-Phraya, by Michael Casey

Departure on the Chao-Phraya was first performed by Michael Casey on tacet trombone and electronics in the Music Department at City University, London, on April 5, 2004.

The piece used the SoundSpotter system in SPOT mode, matching to a fixed extant source buffer, operating in the Pure Data computer music environment on a

755-MHz Dell laptop computer running the Windows 2000 operating system. The source audio consisted of an edited collage of ten minutes of field recordings taken on the Chao-Phraya River in Bangkok, Thailand, in March 2003. The source audio file consisted of the original edited material as well as transformations of the material using band-limited resampling and phase vocoder timescale modifications. The total duration of source audio including the modified material was 20 minutes.

A score for the work, composed by Casey in 2002, was performed on a trombone utilizing a Yamaha Silent Brass mute with an internal microphone transducer. When inserted into the bell of the trombone, the mute eliminates most of the direct acoustic of the trombone and instead passes the sound through a transducer embedded in the mute. This transducer is attached via a small cable to a battery-operated preamplifier worn by the performer; the amplified microphone signal is fed to the input of SoundSpotter via a professional sound card. The audience hears the resulting SoundSpotter output, but they hear little of the target signal input because of the silent mute. Thus, the intention in this work is to make the trombone a mouthpiece to a database of source material; the instrument is the combination of trombone and SoundSpotter, producing the sound using the musical feedback loop between SoundSpotter and performer.

The soundspotting parameters were fixed for each of three sections of the work; a slow introduction utilized sequence lengths of ten feature vectors, the faster middle section utilized sequence lengths of three feature vectors, and the slower ending used sequences of seven feature vectors, with sample rate of 44.1 kHz and hope size of 2,048 samples. The basis range over MFCC features was set to start at dimension 9 and end at dimension 54; this range was chosen as a trade-off between computational expense (using a limited range of the available features for matching) and sensitivity to both timbral and pitched components during matching.

SueMe No. 1, by Michael Casey with Roger Dannenberg

SueMe No. 1 was first performed by Casey (tacet trombone and electronics) and Roger Dannenberg (trumpet) at Goldsmiths College, University of London, on September 15, 2005.

The soundspotting source materials for this work consist of the U.K. official singles' chart number 1s from 1960 to September 2005 downloaded from a well-known Internet music service. Not all of the number 1 singles were available, but more than half were. Because the total duration of all these singles was outside the range of match capability at the time, the database of source material was constrained in several unique ways. First, a number of rehearsal performances using small portions of the database were undertaken to collect the indices of those segments in the source database that matched the target, an improvised trombone performance. The source material was collectively edited to contain the only the audio segments with indices that were matched during the rehearsals. This constrained the database to about 10% of the original material, thereby reducing the audio to a manageable duration. Furthermore, during performance the database was also constrained by matching in sequential sections (consisting of roughly a decade of music), moving the start and end points of the search range continuously by a year in the life of pop music every 15 s. For the final section of the piece, the last 2 min 30 s, a different source was employed, that of the 4-min solo electric guitar performance by Jimi Hendrix at Woodstock in 1970, providing an out-of-chronology dramatic ending to the work.

The soundspotting target consisted of an improvisation by two performers using two different acoustic instruments mixed into a single live target; the first was a tacet trombone, and the second was a trumpet. The trombone player doubled as a SoundSpotter operator so spent some of the performance changing parameters to the soundspotting process.

Erinnerungsspiel (Memory Games), by David Gorton

First performed by Christopher Redgate (oboe) and Casey (electronics), at Goldsmiths College, University of London, on November 11, 2006, *Erinnerungsspiel (Memory Games)* was also recorded at Coombehurst Studio, Kingston University, April 11, 2007, and produced for CD in March 2008 at the U.K. Royal Academy of Music with the assistance of Professor Milton Mermikides (electronics). David Gorton produced a score for the work, the opening of which is shown in fig. 20.9.

This piece uses the SoundSpotter system operating in the Max/MSP or Pd environments. Audio input is gathered from the oboe via a microphone and a MIDI (musical instrument digital interface) input from a MIDI foot controller pedal. *Errinerungspiel* was the first soundspotting work to use a source that was gathered from a live target (i.e., in LIVESPOT mode). The technique was suggested by the composer, David Gorton, and I implemented it in SoundSpotter. The instructions for the work are as follows:

> The piece is made up of eight separate sections which are labelled: a1, a2, b1, b2, g1, g2, d1, and d2. The performer must choose an order in which to play the sections, with the conditions that the piece must begin and end with sections labelled 1, and that no two consecutive sections may share the same alphabetical label. During the first twenty seconds of the piece the volume of the computer output should be faded up from nothing until a point that is clearly audible, but is still subservient to the volume of the solo oboe. This output must then be faded back to nothing during the penultimate bar of the piece. During the piece the SoundSpotter system will have at its disposal an accumulating memory of what the performer has played up to each moment, and will respond with these accumulating resources through time by a scale of similarity/dissimilarity to the currently performed musical surface. The similarity/dissimilarity scale is controlled by the foot pedal, and should be set to the maximum level of similarity at the start of the piece. The performer is then free to control the pedal ad libitum throughout the piece, thus stimulating different kinds of response from the computer system. The result is a two-way dialogue between the performer and SoundSpotter, with the computer

alpha-1

0=*p*, *mf*, *f*

♩=c.102

Figure 20.9 Opening of David Gorton's *Errinerungspiel* for oboe and SoundSpotter. This was the first SoundSpotter work to employ live matching by which the source database grows online as the performance unfolds.

acting in response to the performer, and conversely, the performer acting in response to the computer, both through the use of the foot pedal, and through the shaping of the surface of the musical material. The latter may be aided through the use of flexible dynamic markings, where 0 indicates a mean dynamic taken from a choice at the heading of each section, +1, +2, +3, etc. indicates increasing dynamic levels relative to the mean, and −1, −2, −3, etc. indicates decreasing dynamic levels relative to the mean." (David Gorton, *Erinnerungsspiel*, 2006)

4. SOUNDSPOTTING HITCHCOCK AND MARILYN MONROE

An extension to the basic SoundSpotter system is to provide the facility to play back video in synchrony with the selected audio grains. The video is chosen and the sound track extracted. At performance time, SoundSpotter provides the time index of the chosen fragment. A low-latency random-access video player is triggered at each spot grain boundary and proceeds at the video frame rate, playing the chosen audio in synchrony, until the next spot grain is triggered. A demonstration of the system was given at the International Computer Music Conference in Denmark in 2007, with the source material consisting of entire films by Alfred Hitchcock, *The Birds, Vertigo*, and *Psycho* among them. The target in this case was a live microphone into which the user vocalized. A version of the same system was also publicly presented at the Royal Academy of Music in London in November 2007 with a cello used as the target. Here, the cellist improvised with the audiovisual content of the film to construct new musical-dramatic pathways through the existing narratives.

In his work "Soundspotting Marilyn," composer Beau Sievers used a source database consisting entirely of segments of Marilyn Monroe speaking (taken from her films). The target was a synthetic speech generator that was used to create synthetic utterances to be reconstructed from the source database of Marilyn Monroe's voice (see fig. 20.10). This work is an example of how soundspotting can be used to map synthetic audio into a natural source, thus opening new possibilities for applying audio synthesis techniques.

5. CONCLUSION

In this chapter, a new kind of process music was described, as was an open source software implementation called SoundSpotter. The components of the system are simple, consisting of source material, a target signal, and a matching algorithm that operates in real time. Within the constraints of this relatively simple arrangement

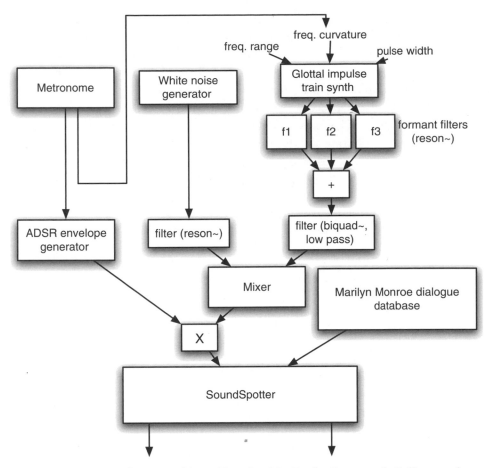

Figure 20.10 System diagram of SoundSpotting Marilyn by Dartmouth College graduate student Beau Sievers. The system uses a speech synthesis algorithm to generate synthetic utterances as the target signal for soundspotting. The source database consists of a large collection of Marilyn Monroe's talking scenes from a number of her films. The result is a reconstruction of the synthetic vocal utterances via the distinctive voice of Marilyn.

of technologies lies a space of musical potentialities that remains, largely, unexplored. This chapter presented aspects of the space of musical possibilities in relation to prior experimental music works and by describing a series of early SoundSpotter works. It is hoped that musical further possibilities will emerge not only by experimentation and rearrangement of the existing concepts, but also by combination with other musical processes. A new musical frontier has presented itself, and it is the preserve of composers and musicians to create the new processes that will emerge beyond this frontier. By way of conclusion, the following is a brief summary of current and ongoing research into soundspotting that will likely be available in future generations of software.

An important area of research in the last decade or so has been machine listening; the goal is to make computer systems that are capable of humanlike hearing and decision making; this includes speech, everyday audio, and music audio. The promise of machine-listening systems is that we might be able to use information about music signals to make control decisions automatically for soundspotting systems. These control decisions would affect the musical outcome of the soundspotting process, so the machine listener becomes a collaborating musician. An example of machine listening that has already been described is tempo and beat tracking. These processes are complex and subtle and rely on sophisticated knowledge and research into how humans perceive tempo and beats and how we can model these processes using algorithms. The nature of beat tracking is such that it is difficult to get a perfectly accurate pulse from music with many layers of onsets and rhythms or for music in which the beat is not roughly stationary. However, advances in beat-tracking systems are occurring steadily, so the availability of robust beat trackers is likely to increase in the near term.

Another example of machine listening applied to musical control is the Cellorometer designed by Milton Mermikides of the Royal Academy of Music for Gorton's second cello sonata. The Cellorometer is a piece of software, constructed in the Max/MSP computer music environment, that tracks the event density of a cello performance over time. The system measures onsets and counts the average number of onsets in a fixed-length window over time, smoothing the result so that short, abrupt changes lead to gradual changes in the measurement. The system is built on the bonk~ object in Max/MSP, which is an onset detector with fine-tuning controls. The Cellorometer is employed in soundspotting performances to control the match sequence length automatically; sections of the target signal, in this case a performance of a score, that are frenetic or rapidly changing are matched using short sequence lengths. Conversely, sections that are sparse or consist of long, slowly changing events are matched by long sequences. Thus, the matching behavior of SoundSpotter is automatically adjusted to the musical context.

An unexplored direction in soundspotting is the use of multiple simultaneous SoundSpotter instances. All of the works described use either a single source and single SoundSpotter instance or many sources and a single SoundSpotter. Given the rapid increase in the computational power of consumer electronics devices, such as laptop computers and mobile phones, there is enough resource to run concurrent SoundSpotter instances. The possibilities here are numerous; for example, a target signal can be separated into different frequency bands and each filtered target routed as the input to a different SoundSpotter instance drawing on different source material. Splitting a target signal can be performed using traditional band-pass filtering techniques, but it could also be achieved using more advanced methods such as independent subspace analysis. The idea is that a complex target signal could be split into a number of simpler sound atoms, each of these sound atoms could be matched against separate sound-appropriate source buffers, and the result could be recombined to create a polyphonic match to the complex target.

Yet another possibility afforded by the use of concurrent SoundSpotter instances is the idea of *multitrack soundspotting*. Here, a number of separate targets are matched by separate SoundSpotters, and the output is remixed to preserve the relative strengths of each of the target signals in the matched output mix. This arrangement is suitable for arrangement strategies such as reorchestration or remixing, in which the musical information content of a source can be left intact but the details replaced using matching into a different domain of audio.

Extensions of soundspotting to the audiovisual domain have already appeared. Videospotting has been demonstrated in public using the SoundSpotter framework (Casey and Grierson 2007). To perform videospotting, a source audio track is first separated from a video source (in the latter case, digital DVD distributions of the films of Alfred Hitchcock). The separated audio track is then imported into SoundSpotter as source material. A target signal is applied and audio output in the usual soundspotting sense, but also the matching frame index is converted to a time index and sent to a concurrent software video player engine that rapidly seeks the corresponding frame in the video and runs the matching sequence of video frames for the audio match. The enhancement of adding visual material to the soundspotting process is dramatic and offers possibilities for many digital art performance and research scenarios.

The final direction that is presented here is a significant reduction in the computational complexity of audio matching. A number of recent research papers and software developments have resulted in new near-constant time-matching algorithms that eliminate the dependence on the size of the source database for real-time matching. By using a technique called locality-sensitive hashing (LSH), databases consisting of hundreds or thousands of hours of audio material can be searched in real time for soundspotting applications (Slaney and Casey 2008). This change in scale of possible source material affords matching on an unprecedented amount of material; the potentials for this avenue of investigation include matching to the entire history of a musical corpus (such as pop or jazz music) or an entire corpus of film material, such as all the movies of the 1940s or 1,000 hours of content from YouTube. Whether there is creative merit in affording such a scale of audio matching remains to be seen and will be answered by a new generation of artists and composers who have such tools at their disposal.

BIBLIOGRAPHY

Bogert, B. P., M. J. R Healy, and J. W. Tukey. 1963. The quefrency analysis of time series for echoes: Cepstrum, pseudo-autocovariance, cross-cepstrum, and saphe cracking. In *Proceedings of the Symposium on Time Series Analysis*, ed. M. Rosenblatt. New York: Wiley, pp. 209–243.

Casey, M. 2001. MPEG-7 sound-recognition tools. *IEEE Transactions on Circuits and Systems for Video Technology* 11(6): 737–747.

Casey, M. 2002. Sound classification and similarity tools. In *Introduction to MPEG-7: Multimedia Content Description Interface*, ed. B. S. Manjunath, P. Salembier, and T. Sikora. New York: Wiley, p. 317.

Casey, M. 2003. Sound replacement, beat unmixing and audio mosaicing; creative uses of MPEG-7 audio. In *Conference on Digital Audio Effects*, tutorial (DAFx). London. http://www.elec.qmul.ac.uk/dafx03/proceedings/, accessed March 30, 2009.

Casey, M. 2004. SoundSpotter download page. http://www.sourceforge.net/projects/mp7c, accessed April 25, 2008.

Casey, M. 2005. Acoustic lexemes for organizing Internet audio. *Contemporary Music Review* 24(6): 489–508.

Casey, M., and M. Grierson. 2007. SoundSpotter and Remix-TV: Fast approximate matching for audio-visual performance. In *Proceedings of the International Computer Music Conference* (ICMC), Copenhagen, Denmark, pp. II, 491–494.

Casey, M., C. Rhodes, and M. Slaney. 2008. Analysis of minimum distances in high-dimensional musical spaces. *IEEE Transactions on Audio, Speech and Language Processing* 16(5): 1015–1028.

Collins, N. 2007. Audiovisual concatenative synthesis. In *Proceedings of the International Computer Music Conference* (ICMC), Copenhagen, Denmark, pp. 389–392.

Dannenberg, R. B. 1984. An on-line algorithm for real-time accompaniment, *in Proceedings of the International Computer Music Conference* (ICMC), pp. 193–198.

Dixon, S. 2001. An interactive beat tracking and visualisation system. in *Proceedings of the International Computer Music Conference* (ICMC), Havana, Cuba, pp. 215–218.

Dolson, M. 1986. The phase vocoder: A tutorial. *Computer Music Journal* 10(4): 14–27.

Eno, B. 1975. *Discrete Music* (liner notes). Editions Eg Records.

Eno. B. 1999. Foreword. In *Experimental Music: Cage and Beyond*, by M. Nyman, 2nd ed. Cambridge: Cambridge University Press.

Koenig, S. 2006. http://www.popmodernism.org/scrambledhackz/, accessed April 25, 2008.

Lazier, A., and P. Cook. 2003. MOSIEVIUS: Feature driven interactive audio mosaicing. *Conference on Digital Audio Effects* (DAFx), London. http://www.elec.qmul.ac.uk/dafx03/proceedings/, accessed March 30, 2009.

Mathews, M. V., J. Miller, F. R. Moore, J. R. Pierce, and J. C. Risset. 1969. *The Technology of Computer Music*. Cambridge: MIT Press.

Nyman, M. 1974. *Experimental Music: Cage and Beyond (Music in the Twentieth Century)*. London: Macmillan.

Oswald, J. 1985. "Plunderphonics, or audio piracy as a compositional prerogative." Paper presented at Wired Society Electro-Acoustic Conference, Toronto, 1985. http://www.plunderphonics.com/xhtml/xplunder.html, accessed April 25, 2008.

Pachet, F., P. Roy, and D. Cazaly. 2000. A combinatorial approach to content-based music selection. *IEEE MultiMedia* 7(1): 44–51.

Peeters, G., S. McAdams, and P. Herrera. 2000. Instrument sound description in the context of MPEG-7. In *Proceedings of the International Computer Music Conference* (ICMC2000), Berlin. http://citeseerx.ist.psu.edu, accessed March 30, 2009.

Portnoff, M. R. 1976. Implementation of the digital phase vocoder using the fast Fourier transform. *IEEE Transactions on Acoustics, Speech, and Signal Processing* ASSP-24(3): 243–248.

Puckette, M. 1997. Pure Data: Recent progress. In *Proceedings of the Third Intercollege Computer Music Festival*, Tokyo, Japan, pp. 1–4.

Quackenbush, S., and A. Lindsay. 2001. Overview of MPEG-7 audio. *IEEE Transactions on Circuits and Systems for Video Technology* 11(6): 725–729.

Raphael, C. 1999. A probabilistic expert system for automatic musical accompaniment. *Journal of Computational and Graphical Statistics* 10(3): 487–512.

Raphael, C. 2001. A Bayesian network for real-time music accompaniment. *Advances in Neural Information Processing Systems* (NIPS) (14). http://citeseerx.ist.psu.edu, accessed March 30, 2009.

Reich, S. 1968. Music as a gradual process. In *Writings about Music, 1965–2000*. New York: Oxford University Press, 2002, p. 34.

Schwarz, D. 2000. A system for data-driven concatenative sound synthesis. In *Proceedings of the Conference on Digital Audio Effects* (DAFx), Verona, Italy, pp. 97–102.

Schwarz, D. 2006. Concatenative sound synthesis: The early years. *Journal of New Music Research* 35: 1, 3–22.

Silvers, R., and M. Hawley. 1997. *Photomosaics*. New York: Henry Holt.

Slaney, M., and M. Casey. 2008. Locality sensitive hashing for finding nearest neighbours. *IEEE Signal Processing Magazine* 25(2): 128–131.

Smaragdis, P., and M. Casey. 2003. Audiovisual independent components. In *Proceedings of the International Symposium on Independent Component Analysis and Blind Source Separation* (ICA), Nara, Japan, pp. 709–714.

Sturm, B. L. 2004. MATConcat: An application for exploring concatenative sound synthesis using MATLAB. In *Proceedings of the International Computer Music Conference* (ICMC2004), Miami.

Turing, A. 1936. On computable numbers, with an application to the Entscheidungsproblem. *Proceedings of the London Mathematical Society* Series 2: 230–265.

Vercoe, B. 1984. The synthetic performer in the context of live performance. In *Proceedings of the International Computer Music Conference* (ICMC), pp. 199–200.

von Helmholtz, H. 1865. *Die Lehre von den Tonempfindungen als physiologische Grundlage für die Theorie der Musik.*, 6th ed., Braunschweig: Vieweg, 1913; trans. A. J. Ellis as *On the Sensations of Tone as a Physiological Basis for the Theory of Music*, 1885. Reprinted New York: Dover, 1954.

Xiang, P. 2002. A new scheme for real-time loop music production based on granular similarity and probability control. In *Proceedings of the Conference on Digital Audio Effects* (DAFx), Hamburg, Germany, pp. 89–92.

Zils, A., and F. Pachet. 2001. Musical mosaicing. Paper presented at Digital Audio Effects Conference (DAFx), University of Limerick.

SOUNDING OUT

CHAPTER 21

INTERACTIVITY AND IMPROVISATION

GEORGE E. LEWIS

UNDERSTANDING computer-based music-making as a form of cultural production obliges a consideration of the discourses that mediate our encounters with the computer itself. Increasingly, new imaginings of history, culture, and artistic practice are finding the computer at their centers, and particularly since the mid-1980s, digital technologies have served as a critical site for interdisciplinary exploration, accelerating the blurring of boundaries between art forms. In turn, these new imaginings are being driven by the advent of new and more powerful forms of computer interactivity that challenge traditional conceptions of human identity and physicality.

Musicians were among the first to design and perform with what I now call *creative machines*,[1] devices that operate in dialogue with and contribute to real-time, real-world musical utterance. At the time of this writing, people have been living with creative art machines for nearly four decades; even so, the conventionally published scholarly literature theorizing the nature and impact of interactive computer music systems is still relatively slim, although many personal statements by composers are available (often disseminated via the World Wide Web). Similarly, while technological documentation of the embrace of interactive technologies abounds in journals devoted to academic computer music, the absence in the public imaginary of memes emerging from the intersection of computer music and the interactivity that members of the field pioneered has become a consequence of the relative absence of theorization and reflection on these issues in the computer music world.

At the uninterrogated core of common notions of interactivity as it is practiced in the digital domain, we find the primordial human practice of improvisation. In the contemporary arts since 1950, issues concerning the nature and practice of improvisation repeatedly emerge, but terms such as "happening," "action," and "intuition" often mask the presence of improvisation in traditional media such as dance, theater, and music. The need to exnominate improvisation here is due largely to the problematic status of improvisation, not only in the high-culture, pan-European art practice that most theorists and researchers assume as a primary cultural and historical background for art production, but also in everyday constructions of morality and integrity that are active in many Western social spheres.

After an absence of about a century, the early 1950s return of improvisative modes of real-time music-making to Western classical music not only explored chance as a component of composition, but also rekindled aesthetic contention around the nature, purpose, structure, and moral propriety of improvised forms and practices.[2] According to cultural historian Daniel Belgrad, in the United States these debates were part of an emerging "culture of spontaneity" that crucially informed the most radical American artistic experimentation in the mid-20th century, from the beats and abstract expressionism to the transgressive new music of Charlie Parker, Thelonious Monk, and the musical New York School of John Cage, David Tudor, Morton Feldman, Earle Brown, and Christian Wolff.[3] In 1960s and 1970s Europe, debates over improvisation, in particular "free jazz," were widespread, and the practices were seen by many as symbolic of a dynamic new approach to social order that would employ spontaneity to unlock the potential of individuals and to combat oppression by hegemonic political and cultural systems.[4]

As improvisation becomes the subject of a burgeoning area of inquiry in the arts, humanities, and sciences, we find practitioners of interactive computer music in the new century situated at this core nexus of improvisation and interactivity, combining sonorous and sensuous experiences with critical spaces for considering the nature of human interaction. Here, the most important unacknowledged lesson the interactive digital arts have taught us concerns the centrality of both improvisation and interactivity to the practice of everyday life. Increasingly, theorizing the nature of these two practices is becoming an interdisciplinary affair, combining the insights of artists, cultural theorists, and technologists.[5]

One may find ironic the historical rupture separating the notion of interactivity on offer since the mid-1980s from the practices that arose in the computer music communities beginning in the early 1970s.[6] The advent of relatively portable mini- and microcomputers spurred the development of "interactive" or "computer-driven" works that displayed a great diversity of approaches to the question of what interaction was and how it affected viewers, listeners, and audiences. In 1981, Joel Chadabe, one of the earliest pioneers, developed the term *interactive composing* to describe the practice.[7]

The early interactive composing instruments of Chadabe, Salvatore Martirano, and others "made musical decisions as they responded to a performer, introducing the concept of shared symbiotic control of a musical process."[8] Much of this work, as with the pioneering microcomputer work of David Behrman and the League of Automatic Music Composers, arose in itinerant art worlds rather than the institutional spaces that had previously dominated computer music-making.[9] The new software-driven behaviors blurred the boundaries between human and machine music-making and called conventional notions of human identity into question while establishing a critical space to explore communication not only, or even primarily, between people and machines but also between people and other people.

Blunting the social impact of the work, however, was the tardiness of most of these composers in coming to terms with the full implications of their improvisations. This tardiness asserted itself along at least two axes. First, the early interactive composers, whether institutionally based or itinerant, tended to see themselves as heirs to a tradition of vanguard classical music that eschewed contact with popular culture, political concerns, and the social world generally. This recusal from the social and cultural world ultimately militated against engaging a wider audience in dialogue surrounding the fascinating questions being raised by the technology.

Second, the absence of a strong theoretical base, particularly in terms of race, gender, and economics, left the early interactive musicians unprepared either to contextualize their issues beyond the frame of pan-European composition, or to theorize their own practices of improvisation. Chadabe's observation that David Behrman's work "was electronic, but it had the feeling of improvised music"[10] stood in sharp contrast and direct challenge to pan-European contemporary music's widespread disavowal of improvisation, yet the term *interactive composing* extended the traditional discursive masking of improvisation's presence. Little in the way of sustained or focused discourse emerged from the community to counteract the massive investment in the disapprobation of improvisation, and as a result, the questions raised by this innovative work would be left to a later generation of interactivity artists and theorists whose activities became subsumed within the field of "new media"—an area within which this earlier history of interactivity remains essentially unknown and unreferenced, and one that has proved similarly reticent regarding theoretical or ethnographic engagement with improvisation.[11]

Even given its theoretical lacunae, the practice of this new kind of live computer music blurred the boundaries between human and machine music-making and called into question received notions of human identity. The "structure" of the pieces was difficult to separate from the enabling technologies. At least privately, these early experimenters realized that integrating improvisation with technology as an articulated object comprising research, theorizing, and performance could project new models for the study of meaning and sociality, where critically oriented aesthetic experience bridges gaps between fields of inquiry.[12] The presence of contingency and partial perspective in the music promoted sharp questioning of the notion of hierarchical control of musical process, a dynamic that had developed in part from the absence of improvisation in Western music since the late 19th century.

One recent example of the growth of improvisation-imbued interactive practices is the Live Algorithms for Music (LAM) research network (www.livealgorithms.org), an initiative created in 2004 by computer scientist Tim Blackwell and composer Michael Young of Goldsmiths College in London. According to Young and Blackwell, LAM's vision foregrounds "the development of an artificial music collaborator. This machine partner would take part in musical performance just as a human might; adapting sensitively to change, making creative contributions, and developing musical ideas suggested by others. Such a system would be running what we call a 'live algorithm.'"[13]

Blackwell and Young described a "live algorithm" as having the ability to "collaborate actively with human performers in real-time performance without a human operator," making "apt and creative contributions to the musical dimensions of sound, time and structure" through the deployment of "a *parametric representation* of the aural environment which changes to reflect interaction between machine and environment." In LAM-influenced work, free improvisation becomes a central component in a conception of "strong" interactivity, which is characterized by LAM researchers as "autonomous," "interactive," "idiosyncratic," and "comprehensible," properties analogous to those ostensibly found in human performance (see http://www.livealgorithms.org/). In contrast, "weakly interactive" or "reflex" systems, in which, for instance, "incoming sound or data is analysed by software and a resultant reaction (e.g., a new sound event) is determined by pre-arranged processes," are said to merely manifest "an illusion of integrated performer-machine interaction."[14]

Given their backgrounds in computer science and artificial intelligence (AI) research, it is perhaps understandable that LAM researchers use the terms *strong* and *weak* interactivity in ways redolent of the computer science discourse of strong and weak AI. More salient for the purposes of this essay, however, are the ways in which both conceptions of computer interactivity can be shown to embody an aesthetic crucially informed by social processes. In both strong and weak modes, moreover, the computer provides the interdisciplinary, interartistic, or synesthetic medium of exchange.

This ranges well beyond the older view of computer music as having as its primary goal the synthesis and organization of "new sounds,"[15] as well as deemphasizing strategies of hierarchical control of musical process, normally associated with the composition of contemporary classical music. Instead, interactivity suggests a new model for the *Gesamtkunstwerk*, one wary of hubris and disinclined to overweening centralization strategies. Collaborative and heterophonic, machine and human subjectivity become blended in the construction in a cyborg-inflected double consciousness.

Improvising computer programs—creative machines—both problematize and clarify constructed distinctions between human and machine in ways that illustrate the radical position of anthropologist Lucy Suchman that "I take the boundaries between persons and machines to be discursively and materially enacted rather than naturally effected and to be available . . . for refiguring."[16] Performances with creative machines are not simulations of "actual" musical experience, but a form of "making music together." Challenging the traditional improvisation-composition binary in Western thinking on music, sociologist Alfred Schutz, in his 1964 meditation on collective music-making maintained that "the system of musical notation is...accidental to the social relationship prevailing among the performers. This social relationship is founded upon the partaking in common of different dimensions of time simultaneously lived through by the participants."[17]

Schutz performed a critical shift in disconnecting improvisation from the mystificatory, romantic notion of artmaking that tends to deform discussions of the practice. The clear implication of his important essay is that improvisation engages local agency, history, contingency, memory, identity, and embodiment. In this way, an improvised music can directly address issues surrounding the practice of everyday life itself, and working with improvising machines becomes a way of creating a politically inflected, critically imbued aesthetic space in which, following Schutz, "a study of the social relationships connected with the musical process may lead to some insights valid for many other forms of social intercourse."[18]

Even so, Schutz's view that "making music together [presupposes] a face-to-face relationship, that is, a community of space"[19] is problematized by the creative musical machine, an entity that did not exist in its present form in Schutz's time. Much contemporary practice with interactive music technologies embeds not a face-to-face animating metaphor but a dramaturgy founded, first, on empathy in the relation among bodies and intentions, and, second, on the creation of a community of differences between one ear and another.

In her analysis of strong AI, Suchman contended that dominant discourses and research directions in the field continue to assume a Euroamerican model of human subjectivity.[20] Computer music, with its strong relationship with computer science, has long assumed a similar posture, but once that reading and its associated aesthetic assumptions are abandoned, what appears is a much wider range of readings in music regarding what constitutes "intelligibility" of machine response as compared with research in natural-language processing or machine vision, areas that have received far greater attention in the scientific community than the machine parsing of acoustic utterance. For example, even Suchman was surprised to learn that AI-based conversational agents "make evident the greater contingency of competent machinic hearing."[21] However, a theory of listening and interpretation is at the root of any design strategy for interactive music machines. Listening itself is an improvisative act engaged in by everyone—an active engagement with the world, where we sift, interpret, store, and forget in parallel with other actions and intentions and fundamentally articulated with them.

In such an environment, contingency becomes not only routine, part of the everyday, but also a factor that must be taken into account. Here, new ethnographies of improvisation that move beyond the 1950s models of jazz-making that still dominate discourses in sociology and cognitive psychology would ask researchers to look at the important questions about how order, agency, and subjectivity are attained, leading to new models of "the expert" that do not depend on the simulation of formulaic models of music for proof of concept.

Over the past twenty years, with the mainstreaming of interactivity as a consumer product, it has become clear that the foundations of a given interactive practice may be located in particular socially and economically articulated networks. As interactivity becomes identified with information storage and retrieval strategies that late capitalism has found useful in its encounter with new media, the notion of "information" itself risks becoming colonized, a metonym for a hierarchical power relationship whose attractiveness amounts to a quiet reversal of the notion that the user is "empowered" by interactivity.

Developing new interfaces for musical expression (to borrow the name of an important yearly conference) has the potential to disrupt this process by encouraging intervention in the ongoing flow of sonic and visual images, promoting recombinancy, and redefining users as fellow travelers in an interactive matrix in which power and influence are dynamically allocated and shared. In particular, strong interactivity, with its privileging of an aesthetic of variation and difference at variance with simpler paradigms of information retrieval and control, promotes self-organizing, interactive behavior that operates both independently and in dialogue with the viewer-auditor's constructing auditory "gaze."[22]

The result is not the quasi-subjectivity of the nominally static artwork envisioned by Mikel Dufrenne in his 1953 *Phenomenology of Aesthetic Experience*, but an experience with apparent machine subjectivity that replaces the objectifications of the old Turing test with the phenomenology of the cyborg.[23] Interactive environments that incorporate a dialogic imagination oblige the reconsideration of the aesthetic and music-structural agency of the creative machine. Just as actor-network theory makes no distinction between human and nonhuman nodes in a given network, creative machines become full actors with an articulation of agency and a reception of affect that ranges both within and beyond the moment of the immediately staged concert, workshop, or other approved "performance."

These musings make common cause with Suchman's assertion that human interactions succeed not due to the abilities of any one participant to construct meaningfulness, but to the possibility of mutually constructing intelligibility in and through interaction.[24] The improvised, interactive encounter becomes a *negotiation*, in which decisions taken by the computer have consequences that must be taken into account by all parties to the exchange. The experience of interacting with or being an audience member for this kind of encounter has the potential for calling forth the same kinds of communicative intersubjectivities as any other music-making process might. It is here that improvising (i.e., living) with creative machines exemplifies the working out of social networks, transforming not only performers, improvisors, composers, and audiences, but also the discursive and social environment in which performance, improvisation, composition, and cognition and reception take place.

Finally, as the computer artist Paul DeMarinis pointed out to me many years ago, at every stage in the computer music-making process, one is standing on the shoulders of other hard-working individuals who created the firmware, drivers, and operating systems that permit one's little program to run relatively painlessly.

Thus, computer music, like any species of cultural production, is created not by lonely romantics, but by vertically and horizontally articulated social networks that function epistemologically. The knowledge-producing and knowledge-vetting functions exercised by these networks are naturally inflected by characteristics such as race, gender, geography, cultural background, economics, and the increasingly globalized socialities that arise from those.

In particular, these socialities have trenchant implications for the development of new discourses that can take computer music beyond the limited goal of producing "art" and "art music," fueled by newer understandings of the practice of improvisation as crucially informed by the quotidian. Realizing that we learn as much about improvisation by observing and analyzing simple, everyday acts and collaborations as we do from analyzing the "truly creative" allows us to see creativity as a birthright on which all humans draw and on which (for well or ill) the fate of Earth depends.

NOTES

1. G. E. Lewis, "Living with creative machines: An improvisor reflects," in *AfroGEEKS: Beyond the Digital Divide*, ed. A. Everett and A. J. Wallace (Santa Barbara: Center for Black Studies Research, 2007), 83–99.

2. G. E. Lewis, "Improvised music after 1950: Afrological and Eurological perspectives," in *The Other Side of Nowhere: Jazz, Improvisation, and Communities in Dialogue*, ed. D. Fischlin and A. Heble (Middletown, CT: Wesleyan University Press, [1996] 2004), 131–162. Western music's break with improvisation is routinely portrayed as gradual and even inevitable, but in fact it constituted a radical rupture with over a half millennium of canonical practice. The extreme understatement with which the historiography of Western music treats this rupture justifies my ironic characterization as a "Quiet Revolution." The slowly growing body of scholarship that retheorizes the decline of improvisation in this period in pan-European music includes R. Moore, "The decline of improvisation in western art music: An interpretation of change," *International Review of the Aesthetics and Sociology of Music* 23(1) (1992): 61–84. Also see A. Sancho-Velasquez, "The legacy of genius: Improvisation, romantic imagination, and the Western musical canon" (Ph.D. dissertation, University of California at Los Angeles, 2001).

3. D. Belgrad, *The Culture of Spontaneity: Improvisation and the Arts in Postwar America* (Chicago: University of Chicago Press, 1998).

4. See H. Bourges, *The Student Revolt: The Activists Speak*, trans. B. R. Brewster (London: Cape, 1968); C. Deliège, "Indétermination et Improvisation," *International Review of the Aesthetics and Sociology of Music* 2(2) (1971): 155–191; V. Globokar, "Reflexionen über Improvisation," in *Improvisation und neue Musik: Acht Kongressreferate*, ed. R. Brinkmann (Mainz: Schott, 1979), 25–41; A. Willener, *The Action-Image of Society: On Cultural Politicization* (London: Tavistock, 1970).

5. Among the panoply of newer scholars working on improvisation are Raymond MacDonald and R. Keith Sawyer (psychology); Larry Silverstein (clinical psychology); Georgina Born (anthropology); Michael Silverstein (linguistics); David Rothenberg,

Arnold Davidson, and Eric Lewis (philosophy); Susan Leigh Foster (dance); Jason Stanyek (ethnomusicology); Paul Ingram and Damon Phillips (organizational science); Ajay Heble (literary theory); Ellen Waterman (sound art); and David P. Brown (architecture). For a prescient early survey of improvisation and the arts, see Hazel Smith and Roger Dean, *Improvisation, Hypermedia, and the Arts since 1945* (Amsterdam: Harwood Academic, 1997). The most frequently cited source on improvisation in recent years was written by a committed musical experimentalist; see Derek Bailey, *Improvisation: Its Nature and Practice in Music* (Ashbourne, UK: Moorland, 1980). For the most part, however, it is hardly surprising that the rekindling of interest in improvisation by a new generation of 21st century scholars was foreshadowed by the 1990s advent of the new jazz studies. Two influential early anthologies are K. Gabbard, *Jazz among the Discourses* (Durham, NC: Duke University Press, 1995); and K. Gabbard, *Representing Jazz* (Durham, NC: Duke University Press, 1995).

    6. For a canonical account of the "origins" of interactivity, see E. Huhtamo, "From cybernation to interaction: A contribution to an archaeology of interactivity," in *The Digital Dialectic: New Essays on New Media*, ed. P. Lunenfeld (Cambridge: MIT Press, 1999), 96–110.

    7. J. Chadabe, *Electric Sound: The Past and Promise of Electronic Music* (Upper Saddle River, NJ: Prentice Hall, 1997), 293.

    8. Ibid., 291.

    9. D. Behrman, "'Keys to Your Music': Zur Konstruktion computergesteuerter interaktiver Klanginstallationen," *MusikTexte: Zeitschrift für neue Musik* 85 (2000), 40–42; J. Bischoff, R. Gold, and J. Horton, "Music for an interactive network of microcomputers," *Computer Music Journal* 2(3) (1978): 24–29; C. Brown and J. Bischoff, "Indigenous to the net: Early network music bands in the San Francisco Bay Area" (2002), http://crossfade. walkerart.org/brownbischoff/; J. Horton, "Unforeseen music: The autobiographical notes of Jim Horton," *Leonardo On-Line* (2002), http://leonardo.info/lmj/horton.html; Hermann-Christoph Müller, "Einheit von Klang und Technik: Die Musik des US-amerikanischen Komponisten David Behrman," *MusikTexte: Zeitschrift für neue Musik* 85 (2000): 31–36.

    10. Chadabe, *Electric Sound*, 297.

    11. One of the early attempts to engage improvisation in the field of new media was B. Laurel, *Computers as Theatre* (New York: Addison-Wesley, 1993). For an early artist-written account of improvisation in chat spaces, see A. LaFarge, "A world exhilarating and wrong: Theatrical improvisation on the Internet," *Leonardo* 28(5) (1995): 415–422.

    12. For a fuller discussion of this history, see Lewis, "Living with Creative Machines."

    13. T. Blackwell, *Live algorithms for music research network—Final report March 2007* (2007), 1. Unpublished report to the Engineering and Physical Sciences Research Council, UK.

    14. See the Live Algorithms for Music Web page, http://www.livealgorithms.org/. Also see T. Blackwell and M. Young, "Live algorithms," *Artificial Intelligence and Simulation of Behaviour Quarterly*, no. 122, Autumn (2005): 7–9; G. E. Lewis, "Live algorithms and the future of music," *CT Watch Quarterly* 3(2) May (2007), http://www.ctwatch.org/quarterly/ articles/2007/05/live-algorithms-and-the-future-of-music/. Blackwell and Young, "Live algorithms," 7.

    15. P. Théberge, *Any Sound You Can Imagine: Making Music/Consuming Technology* (Hanover, NH: Wesleyan University Press, 1997).

    16. L. Suchman, *Human-Machine Reconfigurations: Plans and Situated Actions*, 2nd ed. (Cambridge: Cambridge University Press, 2007), 12.

    17. A. Schutz, "Making music together: A study in social relationship, in *Schutz, Collected Papers 2: Studies in Social Theory*, ed. A. Brodersen (The Hague: Martinus Nijhoff, 1964), 177.

18. Ibid., 159.

19. Ibid., 177.

20. See the discussion "Figuring the Human in AI and Robotics," in L. Suchman, *Human-Machine Reconfigurations: Plans and Situated Actions,* 2nd ed. (Cambridge: Cambridge University Press, 2007), 226–240.

21. Ibid., 247 n. 8.

22. See the account of my approach to constructing and interacting with creative machines in G. E. Lewis, "Too many notes: Computers, complexity and culture in *Voyager,*" *Leonardo Music Journal* 10 (2000): 33–39.

23. M. Dufrenne, *The Phenomenology of Aesthetic Experience (Northwestern University Studies in Phenomenology and Existential Philosophy),* trans. E. S. Casey (Evanston, IL: Northwestern University Press, 1973).

24. Suchman, *Human-Machine Reconfigurations: Plans and Situated Actions,* 2nd ed. (Cambridge: Cambridge University Press, 2007), 12.

BIBLIOGRAPHY

Bailey, D. 1980. *Improvisation: Its Nature and Practice in Music.* Ashbourne, UK: Moorland.

Behrman, D. 2000. "Keys to Your Music": Zur Konstruktion computergesteuerter interaktiver Klanginstallationen. *MusikTexte: Zeitschrift für neue Musik* 85: 40–42.

Belgrad, D. 1998. *The Culture of Spontaneity: Improvisation and the Arts in Postwar America.* Chicago: University of Chicago Press.

Bischoff, J., R. Gold, and J. Horton. 1978. Music for an interactive network of microcomputers. *Computer Music Journal* 2(3): 24–29.

Blackwell, T. 2007. *Live algorithms for music research network—Final report March 2007.* Unpublished report to the Engineering and Physical Sciences Research Council (United Kingdom), pp. 1–6.

Blackwell, T., and M. Young. 2005. Live algorithms. *Artificial Intelligence and Simulation of Behaviour Quarterly* 122 (Autumn): 7–9.

Bourges, H. 1968. *The Student Revolt: The Activists Speak,* trans. B. R. Brewster. London: Cape.

Brown, C., and J. Bischoff. 2002. Indigenous to the net: Early network music bands in the San Francisco Bay area. http://crossfade.walkerart.org/brownbischoff/, accessed June 21, 2008.

Chadabe, J. 1997. *Electric Sound: The Past and Promise of Electronic Music.* Upper Saddle River, NJ: Prentice Hall.

Deliège, C. 1971. Indétermination et Improvisation. *International Review of the Aesthetics and Sociology of Music* 2(2): 155–191.

Dufrenne, M. 1973. *The Phenomenology of Aesthetic Experience (Northwestern University Studies in Phenomenology and Existential Philosophy),* trans. E. S. Casey. Evanston, IL: Northwestern University Press.

Gabbard, K. 1995a. *Jazz among the Discourses.* Durham, NC: Duke University Press.

Gabbard, K. 1995b. *Representing Jazz.* Durham, NC: Duke University Press.

Globokar, V. 1979. Reflexionen über Improvisation. In *Improvisation und neue Musik: Acht Kongressreferate,* ed. R. Brinkmann. Mainz: Schott, pp. 25–41.

Horton, J. 2002. Unforeseen music: The autobiographical notes of Jim Horton. *Leonardo On-Line*. http://leonardo.info/lmj/horton.html, accessed June 23, 2008.

Huhtamo, E. 1999. From cybernation to interaction: A contribution to an archaeology of interactivity. In *The Digital Dialectic: New Essays on New Media*, ed. P. Lunenfeld. Cambridge: MIT Press, pp. 96–110.

LaFarge, A. 1995. A world exhilarating and wrong: Theatrical improvisation on the Internet. *Leonardo* 28(5): 415–422.

Laurel, B. 1993. *Computers as Theatre*. New York: Addison-Wesley.

Lewis, G. E. 2000. Too many notes: Computers, complexity and culture. *Voyager. Leonardo Music Journal* 10 (2000): 33–39.

Lewis, G. E. 2004. Improvised music after 1950: Afrological and Eurological perspectives. In *The Other Side of Nowhere: Jazz, Improvisation, and Communities in Dialogue*, ed. D. Fischlin and A. Heble. Middletown, CT: Wesleyan University Press, pp. 131–162. Originally published as Lewis, G. Improvised Music after 1950: Afrological and Eurological perspectives. *Black Music Research Journal* 16(1) (1996): 91–122.

Lewis, G. E. 2007a. Live algorithms and the future of music. *CT Watch Quarterly* 3(2), May. http://www.ctwatch.org/quarterly/articles/2007/05/live-algorithms-and-the-future-of-music/, accessed June 21, 2008.

Lewis, G. E. 2007b. Living with creative machines: An improvisor reflects. In *AfroGEEKS: Beyond the Digital Divide*, ed. A. Everett and A. J. Wallace. Santa Barbara: Center for Black Studies Research, pp. 83–99.

Moore, R. 1992. The decline of improvisation in Western art music: An interpretation of change. *International Review of the Aesthetics and Sociology of Music* 23(1): 61–84.

Müller, H.-C. 2000. Einheit von Klang und Technik: Die Musik des US-amerikanischen Komponisten David Behrman. *MusikTexte: Zeitschrift für neue Musik* 85: 31–36.

Sancho-Velasquez, A. 2001. "The legacy of genius: Improvisation, romantic imagination, and the Western musical canon." Ph.D. dissertation, University of California at Los Angeles.

Schutz, A. 1964. Making music together: A study in social relationship. In *Schutz, Collected Papers 2: Studies in Social Theory*, ed. Arvid Brodersen. The Hague: Martinus Nijhoff, pp. 159–178.

Smith, H., and R. T. Dean. 1997. *Improvisation, Hypermedia, and the Arts since 1945*. Amsterdam: Harwood Academic.

Suchman, L. 2007. *Human-Machine Reconfigurations: Plans and Situated Actions*. 2nd ed. Cambridge: Cambridge University Press.

Théberge, P. 1997. *Any Sound You Can Imagine: Making Music/Consuming Technology*. Hanover, NH: Wesleyan University Press.

Willener, A. 1970. *The Action-Image of Society: On Cultural Politicization*. London: Tavistock.

....

FROM OUTSIDE THE WINDOW: ELECTRONIC SOUND PERFORMANCE

....

PAULINE OLIVEROS

All musical instruments are tools that map human motoric input on an acoustic output.

> —Godfried-Willem Raes

How can I translate the sense of corporeal fallibility and virtuosity present in acoustic performances into performances of electronic sounds that have no previously established gestural analog?

> —P. Musselman

Although I have been working with a personal computer since 1983 and feel more or less married to the computer, I have remained an outsider to the world of computer music. This is probably because in the 1960s I eschewed synthesis and found my own way to generate electronic sound. Rather than adding up sine waves to create sounds and cutting and splicing tape together to make a piece out of those sounds to be played back on tape, I found a way that allowed me to perform my music in real time in the so-called classical electronic music studio. I needed to map my "human motoric input" onto the machine and "feel my corporeal fallibility and virtuosity" in the process.

The San Francisco Tape Music Center was home base in the 1960s for all kinds of musical adventures and experiments for my colleagues and me. The studio consisted of a small variety of electronic test equipment, a large telephone style patch bay, amplifiers, speakers, and two professional Ampex stereo tape machines. Those tube oscillators with the big frequency dial on the front did not seem inviting for performance. The instruments were made for setting frequencies for scientific tests. Furthermore, there were switches to shift the range of frequency as the dial could not cover the whole frequency range that was accessible on the oscillator.

After staring for a long time at the large Hewlett-Packard war surplus test oscillators[1] and wondering how I could make any music with them, an idea popped into mind: my accordion[2] teacher Willard Palmer[3] had taught me to listen to difference tones. If I played an interval in the high register of my instrument and pulled hard on the bellows, I could hear the difference tones. I had always wondered how it would be to hear just the difference tones without the generating tones.

I noticed that the oscillator frequency range went from 1 Hz to 500 kHz—below and above the range of human hearing, respectively. I set two of our three oscillators to around 40 kHz and 39,950 Hz. I patched them through to the sound system expecting to hear the difference. At first there was nothing. I thought, "There must be something—maybe the amplitude is too low." I placed line amplifiers in the patch, and sure enough I heard my first difference tone low, clear, and rich in quality. I was startled, delighted, and thrilled with the 50 Hz sound. It felt rather magical drawing down this tone from sound vibrations that I could not hear. I touched the dial tentatively and discovered immediately that I could now sweep the audio range by barely turning the dial. "Now," I thought, "how do I use this to play music?"

I had discovered tape head delay and that I could use more than one tape machine to add distance between playback heads for longer time delays.[4] I could route the tracks via a patch bay (there were no mixers available then) in a variety of configurations. I fed the output of the oscillators into the first tape machine, listening and tuning the configuration or signal routing to build my performance instrument. The bias frequencies of the tape machines also modulated the sounds I was getting from the heterodyning of the oscillators. I could send sounds into track 1 of the stereo tape, hear both the record head and playback head with the brief delay, then hear the sound come back from a second playback machine when the tape passed over to the distant supply reel. I could patch the tracks back to the first machine so that new loops were created. Feedback and canonical form became a core element of my electronic music.

In my experience with long practice sessions playing my accordion, I had noticed that my hands usually had a very pleasant tingling sensation that I enjoyed—an aftereffect of mapping "motoric input onto an acoustic output" or my fingers extended to accordion keys and buttons extended to valves so bellows action could blow air through reeds to make sounds.

Soon, through improvisation I was creating my first electronic music. In creating my electronic instrument with the oscillators, the huge dials that had seemed so unfriendly to performance now became receivers for the musical knowledge embodied in my hands and fingers. I had created a very unstable nonlinear music-making system: difference tones from tones set above the range of hearing manipulated by the bias frequency of the electromagnetic tape recording, feedback from a second tape machine in parallel with newly generated difference tones as I responded instantaneously with my hands on those dials to what I was hearing from the delays and as the sounds were all being recorded on magnetic tape.

I had created a new musical instrument that included my "human motoric input" mapped onto the machine for analog output to speakers. This meant that I could play my electronic music in real time without editing or overdubbing. The first pieces made at the San Francisco Tape Music Center were called "Mnemonics I–V" (1965). My first electronic music record release was *I of IV* (1966)[5] (LP record, CBS Odyssey 32 16 0160) made at the University of Toronto Electronic Music Studio. An enthusiastic reviewer lauded the sound of the piece and at the end turned negative and said that because it was made in real time it must have just been thrown together. Clearly, according to the reviewer, I was an outsider throwing music together rather than constructing it carefully.

In 1966, the Buchla Modular synthesizer rendered the classical electronic music studio obsolescent.[6] I made some real-time pieces performing the Buchla with my delay system. I missed the sound of those tube oscillators. Transistor oscillators had a very different sound quality and feeling. Around 1967, I began to play my accordion with the tape delay system. I needed a trusty performance sound source. I played concerts dragging around a couple of Sony 777[7] tape recorders for my delay system. Eventually, in 1983 I replaced the tape machines with Lexicon PC42[8] digital delay processors—one for each hand. I called the evolving instrument the Expanded Instrument System (EIS).[9] I applied what I had learned from playing the oscillators with delays to my accordion playing. I wanted more and more delay processors. This desire led inevitably to the adoption of computer control of the processors. There was no way to manage all the knobs and switches that I wanted to manipulate while performing. I was not interested in studio techniques for constructing a composition. Clearly, my devotion was to improvisational real-time performance.

My adoption of a computer version of my EIS was slowed until 16-bit CD-quality sound became more readily available around 1991. I was reluctant to give up the warm sound of the Lexicons, just as I had been reluctant to give up the sound of those beautiful tube oscillators of the 1960s.

The Lexicon PCM42s had special performance features designed by Gary Hall[10] that I liked as well as the excellent sound reproduction that led me to choose them in the first place. Unlike the tape machine delay system, the digital delay processors allowed for capturing phrases for looping, modulation of delayed material with sine and square waves, and voltage control of clock time for pitch bending. My feet on accelerator-type pedals became sensitized much as my hands and fingers had for motoric mapping to acoustic output. I became very adept at foot-controlled pitch bending with both feet as I was performing new material with my fingers.

I worked in a residency at the Banff Center for three weeks on the Lightning Box—a project with programmer Cornelia Colyer[11] to develop what I called superfoot. I wanted a program that could control the Lexicons like I was doing with my feet only going beyond what I could do physically with my feet. The program would modulate the delays as if my foot was moving at impossible rates and configurations. The first execution of that program was quite thrilling to me as I had extended my motoric input into the computer and imagined something beyond what I could physically accomplish. This was a start toward what eventually became part of the EIS. I created recipes or algorithms that could process delayed input and the delays as well. Rather than knobs and switches, there was a program to control what I could not manage. The program behaved as though it was subject to "human corporeality and fallibility." The recipes or algorithms that I designed for the EIS had assimilated my way of managing the knobs and switches.

I continue to make music in real time with my accordion and with a variety of small instruments and the EIS on the computer. Currently, the program is learning to learn. I want a real-time digital partner that interacts with my input in a humanly motoric way even though the ways may be distinctly beyond human capability. It seems important to me after more than forty years of dealing with my way of making electronic music both analog and digital that we need to find a way to work with nonhuman forms that present us with musical intelligence and new challenges. I remain outside the window.

Since 1990, another window has attracted my attention—telematic performance. The history of this odyssey is described in my forthcoming article, "From Telephone to High Speed Internet: A Brief History of My Tele-Musical Performances."[12] The Telematic Circle,[13] a group of associates interested in telematic performance, has gathered. Performing with musical partners in different locations opens an entirely new window—a new venue. The space between locations is new territory. How to navigate this space and make it as palpable as performing in the same room is a complex and challenging task.

Working together with colleagues Chris Chafe, director of CCRMA (Center for Computer Research in Music and Acoustics)[14] at Stanford University, and Jonas Braasch, director of CARL (Computer Audio Research Laboratory)[15] at Rensselaer Polytechnic Institute, has brought us partway to a satisfying realization of telematic performance. Chafe's open source software JackTrip[16] has provided us with low-latency, eight-channel, CD-quality audio transmission; Jeremy Cooperstock's UltraVideo Conferencing[17] software gives us digital video (DV) quality video; and Braasch's ViMic[18] software makes virtual room simulation possible. My improvisation ensemble Tintinnabulate has jammed together with Chafe's Sound-Wire[19] ensemble for two years. These sessions have given us an enormous amount of artistic and technical data in a synergistic effort. The result of some years of exploration from video telephone to the high-speed Internet has attracted a National Science Foundation grant to research and produce "A Robust Distributed Intelligent System for Telematic Applications". This system will incorporate ViMic and the Expanded Instrument System along with an avatar/agent that will be able to give conducting cues to ensembles across the network and learn from the performances to develop creative solutions in improvisational situations.

For the next two years, Braasch and I as coprincipal investigators and Doug Van Nort, postdoctoral research associate, will engage in designing this intelligent system as we continue to make music with our partners in the Telematic Circle. The main objective of this work is to improve communications with distant partners and to open the window much wider for all that would like to participate.

Stay tuned and keep the windows open! I might like to look in.

NOTES

1. Hewlett-Packard HP200C Wide Range Precision Audio Oscillator Vacuum Tube Type (7 KB). Features include the following: 1- to 500-kHz precision oscillator; 600-ohm balanced, unbalanced output; low-distortion sine wave output; highly stable bridge circuit; excellent choice for audio work; and made in the United States.

2. Pauline Oliveros, The accordion (& the outsider), *The Squid's Ear*. http://www.squidco.com/cgi-bin/news/newsView.cgi?newsID=429, accessed March 30, 2009.

3. Willard A. Palmer, http://www.willardpalmer.org/.

4. Pauline Oliveros, "Tape delay techniques for electronic music composers," in *Software for People (Selected Writings 1963–1980) by Oliveros* (New York: Midpoint Trade Books, 1984), p. 276.

5. From the liner notes from LP Odyssey 32 16 0160: "*I of IV* was made in July, 1966, at the University of Toronto Electronic Music Studio. It is a real time studio performance composition (no editing or tape splicing), utilizing the techniques of amplifying combination tones and tape repetition. The combination-tone technique was one, which I developed in 1965 at the San Francisco Tape Music Center. The equipment consisted of twelve sine-tone square-wave generators connected to an organ keyboard, two line amplifiers, mixer, Hammond spring-type reverb and two stereo tape recorders. Eleven generators were set to operate above twenty thousand cycles per second, and one generator at below one cycle per second. The keyboard output was routed to the line amplifiers, reverb, and then to channel A of recorder 1. The tape was threaded from recorder 1 to recorder 2. Recorder 2 was on playback only. Recorder 2 provided playback repetition approximately eight seconds later. Recorder 1 channel A was routed to recorder 1 channel B, and recorder 1 channel B to recorder 1 channel A in a double feedback loop. Recorder 2 channel A was routed to recorder 1 channel A, and recorder 2 channel B was routed to recorder 1 channel B. The tape repetition contributed timbre and dynamic changes to steady state sounds. The combination tones produced by the eleven generators and the bias frequencies of the tape recorders were pulse modulated by the sub-audio generator." http://www.stalk.net/paradigm/pd04.html EIS; http://depthome.brooklyn.cuny.edu/isam/mockus.html (at the City University of New York).

6. Buchla Modular Synthesizer, http://www.synthmuseum.com/buchla/buc10001.html.

7. Sony TC 777, http://www.sony.net/SonyInfo/CorporateInfo/History/sonyhistory-a.html.

8. Lexicon PC42 delay processors, http://emusician.com/dsp/emusic_max_factor/.

9. P. Oliveros, The Expanded Instrument System: Introduction and brief history, included in *The Future of Creative Technologies, Journal of the Institute of Creative Technologies,* De Montfort University, Leicester, UK, June 2008.

10. Gary Hall, http://emusician.com/dsp/emusic_max_factor/.

11. Cornelia Colyer, http://www.jstor.org/pss/1575535.

12. From telephone to high speed Internet: A brief history of my tele-musical performances, Presented at the International Society of Improvised Music second annual conference during the Telematic Panel, December 14, 2007, at Northwestern University, Evanston, IL. Forthcoming publication in *Leonardo Music Journal.*

13. The Telematic Circle was formed in 2007 as an association of institutions and individuals interested in telematic music performance. See http://www.deeplistening.org/site/telematic for further information.

14. CCRMA, The Stanford University Center for Computer Research in Music and Acoustics (http://ccrma.stanford.edu/), is a multidisciplinary facility where composers and researchers work together using computer-based technology both as an artistic medium and as a research tool.

15. Jonas Braasch, director of Communication Acoustics Research Laboratory (CARL) at Renssalaer Polytechnic Institute, http://symphony.arch.rpi.edu/acoustics/bio.html.

16. JackTrip is a Linux-based system used for multimachine jam sessions over Internet2. It supports any number of channels (as much as the computer/network can handle) of bidirectional, high-quality, uncompressed audio signal steaming, http://ccrma.stanford.edu/groups/soundwire/software/jacktrip/.

17. Jeremy Cooperstock's UltraVideo Conferencing, http://ultravideo.mcgill.edu/.

18. Jonas Braasch's ViMic (Virtual Microphone), http://symphony.arch.rpi.edu/~braasj/JonasBraaschResearch.html.

19. SoundWire ensemble, http://ccrma.stanford.edu/groups/soundwire/.

CHAPTER 23

EMPIRICAL STUDIES OF COMPUTER SOUND

FREYA BAILES
AND ROGER T. DEAN

In this chapter, we discuss computer-generated sound as the object of empirical study, particularly in perceptual, cognitive, and computational research. The purpose of such study begins with the musicological, taken broadly as understanding the structure of music and its impact on listeners, as well as the creative and performative roles of those who realize the music. It continues with the use of computer-generated sound as material for studies on sonic cognition and temporal perception more broadly. One of the advantages of computer sound is its susceptibility to minute control, in the way that scientific empiricists favor, an opportunity largely lacking in cognitive experiments with culturally constrained sonic structures such as those of Western tonal music, the subject of by far the greatest research attention to date.

We focus on computer sound that is fundamentally musical or intended as such but make occasional references to the literature on other computationally generated (or manipulated) sounds. Some such sounds are used to bridge the gap between natural phenomena such as object looming and musical phenomena such as crescendi and diminuendi. When an object that generates sound approaches (looming), the sound can be an important influence on our biological responses and our response of avoidance when necessary; it is of critical interest to understand whether such evolved organismal responses have a counterpart in our dealings with music, and if so how they can be harnessed to expressive or affective intents and impacts. We keep in mind that while repeated exposure to sounds may be necessary to facilitate their perception, many organisms, including humans, are extremely adaptable in their perceptual and cognitive responses, and this is an essential feature of surviving in ever-changing environments.

1. COMPUTER COMPOSITION AND ITS IDEAS AND IMPLICATIONS

As indicated, computer sound (sound generated or mediated by computers) can be special; the technological means and compositional ends are mutually determinative to an unprecedented level. As Hamman (2002) argued, this potential for mutual determination (or at least, influence) is "one of the most important empirical insights generated by early electroacoustic music" (p. 103). Moreover, the technological means permit infinite transformation and establishing a continuum, for example, between the sound of a snail moving and that of Michael Jackson singing or John Oswald manipulating Beethoven. Thus, one might expect that the affective correlates of computer music could be as broad as those of any other sound.

It has been asserted that formalism in electronic composition is inherently empirical rather than theoretical (Hamman 2002) since the concern is with the interaction of sound materials themselves. In early computer music, "musical thought was no longer bound solely to a *transcendental* musical object—the musical object *per se* arose as a consequence of the particularity of the techniques for its production" (p. 103). If so, then such computer music is aligned with the rejection of "grand meta-narratives" by poststructural thought in general and Lyotard in particular (1994). Perhaps techniques in computer music at large have such flexibility that one can mold them to any musical purpose. In accord with our assumption that we need to understand empirically how such molding could be designed and could work, Simon Emmerson indicated that computer music is an experimental tradition, "one which seeks to find new solutions, to test, to research and to modify assumptions accordingly" (1986a, p. 2).

Pierre Schaeffer signaled many of the exploratory approaches open to composers with his ideas about musique concrète. "It was around 1948 . . . that I wished to . . . do a program . . . with music entirely composed of 'noises,' that is, sounds not made by musical instruments or by the human voice" (Malina and Schaeffer 1972, p. 255). As he went on to argue, "Listening to live orchestral music is essentially deductive listening, it is strongly deduced from vision, whereas listening to the radio or a phonograph is inductive or acousmatic listening" (p. 256). Using Peircean terms (although perhaps derived more directly from Saussure), he distinguished a sound that is a "sign . . . supported by meaning" (such as a word) from a sound that is an "index. One searches for the cause of the particular sounds"

(p. 256). Liberated by this understanding, Schaeffer "found it easier to synthesize sounds and to connect them than did many others interested in music made of such sounds" (p. 256). He concluded, "It is necessary to translate the physical nature of sound into its psychological qualities" (p. 258). Even in 1972, he was happy to add that "we are now at the inter-disciplinary stage of finding a language to express mathematically the psychological characteristics of sound" (p. 258) an aspiration that still remains distant in 2009.

Denis Smalley (1986) elaborated ideas of continuous relationships between different and mutually transforming sounds in his theory of "spectro-morphology": "Spectro-morphology is an approach to sound materials and musical structures which concentrates on the spectrum of available pitches and their shaping in time. In embracing the total framework of pitch and time it implies that the vernacular language is confined to a small area of the musical universe" (p. 61). The "vernacular" is Western tonal music, but the comment also applies to traditional musics. While Smalley refers to "pitch," his fundamental concern is with timbre and spectrum as his term *spectro-morphology* implies. Pitch (when discernable) is a consequence of spectrum and a correlate of timbre. Smalley provided a detailed typology of sounds, which is in essence a metaphorical and metonymic system in which the names he provides are in Peircean terms sometimes "indices" (with a connection to the sound), other times "symbols" (with only arbitrary association). His elaborate system provides considerable guidance to a composer in formulating ways to form semiotic links in their composition (see discussion throughout Emmerson 1986b) and has been influential in principle even more than in detail. As Smalley said (p. 81): "So we return to aural discrimination and perception as the supreme musical tools. It is not a scientific knowledge which is required but an experiential knowledge. The composer has to surmount all the preoccupations and distractions of the fabrication process to become the subject of his or her own musical experimentation—the universal listener, the surrogate for all listeners." But, Smalley also respected the "researcher's" aural judgment (p. 93): "Spectro-morphological thinking is the rightful heir of Western musical tradition. Spectro-morphology reaffirms the primacy of aural perception which has been so heinously ignored in the recent past, and warns composers, researchers and technologists that unless aural judgement is permitted to triumph over technology, electroacoustic music will attract deserved condemnation."

All these approaches to compositional thought display a strong relation with the ideas of Gaver (1993a, 1993b) concerning ecological acoustics: in "everyday" listening, we attend to sounds for the information about physical sources they can bring, as in Schaeffer's description of an index, while in "listening to a string quartet, we might be concerned with the pattern of sensations the sounds evoke (musical listening)" (1993b, p. 2). As John Cage might emphasize, one can sometimes listen to particular sounds in either manner. The greater the ecological frequency of an environmental sound, the more readily it will be associated with its physical source (Ballas 1993) and, conversely, the more difficult it may be to reappropriate as one of Schaeffer's bruits, unless that physical association remains relevant. Conversely, unfamiliar sounds, especially in certain listening contexts such as the concert hall or that of the domestic speaker system, are unlikely to be analyzed as potential physical objects, more as sound itself. Eric Clarke also considered these relationships in detail in a recent book (2005). Composition already uses a vast array of the potential psychological approaches to sound as meaning and expression, but our understanding of how these really operate, especially with listeners rather than composers, is rather rudimentary.

2. COMPUTER SOUNDS AND INTERFACES

There are a number of advantages to computer technology when experimenting with sound. For instance, spatial effects can be generated (reviewed in outline by Toiviainen in 2008 and covered in more detail in other chapters of this book), and various spatial cues (distance, binaural, pinna) may be used in virtual reality sonic environments (McAdams et al. 2004). Alternative tuning systems are also possible through computers (reviewed in Sethares 1998, Toiviainen 2008). As Schaeffer argued:

> The structure of sound is one of the most amazing traps that nature has ever invented to make man believe that music has a mathematical basis: octaves correspond to the powers of two, harmonics are like the set of integers, there is the cycle of fifths (except that the cycle of fifths is not quite closed and our ear does not notice it). This cycle of fifths is called "temperament" and leads to the *tempered* musical scale but one quickly forgets this little detail about the tempered scale; one forgets that one has cheated with mathematics, in the West, at least. (Malina and Schaeffer 1972, p. 258)

In a forthcoming article (Dean et al. forthcoming), we have proposed several new tuning systems that are not equal tempered and do not contain any precise octave or other repeating patterns. The scales are based on the prime number series, ensuring so-called just tunings. However, rather than subdivide the octave or pairs of octaves into a prime number of equal divisions, we subdivide the whole audible range (roughly that of the piano keyboard) into intervals based on the first 41, 51, 61, 71, 81, or 91 primes. The second author of this article has realized an electroacoustic performance piece "Ubasuteyama" (released on the Wirripang label, 2008) with the 91-prime scale performed via Max/MSP (Max Signal Processing) and with inharmonic timbres, whose partials also use some prime number ratios. However, as argued by Wendy Carlos, Bill Sethares, and others (Carlos 1987, Sethares 1998), it may be valuable to adapt the timbres used with such scale-tuning systems to reflect the frequency ratios of the scale more fully, and computers allow for this possibility.

Computer musicians are often interface experimenters (cf. chapter 11, this volume), and more broadly, a further characteristic of the computer music domain is the emergence of individual musicians as practice-led researchers. Practice-led researchers in the arts, in an ideal description, might be those who create artistic works by a process that involves fundamental research about subject or technique and who allow the resulting artistic work to feed back into an ongoing fundamental research stream. The artistic work might become the subject of an empirical study, whose results further inform the research process and in turn future artistic works. This is not to subsume the artistic expression under research or vice versa but to indicate an ideal reciprocity and repeating cyclic process (see Smith and Dean 2009).

An example of the practice-led research process just summarized may be found in the work of Jordà (2002), who used his improvisation interface FMOL (F@ust music online) not only to produce computer sound but also to raise research questions concerning computer improvisation. Similarly, Manfred Clynes has been at the forefront of research into expressive gesture and sound, with his theory of "sentics." In one study, he used emotional body movements to modulate the frequency and spectral envelope of a soundwave, which listeners were able to identify correctly for emotional content (Carterette 1989). However, his work is unusual in reaching beyond the development of an idiosyncratic interface or technique, as often very little can be generalized for use by other sound artists or even encapsulated by cognitive science. One can hope this situation changes, and certainly academe provides an environment in which it could. For instance, empirical research by Folkestad (1996) addressed how children use computers to compose music. Applying techniques from situated cognition, he gathered MIDI (musical instrument digital interface) data from participant compositions to look at stages of the compositional process, interviewed participants, and observed them at work. This approach can reveal much about interfaces themselves but equally about useful educational and creative processes. Computers as interactive music systems can be used as an empirical basis to study human behavior in interacting with machines and with other beings and to infer underlying cognition. Laske (1979) made this point, arguing that "in an interactive task environment, [user] behavior can be empirically documented. Interactive computer music systems are thus excellent experimental environments for studying the functional ability of memory" (p. 43).

3. EARLY ATTITUDES AND APPROACHES TO COMPUTER SOUND

Writing in 1969, Karbusický concluded his article on listener perceptions of a computer composition by Eimert by saying "especially in the case of 'experimental music,' which has not yet struck deep roots in society, well-timed analyses of its apperception by listeners are of the greatest significance" (p. 44). Yet, it would be another twenty years until a symposium on the subject of the structure and perception of electroacoustic sound and music took place. An explicit aim of that event (Nielzén and Olsson 1989) was to confront composers with scientists to further the understanding and development of research in computer music. The symposium proceedings are telling of incomprehension regarding whether, and how, computed sound should be explored, with a conservative emphasis on perceptual and aesthetic limitations that militate against experimentation.

For instance, Carterette (1989), in addressing perception and physiology in the hearing of computer sound, assumed that it "will be heard as pleasing or aesthetic like any natural sound. Computer music bestows a great and wonderful power on the composer or performer but does not set him free to flaunt his music or flout the listener's ear" (p. 83). He further assumed that only a limited subset of computer sounds could ever play a musical role, namely, those that are neither too "pure" nor too "noisy." It is notable how extremely these assumptions contrast with the general emphasis of Schaeffer and others on the suitability of all sound objects in composition. Carterette's assertions are empirically testable, but no attempt is made here or elsewhere to do so.

Sloboda (1989), considering both sonic familiarity and cognitive adaptability, represented a psychologist's perspective at the symposium on electroacoustic sound, suggesting of musical reception that "change through evolution seems to characterise almost every historical phenomenon from the differentiation of species to the growth of ideas. Psychologists may be able to remind composers that people need preparation before they can handle radical change" (p. 8). But for an individual listener, "change' in what they hear may at any moment be extremely abrupt, for example, when they first hear music of an unfamiliar culture, tuning system, or genre. Accordingly, organismal adaptability, a key feature mentioned here, can operate within minutes and hours as well as over evolutionary timescales.

For example, Kessler et al. (1984) showed that both Balinese and American listeners could make use of the frequency of occurrence of particular sounds (tones within scales) to adapt quickly to culturally remote melodic structures. It could be that mere exposure to the statistical regularities of a new sound system is enough to establish a new statistical short-term memory, which then can eventually be incorporated in long-term memory as one of its "schema" (Leman 2001).

There has indeed been a recent emergence of evidence for statistical learning in the auditory domain. Saffran et al. (1996) used artificial language to demonstrate that adults learn to differentiate "words" from "nonwords" based on the frequency of occurrence of pseudophonemes in an auditory stream. Similar findings have also been reported with artificial strings of tone sequences (Saffran et al. 1999), and Kuhn and Dienes (2005) reported the implicit learning of nonadjacent pitch relationships in melodies. Thus, one of the key issues is the durability of a newly learned, potentially adaptive response. In other words, when does it change from being a temporary association to becoming a long-term schema? In agreement with Huron (2001), we would argue:

> Those who believe that perceptual mechanisms are largely fixed and immutable are in danger of underestimating human capabilities and therefore of

impeding the development of musical culture. Conversely, those who believe that perceptual mechanisms are highly adaptable are in danger of overestimating human adaptability and therefore of encouraging activities that are irrelevant. to human needs. Although questions concerning the adaptability of human perception may invite opinions, these questions more properly invite further empirical investigation. (p. 55)

An approach to music that sometimes and in some cultures aims to create novel and stylistically unfamiliar work is improvisation (Smith and Dean 1997), and computers are now fast and flexible enough to be well suited to musical improvisation (Dean 2003). Jordà (2002) wrote that "Improvisation using computers still seems a burgeoning and under explored multidisciplinary area where the design of new controller interfaces, real-time sound synthesis and processing techniques, music theory, cognitive science, algorithmic composition techniques, and existing models of improvisation (computer and non-computer based) can converge, in order to bring new interactive music-making paradigms" (p. 1). This promising multidisciplinary agenda was advanced seven years ago; since then, no concerted research to our knowledge has used empirical methodologies to investigate computer improvisation, something that we are currently seeking to address.

Brattico and Sassanelli (2000) raised important questions regarding the perception and cognition of sounds that have been artificially generated: "How can listeners react to them and how can sounds acquire a semantic value if they are neither physically nor culturally constrained?" (p. 108). Concerned with the ambiguity of source identification in electroacoustic music, specifically Trevor Wishart's work, they argued that listeners must adopt their own listening strategies. They drew on writing by Wishart and György Ligeti to emphasize the potential of the human voice in electroacoustic works to communicate affect universally (an emphasis developed in chapter 14, this volume). Unfortunately, it is left to others to determine quite how listeners perceive and cognize this music and to question the extent of the obstacles to listener reception that they imply.

Others come tantalizingly close to an examination of listener perceptions of specifically computer-generated music. McAdams, Depalle et al. (2004) studied the perception of musical similarity in thematic material from Reynolds's *Angel of Death*. This piece combines piano, chamber orchestra, and computer-processed sound sections. The researchers were not concerned with the perception of the computer-processed sound per se but incidentally noted that solo computer sections were rated as high in emotional force by listeners.

A recent edited book about empirical musicology (Clarke and Cook 2004) usefully suggested methods to analyze audio rather than notated score. However, the index made only five references to electronic music, and the most substantial mention of electroacoustic composition was made by McAdams et al. (2004), who observed a lack of perceptual research into sound texture that is particularly relevant to such works. Since then, Toiviainen (2008) has reviewed the subject of the psychology of electronic music. While he underscored the relevance of psychology for electronic music, the chapter merely provided "an introduction to perceptual and cognitive processes of music that are fundamental for understanding electronic music" (p. 218) and did not report empirical means to understand computer sound better.

We present some brief comments on empirical approaches, such as computational analyses of music, including computer music in another section, but the field remains grossly underexplored, except possibly from the point of view of music information retrieval.

Toiviainen concluded his 2008 chapter with an assertion similar to that expressed by the presenters at the 1989 symposium, namely, that computer technology makes it "possible to produce musical material that exceeds the capacity of the human perceptual system. Therefore, for an electronic musician, being aware of the capabilities and limitations of human auditory processing is crucial for efficient communication of musical ideas and exploration of new grounds" (p. 231). This assertion is based on a number of assumptions. One assumption, that excessive complexity can be produced at all, is probably correct, and as a "stringent" criterion, listeners cannot follow more than about three or four musical streams in polyphonic classical music (Huron 2001) or in synthetic sound streams such as studied by Bregman (1990). However, this is quite a different criterion from one that would question whether the addition or subtraction of one stream would be noticeable by a listener (a more "relaxed" criterion). The second assumption in his comment is rather contrary to the intuitions of most acoustic instrumentalists: he implied that computer-generated sound is more complex than that of, say, the oboe or the double bass. But, the complexity of timbre and envelope during realization of a score using these instruments provides a massive amount of "information" besides that in the notation. Accordingly, it is not obvious that computer music and digital instruments necessarily produce music that is in any relevant sense more "complex" or informationally redundant than instrumental music.

4. COMPUTER MODELS OF MUSIC AND MUSIC GENERATION

Leaving the lack of empirical investigation of computer sound to one side, computers have been used instead to model cognitive processing of sound or to attempt to capture symbolic relationships in sound. "There is a particularly interesting convergence between the fields of music cognition and interactive composition: as music cognition research becomes increasingly concerned with processes that could account for musical competence in a real musical environment, it gives rise to algorithms that can be adapted and used by composers and improvisers in performance" (Rowe 2001, p. 9). In this situation, musicians may benefit from the generation of algorithms by researchers in music cognition; these algorithms are originally devised to explain real-time performance and are not necessarily intended for the computer generation of a performance. Rowe was optimistic of realizations that have yet to be extensively produced but have great potential. Furthermore, it is necessary to distinguish, as Wiggins et al. do in detail in chapter 19 of this book, between computational models of structure and corresponding generative algorithms on the one hand and computational models of music cognition on the other. The former can be considered "descriptive," in that the algorithm simply embodies a description of a style that has preexisted and been analyzed from statistical (and perhaps additional) points of view. The algorithm may then reproduce those features in new music that it generates, but the scope of the generated features cannot go beyond those of the source material. On the other hand, a computational model of music cognition might ideally be capable of revealing features of music that have not already become familiar, or even occurred, so that it is "exploratory" and potentially more fully "generative." This complex issue is intrinsic to studies of machine creativity just as much as to our present concern of music generation.

The interaction between modeling capabilities and computer-generated music is epitomized by "virtual music" (Cope 2001), primarily an example of descriptive approaches. This is machine-created composition that attempts to replicate a given musical style, and such style simulation has been the chief concern of Cope's Experiments in Musical Intelligence program. However, Hamman (2002) argued that computers are most useful for the generation of unknown models rather than in modeling historical styles. Such "unknown models" are most commonly novel structural algorithms, but they could also well include some generated directly by a computational model of aspects of temporal cognition (such as the elaborate production model ACT-R developed by Anderson and colleagues [2004]).

The cognitive processing of musical style is complex, but it remains a useful approach to generate a model founded on stylistically grammatical rules capable of outputting computer-generated compositions for comparison with authentic compositions. An important complement to this work is an empirical test of a model by examining listener perceptions of the alternative versions. Storino et al. (2003) asked expert and nonexpert listeners to indicate which aria of a pair was written by the composer who had composed arias they had previously heard in an exposure phase. This was the Baroque composer Giovanni Legrenzi, with the foil aria corresponding to the compositions of a computer program called Legre. The work revealed a role for musical expertise in the ability to distinguish the computer output from the authentic Legrenzi composition, with Baroque music specialists the most accurate. Turing tests assess whether a computational output is distinguishable from a human output, a test that conversational agents have yet to perform well. Arguably, tests that invite comparisons of relatedness, quality, or preference are more useful (e.g., the Legrenzi study or one concerning "interesting" Baroque pieces vs. less-interesting ones). Wiggins et al. also discuss this issue in chapter 19 of this volume.

Computational modeling of certain types of music (such as Western tonal music) frequently involves the generation of musical output that is subsequently analyzed by a music theorist. Temperley (2001) provided an example of such an approach, and while his work is more computational than experimental, his concern was to understand music cognition beyond the level of idiosyncratic play. An alternative branch of computational modeling is that of neural networks. In music, this line of research has similarly sought to compare possible neural processing of musical dimensions with plausible computational structures. Bharucha (1999) is well known for his modeling of particularly tonal relationships by computational "neural networks." This work would not be possible without the combined focus of computational power and musical output. It also shows the remarkable short-term adaptability of neural networks, let alone human brains.

Also at the forefront of computational approaches to understanding music cognition is research on expressive parameters of human performance. The Dutch Music, Mind, Machine group is a good example of a concentrated exploration of components of musical expression, including the use of sonic output from generative models as empirical material (e.g., Honing 2001). Similarly, the KTH (Royal Institute of Technology) rule set, generated in Sweden, is a set of computational rules for controlling the playback of sequenced material to make it seem lively, or expressive in particular ways, and it has been derived from cognitive studies of features that correlate with listener responses in affective terms. Correspondingly, the outputs of the KTH rule set have been subject to some cognitive evaluation, and the data generally demonstrate its positive impact. Livingstone et al. (2007) used the KTH set as part of a generative algorithm so that musical material generated afresh from an algorithmic process can itself be subject to the KTH rules to give it an additional expressive component.

5. SONIFICATION: COMPUTATIONAL REPRESENTATION OF NONMUSICAL DATA IN SOUND

Sonification requires mention here as an example of using computer sound for a specific and empirically assessable functional purpose. Music may or may not have explicit or even implicit communicative and expressive purposes, but in any case, the meaning generated by a listener is a result of the creator's input, the sonic realization, and the listener's efforts. In partial contrast, the term *sonification* was introduced to distinguish sonic representation of a preexistent objective data set for the purposes of its efficient communication, unconnected with music (e.g., seismic data concerning oil exploration), from other kinds of sound generation. Of course, there is a continuum between all these forms of sonic creation, and a rigorously algorithmic composer may be said to sonify the algorithm he or she uses. Furthermore, a composer may use a data set for a musical purpose, rather than for information display and analysis, and may do so just as rigorously (with as little additional intervention) as a sonifier. However, the composer's purpose is not the display of objective data or comprehension of that data, and rarely is the purpose even comprehension of the algorithm rather than of its expression in the sonic output.

From the perspective of the present chapter, an important issue is that sonification can use objective data, and granted the intention is the display and interrogation of the data, then a new set of empirical assessments becomes possible, for example, to what degree is precision of display achieved and to what extent was the mode of display facilitating rather than hindering the data interrogation. These can be tested precisely, and it is interesting that in spite of the practical potential and in some cases present value (in the oil industry or in warning systems), such testing has been very limited. Warning systems are a specialized case, often best served by a limited palette of auditory "icons," which are really either indices or icons, and contain or develop a relationship with the warning to be conveyed. Quite a few empirical studies of their perception have been presented (Brewster et al. 1993, Lucas 1994, Coward and Stevens 2004) but very little has been done empirically to study wider ranging and notably continuous real-time displays.

6. Emphasizing the Listener's Experience of Computer Music

Electroacoustic music has posed a challenge to traditional music theoretic accounts of pitch relations since these are often irrelevant to the work or they emphasize abstract, syntactic sound properties while neglecting more referential or "extramusical" components. Arguably, such accounts are alienated from and alienating for the listener. In response, Windsor (1997) argued for an alternative approach to understanding computer music by exploring the way in which structural components of the sound contribute to meaning. This necessarily emphasizes the importance of the listener's perception of the music, a sentiment pre-dated by Ward (1989), who wrote: "In the field of music, experiential reality is the only important reality" (p. 101). Emmerson (1986a) pointed out that academic discourse concerning electroacoustic music has focused primarily on analyses of musical techniques and means, neglecting more aesthetic concerns. As we have noted, an equally neglected topic is the empirical investigation of listener perceptions of computer music, and this in spite of Emmerson's asserted importance of the listener as arbiter.

Landy and his Intention/Reception (I/R) project, briefly discussed in chapter 25 of this book and elaborated more in Landy (2006), is a notable exception, and his work emphasizes the importance of the composer providing verbal cues to aid the listener and notes how advantageous such cues seem to be. He developed (2006) earlier arguments on the relationship between verbal description and listener response proposed by Cook (1998). In the I/R methodology, electroacoustic composers are invited to fill out a Composer Intention Questionnaire concerning a particular composition, and listeners are invited to fill out a Real-Time Questionnaire while listening to several repetitions of this composition, as well as providing a more detailed reflection of their impressions of the music between the first and second hearings (Weale 2006). To investigate the hypothesis that title and dramaturgic information aid accessibility to the work, the introduction of this information was staggered between successive hearings. The project constitutes a rare test of listener reactions to computer music.

There are happily some other exceptions to our generalization that computer music has been neglected as empirical subject or tool, some in which reflection regarding how listeners perceive computer music has even guided the treatment of computer sound, and we now turn our attention to these.

7. ONGOING EMPIRICAL TARGETS FOR STUDIES OF COMPUTER MUSIC

In this section, we illustrate the small number of studies specific to the perception of computer-generated sounds intended or suitable for musical use. We do not elaborate on studies in which computer-controlled sounds have been used to investigate psychoacoustic phenomena, such as the complex issue of perceptual loudness, acoustic looming (Neuhoff 2001, Olsen et al. 2007), or just noticeable differences in pitch (de Cheveigné 2005). In particular, there are some fascinating studies of pitch, dissonance, and timbral roughness using synthetic sounds (Mathews and Pierce 1980, Sethares 1998), leading to the idea that instrumental timbres may usefully be adapted specifically to the tuning system in which they will be used (see Dean et al. forthcoming).

One of the earliest empirical investigations of the perception of computer music is a sociological survey of listener response to sections of Herbert Eimert's *Epitaph for Aikichi Kuboyama* (Karbusický 1969). An impressive 4,500 respondents described what notions or images were evoked by listening to the music. Karbusický wrote that "in electronic music new and unwonted sounds are produced that differ substantially from the conventional, 'stylised' sounds obtained from instruments. This 'inhumanness' of the new material obviously evokes such notions of catastrophes, strange sounds, and cosmic happenings" (pp. 33–34). Other listeners sought to establish a relationship between the electronic sounds and their normal sound environment. Karbusický argued that "the imaginative faculty of listeners to electronic music is largely influenced by its utilization in the mass media, above all as background music for science fiction programmes" (p. 35). It seems that social conventions surrounding the meaning of computer sounds were forged, and the electronic material was neither autonomous nor a neutral sonic structure. Examining associations between reported musical preference and responses to the piece, Karbusický observed that those who liked listening to jazz associated the music with joy, while those who enjoy classical and romantic music referred to "cosmos" interpretations. Those who enjoyed listening to Webern did not report such extramusical associations. It is difficult to project back to 1969, even if one was alive then. The novelty of electronic sound in popular culture, and on TV and in cinema, and its association with sci-fi therein, has surely worn off, although the classic *Doctor Who* TV series still makes ongoing appearances in some countries, with electronic sound that is only slightly updated from the original. (The late British-Australian electronic music composer Tristram Cary wrote music for *Doctor Who* from 1964 until at least 1972.) We would anticipate that when a similar study is done in the present cultural environment, responses would be very different.

Bücklein (1981) investigated the perception of fluctuations in the transfer functions of electroacoustic systems. He found that listeners to speech, music, and noise stimuli better perceived peaks in the frequency response than valleys, a finding that is relevant to asymmetries of perception in computer music. Computers have allowed the generation of artificial sounds that inform us of perceptual phenomena that would otherwise remain undiscovered (Ward 1989, Bregman 1990).

For instance, Deutsch (1989) described the generation of Shepard tones, in which the amplitudes of the sinusoidal components of a tone are determined by a bell-shaped spectral envelope. While the chroma or pitch class of these tones is clearly modulated by raising or lowering the frequency of the components, pitch height is perceived to change ambiguously as either rising or falling. Such sounds probably never occur in the natural environment, and their generation has led to a number of empirical studies of pitch perception, dubbed the tritone paradox and the semitone paradox.

Others have begun with familiar acoustic sounds, using computers for analysis and synthesis. For instance, Gordon and Grey (1978) were interested in empirically testing listener perceptions of spectral modifications to orchestral instrument tones. Such synthesized stimuli allow for the precise control of the parameters of interest. Warren and Verbrugge (1984) took advantage of sound-processing techniques to conduct seminal research into the auditory perception of breaking and bouncing glass. Comparing listener perceptions of natural sounds with computer-constructed material, they demonstrated the importance of time-varying properties of the auditory signal for correct categorization of breaking and bouncing sounds. There was a remarkable facility to identify "breaking" within sounds that were radical transformations of natural breaking sounds. This could also be viewed as a demonstration of diverse means to "sonify" the processes of breaking and bouncing.

There is still considerable scope for empirical investigations of listener perceptions and responses to computer sound. In the light of our comments, it is
understandable that research has often been driven by personal compositional
goals and analyses of the mutual impact of technology and sonic possibility.
Those who have paused to question what listeners perceive and how they react to
computer-generated sound have generally contributed on a theoretical rather than
an empirical level. There remain key questions concerning perceptual, cognitive,
and affective response to computer sound, important not least for the efficient
design of computer-generated sound capable of communicating structural and
affective expression. Here, we outline key areas that seem to us to be the most
fruitful, several of which we are directly engaged in at present.

First, we think back to some of the typical properties of computer music that
have been described, such as the structural importance of texture and timbre rather
than the note-based compositional features found in Western tonal music (such as
tonal relations and metric structure). We summarize important research targets in
terms of sequentially increasing complexity, moving from timbre, texture, and
sonic objects to segmentation and structure and then pointing to the issue of
relationships between all the preceding components and affect. Note that each
component necessarily involves several parties: both composer or improviser and
listener.

Timbre perception is little understood, and the perception of musical texture
in computer music has only just begun to be considered (Van Nort 2007). This is
an obvious area for future research, through which we should learn more about the
structural perception and cognition of timbral and textural relations and their
temporal trajectory. Listeners can be expected to respond differently to certain
sonic structures (timbre, texture) in terms of perceived musical expression and
their own affective response. This leads to important questions of interest to both
psychologists and those concerned with music reception: just how adaptable are
our mental schemata (frameworks) concerning the perception of computer sound?
What may be the cognitive and affective consequences for a listener who lacks
perceptual fluency in the genre?

We have already begun to explore the perception of computer-generated music
using experimental methods to determine what listeners hear with respect to the
algorithmic composition of the stimuli and what affective expression is communicated to them through these algorithmic structures. Our work has been motivated
by both personal compositional goals and a broader concern with cognitive science.
Given the dearth of knowledge regarding whether listeners perceive even the most
basic algorithmic devices in computer music, our investigations began by examining
perceptions of sound segmentation in computer-generated stimuli (Bailes and Dean
2007a, 2007b). In summary, we find that even musically naïve listeners are able to
detect sound segmentation in stimuli that range from sine tones to filtered noise to
more heterogeneous timbre segments. In addition, asymmetrical perceptions have
been revealed by this work: when one sound changed to another and this involved
the thickening of the timbral texture (e.g., the addition of partials to the spectrum),

listeners tended to perceive such an increase in texture more readily than the converse decrease in texture at the point of segmentation. Such a finding is compatible with the data of Bücklein (1981) and can be used to shape computer composition; it also deserves further study for its possible links to the phenomenon of auditory looming, by which increases of loudness may be more readily perceived than decreases of the same magnitude (Neuhoff 2001, Olsen et al. 2007).

Ongoing work in our laboratory is systematically exploring the influence of different types of sound transitions (cross-fades and convolution) on listener perceptions of change in computer sound and expressed affect. Contextual factors such as sound duration have a different impact on listener ratings of perceived affect. In addition, an influence of familiarity with the experimental sounds seems to be implied by the systematic rating of processed water and drum sounds as expressing a positive valence, while noise-based stimuli are reported to express a negative valence.

On the premise that computer sounds reminiscent of environmental or natural sounds may be perceived as particularly evocative, we have also conducted survey research exploring listener responses to sounds that are a hybrid between human speech and noise, with no detectable phonemes, and that we term NoiseSpeech (Dean and Bailes 2006). As others have written, "an electronic voice can mouth coherent or incoherent phonemes, syllables or phrases which mediate between music and language at many levels of emotion and communication" (Carterette 1989, p. 84). The example given is of Stockhausen's *Gesang der Jünglinge*, in which a treble voice is distorted to break the normal physical rules of vocal production. We have demonstrated (Bailes and Dean forthcoming) that listeners indeed cluster such NoiseSpeech sounds with genuine speech sounds when asked to discriminate sonic character in terms of attributes explicitly incorporated in the range of sounds studied (piano, drums, speech) and one "dummy" attribute that did not belong to the sound stimuli (water). Remarkably, this clustering was observed even with NoiseSpeech sounds that comprised time-invariant formants superimposed on noise (although speech is characterized by highly time-variant formants). In other work, we are currently determining whether such NoiseSpeech communicates affect in line with its perception as speech related and similarly whether NoiseSong is perceived according to similar categories, and similarly communicates affect, for naïve listeners.

As we illustrated in this section, questions of empirical importance for psychology and for computer music composers abound at the levels of sound unit or component; sound structural segmentation; larger-scale perception of structure, event, and prediction; and the relationship of all the preceding to musical affect. Synthesizing John Locke's 17th-century ideas on sound perception, we believe that computers present an "unparalleled opportunity for creating 'new' and 'complex' ideas by the application of algorithmic 'simple ideas' in tandem and in collision, to bring out statistical patterns that may not have occurred ecologically" (Dean and Bailes 2007, p. 94) and that accordingly pose important empirical questions. We hope this survey will encourage more participants in this research field.

BIBLIOGRAPHY

Anderson, J. R., D. Bothell, M. D. Byrne, S. Douglass, C. Lebiere, and Y. Qin. 2004. An integrated theory of the mind. *Psychological Review* 111(4): 1036–1060.

Bailes, F., and R. T. Dean. 2007a. Facilitation and coherence between the dynamic and retrospective perception of segmentation in computer-generated music. *Empirical Musicology Review* 2(3): 74–80.

Bailes, F., and R. T. Dean. 2007b. Listener detection of segmentation in computer-generated sound: An exploratory experimental study. *Journal of New Music Research* 36(2): 83–93.

Bailes, F., and R. T. Dean. Forthcoming. When is noise speech? A survey in sonic ambiguity. *Computer Music Journal.*

Ballas, J. A. 1993. Common factors in the identification of an assortment of brief everyday sounds. *Journal of Experimental Psychology: Human Perception and Performance* 19: 250–267.

Bharucha, J. J. 1999. Neural nets, temporal composites, and tonality. In *The Psychology of Music,* ed. D. Deutsch. San Diego: Academic Press, pp. 413–440.

Brattico, E., and F. Sassanelli. 2000. Perception and musical preferences in Wishart's work. *Journal of New Music Research* 29(2): 107–119.

Bregman, A. S. 1990. *Auditory Scene Analysis: The Perceptual Organization of Sound.* Cambridge: MIT Press.

Brewster, S. A., P. C. Wright, and A. D. N. Edwards. 1993. "An evaluation of earcons for use in auditory human computer interfaces." Paper presented at INTERCHI '93, April 24–29, Amsterdam, the Netherlands.

Bücklein, R. 1981. The audibility of frequency response irregularities. *Journal of the Audio Engineering Society* 29(3): 126–131.

Carlos, W. 1987. Tuning: At the crossroads. *Computer Music Journal* 11(1): 29–43.

Carterette, E. C. 1989. Perception and physiology in the hearing of computed sound. In *Structure and Perception of Electroacoustic Sound and Music,* ed. S. Nielzénand O. Olsson. Amsterdam: Excerpta Medica, pp. 83–99.

Clarke, E., and N. Cook, eds. 2004. *Empirical Musicology: Aims, Methods, Prospects.* New York: Oxford University Press.

Clarke, E. F. 2005. *Ways of Listening: An Ecological Approach to the Perception of Musical Meaning.* New York: Oxford University Press.

Cook, N. 1998. *Analysing Musical Multimedia.* Oxford: Clarendon Press.

Cope, D. 2001. *Virtual Music: Computer Synthesis of Musical Style.* Cambridge: MIT Press.

Coward, S. W., and C. J. Stevens. 2004. Extracting meaning from sound: Nomic mappings, everyday listening, and perceiving object size from frequency. *The Psychological Record* 54: 349–364.

Dean, R. T. 2003. *Hyperimprovisation: Computer Interactive Sound Improvisation; with CD (R) of Sound Works, Intermedia, and Performance Software Patches.* Middleton, WI: A-R Editions.

Dean, R. T., and F. Bailes. 2006. NoiseSpeech. *Performance Research* 11(3): 85–86.

Dean, R. T., and F. Bailes. 2007. "Human understanding" in imagining and organising sound: Some implications of John Locke's essay for ecological, cognitive and embodied approaches to composition. *Organised Sound* 12(1): 89–95.

Dean, R. T., F. Bailes, and D. Brennan. Forthcoming. Microtonality, the octave, and novel tunings for affective music. In *Music of the Spirit,* ed. B. Crossman and M. Atherton. Sydney: Australian Music Centre.

de Cheveigné, A. 2005. Pitch perception models. In *Pitch. Neural Coding and Perception*, ed. C. J. Plack, R. R. Fay, A. J. Oxenham, and A. N. Popper. New York: Springer, pp. 169–233.

Deutsch, D. 1989. Some new musical paradoxes. In *Structure and Perception of Electroacoustic Sound and Music*, ed. S. Nielzén and O. Olsson. Amsterdam: Excerpta Medica, pp. 61–81.

Emmerson, S. 1986a. Introduction. In *The Language of Electroacoustic Music*, ed. S. Emmerson. New York: Harwood Academic, pp. 1–4.

Emmerson, S. 1986b. *The Language of Electroacoustic Music*. New York: Harwood Academic.

Folkestad, G. 1996. *Computer Based Creative Music Making: Young People's Music in the Digital Age, Göteborg Studies in Educational Sciences*. Göteborg, Sweden: Acta Universitatis Gothoburgensis.

Gaver, W. W. 1993a. How do we hear in the world? Explorations in ecological acoustics. *Ecological Psychology* 5(4): 285–313.

Gaver, W. W. 1993b. What in the world do we hear? An ecological approach to auditory event perception. *Ecological Psychology* 5(1): 1–29.

Gordon, J. W., and J. M. Grey. 1978. Perception of spectral modifications on orchestral instrument tones. *Computer Music Journal* 2(1): 24–31.

Hamman, M. 2002. From technical to technological: The imperative of technology in experimental music composition. *Perspectives of New Music* 40(1): 94–120.

Honing, H. 2001. From time to time: The representation of timing and tempo. *Computer Music Journal* 25(3): 50–61.

Huron, D. 2001. Tone and voice: A derivation of the rules of voice-leading from perceptual principles. *Music Perception* 19(1): 1–64.

Jordà, S. 2002. Improvising with computers: A personal survey (1989–2001). *Journal of New Music Research* 31(1): 1–10.

Karbusický, V. 1969. Electronic music and the listener. *The World of Music* 11(1): 32–44.

Kessler, E. J., C. Hansen, and R. N. Shepard. 1984. Tonal schemata in the perception of music in Bali and in the West. *Music Perception* 2(2): 131–165.

Kuhn, G., and Z. Dienes. 2005. Implicit learning of nonlocal musical rules: Implicitly learning more than chunks. *Journal of Experimental Psychology: Learning, Memory, and Cognition* 31(6): 1417–1432.

Landy, L. 2006. The Intention/Reception project. In *Analytical Methods of Electroacoustic Music*, ed. M. Simoni. New York: Routledge, pp. 29–54.

Laske, O. E. 1979. Considering human memory in designing user interfaces for computer music. *Computer Music Journal* 2(4): 39–45.

Leman, M. 2001. Modeling musical imagery. In *Musical Imagery*, ed. R. I. Godøy and H. Jørgensen. Lisse: Swets and Zeitlinger, pp. 57–76.

Livingstone, S. R., M. Ralf, A. R. Brown, and A. Loch. 2007. Controlling musical emotionality: An affective computational architecture for influencing musical emotions. *Digital Creativity* 18(1): 43–53.

Lucas, P. A. 1994. "An evaluation of the communicative ability of auditory icons and earcons." Paper presented at Second International Conference on Auditory Display ICAD '94, November 7–9, Santa Fe, NM.

Lyotard, J. 1994. *The Post-modern Condition: A Report on Knowledge*. Manchester: Manchester University Press.

Malina, F. J., and P. Schaeffer. 1972. A conversation on concrete music and kinetic art. *Leonardo* 5(3): 255–260.

Mathews, M. V., and J. R. Pierce. 1980. Harmony and nonharmonic partials. *Journal of the Acoustical Society of America* 68: 1252–1257.

McAdams, S., P. Depalle, and E. Clarke. 2004. Analyzing musical sound. In *Empirical Musicology: Aims, Methods, Prospects*, ed. E. Clarke and N. Cook. New York: Oxford University Press, pp. 157–197.

McAdams, S., B. W. Vines, S. Vieillard, B. K. Smith, and R. Reynolds. 2004. Influences of large-scale form on continuous ratings in response to a contemporary piece in a live concert setting. *Music Perception* 22(2): 297–350.

Neuhoff, J. G. 2001. An adaptive bias in the perception of looming auditory motion. *Ecological Psychology* 132: 87–110.

Nielzén, S., and O. Olsson, eds. 1989. *Structure and Perception of Electroacoustic Sound and Music*. Amsterdam: Excerpta Medica.

Olsen, K. N., C. Stevens, and J. Tardieu. 2007. "A perceptual bias for increasing loudness: Loudness change and its role in music and mood." Paper presented at Inaugural International Conference on Music Communication Science, December 5–7, 2007, Sydney, Australia.

Rowe, R. 2001. *Machine Musicianship*. Cambridge: MIT Press.

Saffran, J. R., E. K. Johnson, R. N. Aslin, and E. L. Newport. 1999. Statistical learning of tone sequences by human infants and adults. *Cognition* 70: 27–52.

Saffran, J. R., E. L. Newport, and R. N. Aslin. 1996. Word segmentation: The role of distributional cues. *Journal of Memory and Language* 35: 606–621.

Sethares, W. 1998. *Tuning, Timbre, Spectrum, Scale*. London: Springer-Verlag.

Sloboda, J. A. 1989. Music psychology and the composer. In *Structure and Perception of Electroacoustic Sound and Music*, ed. S. Nielzén and O. Olsson. Amsterdam: Excerpta Medica, pp. 3–12.

Smalley, D. 1986. Spectro-morphology and structuring processes. In *The Language of Electroacoustic Music*, ed. S. Emmerson. London: Macmillan.

Smith, H., and R. T. Dean, eds. 2009. *Practice-Led Research, Research-Led Practice in the Creative Arts*. Edinburgh: Edinburgh University Press.

Smith, H. A., and R. T. Dean. 1997. *Improvisation, Hypermedia and the Arts since 1945*. London: Harwood Academic.

Storino, M., E. Bigand, R. Dalmonte, and M. Baroni. 2003. "Style processing." Paper presented at 5th Triennial ESCOM Conference, September 8–13, Hanover University of Music and Drama, Germany.

Temperley, D. 2001. *The Cognition of Basic Musical Structures*. Cambridge: MIT Press.

Toiviainen, P. 2008. The psychology of electronic music. In *The Cambridge Companion to Electronic Music*, ed. N. Collins. New York: Cambridge University Press, pp. 218–231.

Van Nort, D. 2007. Texture perception: Signal models and compositional approaches. In *SMPC 2007*. Montreal: Concordia University, pp. 73–74.

Ward, W. D. 1989. Physiology of hearing. In *Structure and Perception of Electroacoustic Sound and Music*, ed. S. Nielzén and O. Olsson. Amsterdam: Excerpta Medica, pp. 101–107.

Warren, W. H., and R. R. Verbrugge. 1984. Auditory perception of breaking and bouncing events: A case study in ecological acoustics. *Journal of Experimental Psychology: Human Perception and Performance* 10(5): 704–712.

Weale, R. 2006. Discovering how accessible electroacoustic music can be: The Intention/Reception project. *Organised Sound* 11(2): 189–200.

Windsor, L. W. 1997. Frequency structure in electroacoustic music: Ideology, function and perception. *Organised Sound* 2(2): 77–82.

PART V

CULTURAL AND EDUCATIONAL ISSUES

CHAPTER 24

TOWARD THE GENDER IDEAL

MARY SIMONI

The basic discovery about any people is the discovery of the relationship between its men and its women.

—Pearl S. Buck

1. Toward the Gender Ideal: Milestones

Since the early days of music technology, the accomplishments of men have established the pillars of the field: synthesis, composition, performance, and audio engineering. The frequency at which the achievements of men are cited in established historical references dwarfs the contributions of women. Even today, we readily observe an imbalance between men and women who enter the field as students and persist throughout a career. Such disproportionate participation and persistence in music technology by males and females has piqued the interest of several researchers since the late 20th century (McCartney 1995, Simoni 1995). The disparity in participation by gender has led to such countermeasures as concert series and publications that exclusively showcase contributions of women (Burns 2002, Canadian Electroacoustic Community 2006, Hinkle-Turner 2006) or organizational alliances between professional associations such as the International Computer Music Association and the International Alliance for Women in Music.

The juxtaposition of research in gender and music technology with the history of feminism and civil rights proves insightful since milestones in these social movements are contemporary with the advent of music technology. Before beginning to explore the connections among these historical events, it is important to establish some definitions. First, according to Hoffert (2003), *gender* is "the cultural meaning given to an individual's sex; a social condition based on anatomical characteristics." Second, and for the purposes of this study, *music technology* is defined as the use of electronic technologies in the conception, performance, notation, cataloging, recording, and production of music. Third, *feminism* is the belief that men and women are inherently equal and thus deserve equal rights and opportunities. The social movement to promote equality of the sexes is called *feminism*. Last, *civil rights* are the fundamental rights of the individual, such as liberty, due process, equal protection under the law, and freedom from discrimination. Any civil rights movement is concerned with restoring these fundamental rights.

The first wave of feminism occurred in the late 19th and early 20th century and culminated in the attainment of women's suffrage around the world, including New Zealand, Australia, Finland, the United States, and the United Kingdom. The motto of the 1868 American periodical *The Revolution*, published by the prominent suffragist Susan B. Anthony, summed the first-wave feminist view succinctly (McPhee and Fitzgerald 1979, p. 168): "Principles, not policy; justice, not favor; men, their rights and nothing more; women their rights, and nothing less."

The second wave of feminism began in the early 20th century and called for an end to the legal and social discrimination against women. As stated by British feminist Alison Neilans (Strachey 1936, p. 176), "The feminist goal is an equal moral standard; that law, custom and public opinion should accord to women as a natural and inalienable right the same liberty of action and the same standard of responsibility, neither more nor less, that are accorded to men." Historically, the second wave of feminism overlaps with both the beginning of music technology and the global burgeoning of the civil rights movement.

Civil strife, beginning in the mid-20th century and continuing to this day, paints the countless ugly faces of discrimination: religious, cultural, ethnic, racial, political, and sexual to name but a few. Notable bursts of civil turmoil include the Northern Ireland sectarian conflict, the fight against apartheid in South Africa, and the civil rights movement in the United States. Despite the influential work of peace activists such as Dr. Martin Luther King Jr., Mohandas Gandhi, and the Dalai Lama, the quest for global civil rights is scarred by the carnage of terrorists. Notable episodes include the march on Selma, Alabama, in the United States; the Omagh bombing in Northern Ireland; the genocide of Rwanda; and today's improvised explosive devices of sectarian Iraq.

Without question, global civil rights movements set the stage for the third wave of feminism. This wave of feminism unites women across the world in challenging the second-wave feminists, claiming their philosophy applies mostly to the experiences of English-speaking middle-class women. As transgender activist and author Leslie Feinberg vigorously proclaimed in the *Trans Liberation* (1998, p. 141), "The ranks of rebellions and revolutions that have shaped human history have been made up of people like you and me.... The people who make a difference are those who fight for freedom—not because they're guaranteed to succeed—but because it's the right thing to do."

One branch of feminism, known as *difference feminism*, asserts that the fundamental natures of men and women are ontologically different. Since the late 20th century, difference feminism has evolved to a position of integral complementarity; that is, women and men are considered integral whole beings who, when combined, form a gestalt. *Equity feminism*, a term first used by Christina Hoff Sommers (1994), signals solidarity among women and strives to restore the tenets of equality characteristic of the first wave of feminism. As the feminist movement has matured, feminist theory has become increasingly factionalized, and in some cases, misguided feminism has had the detrimental effect of polarizing the sexes (Sommers 2000). Nevertheless, feminists persist in the belief that just as people of all races and ethnicities should work together to promote civil justice, so must men and women work together to put an end to gender bias. As influential journalist and women's activist Gloria Steinem stated, "We are talking about a society in which there will be no roles other than those chosen or those earned. We are really talking about humanism." Steinem's fundamental value of equal opportunity and justice for all people is the orthodox litmus test for both feminism and civil rights (Wikipedia n.d.).

The catalyst that has sparked and continues to bolster the feminist and civil rights movements is a perceived injustice caused by a disparity of power—both formal and informal. Formal power is obtained by holding a position of authority, whereas informal power is usually ascribed to an individual because of the perceived value of the contributions of that individual in a specific context. A disparity of power manifests itself in many ways; some behaviors support equity, while others subvert it. As an illustration of the correlation of formal and informal power, consider the influx of electronic appliances into Western households in the mid-20th century. These appliances brought with them a bifurcation of power; women were consulted as expert consumers who influenced the design of household appliances that were typically engineered and built by men (Oldenziel 2001). Informal power was ascribed to women because of their ability to describe the quality of interactions *with* machines, whereas men held formal power as the designers and engineers *of* the machines. Concurrent with the development of household appliances and the gender roles associated with the use of machines arrived the dawn of music technology. It is not surprising that women such as Laurie Spiegel and Joan E. Miller made considerable contributions to early research in music technology, but their names seldom appear in historical accounts of the period. The story of Joan E. Miller, likely a female, remains an enigma. She is listed as the first of Max Mathew's collaborators in the historically significant book *The Technology of Computer Music* (Mathews et al. 1969). Yet, after the publication of this influential book, Miller seems to have lapsed into obscurity.

To this day, people perceive some fields of music technology, notably audio engineering, as male dominated. Presumably, audio engineering persists as a gendered field because it is often portrayed with masculine images that connote control and power. The fact that the record industry has a reputation of overt sex discrimination may also impart an unwelcoming milieu for women. One of the most notable instances of blatant gender discrimination in the recording industry occurred when Decca Records declined to hire Delia Derbyshire as a recording engineer in 1959 simply because she was a woman. From the audio engineer's subtle control over the mix during a recording session to the physical demands of moving equipment, audio engineering reveals an intricate interaction between both informal and formal power (Sandstrom 2000). Such an imbalance of power continues to propel the feminist's pursuit of equity between men and women. As Roseanne Barr remarked (Brainy Quote n.d.), "The thing women have yet to learn is nobody gives you power. You just take it." These words of gritty advice speak to those females who have been inculcated to seek assurance before engaging in a behavior.

2. THE SURVEY

The goal of the survey was to explore questions of gender and its relationship to music technology experience, behavior, and perception and from there begin to quantify and analyze contemporary trends in gender differences. The survey was grouped into seven sections: (1) "About This Survey," (2) "Demographics," (3) "Experience with Music Technology," (4) "Behaviors around Music Technology," (5) "Gendered Perception of Music Technology Behaviors (Self)," (6) "Gendered Perception of Music Technology Behaviors (Others)," and (7) "Concluding Remarks."

A. Methodology

The survey's target population was the international community of music technologists. An e-mail invitation was sent to members of the International Computer Music Association, the Society for Electroacoustic Musicians in the United States, the Canadian Electroacoustic Community, the Sonic Arts Network, and the Australasian Computer Music Association. An invitation to participate in the survey was posted to several Facebook (http://www.facebook.com) groups, including the 2008 International Computer Music Conference, Performing Arts Technology, Ars Electronica, and Computer Music. Electronic communication was used to solicit responses because this mode of communication is the norm for the target population. Respondents determined whether they would participate in the survey, and because of this self-selection, the respondents may be viewed as having an interest (or bias) in the survey topic. In addition, electronic invitations to complete the survey may have been forwarded from members of the target population to someone who may not be a member of the target population. The online survey was publicly available during March 2008.

B. Respondent Demographics

A total of 450 respondents initiated the survey, and of those, 342 completed the survey (76%). Respondents were not required to answer the questions, with the exception of "I agree to participate in this survey," so the number of respondents N varies for each question. Respondents from twenty-six countries participated in the survey, and they ranged in age from 18 to 91 years. Most respondents identified their gender as either male or female (98.4%), with the remaining respondents identifying their gender as homosexual, gender queer, or transsexual. Of the 379 respondents who identified their gender as male or female, 186 were female (49.1%) and 193 were male (50.9%). For the purposes of this study, the gender categories were limited to female and male. Table 24.1 summarizes female-male gender participation by geographic region and age group.

Given the target population, it is not surprising that most respondents use music technology as part of their occupation (86.2%) as well as for leisure (88.3%). The various occupations of the respondents spanned a broad continuum from student to retiree and included such occupations as composer, sound artist, dancer, instructor, instrument designer, network administrator, information analyst, broadcast engineer, audiovisual technician, computer programmer, librarian, or manager. Of 326 respondents, males were slightly more likely (51.5%) than females (48.5%) to use music technology as part of their occupation. The survey had approximately equal participation by males and females overall, with equitable participation by men and women engaged in music technology as an occupation.

To gain insight into the depth and range of experience of the survey population, respondents were asked how many years they studied music technology, mathematics, computer science, and engineering as well as played music. Table 24.2 shows the years of study of music technology, music, mathematics, and computer science or engineering grouped by gender. As for the study of music technology, the data show that males lead females by an average of over three years of study. However, females lead males in the study of music by just over one year. The mean years of mathematics study for males and females is comparable, with a noteworthy difference in the variability, or standard deviation, of years of study. A gap of almost two years describes the mean difference between males and females and their study of computer science or engineering, with an increase in the standard deviation for males.

C. Respondent Experience

Respondents were asked about the range and frequency of their experiences with music technology by category: The categories were using a computer to create

Table 24.1 Respondents by geographic region, age group, and gender

Geographic region	Age group	Female			Male			Total	
		Count	Region %	Global %	Count	Region %	Global %	Count	Global %
North and South America	18–25	45	17.44	11.87	38	14.73	10.03	83	21.90
	26–35	42	16.28	11.08	22	8.53	5.80	64	16.89
	36–45	18	6.98	4.75	21	8.14	5.54	39	10.29
	46–55	25	9.69	6.60	23	8.91	6.07	48	12.66
	56+	10	3.88	2.64	14	5.43	3.69	24	6.33
	Total	140	54.26	36.94	118	45.74	31.13	258	68.07
Europe	18–25	14	15.73	3.69	15	16.85	3.96	29	7.65
	26–35	5	5.62	1.32	20	22.47	5.28	25	6.60
	36–45	7	7.87	1.85	9	10.11	2.37	16	4.22
	46–55	3	3.37	0.79	10	11.24	2.64	13	3.43
	56+	2	2.25	0.53	4	4.49	1.06	6	1.58
	Total	31	34.83	8.18	58	65.17	15.30	89	23.48
Africa, Asia, and Oceania	18–25	2	6.25	0.53	4	12.50	1.06	6	1.58
	26–35	7	21.88	1.85	7	21.88	1.85	14	3.69
	36–45	4	12.50	1.06	5	15.63	1.32	9	2.37
	46–55	2	6.25	0.53	1	3.13	0.26	3	0.79
	Total	15	46.88	3.96	17	53.13	4.49	32	8.44

Table 24.2 Respondents' years of study by gender

| | | Years studied in the field of: | | | |
		Music technology	Music	Mathematics	Computer science and/or engineering
Female	Mean	12.53	25.13	9.57	2.95
	N	186	186	179	177
	Standard deviation	11.58	13.97	7.54	6.13
Male	Mean	15.73	23.91	9.52	4.61
	N	191	191	183	184
	Standard deviation	11.69	13.90	10.56	8.45
Total	Mean	14.15	24.51	9.55	3.80
	N	377	377	362	361
	Standard deviation	11.73	13.93	9.18	7.44

musical compositions, using a computer to record and/or produce the music of others, using a computer to record and/or produce the respondent's own music, using a computer to facilitate musical performance, using a computer as a musical instrument, using a computer to catalogue the respondent's music collection, using a computer to create audio for computer games, using a computer to create sound and scores for music video and/or film, and using a computer to teach the respondent new things about music technology. For each of these categories, respondents estimated their frequency of computer use as not at all, rarely, sometimes, often, and all the time. An important finding among these experiences by gender indicates a majority of the respondents were using computers to create musical compositions all of the time (56%), and of these respondents, males were more likely to engage in this activity (58%) than females (42%). Similarly, a majority of respondents catalogued their music collection all of the time (51.6%), with males more likely to engage in this activity (57.4%) than females (42.5%). An overwhelming number of respondents never used computers to create audio for computer games (87.7%), and of these respondents, females were less likely to engage in this activity (53.6%) than males (46.4%). By and large, males seemed to be using computers more often and for a broader range of uses than females with a few minor exceptions; notably, females (57.8%) slightly led males (42.2%) in their use of music technology to create sound and scores for video or film.

Based on the number of years of experience as well as range and frequency of music technology experiences, the respondents were grouped into three experience levels: novice, intermediate, and advanced. Table 24.3 summarizes the gender

Table 24.3 Respondents grouped by geographic region, experience level, and age

Geographic region		Experience level				Age groups					
		Novice	Intermediate	Advanced	Total	18–25	26–35	36–45	46–55	56+	Total
North and South America	Female	54	34	27	115	45	42	18	25	10	140
	Male	18	43	46	107	38	22	21	23	14	118
	Total	*72*	*77*	*73*	*222*	*83*	*64*	*39*	*48*	*24*	*258*
Europe	Female	9	10	8	27	14	5	7	3	2	31
	Male	16	15	18	49	15	20	9	10	4	58
	Total	*25*	*25*	*26*	*76*	*29*	*25*	*16*	*13*	*6*	*89*
Africa, Asia, and Oceania	Female	5	3	5	13	2	7	4	2	0	15
	Male	9	7	1	17	4	7	5	1	0	17
	Total	*14*	*10*	*6*	*30*	*6*	*14*	*9*	*3*	*0*	*32*

distribution based on experience level and geographic region. In the Americas, females were three times more likely than males to be in the novice group. In both the Europe and Asia, Africa, and Oceania groups, the trend is reversed, with more males grouped as novices. Across all geographic regions, more males than females are grouped as having an intermediate level of experience. Most of the advanced users were male in the Americas and Europe, with a noteworthy group of five advanced females of six (83.3%) in the Asia, Africa, and Oceania region.

In the novice group, females outnumbered males across all age groups except for those in the most senior category (56+ years), in which they equaled the number of males (three). Such a distribution suggests that should these novice females persist in the field, at some point in the future we may observe equitable participation by females and males. The number of males was greater than females across all age groups in both the intermediate and advanced levels.

3. Behaviors around Music Technology

When the respondents were queried regarding the gender of most of the people they communicated with about music technology, 127 females (74.2%) reported that they most often communicated with males, whereas 15 females (8.7%) reported that they most often talked with other females. The remaining females reportedly never communicated with anyone about music technology (17.1%). Of the male respondents, 139 (76.4%) said that they were more likely to communicate with other males, whereas only 7 (3.8%) reported that they were more likely to talk with females. The remaining males reportedly never communicated with anyone about music technology (19.8%). A small percentage of females (1.8%) reported that they had never thought about the gender of those with whom they communicated, whereas none of the men reported uncertainty. Clearly, the data present evidence that both males and females were more likely to talk with males about music technology. Similar trends can be observed in gender relationships among collaborators; both females and males were significantly more likely to collaborate with men. Surely, this evidence of male-patterned communication and collaboration is unusual. It seems unlikely that these patterns in communication and collaboration are seditious symptoms of subversion like those observed by Australian feminist and author Germaine Greer (Quoteopia n.d.). She asserted, "The sight of women talking together has always made men uneasy; nowadays it means rank subversion." Further research is needed to understand the intrinsic reasons for gender disparity in communication and collaboration norms.

Respondents were also asked if gender played a role in how they learned about music technology. Gender seems to have played more of a role for females (49.7%) than males (30.1%). An overwhelming majority of females (82.8%) are engaged in formal instruction about music technology taught by males, in sharp contrast to only seven males (3.9%) who reported that they were taught by females. Males were over twice as likely (15.2%) not to consider the gender of their instructor in comparison with the female respondents (7.1%). Similar trends can be observed in mentoring; males mentored nearly all females (73.6%).

Given the prominent role of males in communicating, collaborating, and teaching music technology, it is important to identify if there were perceived discriminatory practices around gender (Table 24.4). Both female and male novices reported that they had never thought about gender discrimination and were essentially equally split between those who had observed discrimination (42.2%) and those who had not (39%). A disturbing trend emerged with intermediate females: These women were more attuned to the likelihood of gender discrimination, and those who had experienced discrimination outnumbered those who had not by a factor of two. The findings are even more dismal among the advanced females, who were unequivocally aware of gender discrimination, with a significant number of women (84.6%) having witnessed it. As aptly stated by Caroline Bird (1968): "Hypocritical insistence that opportunity is really equal is the cruelest form of discrimination. It implies that the loser in any contest has lost through his own inabilities. And while women and blacks realize that the cards are stacked against them, they are compelled by the prevailing rhetoric to act as if they had actually lost out in fair competition." We must be alert that subtle discrimination varnished by the rhetoric of equality may confuse the value an individual may credit to their contributions. Such confusion may lead to doubt in one's abilities that, over time, erode the individual's resolve to persist in the field.

Due to the pervasive gender imbalance in most music technology educational settings, it is important to ascertain the effect of gender disparity on female and male students. The respondents were asked if they were sometimes uncomfortable being the only female in a group of males or the only male in a group of females. Table 24.5 details the results of this question grouped by gender and experience level. It is interesting to note that most novice females (58.5%) were not uncomfortable being the only female in a group of males. Similarly, the majority of novice males (66.7%) were also not uncomfortable being the only male in a group of females. A gender difference emerged at the intermediate level; a majority of females (53.3%) were uncomfortable being the only female in a group of males, but only a small minority of males (14.5%) were uncomfortable being the only male in a group of females. A gender difference was similarly evident at the advanced level, with all females having assessed their comfort as a member of all-male groups. The female response was equally split: 50% were comfortable and 50% were uncomfortable. Succinctly put, given a class comprised of all males and one female, there was a 50/50 chance that the female was uncomfortable in the learning environment. This finding suggests teachers should consider pedagogical techniques that mitigate this problem.

Table 24.4 Have you ever observed discriminatory practices around gender in the field of music technology?

Gender	Experience level	Yes		No		Never thought about it		Total
		N	%	N	%	N	%	N
Female	Novice	25	39.1	12	18.8	27	42.2	64
	Intermediate	28	63.6	3	6.8	13	29.5	44
	Advanced	33	84.6	0	0.0	6	15.4	39
	Total	*86*	*58.5*	*15*	*10.2*	*46*	*31.3*	*147*
Male	Novice	10	24.4	8	19.5	23	56.1	41
	Intermediate	19	30.2	2	3.2	42	66.7	63
	Advanced	21	33.3	2	3.2	40	63.5	63
	Total	*50*	*29.9*	*12*	*7.2*	*105*	*62.9*	*167*
All	Novice	35	33.3	20	19.0	50	47.6	105
	Intermediate	47	43.9	5	4.7	55	51.4	107
	Advanced	54	52.9	2	2.0	46	45.1	102
	Total	*136*	*43.3*	*27*	*8.6*	*151*	*48.1*	*314*

Table 24.5 Are you sometimes uncomfortable being the only female in a group of males or the only male in a group of females?

Gender	Experience level	Yes		No		Never thought about it		Total
		N	%	N	%	N	%	N
Female	Novice	26	40.0	1	1.5	38	58.5	65
	Intermediate	24	53.3	2	4.4	19	42.2	45
	Advanced	20	50.0	0	0.0	20	50.0	40
	Total	70	46.7	3	2.0	77	51.3	150
Male	Novice	7	17.9	6	15.4	26	66.7	39
	Intermediate	9	14.5	5	8.1	48	77.4	62
	Advanced	4	6.3	6	9.5	53	84.1	63
	Total	20	12.2	17	10.4	127	77.4	164
All	Novice	33	31.7	7	6.7	64	61.5	104
	Intermediate	33	30.8	7	6.5	67	62.6	107
	Advanced	24	23.3	6	5.8	73	70.9	103
	Total	90	28.7	20	6.4	204	65.0	314

4. Gendered Perception of Music Technology Behaviors

> Let it not be said, wherever there is energy or creative genius, "She has a masculine mind."
>
> —Fuller 1845, p. 43

Gendered perception of behavior relates the respondent's attribution of femininity or masculinity to that behavior. Respondents were given a series of questions, each about a behavior related to music technology, and asked to gauge their gendered perception of that behavior. These questions began with "I think..." Following these questions, respondents were asked the same succession of questions, but this time were asked to conjecture what others thought of the behavior. These questions began with "Most people think..." Figure 24.1 depicts excerpts from the survey for gendered perception of music technology behaviors or self and others. Responses were assigned a numerical value of $+2$ (very masculine), $+1$ (kind of masculine), 0 (neither masculine nor feminine), -1 (kind of feminine), or -2 (very feminine).

Box 24.1 documents the eleven paired gender perception questions. The purpose of this parallel questioning of self and others was to reveal any discrepancy in the way females and males think of a behavior in comparison with what they believe others think of that behavior.

An analysis of the cumulative responses to the gender perception questions evinces a remarkable convergence between females and males on the first pair of

---

Gendered Perception of Music Technology Behaviors (Self)

1. I think playing a traditional musical instrument is

○ Very masculine
○ Kind of masculine
○ Neither masculine nor feminine
○ Kind of feminine
○ Very feminine

Gendered Perception of Music Technology Behaviors (Others)

1. Most people think playing a traditional musical instrument is

○ Very masculine
○ Kind of masculine
○ Neither masculine nor feminine
○ Kind of feminine
○ Very feminine

Figure 24.1 Excerpt from survey "I (Most people) think playing a musical instrument is ..."

Box 24.1 Paired gender perception questions

1. I (Most people) think playing a traditional musical instrument is . . .
2. I (Most people) think composing popular music is . . .
3. I (Most people) think using a computer to create musical compositions is . . .
4. I (Most people) think using a computer to record and/or produce the music of others is . . .
5. I (Most people) think using a computer to record and/or produce my own music is . . .
6. I (Most people) think using a computer to facilitate musical performance is . . .
7. I (Most people) think using a computer as a musical instrument is . . .
8. I (Most people) think using a computer to computer to catalog a music collection is . . .
9. I (Most people) think using a computer to create audio for computer games is . . .
10. I (Most people) think using a computer to create sound and scores for video and/or film is . . .

---

questions: "I think playing a musical instrument is . . . " and "Most people think playing a musical instrument is . . . " Of the 139 female respondents, 129 (92.8%) thought playing a musical instrument was neither feminine nor masculine or gender neutral. Of these 129 females, 85 (65.9%) thought most people would agree. Of the 151 male respondents, 141 (93.4%) thought playing a musical instrument was neither feminine nor masculine. Of these 141 males, 112 (79.4%) thought most people also considered playing a musical instrument as gender neutral. A normal distribution with the mean and median near gender neutrality (neither masculine nor feminine or a mean of 0) emerges for perception of self and others regardless of the respondent's gender (fig. 24.2). This normal distribution around gender neutrality is a viable and convenient way to quantify the gender ideal: regardless of a particular behavior, most individuals perceived the behavior as neither feminine nor masculine, and they thought most people would agree. This distribution is referred to as a normal distribution of the gender ideal.

I think . . .   Most people think . . .

The concept of a normal distribution of the gender ideal facilitates the assertion of a null hypothesis H_0 and an alternate hypothesis H_a when describing evidence of gender bias in perception. For this survey population, the null hypothesis states that for any behavior, the perception of individuals and the perception of others is gender neutral; that is, behavior is neither masculine nor feminine and has a mean response of 0. The alternative hypothesis states that for any behavior, the perception of individuals and the perception of others is not gender neutral. Stated mathematically:

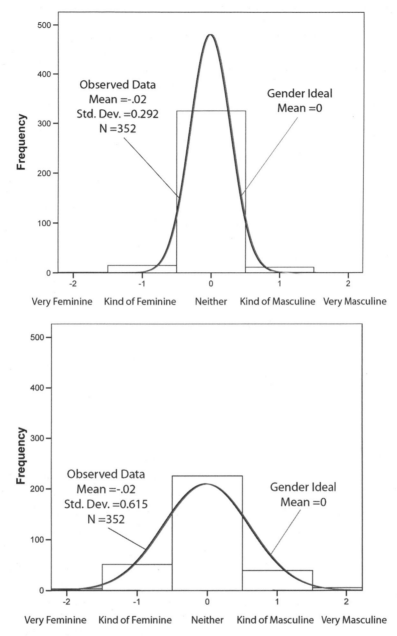

Figure 24.2 Playing a traditional musical instrument. (A) "I think...";
(B) "Most people think..."

Null Hypothesis
H_0: mean $= 0$ *gender neutral perception of self and others*

Alternate Hypothesis
H_a: mean $\neq 0$

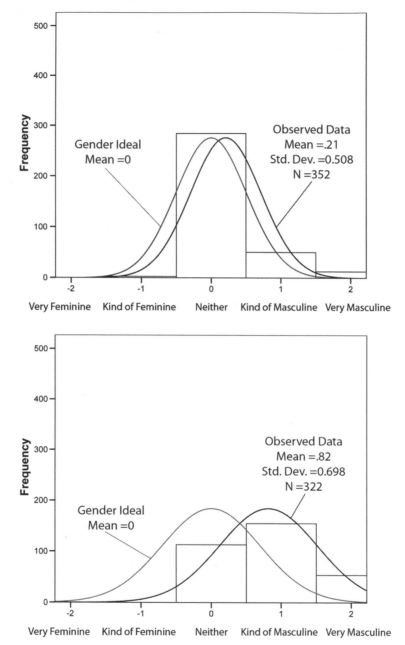

Figure 24.3 Using a computer to create musical compositions. (A) "I think…";
(B) "Most people think…"

For the first paired gender perception questions, "I (Most people) think playing a musical instrument is…," the null hypothesis was true for both individuals and others.

Another pair of gender perception questions that invites further examination is the use of a computer to create musical compositions (fig. 24.3). The cumulative mean of all respondents to the question "I think using a computer to create musical compositions is … " is slightly biased toward kind of masculine (0.21). The cumulative mean becomes increasingly masculine when considering the perception of others (0.82). This finding seems incongruous for those female respondents who reportedly used computers to create musical compositions all of the time (23.5% of the respondents). It is possible that the gender identity of these females concedes toward masculine, whereas it seems that males need not make an identity adjustment. For these paired questions, the alternate hypothesis was true, signaling a masculine bias in the perception of using a computer to create musical compositions.

I think …   Most people think …

Since there is a documented history of gender discrimination in the recording industry, an account of the respondent's current perceptions toward recording and producing the music of others may elucidate progress in the field. The cumulative mean of gendered perception of self (fig. 24.4) is slightly biased toward kind of masculine (0.25) and is approximately comparable to the masculine bias in computer music composition (fig. 24.3). The masculine predilection increases when considering the perception of others (0.92). Admittedly, a touch of gender bias is probably better than overt discrimination. Yet, these data suggest that much work lies ahead to cultivate a normal distribution of the gender ideal in recording and producing the music of others. Unfortunately, for the purposes of this study, the alternative hypothesis is true, indicating masculine bias in using a computer to record or produce the music of others.

I think …   Most people think …

Of all the paired gender perception questions, the most prominent penchant toward masculinity is observed in creating audio for computer games (fig. 24.5). The respondents' answer to the question, "I think creating audio for computer games" resulted in a cumulative mean of 0.46, conspicuously skewed toward masculine. When the respondents considered the perception of others, the proclivity toward masculinity increased to a cumulative mean of 1.15. For the only time in this survey, the cumulative mean extends beyond "kind of masculine" to "very masculine." Oddly enough, 87.6% of the respondents reported that they had never used a computer to create audio for computer games. Even with an overwhelming majority of the respondents not having personally engaged in the behavior, the alternative hypothesis is undeniably true.

I think …   Most people think …

As a matter of fact, it is highly unlikely that the null hypothesis is true for any of the gender perception questions with the exception of playing a musical instrument (table 24.6). These results statistically demonstrate that the alternative hypothesis is unequivocally true: Music technologists had a tendency toward masculine bias in perception of self and others for activities that are essential to the field.

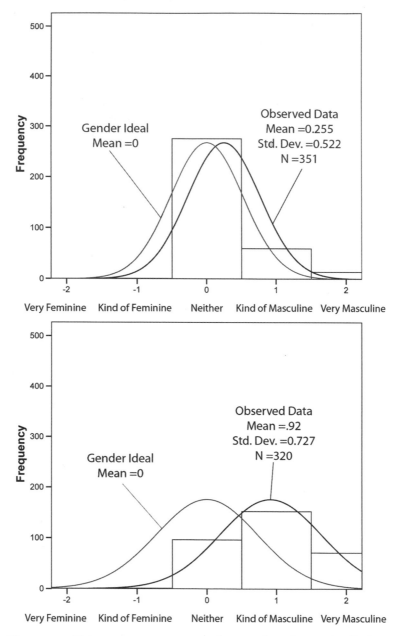

Figure 24.4 Using a computer to record or produce the music of others.
(A) "I think..."; (B) "Most people think..."

Another interesting line of inquiry for the paired gender perception questions was to ascertain the gender gap between perception of self and others. In observing the responses between the paired gender perception questions, the data reveal that respondents attributed a greater masculine bias to perception of others than perception of self (mean > 0.00). The only exception to this observation is that males thought playing a musical instrument was more feminine than they

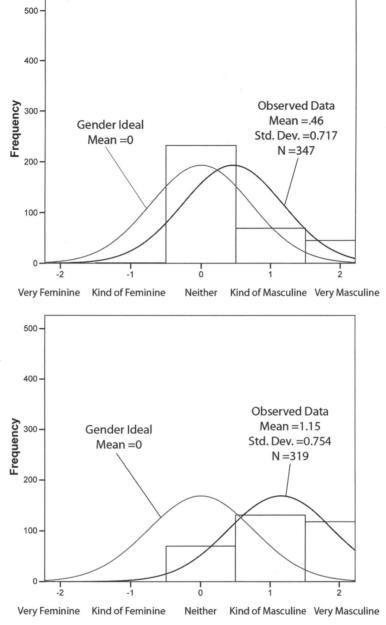

Figure 24.5 Using a computer to create audio for computer games.
(A) "I think ... "; (B) "Most people think ... "

themselves did (mean < 0.00). The mean discrepancy facilitates evaluating the extent of masculine or feminine bias that the respondents attributed to the perception of others. A preponderance of positive mean discrepancies indicates that the respondents thought that other people thought a particular behavior was more masculine than they did. Table 24.7 shows the mean discrepancy first

Table 24.6 One-sample *t* test on the null hypothesis, test value = 0

	t	df	Sig. (2-tailed)	Mean	95% confidence interval of the difference	
					Lower	Upper
I think...						
Playing a traditional musical instrument is...	−1.10	351	$p > .25$	−0.02	−0.05	0.01
Composing popular music is...	3.68	351	$p < .0001$	0.08	0.04	0.12
Using a computer to create musical compositions is...	7.77	351	$p < .0001$	0.21	0.16	0.26
Using a computer to record and/or produce the music of others is...	8.89	350	$p < .0001$	0.25	0.19	0.30
Using a computer to record and/or produce my own music is...	4.84	349	$p < .0001$	0.11	0.07	0.16
Using a computer to facilitate musical performance is...	7.00	351	$p < .0001$	0.16	0.12	0.21
Using a computer as a musical instrument is...	7.37	347	$p < .0001$	0.20	0.15	0.25
Using a computer to catalog a music collection is...	3.60	343	$p < .0001$	0.08	0.03	0.12
Using a computer to create audio for computer games is...	11.82	346	$p < .0001$	0.46	0.38	0.53
Using a computer to create sound and scores for video and/or film is...	6.21	349	$p < .0001$	0.14	0.10	0.18
Teaching myself to learn new things about music technology is...	4.51	351	$p < .0001$	0.10	0.05	0.14
Most people think...						
Playing a traditional musical instrument is...	−0.72	322	$p > .25$	−0.02	−0.09	0.04
Composing popular music is...	11.16	319	$p < .0001$	0.41	0.34	0.49
Using a computer to create musical compositions is...	21.01	321	$p < .0001$	0.82	0.74	0.89
Using a computer to record and/or produce the music of others is...	22.52	319	$p < .0001$	0.92	0.84	1.00
Using a computer to record and/or produce my own music is...	17.03	321	$p < .0001$	0.64	0.56	0.71
Using a computer to facilitate musical performance is...	17.53	318	$p < .0001$	0.70	0.62	0.78
Using a computer as a musical instrument is...	18.92	321	$p < .0001$	0.78	0.70	0.86
Using a computer to catalog a music collection is...	6.39	320	$p < .0001$	0.21	0.15	0.28
Using a computer to create audio for computer games is...	27.25	318	$p < .0001$	1.15	1.07	1.23
Using a computer to create sound and scores for video and/or film is...	15.64	317	$p < .0001$	0.61	0.53	0.68
Teaching myself to learn new things about music technology is...	13.82	320	$p < .0001$	0.51	0.44	0.59

Table 24.7 Summary comparison of "I think " versus "Most people think"

"I think" versus "Most people think" discrepancy	Female			Male			Total		
	Mean discrepancy	N	Standard deviation	Mean discrepancy	N	Standard deviation	Mean Discrepancy	N	Standard deviation
1 Playing a traditional musical instrument is...	0.01	159	0.64	−0.01	164	0.53	0.00	323	0.58
2 Composing popular music is...	0.45	158	0.74	0.25	162	0.56	0.35	320	0.66
3 Using a computer to create musical compositions is...	0.69	157	0.84	0.55	165	0.68	0.61	322	0.76
4 Using a computer to record and/or produce the music of others is...	0.75	155	0.74	0.64	164	0.68	0.69	319	0.71
5 Using a computer to record and/or produce my own music is...	0.62	157	0.71	0.45	163	0.62	0.53	320	0.67
6 Using a computer to facilitate musical performance is...	0.62	155	0.72	0.49	164	0.62	0.55	319	0.68
7 Using a computer as a musical instrument is...	0.64	157	0.73	0.53	162	0.64	0.59	319	0.69
8 Using a computer to catalog a music collection is...	0.22	154	0.61	0.07	161	0.43	0.14	315	0.53
9 Using a computer to create audio for computer games is...	0.77	157	0.78	0.67	160	0.70	0.72	317	0.74
10 Using a computer to create sound and scores for video and/or film is...	0.55	156	0.65	0.43	160	0.62	0.49	316	0.63
11 Teaching myself to learn new things about music technology is...	0.53	159	0.71	0.30	162	0.65	0.41	321	0.69

Table 24.8 Numerical ordering of mean discrepancy of paired gender perception questions

		"I think" versus "Most people think" mean discrepancy								
		0	0.1	0.2	0.3	0.4	0.5	0.6	0.7	0.8
Male	Question number	1	8		2, 11	10, 5	6, 7, 3	4	9	
Female	Question number	1		8		2	11	10, 6, 5, 7	3, 4	9

grouped by gender, then for the total survey population. A careful inquiry is advised to begin to understand why music technologists ascribed masculine bias to the imputed perception of others in comparison to perception of self.

Perhaps the most disconcerting observation reported in table 24.7 is that the mean discrepancy of females is always greater than the mean discrepancy of males. This larger mean discrepancy indicates that females attributed a greater masculine bias to these activities than the males. These findings suggest that females may be reinforcing gender bias through their perception of self and others.

The mean discrepancy detailed in table 24.7 reveals a stunning similarity: regardless of gender, females and males tended to agree on the rank ordering of the discrepancy by behavior. Table 24.8 presents the mean discrepancy by gender for the eleven paired gender perception questions on a continuum ordered from least to greatest discrepancy; the mean discrepancy was rounded to the nearest 0.1. There is a slight reordering of the questions between females and males in the middle of the continuum regarding using a computer to record or produce the respondent's music, using a computer to facilitate musical performance, and using a computer to create sound and scores for video or film. Even though females led males in their use of computers to create sound for scores and films, the female mean discrepancy is tipped toward masculine. Anchoring both ends of the continuum is a perceptual accord for playing a musical instrument, in sharp contrast to a masculine-biased divergence imputed to others for creating audio for computer games.

5. TOWARD THE GENDER IDEAL

Now that there is a statistical basis that demonstrates that the field of music technology has challenges around perception of gender, the compelling question is how to mitigate the inequity. Some of these challenges may dissipate as the number of females persists in the field, creating a pipeline that promotes equitable participation. Other challenges may diminish simply by increasing our awareness of and sensitivity to the issue. Some of the thorniest problems, particularly those around the discrepancy of gendered perception of self and others and discrimination, call for further study.

The pipeline of novice females who reside in the Americas shows the potential for gender equity should these females persist in the field. The predominance of novice males in Europe as well as the Asia, Africa, and Oceania regions suggests that more effort should be expended to recruit females. Regardless of experience level, teachers and mentors should ensure that students are comfortable in their learning environment and realize that gender plays a significant role, more so for females than males. Intermediate and advanced music technologists should be cognizant of their own proclivities for gender bias in communication and collaboration and strive for gender balance. It is quite likely that gender balance in communication and collaboration will spread as gender balance increases. Should females persist to the advanced level, there exists the potential that gender balance in teaching and mentoring will follow.

Another implication of this study results from the gender-neutral perceptual accord between self and others, regardless of gender, with respect to playing a musical instrument. This perceptual accord may suggest that the longer a behavior is assimilated into a culture as a societal norm, and that the behavior is exemplified by a multitude of accomplished female and male role models, the greater the likelihood that a normal distribution of the gender ideal will result. The ramification of this postulation hints that music technologists should cultivate gender balance among the field's role models.

Awareness of self and others is an essential ingredient that shapes perception and guides our daily actions. We must be aware of external stimuli, particularly imagery and language, intended to influence our perception of gender. The rhetoric that reinforces gender bias erodes the confidence in one's own abilities. An entente that accepts the gender identity of the individual in relation to others is imperative for the individual to be a productive and participating member of a community. The most insidious case for alarm is discrimination: it is through vigilant awareness that we can arrest its deleterious consequences.

Without question, this study unveiled questions that call for further research. First, a careful inquiry will foster insight into the impact of the imputed perception of others on the gendered perception of self. It may be likely that certain behaviors are more likely to occur or not given a discrepancy between gendered perception of self and others. Similarly, it would be intriguing to discover the root cause that tips the perception of music technology behaviors toward masculine. Furthermore, we should discover why females are more likely to observe gender discrimination the longer that they persist in the field and why males tend not to observe gender discrimination. It would be climacteric to identify the nature and extent of the discrimination and determine if there are social, organizational, or institutional norms that purvey circumstantial opportunity for gender discrimination.

This study does nothing more than posit a milestone against which we may benchmark our progress. Just as feminist and civil rights leaders were called to action in the name of justice, so must music technologists purport a community with a foundation that is built on equity. The next step leads to intervention strategies that advance the community toward the gender ideal.

Acknowledgments: This research is made possible through the support of the University of Michigan School of Music, Theatre, and Dance; the James A. and Faith Knight Foundation; the Center for Statistical Consultation and Research at the University of Michigan; and my research assistants, Isaac Delongchamp, Sarah Dowd, and Shannon Dowd. I thank Kevin Austin for his assistance in the international distribution of the survey. The Institutional Review Board in the Behavioral Sciences approved the survey (HUM00018465).

BIBLIOGRAPHY

Bird, C., with S. Briller. 1968. *Born Female: The High Cost of Keeping Women Down.* New York: McKay.

Brainy Quotes. n.d. Roseanne Barr quotes. http://www.brainyquote.com/quotes/authors/r/roseanne_barr.html, accessed March 29, 2009.

Burns, K., ed. 2002. *Women and Music in America since 1900: An Encyclopedia.* Westport, CT: Greenwood Press.

Canadian Electroacoustic Community. 2006. The international women's electroacoustic listening room project: Voices on the edge. http://cec.concordia.ca/econtact/8_2/Madsen.html, accessed March 29, 2009.

Feinberg, L. 1998. *Trans Liberation.* Boston: Beacon Press.

Fuller, S. M. 1845. *Woman in the Nineteenth Century.* London: Clarke.

Hinkle-Turner, E. 2006. *Women Composers and Music Technology in the United States: Crossing the Line.* Burlington, VT: Ashgate Press.

Hoffert, S. D. 2003. *A History of Gender in America: Essays, Documents, and Articles.* Upper Saddle, NJ: Prentice Hall.

Mathews, M., with J. E. Miller, F. R. Moore, J. R. Pierce, and J. C. Risset. 1969. *The Technology of Computer Music.* Cambridge: MIT Press.

McCartney, A. 1995. Inventing images: Constructing and contesting gender in thinking about electroacoustic music. *Leonardo Music Journal* 5: 57–66.

McPhee, C., and A. Fitzgerald, comps. 1979. *Feminist Quotations: Voices of Rebels, Reformers, and Visionaries.* New York: Crowell.

Oldenziel, R. 2001. Man the maker, woman the consumer: The consumption junction revisited. In *Feminism in Twentieth-Century Science, Technology, and Medicine,* ed. A. Creager. Chicago: University of Chicago Press.

Quoteopia. n.d. Germaine Greer quotes. http://www.quoteopia.com/famous.php?quotesby=germainegreer, accessed March 29, 2009.

Sandstrom, B. 2000. Women mix engineers. In *Music and Gender,* ed. P. Moisala and B. Diamond. Chicago: University of Illinois Press.

Simoni, M. 1995. A survey of gender issues related to computer music and strategies for change. In *Proceedings of the 1995 International Computer Music Conference.* San Francisco: International Computer Music Association.

Sommers, C. H. 1994. *Who Stole Feminism? How Women Have Betrayed Women.* New York: Simon and Schuster.

Sommers, C. H. 2000. *The War against Boys: How Misguided Feminism Is Harming Our Young Men.* New York: Simon and Schuster.

Strachey, R., ed. 1936. *Our Freedom and Its Results.* London: Hogarth Press.

Wikipedia. n.d. Gloria Steinem. http://en.wikipedia.org/wiki/Gloria_Steinem, accessed March 29, 2009.

CHAPTER 25

SOUND-BASED MUSIC 4 ALL

LEIGH LANDY

As a composer and enthusiast of various forms of contemporary music trained in the 1970s, I am used to writing about the inevitable frustrations of someone who is passionate about his music but also someone who works in a society that has largely ignored such forms of music.[1] In other words, there has been a clear tension between the amount of effort that goes into the creation of certain types of contemporary music and the related societal impact. I believe that for decades many of our societies have suffered from what I would call a manipulated imbalance of appreciation regarding various types of music and have always felt that much contemporary music, including new and innovative forms of music that are reliant on new technologies, have been harshly treated. In contrast, this text possesses a positive spin in that we shall discover how the increase of accessibility of tools and of interest can be related. To understand the evolution that contributed to this change, we need to investigate the circumstances that led to certain types of music's isolation and then look into how the increased availability of digital means of music appreciation, music-related knowledge, and music-making has been effective in terms of increasing the accessibility of the music. Related to these developments is a parallel evolution in which certain common forms of music classification are becoming less relevant to certain repertoires, thus breaking down barriers that prevented people from discovering certain types of contemporary music. Alex Ross has described his view of the blurring of boundaries as follows: "One possible destination for twenty-first-century music is a final 'great fusion': intelligent pop artists and extroverted [art music] composers speaking more or less the same language" (2007, p. 542). In particular, in the case of the focus of this chapter, sound-based music, that is, music in which sounds, *not* notes, form the basic unit,[2] the separation of art music and popular music is clearly becoming less relevant as the distinction becomes less audible in a great number of sound-based works and the means of production converge, opening up this type of music to a much larger community than the one it has known in the past.

1. CONTEXT XX

Our tale commences in the previous century (also known as XX) when two developments strongly affected the lot of most contemporary music: the commercialization and the industrialization of music. The launch of an era of technological progress, namely, the "age of mechanical reproduction" as Walter Benjamin called it (see, e.g., Benjamin 1992), changed how music was to be produced, disseminated, and most importantly, listened to forever. Stating the obvious, just over a century ago, to hear music one had to be present where the music was being made. Today, one can hear anything at any time at the push of a button (or other interface) thanks to the industrialization of music. Then, there is the influence of commerce. The commercialization of music in the 20th century led to a seismic shift in musical interest in many parts of the world.[3] The reductionist version of this shift is that many forms of traditional, noncommercial aurally transmitted folk music and, to a lesser extent, art music—in particular its contemporary forms—declined in interest as the interest in more trendy and more globalized forms of popular music climbed rapidly.

However, the era of analog mechanical reproduction and the age of digital mechanical reproduction have had dissimilar effects in terms of community forming. Therefore, today's context is fortunately evolving away from the pattern described in this first part of the chapter, at least as far as new forms of music-making are concerned. The growth of the power of the music industry, a product of the ability to reproduce music, is one of three contextual threads related to musical marginalization, alongside that of music education and the attitudes of many of the musicians involved with contemporary music.

The focus in this first part of the chapter is on contemporary art music. I believe the wider repertoire, that is, that including vocal and instrumental contemporary music, is important to discuss here as what is commonly known as electroacoustic music and computer music both inherited great challenges from contemporary music's demise. I then focus on digital music-making, followed more specifically by sound-based music.

A. The Communications Media, in Particular Broadcast Media, and the Recording Industry

One of the questions I have often asked of undergraduate students in countries where I have lectured is: "How many of you know much traditional folk music from your area?" This question is often met with laughter, and normally very few hands are raised. Although for centuries this type of communal music formed part of community behavior, it has become an object of ridicule in many quarters of today's societies. In fact, in many of these countries folk music has had to be reborn as a form of commercial music. Granted, there are countries where folk music has hardly been affected; most of these have not undergone such huge technological changes as in the countries where I have worked.

Perhaps many readers feel sympathy with the students when reading this often-encountered description. I, for one, am not a proponent of preserving part of one's culture for the sake of it. Still, the loss of music that is a form of celebration of local or regional identity, and its replacement by products offered as part of our consumer society, does raise issues concerning who is empowered in terms of musical knowledge, choice, and musical behavior in general. The virtual erasure of a type of music as old as human existence is no trivial matter.

The fact is that as soon as the recording and broadcasting industries took hold of music dissemination to a large extent, music appreciation and music-making would inevitably change radically. Other than in countries with state broadcasters who are contracted to represent the entire spectrum of music in a balanced manner—and these are few and far between—music on offer is based on numbers of listeners, advertising income, and similar factors (not to mention political factors in some countries). Similarly, the number of nonprofit recording companies is highly restricted. The fact that such companies often request a subsidy from the musicians or their organizations for their recordings comes as no surprise.

This combination of revenue or statistics-based broadcasting and profit-motivated recording led to the empowerment of those industries. The critic of this era, controversial as he may be these days, Herbert Marcuse, often complained that such empowerment was to lead toward a quantity as opposed to a quality culture (see, e.g., Marcuse 1964). This has proven true to a large extent but looks to change in our young new century.

How was this commercial empowerment reflected within the spectrum of contemporary art music during this period? In those areas possessing highly subsidized musical cultures, whether through state or other forms of support, contemporary music seems to have been able to offer a reasonable amount of activities and, indeed, recordings. Still, one should take into account the fact that the number of participants grew during that period, reflecting the increase of population. The number of events, however, did not increase in a similar proportion. The number of art music concerts focused on or containing contemporary works was far outweighed by that of the key historical periods, baroque, classical, and romantic. Only the older works of the Middle Ages and Renaissance were treated as somewhat exotic, much like a good deal of the contemporary repertoire. In this regard, I have often spoken of the late 20th century's "rainbow of appreciation in Western art music history," with the two far/lower ends less visible than the middle.

I remember when I was a student that a comic was published mocking the contemporary music scene. This comic was by Matt Groening (before he became famous with *The Simpsons*); in his work, one composer asked another one whether he was sick and tired of performing his music "before 47 spectators" (Groening 1997).[4] In a similar vein, the French critic, festival organizer, and politician Maurice Fleuret was alleged to have described a contemporary music practice in the 1970s and 1980s in terms of Kleenex—use once and throw away—thus suggesting that a work's première was also its dernière. Such remarks typify the odd situation known to many late-20th-century contemporary music composers: few performances, few recording opportunities, and even fewer broadcasts.[5] Contemporary musicians who formed exceptions, such as most minimalist composers, were those whose music contained elements that were also available in accepted genres emanating from the music industry, including harmonies and rhythms from jazz and folk music's commoditized version, world music.

We must not forget that as we approached the end of the XX century we also became part of what is commonly called the "image culture." Television, of course, was never that interested in contemporary music. When it was, it tended to create clumsy MTV-like broadcasts of works with many cuts between the cameras in an attempt to avoid the viewer's becoming bored with a still image, leading to generally unrewarding visual experiences. This in itself is one of the major reasons why people never became acquainted with this repertoire.

It is my firm belief that, other than through the influence of a youth's parents, music teacher, or the fact that a friend was acquainted with contemporary music, it was nearly impossible for a young person to become aware of its existence. Another complaint that I have often uttered is that we are immediately informed when a football player or rock star is injured or some such, but most people would not have a clue if a major work of art music had been composed in their country. In fact, in contrast to the 19th century, the notion of a "major work" seems to have diminished in stature somewhat as the 20th century evolved, although most colleagues in the field would probably leap to offer some exceptions. In a sense, contemporary music found means to survive in spite of the broadcast and recording media.

B. Music Education

As stated, few preuniversity children were introduced to any form of contemporary art music and other forms of innovative music. This is still true today. How then can they be expected to discover it?[6]

Music education is a difficult subject as in some countries it forms part of the "rest of" group of subjects after reading, grammar, writing, mathematics, science, and history. Some countries have dropped music from the list of compulsory subjects at the primary level, and in many secondary schools students can opt out of musical study. So, what can one propose in such a situation? Beyond demonstrating the obvious skills that music-making offers a young person, one thing is to build from the known to the unknown; this may, for example, involve a greater emphasis on popular music at schools. Another is to offer children the widest repertoire possible at a young age to allow them to be more aware of the choices that exist. To achieve this, educators need to be convinced that people *can* enjoy this wider repertoire. One example of an approach supporting this goal, the Intention/Reception project, is introduced in this chapter. Finally, there exist new technological tools that can facilitate musical creativity. I return to this point in the discussion regarding the EARS Pedagogical project. Fortunately, there are signs of a growing interest in terms of dealing with inexperienced listeners of various ages (see, e.g., Brown 2007, Hugill 2007, and chapter 26, this volume).

Attempts have been made to modernize music curricula in schools. Many have been approved by governments and were later to fail for financial reasons or due to the reticence of teachers responsible for music. What then will cause these useful changes to occur? Part of this answer must come from parents and the general public expectation for their nations' education to reflect and support musical diversity. The other must come from education itself, probably led by those in higher education who believe that the music they are teaching and eventually making is worthy of a broader community of interest; thus, these educators must find means to lobby through constructive changes that are more representative of music in society today and help pave the way to a better musical balance tomorrow.

One can study any type of music at universities these days. In the United Kingdom, music technology and popular music students now outnumber "traditional" music students at university level. Thus, the market economy is reflected within the university sector for better or worse. With such a broad presence within higher education institutions, why is there such a gap elsewhere in education and in our societies at large? This gap is relevant to people both young and old.

One of the main reasons for the isolation of contemporary music has been a generally elitist attitude, including within the university sector where contemporary music is offered. Contemporary music is often learned music, just like a good deal of Western art music of the past. The problem has been that one has had to become even more learned than in past centuries to appreciate many of these new forms of music. (Just think of many works composed as part of the quest for new forms of musical complexity.) Has this led to a situation where one needs to leave one's cultural passport at campus gates? Who from the universities is going to be able to facilitate the creation of broader audiences in such circumstances?[7] Actually, things are not quite as black and white as they are being portrayed, as demonstrated in the following section.

C. The Separation of Art from Life in Many Forms of Contemporary Music

Thus far, the massive sea change of appreciation has largely been attributed to the cultural or creative industries—unthinkable terms before the previous century—and our education systems. Contemporary musicians, including many of those working in higher education, also share a good deal of the guilt for the marginalization of their music. The basis of the accusation is as follows: There has always been an element of avant-gardism in art history. It has varied throughout the ages and reached a climax with figures such as Charles Ives in the first half of the 20th century. These were artists whose music really was ahead of their time. Things caught up in a way as the "anything goes" trends of the latter half of the century meant that there was a public for anything, regardless of how small it might be.[8] An attitude in the late 20th century was one of laisser aller and see what happens. This attitude has allowed marginalization to grow deep roots.

In traditional societies, art was always not only part of life, but also integrated into one's daily activities. In high art traditions, art-making and appreciation follow their own rituals; however, the integration of art music with most aspects of our daily life has diminished over the centuries. Contemporary musicians, aware of their work being marginalized, in general have not demonstrated a great interest in addressing this increasing separation. This is ironic as potential listeners often need to make connections with the known when trying something novel. It is even odder when we consider the fact that music involving sounds related to daily existence can offer an immediate link to life.

However, not all of this music is that complex, is that detached from life, or needs a learned public. Works ranging from certain instrumental pieces by György Ligeti to many sound-based works by Bernard Parmegiani offer immediate access to listeners with no background in these repertoires. My view for the last decade and a half has been that when music is suffering from marginalization, offering a helping hand may aid in reaching greater levels of appreciation. This helping hand may take on the simple form of educational and community arts outreach. It may also involve offering the listener something to hold on to in their works[9] to help them over the threshold into the musicians' own sonic worlds as have the two composers mentioned. Even the sharing of artistic intention, when it can be articulated, is a form of communication with potential listeners. Most composition students, however, are taught how to compose, not to share the "why" of a work or to engage with potential listeners. This attitude of not offering a helping hand to these listeners has contributed at least as much to the music's marginalization as anything else.

In terms of technology-driven music during this period, a key factor, at least until the 1990s, was the fact that most equipment was not affordable to individuals. It was those musicians attached to universities and studios who gained access to most equipment, another form of elitism. In a sense, outreach activities involving music technology were counterproductive at that time as one could only introduce a means of working and then take that means of working away at the end of a workshop or residency. Today, in contrast, it is more likely that what one takes into a residency is consistent to a large extent with what is already available to those participating. People like to be introduced to things that they can continue to make themselves after all. This leads us across the century border.

2. CONTEXT EARLY XXI

The first part of this chapter described a context we are gradually leaving behind as our digital tools become increasingly available. This second part focuses on the consequences of the availability of many of these tools and is followed by a section focusing on how these consequences can play a favorable role in the development of one form of contemporary music, namely, sound-based music.

Music Communities + Tools = Increased Awareness

The music business may be as large as it has ever been, but it is changing extremely rapidly during this first decade of the 21st century. The key reason for this is the Internet coming of age. Our focus in this part of the chapter is not about how musical industries are reacting to the changing technology; instead, it is on the roles of the technology itself.

Although computer-based communication has been around for quite some time, it is only in recent years that one has discovered the vital and wide-ranging potential our computers and other digital objects offer in terms of communication. For the purposes of this section, I divide the discussion in three, concentrating on music appreciation, information/knowledge related to music, and music-making. The hypothesis here is that through increased digital communication many sorts of music are becoming more accessible to more people than was the case even a decade ago. Through the increase of this information and the related means of communication, awareness is increasing, and consequently communities are being formed, some more spread out geographically than previously and some with new foci. This in turn is supporting new means of appreciation and music-making, thus enhancing today's broad horizon of musical opportunities. The following discussion is not meant to be exhaustive but instead to demonstrate new means, some quite radical, related to music and information related to music.

Just a decade ago, we listened to music on CDs and on the radio, learned about concerts and broadcasts in the printed media (e.g., newspapers and journals), and performed music with others involving physical presence. All of this is still available today.

Today, we can also listen to music on the Internet or download it onto our iPods, learn about concerts on the Web or be informed about them on various bulletin board systems or by way of user groups, and perform music virtually. In fact, in the first two cases a significant percentage is involved. In other words, a large amount of music is reproduced involving digital transmission without it ending up on a commercial read-only product; much information concerning music is passed along without the necessary involvement of paper. It is solely the third of the three, that is, virtual Internet-based music-making, that is still in its infancy, but it is growing rapidly.

Music Appreciation

For some, an investment in a CD is reasonably considerable. In some CD shops, one is provided with the opportunity to listen to certain CDs before purchasing them, but this is an exception, not the rule. Today, when purchasing many CDs, online listeners are often offered the chance to hear a number of tracks beforehand. More important, one need no longer think in terms of complete CDs unless that is the specific desire. Individual pieces can be purchased, be it in an encoded form that is currently not as high quality as CD audio.[10]

People who make noncommercial music are often allowing their works to be shared at low or even no cost whether it is downloaded from iTunes or its equivalent or from the artists' own Web sites or those of an organization with which they are affiliated. One can also listen to huge amounts of music on Web sites, including MySpace or YouTube (eventually involving visuals). Search engines can access music by way of the clever usage of keywords; they are particularly helpful when one is looking for a type of music, not a particular musician. This greater availability of information and the easier means to access information allow interested individuals the opportunity to discover and join evolving communities with relative ease and without great (or any) expense. Furthermore, one can listen in on an Internet performance or even participate in one. This is introduced under the discussion of music-making. Never wanting to miss a trick, stakeholders in the commercial sector, such as Amazon, have cleverly followed this trend by increasing the proportion of investment into lower-turnover items as well as independent labels and artists reflecting this widening of choice. This approach is known as the *long tail*, reflecting an image known to some probability distributions.

Even radio listening used to be limited to what was presented and when. Now, one can listen to most radio stations—and not just those that an antenna can receive—online, not to mention the plethora of new Internet broadcasters. Many of these offer a "listen anytime" option, allowing people to listen to music (or any other audio information) at their convenience. Internet broadcasters in general have a narrower focus than most radio stations, thus catering to a better-defined community of listeners. Again, greater information availability means greater access opportunities.

All of this has implied the possession of a computer with an Internet connection. Clearly, products based on our mobile technology are becoming increasingly sophisticated, so their role and that of new objects that are currently in the minds of their inventors will inevitably increase. There are entire urban areas that offer Wi-Fi. These developments mean that we will be able to access much of this information anytime, anywhere.

Information/Knowledge Related to Music

The arrival of the new millennium was by no means the starting point of any of the developments described here. Some technologies had been in development or simply less universally available for decades. Where music has witnessed some striking evolutions straddling century boundaries, the arrival of this new century was perhaps more exciting due to the increase of the availability of music and music-related information than to stylistic change. What is evident in the first decade of the 21st century is threefold: the amount of information on offer has increased enormously, as have the means of sharing that information and the number of people sharing and benefiting from this evolution. For example, new forms of virtual communities were already evolving in the 1980s (see, e.g., Rhein-gold 2000).[11] A population thousands of times the size of the 1980s user groups now appreciates what was being developed at that time. Bulletin boards; online forums; information portals; wikis; blogs; multiuser domains, including social networking sites; personal, group, academic, and organization Web sites; as well as the music and music-making tools themselves can be found online.

We live in an era of lifelong as well as online learning.[12] Although not everything found online goes through the stringent peer review process of research publications, one can become aware of, gain access to, and eventually gain expertise in virtually any sort of music based on what is available digitally today and evolves from virtual communities sharing common musical interests.

Music-Making

The third aspect of our trilogy takes us one step further along the path from appreciation and understanding to creative involvement. This final area, as said, is relatively less developed than the other two but will inevitably gain in importance as our computer and other digital systems become more powerful and affordable. The fact that a sophisticated sound synthesis engine based on Csound is planned for the Massachusetts Institute of Technology (MIT) Media Lab's $100 laptop is just one indication of this inevitability.

Due to the emergence of Internet music-making (see, e.g., Vol. 24, issue 6, of *Contemporary Music Review* [2005], Barbosa 2003, Weinberg 2005), I have often suggested that a good deal of tomorrow's folk music is likely to take place online. New forms of distributed performance, many based on existent forms of music, are being developed or are already available. As technology advances, the ability to view others participating will increase; currently, most Internet music-making involves audio only and utilizes unique user interfaces.

Traditional forms of note-based music will continue to evolve as they always have. The addition of digital forms of music-making has simultaneously expanded the horizon of opportunities as well as supported those evolving distributed communities of interest.

Digital music-making on offer can be made in real time or non-real-time environments, can be note or sound based, and may involve single or multiple users. It may involve new forms of traditional instruments, new devices or inter-faces evolving from these traditional instruments, or totally new types of instruments.[13] When music software is to be used, the new notions of freeware and shareware are more rule than exception these days, underscoring another form of support for accessibility. Copyleft has joined copyright, aiding yet another form of music becoming accessible.[14]

The often-heard term *interactivity* is more than a trend. It is a word supporting human/machine and human/human (by way of a machine) musical communication. It has been responsible for the development of all sorts of potential musical tools.

Interactive sound installations represent an interesting example. They have rarely met with the same resistance that certain forms of contemporary music have faced. Perhaps this is due to the fact that, similar to an artwork, one can choose when to visit them and for how long. Regardless, such installations are a symbol of a major trend catalyzed by digital and, indeed, postdigital technologies, namely, the facilitation of new forms of participation. The firm boundary between "maker" and "taker" of music familiar to us through the culture of concert performance or broadcast and CD listening (but not most forms of folk music or music in club culture, where participation takes place by way of joining in the music or dancing) is being redefined. These new aspects of participation often lead to greater interest, eventually appreciation, and as a consequence, further desire to be involved with creativity in a given form of artistic endeavor.

In this section of the chapter, the naming of specific examples has been avoided as so much is rapidly evolving that readers of this volume in a few years would simply replace the examples with more recent ones with which they are acquainted. What is clear is that as digital technology evolves, our abilities to create and participate in communities based on musical interest evolve in parallel.[15] Given the information available in digital form, interested parties can discover music, musical knowledge, creative musical opportunities, and communities associated with all of these with relative ease. This is the information revolution that has moved so many of those marginalized experiments of the second half of the 20th century forward. As the number of Internet broadcasts and archives grow and are shared freely, the number of interested parties will grow in turn, thus leading to the most crowded "radio dial" in history. One need no longer tune into a radio station in the hope that at least something of one's liking is played but can tune into an Internet site with most of the repertoire of interest. As a consequence, one no longer speaks of the margins of music but instead of a new balance between the music born of industry and the music born of digital communities. This balance is, in my view, much healthier than the one created in the 20th century and more "natural," similar to those local communities that evolved in previous centuries.

One of the types of music to have reached a broader audience than during the period of marginalization is sound-based music. One reason for the broadening of the audience is that techniques related to this kind of music eased their way across the art/popular music divide during the late decades of the 20th century so that today new forms of music and music-making are evolving that are very much an art form of their own, often allowing people to create a bridge between their art and life.

3. Sound-Based Music

Of the three revolutions presented in this chapter—technological (mechanical reproduction), musical (sound-based music often employing new technologies), and related to information (digital online communication)—the musical one is the focus of this final part. Thus, new or relatively new forms of music-making consisting primarily of sounds, not notes, are discussed. I treat this body of work as a case in point regarding drawing innovative forms of music out of isolation while creating new communities of interest and involvement. Sound organization ranges from forms of sound design for film and other artistic media, to sound art found in installations and galleries, to the broad spectrum of music that falls under the umbrella term *electroacoustic music*.[16] Sound organization can be heard in many computer games, advertisements, and some commercial television programs and films; it is not only an activity of the experimental new media arts. This being the case, most people will have been confronted with forms of sound-based music whether consciously or otherwise. Given the opportunities for making this exciting body of work available to people of all ages, perhaps demarginalizing things need not be so difficult after all.

A. Sound-Based Music: Reconnecting Life to Art

In this chapter, the notion of offering listeners things to hold on to was suggested. This can range from a tangible musical aspect to more emotion-derived experiences to the relationship between sound and image to something related to the listener's own life. Sound-based music offers the opportunity to relate art with life by way of employing sounds that the listener can associate with real-world experience. This particular point of view sits uncomfortably with one of the key notions of one of the great pioneers and theorists of musique concrète and the associated forms of sound-based music that followed it, Pierre Schaeffer. He was of the belief that the music he helped to found worked best when the listener followed a strategy of reduced listening (*écoute réduite*).[17] He believed that listening to a sound's quality led to a successful listening experience as opposed to paying attention to its source or cause. William W. Gaver spoke of a separation between musical listening and everyday listening, whether it concerns a work of musique concrète or a stroll in the countryside (1993). There is much to be said about the reduced listening strategy; much of it would be positive. However, in a chapter supporting access to sound-based music, this is not the best path to follow as people, in particular listeners new to forms of sound-based music, like to make links with their own aural experience, thus including links to real-world sounds if they are perceived.

Just like anything in life, being confronted with something entirely new can be challenging for people of all ages. In general, something must link that which is new with something that is familiar; alternatively, they should be provided with something to hold on to in order to guide them into this new terrain. A research project with which I have been associated for some time, called the Intention/ Reception project, has investigated just this sort of issue in terms of sound-based music while also looking into accessibility issues (see, e.g., Landy 2006, Weale 2006). What this research has demonstrated is that inexperienced listeners indeed do largely prefer to be offered things to hold on to, whether they are musical, related to sound sources and sonic contexts, or even a musician's intention. It has also demonstrated with some highly remarkable statistics that the potential audience for sound-based music is much larger than most people would imagine. Of the pieces chosen thus far, all of which make sonic references to the real world, some very directly, others most subtly, participants belonging to the inexperienced listeners' groups have consistently stated (between 59% and 80% of responses thus far) that they would like to hear another work of this sort in the future. The Intention/Reception methodology is called on in the discussion in this chapter of a planned curriculum for young people.

Sound-based music's content thus offers opportunities that are perhaps more evident than in note-based forms of music in terms of linking life to art and thus offering novel forms of access to new and innovative types of musical expression.[18] It is clear that the most difficult threshold in terms of any type of unknown music is the threshold of entrance. Once a person has discovered an interest in a type of music, a curiosity may develop to discover more about it and, eventually, participate in it. Given the new forms of access discussed in the second part of this chapter and everyone's association with sounds from the real world, various forms of sound-based music may offer fewer threshold challenges than other innovative forms of music. There are, of course, certain forms of sound-based music that are equally complex or unusual in the sense of their being removed from better-known forms of music, by which appreciation may be just as challenging as those types of note-based music for which access is not evident. Communities may form around these types of music, but not necessarily for newcomers; these are thus communities based on an acquired taste.

B. How These New Developments Are Being Reflected and Will Play an Increasing Role in Music Education

In fact, the threshold issue in terms of sound-based music need not be difficult at all as most young people today have access to digital games, many of which incorporate user-driven forms of algorithmic sound sequences. Almost every child who is provided with a user-friendly opportunity to make music with sounds, whether with simple daily objects or on a computer, is open to experiment and work creatively. Yet, most schools do not offer anything to do with this music yet.

Attempts to combat this state of affairs are taking place on several fronts, in particular by taking results such as those gained in the Intention/Reception project and using them as a lobbying tool so that people in education, commerce, and industry take this important information into account; by creating educational tools for young people; and by writing new, more liberal and balanced music curricula reflecting the reality of today's musical communities.

As this book goes to press, two developments are ongoing that represent initiatives involving tools and curricula relevant to this discussion: the EARS (ElectroAcoustic Resource Site) Pedagogical project and a new UK curriculum for fourteen year olds in Music and Technology. These will now be presented briefly.

The EARS Pedagogical Project

The ElectroAcoustic Resource Site (EARS; www.ears.dmu.ac.uk) was born of the need to have a presence on the Web dealing with the terminology related to this body of work (and extended to cover all of sound-based music) as well as to serve as a means of finding information related to the subject of electroacoustic (and thus sound-based) music studies. This project has demonstrated its value given its high usage statistics and the support the project has received in terms of its internationalization, for example, its multilingual content, over the years.

What is more relevant to this discussion is a recent development within the EARS project, namely, the EARS Pedagogical project. This tripartite project was influenced by the Groupe de Recherches Musicales's CD-ROM, *La musique électroacoustique* (INA/GRM-Hyptique 2000).[19] This wonderfully produced French language publication is divided into three parts: listening, understanding, and doing. The same segmentation forms the basis of this new project. The Intention/Reception project's methodology, which supports sound-based music appreciation, is being updated to form the first of the three integrated parts of this educational project. EARS II, which initially will possess fewer terms than the current EARS, will employ definitions that can be understood by children (of age 10 and upward initially) or others with no subject-specific knowledge and, more importantly, will employ every aspect of hypermedia relevant to individual terms. EARS II will function as a tool for understanding concepts, whether they are historical, theoretical, or related to technological aspects. Users of all ages will be invited to try out concepts through interactive interfaces.[20] Sound and movie examples related to terms will be provided, as will hyperlinks for those interested in pursuing concepts further. A new software program called Sound Organiser is being developed in collaboration with the Groupe de Recherches Musicales in Paris that employs a strategy borrowed from computer games, namely, that of levels, in this case, learning levels. As an individual gains an ability related to a certain skill, he or she may progress to the next level, at which further opportunities are introduced. Challenges are presented to make the learning curve enjoyable. At higher levels, a distributed network version is envisioned for multiple users to make sound-based works in real time together wherever they happen to be.

An integrated curriculum will allow people learning by way of the EARS Pedagogical project to become introduced to new types of music as new concepts are presented and new forms of, for example, sound manipulation are included at the next level of the Sound Organiser. Once a certain level of expertise is gained, users may decide to graduate to current less-user-friendly, but more "complete," software programs.

This project illustrates a holistic way of becoming acquainted with, learning concepts about, and being creatively involved with sound-based music. One can envision user groups for young people evolving with certain musical tendencies or involving certain themes. Art and life can certainly find new points of intersection in a socially innovative and culturally exciting new form of artistic endeavor that ideally will build bridges between people of all ages across the globe.[21]

An Alternative Music and Technology Curriculum

Music teacher and postgraduate student Alexis Ffrench was asked by a leading music examination company in Britain to write an alternative curriculum for schoolchildren. The invitation was due to the fact that he had criticized the current GCSE (General Certificate of Secondary Education) and A-level curricula (for ca. 14- to 16- and 16- to 18-year-old students, respectively) of a competing company as too traditional and too narrow. It is this last company's curricula that are being used by most schools in England and Wales currently. As this chapter was written (late 2007/early 2008), his proposed GCSE curriculum[22] was being tested in a small number of U.K. schools.

There are various revolutionary and refreshing aspects of this proposal, most of which are relevant to this text. First, it recognizes that people can achieve a high level of musicianship without being musically "literate" through the use of the five-line score. Ffrench's curriculum thus contains two paths, and the same high level of achievement can be attained in either. This being the case, Ffrench therefore recognized both aural and written musical traditions. In fact, he also recognized a third and more recent means of making music called the electroacoustic paradigm by François Delalande (2001) and my sound-based music paradigm by myself (Landy 2007b and introduced at greater length in 2007a). It is with this in mind that the curriculum is called Music and Technology and not just Music or Music Technology.

Ffrench believes in young people being introduced to the widest repertoire possible, including, for example, Black African, South and East Asian traditions, jazz, popular music, musical theater, and Western art music. He also introduces people to sound-based music in this curriculum through sections dealing with the soundscape and its associated field of acoustic communication as well as other forms of music employing new technologies. Students are not, of course, expected to achieve the same level of knowledge or musical expertise in all of these areas, but instead a basic awareness is expected, and following this, various studies leading toward specialization in one or more of these areas can be pursued.

If young people were to be presented with such a wealth of music and creative musical opportunities, their ability to make choices beyond those presented by the mass media would be enhanced. It is for this reason that one hopes that such curricula will be implemented in as many places as possible in the not too distant future. By introducing these students to sound-based music and opening curricula like this to readily available sound-based music tools such as those of the EARS

Pedagogical project, threshold issues will be dealt with in an early phase of these children's lives, and the opportunity to become involved in this form of music or any other will be made that much greater.

C. Sound-Based Music 4 All

This new century is going to be very exciting due to the revolutions related to digital communication. Book, journal, and music score publishers are all trying to figure out what their businesses will be like in a decade or two. The same can be said of our music recording industry, and broadcasting is redefining itself as well. For example, the transformation of the BBC in recent years in terms of its forms of Web-based communication has been massive.

All of this is going to lead to a much healthier map of music. For those interested in the music of sounds, a very dynamic future is predicted. When doing the research that led to my coining the term *sound-based music paradigm*, it became clear that an important wall previously segregating audiences of art and popular music was much less visible, that is, audible, and hence much less relevant when discussing the music of sounds.[23] A large portion of new media or digital art is innovative, and the innovative spirit found in sound-based music is shared by people who have roots in popular as well as art music traditions. The means of creating a work are largely shared, as is the technology and potential source material. Frankly, today some of the largest audible divisions in this body of music are those inherited from the past—the employment of a beat or not and a focus on noise textures, on loudness, on complexity; however, what appears in a given sound-based work need not place it as either popular or art music. Many such works are simply sound-based pieces.

That sound-based music can and will grow in the years ahead is clear as these tools become better known and become more accessible in developing countries and as education and means of broadcast and dissemination improve. People of all ages, abilities, and backgrounds will be able to share sounds and sound-based works as well as participate together in sound-based performance. It is already available to all, but many still are unaware of its existence. As tools evolve, education and dissemination improve, and new media arts become more widely embraced by society at large, communities will grow, and new ones will evolve. This is a far cry from the significant cold shoulder our cultures provided most forms of innovative musics not that long ago.

NOTES

1. See, for example, Landy 1990 and 1991 for two early discussions related to marginalization. Of course, I am not alone in this quest; an example of an important text on

this subject is the work of Duteutre (1995). A more optimistic view can be found in the 2007 work of Ross.

2. The term *sound-based music* was introduced in Landy 2007b and further developed in Landy 2007a and encompasses most electroacoustic music as well as sonic art and sound art. Terms associated with sound-based music include acousmatic music; soundscape composition; ambient music; sound-based electronic music; electronica (e.g., glitch, lowercase sound, noise music); sound-based formalized music; sound-based new performance (e.g., laptop music, new devices devised for sound-based music); sound art; sound installations; sound-based Internet music; turntablism; and a variety of forms of sound-based music rooted in experimental popular music, among others. Some authors prefer to separate sound design, sound art, and the like from music. Douglas Kahn described these tensions in his book *Noise Water Meat* (1999) and supported the view presented here that creative works focused on the organization of sound form a subset of music.

3. Jacques Attali's book *Noise* (1985) contains a post-Marcusian argument concerning the power of the industrialization of music and offers a foundation for any discussion concerning music's being evolved from its more traditional roles into a major commodity.

4. This is a number that might have been satisfying for folk musicians, but most of them would have been able to perform more often than most contemporary musicians.

5. Such ironic remarks do not restrict themselves to the past. In a recent music review concerning the Huddersfield Contemporary Music Festival, music critic Anna Picard wrote: "One could admire an audience that travels to hear music that many would travel equally far not to hear" (*Independent on Sunday*, December 2, 2007, p. 56).

6. France forms an exception with its rotation of baccalaureate exam pieces, including works by Jean-Claude Risset (electroacoustic) and Jimi Hendrix (experimental pop) over recent years. These works are, of course, introduced at the end of the study as one gains entrance into the music of today.

7. This elitism has been reduced in recent years due to some universities' outreach programs and others becoming involved with issues concerning accessibility issues related to innovative forms of music.

8. I am consciously avoiding the terms modernism and postmodernism here, as their usage, particularly in music, is too ambiguous for this discussion.

9. I introduced the phrase the *something to hold on to factor* in timbral music (Landy 1994).

10. The price comparison approach here is dangerous, of course. The sum of MP3 files on a downloaded CD could cost more than a 44.1k CD purchased as an object. There are therefore issues of quantity and sound quality here, but the fact remains that more music is accessible to a wider public than ever.

11. Nonlocalized communities have, of course, existed for a considerable period. Musicians interested in a certain type of music, for example, could share the same periodicals focused on their particular genre, meet at conferences and festivals, purchase the same recordings, and so on over most of the 20th century. The key differences with the virtual communities described here are the increased amount of information and the decreased amount of expenditure to access the information.

12. Even instrumental lessons and master classes are taking place now involving telepresence, but this is still an expensive and thus fairly inaccessible technology.

13. People associated with the Drake Project (www.drakemusicproject.org) have been involved with the creation of instruments for people with special needs, something they call "assistive music technology." This exemplifies how new technologies are making

music-making accessible to those who for whatever reason may not have been able or willing to make music previously.

14. Copyleft is the opposite of copyright, that is, the freeing of any rights related to the work in question. People can designate the level of rights related to their work these days. See, for example, creativecommons.org, accessed November 29, 2007.

15. It goes without saying that not all technological developments are a form of progress in the sense of moving an art form forward; many are not terribly useful, some may even take us backward. During our current Google epoch, we are very much a culture of "seek and ye shall find," and it is this that is being celebrated here.

16. A few remarks might be added here concerning where to draw the line between sound-based music and sounds that when organized are not music. I believe that this distinction is a personal one and prefer to avoid the discussion in the present text for that very reason.

17. For a definition of this term and to find resources related to this term, please refer to http://www.ears.dmu.ac.uk/spip.php?rubrique219, accessed November 29, 2007.

18. It is, of course, true that the live musician in note- or sound-based music is something to hold on to for the viewer, that is, as opposed to the case of CD listening. What is being addressed here is musical content; clearly, a good deal of contemporary note-based music is proving challenging to many listeners internationally.

19. Another initiative worthy of mention in the area of sound generation for young people is NOTAM's (Norwegian Network for Technology, Acoustics, and Music) software DSP. The most recent version can be found at http://www.notam02.no/DSP02/en/, accessed January 19, 2008.

20. A second, full-scale version for undergraduate students is currently in its planning phase.

21. Similar to the original EARS project, the intention is to offer all three aspects in as many languages and using as many local/regional sounds and music examples as possible. The latest articles related to EARS and Pedagogical EARS can be found at http://www.ears. dmu.ac.uk/spip.php?page=articleEars&id_article=3597, accessed November 29, 2007.

22. An A-level curriculum is proposed as a second phase of this development.

23. In Landy 2007a, several musical examples are presented to illustrate this conclusion. Artists such as Aphex Twin and Squarepusher may have roots in popular music, but some of their works could have been realized by someone with an art music background; the works are hard to place in traditional art versus pop categories. Many electronica works and pieces of noise music are equally difficult to place or simply reside in both due to certain aspects of their content. Furthermore, soundscape compositions often demonstrate little influence from either tradition. These and other examples support the notion of a sound-based music paradigm, a "supergenre" that takes aspects related to production, reception, and knowledge of this body of works into account.

BIBLIOGRAPHY

Attali, J. 1985. *Noise: The Political Economy of Music*. Manchester: Manchester University Press (originally published in 1977 as *Bruits; essai sur l'économie politique de la musique*. Paris: Presses Universitaires de France).

Barbosa, A. 2003. Displaced soundscapes: A survey of network systems for music and sonic art collaboration. *Leonardo Music Journal* 13: 53–59.

Benjamin, W. 1992. The work of art in the age of mechanical reproduction. *Illuminations*. London: Fontana, pp. 211–244.

Brown, A. 2007. *Computers in Music Education: Amplifying Musicality*. New York: Routledge.

Delalande, F. 2001. *Le son des musiques: Entre technologie et esthétique*. Paris: INA/GRM Buchet/Chastel.

Duteutre, B. 1995. *Requiem pour une avant-garde*. Paris: Éditions Robert Laffont.

Gaver, W. W. 1993. What in the world do we hear? An ecological approach to auditory event perception. *Ecological Psychology* 5(1): 1–29.

Groening, M. 1997. *The Huge Book of Hell*. New York: Penguin.

Hugill, A. 2007. *The Digital Musician*. New York: Routledge.

INA/GRM-Hyptique. 2000. La musique électroacoustique. *Colletion Musiques Tangibles* 1. CD-ROM. Éditions hyptique.net.

Kahn, D. 1999. *Noise Water Meat: A History of Sound in the Arts*. Cambridge: MIT Press.

Landy, L. 1990. Is more than three decades of computer music reaching the public it deserves? *International Computer Music Conference Glasgow Proceedings*, pp. 369–372.

Landy, L. 1991. *What's the Matter with Today's Experimental Music? Organized Sound too Rarely Heard*. Chur, Switzerland: Harwood Academic.

Landy, L. 1994. "The something to hold on to factor" in timbral composition. *Contemporary Music Review* 18(2): 49–58.

Landy, L. 2006. The Intention/Reception project. In *Analytical Methods of Electroacoustic Music*, ed. M. Simoni. New York: Routledge, pp. 29–53 plus appendices on the book's DVD.

Landy, L. 2007a. *La musique des sons/The Music of Sounds*. Paris: Sorbonne MINT/OMF.

Landy, L. 2007b. *Understanding the Art of Sound Organization*. Cambridge: MIT Press.

Marcuse, H. 1964. *One-Dimensional Man*. Boston: Beacon Press.

Rheingold, H. 2000. *The Virtual Community: Homesteading on the Electronic Frontier*. Cambridge: MIT Press (originally published 1993 by Addison Wesley).

Ross, A. 2007. *The Rest Is Noise: Listening to the Twentieth Century*. New York: Farrar, Strauss and Giroux.

Weale, R. 2006. Discovering how accessible electroacoustic music can be: The Intention/Reception project. *Organised Sound* 11(2): 189–200.

Weinberg, G. 2005. Interconnected musical networks: Toward a theoretical framework. *Computer Music Journal* 29(2): 23–39.

CHAPTER 26

FRAMING LEARNING PERSPECTIVES IN COMPUTER MUSIC EDUCATION

JØRAN RUDI AND
PALMYRE PIERROUX

MUSIC can be said to be a construction of the human imagination and the creative processes of the composer, the performer, and the listener. Crafting, interpreting, and appreciating a work all require recognition, reflection, and a personal resonance in response to the sounding material or the ideas embedded in it. From this perspective, teaching music becomes a complex issue. This is particularly the case for teaching computer music, which, in addition to training students and developing their knowledge of musical form and how it is crafted, often entails engaging students at the conceptual level in reflecting on what *counts* as music.

Yet, as with any music field or genre, education in computer music is essentially focused on advancing knowledge and an acceptance of some core disciplinary concepts and values. As with other genres, computer music education needs to be designed for different developmental levels and curricular plans, taking into account the institutional and social aspects of formal and informal learning contexts. However, the strong technical tool focus in computer music also has the potential to build on and extend students' everyday experimentation with new technologies and musical encounters in ways that are meaningful and relevant to them. We propose in this chapter that such an understanding is key to the teaching and learning of computer music and will advance its potential as a disciplinary field in the future. This is because computer music is related to all kinds of digital literacies and media consumption prevalent today. We seek a broader integration of computer music in educational contexts, and we investigate means of making computer music relevant as a discipline by drawing more directly on young people's increasingly complex digital literacies related to music.

The overall focus of this chapter is a discussion of approaches to learning and teaching computer music, with a particular focus on pedagogical design and the use of learning technologies among nonspecialists and young people in secondary and upper secondary school levels. The discussion is organized in three parts. It begins with a framing of computer music as a discipline taught at secondary and upper secondary levels and provides an overview of its core areas or knowledge domains. These are described as (1) listening, (2) physics, (3) signal processing, and (4) musical form. These core areas are understood as relevant to learning contexts within but also outside formalized educational settings. The second part of this chapter discusses learning perspectives and presents a frame for conceptualizing learning with digital technologies. In the third part, we discuss recent approaches to designing and implementing computer music technologies, with a particular focus on DSP, an online learning platform designed by NOTAM (Norwegian Network for Technology, Acoustics, and Music) that adopts an exploratory instructional approach to computer music. The technology design and pedagogical approach have been further developed through several years of work with DSP in workshops for upper secondary school students in Norway.

1. FRAMING COMPUTER MUSIC AS A DISCIPLINE

Computers are by far the most common tools in any music production today; as a result, there is a huge variation in what is called *computer music*. As the term has become more imprecise, different approaches have recently been suggested to define computer music as a genre. Natasha Barrett, for example, described computer music as "including all that is not purely acoustic music, based on instrumental models, nor overtly commercially oriented" (2007, p. 232). Other researchers proposed analyzing technology-based sonic expressions and arriving at a taxonomy of computer music that is based on descriptions of the aesthetic characteristics. This has been discussed as a possible approach by Landy (2007), for example, as a means of addressing the wide distribution of technological tools and signal-processing methods that have emerged over the past ten to fifteen years through commercialization, among other trends.

Highly advanced tools are available at low cost, and electronic sounds and more comprehensive abstract sonic expressions crafted with electroacoustic methods are commonplace, found in all rich media environments. Broad access to advanced tools bypasses the traditional limitations of access that are based on economy and education, and in this sense the playing field has become more even—one can talk about a real democratization. Briefly summarized, the long trend that we see emerging from the use of commercial and social technologies on the Internet is the sustainability of niche cultures that are less dependent on the retail industry, publishing houses, and record companies. This is because of the inexpensive distribution means and the ease of network-building that is possible over the Internet. Niches have their roots in small interest groups and subcultures, and the low cost of making music available through the Internet has had the effect of making these niche expressions commercially interesting. In fact, the economic yield for large Internet retailers of music and books shows that the sum generated by very small titles amounts to nearly the same as what is generated by the "blockbuster industry" (Anderson 2006). This is due in part to the increased availability and visibility of niche products during recent years, encouraged by the tremendous growth in social networking technologies on the Internet, such as blogs and wikis. Such social software makes self-publishing of user-generated content and file distribution quite easy, with niche products marketed through social networks that largely bypass such traditional gatekeepers of content and economy as record companies and publishing houses.

Together, the possibility for self-publication and a market presence has facilitated flourishing of electroacoustic art outside traditional education institutions and mediation channels. However, the democratization process briefly outlined is nonetheless largely driven by commercialization and the commercial drive for globalization, supported by the Internet. This emphasis on commercialization means that recent advances in research and engineering are not fully exploited in the music market as a whole, with the result that quite similar types of tools now dominate entry level music production nearly everywhere. Although this near uniformity may foster a general digital literacy in music production, there are also creative consequences, bringing about aesthetic changes and a refocusing of the field that is much more oriented toward popular music.

While such shifts do not reduce the value of the cultural heritage found in the electroacoustic tradition of computer music, they are nonetheless significant in terms of a convergence of tools and methods between art genres. Furthermore, this convergence has pedagogical implications as the expansion of computer music techniques and signal-processing methods into popular music genres and aesthetics has increasingly become part of students' digital literacy (Tyner 1998, Brown 2007), or rather "multiple literacies" (Gee 1990, Group 1996, Roth 2006). In other words, computer music as a discipline taps into the multiple literacies that students develop in convergences among signal-processing techniques, online and off-line social networks, niche music markets and interests, multimedia mixing tools, and popular music aesthetics. The concept of multiple literacies thus extends beyond reading, writing, and digital skills taught in formal school settings. Instead, multiple literacies is a term describing actions and emergent forms of knowledge as people are apprenticed into (digital) practices as part of a social group (Gee 1990). In the following, we describe some of core areas in computer music that transverse and intersect with such everyday multiple literacies, and we reflect on how these knowledge domains may be incorporated in pedagogical designs.

2. CORE AREAS IN COMPUTER MUSIC

The goal of any musical training is to strengthen musical skills among the students. Students should develop language to describe and discuss music, they should recognize and identify formal qualities, and at best they should also be able to create musical value through personal expression and crafting of musical form. To reach these goals successfully in computer music, students need skills in understanding musical structure, practical knowledge about software and hardware tools, and familiarity with production aspects of computer music composition. Since composing computer music most often involves direct aural feedback to the composer in the process, the students also need listening skills beyond normal identification of pitch, tone, and interval and a consciousness of the importance of spatial distribution and development of musical material. Basic knowledge in acoustics and about the physical properties of sound is also beneficial. As a means of further articulating the disciplinary content of computer music as a secondary and upper secondary school subject, we identify the following four knowledge domains or core areas: listening, physics and psychophysics, signal processing, and musical form.

A. Listening

Computer music is real time in the sense that the composer gets nearly immediate-sounding results when working with software and hardware. This sets it apart from working with notated music of the more traditional kind, which generally requires the composer to wait to hear the work until rehearsals start for the premiere. This technological aspect of composing computer music, combined with the normal use of material without pitch—recorded or synthesized—brings listening into the composition process at an early stage. Listening is a precondition for the entire process, and the use of abstract material immediately actuates questions about what the sounds are, what we are listening to, and what the meaning is.

The traditional way of listening to computer and electronic music has its roots in Pierre Schaeffer's (1966) late ideas of reduced listening to sounds only as they appear, isolated from their source, and considered only by their emergent qualities. Following Schaeffer, Denis Smalley (1986) developed a large taxonomy for categorizing sounds based on their spectral development and movement. Another listening approach was developed by Simon Emmerson (1986), who distinguished between abstract and abstracted syntax, aural and mimetic discourse. Emmerson opened for contextual listening, allowing the sounds' origins to be considered significant for reflection on the music. This focus on contextual listening was emphasized further by Murray Schafer (1977) and others in the genre *soundscape composition,* for which the founding idea is that any environment exposes itself through sound and can be presented through careful selection and recomposition of recorded material. These mentioned perspectives are complemented by the term *imaginary listening* (d'Escrivan 2007), which describes how sound in film, for example, is used to reveal events that are happening off screen or recorded sounds are treated to add drama to other objects and events than their source.

Common to all these perspectives is the focus on listening as a process and on the construction of meaning as a process that all participants in a musical experience share, including the composer, the performer, and the listener. Hearing thus becomes an acoustical phenomenon, while listening is an action (Barthes 1991). Careful listening reveals that silence does not exist, and that attention to sound, in an ecological perspective, makes us aware of crucial characteristics of our situation, in art or outside, personal and social. John Cage described the sounds in the world as musical, and in an interview, sound artist Bill Fontana stated: "From a musical point of view, the world is musical at any given moment" (Rudi 2005, p. 97). In Fontana's works, microphone placement translates to listening perspective, and he uses the recording equipment to focus and select some perspectives over others. We can say that use of technology changes the way we listen, and as such, we listen to mediated versions of someone else's intentionality.

The listening experience gets better with training, and the more experienced a listener is, the richer the experience. There is a body of research suggesting that as a listener's experience grows, the focus shifts from sound and source identification to pattern recognition and logic. Given that the types of listening described involve so much more than the focus on pitch, interval, and harmony that dominates most music education, listening literacies receive particular attention in computer music as a knowledge domain.

B. Physics and Psychophysics

Sound has physical properties, and the science of acoustics describes sound and sound propagation in space and through different materials. Issues such as absorption, reflection, and resonance are important in understanding the characteristics of signals as they fill, and move in, our surroundings. Further, knowledge of how sound can be analyzed and represented belongs to the discipline of computer music and is the basis for digital-recording techniques and signal processing. Different types of signal representation allow for different types of processing and in turn influence the construction of user interfaces, especially graphical interfaces for screen, but also physical interfaces for control and performance.

We often experience meaning as immediately embedded in sounds, as we recognize them, their presumed source, and their place and movement around us. These immediate interpretations go beyond our objective, acoustic reality, and form important parts of the specifically human species response and adaptation to acoustic nature and culture, or what is called *psychoacoustics*. This discipline includes issues of sound separation and interpretation of simple and complex, similar-sounding, and simultaneous audio streams and investigates our ability to recognize sounds and their placement. Our auditory system gives preference to certain types of signals and can thus be said to amplify some at the cost of others. In more specific musical contexts, there are issues of sound, melody, and music recognition when tone quality, pitch, masking, and time differences vary. Timbral matching allows us to "name that tune in no notes." Bregman (1990) collapsed these topics into what he called "auditory scene analysis." In education, this core area in computer music can provide critical awareness, reflection, and sensitivity to relationships among physics, acoustics, and the meaning of sounds in our natural and cultural environment.

C. Signal Processing

Recording, synthesizing, changing, and combining sounds in the digital domain are types of signal processing; the computer develops the sound in one way or another. Teaching computer music must therefore include information about how a computer works with sound and give some insight into the many synthesis and signal-processing types that are commonly employed. Directly linking knowledge of sound and how it can be taken apart, processed, and reconstructed using different signal-processing methods is essential to this core area. Explicitly linking the physical properties of sound with its numerical representation is also a means of conveying how creative ideas can be presented in different ways, for example, as expressions in mathematics and physics. This cross-disciplinary knowledge is at the core of old school computer music and expresses the principles of signal processing as a core area.

D. Musical Form

A central feature in most music education is to support students' appreciation of different types of music and their recognition and familiarity with the formal characteristics of different kinds of expressions. The underlying pedagogical aim is to expand the student's ability to find music in all acoustic art, to develop their skills in listening and analysis, and perhaps also to enable them to better enjoy musical styles with which they are less familiar.

In comparison to music that is built on instrumental models, computer music poses a challenge to students in that there is little focus on pitch structures, melodic material, or rhythm. The basic building blocks most listeners are used to are essentially missing, including recognizable genres. Pitch-based music dominates our hemisphere, to the point at which the representation of the music as notes is often described as the music itself. Edgard Varèse coined the description of music as "organized sound," and in computer music, this focus on timbral development as essential in composition is sustained. However, musical forms and their organization may be more difficult to comprehend and recognize on a concrete level because the forms are often inspired by the sounds themselves. The spatial distribution and performance of the elements is often a crucial component of computer music works and represent another departure from the more familiar pitch-space.

Once students begin to hear electronic sounds as musical, there is the hurdle of shaping credible forms, which demands a new level of abstraction. Musical forms take on different sizes and appear on many levels, in dominating or supporting roles, and structural terms such as foreground/background and micro-/meso-/macrolevels may be used to articulate compositional features (Roads 2001). In computer music, musical forms are often constructed in unconventional ways, from features and principles extracted from the sounds themselves or developed by algorithmic means. Both of these approaches differ from most methods based in tonal or rhythmic ideas.

Media today are filled with computer-processed material, and people are familiar with electronic sound quality and the abstract and abstracted discourse the material contains. In other words, this is part of an everyday digital literacy, not framed as a specific musical competence. Relating understandings of computer sounds to compositional forms in computer music involves resonance and recognition and depends on "something to hold on to" (Landy 1994). To meet this challenge of relating everyday knowledge of electronic sounds to musical form in computer music, a fundamentally broadened aesthetic understanding and discourse is needed.

3. COMPUTER MUSIC ACROSS DISCIPLINES

Music education at secondary and upper secondary levels is typically not a significant part of a school's curriculum, and work with music technology may constitute a brief part of a semester, if it is made available at all. This negligence reflects the precarious and peripheral role of the arts in education in general, a situation worsened by the relatively limited empirical research on the arts compared, for example, to science education in schools.

Such limitations pose a real challenge for computer music since the field, as we have seen, is quite comprehensive, focusing on composition and technology with underpinnings in acoustics, psychoacoustics, recording, synthesis, and signal processing. A natural ambition for computer music educators is to increase musical work with technology by integrating and relating this work across knowledge domains and other school subjects. Computer music is relevant to the study of music history, for example, as its aesthetics are best understood as springing from the Western art music tradition and from the desire to break away from some of its conventions. Digital representation of music's physical properties also allows for interesting tasks in mathematics and physics classes, especially if clear links to the perception and understanding of musical properties can be maintained. Music has wittingly been described as a special instance of applied physics, reducing music to the physical properties of sound only and thus actuating the question of musical representation. These are two instances in which computer music and electro-acoustic techniques can serve as point of departure for a cross-disciplinary revitalization and competence building in art education, particularly in light of the large convergence in media technology.

The significance of music and arts education for human development raised by John Dewey in the early part of the 20th century is a large and ongoing discussion that exceeds the scope of this chapter. In cognitive psychology, for example, arguments are made for the transfer of conceptual development across subjects based on studies of music lessons for IQ enhancement (Schellenberg 2004) or of aesthetic understanding for critical thinking (Housen 2001–2002). Often, assessment issues raised by such studies are framed by interests at the policy level and by the need for empirical studies that demonstrate a causal relationship to students' achievement (Gadsden 2008). In this chapter, we point to the need for research that is framed more broadly, addressing social as well as cognitive dimensions and questions of how learning and teaching in the arts, like other subjects, are linked to issues of identity, multiple literacies, life experiences, and contexts outside formalized educational settings.[1]

4. LEARNING PERSPECTIVES AND COMPUTER MUSIC

Perspectives on learning in computer music are largely undeveloped, and there is a strong need for empirical research of pedagogical approaches to the discipline. A recent contribution to the field was provided by Brown (2007), who addressed the use of computers in music education in general, pointing to their potential in four main areas: music production, presentation, reflection, and implementation. Brown adopted a constructivist perspective on learning, a broad term that draws mainly on the thinking of Jean Piaget, Dewey, and Jerome Bruner and emphasizes the active role of the individual learner in constructing knowledge through experience, inquiry, and discovery. Another constructivist position that has been significant for education in the arts is Howard Gardner's (1984) theory of multiple intelligences, with musical intelligence identified as one of seven types. Gardner's view has been popular for contributing to awareness of the richness and complexity of human cognition and represents in this sense a continuation of Dewey's (1934) views on aesthetic knowing, which emphasizes the development of individual perceptual processes and cognitive faculties through immediate, somatic experience (Shusterman 2000, Pierroux 2003).

This emphasis on identifying learning with individual cognition and the development of mental schemata is what most clearly distinguishes constructivism from sociocultural perspectives, which focus on the development of cognition through human activity in a system of social relations and cultural tools. Based on the work of Russian psychologist Lev Vygotsky (1978, 1986), and developed over recent generations, sociocultural perspectives adopt the position that "mind is no longer to be located entirely inside the head; higher psychological function are transactions that include the biologically individual, the cultural mediational artifacts, and the culturally structured social and natural environments of which persons are a part" (Cole and Wertsch 1996, p. 253).

Such an understanding of the significance of human activity, cultural tools, and social context for learning has implications for understandings of what computer music is, for pedagogical approaches to computer music in schools, and for the design of learning technologies for computer music. This broader understanding of human development is needed for framing approaches to teaching computer music since, as mentioned, the core areas comprising the knowledge domain are closely linked to ongoing changes in social practices and multiple literacies outside formal school settings. In education research, for example, ethnographic methods are useful in analytical accounts of the mediating role of social interaction, the situated context, and the institutional setting in learning processes (Rasmussen et al. 2003, Roth 2006, Pierroux forthcoming). In other words, as mentioned, an articulated learning perspective and empirical studies are needed that will make apparent connections between literacies in musical form, acoustics, signal processing, and listening to integrate computer music better in different educational settings.

5. DESIGN APPROACHES TO LEARNING TECHNOLOGIES

Computers have been used in different ways to create environments for learning for the past twenty years. Current developments in learning systems may be grouped in terms of supporting students' activities through investigative elements (inquiry or discovery learning), play (gaming), production (modeling, composition, wikis), and collaboration (synchronous and asynchronous systems). In environments designed for inquiry in science learning, for example, investigative elements include simulating and modeling aspects of natural phenomena, tools for analyzing or visualizing data, and ways of modeling learners' theories and hypotheses to study the consequences (van Joolingen et al. 2007).

Brown (2007) likewise distinguished between different learning technologies and e-learning according to types of interaction or educational support that they provide. Technologies designed specifically for educational purposes are characterized as interactive software, asynchronous communication, asynchronous collaboration, synchronous collaboration, and Web content creation. However, rather than defining the learning by the technology, we suggest that a more useful approach may be to conceptualize these as features or components that may be integrated into environments according to an overall pedagogical design intent.

While design approaches may vary, there is generally a pedagogical aim to change and improve students' conceptual understanding of disciplinary issues related to specific knowledge domains (Krange and Ludvigsen 2008). In computer music, these domains have been described here as listening, physics, signal processing, and musical form. However, in addition to disciplinary knowledge, there is a creative and productive aspect to learning in the arts that brings gaming, experimenting, and discovery to the foreground in learning technologies designed for music education, particularly computer music. Instructional approaches that prioritize modeling and procedural knowledge may be unable to support learners in their creative and experimental work with sound and musical forms and in then relating these to core disciplinary concepts. This is because guided instructional design often solely entails a set of "forced" or "obligatory" sequence of steps or problems that must be solved before learners are allowed to move on to the next task (Pickering 1995). IRCAM's (Institut de Recherche et Coordination Acoustique/ Musique's) software 10 Jeux d'ecoute (2000) is an example of an instructional perspective that emphasizes the use of forced moves, structured around computer music' core areas and taking students through ten fixed audio games.

In contrast, as discussed in greater detail in the following section, environments designed with a more experimental approach combine forced moves that support discovery and inquiry learning through investigative elements but also emphasize direct engagement by integrating game features or composition tools with more "open" or "optional" moves. As Smith and Dean (2002) pointed out, a nonlinear interaction with information is often desirable when encouraging learners to generate new ideas and interpretations in educational contexts. Thus, a balance between forced and open moves in design also represents an epistemological stance and is at the crux of designing "technological" learning scaffolds.

Although there is a relatively long history of digital learning environments and research on effectiveness and efficiency, findings from evaluation and analysis of their use suggest some recurring issues. First, there is a problem in designing for the complexity of social interaction and actual use in different settings, which tend to have a significant impact on how the learning technologies are taken up by students. Chief among the concerns here is the role of the teacher, or more capable peer, whose guidance is key to learning. The second finding that runs through much of the research relates to the tension mentioned between guided instruction, which provides information and fully explains the concepts that students are expected to learn in a procedural, task-solving approach, and "minimal guidance" designs that engage and support learners in abstract, conceptual thinking by drawing on their unique prior experience as they collaboratively and experimentally construct knowledge and solve tasks (Kirschner et al. 2006). Issues here revolve around the level and types of guidance, the complexity of the task, the types of representations used, and the use of modeling versus experimental activities. The general concern is that if the task and the information to which inexperienced or less-able learners need to relate to solve the problem are too complex and there is only a minimum of guidance, then the "problem-solving" activity will hinder abstract and conceptual thinking related to the knowledge domain. Approaches to these challenges are discussed next in relation to learning in computer music.

6. Some Examples of Music Software as Learning Tools

In addition to a small number of learning technologies specifically designed for computer music education, there are an increasing number of tools on the "open market" developed for musical purposes as software and computers become more powerful. Most of these are professional or semiprofessional tools, but an increasing number are also designed for nonspecialists. Some software tools focus on music appreciation and train recognition of sound and form, some train recognition of specific musical repertoire, some are technically oriented toward signal-processing methods, while others are oriented toward experimentation and creative work within varying sets of constraints. The last are very diversified, with programs ranging from a simple combination of ready-made samples, to more open-ended programs by which users can create and process sounds and do their own sampling. Sequencers and sequencer-like software have become the most common production tools, integrating both signal processing and definition of timeline in larger-scale forms. However, the sequencer model conceptualizes the musical narrative as a linear and pitch-based movement, with little emphasis on principle-driven musical development or spatial composition.

In terms of learning resources, some Web sites include texts that describe theoretical aspects of sound and sound processing, often including simple demos of some principles by which one can change a parameter and hear and see the result. An example of this approach can be found on the BBC's Web site Music Sense,[2] although it is oriented toward traditional concepts such as pitch, interval, chords, and scales. The ambitious education project by the Massachusetts Institute of Technology aimed at the developing world, One Laptop Per Child (OLPC),[3] is particularly interesting in that it is developed according to principles of collaborative learning and sharing. Adaptation of the free and open source Linux operating system allows students to select, share, and view activities and networking opportunities at group, local (neighborhood), and global levels. A suite of simple learning activities in math, art, reading, and music is preinstalled and available for continual development as open source software in the OLPC wiki.

Among the preinstalled OLPC activities is a music program called TamTam,[4] which is a suite of four programs with Csound as the audio engine. Students at different developmental levels may collaboratively play, perform, edit, record, and share music using one of these programs. The musical focus of TamTam is largely on pitch and rhythm, complemented for more advanced students by a "synthlab", in which the workflow design is modeled on Max/MSP (Max Signal Processing). For composition, the paradigm is piano roll representation in a sequencer interface. A certain level of assessment by teachers is also possible through a visualization tool that renders individual student activities in a journal feature.

In addition to such integrated approaches to digital learning tools and music software, there are educational texts on the Internet that describe how to construct specific musical forms, often using a particular software, such as Audacity.[5] An example of this, written by Bruno Bossis,[6] can be found on the UNESCO (United Nations Educational, Scientific, and Cultural Organization) Digi-Arts Web site.[7] The Web site describes its aim as the "development of interdisciplinary activities in research, creativity and communication in the field of media art"[8] and contains theoretical and historical texts, tutorial texts for free software, step-by-step exercises, and links to other Web sites with software. The design of this Web site is a good example of a guided instructional approach, explaining musical history, physics, and signal processing at an advanced level and with little emphasis on exploration or the creativity of the viewers/users. In the pedagogical approaches listed in this chapter, instruction tends to follow a procedural track by which one specific task needs to be completed before the next step can be taken.

An example of a gaming approach to learning pitch and rhythm with minimal guidance is Morton Sobotnick's Creating Music software for children,[9] which includes the use of open sketchpads in working with pitch-based music. Here, users can set their own pitches and change timbre for playback of these pitches. Musical staffs and conventional notation for accurate pitch and rhythm are not used on this Web site. Instead, the sketchpad window is quantized, so the results stay within the conventional bounds without requiring effort to do so. An example of a Web site that encourages experiments with other tuning systems is NOTAM's Portable Pure Tuning.[10] This Web site contains a pure tuning automat software for downloading and informative texts about principles and research behind the pure tuning system.

There are also examples of Web sites designed to support both creative processes and the mediation of musical productions, such as school performances. An example of the latter is Sonic Postcards,[11] at which Internet technology is used to disseminate musical results. The Web site has been developed with a teacher's kit, intended to build competence and deepen the teacher's understanding of the project. Such tutorials, however, have their limitations as educational tools. The availability of theoretical texts on different levels is an important step in reaching out beyond specialist circles, but it is not really sufficient as a scaffold for learning in nonexpert classrooms settings.

In sum, as Brown (2007) pointed out, many of the features in generally available technologies can scaffold learning experiences in music education, including software that provides accompaniments for performance; allows playback during the compositional process; generates analysis, feedback, and error adjustments for compositions; enables real-time networking between composers for developing ensemble skills; and provides online discussion forums and peer group support environments.[12] However, these are often technology-led solutions and lack pedagogically informed frameworks for activities and tasks for use in real learning settings. In recent years, this problem has been recognized in many disciplines, and the development of learning technologies for specific educational settings has begun to gain momentum.

A. DSP as Learning Tool

To illustrate the educational approach outlined in the beginning of this text as a combination of crafting, interpreting and appreciating music, and critical reflection on what counts as music, we consider in greater detail NOTAM's software DSP.[13] The software attempts to address the need for specific learning technology for computer music and was first introduced at the International Computer Music Conference (ICMC) in 1997 (Rudi 1997). The software was developed in response to national curriculum changes in secondary schools in Norway; composition became an obligatory part of music education, and the use of technology while composing was encouraged. At the time, there was a lack of suitable educational music technology available for Windows and Mac OS other than simple sequencers, and the limitations of a pitch-based approach made it attractive to come up with another solution for teaching composition.

The application DSP is for composition and signal processing, with a simple user interface and a help system that can be accessed from any point inside the application. It makes use of the most common synthesis and signal-processing methods and is in keeping with most established graphical user interface (GUI) conventions to ensure a user-friendly interface (Rudi 2007). A normal student at secondary and upper secondary levels intuitively understands how to use the software as he or she is led directly into the creative workflow of the software, with the signal generation and processing automatically moving results into a mixer. This means that the student is immediately working on a first composition. Particular attention has been paid to the graphic design of an appealing GUI, motivating younger users through the professional look and feel of the software. The pedagogical design supports a discovery, inquiry learning approach, employing what Erstad (1999) described as a "student-centered" perspective. During the design process, emphasis was placed on tasks and activities that would require little formal training of the students, an approach that has also been discussed by Regelski (2004).

B. DSP in Learning Settings

For the nonspecialist groups with which NOTAM has been involved, a workshop model has invariably given good results. Workshop teachers lead the activities, and in school projects the class teacher is involved as well. The presence of workshop leaders and teachers with specialized disciplinary knowledge is a key aspect of the success of the educational design employed by NOTAM in DSP workshops. Recent studies in education science affirmed that teacher interventions in student group work is often key to assisting students in understanding the disciplinary nature of a task, particularly when learning technologies are involved (Rasmussen et al. 2003). At the same time, classroom teachers scaffold their own knowledge in workshop settings through working alongside specialists in electroacoustic thinking and techniques.

In the DSP workshop model, a normal school computer lab setup is adequate, and students are typically teamed up two or three per machine to collaborate in solving the aesthetic and technical problems they encounter during the workshop. This is another important principle in sociocultural perspectives on learning as discourse and interaction are viewed as central to the construction of meaning and knowledge in classroom settings (Wells 1999, Wegerif 2001, Arnseth and Ludvigsen 2006). The teacher introduces the tasks to the students by saying that they will be working with invited instructors to complete a class project in composition and performance. The basic technologies are the DSP software, software for sample editing, microphones, and recording equipment. In some workshops for festivals or other performance-oriented events, the computer work may be combined with actual instruments, homemade electronics, found objects, and combinations of microphones and effect processors for greater diversity and more interesting stage performances. The NOTAM workshops involve collaborations with external partners with relevant teaching skills and experience for the specific age group involved, and the workshops are often partially financed through national initiatives.

The pedagogical approach aims to integrate knowledge from the core areas in response to students' questions, which invariably arise after a period of exploring, experimenting, and getting to know the tools. At the onset of every workshop, students are immediately engaged in experimentation and constructive investigation, mediated by the program's open construction, which includes all elements needed for music production. Students' general digital literacy makes this a low-threshold entry into the workshop, and we have found that computer skills have improved dramatically since we started these workshops some ten years ago. Significantly, after having learned how things work, and after having made and processed a number of sounds, students have established some basic skills and begin to question and look for some kind of direction, either theoretically or in the form of concrete tasks. This pattern corresponds with findings in educational research and is the basis for exploratory approaches in inquiry-based designs for learning technologies (van Joolingen et al. 2007). A period of creative exploration is also generally acknowledged as fundamental to learning approaches in the arts.

In the DSP workshop model, learning scaffolds thus include disciplinary knowledge and tasks introduced in situ by the teachers, the collaborative meaning making of the students as they creatively engage with the software, "help" texts that describe algorithms employed by the program, theoretical texts dealing with physics and aesthetics, and an animated demo piece that is available as a "worked example" to guide students step-by-step through analytical approaches to sound material. In addition, DSP contains extensive resources for teachers with suggestions for interdisciplinary classroom projects.

Creative work is supported by the listening activities in the DSP program as students find and record sounds that hold meaning for them and place them in new contexts to express something specific and thus give the sounds new significance. Recording their own material facilitates students' reflections on their sounding environment, a kind of attention that is also emphasized by workshop leaders when introducing the project. Through artistic exploration, the students create musical values, rendering forms to which they have assigned meaning. The contexts for the workshops are important for the kinds of meanings that emerge, whether school projects with a duration of several weeks or projects designed to produce a result in a matter of a couple of hours. Although time constraints determine the amount of free experimentation, the approach is the same, building on students' everyday digital literacies and creative impulses.

Observations and feedback from participants over an extended period suggest that through collaborative creative work students engage with the core areas in computer music as well as acquire software-specific computer skills, practical skills for stage performance, and general audio technical skills. We have observed that there is a concentration on creative work in the DSP workshops, and that problems that arise in connection with this work are solved collaboratively, through student discourse and interaction and through the support of the teachers. Student concentration is centered on the disciplinary domain of music rather than on mastering the technology. However, as with the other technologies described, empirical studies of use in schools and workshop settings will need to be designed and conducted to provide a richer account of how the DSP platform, participants' interactions and previous knowledge, and institutional factors mediate students' learning in the core areas of computer music.

C. Design Development

In 2003, DSP was migrated from Windows and rewritten in Java for cross-platform availability. The software was renamed DSP02[14] and first developed to run in a browser from a comprehensive Web site that contains texts, examples, and tutorials. When it was found that many users experienced problems with an online Internet solution, the program was changed to become a stand-alone application. Now, DSP02 may be downloaded free from the Web site and runs independently from a browser as a Java applet without being connected to the Internet. Some additional functionality has been developed, and the software has to date been translated into seven languages. The software itself adapts to any of these according to the language used in the operating system of the computer. The graphic interface was redesigned in 2003, and the engine now utilizes Phil Burk's Jsyn library.[15]

The DSP software is now more than ten years old and is in use around the world, with several hundred downloads every month. Although the educational approach incorporated into DSP is apparently easily implemented in a range of learning settings, the software design would certainly benefit from new methods that capitalize on current social networking features to support collaboration and dissemination. Future design developments are currently being explored through analyses of DSP projects in Norwegian school settings and informal learning workshops that use wiki platforms and learning management systems for communication and file exchange, such as The Music Workshop,[16] in which DSP is used in combination with the Blender[17] software from NOTAM.

Advances in Internet technology accentuate the need for adapting the educational material and to incorporate the social aspects of electronic learning environments. We also see the need for collaboration with textbook publishers to make the learning resources available in other kinds of settings. An important aspect of such initiatives is the desire to integrate computer music into the social fabric on a broader scale and to disseminate student activities. Similar approaches to dissemination of student work with music include the Beacon project[18] at Museu de Arte Contemporânea de Niterói in Brazil and its Norwegian equivalent, Kunstfyret.[19] Repositories of diverse projects can serve as a learning resource, and results from DSP use are shared on the Web site, including Norwegian school workshops Lydoku[20] and Sound Treasure Hunt[21]; and music festivals such as St. Olav Festival 2008,[22] Ultima,[23] and the Hauge/Tveit Jubilee in 2008.[24] Importantly, the diverse settings also contribute to expanding the use of the software into other sonic arts, including soundscape composition, text/sound art, and remix performances.

7. CONCLUSION

In the DSP case described, envisioned design improvements incorporate features for teachers' assessment needs as well as for organizing student and teacher activities. In terms of the latter, this means linking DSP more closely with students' and teachers' literacies in social software, allowing participants to shape and share the learning environment, collaboratively adding to and modifying materials, and making connections across local and global levels of knowledge building. As for assessment, an important issue at stake for teachers when using collaborative, open learning environments is the need for visualizations of student contributions at both individual and group levels (Lund et al. 2007, Pierroux et al. 2008).

Importantly, increased use of social software in learning technology designs and a sociocultural perspective on computer music literacies will require new methods and a broader unit of analysis in music education research. It entails a shift from a primary research focus on assessing relations between music and individual cognition and affect to studies of how knowledge is constructed across such shared communities and made relevant in students' music literacies in specific settings. Such a shift has political as well as theoretical implications. Traditionally, learning research has investigated the significance of music and art education in terms of factors in affective and cognitive development and critical thinking. Findings from such research often argue for the transfer effect of cognitive development across other subject areas and thus become a political tool to promote better integration of the arts into national curricular plans.

While acknowledging the usefulness of psychological studies of music and human development, the argument made in this chapter for computer music education is another. The point to be made here is that there is an inextricable link between the cultural historical development of computer music as a genre and learning technologies like DSP, which as a tool has material as well as ideational aspects. Digital tools change in keeping with cultural, historical, and literacy practices in formal and informal learning settings, and there is at the same time a reflexive relationship between these tools and changes in computer music as a musical genre. It is here, we propose, that the future framing of learning perspectives in computer music education lay, in greater awareness of this reflexivity between tools and the development of human ideas and creativity.

Relating core areas in computer music to everyday multiple literacies entails developing a language of aesthetics for abstraction, distortion, and simulation in contemporary music and sounding materials. In addition, music education needs to be updated with digitally based methods and principles that draw on simpler commercial music software and technologies. This means that developments in the teaching and learning of computer music hinge on creating a better balance between the sharper research edge in computer music and more commercially driven standard solutions to music technology.

Computer music education will have a larger impact if included in the broader fabric of society and texture of everyday life. Moreover, changes in educational approaches to computer music are needed to meet the demands of public institutions and funding bodies to reach larger audiences. We propose that better integration of computer music in secondary and upper secondary education is possible by adapting teaching methods and core knowledge to diverse collaborative learning settings; by designing for students' creativity and digital literacies in exploratory, inquiry-based activities; and by incorporating social software features as pedagogical scaffolds in computer music learning technologies.

NOTES

1. See Gadsden (2008) for a recent review of such approaches.
2. BBC, Music Sense. http://www.bbc.co.uk/music/parents/activities/musicsense/index.shtml, accessed October 14, 2008.

3. Laptop.org, One Laptop Per Child (OLPC). http://www.laptop.org/en/laptop/start/, accessed September 30, 2008.

4. Laptop.org, TamTam. http://wiki.laptop.org/go/TamTam, accessed October 10, 2008.

5. Audacity. http://audacity.sourceforge.net/, accessed October 10, 2008.

6. UNESCO, Bruno Bossis. http://portal.unesco.org/culture/en/ev.php-URL_ID=27220&URL_DO=DO_TOPIC&URL_SECTION=201.html, accessed September 29, 2008.

7. UNESCO, Digi-Arts. http://portal.unesco.org/culture/en/ev.php-URL_ID=1391&URL_DO=DO_TOPIC&URL_SECTION=201.html, accessed October 1, 2008.

8. Ibid.

9. Morton Subotnick, Creating Music. http://www.creatingmusic.com/, accessed October 1, 2008.

10. NOTAM, Portable Pure Tuning. http://www.notam02.no/renstemming/index-e.html, accessed September 15, 2008.

11. Sonic Arts Network, Sonic Postcards. http://sonicpostcards.org/, accessed October 15, 2008.

12. See, for example, Smartmusic. http://www.smartmusic.com/; Exploding Art Music Productions, Exploding Art. http://www.explodingart.com/jam2jam.html; Empire Interactive Limited, E-jay. http://www.ejay.com/News.aspx?newsid=21, all accessed October 15, 2008.

13. NOTAM, DSP. http://www.notam02.no/DSP, accessed September 1, 2008.

14. NOTAM, DSP02. http://www.notam02.no/DSP02, accessed September 1, 2008.

15. SoftSynth. http://www.softsynth.com/jsyn/, accessed September 1, 2008.

16. Drivhuset, Musikkverksted (Music Workshop). http://www.musikkverksted.no/, accessed September 1, 2008.

17. See Drivhuset, Blender under *verktøy*. http://www.musikkverksted.no/musikk/, accessed September 1, 2008.

18. Museu de Arte Contemporânea de Niterói. http://www.macniteroi.com.br/index.php?op=noticias&notice_id=08, accessed September 1, 2008.

19. Tony Larsson, Art Lighthouse. http://www.oslofjorden.org/skole/kunstfyret.shtml, accessed September 1, 2008.

20. Drivhuset, Music Workshop. http://www.drivhuset.musikkverksted.no/lydokuH07/index.html, accessed September 1, 2008.

21. Drivhuset, Sound Treasure Hunt. http://drivhuset.musikkverksted.no/lydskattejakten/, accessed September 1, 2008.

22. St. Olav Festival. http://www.olavsfestdagene.no/, accessed September 1, 2008.

23. ULTIMA. http://www.ultima.no/, accessed September 1, 2008.

24. HT08 AS, Hauge Tveit. http://www.ht08.no/Default2.aspx?pageid=748, accessed September 1, 2008.

BIBLIOGRAPHY

Anderson, C. 2006. *The Long Tail*. New York: Hyperion Books.

Arnseth, H. C., and S. Ludvigsen 2006. Approaching institutional contexts: Systemic versus dialogic research in CSCL. *International Journal of Computer-Supported Collaborative Learning* 1(2): 167–185.

Barrett, N. 2007. Trends in electroacoustic music. In *The Cambridge Companion to Electronic Music*, ed. N. Collins and J. d'Escrivan. Cambridge: Cambridge University Press, pp. 232–253.

Barthes, R. 1991. *Responsibility of Forms*. Berkeley: University of California Press.

Bregman, A. S. 1990. *Auditory Scene Analysis*. Cambridge: MIT Press.

Brown, A. R. 2007. *Computers in Music Education*. New York: Routledge.

Cole, M., and J. V. Wertsch 1996. Beyond the individual-social antimony in discussions of Piaget and Vygotsky. *Human Development* 39(5): 250–256.

d'Escrivan, J. 2007. Electronic music. In *The Cambridge Companion to Electronic Music*, ed. N. Collins and J. d'Escrivan. Cambridge: Cambridge University Press, pp. 156–170.

Dewey, J. 1934. *Art as Experience*. New York: Perigree.

Emmerson, S. 1986. The relation of language to materials. In *The Language of Electroacoustic Music*, ed. S. Emmerson. New York: Harwood, pp. 17–39.

Erstad, O. 1999. *Teknologibaserte læringsmiljø og mediepedagogiske utfordringer* [Technology-Based Learning Environments and Media Education Challenges]. Oslo: University of Oslo, ITU.

Gadsden, V. L. 2008. The arts and education: Knowledge generation, pedagogy, and the discourse of learning. In *Review of Research in Education*, Vol. 32, ed. G. Kelly, A. Luke, and J. Green. Washington, DC: American Education Research Association, pp. 29–61.

Gardner, H. 1984. *Frames of Mind: The Theory of Multiple Intelligences*. London: Heinemann.

Gee, J. P. 1990. *Social Linguistics and Literacies. Ideology in Discourses*. London: Routledge.

Group, T. N. L. 1996. A pedagogy of multiliteracies: Designing social futures. *Harvard Educational Review* 66(1): 60–92.

Housen, A. 2001–2002. Aesthetic thought, critical thinking and transfer. *Arts and Learning Research Journal* 18(1): 99–131.

IRCAM. 2000. 10 Jeux d'écoute. DVD, CD-ROM. Paris: IRCAM, Editions Hyptique.

Kirschner, P. A., J. Sweller, and R. E. Clarke 2006. Why minimal guidance during instruction does not work: An analysis of the failure of constructivist, problem-based, experiential, and inquiry-based teaching. *Educational Psychologist* 41(2): 75–86.

Krange, I. and S. A. Ludvigsen 2008. What does it mean? Students' procedural and conceptual problem solving in a CSCL environment designed within the field of science education. *Journal of Computer Assisted Learning* 3: 25–52.

Landy, L. 1994. The "something to hold onto factor" in timbral composition. *Contemporary Music Review* 10(2): 49–60.

Landy, L. 2007. *Understanding the Art of Sound Organization*. Cambridge: MIT Press.

Lund, A., P. Pierroux, I. Rasmussen, and O. Smørdal. 2007. Emerging issues in wiki research: Knowledge advancement and design. *Proceedings of the CSCL 2007 Conference*, New Brunswick, NJ, July 16–21.

Pickering, A. *The Mangle of Practice: Time, Agency, and Space*. Chicago: Chicago University Press.

Pierroux, P. 2003. Communicating art in museums. *Journal of Museum Education* 28(1): 3–7.

Pierroux, P. Forthcoming. Guiding meaning on guided tours. Narratives of art and learning in museums. In *Inside Multimodal Composition*, ed. A. Morrison. Cresskill, NJ: Hampton Press.

Pierroux, P., I. Rasmussen, A. Lund, O. Smørdal, G. Stahl, J. A. Larusson, and R. Alterman. 2008. Supporting and Tracking Collective Cognition in Wikis. *Proceedings of the ICLS 2008 Conference*, Utrecht, June 24–28.

Rasmussen, I., I. Krange, and S. Ludvigsen. 2003. The process of understanding the task: How is agency distributed between students, teachers, and representations in technology-rich learning environments? *International Journal of Educational Research* 39: 839–849.

Regelski, T. 2004. *Teaching General Music in Grades 4–8. A Musicianship Approach.* Oxford: Oxford University Press.

Roads, C. 2001. *Microsound.* Cambridge: MIT Press.

Roth, W.-M. 2006. Literacies, from a dialectical perspective. *Mind, Culture and Activity* 13 (4): 279–282.

Rudi, J. 1997. "DSP—for children." *Proceedings of the International Computer Music Conference (ICMC)*, Thessaloniki, Greece, September 25–30.

Rudi, J. 2005. "From a musical point of view, the world is musical at any given moment": An interview with Bill Fontana. *Organised Sound* 10(2): 97–102.

Rudi, J. 2007. Computer music composition for children. *Signal Processing Magazine, IEEE* 24(2): 140–143.

Schaeffer, P. 1966. *Traité des objets musicaux.* Paris: Seuil.

Schafer, R. M. 1977. *The Tuning of the World.* Toronto: McClelland and Stewart.

Schellenberg, G. E. 2004. Music lessons enhance IQ. *American Psychological Society* 15(8): 511–514.

Shusterman, R. 2000. *Pragmatist Aesthetics.* Lanham, MD: Rowman and Littlefield.

Smalley, D. 1986. Spectro-morphology and structuring processes. In *The Language of Electroacoustic Music*, ed. S. Emmerson. New York: Harwood, pp. 61–93.

Smith, H., and Dean, R. T. 2002. The egg the cart the horse the chicken: Cyberwriting, sound, intermedia [Electronic Version]. *Interactive Multimedia Electronic Journal of Computer-Enhanced Learning*, 4. http://imej.wfu.edu/articles/2002/1/01/index.asp, accessed April 26, 2008.

Tyner, K. 1998. *Literacy in a Digital World.* Mahwah, NJ: Erlbaum.

van Joolingen, W. R., T. de Jong, and A. Dimitrakopoulou. 2007. Issues in computer supported inquiry learning in science. *Journal of Computer Assisted Learning* 23: 111–119.

Vygotsky, L. S. 1978. *Mind in Society. The Development of Higher Psychological Processes.* Cambridge: Harvard University Press.

Vygotsky, L. S. 1986. *Thought and Language.* Cambridge: MIT Press.

Wegerif, R. 2001. Applying a dialogical model of reason in the classroom. In *Rethinking Collaborative Learning*, ed. R. Faulkner, D. Miell, and K. Littleton. London: Free Association Press, pp. 119–139.

Wells, G. 1999. *Dialogic Inquiry. Toward a Sociocultural Practice and Theory of Education.* Cambridge: Cambridge University Press.

A CHRONOLOGY OF COMPUTER MUSIC AND RELATED EVENTS

PAUL DOORNBUSCH

PRE-1980 events are included with less detail as the focus for this volume is on later events. In addition, this concentrates on computer music and includes only those details of analog electronic music as are important for computer music or to set a context. Please see the references for a more detailed treatment of earlier events and of analog electronic music.[1]

Acknowledgments: Many colleagues and friends have assisted in this chronology; they include Clarence Barlow, Natasha Barrett, Richard Barrett, Paul Berg, Phil Burke, Max Burnet, Warren Burt, Nicolas Collins, Perry Cook, Nick Didkovsky, Richard Dudas, Tom Erbe, Ricardo Dal Farra, Kelly Fitz, Adrian Freed, Christian Haines, Paul Lansky, alcides lanza, Mats Lindström, Cort Lippe, Jean Piché, Larry Polansky, Miller Puckette, Curtis Roads. Jo Scherpenisse, Andrew Sorensen, Ken Steiglitz, Kees Tazelaar, Peter Thorne, Matt Wright, David Zicarelli, and the editor of this publication, Roger Dean—my gratitude and many thanks to everyone for helping to make this as complete and accurate as possible.

Computer Music Chronology, 1939–2009

Year	Selected significant musical events	Main technological events	Computer music events
1939	John Cage performs *Imaginary Landscape No. 1*, the first performance to include live electronics.[2]		
1943		High-quality, stereo, magnetic tape recorder.[3]	
1944			Grainger-Cross Free Music Machine (graphical, optical control of synthesis) developed by Percy Grainger and Burnett Cross.
1945		German, high-quality, tape recorder technology spreads to the rest of Europe and the United States.	
1947		Bell Labs develops the solid-state transistor.	Hugh Le Caine begins developing the Electronic Sackbut electronic instrument.
1948	Pierre Schaeffer creates *Étude aux chemins de fer*, the first piece of musique concrète.[4]	Manchester Mark 1 (Baby)—first stored-program computer. Harry Chamberlin builds tape-playback instrument, a precursor of the modern sampler.	Music for Magnetic Tape project created by Louis and Bebe Baron in New York. Norman McLaren painstakingly draws optical waveforms on film soundtracks.
1951	John Cage starts working on *Williams Mix* (for multichannel tape). Pierre Schaeffer and Pierre Henry compose *Symphonie pour un homme seul* (for spatialized playback of multiple analog disks).		CSIRAC (0.0005 MIPS[5]) plays in real-time some standard, popular, tunes of the day—the first computer to play music.[6] Ferranti Mark I computer plays music (popular melodies) and is recorded by the BBC—the oldest surviving recording of a computer playing music. Groupe de Recherches de Musique Concrète (GRMC) founded at the RTF, Paris.

Year	Selected significant musical events	Main technological events	Computer music events
			Jikken Kobo (Experimental Workshop) founded in Tokyo by Joji Yuasa, Toru Takemitsu, and other composers and artists.
			WDR (Westdeutscher Rundfunk—West German Radio) studio founded in Köln, Germany.
1953	Karlheinz Stockhausen composes *Studie I.*	IBM 701 shipped (its first large computer based on vacuum tubes) and its first magnetic tape device. Les Paul commissions Ampex to build an eight-track tape recorder.	GRM organizes a festival of mostly electronic music, named the First International Ten Days of Experimental Music, at UNESCO, Paris.
1954	Mauricio Kagel uses sounds and tape as part of his sonorization for an industrial exhibition in Mendoza. Karlheinz Stockhausen composes *Studie II.*	IBM 704 introduced with the first IBM operating system. IBM completes the specification for the first high-level computer language, FORTRAN (FORmula TRANslation).	NHK studio established in Tokyo, Japan.
1955	Toshiro Mayuzumi composes *Music for Sine Waves by Proportion of Prime Numbers, Music for Modulated Waves by Proportion of Prime Numbers,* and *Invention for Square Waves and Sawtooth Waves* (all for tape). Edgar Varèse's *Déserts* (for wind, percussion, and tape) is premiered. Iannis Xenakis premieres *Metastasis* (for orchestra). Iannis Xenakis publishes *The Crisis of Serial Music,*	Ampex releases the first commercial eight-track tape recorder. Hugh Le Caine builds the Special Purpose Tape Recorder, a multitape playback instrument, a precursor of the sampler; it had six tapes, later expanded to ten.	Columbia University Electronic Music Center established by Otto Luening and Vladimir Ussachevsky. Lejaren Hiller and Leonard Isaacson start work on the *Illiac Suite*—first computer composition experiments. NKH Electronic Studio is founded in Tokyo by Toshio Myuzumi. Studio di Fonologia Musicale of the RAI in Milan is founded by Luciano Berio and Bruno Maderna.

(*continued*)

Year	Selected significant musical events	Main technological events	Computer music events
	criticizing serial composition.		
1956	Louis and Bebe Baron produce *Forbidden Planet* (tape, for film). Karlheinz Stockhausen completes *Gesang der Jünglinge* (for five-track tape, later reduced to four tracks).	Ampex releases the first commercial videocassette recorder. IBM 704 mainframe released (0.0064 MIPS).	The Centre for Electronic Music is established at the Philips Research Laboratories.
1957	Kid Baltan composes *Song of the Second Moon* (for tape). G. M. Koenig composes *Essay* (for tape). Karlheinz Stockhausen premieres *Gruppen* (for three orchestras). Iannis Xenakis premieres *Pithoprakta* (for orchestra)	IBM introduces the first compiler for FORTRAN.	Columbia University receives the RCA Mark II Synthesizer (with digital control of analog synthesis). Max Mathews writes MUSIC I—first computer sound synthesis program. Lejaren Hiller and Leonard Isaacson complete the *Illiac Suite.* Taller Experimental de Sonido (Experimental Sound Workshop) established at the Catholic University in Santiago, Chile.
1958	José Vicente Asuar composes *Variaciones Espectrales* (for tape). Luciano Berio composes *Thema—omaggio a Joyce* (for tape) and *Sequenza I* (for flute). Film *Forbidden Planet* is released with an all-electronic soundtrack. Philips Pavilion opens in Brussels with Edgar Varèse's *Poème électronique* (for tape) and Iannis Xenakis's *Concrète P.H.* (for tape).	Digital Equipment Corporation (DEC) founded. First integrated circuits developed at Texas Instruments. LISP language developed.	BBC Radiophonic Workshop founded by Daphne Oram and Desmond Briscoe. Mostly famous for the electronic sounds in television shows such as *Doctor Who.* Cooperative Studio for Electronic Music is privately established at Ann Arbor, Michigan, by Robert Ashley and Gordon Mumma. Columbia-Princeton Electronic Music Center founded.

Year	Selected significant musical events	Main technological events	Computer music events
	Toru Takemitsu composes *Dialogue* (for tape). Vladimir Ussachevsky composes *Linear Contrasts* (for tape).		Estudio de Fonología Musical of the University of Buenos Aires founded. Studio Für Elektronische Musik founded in Munich by Siemens AG. University of Illinois Electronic Music Studio founded. José Vicente Asuar founds the Electronic Music Studio in Chile.
1960	Luciano Berio completes *Visage* (for tape) and *Momenti* (for four-track tape). John Cage completes *Cartridge Music* (for amplified small sounds). Luigi Nono composes *Omaggio a Emilio Vedova* (for four-track tape). Karlheinz Stockhausen completes *Kontakte* (two versions; for electronic sounds and sound projection and for electronic sounds, piano, and percussion). Vladimir Ussachevsky composes *Wireless Fantasy* (for tape).	AT&T announces its Dataphone, the first commercial modem. IBM 7090 ships (fully transistorized mainframe).	Studio voor elektronische muziek (STEM) is founded in Utrecht University with the gift of the Philips studio. Raymond Scott developes the Electronium analog composition machine. University of Toronto Electronic Studios opened.
1961	Merce Cunningham premieres *Aeon* (ballet) with music by John Cage. György Ligeti's *Atmosphères* is premiered (for orchestra). Max Mathews composes *The Second Law* (for computer synthesized tape), a study using pitched and unpitched noises for the first time.	The first industrial robot, UNIMATE, began work at General Motors.	Israel Center for Electronic Music opens at the Hebrew University, founded by Joseph Tal. Max Mathews uses physical modeling synthesis in MUSIC to create *Daisy Bell* (a.k.a. *Bicycle Built for Two*) vocal synthesis on an IBM 704. Robert Moog and Herbert Deutsch develop an analog

(continued)

Year	Selected significant musical events	Main technological events	Computer music events
	James Tenney composes *Analog #1: Noise Study* using computer synthesized noise. Horacio Vaggione composes *Ensayo sobre mezcla de sonidos, Cemeronia*, and *Cantata I* (for tape).		synthesizer. James Tenney, a recognized composer, joins Bell Labs to work with Max Mathews.
1962	G. M. Koenig composes *Terminus 1* (for tape). Luigi Nono composes *Djamila Boupachá* (for soloists and orchestra). Iannis Xenakis completes the *ST* series of works (for string quartet, ensemble, and orchestra) using his stochastic composition computer program. Iannis Xenakis completes *Bohor* (for eight-track tape).	Students at MIT develop the first interactive computer game, SpaceWar.	James Tenney writes the PF2 program, used to write his *Four Stochastic Studies*. Iannis Xenakis completes a program for stochastic music composition on an IBM 7090.
1963	Pierre Henry composes *Variations pour Une Porte et Un Soupir.* Toru Takemitsu composes *Arc* (for piano, orchestra, and electronic sounds).	Compact Cassette (analog tape format) introduced by Philips.	
1964	Milton Babbitt completes *Philomel* (for soprano and tape). Luigi Nono composes *La fabbrica illuminata* (for voice and tape). Giacinto Scelsi composes *String Quartet No. 4* (for string quartet and electronics). La Monte Young completes *A Well Tuned Piano* (for just-intuned solo piano). Karlheinz Stockhausen composes *Mikrophonie I* (for instruments and live electronics).	ASCII standard introduced. BASIC computer language is developed at Dartmouth College. First computer mouse is prototyped after being invented the previous year by Douglas Engelbart. IBM introduces the System/360.	G. M. Koenig takes over STEM in Utrecht (with Frank de Vries), giving it a new direction, and writes *Project 1*, for aleatoric serial composition. Laboratory of the Centro Latinoamericano de Altos Estudios Musicales (CLAEM) of the Di Tella Institute, Argentina, is founded by Alberto Ginastera. McGill University Electronic Music Studio (EMS) founded in Montreal by István Anhalt. Stockholm Elektron Musik Studion (EMS) is founded.

Year	Selected significant musical events	Main technological events	Computer music events
			Robert Moog and Don Buchla separately release modular analog synthesizers.
1965	Mario Davidovsky composes *Electronic Study No. 3, In Memoriam Edgar Varèse* (for tape). Steve Reich composes *It's Gonna Rain* (for tape). Karlheinz Stockhausen composes *Solo* (for melody instrument and feedback loop).	DEC PDP-8 released. Dolby A noise reduction system introduced. Hi-Fi equipment commercially released.	
1966	Dave Behrman completes *Wave Train* (piano resonance with feedback). Luciano Berio completes *Sequenza III* (for female voice). Herbert Brün composes *Non Sequitier VI* (for tape). Luigi Nono completes *A floresta é jovem e cheja de vida* (for soprano, three recitants, clarinet, copper plates, and eight-track tape). Karlheinz Stockhausen completes *Hymnen* (for four-track tape). Iannis Xenakis completes *Terretektorh* (for large orchestra spread out in space).	E-mail applications arrive for users on closed, proprietary, networks.	Center for Electronic and Computer Music (CECM) established in Paris and at Indiana University, by Iannis Xenakis. Electronic Music Studio founded at Victoria University in Wellington. Estudio de Fonología Musical of Instituto Nacional de Cultura y Bellas Artes (INCIBA) founded in Venezuela. G. M. Koenig writes *Project 2*, allowing greater control over the composition process.
1967	Iannis Xenakis completes *Polytope de Montréal* (for four small orchestras and show for Expo 67).	Hugh Le Caine builds the Serial Sound Structure Generator, a complex analog sequencer for serial music.	Electronic Music Studio founded at the Royal College of Music, London, by Tristram Cary. STEM at Utrecht University changes its name to the Institute of Sonology. STEIM is formed in Amsterdam.

(continued)

Year	Selected significant musical events	Main technological events	Computer music events
1968	Robert Ashley completes *Purposeful Lady Slow Afternoon* (for tape). John Cage and Lejaren Hiller compose *HPSCHD* (for up to seven harpsichords and up to fifty-one tapes). Wendy Carlos releases *Switched on Bach* (record). Luigi Nono composes *Contrappunto dialettico alla mente* (for tape). Karlheinz Stockhausen completes *Stimmung* (for six amplified vocalists).		*Leonardo Journal of the Arts, Science, and Technology* first published. MUSIC V released and written in FORTRAN so it is ported to many computers. Jean-Claude Risset at Bell Labs creates a catalog of sound synthesis with MUSIC V instruments. Lejaren Hiller joins the Computer Music Studios in the University at Buffalo (State University of New York).
1969	Luciano Berio composes *Sinfonia* (for eight amplified voices and orchestra). Toshi Ichiyanagi composes *Tokyo 1.9.6.9* (for tape). G. M. Koenig composes *Funktion Blau, Funktion Indigo, Funktion Violett, Funktion Grau* (for tape). Bruno Maderna composes *Quadrivium* (for percussion quartet and orchestra). Iannis Xenakis composes *Kraanerg* (dance work for orchestra and four track tape).	First ARPANET (Advanced Research Projects Agency Network) links between the University of California at Los Angeles, University of California at Santa Barbara, and the University of Utah and also including the (private) Stanford Research Institute. First of the DEC PDP-15 family released. Digital tape-recording experiments begin. RS232 serial communication standard developed. UNIX developed.	CEMS (Coordinated Electronic Music Studio) system installed in the Electronic Music Studio at the State University of New York at Albany. Electronic Music Studio established at the University of Adelaide, Australia. Max Mathews builds the GROOVE synthesizer, the first digital control of analog synthesis. Peter Zinovieff uses a PDP-8 to control analog synthesis in MUSYS III.
1970	César Bolaños composes *Sialoecibi* (for piano and one reciter-mime-actor), and *Canción sin palabras* (for piano with two performers and tape). Mario Davidovsky composes *Synchronisms No. 6* (for piano and tape) and is awarded the Pulitzer Prize for it in 1971.	ARPANET expands with more connected locations. First of the DEC PDP-11 family released. The first version of the UNIX operating system runs on a DEC PDP-7. Lexicon releases the first digital delay unit.	Institut de Recherche et Coordination Acoustique/ Musique (IRCAM) is founded and planning started. Electronic Music Lab established at Mexico's National Conservatory of Music. Princeton "Underground Laboratory" Electronic

Year	Selected significant musical events	Main technological events	Computer music events
	Charles Dodge completes *Earth's Magnetic Field* (for tape), mapping data into musical parameters.		Music Studio established by Godfrey Winham and Ken Steiglitz.
	Kraftwerk emerges as the first fully electronic pop band.		
	Alvin Lucier completes *I Am Sitting in a Room* (for tape).		
	Iannis Xenakis completes *Hibiki-Hana -Ma* (for twelve-track tape).		
1971	Emmanuel Ghent completes *Phosphones* (for tape, on GROOVE).	C computer language is developed by Kernighan and Ritchie of Bell Laboratories.	Electronic Music Studio at the Academy of Music and Dance in Jerusalem founded by Tzvi Avni.
	Karlheinz Stockhausen completes *Mantra* (for two pianists, sine wave generators, ring modulators, and tape).	DEC PDP-11/ 45 released (0.76 MIPS).	SSP (sound synthesis program) implemented by Koenig for real-time digital instruction synthesis.
	Iannis Xenakis completes *Persèpolis* (for eight-track tape).	Denon demonstrates 18-bit PCM (pulse code modulation) digital stereo recording with a video recorder.	University of Natal, Durban, South Africa Electronic Music Studio opens.
		First microprocessor is developed, the Intel 4004.	Barry Vercoe ports MUSIC 360 (a derivative of MUSIC IV) to the PDP-11 and improves it, creating MUSIC 11.
1972	Charles Dodge completes *Speech Songs* (for computer synthesized tape).	ARPANET widely introduced.	Barry Truax develops POD4 and POD5 (fixed-waveform synthesis) for the PDP-15 at the Institute of Sonology.
	György Ligeti composes *Double Concerto* (for flute, oboe, and orchestra).	First e-mail is sent and an open e-mail application demonstrated.	Centre d'Etudes de Mathematiques et Automatiques Musicales (CEMAMu), is founded near Paris by Iannis Xenakis.
	Iannis Xenakis completes *Polytope de Cluny* (for eight-track tape with a computer-controll ed light show), and it opens in Paris.	IBM introduces the 8-inch floppy disk. Intel 8008 introduced, first commercial 8-bit microprocessor.	Centro de Investigaciones en Communication Massiva, Artes y Technologia (CICMAT) established in Buenos Aires

(*continued*)

Year	Selected significant musical events	Main technological events	Computer music events
			from CLAEM studio.
			Herbert Brün starts work on the SAWDUST stochastic synthesis software.
1973	David Tudor creates *Rainforest IV* (for spatially mixed live sounds of suspended sculptures and found objects).	Ethernet developed at Xerox Palo Alto Research Center (PARC). First ARPANET connection to Europe. Part of UNIX is rewritten in the C language.	Estudio de Fonología Musical of Instituto Nacional de Cultura y Bellas Artes (INCIBA) re-established in Venezuela. Gmebaphone (tape music spatialization system) created at GMEB, Bourges, France. W. Kaegi and Stan Templaars develop VOSIM synthesis at Sonology. Barry Truax develops POD6 for real-time digital FM synthesis. MIT Electronic Music Studios (EMS) established, to become part of MIT Media Lab in 1985. STEIM focuses on electronic music performance with the arrival of Michel Waisvisz.
1974	Pauline Oliveros completes *Sonic Meditations* (for voices and other sounds). Giacinto Scelsi composes *Aitsi* (for electronically prepared piano). First International Computer Music Conference, Michigan, USA.	X.25 networking common in U.K. universities. TCP (network protocol) proposed as common network transport, first use of the word "Internet." Xerox PARC designs a computer with a mouse. Mellotron is built, first commercial instrument "sampler" with a keyboard playing loops of analog tape.	Acousmonium (tape music spatialization system) created at GRM, Paris. Ambisonics (spatial audio reproduction) developed by Michael Gerzon, Peter Fellgett, and Duanne Cooper. Electronic Music Studio at the Rubin Academy of Music at Tel-Aviv University established by Yizhak Sadai.

Year	Selected significant musical events	Main technological events	Computer music events
			Yamaha licenses frequency modulation synthesis from John Chowning.
			Curtis Roads implements granular synthesis with MUSIC V.
1975	Milton Babbit completes *Phonemena* (version for soprano and tape). Luciano Berio completes *Chants parallèle* (for tape).	Altair 8800 microcomputer released, first mass-produced microcomputer and computer kit. EMT releases the first digital reverb unit. Homebrew Computer Club formed in San Francisco. Micro-Soft (later Microsoft) founded. MOS Technology (later Commodore) KIM-1 microcomputer released. (0.2 MIPS)	Center for Computer Research in Music and Acoustics (CCRMA) founded at Stanford University. Electronic Music and Video Studios established at La Trobe University, Melbourne, Australia. Princeton "Underground Laboratory" becomes the Winham Sound Laboratory. Synclavier prototype of working all-digital synthesizer.
1976	Luciano Berio composes *Coro* (for forty voices and orchestra). Herbert Brün composes *Dust* (for computer-generated tape). Brian Ferneyhough completes *Time and Motion Study II* (for amplified cello, tape delay system, and modulators). Philip Glass premieres *Einstein at the Beach* (an opera for ensemble, chorus, and soloists). Steve Reich composes *Music for 18 Musicians* (for ensemble and four female voices). Barry Vercoe composes *Synapse* (for viola and computer). Iannis Xenakis composes	Apple Computer Company founded. Digital Equipment Corporation introduces the DEC VAX 11/780, a popular minicomputer.	Dave Behrman uses a KIM-1 in performance of *On the Other Ocean* at Mills College. Paul Berg develops the PILE synthesis language for real-time instruction synthesis on a PDP-15 at the Institute of Sonology. Fairlight CMI prototype, Quasar M8, working. Giuseppe Di Giugno develops the 4A synthesizer at IRCAM. Jim Horton uses a KIM-1 in performance at the Exploratorium in San Francisco. Laurie Spiegel creates the VAMPIRE system for real-time video and sound.

(continued)

Year	Selected significant musical events	Main technological events	Computer music events
	Psappha (for solo percussion).		
1977	Luc Ferrari completes *Presque Rien N°2* (for tape).	Apple II released (0.23 MIPS).	The *Computer Music Journal* is first published in Menlo Park, California.
	György Ligeti composes *Le Grand Macabre* (opera).	BSD UNIX released.	Digital control of analog studio at the Institute of Sonology.
	Gareth Loy composes *Nekyia* (for four-track tape, rendered on the Samson Box).	Commodore PET microcomputer released.	IRCAM is opened.
	Alvin Lucier completes *Music on a Long Thin Wire* (for amplified wire and electromagnetic excitor).	Tandy announces the TRS-80 microcomputer.	George Lewis plays with an improvising KIM-1 at Mills College.
	Trevor Wishart completes *Red Bird* (for tape).		Peter Samson completes the Systems Concepts (Samson Box) digital synthesizer, a MUSIC IV implementation in hardware.
	David Wessel composes *Anthony* (for tape).		Iannis Xenakis develops functioning UPIC at CEMAMu.
	Iannis Xenakis completes *La Legende d'Eer* (for seven-track tape).		
1978	Paul Lansky composes *Six Fantasies on a Poem by Thomas Campion* (for computer-synthesized tape).	Atari 800 microcomputer released.	William Buxton has the SSSP software on a PDP-11 controlling sixteen digital oscillators.
	Luigi Nono composes *Con Luigi Dallapiccola* (for percussion and electronics).	5.25-inch floppy disks become an industry standard.	Di Giugno completes the 4C synthesizer.
	Iannis Xenakis completes *Mycenae-Alpha* (for tape) on the UPIC and opens *Le Diatope* in Paris.	Stereo PCM audio adaptors for VCR tape recorders introduced.	League of Automatic Music Composers formed.
		TCP splits into TCP/IP, and allows for the creation of UDP (User Datagram Protocol), a network protocol designed low delay and useful for streamed data.	Synclavier enters production.
1979	Robert Ashley completes *Automatic Writing* (for tape).	CompuServe offers electronic mail to personal computer users.	The International Computer Music Association is founded by Thom Blum, Curtis Roads, and John Strawn. Fairlight CMI I released.
	Iannis Xenakis completes *Pleides* (for six percusionists).	Motorola 68000 microprocessor introduced.	

Year	Selected significant musical events	Main technological events	Computer music events
			F. Richard Moore founds the Computer Audio Research Lab at the University of California at San Diego, and also develops the software CMUSIC.
1980	Clarence Barlow completes *Çogluotobüsisletmesi* (versions for piano and computer rendition). John Cage composes *Roaratorio* (for electronic tapes, speaker, and Irish folk musicians). Charles Dodge composes *Any Resemblance Is Purely Coincidental* (for piano and tape). Trevor Wishart completes *Anticredos* (for six amplified voices and percussion).	EMT releases the first commercial digital hard-disk audio recorder. Multitrack digital tape recorders introduced. Sinclair ZX80 microcomputer released. TCP/IP accepted as superior network protocol for the Internet. Technics 1200 turntable released and becomes the standard DJ turntable.	FOF formant synthesis developed at IRCAM. The *Computer Music Journal* moves to the MIT Press, legitimizing computer music research.
1981	Larry Austin composes *Canadian Coastlines: Canonic Fractals for Musicians and Computer Band* (for instruments and tape). Pierre Boulez premieres *Répons* (for ensemble and live electronics). Herbert Brün composes *i toLD You so!* (for computer-generated tape). Nicolas Collins composes *Second State* (for microcomputer-controlled feedback). David Rosenboom completes *Departure* (for SATB voices). MTV starts on commercial television.	IBM PC introduced. First optical storage disk system introduced by Philips. 3.5-inch floppy disks released by Sony.	Electronic Music Studio founded at Seoul National University. Estúdio da Glória established in Rio de Janeiro, Brazil. Giuseppe Di Giugno completes the 4X synthesizer. Yamaha GS1 and GS2 digital synthesizers released.
1982	Nicolas Collins composes *Is She/He Really Going Out*	Acorn BBC Micro computer released.	Birmingham ElectroAcoustic Sound

(*continued*)

Year	Selected significant musical events	Main technological events	Computer music events
	With Him/Her/Them (for circuits, radios, prepared tapes, and computer-controlled mixer). G. M. Koenig composes *3 ASKO Pieces* (for small orchestra). Luigi Nono composes *Donde estas hermano?* (for two sopranos, mezzo-soprano, and contralto) and *Quando stanno morendo* (for female voices, cello, bass flute, and live electronics). Dennis Smalley composes *Vortex* (for tape).	Commodore 64 computer released. First CD released. Sony releases the PCM-F1, a consumer adaptor for VCRs for high-quality (CD-quality) stereo digital recording.	Theatre (BEAST, tape music spatialization system) is created. Emu-Emulator commercial sampler synthesizer released. HMSL (Hierarchical Music Specification Language) music programming language released (for an S-100 computer controlling a Buchla synthesizer). Laboratorio de Investigación y Producción Musical (LIPM) established in Buenos Aires from the CICMAT studio.
1983	Jean-Baptiste Barrière composes *Chréode* (for computer-generated tape). François Bayle composes *Le Sommeil d'Euclide* (for tape). Luigi Nono composes *Omaggio a György Kurtág* (for contralto, flute, clarinet, tuba, and live electronics) and *Guai ai gelidi mostri* (for two voices, ensemble, and live electronics). Roger Reynolds completes *Archipelago* (for large ensemble and eight-channel computer-generated tape). Jean-Claude Risset composes *L'autre Face* (for soprano and tape). Karlheinz Stockhausen completes *Samstag Aus Licht* (opera). Tamas Ungvary composes *Gypsy Children's Giant Dance with Ili Fourier* (for	ARPANET converts to TCP/IP protocol—the modern Internet backbone is created. ARPANET splits into MILNET (for military communications) and ARPANET (for civilian applications). Fiber-optic cable is used for long-distance audio transmission. First CD players released worldwide. IBM PC/XT released (0.25 MIPS).	MIDI 1.0 specification released. First MIDI synthesizers appear. Yamaha releases DX7 FM synthesizer—first mass-market all-digital synthesizer, with MIDI.

Year	Selected significant musical events	Main technological events	Computer music events
	ensemble and computer sounds).		
1984	Luciano Berio composes *Sequenza X* (for trumpet and piano resonance) and *Orpheo II* (opera for voice, orchestras, and tapes). Paul Lansky composes *Idle Chatter* (for computer-synthesized tape). Mesias Maiguashca composes *Fmelodies II* (for ensemble and tape). Luigi Nono composes *A Pierre* (for contrabass flute, contrabass clarinet, and electronics). Bernard Parmegiani composes *La Creation Du Monde* (for tape).	Apple Macintosh released (68000 processor, 0.5 MIPS). CD-ROM computer storage introduced. William Gibson's *Neuromancer* novel is published. TCP/IP starts spreading to Europe.	Roger Dannenberg and Barry Vercoe demonstrate automatic accompaniment at the ICMC. Paul Lansky develops Cmix. Platypus workstation plug-in DSP card completed. Steinberg releases Pro-16 multitrack MIDI sequencer. Yamaha releases the CX5M Music Computer (Z80 based), with built-in FM synthesis modules and composition software. Michel Waisvisz develops The Hands controller. MIDIForth MIDI composition software released. Waseda University (Tokyo) designs WABOT-2, a piano playing robot that reads scores.
1985	Lars-Gunnar Bodin composes *Anima* (for female voice and tape). Luigi Nono completes *Prometeo* (for multiple orchestras, two conductors, narrators, spatially placed groups of instrumental and vocal soloists, and live electronic sound distribution). Pauline Oliveros composes *Wanderer* (for accordion orchestra). Jean-Claude Risset composes *Sud* (for four-track tape). David Rosenboom completes *Zones of*	Atari 520ST released (0.5 MIPS). Commodore Amiga 1000 computer released (0.5 MIPS). Digital mixing consoles are released. Microsoft releases Windows 1.0.	Les Ateliers UPIC is founded near Paris by Iannis Xenakis to promote the research of CEMAMu, especially the UPIC System, and to teach professionals and amateurs alike to use the UPIC. Barry Vercoe creates Csound from the MUSIC 11 base at MIT. Kyma environment released for Platypus. Ensoniq Mirage sampler released. The Hub computer network ensemble formed. George Lewis starts work on Voyager for the

(*continued*)

Year	Selected significant musical events	Main technological events	Computer music events
	Influence (for percussion and electronics). Kaija Saariaho completes *Jardin Secret I* (for tape). Giacinto Scelsi composes *String Quartet No.5* from *Aitsi* (for string quartet and electronics). Denis Smalley composes *Clarinet Threads* (for amplified clarinet tape). Horacio Vaggione completes *Thema* (for amplified bass saxophone and computer-generated tape).		Macintosh. Laurie Spiegel develops Music Mouse. MIT Media Lab is founded. Electronic music labs established at the Escuela Superior de Música del Instituto Nacional de Bellas Artes (INBA) and at Centro Independiente de Investigacion y Multimedia (CIIM), Mexico.
1986	Richard Karpen composes *Eclipse* (for computer-created sound). G. M. Koenig composes *Beitrag* (for orchestra). Trevor Wishart completes *Vox 5* (for tape).	Dolby SR noise reduction system introduced. R-DAT (digital audio tape) specification released and machines released in Japan. First RISC (reduced instruction set computing) computers introduced by IBM and MIPS.	Akai S900 sampler released and becomes a mass-market sampling module. Music Box MIDI algorithmic composition software released. Nicolas Collins creates *Trombone Propelled Electronics*, trombone-based DSP controller. Composers Desktop Project (CDP) started with porting CMUSIC to an Atari ST. The Computer and Electronic Music Studio founded in Beijing by Yuanlin Chen. FURT electronic music duo forms. Institute of Sonology moves from Utrecht University to the Royal Conservatory of The Hague, Netherlands. Miller Puckette develops Patcher at IRCAM to control the 4X. Music Kit music and DSP programming library

Year	Selected significant musical events	Main technological events	Computer music events
			released by NeXT Computer.
			Soviet Computer Music Centre established in Moscow.
			David Zicarelli develops M.
1987	John Adams premieres *Nixon in China* (opera).	Intel 80386 computers released (2 MIPS).	C-Lab Creator MIDI sequencer released for Atari.
	Robert Ashley completes *el/Aficionado* (opera for solo voices, chorus, solo piano, and electronics).	Consumer DAT decks released. Motorola 68030 microprocessor released.	George Lewis completes Voyager software for interactive improvisation.
	Richard Karpen composes *Il Nome* (for soprano and computer-created sound).		HMSL music programming language becomes widely available on common computers.
	G. M. Koenig composes *String quartet 1987*.		Max Mathews develops the Radio Baton controller.
	Thierry Lancino completes *Aloni* (for contralto, boys choir, ensemble, and electronics).		
	Luigi Nono composes *Post-prae-ludium no.1 'per Donau* (for tuba and live electronics).		
	David Rosenboom completes *Systems of Judgement* (for computer music systems and various instruments).		
	Denis Smalley composes *Wind Chimes* (for tape).		
	Alejandro Viñao composes *Toccata del Maga* (for ensemble, samples, and real-time electronics).		
1988	John Cage composes *Europera* (opera; for singers, orchestra, and tape).	ARPANET and 10% of its computers are partly disabled by the first worm "virus," which flooded the network and computers.	Korg M1 released, first music workstation.
	Mario Davidovsky composes *Synchronisms No. 9* (for violin and tape).	NeXT workstation introduced.	SensorLab (sensor to MIDI interface) development starts at STEIM and occasional prototypes released.
	Kaija Saariaho composes		Wave Field Synthesis

(*continued*)

Year	Selected significant musical events	Main technological events	Computer music events
	Petals (for cello with live electronics) and *Stilleben* (for tape).		(spatial audio reproduction) theory developed at the University of Delft.
1989	Luigi Nono completes *La Lontananza Nostalgica Utopica Futura* (for solo violin, eight tapes, and ten music stands). Marco Stroppa composes *Traiettoria* (for piano and computer-generated tape).	Intel i486 computers released (8.7 MIPS). Digidesign Sound Accelerator DSP card for Apple Macintosh released.	Opcode Max released. Digidesign Turbosynth and Sound Tools (first DAW) released. Steinberg releases Cubase 1.0 graphical MIDI sequencer for Atari. C-Lab Notator MIDI notation and sequencer released. Zentrum für Kunst und Muzik (ZKM) is founded.
1990	Ricardo Dal Farra composes *Interacciones* (for real-time interactive computer-generat ed sounds and images). Paul Lansky composes *Night Traffic* (for computer-generat ed tape). Takayuki Rai composes *Sparkle* (for bass clarinet and tape).	Apple IIfx released (10 MIPS). Windows 3.0 released, first commercially successful version. Sony introduces the writeable CD. Dolby proposes five-channel surround sound for home cinema. MPEG-1 Audio Layer III (MP3) becomes a standard.	Don Buchla develops the Thunder controller. Cubase 1.0 sequencer released for Macintosh. IRCAM ISPW released with MaxFTS. Graphical Kyma software released for updated DSP hardware called Capybara. Flute-playing robot project started at Waseda University. Laboratory for Analysis and Synthesis of Image and Sound (OASIS) founded at the Universidade Federal de Minas Gerais (UFMG) in Brazil. Laboratorio Colombiano de Música Electrónica Jacqueline Nova, first founded in the Universidad Autónoma de Manizales, Columbia.
1991	Nicolas Collins creates *Broken Light* (for string quartet and modified CD players).	Alesis ADAT introduced, the first consumer digital multitrack recorder. Apple releases the	Buchla develops the Lightning controller. Gabinete de Electroacústica para la

Year	Selected significant musical events	Main technological events	Computer music events
	Karel Goeyvaerts composes *Aquarius* (for instrumental ensemble). Iannis Xenakis completes *GENDY3* (for tape, created solely with dynamic stochastic synthesis).	QuickTime multimedia format and the influential PowerBook series of laptop computers. First World Wide Web software released by CERN (Organisation Européenne pour la Recherche Nucléaire), HTTP protocol developed. Linux project started. Mac OS 7 released. Sony MiniDisk released.	Música de Arte (GEMA) founded at the University of Chile. Laetitia Sonami develops first Lady's Glove. *Leonardo Music Journal* first published by MIT Press. Iannis Xenakis completes GENDYN program for dynamic stochastic synthesis. Pro Tools 1 DAW released. Steinberg releases Cubase Audio DAW software. SoundHack DSP sound manipulation software released. Symbolic Composer (algorithmic composition software) introduced.
1992	Mario Davidovsky composes *Synchronisms No. 10* (for guitar and electronic sounds). alcides lanza composes *vôo* (for actress-singer, electroacoustic sounds, and DSP). Bob Ostertag composes *All the Rage* (for sting quartet and sounds, transcribed from riot recordings). Kaija Saariaho composes *Amers* (for ensemble and live electronics). Marco Stroppa composes *In cielo, in terra, in mare* (a radiophonic opera). Horacio Vaggione composes *Kitab* (for bass clarinet, piano, contrabass, and computer-process ed and controlled sounds).	First PowerPC processor (601) released. IBM releases their first ThinkPad laptop computer. C-Lab programmers form Emagic. Digital Compact Cassette (digital tape format) introduced by Philips and Matsushita. Windows 3.1 released.	AC Toolbox (algorithmic composition software) introduced. Laboratório de Música e Tecnologia (LaMuT) established in Rio de Janeiro, Brazil. Lemur DSP sound manipulation software released. SensorLab (sensor to MIDI interface) released by STEIM.

(continued)

Year	Selected significant musical events	Main technological events	Computer music events
1993	Karlheinz Essl composes *Entsagung* (for ensemble and live electronics). Cort Lippe composes *Music for Sextet and ISPW* (for flute, bass clarinet, trombone, violin, cello, piano, and computer). Daniel Teruggi composes *Sphaera* (for tape). Laptop Music and Noise Music practices emerge from the combination of available technology and application of the tools and aesthetic of computer music to more popular ends.	First graphical Web browser application released, Mosaic (later to become Netscape Navigator).	Emagic Notator Logic MIDI sequencer and DAW released for the Macintosh with Digidesign hardware. The Center for Electroacoustic Music of China founded in Beijing by Zhang Xiaofu. *Leonardo Electronic Almanac* journal first published by MIT Press. Norwegian Network for Technology, Acoustics, and Music (NOTAM) is founded. Sensorband forms. Yamaha releases VL1 and VP1 digital physical modeling synthesizers.
1994	Takayuki Rai composes *Kinetic Figuration* (for MIDI piano, synthesizer, and computer). Curtis Roads completes *Clang-Tint* (for fixed media). Kaija Saariaho composes *Six Japanese Gardens* (for percussion and electronics). David Tudor creates *Soundings: Ocean Diary* for Merce Cuningham (live electronic sounds for ballet). Trevor Wishart completes *Tongues of Fire* (for tape). Iannis Xenakis completes *S.709* (for tape, created solely with dynamic stochastic synthesis).	Apple switches to PowerPC processors. Netscape Navigator Web browser released. First modern Web search engine appears, WebCrawler. First WWW conference and WWW becoming common. DVD disks and players introduced. Sun Microsystems releases Java 1.0a computer language. Yamaha introduces the first consumer digital mixer.	Emagic releases Logic 4 with Audiowerk interface, making DAW software possible without additional DSP hardware. IRCAM introduces AudioSculpt DSP sound manipulation software. Princeton Sound Kitchen formed from the 1970s Winham Lab.
1995	Jean Piché composes *The Dangerous Kitchen* (for	ARPANET renamed as Internet.	Bar Ilan University Computer Music

Year	Selected significant musical events	Main technological events	Computer music events
	voice and interactive computer system). David Rosenboom completes *On Being Invisible II* (for soloist, brainwaves, and computer-assisted electronic music system).	Intel Pentium Pro computers released (400 MIPS). Internet becomes widely available. Mac OS 7.5 released. Nagra introduces a "solid-state" audio recorder. Windows 95 released.	Laboratory founded in Israel. Clavia Nord Lead synthesizer released, using physical modeling to digitally reproduce analog synthesis. Cynthia (a graphical interface to Csound) released. LiSa (live sampling) software released by STEIM. Synthesis Toolkit (STK) released.
1996	Ricardo Dal Farra composes *Tierra y Sol* (for tape). Mille Plateaux releases *In Memoriam Gilles Deleuze*.	First experimental recordings made with 24 bits and 96-kHz AD and DA converters.	Don Buchla develops Lightning II controller. Cecilia (a graphical companion to Csound, developed from Cynthia) released. Native Instruments' Generator version 0.96 (synthesis software) released. *Organised Sound Journal* is first published by Cambridge University Press. PatchWork (algorithmic composition software) introduced. Princeton Sound Lab is formed. Steinberg release VST plug-in software. SuperCollider released by James McCartney.
1997	Richard Barrett composes *Opening of the Mouth* (for two vocalists, instrumentalists, and electronics). G. M. Koenig composes	Apple Macintosh G3 released (600 MIPS). Mac OS 8 released. DVD-Audio standard developed.	Cloud Generator granular synthesis software released by John Alexander and Curtis Roads. Csound becomes real-time on PC hardware.

(continued)

Year	Selected significant musical events	Main technological events	Computer music events
	Per Flauti (for two flutes). Takayuki Rai composes *Impulse* (for percussion and computer). Kees Tazelaar completes *Depths of Field* (for eight-channel fixed media).		Image/ine (image processing and MIDI) software released by STEIM. Max/MSP released. Open Sound Control (OSC) released. Pure Data released. Steinberg release VST and ASIO as open standards.
1998	Cort Lippe composes *Music for Hi-Hat and Computer* (for Hi-Hat and live DSP). David Rosenboom completes *Bell Solaris* (for piano). Horacio Vaggione composes *Agon* (for multichannel tape).	Intel releases the Pentium II processor (800 MIPS). First portable MP3 players introduced. Windows 98 released.	Native Instruments/ Reaktor (synthesis software) released. OpenMusic (algorithmic composition software) introduced. Symbolic Sound releases the significantly expanded Capybara 320.
1999	alcides lanza composes *ontem* (for actress-singer, tablas, percussion electroacoustic sounds, and live DSP). Cort Lippe composes *Music for Cello and Computer*. Curtis Roads completes *Half-Life* (for fixed media). Alejandro Viñao composes *Epitafios* (for mixed choir and computer).	Apple Macintosh G4 released (825 MIPS). Mac OS 9 released. CD-R drives become standard part in PCs. DVD-Audio (high resolution digital audio) standard finalised. Super Audio CD (SACD) high resolution CD format introduced by Sony and Philips.	Cubase VST 2 released with VSTi interface for virtual software instruments and synthesizer plug-ins. Dr. Erol Üçer Center for Advanced Studies in Music (MIAM) established in Istanbul. Pro Tools LE released.
2000	Natasha Barrett composes *Utility of Space* (fixed media, versions for stereo playback and ambisonic playback). Nicolas Collins coordinates *Fiber Jelly* for networked computer ensemble, with Justin Bennett, Kaffe Mathews, Scanner, Anne Wellmer,	1-GHz Intel Pentium III computers released (1,800 MIPS). Windows ME released.	Haifa University Electronic Music Studio founded by Arie Shapira. Les Ateliers UPIC changes its name to CCMIX (Center for the Composition of Music Iannis Xenakis) under the directorship of Gerard Pape. Loris DSP sound

Year	Selected significant musical events	Main technological events	Computer music events
	Zeitblom. Brian Ferneyhough completes *The Doctrine of Similarity* (for voices and ensemble). Jean Piché composes *A Cervantes* (for saxophone and interactive computer system).		manipulation software released. Propellerhead Software's Reason 1.0 virtual synthesizer/sampler released.
2001	*Improvised Music from Japan* released, showing off the burgeoning Japanese electronic improvisation scene. Gerard Pape composes *The Ecstasy of St. Theresa* (for nine voices and live electronics). Jean Piché composes *eXpress* (for fixed-media, three-channel video, and stereo sound). Takayuki Rai composes *Lucent Aquarelle* (for harp and computer). Benjamin Thigpen composes *balagan* (for eight-channel fixed media). Roger Reynolds completes *The Angel of Death* (for solo piano, chamber orchestra, and six-channel computer-process ed sound). Horacio Vaggione composes *Sçir* (for bass flute and tape). First annual NIME conference, Seattle, Washington, USA.	Mac OS X (UNIX based) released. Windows XP released. Apple iPod released.	Ableton Live, Version 1 (loop-based sequencer software) released. Composers Desktop Project 4 released with full functionality and graphical interface. Curtis Bahn develops the SBass controller. Electronic Music Unit (studios) established at the University of Adelaide. JMSL (Java Music Specification Language) music programming language, based on HMSL, is released. PulsarSynthesis software released by Alberto de Campo and Curtis Roads.
2002	Paul Doornbusch composes *Continuity 3* (for		JunXion (Sensor to MIDI) software released by

(continued)

Year	Selected significant musical events	Main technological events	Computer music events
	percussion and computer). Jean Piché composes *Bharat* (for fixed media, three-channel video, and stereo sound). Kaija Saariaho completes *From the Grammar of Dreams* (for soprano and mezzosoprano).	Apple buys Emagic and takes control of Logic DAW software.	STEIM. SuperCollider becomes Open Source. SuperCollider 3 released.
2003	Richard Barrett composes *DARK MATTER* (for eighteen performers and electronics). Ricardo Dal Farra completes *Civilizaciones* (for six percussion players and live electronics). alcides lanza composes *aXents* (for chamber ensemble and computer synthesized sounds). Karlheinz Stockhausen completes the opera cycle *Licht.* Kees Tazelaar composes *Sternflüstern* (for fixed media). Horacio Vaggione composes *Gymel* (for tape).	Apple Macintosh G5 released (3,100 MIPS). Apple introduces iTunes.	ChucK live coding software released by Perry Cook and Ge Wang. Sonic Arts Research Centre (SARC) opens in Belfast.
2004	James Dillon completes *Philomela* (opera). Brian Ferneyhough completes *Shadowtime* (opera for soloists, small orchestra, and tape).	iPod becomes dominant portable media player and iTunes the dominant online music distributor.	Apple releases Garageband, consumer DAW software. EmissionControl granular synthesis software released by David Thall. SoundHack Spectral Shapers DSP sound manipulation plug-ins introduced.
2005	Curtis Roads completes *POINT LINE CLOUD* (for fixed media).	Mac OS X 10 Server released.	Impromptu live coding software released by Andrew Sorensen.

Year	Selected significant musical events	Main technological events	Computer music events
	Benjamin Thigpen composes *0.95652173913* (for eight-channel fixed media). Horacio Vaggione completes *Taléas* (for recorders and electroacoustics).		Princeton Laptop Orchestra (PLOrk) founded. SPEAR phase vocoder (DSP) software released.
2006	Natasha Barrett composes *Crack Process* (for percussion, trumpet, electric guitar, and computers with real-time processing and motion tracking). Gerard Pape composes *Héliophonie I* (for eight-track tape and video). Kaija Saariaho composes *Tag des Jahrs* (for mixed choir and electronics).	Intel Core 2 Duo computers released (7,100 MIPS). Apple switches its computers to Intel processors and includes support for multiple operating systems.	The Game of Life Foundation (Netherlands) develops a 192-speaker system, the first portable Wave Field Synthesis system, exclusively for the presentation of electronic music.
2007	Cort Lippe composes *Music for Snare Drum and Computer* (for Snare Drum and live DSP).	Windows Vista released. Mac OS X v10.5 released.	Apple release Logic 8, DAW software, capable of handling 255 audio tracks without additional DSP hardware. Cercle pour la Libération du Son et de l'Image (CLSI, a laptop orchestra) is formed in Paris. Waseda University achieves a natural-sounding, flute-playing anthropomorphic robot, with vibrato.
2008	Cort Lippe composes *Music for Tuba and Computer*, premiered January 2009 at ZKM, Karlsruhe Germany. Gerard Pape composes *Héliophonie II* (for eight computers and video).	Multicore computers are common with 3-GHz Intel Xenon processors, such as Apple's Mac Pro (50,000+ MIPS).	DAW software is very common, sometimes a commodity, as are plug-ins for DSP effects and synthesis. Downloaded music tops the *Billboard Magazine*'s Classical Chart after it decides to allow

(continued)

Year	Selected significant musical events	Main technological events	Computer music events
			download-only music.
			Keith McMillan Instruments releases the K-Bow sensor mechanism for a string player's bow and StringPort string-to-USB 2 controller interface for guitar players, making sensor control of synthesis more commercial and feasible for standard musicians.
			Max/MSP 5 released with a greatly improved user interface.
			Stanford Laptop Orchestra founded.
2009	Rand Steiger premieres *Cryosphere* (for orchestra and electronics) at Carnegie (Zankel) Hall, New York.	Computing hardware continues to break previous performance limitations, mostly by running more CPU cores in parallel. Mac OS X v10.6 released.	At least 1,000 computer music studios exist in universities and institutions around the world, many engaged in research. Since most personal studios are also computer music studios, there are hundreds of thousands to millions, worldwide.
			Symbolic Sound release significantly updated hardware, Pacarana, for the graphical Kyma X synthesis system.

NOTES

1. The second column of the chronology reflects a (sometimes personal) collection of music that are pieces made (mostly) with the use of a computer or significant other works (usually including electronics) often of interest to computer music practitioners. It is not a particular filtering or censorship of the available music; the list is limited as there is far too much to include. While some of the pieces may appear to be instrumental in nature, these have (mostly) been composed with algorithmic techniques using computers. The completeness and inclusiveness of a list such as this is always an issue. While every attempt has been made to make this as inclusive, complete, and accurate as possible, there will inevitably be omissions (if for no other reason than a complete list would fill a volume) that someone thinks are significant. While it is hoped that all of the significant and important events have been included, any omissions are unfortunate and possibly due to a lack of available documentation and not the lack of research effort or an attempt at filtering or censorship.

2. There was some activity before 1939, such as Stephan Wolpe using eight gramophones at different speeds at a Dada performance in 1920. Darius Milhaud (1922), Percy Grainger, and Edgar Varèse (1936) all experimented with gramophone record manipulation, and Varèse suggested in 1940 that Hollywood set up an Optical Sound Studio. Also, Ernst Toch and Paul Hindemith created gramophone studies, however the results of these developments have been lost and there remains only sketchy written reports. Additionally, there were people working with film soundtracks who were making sound collages, but while this work was interesting the consequences of it were minimal.

3. Steel band and wire recorders had existed for some time already, and German engineers had developed a coated plastic tape for magnetic recording, but it was not very high quality. In 1943, the use of high-frequency bias was accidentally discovered, which gave a dramatic improvement in the quality of recording. The Allies during World War II were surprised by the length of German broadcasts, which sounded as if they were live, as they did not know about the high quality of the new magnetic tape recorders. This technology spread after the war.

4. Halim El-Dabh, born in Egypt and educated in Egypt and the United States, created a piece of music by recording on a wire recorder in 1944. Titled *Ta'abir al-Zaar*, there is an excerpt titled "Wire Recorder Piece" now available on CD, and it may well be the first piece of music created by manipulating recordings, or "musique concrète". There are other examples of people making earlier works with optical soundtracks on film and so on. Some examples of these are; in Germany, Walter Ruttman and Fritz Bischoff created works in 1928. In Russia, G. V. Alexandrov created pieces from 1930, as did Dziga Vertov from 1931 (although some say he started in 1916). Jack Ellit, an Australian working in London with experimental New Zealand filmmaker Len Lye, created works such as *Journey #1* using optical film technology from about 1930. However, again there was little in the way of musical consequences of this work.

5. MIPS (millions of instructions per second) is a measure of the raw computing power of the CPU (central processing unit) of a computer, an indication of how many instructions it can perform in a given time. Generally, MIPS is regarded as a very poor measure of computing power as it does not take into account other important factors, such as the instruction mix (some instructions take more time than others) and data input and output capabilities. However, for the simplistic use here of giving some indication of the

changes in raw computing power over time, it is adequate. There was also a microprocessor manufacturer named MIPS Technologies.

6. CSIRAC played music at least several months before the Ferranti Mark I and possibly much earlier. Unfortunately, there is no other surviving evidence about the Ferranti music apart from the recording. There are various brief, anecdotal, reports of computers playing music in a range of ways at about the same time as CSIRAC. These include an assortment of sound-producing mechanisms, incorporating attaching a speaker to a serial bus or part of the computer, placing radio equipment near the computer and playing sounds through the radio's speaker via radio-frequency interference, and programming computers to print on large electromechanical printing machines such that the rapid printing created tones, among other methods. Unfortunately, there are no surviving recordings of these activities, and so far there is no surviving evidence from the time. It is important to note that these early attempts at making computers play music did not use a digital-to-analog converter (DAC) or predetermined synthesis waveforms. The developments initiated by Max Mathews and John Pierce have the distinction of being the first musical use of a DAC as well as going beyond what was previously the playback of standard or popular melodies to investigating the very rich musical possibilities offered by the computer. Thus it is Mathews and Pierce, whose work led to the great musical consequences and advances of computer music, who are the rightful fathers of the genre, as their work has had the significant consequences.

BIBLIOGRAPHY

Chadabe, J. 1997. *Electric Sound: The Past and Promise of Electronic Music.* Upper Saddle River, NJ: Prentice Hall.
Collins, N., and J. d'Escriván. 2007. *The Cambridge Companion to Electronic Music.* Cambridge: Cambridge University Press, pp. xiv–xxi.
Manning, P. 2004. *Electronic and Computer Music.* Oxford: Oxford University Press.
De Montfort University. ElectroAcoustic Resource Site. http://www.ears.dmu.ac.uk/spip. php, accessed May 15–18, 2008.
The EMF Institute. The EMF Institute Big Timeline. http://emfinstitute.emf.org/ bigtimelines/bigtimeline.html, accessed May 15–18, 2008.

Much information is also available in the following journals: *Computer Music Journal, Leonardo, Leonardo Music Journal,* and *Organised Sound.* In addition, there are snippets of information in online forums, Web sites, and community mailing lists, such as the International Computer Music Association, CEC-Conference (Canadian Electroacoustic Community), Electronic Music Foundation, and so on.

INDEX

....

Page numbers followed by *f*, *t*, or n refer to figures, tables, or footnotes, respectively.